Contents

Sienese landscape.

Principal sights

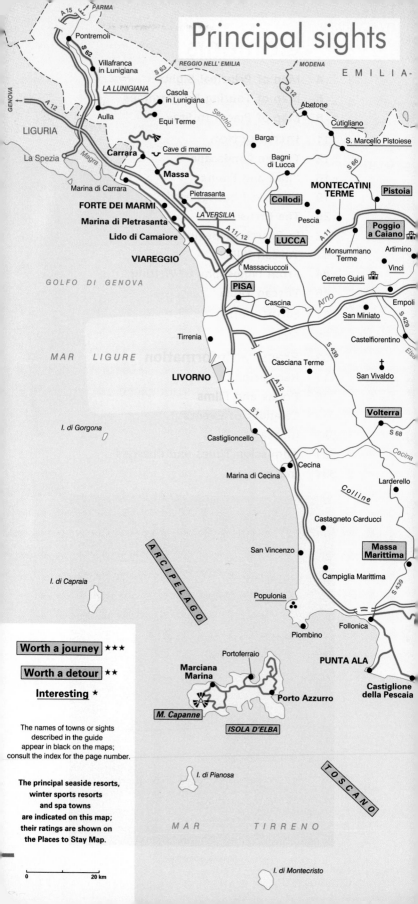

A 15 PARMA
Pontremoli
S 62
Villafranca
in Lunigiana
S 63 REGGIO NELL' EMILIA MODENA EMILIA-
LA LUNIGIANA
Casola S 12
in Lunigiana Abetone
Aulla Equi Terme Serchio Cutigliano
LIGURIA Barga S. Marcello Pistoiese
La Spezia Magra Bagni S 66
Carrara Cave di marmo di Lucca
Massa MONTECATINI
Pietrasanta **Collodi** TERME **Pistoia**
Marina di Carrara Pescia
FORTE DEI MARMI LA VERSILIA **Poggio**
Marina di Pietrasanta A 11/12 **a Caiano**
Lido di Camaiore **LUCCA** A 11 Artimino
VIAREGGIO Monsummano Vinci
Terme
Massaciuccoli Cerreto Guidi
GOLFO DI GENOVA **PISA** Empoli
Arno S 429
Cascina San Miniato
Tirrenia Castelfiorentino Elsa
MAR LIGURE San Vivaldo
Casciana Terme
LIVORNO S 439 **Volterra**
A 12 S 68
I. di Gorgona Cecina
Castiglioncello Colline
Cecina Larderello
Marina di Cecina
I. di Capraia Castagneto Carducci
A S 1
R **Massa**
San Vincenzo **Marittima**
C Campiglia Marittima S 439
I Populonia
P Follonica
E Piombino
L
A **PUNTA ALA**
G Portoferraio
O **Marciana** **Castiglione**
Marina **della Pescaia**
M. Capanne **Porto Azzurro**
ISOLA D'ELBA
T
O
S
I. di Pianosa C
A
N
O
MAR TIRRENO
I. di Montecristo

Worth a journey ★★★

Worth a detour ★★

Interesting ★

The names of towns or sights
described in the guide
appear in black on the maps;
consult the index for the page number.

**The principal seaside resorts,
winter sports resorts
and spa towns
are indicated on this map;
their ratings are shown on
the Places to Stay Map.**

0   20 km

Touring programmes

1. Famous towns and cities = 300 km - 186 miles (12 days including 4 in Florence)
2. Marble mountains: cultural centres and wildlife - 300 km - 186 miles
3. North of Florence - 200 km - 124 miles
4. Casentino and Pratomagno: wildlife and monasticism - 250 km - 155 miles
5. Upper Tiber Valley and Chiana Valley - 25 km - 155 miles
6. Siena and the Sienese Hills - 200 km - 124 miles
7. Tuscan mining district (the metalliferous hills and the Isle of Elba) - 400 km - 248 miles
8. Southern Tuscany - 450 km - 279 miles

For a more detailed description of the tours see the Practical Information Section - Touring in Tuscany

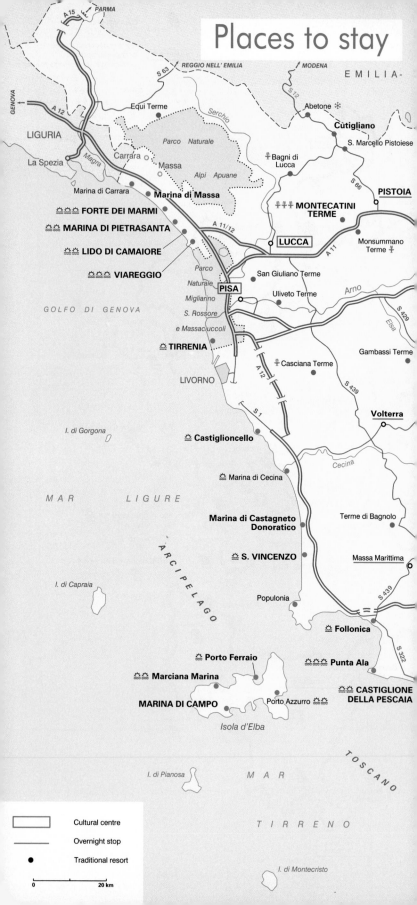

Places to stay

PARMA
A 15
S 63
REGGIO NELL' EMILIA
MODENA
EMILIA-
Abetone ※
GENOVA
A 12
Equi Terme
Serchio
Cutigliano
S. Marcello Pistoiese
LIGURIA
Parco   Naturale
S 12
Bagni di
Lucca
Magra
Carrara ○
Massa
S 66
La Spezia
○
Alpi   Apuane
PISTOIA
Marina di Carrara
⚨⚨⚨ MONTECATINI
TERME
⚨ Marina di Massa
⚨⚨⚨ FORTE DEI MARMI
A 11/12
⚨⚨ MARINA DI PIETRASANTA
LUCCA
Monsummano
Terme ⚨
⚨⚨ LIDO DI CAMAIORE
A 11
⚨⚨⚨ VIAREGGIO
Parco
San Giuliano Terme
Naturale
PISA
Migliarino
Uliveto Terme
Arno
S 429
GOLFO DI GENOVA
S. Rossore
e Massaciuccoli
Elsa
⚨ TIRRENIA
Gambassi Terme
Casciana Terme
LIVORNO
A 12
S 439
I. di Gorgona
S 1
Volterra
○
⚨ Castiglioncello
Cecina
⚨ Marina di Cecina
MAR   LIGURE
Terme di Bagnolo
Marina di Castagneto
Donoratico
I. di Capraia
⚨ S. VINCENZO
Massa Marittima
A R C I P E L A G O
Populonia
S 439
⚨ Follonica
⚨ Porto Ferraio
⚨⚨⚨ Punta Ala
S 322
⚨⚨ Marciana Marina
⚨⚨ CASTIGLIONE
DELLA PESCAIA
MARINA DI CAMPO
Porto Azzurro ⚨⚨
Isola d'Elba
T O S C A N O
I. di Pianosa
M A R
T I R R E N O
I. di Montecristo

☐	Cultural centre
—	Overnight stop
●	Traditional resort

0   20 km

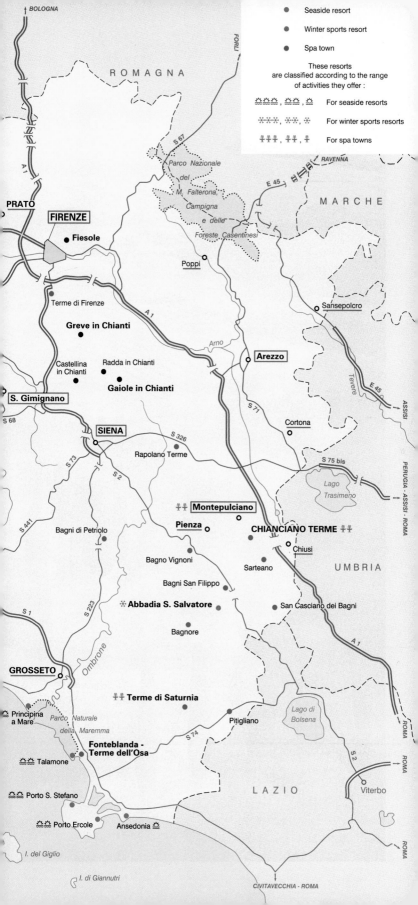

Orcia Valley.

Introduction

P. Somelet/DIAF.

Tuscan Landscape

The name Tuscany, first used in the 10C, is derived from the Latin word *Tuscia,* which was employed from the 3C onwards to describe the region then known as Etruria, the territory of the Etruscans (also known as Tusci), situated between the Tiber and the Arno.

Mountains, hills, inland basins and low coastal plains with very varied types of soil are dotted across this mainly highland region, which has some of the largest stretches of woodland in Italy and an abundance of rivers and streams that run down the western slopes of the Apennines and into the Mediterranean.

A VARIED LANDSCAPE

The north-eastern boundary of Tuscany is clearly defined. It consists of the **Apennines** which curve across the Italian peninsula from Liguria on the Tyrrhenian coast of the Mediterranean Sea to the Adriatic coast. This backbone of hills constitutes a watershed. The geological relief on the northern slopes (where the foothills lie perpendicular to the central ridge) is fairly simple but on the south-facing Tuscan side, there is a series of secondary ranges (low mountains and hills) lying parallel to the main range, creating valleys and inland basins containing the major cities-Florence, Siena and Arezzo.

Like the Apennines, these low mountains are comparatively young, dating only from the Tertiary era, and they consist predominantly of clay and schist, the one exception being the hard and immaculate marble of the **Apuan Alps**. The soil is soft and the very violent, heavy rainstorms often lead to flooding in the areas near the river beds (roads, fields and villages), frequently causing dramatic landslides *(frane)* or deep gorges *(calanchi)* which alternate with the crags *(balze)* caused by erosion in the Volterra region. Less extensive landslides have formed jagged peaks *(crete)* among the hills of the Siena region and the Orcia Valley.

Countless rivers and streams rise in the Tuscan Apennines, where the highest peak is Mount Cimone (alt 2165m-7103ft). The range is fringed by small lush valleys – (from north to south) the **Lunigiana** region traversed by the River Magra; the **Garfagnana** region watered by the Serchio; the **Mugello** region containing the Sieve (a tributary of the Arno); the **Casentino** region traversed by the upper reaches of the Arno; the north end of the **Val Tiberina,** where the River Tiber *(Tevere)* rises on the border with Umbria.

Further from the Apennine backbone are folds of soft sandstone and schist forming a series of uplands that vary in appearance from the gently-rolling Florentine countryside to the bare limestone peaks of the Sienese Hills. Numerous rivers – Elsa, Cecina, Ombrone – also rise in these upland regions.

Near the coast the landscape opens out into a wide coastal plain, formed mainly by alluvial deposits from the numerous rivers of Tuscany, which extends into the sea where the seabed is relatively flat and the water shallow. The Tuscan Archipelago and Monte Argentario peninsula are the last outcrops of the Apennine folds extending into the sea.

The chief delight of the Tuscan countryside is that its great variety is on a human scale and clothed in abundant vegetation from the coniferous forests of the high mountains to the olive groves, vineyards and verdant pastures in the valleys.

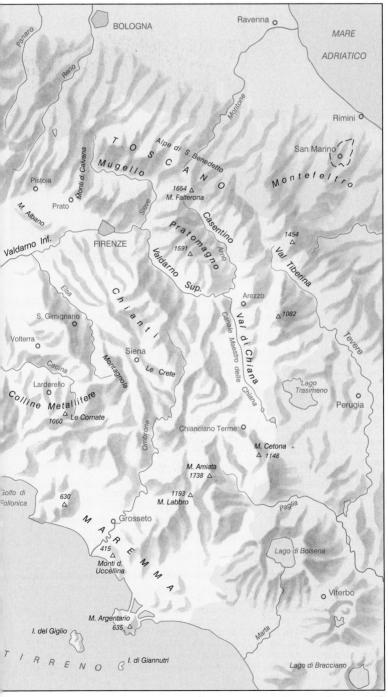

FAMILIAR SCENES AND LESSER-KNOWN LANDSCAPES

Apuan Alps – The Apuan Alps north of the Arno are glistening mountains composed of the white marble that has made the name of Carrara so famous. Blocks and slabs of marble can be seen piled up on the wharves of Marina di Carrara.

At the foot of the mountains lies the splendid sandy shoreline of **Versilia,** where from June to September the serried rows of beach furniture stretch as far as the eye can see. Viareggio is undoubtedly the most popular resort. The very mild climate is ideal for flower growing.

At the southern end of this flat coastal area lies Livorno (Leghorn), the only real commercial port in Tuscany, with major shipyards and oil refineries.

Vinci and the Montalbano hills.

Arno Basin – The River Arno (241km – 150 miles long), the major Tuscan river, rises on Mount Falterona on the border with Romagna *(Michelin map 430 K 17)* and irrigates the alluvial land on either side of its long course. After flowing through the **Casentino** region, it skirts the south end of the **Pratomagno** range in a deep meander where it is joined, not far from Arezzo, by the fast-flowing **Chiana River,** one section of which has been canalised (Maestro Canal). The river then flows north through the **Upper Arno Valley** *(Valdarno superiore),* its course bounded to the west by the Chianti Hills.

When the river reaches Florence, the valley suddenly opens out into the **Lower Arno Valley** *(Valdarno Inferiore),* widening until it reaches the sea. Most of the agricultural and industrial activity is concentrated in this area; it is also the most densely-populated part of the region. The main sectors of employment are intensive and specialised farming (especially around Pistoia where the maritime climate has favoured the planting of huge nurseries producing fruit trees and house plants), chemical industries and glass-making in Pisa (where St-Gobain has a factory), textiles in Prato and engineering in Florence (where there is still an industrial infrastructure based on old crafts – leather goods, shoes, etc).

As well as being the main economic centre of Tuscany, **Florence** is also the regional political capital, a role which is reflected in the wide circulation of its daily newspaper *La Nazione* throughout central Italy. It is also the cultural and artistic symbol of the region. Florence is a city

Val di Chiana

The course of the River Chiana, which originally flowed south into the Tiber and not north into the Arno, was reversed in the 16C. In Antiquity the Etruscans of Chiusi kept a close watch on the river, as it provided an easy link with Rome. As the local population abandoned the region during the Middle Ages and as the incline of the plain is very gentle, the river water was gradually dammed up by the deposit of alluvium and eventually stagnated. The Chiana Valley then turned into a vast and unhealthy area of marshland. In 1551 most of the water was drained off through a canal *(Canale Maestro Chiana)* which ran north into the Arno. The Chiani, a small arm of the former river to the south, still flows into the Tiber, as a tributary of the Paglia.

of worldwide artistic and architectural renown, and it shares its prestige with its old rival Pisa and other major centres within the basin such as Lucca, Pistoia and Prato, which have succeeded in retaining their interest as small historic towns despite being highly industrialised.

The Florentine Countryside and Chianti District – Pure light, flowing lines and serenity are the main characteristics of the famous landscapes that can be admired in the works of the Florentine Primitives. The silvery rippling hillsides covered with olive groves, interspersed with mulberry bushes and rows of vines, slope gently down to fields of maize or corn. The hilltops, where the dark slender outlines of cypress trees occasionally contrast with clumps of oak or chestnut trees, provide the setting for fortified villages such as Monteriggioni or for majestic old farmhouses *(villas)* dominated by a large central tower used as a dovecote.

A hazy mist often hangs over the region, sometimes persisting throughout the day, softening the distant outlines and drawing a veil of pearly light over the rolling hills and colours of the landscape.

South of Florence, on the threshold of southern Tuscany, rise the Chianti Hills extending between the main Siena road and the *Autostrada del Sole*, the motorway which runs through the Arno Valley. This jolly, friendly region consists of impressive clay hills bearing the famous Chianti vineyards producing the highly-esteemed vintages that are named after the famous families who own them.

To the west is San Gimignano which has remained almost unchanged since the Middle Ages. It has numerous towers in which some are quick to see the forerunner of the skyscraper.

Sienese Hills – The hills south of Chianti are devoid of vegetation, revealing their pale golden soil which turns to grey beyond Siena. This city is set in the heart of this serene pastoral landscape. Like Florence and Pisa, Siena, the home of the Palio horse race, constitutes a major tourist attraction.

The Asciano road leading southeast to Monte Oliveto Maggiore passes through strange limestone landscapes. This is the region of the Sienese *Crete,* line upon line of desolate, arid, chalky hills streaked with deep ravines created by the surface water draining down from the peaks.

Metalliferous Hills – Between the Florence region and the sea is a zone of low, stocky yet disturbing hills. As their name suggests, they are rich in iron ore and also contain deposits of other minerals – lead, copper, zinc. In the area around Larderello, white steam from the hot springs *(soffioni)*, which are rich in borax, a mineral used in the production of pharmaceuticals, is emitted from the bowels

of the earth giving the landscape a dreamlike appearance. The springs, which colour the landscape red, are used to produce electricity in geothermal power plants.

The Island of Elba offshore belongs to the same mountain system. Its iron mines produce ore that is sent to the mainland to feed the blast furnaces of Piombino. Ferries to the island leave from Piombino harbour.

Maremma and Southern Tuscany – On the southern boundary with Latium are the first volcanic mountains of central Italy, the highest being Mount Amiata (1738m – 5702ft). The mountains are rich in cinnabar, which is used to produce mercury; Italy is one of the world's leading suppliers of this metal.

The austere landscape provides the backdrop to the Maremma, a region of melancholy beauty, erstwhile land of evil spells and dark legends but now an area of quiet

Uccellina Hills in the Maremma.

15

rusticity. It has herds of horses and buffalo, once raised there in the wild under the watchful eye of herdsmen *(butteri)*. Under the agrarian reforms introduced in 1950, these regions, which were formerly the property of a few big city landowners, benefitted from land improvement which completely altered their appearance. They were re-allocated to farmers from other regions, whose farmsteads are now dotted across the area. The land is cultivated in a more rational manner – cereal and fodder crops, market-gardening, rice, sunflowers – and modern farming co-operatives have been set up in the region. Cattle is raised for dairy products, supplying cities such as Florence or Rome, and sheep farming has produced a delicious ewe's milk cheese called *pecorino*.

TUSCAN TOWNS AND VILLAGES

From the surrounding hillsides, the first striking feature of a village or town is often uniformity of colour. All the buildings are the colour of well-baked bread, with varying shades of brown or grey. Façades built of stone or locally-produced brick are still common, and the traditional small roof tiles have withstood the passage of time. Some of the old towns are encircled by ramparts, with the modern districts spreadeagled across the countryside beyond.

The maze of streets, staggered teetering rooftops, the odd crenellated façade, a belfry and the distinct white marble of a church and its belltower *(campanile)* form an intricate picture and create an impression of towns shaped by their history and the anonymous lives of the citizens.

In the centre of Tuscan towns, medieval and Renaissance houses (occasionally refurbished or restored) stand side by side. The façades still have interesting features such as rings where horses were once tied up, the upper sections still include standard holders and wrought-iron lanterns, and along the lower parts of certain dwellings run the stone benches that have been a traditional feature of such communities since the Middle Ages when social life centred on the street.

Almost every small town has its administrative building *(palazzo dei priori* or *palazzo del podestà* or *palazzo comunale)* often decorated with the coats of arms of the wealthy families who held the reins of local government. These shields sometimes cover the entire façade, as is the case in Volterra, Colle di Val d'Elsa and Scarperia. Merchants' loggias give the streets an attractive air with their open arcades on the corner of a building or below a simple façade, sometimes but not always overlooking a square.

Unlike the cities, these old towns and villages, many of them perched on hilltops, huddle around their historic streets. Bounded by old walls or one last row of houses, they stand out sharply against the surrounding carefully-cultivated countryside.

*The **Michelin Green Guide Rome** describes the Eternal City :*
– the best-known sights
– the districts steeped in 3 000 years of history
– the art treasures in the museums and galleries

Flora and Fauna

Tuscany is the most thickly-wooded region in Italy. The forests (approximately 1 000 000 ha), of which 25 % consists of mature trees, contains an extremely wide variety of vegetation, from subtropical species in certain coastal areas and on the islands to alpine plants on the upper slopes of the Apennines. The region has a vast number of wild, unspoiled areas – two national parks and three nature reserves – and is also famous for its landscape, carefully tended by

Umbrella pine.

16

the hand of man over thousands of years, where vines, olive groves and fields of cereal crops create the backdrop to humble farms and magnificent abbeys alike.

Terraced vegetation – Near the sea, pine trees reign supreme, spreading out into expanses of well-protected pine forests (Versilian and Etruscan Rivieras and the Maremma). Two varieties predominate – the **maritime pine,** which has a conical head and long straight trunk, and the **umbrella pine** with its flattened crown. The umbrella pine grows well in very poor soil where it does not have to compete with other types of plant (unlike the maritime pine which mingles happily with holm or cork oaks) and can therefore be found on the sandy soil of the coastline and the hillsides of the hinterland standing alone or blending harmoniously and gracefully with the cypress trees. It has been cultivated since ancient times for its edible oil-bearing pine kernels.

The **cypress** takes to all types of soil and has been widely planted by man for its ornamental appearance and effectiveness as a windshield for crops. It can be found in the lower regions of the Mugello Valley, the Sienese hills, the Orcia Valley and, more especially, on the hills of the Chianti region of which it is one of the symbols, together with the vine and the olive tree.

Cypress tree.

For many centuries, low-altitude areas were covered in coppices, artificially-maintained woodland consisting of small trees that were periodically cut back for use mainly as fire-wood. Many coppices have now declined after some thirty years of neglect, giving way to *macchia* vegetation consisting of trees and shrubs, mostly evergreens, such as the **holm oak,** or sub-evergreen species, like the **cork oak**; the leaves of the latter are deciduous but may last for more than one year and the dark or grey-green foliage and twisted trunks of the trees give the landscape a wild, untamed appearance. The *macchia* vegetation also includes a wide range of thorny and aromatic bushes with tough, glossy leaves – heather, bramble, butcher's broom (knee-holly), hawthorn, broom, juniper and rosemary. In places where the *macchia* itself peters out, there is a poorer version of the vegetation known as *gariga* which is generally found in particularly arid

Olive tree.

areas where only xerophilous plants (plants adapted to drought, sun and cold) such as lentiscus, myrtle, cistus and rosemary are able to survive.

Growing near these plants are agaves and prickly pears (common on the island of Elba), both of which were imported from America in the 16C.

In the low-lying areas there is also a significant amount of natural pasture-land and meadow as well as land devoted to cereal crops, market gardening, vegetable farming and horticulture. Intensive cropping extends up to the limit beyond which olive trees will not grow (alt 600-700m – 1970-2300ft). Together with **vines, olive trees** are the main plants on the hillsides. They are grown for the production of table olives, hand-picked from the tree, and of olive oil, pressed from ripe fruit collected in nets on the ground.

Chestnut trees, which can grow at altitudes of up to 1000m-3280ft, can be found throughout Tuscany, even a short distance above sea-level. It is especially characteristic of the woodland on the island of Elba and is also common in the Mugello Region, and on Monti Pisani and Monte Amiata.

Sweet chestnut tree.

In the undergrowth there are blackberries, wild asparagus (on Amiata) and numerous fungi, including truffles which grow freely among the roots of the holm oak.

Beeches and **fir trees** mark the upper tree line (altitude 1000-1700m – 3280-5580ft) – on Monte Amiata and the Apennines. Magnificent coniferous forests cover the area around Camaldoli, Vallombrosa and Abetone. The thickest chestnut groves are to be found in the Mugello and Casentino Regions. Beeches can be found growing alongside numerous other varieties such as maple, ash, hornbeam, Turkey oak and poplar.

Beyond the highland forests, the landscape clears to give way to sun-drenched pastures such as those in the Garfagnana region.

Fauna – Because of its thriving and varied plant life, Tuscany has retained a wide variety of fauna. Here as elsewhere, however, wildlife is under threat from hunting, pollution and the changes imposed by technological progress – town planning, roads, railways, riverbank and coastal developments, not to mention the recent reclamation of former marshland which was the haunt of a particular type of wildlife that is now scarce despite the creation of nature reserves which seek to protect and preserve it.

Among the **large mammals**, the bear and lynx have died out in Tuscany, but wolves can still be found in the Apennines (they have even returned to the Garfagnana region) and the upper valley of the Tiber. Stags were imported during the era of the grand dukes from Styria, east of the Austrian Alps, and have survived in the Casentino Valley; they can also be found in the Maremma region along with other members of the deer family such as the roe-deer and fallow-deer; the latter were imported from Asia Minor during Ancient Roman times. There are also very large numbers of deer in the pine forests of San Rossore, Migliarino, Capalbio and Monte Argentario. Another of the ungulates of Tuscany is the wild goat, unfortunately an endangered species, which now survives only on the island of Montecristo where it is highly protected. The wild boar, however, the emblem of the Maremma, inhabits many areas of scrubland and pine forest in Tuscany. It may be the bane of farmers' lives but it plays an important role in keeping vegetation under control as it turns over the soil with its snout in search of roots, acorns, bulbs, larvae and insects, and thus leaves traces of its passage or its presence in an area.

The most common **small mammals** in the region are the hare and the wild rabbit, which is particularly prolific as it produces three to four litters of four to ten young each year, and the fox, its main predator, which is capable of adapting to all types of environment from sand dunes to rocky areas and from forest to farmland. In the dunes of the Maremma region in particular wild rabbits are preyed upon by polecats, weasels, martens and stone martens and even a number of nocturnal birds of prey. Indeed it is the presence of large numbers of rabbits that ensures the survival of these predators. The pine forests are also home to martens and stone martens as well as hedgehogs, porcupines and badgers. Wildcats and polecats can be seen in the shrubby rocky areas of the Maremma region.

The otter lives in the swamps *(paludi)* and on the banks of the major rivers, co-existing with the Old World beaver which has a cylindrical tail unlike its South American cousin whose tail is flat. For a long time the otter was prized for its fur but it is now an endangered species, which has survived in the Garfagnana and Maremma regions but has also suffered as a result of land development along the river banks; beavers, on the other hand, have adapted to such changes.

Owing to its varied relief and abundance of rivers and streams, Tuscany harbours numerous **species of birds,** including migrants such as passerines (thrushes, swallows, magpies, nightingales, kingfishers), birds of prey (golden eagles, sparrow-hawks, falcons, buzzards, kites, owls), web-footed species (cormorants, mallard ducks, coots, seagulls, wild geese) and waders (herons, oyster catchers, cranes, egrets, storks).

Unlike the waters along the coast and round the islands which have abundant **fish stocks**, the rivers are sparsely populated.

Livestock farming includes the white beef cattle of the Val di Chiana, a long-established breed known as *chianina*; its extremely tender meat is famous throughout Italy.

Padùle

In Tuscany a swamp *(palude)* is called *padule* (inversion of the final consonants). Although the swamps have all but disappeared as a result of land improvement in unhealthy areas, the region still includes the Padule di Raspollino (northwest of Grosseto), the Padule di Fuccecchio (between Florence and Pisa) and the entire area around the Massaciuccoli Lake, which is considered locally as a *padùle*.

Historical Background

Major historic events are shown in italics

Antiquity – Tuscany known as Etruria

753 BC	*Legendary date of the founding of Rome by Romulus.*
Late 8C	Appearance of Etruscans in central Italy.
2nd half of 7C	Occupation of the Latin country by Etruscans.
Late 7C-Late 6C	Rome governed by sovereigns from Etruria (Tarquin dynasty), whose reign marked the height of **Etruscan expansion**.
509	Fall of Tarquinius Superbus. Beginning of the decline of Etruscan power. *Founding of the Roman Republic.*
3C	Etruscan submission to Roman rule. Volterra conquered in 295. Perugia and Arezzo rallied to the Roman camp in 294. Fall of Etruria's religious capital, Volsinii (now Orvieto in Umbria) in 265 marking the end of Etruscan independence.
AD 330	*Byzantium chosen by Constantine the Great as the capital of the Roman Empire and renamed Constantinople in his honour.*
395	*Division of the Roman Empire into the Eastern and Western Empires with Constantinople and Rome as their respective capitals.*
476	*Fall of the Western Roman Empire.*

Dark Ages and Foreign Invasions

568	Occupation by Lombards (from Northern Europe) of the Po Plain (Lombardy is named after them) and of Tuscany, Umbria and Puglia and Campania in the south. Foundation of duchies; Tuscany centred on the Duchy of Lucca. *Weakening of Byzantine authority over its empire. Beginning of a period of cohabitation with the Kingdom of Lombardy.*
570-774	Long and violent occupation of Tuscany by the Lombards.
751	Surrender of Ravenna.
752	Rome threatened by the Lombards. Appeal by the Pope to Pepin the Short, King of the Franks.
756	Undertaking by Pepin the Short to restore the States occupied by the Lombards to the Pope, marking the beginning of the Pope's temporal power and the birth of the Papal States which were to be of major importance in Italian history until the 19C.
774	Defeat of the Lombards by Charlemagne (son of Pepin the Short). Tuscany under Carolingian rule. Lucca the centre of the new Marches of Tuscany.
9C	Break-up of the Carolingian Empire causing anarchy in Italy and the founding of numerous rival states.
951	Intervention in Italy by King Otto I of Saxony at the request of the Pope.
962	Coronation of Otto I as Emperor by the Pope; foundation of the **Holy Roman Empire of the German Nation**. Exclusive right to appoint the clergy claimed by the Emperor.

Struggle between the Church and the Holy Roman Emperor – The Communes

In the late 11C, in defiance of the Holy Roman Emperor's growing stranglehold on the Papacy, Gregory VII decreed (1075-1076) that no member of the clergy could be appointed to a parish or diocese by a layman and he excommunicated Emperor Henry IV. This gave rise to the **Investiture Controversy,** the source of a lengthy dispute between Papacy and Empire constituting the background to a whole era of Italian history.

This period also saw the rise of the **Communes** *(comune)*, whose role was to become a determining factor in the political life of medieval Italy.

The Communes – The struggle between Imperial power and the Papacy, in which each of the protagonists attempted to foster support from various cities by granting them privileges, was one of the major reasons for the spectacular development of Italian towns in the late 11C. The Crusades and ensuing economic prosperity, especially in Pisa, further accentuated the expansion, creating an unprecedented boom in trade and industry (principally silk and wool) and resulting in the birth of a new class – the merchants.

The Communes flourished and their existence, which was finally officially recognised by both Pope and Emperor, considerably altered political life in northern and central medieval Italy, including Tuscany, changing the face of numerous towns.

The Commune, a self-governing association of citizens, was marked by an unarmed takeover of power by the gentry and wealthy middle classes at the expense of the great feudal landowning nobility.

As the prosperity of the towns grew, so the merchants and less wealthy classes of society gained power. The nobles, meanwhile, were gradually excluded from positions of authority.

In the early years, the Communes were governed by **Consuls**, elected by an Assembly, who held executive and judicial powers. Later, Frederick Barbarossa appointed a governor **(podestà)** as the direct representative of imperial power at the head of each town under Imperial rule. In principal, this magistrate came from outside the town and acted as the head of the army and an arbitrator in legal matters although, like the consuls, he had no legislative power.

When the influence acquired by the Craft Guilds **(arti)** led to a restructuring of towns and cities and brought the "popular" classes to power, a **Captain of the People** *(Capitano del Popolo)* monitored by an increasingly influential assembly was appointed to govern the town jointly with the governor *(podestà)*. In the end the *Podestà* was replaced by the *Capitano*.

The Communes took advantage of the struggle between Church and Empire, adding to its complexity, and the emperor was faced in many instances with violent hostility. All towns took sides in the controversy between the Pope and the Emperor, some fluctuating by choice or by coercion between the factions. In the furious clashes that set Italian towns and cities against one another, economic rivalries and individual enmities accounted for much of the fighting.

Despite these upheavals, the country experienced a major economic and artistic boom during the 13C and the first half of the 14C, stimulated by the power of the Communes which had become not only busy trading towns but also important artistic centres. Universities, which gained fame throughout Europe, were founded in Siena, Pisa and Florence; through Dante the Italian language acquired a glory that was never to wane.

The break-up of the Communes was provoked by the Black Death (1348), which was followed by sporadic outbreaks of plague during the second half of the 14C, by endemic fighting between neighbouring towns and by internal conflict within the towns.

Guelfs and Ghibellines

The names Guelf and Ghibelline *(Guelfi* and *Ghibellini* in Italian), which came into use in Florence in 1215, are derived from the names of the two great German families who disputed the throne of the Holy Roman Emperor in the 12C. The **Ghibellines** were the supporters of the lords of Waiblingen, the cradle of the House of Swabia and therefore of the Hohenstaufen dynasty. The **Guelfs**, who were rivals of the Hohenstaufen family and therefore supporters of the Pope, were members of the Welf dynasty (House of Bavaria). The later division into White Guelfs and Black Guelfs was confined to Florence.

1115	Death of Countess Matilda, Marchioness of Tuscany. Tuscany bequeathed by her to the Papacy as a final gesture after half a century of supporting the Pope.
1122	*Investiture Controversy brought to an end by the Concordat of Worms which gave the Pope the upper hand.*
1125	Annexation of Fiesole by Florence marking the beginning of Florentine expansion in Tuscany.
1152	Crisis of succession in Germany in which the supporters of the House of Bavaria opposed the supporters of the House of Swabia. Election of Frederick of Hohenstaufen, otherwise known as Frederick Barbarossa, supported by the House of Swabia.
1155	Coronation in Italy by the Pope of Frederick Barbarossa as Emperor and Barbarossa's attempt to impose his rule throughout the whole of Italy. Renewal of the struggle between the Papacy and the Empire, complicated by the growing hostility of the Communes. Appointment by Frederick of a governor *(podestà)* to control the Communes that he had forced into submission.

In the 13C the Investiture Controversy was replaced by the issue of primacy between Pope and Emperor. The zeal of the Guelf faction was stimulated by the preaching of the new religious orders (Minim Brothers of St Francis of Assisi, Dominicans).

1227-1250	New episode in the struggle led by Pope Gregory IX and Pope Innocent IV against Frederick II of Swabia (grandson of Frederick Barbarossa), crowned King of Sicily in 1194 and German Emperor in 1220. New victory for the Papacy in 1245; excommunication and dismissal of the Emperor by the Pope.

The Crisis between Pope and Empire

1250	Death of Frederick II marking the beginning of a period of strife.
1251	Founding of a federation of Tuscan Ghibelline towns, headed by Pisa and Siena.
1260	Attempt by King Manfred of Sicily, the legitimised bastard son of Frederick, to conquer the peninsula with the support of the Ghibelline towns. After being defeated at **Montaperti**, Florence, traditionally a Guelf city, which had already been Ghibelline for 13 years during the rule of Frederick II, again supported the Ghibelline faction for a short period.
1263-1266	Appeal by the Pope to Charles of Anjou (brother of St Louis, King of France) who defeated Manfred at Benevento (Campania) in 1266. Death of Manfred in battle and the establishment of the Anjou dynasty in Sicily and Naples, subjecting Italy to a period of French control.
1284	Defeat of Pisa by Genoa at the **Battle of Meloria** causing Pisa to lose its supremacy over Sardinia and Corsica and its prime position on the Mediterranean.
1289	**Battle of Campaldino** near Poppi quashing Ghibelline hopes.
Late 13C	Siena overtaken by Florence as a banking centre and the largest city in Tuscany.

The 14C saw a decline in the power of the Communes *(see above)* and in Florence, as elsewhere in Italy, the rise of the great family of the Medici.

The collapse of imperial rule was followed by an erosion of the power of the Papacy, which was faced with grave difficulties. Italy was in crisis. Foreign influence began to make itself felt within the country, first through the French and later through the Aragonese, both of whom were fighting to gain control of the south. Florence exerted huge power and only Pisa, Lucca and Siena still managed to retain their independence.

1300	Division in Florence between the **Black Guelfs**, who supported foreign intervention, and the **White Guelfs**, who advocated total independence in the name of freedom.
1301	Annexation of Pistoia by Florence.
1309	*Removal of the Popes to Avignon to escape the unrest in Rome.*
1328	Appeal for support by the Ghibellines to Louis of Bavaria; failure of his intervention marking the end of German claims in Italy.
1348	Death of almost one-half (and sometimes more) of the urban population from the Black Death which swept through Italy and spread throughout Europe.
1361	Annexation of Volterra by Florence.
1377	Return of the Papacy to Rome at the instigation of Petrarch and Catherine of Siena.
1378-1417	**Great Western Schism**: Papal re-instatement in Rome opposed by the antipope resident in Avignon and a second antipope in Pisa (1409).
1384	Annexation of Arezzo by Florence.

15C – The Glorious Era of the Tuscan Renaissance

In the 15C Italy experienced a remarkable increase in economic and artistic activity. The medieval era drew to a close and was replaced by the Renaissance which blossomed in Florence, the city of the Medici, where it was a glittering incarnation of a golden age.

1406	Conquest of Pisa by Florence.
1434	Beginning of the Medici oligarchy in Florence, with the arrival in government of Cosimo the Elder *(qv)*.
1454	Political stability in Italy between the great rival States of Milan, Florence, Rome and Naples guaranteed by the **Treaty of Lodi**, which was vigilantly upheld by Lorenzo the Magnificent, ruler of Florence from 1469.

SCALA

15C marriage (Adimari Chest, Galleria dell'Accademia, Florence).

21

1494	Policy of interference in Italian affairs resumed by Charles VIII of France, thus putting the new stability in jeopardy. After a triumphant welcome in Pisa and benign indifference in Florence, he passed through Siena, marched on Rome and entered Naples but was soon forced to retreat.
	His campaign marked the beginning of the Italian wars, which were later resumed by Louis XII, with the same lack of success.
1494-1498	Republic briefly established in Florence by Savonarola *(qv)*.

The Marzocco by Donatello (Bargello, Florence). SCALA

The Marzocco

This figure of a seated lion, gripping the Florentine heraldic lily in its left front paw, symbolises the political power of Florence. It can be seen in the main square of every town and village governed by the city of the Medici and is an impressive testimony to the authority of Florentine rule. It gets its name from Mars, the god of war, represented by an ancient statue at the entrance to the Ponte Vecchio in Florence in the Middle Ages. The statue was destroyed by the floodwaters of the Arno in 1333 and replaced by the townspeople in 1420 in memory of its predecessor by Donatello's everlasting sculpture of a lion, named *Martoco* (little Mars). In 1810 it was moved to the Piazza della Signoria and subsequently replaced by a copy.

Grand Duchy of Tuscany

The **16C** was marked by the rivalry between France and Spain which turned Italy into a battlefield as the two great powers struggled for overall control of Europe.

Florence overtaken by Rome as a centre of artistic creativity in the reigns of the great Pope, Julius II (1503-1513) and the Medici Pope Leo X (1513-1521).

1508-1526	*François I of France at war in northern Italy; victorious at Marignano but forced to renounce his claim to Italy after defeat at Pavia.*
1527	*Italy attacked by Emperor Charles V. The power of the Holy See diminished by the sack of Rome.*
	Re-instatement of Alessandro Medici, the Emperor's own son-in-law, in Florence which became a duchy (1532).
1545-1563	*Council of Trent leading to the Counter-Reformation (or Catholic Reformation).*
1555	French claims in Italy temporarily brought to an end by the failure of the campaign launched by Henri II, whose supporters were defeated by the Emperor's forces at the Siege of Siena *(qv)*.
	Siena forced to submit by Cosimo I, protégé of Charles V. Unification of Tuscany completed, except for Lucca, Piombino and the Garrison State *(qv)*.
1559	Treaty of Cateau-Cambrésis marking the end of the Italian Campaign and the beginning of Spanish domination. Central Italy sandwiched between territories subject to foreign rule – the Duchy of Milan under France to the north and southern Italy, Sicily and Sardinia under Spain to the south.
1569	Tuscany made a grand duchy under the absolute rule of Cosimo I.
17C	Italy in decline and no longer the object of dispute between Spain and France during the reign of Louis XIV.
18C	Instigation by the rulers of a number of Italian States of a form of "Enlightened Despotism", a concept which was spreading throughout Europe from France. It was best embodied in Italy by Grand Duke Peter Leopold of Tuscany (1765-1790), son of Maria Theresa of Austria, who based his style of government on the most innovatory theories of the day.
1713	**Treaty of Utrecht** marking the end of Spanish domination and the beginning of Austrian control. From 1714 to 1748, however, Italy remained at stake between the Habsburgs and the Spanish Bourbons.
1737	End of the Medici line. Grand Duchy of Tuscany granted by the Austrians to François of Lorraine, husband of Maria Theresa and future Emperor of Austria. Under this dynasty, Florence and Tuscany experienced a period of reform and progress.

Napoleonic Empire

1796-1799	Napoleonic campaign ending in the Peace of Campo Formio (1797) by which France annexed Italy. Occupation of Florence.
Early 19C	Annexation of territory by Napoleon. Italians experienced their first period of unity under governmental and military institutions similar to those established in France.
1800-1801	Second Napoleonic campaign leading to the founding of an Italian Republic; Tuscany became the Kingdom of Etruria.
1805-1806	Napoleon, now Emperor of France, proclaimed himself King of Italy, and appointed his stepson Eugène de Beauharnais as viceroy, and gave his sister Élisa *(qv)* control over the newly-formed duchies of Lucca and Piombino. The Kingdom of Naples was ruled initially by his brother Joseph and later by Murat.
1809-1811	As Grand Duchess of Tuscany Élisa moved to Florence. Annexation of the Island of Elba by France.
1814-1815	Collapse of the Napoleonic Empire. The **Congress of Vienna** marked the end of the French occupation of Italy and confirmed the hegemony of Austria, which ruled the North and Centre of the country, including the Grand Duchy of Tuscany, which was returned to the House of Lorraine expanded to include the Island of Elba and the Principality of Piombino. The Duchy of Lucca was granted to the Spanish infanta, Maria Luisa of Bourbon.
	Italy was again divided and subject to the rule of absolute monarchs. An ideological movement began to develop based on a policy of liberalism combined with increasing patriotic awareness. The movement known as **Risorgimento** (from *risorgere* meaning to rise again) was originally led by a cultured elite that was greatly influenced by Romantic ideals. It was later taken over by the liberal and moderate middle classes. An initial phase of brutally-quashed revolts reached a climax in the confusion of the 1848 revolution which ended in failure. This was followed by a period of diplomacy, during which the spiritual leader and driving force was Cavour, which resulted in the unification of Italy in 1870.
1831 onwards	After a number of riots throughout Italy, the rebels banded together under **Mazzini**, whose "Young Italy" movement attracted numerous freemasons and former members of the *Carboneria*, a secret society originating in France, which spread to central and northern Italy from Naples, where it opposed Murat's regime. It was particularly successful in France, where Napoleon III was one of its followers who were known as *Carbonari*.
1848-1849	Introduction by a number of sovereigns, including the Grand Duke of Tuscany, of reforms aimed at establishing a degree of liberalism; increase in the number of rebellions.
February 1849	Republics proclaimed by Mazzini's followers in Rome and Tuscany (the latter lasting only six months) after declaring the abolition of the temporal power of the Pope and expelling Grand Duke Leopold from Florence.
	From 1850 the inflexibility of Mazzini gave way to more moderate theories advocating political solutions.
1850	Mechanisation of the textile industry in Prato.
1852	**Cavour** *entered the political limelight as President of the Council.*
1859	*Napoleon III launched a military campaign, marked by Franco-Piedmontese victories over the Austrians at Magenta and Solferino.*
1860	Decisive year for Italian unification. Unification with Piedmont of the Grand Duchy of Tuscany, the Duchy of Parma and Modena and the Duchy of Emilia and Romagna. In return for these concessions, Nice and Savoy granted to Napoleon III under the Treaty of Turin. Unification with Piedmont of southern Italy through the Expedition of the Thousand Volunteers (Red-shirts) under the command of **Garibaldi**, who landed in Sicily and Naples. Only the Papal States and Venetia unaffected by the unification process.
14 March 1861	Victor Emmanuel II of Savoy proclaimed King of Italy with its capital in Turin.
1865-1870	Capital transferred from Turin to Florence; final transfer to Rome eventually made by Piedmontese troops in 1870.

Tuscany within Unified Italy

1905	Resumption and expansion of the scheme for draining the Maremma region, which was initially launched by the Dukes of Lorraine in the 19C; resulting in the almost complete eradication of malaria.
1915-1918	*First World War*

1919	Earthquake in the Mugello region.
1929	Industrial and mining activity in Tuscany badly hit by the economic recession.
1940-1945	*Second World War*
1943	Central Italy, particularly Tuscany, became a huge battlefield disputed between the Germans in northern Italy and the Allies in southern Italy (they landed in Sicily in July). Major bombing raids on Pisa, Livorno and Grosseto, hence their modern appearance today. German bombing raid on Florence, which destroyed all the bridges except the Ponte Vecchio.
July 1944	Pisa under artillery attack, which set fire to the Camposanto.
12 August 1944	Florence liberated by the Allies.
June 1946	Italy became a Republic, with Tuscany voting massively in favour.
1948	Italy divided into 20 self-governing administrative regions, including Tuscany which is sub-divided into nine provinces – Arezzo, Florence, Grosseto, Livorno, Lucca, Massa-Carrara, Pisa, Pistoia and Siena.
1966	River Arno in flood, causing extensive damage, especially in Florence where certain works of art were damaged beyond repair.
1986	Florence voted European City of Culture.
1988	Cars banished from the centre of major cities such as Florence, Siena, Lucca and Volterra.
1992	Establishment of the Apuan Alps Natural Park following approval by the Tuscany Regional Council in 1985.
27 May 1993	Bomb attack on the Uffizi Gallery in Florence causing the destruction of three paintings and varying degrees of damage to numerous works of art.
1993	Council of Europe environmental protection award received by the Maremma Nature Reserve.
1994	Addition of the Province of Prato to the nine existing provinces.

The Ponte Vecchio during the Arno floods in 1966.

The Etruscans, Ancestors of the Tuscans

In contrast to Eastern Mediterranean countries, the development of a real civilisation occurred rather belatedly in Tuscany and indeed in Italy itself. Around the year 1000 BC, peoples from the North speaking an Indo-European language settled in what corresponds approximately to Tuscany today, in addition to the North of Latium and Umbria. These new arrivals were skilled in the use of iron, and they also cremated their dead, placing the ashes in biconical or hut-shaped clay urns which were then placed at the bottom of pits. This civilisation, which seems to have spread northwards as far as the Po Plain, was called the **Villanovan** culture and was named after a town near Bologna where it was first identified by the discovery of a necropolis.

The Etruscan culture seems to have grown up and developed out of this particular Villanovan settlement. In fact, this initial civilisation is often described as proto-Etruscan.

False Enigma of Etruscan Origins – It was long believed that the Etruscans came from Asia Minor. This, at least, was the view expressed by Herodotus, who described them as Lydians fleeing from their famine-stricken country in a mass exodus led by the king's son, Tyrrhenos. The Greeks gave them the name of *Tyrrhenoi*, and the word has survived to this day in the name of the sea on whose shores their long trek came to an end. This hypothesis is born out by the Orientalising character of their art throughout the 8C-7C BC, their religion based on divination and their language, which bore no resemblance to any of the other Indo-European languages spoken at this time in most regions of Italy but which had some similarities with Aegean dialects. Other experts, however, have found evidence of the presence of this Mediterranean tribe in the Italian peninsula long before the Indo-European invasions. The fact that the Etruscan civilisation followed in the footsteps of the Villanovian culture, often developing on the same sites, has led to suggestions that the two peoples were linked in some way.

Even if the reason for the development of the civilisation remains unclear, the explanation of a sudden mass influx of people has been dismissed, and nowadays the accent is placed first on the gradual introduction of trends in art and philosophy as a result of trading relations, especially with the East, and secondly on various ethnic groups (in-bred and foreign) which eventually flourished forming a brilliant civilisation when the moment was right.

HISTORY AND CULTURE

Etruscan Expansion – The Etruscans appeared in central Italy in the 8C BC. Their power and civilisation reached a peak in the 6C but began to fall into a decline during the following century until they were eventually absorbed by Rome.

Correctly speaking, Etruria, or as it is sometimes called, Tyrrhenian Etruria, covered the area bounded to the east by the Apennines, to the south by the Tiber and to the north by the Arno. In Rome, the west bank of the Tiber was in fact called the *ripa etrusca*. With their powerful fleet of ships, the Etruscans soon established commercial links with the East (Greece, Cyprus, Syria), Gaul, Spain and Africa (Carthage), exporting Tuscan iron and copper, and importing fabrics, jewellery, ivory and ceramics.

They sought to extend their domination southwards where, during the second half of the 7C, they occupied the Latin country, settling on the site of Rome which, for over a century, was governed by the Tarquinian dynasty of Etruscan kings. Early in the 6C they ventured into Campania, making Capua one of their main strongholds but clashing with the Greeks who had settled in southern Italy (known as Magna Graecia) and from whom they were unable to capture Cumae. In the late 6C they spread north throughout much of the Po Plain, founding Bologna (then known as Felsina), which became the main centre of Po Valley Etruria and the port of Spina (now in the Po delta, near Comacchio) from where they could control trade in the Adriatic. Their "empire" stretched as far as Corsica, of which they occupied the east coast after winning the Battle of Alalia (now Aleria) c540 BC.

It was during the 6C that Etruria reached the height of its influence and power as regards territorial expansion, trading relations, the quality of its artistic expression and the spread of its civilisation. During this period Etruria formed a federation of City States, in which each state was called a **lucumonia** from *lucumon* meaning a person exercising a priestly or regal function) that remained united on religious rather than political grounds. Their fall was, in fact, hastened by the fact that they never succeeded in combining their military might against their enemies. It is known that, in theory at least, there were 12 cities but it is difficult to know which were part of the federation since the list seems to have varied.

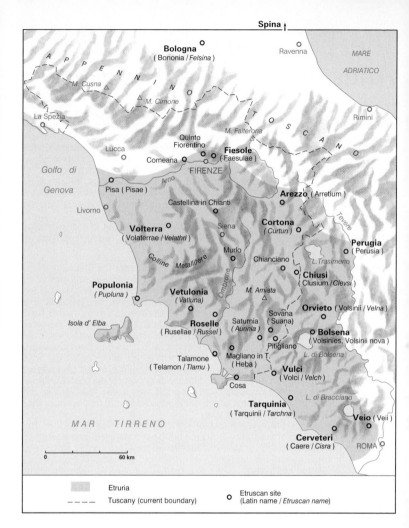

Spina ↑

Bologna (Bononia / Felsina)
Ravenna
MARE ADRIATICO

A P P E N N I N O

M. Cusna
M. Cimone

T O S C A N O

La Spezia
Rimini

M. Falterona

Quinto Fiorentino
Lucca
Fiesole (Faesulae)
Comeana
FIRENZE

Golfo di Genova

Pisa (Pisae)
Arno
Castellina in Chianti
Arezzo (Arretium)

Livorno

Siena
Cortona (Curtun)
Perugia (Perusia)

Volterra (Volaterrae / Velathri)
L. Trasimeno
Tevere

Murlo
Chianciano
Chiusi (Clusium / Clevsi)

Colline Metallifere

Populonia (Pupluna)
Vetulonia (Vatluna)
M. Amiata
Orvieto (Volsinii / Velna)

Isola d'Elba
Roselle (Rusellae / Russel)
Saturnia (Aurinia)
Sovana (Suana)
Bolsena (Volsinies, Volsinii nova)

Ombrone

Talamone (Telamon / Tlamu)
Magliano in T. (Heba)
Pitigliano
L. di Bolsena

Cosa
Vulci (Volci / Velch)

MAR TIRRENO
Tarquinia (Tarquinii / Tarchna)
L. di Bracciano

Veio (Veii)

Cerveteri (Caere / Cisra)
ROMA

0   60 km

▨ Etruria	○ Etruscan site (Latin name / Etruscan name)
- - - - Tuscany (current boundary)	

In the late 6C Tarquinius Superbus, the last Etruscan King of Rome, was driven from power and in the early 7C the Etruscans were cut off from Campania. They made a vain attempt to reach the region by sea but suffered a crushing defeat at the hands of the Greeks off Cumae. Threatened by the Celts in the North, who invaded the Po Valley in the early 4C, and in almost constant conflict with Rome, the Etruscans saw their cities fall one by one during the 3C in the face of the growing power of Rome. The fall of their religious capital Volsinii (now Orvieto in Umbria) in 265 BC marked the end of their period of independence. After submitting to the new masters of the peninsula, Etruria shared the fortunes of Rome and was granted official recognition in 90 BC.

A Healthy Economy – The spread of the Etruscan civilisation was based largely on the success of its traders who distributed the products made by its many craftsmen and farmers to destinations near and far. Etruria was not only rich in metal deposits but was also a fertile land abundantly watered by the numerous streams and rivers rising in the Apennines. The mining of ore – iron, lead, copper and tin – and the related craftwork were based mostly in northern Etruria. The southern part of the country developed an agrarian economy and the Maremma was extensively drained during this period. The two main products much prized by the Mediterranean people were olive oil and wine; the latter was a luxury beverage introduced into Gaul by the Etruscans during the 7C-6C BC. This agrarian economy made possible the accumulation of wealth, particularly in land, which permitted the introduction of Hellenistic art, through trade in craft items such as ceramics, and probably even paved the way for the arrival of Greek artists who introduced monumental painting, evidence of which can be seen in the magnificent painted tombs situated in present-day Lazio (Roman Latium).

The Etruscans – Archeological finds and Greek and Latin texts in which the Etruscan civilisation is mentioned have enabled modern specialists to define the boundaries of Etruria with a high degree of accuracy. There is, however, no known Etruscan literature. The Etruscan **language** can be read without difficulty, as the

26

Etruscans adopted the Greek alphabet in the 7C in order to facilitate trading relations, but its structure and the meaning of certain terms are obscure. It is easy to read short inscriptions but long texts remain more difficult to translate.

Life on Earth and Beyond the Grave – Although the Etruscans were excellent seafarers, a necessary talent in a trading nation, and even formidable pirates, most of them lived in inland towns. Their civilisation was based on an aristocratic society which made use of large numbers of slaves and in which women were held in high regard, an unusual feature in those times which was widely criticised by the Greeks and Romans.

Familiar scenes painted on the walls of tombs *(hypogea)* and the many everyday objects which have been uncovered during excavations, have provided an insight into daily life and beliefs. The Etruscan civilisation was cha-

Montagnola Tomb, Quinto Alto.

racterised by extreme refinement but also by great cruelty. The people took great delight in luxury, adorning themselves with jewellery and rich clothing and surrounding themselves with beautiful furniture and precious objects. They enjoyed dancing and music so much that many activities – chores or games – were carried out to the sound of a musical instrument. On the other hand it is known that funerals were occasionally accompanied by human sacrifices and it seems that some of the bloody spectacles which later became popular in Rome, such as gladiatorial combat, were inherited from Etruscan funeral rites.

Religious practices and worship of the dead played a major role in daily life. The Etruscan gods bore a strong resemblance to those of the Greeks but, in contrast to the religions of Greece and Rome, the Etruscans based their religion on revelations and filled their world with symbols, interpreting anything that went against the norm as an omen; for example lightning played a vital role in their universe. They displayed great faith in divination, through the study of animal entrails *(haruspices)* and the flight of birds *(auspices)*, practices which were later taken over and developed by the Romans. In contrast to their predecessors the Villanovians *(qv)*, whose only form of funeral rite was cremation, the Etruscans practised cremation or burial according to time and place. Like most ancient peoples, they believed in life after death for which sacrifices and offerings were required.

ETRUSCAN ART

Most of the remains that have been found are related to funerary art.

In its early phase (8C) the art form seems to have been strongly influenced by the Orient, from which it borrowed its decorative motifs. This period already provides evidence of the art forms which were characteristic of the Etruscan culture – superb goldware, bronzeware and a type of *bucchero* ceramic ware *(see below)*.

Etruscan art reached the peak of its creative excellence from the 7C to the mid 5C BC. This period saw the arrival of Greek pottery in Etruria, the construction of most of the temples, the execution of the famous paintings in Tarquinia in Lazio, and the production of the most highly-accomplished bronzeware and the finest sarcophagi. During the troubled period of the Roman conquest, Etruscan art lost its strength and character; from the 3C onwards it entered its Hellenistic phase. Under Roman rule Etruria continued to produce works of art for the next 200 years or more but they were mass-produced and, although still attractive, had none of the original vitality. Once, however, Etruscan art had been assimilated by the Romans in the 1C BC, it appeared to lose all individuality.

Etruscan art was long considered to be a mere offshoot of Greek art but as more works are discovered it has been given the acclaim it deserves – that of an art form with a very strong personality based on a fascinating combination of refinement and power, elegant stylisation and violent realism.

Town Planning and Architecture – Etruscans usually founded their urban communities on a hill near a plain watered by a river or stream so that they could farm the land. They protected their towns with huge walls such as those at Roselle *(qv)* and practised a highly-developed degree of town planning. They were remarkable technicians, excelling in bridge building and in the provision of water to towns and for the irrigation of fields.

During the reign of the three Etruscan kings who governed Rome from 616 to 509 BC, they drained the valley where the Republican Forum was subsequently built and, in addition to a number of temples, constructed the Cloaca Maxima, a sewer which is still in use.

Few Etruscan buildings have withstood the passage of time, because the materials used in their construction were relatively fragile, but a few arches and monumental gateways bonded with huge blocks of stone have survived.

The Etruscans knew how to use semicircular arches and passed on their knowledge to the Romans. Their temples were rectangular in shape and raised above ground level. A flight of steps led up to the entrance which was preceded by a colonnade. On the outskirts of the towns were vast graveyards, forming veritable cities of the dead, including streets and in some places squares. The graves were shaped like temples, houses or simple barrows. In volcanic areas they were hollowed out of the tufa cliffs.

Etruscan styles of housing were reflected in the funerary architecture, which has survived in greater quantity, and most of the available information comes from excavations on the sites of aristocratic residences, as in Murlo. Apparently the mansions were built around an atrium flanked by colonnaded porticoes, a style that was later used in Roman houses. The Etruscans also made use of the *compluvium*, a system of sloping roofs which channelled rainwater into the centre of the atrium. In some cases the roofs were decorated like the temples with huge sculptures *(see below)*.

Sculpture – Although most traces of architectural work have disappeared, the most popular art form seems to have been sculpture. Etruscan sculptors did not use marble but preferred clay, often painting it in vivid colours or adorning it with gold leaf. In most work the influence of the Ancient Greeks is obvious.

The great period of Etruscan sculpture was the 6C BC when statuary was an important element in the decoration of temples and even aristocratic residences; it is evident from the remains of the house in Murlo that the roof ridge was decorated with statuary.

Decorative plaques and friezes, ornamented with animals, banqueting scenes, and processions, were made for the same purpose, as were countless antefixes, many of them representing female heads.

Figurative sculpture gave rise to votive statues which were smaller than life-size but represented the deceased in their earthly lives – a warrior in battle, a woman washing. Busts of people are more unusual but, despite the stylised features, they are strikingly realistic owing to the intensity of the facial expressions. Large protruding eyes and enigmatic smiles are characteristic of Etruscan art. So also are the famous figures on sarcophagi, shown reclining in an attitude representative of a guest at a banquet.

The Hellenistic period in Etruscan art was marked by an increase in the number of funeral urns, miniature sarcophagi which always had a representation of the deceased on the lid. On the sides were low-relief carvings of scenes taken mainly from Greek mythology. They are outstanding for the sense of movement that they convey.

Bronzes – The Etruscans excelled in bronzework. Owing to the extensive copper deposits in Tuscany, bronzeware was a major part of the trading economy from the late 7C onwards. Etruscan bronzes, both utilitarian and merely decorative, were highly prized by the Greeks and Romans. The bronze was rolled for dishes, mirrors and fibulae but cast for votive statuettes and statues. The decorative elements were engraved or raised in relief using the *repoussé* technique.

Funerary urn (Museo Archeologico, Chiusi).

Rodolphe Corbel

Under the influence of the Orientals and Greeks, Etruscan bronzes reached perfection during the second half of the 6C and the first third of the 5C but retained some of their own specific characteristics such as the marked elongation of the outlines. The end of the 5C, when the Hellenistic influence was particularly strong, is the date of the masterpiece of animal statuary, the Chimera of Arezzo *(now in the Museo archeologico in Florence)*. Thereafter bronze sculptors turned their attention rather more to the production of monumental statues. During the Hellenistic period there was no longer an authentically Etruscan art form and the famous Arringatore *(also in the Museo archeologico in Florence)* has a somewhat dramatic realism which foreshadows Roman art.

Painting – The splendid remains of Etruscan painting were all found in the graveyards of southern Etruria, which is now in Lazio. The paintings were reserved for the wealthiest members of society and they underline the difference between the mining area of the north, where people enjoyed an average standard of living, and the richer, agricultural south. Although no examples of Etruscan art have been found in Tuscany, the paintings prove that Etruscan artists knew and mastered all the various forms of art. The paintings are also a very precious record of the everyday life and beliefs of the Etruscan people.

In the burial chambers, within the graveyards, the paintings were designed to remind the deceased of earthly pleasures such as games, entertainments, music, dancing, hunting and, more importantly, banqueting which was traditionally the main subject.

Artists used the fresco technique, applying colours – ochre, red made with iron oxides, white produced from lime, coal black and lapis-lazuli blue – on a limewash that was still wet and which "fixed" the colours.

The so-called "archaic" style (6C BC) covered a wide range of topics. During the "classical" period (first half of the 5C), an austere Attic style predominated. Its main features were banqueting scenes, almost to the exclusion of any other subject, less obvious shading, very sophisticated drawing techniques and extreme attention to detail. In the second half of the 5C and during the 4C, outlines were gradually replaced by spots of colour.

Here again, Etruscan artists showed a heightened sense of movement.

Pottery – The Etruscans showed true genius in this field, making pottery in **bucchero**, a terracotta produced from black paste which was then buffed up using a technique that is still not fully understood. Their products, most of them linked to the

Greek Ceramics

Amphorae for storing oil or wine, craters for mixing wine and water, pitchers such as the hydria for water and the oinochoe for wine, drinking vessels *(kanthari)* and other pieces of pottery sold by the Greeks throughout the Mediterranean were imported in huge quantities by the Etruscans. They were decorated with scenes in which mythology and daily life are closely linked; main characteristics vary from one period to another.

Corinthian ceramics, which were usually pale in colour and decorated with exquisite miniatures in the Oriental style constituting either a single subject or a frieze, were replaced in the 7C by **Attic** pottery produced in Athens. The decoration consisted originally of black figures set against a red background and then, from 530 BC onwards, of red figures against a glazed black background; within the figures, the lines and motifs were no longer incised but were painted on with a brush; eyes were shown facing forwards even when the face was shown in profile. By the beginning of the 5C this style had made Athens the main centre of pottery production. In the following century, in Athens and Magna Graecia, exuberant floral motifs and scrolls were painted on the glazed black background in white, yellow and dark red, surrounding a single figure.

Kantharos.

Drinking cup.

Oinochoe.

Krater with scrolled handles.

Amphora.

Hydria.

Chalice type Krater.

consumption of wine during banquets, were exported in huge quantities. They included amphorae, wine pitchers, two-handled drinking cups and goblets. Buccheroware first appeared *c*670 in Cerveteri and was initially characterised by its pure lines and total lack of decoration. Later it was decorated with motifs picked out in dotted lines. Eventually the pottery became more complex in both form and ornamentation and consisted of two types – lightly embossed *(bucchero sottile)* and heavily embossed *(bucchero pesante)*. The lightly embossed was decorated with friezes of repetitive motifs inspired by Greek bronze vases, with a similar sheen. The second group, which appeared after the 7C, had more sophisticated shapes and

was heavier. Pieces were decorated with a single figurative scene in relief. From the 5C onwards buccheroware died out and was replaced by other forms of pottery.

Greek pottery *(see below)* was enormously popular in Etruria. It was imported in huge quantities and reproduced so that it is sometimes difficult to tell which of the many craters, drinking-cups and pitchers in graves were Greek and which were produced locally. In the 5C the artists produced superb cinerary chests to contain the ashes of the deceased. Some of them were shaped like animals

Buccheroware kantharos
(Museo Archeologico, Florence).

(zoomorphic); others were shaped like human figures (anthropomorphic). All were decorated with geometric motifs reminiscent of Inca or Aztec pottery.

Gold and Silverware – Heavy jewellery, often made of gold and showing a high level of skill and sophistication, was worn by both men and women. As craftsmen, Etruscan goldsmiths were unrivalled and they perfected the delicate technique of filigrane work and granulation which had been developed at the end of the third millenium in Troy and later in Greece. The tiny grains of gold were several hundredths of a millimeter in diameter and the method used to produce them has been lost.

Via Francigena

From the late 12C to the early 15C, the economic prosperity noticeable throughout Europe was accompanied by an unprecedented development in trading relations; trade routes became of major importance, particularly the road which linked the rich economic centres on the North Sea coast, via Picardy, Champagne and Lausanne to Italy. As in the Early Middle Ages Flanders was part of France, so, in the 9C, the road was named *Via Francigena* or *Via Francesca*. In Italy it followed the route taken by the road that the Lombards had been forced to build from the 6C onwards through the heartlands of Tuscany in order to gain access to their southern duchies of Spoleta and Benevento from their capital Pavia without passing through the territories owned by Byzantium. The road crossed the Apennines through the Cisa Pass (north of Pontremoli), followed the Lunigiana Gap to Lucca, passed through the valleys of the Elsa, Arbia and Orcia. then skirted the eastern side of Mount Amiata and Lake Bolsena and continued to Rome along the ancient Via Cassia. After defeating the Lombards in 774, Charlemagne used the road to communicate with Rome. It then became a vital route for merchants and travellers and also for pilgrims making their way to the Eternal City or the Holy Land or travelling to Santiago de Compostela in Spain. On their journey they would stop at the many churches along the route; in Lucca they flocked to see the "Volto Santo" whose fame was equalled only by the number of visitors.

In the 13C the *Via Francigena,* which ran through Siena but not Florence, was joined by a second road linking the Arno Valley to the Po Plain and northern Europe.

In Search of Beauty

Although it was in Tuscany that the rich Etruscan civilisation developed, any reference to Tuscan art usually concerns the two major periods in its history – the Middle Ages (Romanesque and Gothic architecture) and, to an even greater extent, the Renaissance.

No outstanding monuments were erected in Tuscany during the **Roman period** and the visible Roman remains indicate only the Romanisation of earlier Etruscan sites or the development of Roman colonies on Tuscan soil. Some of the towns and cities have retained the outline of Roman buildings in their urban development. In Florence the narrow curving streets near Santa Croce follow the perimeter of a Roman amphitheatre and Piazza della Repubblica was laid out on the site of the Roman forum. More substantial Roman remains have been found elsewhere. Fiesole has a Roman theatre and Roman baths; Volterra has a Roman theatre; Arezzo boasts an amphitheatre, and Cosa has Roman ramparts. There are a few patrician villas along the coast – in Massaciuccoli and on the island of Giannutri – suggesting that the Romans appreciated the beauty of the Tuscany coastline.

MAIN FEATURES OF TUSCAN ART

One Region, One Guiding Principle; Three Cities, Three Trends – In Tuscany, as elsewhere in Central and Northern Italy, the Communes played a very important part in local history from the 11C onwards. Three of them – Pisa, Siena and Florence – were in conflict until the 15C when Florence, the city of the Medici, succeeded in acquiring a degree of control over the region as a whole. During this period political rivalries and subdivisions had major repercussions on the Arts. Each city developed its own forms and style, influencing only its immediate neighbourhood and nearby towns.

Pisa, fascinated by the oriental splendours brought back by its seafarers and travellers, created unusual architectural forms showing a frenetic desire for ornamentation. Alternating bands of green and white marble were combined with rows of arcading, which covered whole façades in which almost every feature was carved or inset with colour-ed marble or ceramic motifs.

Siena, on the other hand, favoured Gothic architecture and continued to prefer the delights of its lyrical gentleness throughout the 15C. Sienese architecture, painting and sculpture show a search for delicate, floral beauty imbued with a great sense of freshness. Sienese art may sometimes be rather affected but it is always lively. It may be tender or petulantly joyful but it is never austere nor dogmatic.

Gothic windows, Palazzo Salimbeni, Siena.

Although Florence also showed a liking for multi-coloured marble decoration during the Romanesque period, it was always a city of haughty rigour, of sobriety akin to austerity and of a totally intellectual perfection. In painting its natural tendencies led to transcriptions of reality, with accurate drawing and definitions of a rigorous form of perspective. The sensual nature of light and voluptuous colours, the features that bring warmth to a scene or a landscape, did not interest the artists of Florence, who differed in this respect from the Venetians. Their sole aim was to represent the truth, sublimated only to the representation of perfect beauty; this is the purpose of the famous *sfumato* technique *(qv)* of Leonardo da Vinci, which was not intended as a means of transmitting a feeling but rather as a subliminal way of muting outlines and colours in accordance with the distance between the artist and his subject.

Despite this diversity in the creative arts, Tuscany found a fundamental unity in these three trends – an intellectual view of art which appealed to the head rather than the heart, a beauty perfect in its forms and its tangible reality.

Birth of the "Universal" Artist – It was in Tuscany that this well-rounded being was born, a person who was inherently an artist, able to work in almost all art forms with the same degree of talent, a multi-faceted Humanist who, in many cases, was versed in all the disciplines of human knowledge and who was the prime mover of the Renaissance. Giotto, the artist who worked in the early 14C, was also an architect and town planner. He was followed by men such as Verrocchio, painter, sculptor and decorator; the Pollaiolo brothers, Antonio and Piero, who were painters and sculptors – Antonio was also a bronze-founder and medal-maker; Francesco di Giorgio Martini from Siena, architect, sculptor, painter, bronze-founder, decorator and engineer; Sansovino the sculptor and architect. The two most important artists were Michelangelo, sculptor, painter, architect, town planner and even poet, and Leonardo da Vinci, painter, sculptor, engraver, architect, engineer, and also musician and poet. This long list of outstanding all-rounders could also include Piero della Francesca, a remarkable painter whose research into perspective and optics led him, towards the end of his life, to write two treatises on perspective and geometry.

It was this eclecticism which led to major advances in the technical aspects of each art form. Architects were concerned with the beauty of inner volumes but were also engineers, faced with the problem of translating the physical reality into spatial terms; this is obvious in the dome designed by Brunelleschi for Florence Cathedral. Although some artists concentrated on a single art form, they were in constant contact with their colleagues and, through their mutual admiration of each other's skills, they took an interest in their respective discoveries. Masaccio, the painter who was a friend of Donatello and Brunelleschi, expressed volume with a fullness more usually found in the works of sculptors and he was the first to master the scientific aspects of perspective as taught to him by his friend the architect.

Through this exceptional blossoming of great creative personalities, the concept of the "artist" achieved reality in Tuscany, replacing the anonymous craftsman of medieval times and marking a major turning point in the history of Art.

Decoration of Walls – Walls require decoration and it was in Tuscany that the idea was first mooted of a decoration that would define the wall itself and consequently the space behind it. The uniformity of a façade in which the doors, windows and stone bonding are set within a network of static geometric lines, was defined for the first time in Florence. The same was true of the harmony of an inner courtyard, designed around the symmetry of the four façades. The staircase was removed to the interior of the building so that it no longer disturbed the unity created by the architect.

This search for symmetry in the façade of a building was soon to spread to urban planning and a monument was no longer considered in isolation; it had to harmonise with its surroundings within the space available. Because it is a prominent feature, a street corner required careful decoration, such as a loggia for trading purposes, a monumental shield or a niche. A long façade facing the street required rhythm to articulate the perspective. Squares had to be treated so as to incorporate the existing buildings into a harmonious whole; in the case of a new square, such as the central square in Pienza *(qv)*, uniformity was the desired effect.

Façades became such an obsession in Florence that numerous churches are devoid of any decorative features because of a lack of agreement on, or the necessary funding for, the final masterpiece; San Lorenzo and Santo Spirito have totally plain façades and Santa Maria del Diore and Santa Croce are fronted with 19C pastiches. Even though Tuscans, like the other people of the Mediterranean countries, tend to live outside, interiors were not neglected. Indeed in large buildings they were also seen as a decorative space. Whereas Byzantium made use of mosaics and countries in more northerly climes decorated their cathedrals with lavish stained-glass windows and their country houses and castles with tapestries, Tuscany revealed the full richness of **fresco painting**.

Technique of Fresco Painting – This technique, which takes its name from the Italian *a fresco*, involves painting a mural on a fresh coat of plaster. As the underlayer dries, it absorbs and fixes the colours, causing the surface to solidify, protecting the wall from water and changes of temperature and, therefore, from damage due to the passage of time.

The preparation of the plaster base was very important. The wall was sprinkled with water and covered with a rough base *(arricio)* consisting of one-fifth lime and four-fifths sand, the purpose of which was to ensure that the paint dried more easily and was separated from the wall. It was on this rough base that the preliminary drawing was made. As paper was uncommon and very expensive until the 15C, the underdrawing was done on the wall itself using a reddish-brown pigment called *sinopia (qv)*. In later years, when paper became more readily available, the drawing was made separately and worked up to scale on a "cartoon" on which the outlines of the drawing were marked by perforations. The cartoon was held up against the wall and the outline was transferred to the wall by passing lamp-black across the holes. The drawing could then be recreated on the wall from the black dots.

Small areas of the rough base were then covered with a thin mixture of sand and lime *(intonaco)*, in which lime predominated so that the surface crystallised when drying. This layer was smoothed and polished and remained fresh for only 6 to 7 hours. It was applied over an area known as a *giornata,* meaning a day, which corresponded to the surface that the artist could paint in that time. It could not later be touched up because it would not then have withstood the passage of time.

The *giornata*, which can be identified on some frescoes, varied in size according to the difficulty of the work. As the *intonaco* covered the original drawing, the artist had to work using the rest of the composition as a point of reference or he could again make use of the cartoon on the fresh plasterwork.

The fresco technique required painters to work swiftly, with a sure hand and eye, and imposed two other disciplines. The work produced was the final version and the detail had to be painted without the artist having an overall view of the work. The work could not be done in the order which suited the artist, because frescoes had to be painted from top to bottom lest the painting of the *giornata* spoiled the area painted on the previous days.

The fresco technique could be used to cover the entire surface of a wall and also the vaulting or ceiling above. There are countless examples of frescoes, especially in churches – in Florence in the chancel of Santa Maria Novella, the Brancacci Chapel in Santa Maria del Carmine, in the convent refectories *(qv)* or the cells of San Marco; in Arezzo in the chancel of San Francesco; in San Gimignano in the nave and aisles of the collegiate church and the chancel of Sant'Agostino; in Pisa in the Camposanto and also in the cloisters of Monte Oliveto Maggiore. Fresco painting was also used as a decoration in public buildings, such as the Palazzo Pubblico in Siena, and in private residences like the Palazzo Medici in Florence (Chapel of the Magi) or the Palazzo Davanzati, where the ornamentation is less lavish. By using this technique, the Tuscans showed that walls should be seen in their entirety rather than decorated with a single, isolated piece of ornamentation. The same principle is being applied in the decoration of the pavement in Siena Cathedral, which consists of a set of tableaux in marble, or of the Princes' Chapel in San Lorenzo in Florence, where the floor, walls and ceiling are all decorated with coloured marble.

THE MIDDLE AGES

In the 11C and 12C, a period marked by the beginnings of trade, the countryside of Tuscany took on a different appearance. Economic changes and the relative prosperity that followed led to the building of numerous churches. Most of them were fairly modest affairs, a parish church *(pieva)* built even in the most isolated places, such as the Garfagnana, Lunigiana, Casentino or Pratomagno regions but all testify to the importance of Romanesque art and architecture in Tuscany where it was more ornate and more widespread than elsewhere in Italy. The Middle Ages, between the 11C and 14C, also saw the establishment of many monasteries belonging to traditional Orders, such as the Benedictines or Cistercians, and some belonging to the new Mendicant Orders, such as the Dominicans and Franciscans. The first Franciscan communities were founded in the neighbouring region of Umbria (east) and two of their monasteries in Tuscany were set up by St Francis himself – Le Celle *(qv)* near Cortona and La Verna *(qv)* east of Florence. There were also several new Orders which came into being in Tuscany itself – the Vallombrosans and the Hermit Monks of Camaldoli in the 11C, the Servites, an Order founded on Monte Senario, in the 13C and the Olivetan Order founded on Monte Oliveto Maggiore in the 14C.

The spate of building in the countryside meant that the hilltops were soon occupied by small towns encircled by walls or with fortresses or castles, such as Monteriggioni, Montalcino or Radicofani; more fortresses were built in the Orcia Valley – Montecchio, Poppi etc.

In the towns, cathedrals and a large number of churches were built (or rebuilt), including new Franciscan friaries and Dominican monasteries. The aristocracy began to build houses with overhanging upper storeys and tower-houses. Street corners were enhanced with loggias used for trading activities and, to counterbalance the religious power of the church, an administrative building was erected in the town centre *(palazzo comunale* or *palazzo del podestà)*.

Romanesque Religious Architecture

Except in Pisa, which is a special case, the main feature of Romanesque architecture was its simplicity. The materials used were brick, timber and local stone, often only roughly shaped. The buildings were modest in size – a *pieve* is, by definition, a small parish church designed for the people. The layout was simple. The basilica design dating from the Paleo-Christian era remained as popular here as elsewhere in Italy and the nave, sometimes flanked by aisles, extended into a single or sometimes a triple apse, often without a projecting transept. The roof also was plain, the rafters being visible in most of the churches. The colours provided little contrast, a harmonious blend of brown, pale yellow or grey stonework unbroken by the vivid brilliance of a stained-glass window. In most cases the window openings were screened by a sheet of alabaster or marble which let in only a pale, eerie light.

External Influences – Apart from the traditional **Paleo-Christian** elements that could be seen throughout Italy – basilica-type layout, rafters, a separate belltower or none at all – Tuscan architecture made use of elements from Burgundy, owing to the influence from the end of the 10C onwards of the Benedictine Abbey of Cluny, and from Lombardy, where the large cities had their own style of architecture.

The **Burgundian influence** led first to the inclusion of a crypt, in continuation of a custom already established in the Paleo-Christian era. Crypts can be seen in the Benedictine monasteries of the day – San Salvatore on Mount Amiata, Farneta Abbey or San Miniato in Florence. The use of the Latin Cross design was also common to Benedictine buildings – San Salvatore, Farneta, San Bruzio near Magliano. In Sant'Antimo, which was a Cistercian monastery, the influence of Cluny is obvious in the radiating chancel chapels, the marked difference in height between the nave and the aisles, and in some of the carvings such as the narrative capitals. As the influence of Benedictine monastic life was generally limited in Tuscany, owing to reservations on the part of the bishops and, more cogently, to the founding in Tuscany of austere religious communities – the Vallombrosans and the Congregation of Camaldoli – which required strict obedience to the Rule of St Benedict, so its effect on architecture was equally restrained.

The **Lombard style** is evident in certain architectural features in Tuscany such as arched friezes on the upper sections of buildings and on belltowers, pilaster strips, niches (San Piero a Grado, Sant'Antimo, Gropina, Sant'Appiano in the Chianti region, the parish church in Artimino), the use of single, sometimes clustered, pillars (San Donato in Poggio, San Quirico in Orcia, Sovana, Lucca Cathedral porch), pillars alternating with columns (Sant'Antimo, Gropina, Santa Maria della Pieve in Arezzo), splayed entrances (San Quirico in Orcia, Satreano, Pieve di Corsignano), and even the presence of a lantern-tower above the dome over the transept crossing (Asciano). There was also a more general use of **trans-Alpine** features which spread along the Via Francigena *(qv)* and were to be seen more particularly in southern Tuscany – details such as the use of multifoiled oculi, toothed arching, the exceptional use in Sovana Cathedral of quadripartite vaulting, despite the absence of any other Gothic feature, and the appearance of a non load-bearing arch combined with roof rafters in San Miniato al Monte.

From the second half of the 11C onwards these foreign influences began to wane in the face of the increasing popularity of local designs that showed a high degree of inventiveness.

Façade of San Michele in Lucca (detail).

Pisan Romanesque Style – Through their contacts with Christians in the Middle East and their knowledge of Islamic art forms, the Pisans developed a highly-ornate style that reached its peak in Piazza dei Miracoli where the baptistery, cathedral, belltower (the Leaning Tower) and Camposanto are laid out like a theatrical stage set.

The stylistic elements, which were most characteristic of the cathedral designed by the architect Buscheto and which enjoyed enormous success in areas subjected to Pisan influence, were the green and white striped marble façades with their blind arcading and the open-work galleries and the inset diamond-shaped decoration on the main façades, the use of a colonnade to separate the nave and aisles and the general use externally and internally of elevated arches.

These features can all be seen, to a greater or lesser extent, in the Pistoia and Prato districts, in and around Lucca, in the dioceses of Volterra and Massa Marittima and as far south as Siena and its neighbourhood; Siena Cathedral, which is decorated with alternating bands of coloured marble, was begun in the Romanesque period.

Florentine Romanesque Architecture – The two main examples of this style, which was prevalent in Florence from the 11C to the 13C, are the Baptistery and the church of San Miniato al Monte in Florence. Both were strongly marked by the Paleo-Christian tradition and both are outstanding for their classical design, pure volumes and rigorous geometric structure and decoration. Their façades consist of smooth white marble inset with linear motifs in coloured marble. This style was used again in a building only in the Badia in Fiesole and in the church in Empoli but it was used in the decoration of religious furnishings such as ambos, fonts and pulpits including the one in San Giovanni Maggiore (near Scarperia). The rational structural geometry of these buildings, which consisted of nothing more than simple volumes, can however be seen in churches in areas under Florentine control, such as San Donato in Poggio.

Gothic Architecture

Gothic architecture first appeared in urban centres in the 13C but in a very basic and modest form compared to its equivalent north of the Alps.

Religious Architecture – The Gothic style came from the countries of northern Europe and met with very little success in Italy because it was seen as a form of political submission to the German Emperor and was therefore referred to scathingly as "of the Goths" *(gotico)*. The style was introduced by the Cistercians, as is obvious in the abbey of San Galgano, and was then adopted by the Franciscans, after the building of the basilica in Assisi, and later by the Dominicans. During the 13C and 14C both these Orders built churches in the urban centres so that they could continue their work as preachers. Pointed and ogive arches enabled them to erect more spacious buildings, which in many instances had a single nave – San Domenico and San Francesco in Siena – so that even the poorest members of the congregation could see everything that was going on in the House of God which was to be open to all and devoid of mystery. In most of the other religious buildings of the time, the Gothic style affected only the decoration and not the structure; in Pisa the Gothic lancet windows (15C) in the Camposanto are framed by tall semicircular arches and Santa Maria della Spina is a gem of stone-cutting, full of gables, pinnacles and niches. It is, however, in Florence and Siena that the major buildings from this period are to be found.

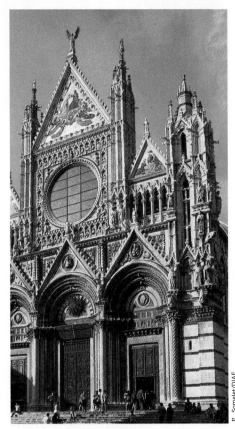

Siena Cathedral was started in the 13C as a Romanesque church with nave and aisles, semicircular arches, black and white striped façades in the Pisan style, and a dome on squinches. In 1284 Giovanni Pisano remodelled the façade in the Gothic style with deep doorways beneath gables, towers with piers and pinnacles, and a plethora of sculptures and coloured decoration – mosaics and marble insets. In the 14C, when the apse was extended above street level and supported on ogive arches, a baptistery dedicated to John the Baptist (San Giovanni) was built underneath. From 1339 onwards a project was launched to enlarge the cathedral, in which the older building would have become the transept of the new one, which would have been the largest Gothic building in Tuscany if the work had been completed *(see SIENA)*. The vast size of the project explains the extreme simplicity of the churches belonging to the Mendicant Orders in Siena; all the effort went into the cathedral to the detriment of any other work.

In **Florence**, on the other hand, it was the Dominican monastery of Santa Maria Novella

West Front of Siena Cathedral.

which marked the introduction of the Gothic style in the last quarter of the 13C. The vast church, with nave and aisles roofed with ogive vaulting, was laid out like a basilica with a flat east end. Shortly afterwards, the Franciscans built a church, Santa Croce, in which the nave was separated from the aisles by great ribbed arches although the roof still consisted of the traditional Paleo-Christian rafters.

The most unusual building is the Cathedral of Santa Maria del Fiore in which the nave and aisles are almost of the same height. Its main features are its powerful design and its simplicity, and the obvious determination to create a vast interior devoid of luxury. It is the horizontal lines, rather than the vertical, that are emphasised although verticality was a dominant feature of Gothic architecture. The same principle is at work in the interior of Santa Maria Novella, which is decorated with horizontal bands, and in Santa Croce, where a gallery along the upper section of the wall breaks the vertical lines. In Florence therefore Gothic architecture was revised and adapted to suit a rational and modest feeling which does not easily express itself in a profusion of slender decorative features.

SCALA

Interior of Santa Croce, Florence.

Lay Architecture – Unlike the churches and cathedrals, lay architecture was more open to the Gothic influence.

The Palazzo Vecchio in Florence, which has all the austerity of a fortress in its almost windowless lower section, has an upper section decorated with double windows, machicolations, crenellations and a fine projecting tower. Its example was followed by the Bargello, which also has a tower.

In Siena the Palazzo del Populo consists of a central section flanked by two lower sections. Its many windows give it a lightness echoed in the tall Mangia Tower.

All over Tuscany are other Palazzi – del Populo or del Podestà – decorated with crenellations and mansions built for wealthy patricians with delightful double or tripartite bays. It was also during this period – the 13C and 14C – that towns such as Siena, San Gimignano, Volterra, Cortona and Arezzo acquired the appearance they have retained to this day.

Medieval Painting and Sculpture

Painting – Tuscan painting had strong links with Greek and Byzantine art. During the 12C a new trend developed, in Pisa and Lucca, of displaying a Crucifix in the sanctuary or in the transept crossing. There were two types of Crucifix. One showed Christ in Triumph, a hieratic and serene representation; the other depicted the Passion of Christ, his body twisted and contorted with pain. An example of the former is the Crucifix by **Berlinghieri** painted for Lucca Cathedral c1220-1230. The latter type was promoted by **Giunta Pisano**, who began to emphasise the pathos of Christ's passion in the 1240's, and by the success of the sermons preached by the Franciscans, whose leader died in 1226.

Giunta adapted the Greco-Byzantine style to suit the new form of iconography, whereas **Margaritone of Arezzo** developed a degree of sensitivity and gentleness in his works, especially in the representation of St Francis himself. This trend towards Greek-style icons died out when the artists working on the decoration of the interior of the baptistery in Florence expressed their skills in mosaics. **Cimabue**, who had worked on the enormous basilica in Assisi at the end of the 13C, showed a new approach within the traditional Byzantine forms. He succeeded in giving his figures an expressiveness that could not fail to move the congregation and induce feelings of tenderness. In addition to several Crucifixes, he painted many *Maestà* – paintings of the Madonna and Child seated on a throne and often surrounded by angels and saints – a subject which, through its tenderness, was characteristic of artistic creativity in Florence and Siena.

SCALA

Maestà by Duccio (Museo dell'Opera Metropolitana, Siena).

Giotto also painted *Maestà* as did **Duccio di Buoninsegna** in Siena. The Sienese School *(see SIENA)* in which the leading figures in the 14C were Simone Martini and the Lorenzetti brothers, played a vital role in the **international Gothic style,** that is the most decorative, refined and florid trend of the Late Gothic period, which also developed in Paris, Avignon and Prague.

Sculpture - A number of works produced in Pisa in the mid-13C had a very real importance for medieval sculpture in Tuscany and even in Italy as a whole. There were promising beginnings - the ambo made by **Guglielmo** (12C) for Pisa Cathedral *(now in Cagliari; see Pisa: Museo dell'opera del duomo)* and works that revealed the Lombard influence such as the anonymous figure of *St Martin* on the west front of Lucca Cathedral (13C).

The real initiator of the new trend was **Nicola Pisano** who carved the pulpit for the baptistery in Pisa in 1260. His powerful style combined Romanesque lions supporting the columns of the pulpit with Gothic trefoiled arches and low reliefs which were copies of Classical architecture. In the pulpit for Siena Cathedral carved by him between 1266 and 1268, he turned resolutely towards the Gothic style.

From then on this type of furnishing became increasingly commonplace throughout Tuscany. In Pistoia in 1270 **Fra Guglielmo** carved the pulpit in San Giovanni Fuorcivitas, which is set against a wall, and **Giovanni Pisano,** Nicola's son, carved the hexagonal pulpit for Sant'Andrea in 1301. Giovanni Pisano also worked on the façade of Siena Cathedral and on the chancel in Massa Marittima Cathedral and in Prato Cathedral, and he carved the huge pulpit (1302-1312) supported on ten columns and a central pillar for Pisa Cathedral. His pupils included Goro di Gregorio, who made a name for himself with the sarcophagus of St Cerbone in Massa Marittima Cathedral, but the best known of all was **Tino da Camaino** from Siena who carved the tomb of Henry VII of Luxemburg *(now in the Museo dell'opera del duomo in Pisa).*

The next generation continued to work in a style that was more and more detached from architecture, so that sculptors acquired greater finesse in their use of the chisel and relied less on an impression of strength and force. In Florence **Andrea da Pontedera,** better known as **Pisano,** created the first of the three bronze doors of the Baptistery (1336) and **Orcagna** carved the Orsanmichele tabernacle (1352-1359).

37

RENAISSANCE

During the days of the Communes, the Arts flourished in all the politically-strong towns and cities in Tuscany. In the 15C, however, the beginning of Florentine domination in the region led to a centralisation of artistic development in the city of the Medici *(see the introduction on Art in the chapter on Firenze)*. It is true that this blossoming in the Arts was encouraged by a very special social climate. The city's economic and financial prosperity, the patronage of its aristocracy and the development of intellectual and philosophical thought all coincided at a time when ancient ruins were being discovered in Rome; the ruins in Greece were not discovered until the 18C. From then on the influence of the Ancient Roman civilisation was seen in every field of art and knowledge, leading to what was known as the **Renaissance** – a taste for Classical rather than Gothic aesthetics, a preference for mythology and lay subjects rather than only the religious, and for tangible and mathematically-measurable reality rather than symbolism. This change in aesthetic values in Florence soon embraced the entire region, before spreading to the rest of Italy and Europe. Many Florentine artists worked outside the city and a few quite outstanding figures were born within the Florence area and developed their artistic skills within the ambit of the city.

Architecture – Brunelleschi made various trips to Rome to study the Ancient Roman remains and to gain an insight into Classical art and architecture. His career was based solely in Florence where he revolutionised every feature of architecture *(see Firenze)*. The Old Sacristy in San Lorenzo (designed 1421-1428) and the Pazzi Chapel in Santa Croce (designed *c*1430) had a major impact because their design was centred on the transept and they were surmounted by a dome. A number of churches followed their example and were laid out like a Greek Cross – in the 15C Santa Maria delle Carceri in Prato, which was begun in 1485 and designed by Guiliano da Sangallo, and Santa Maria del Calcinaio in Cortona, designed by Francesco di Giorgio Martini from Siena; the interior structure of both these churches is enhanced by the Brunelleschi-like use of *pietra serena* which contrasts with the white wall; in the 16C San Biagio in Montepulciano, built from 1518 to 1545 by da Sangallo the Elder (Guiliano's brother), and Santa Maria Nuova in Cortona designed by Vasari.

In the field of **lay architecture**, this period saw the building of **mansions** in towns and cities and **villas** in the country. Michelozzo (1396-1472), who designed the Palazzo Medici in Florence, also converted the family's feudal residences in Trebbio and Cafaggiolo into villas. He worked in Pistoia, Montepulciano and Volterra. Guiliano da Sangallo (*c*1443-1516) designed the Medici villa in Poggio a Caiano, which in its day was the only villa to be surrounded by a garden and park. The ground floor was surrounded on four sides by a portico and the main entrance was embellished with a central portico capped by a pediment, like an Ancient Roman temple. This was the first majestic country villa *(see the chapter on Tuscan Villas)*.

During this period some of the towns and cities acquired their own specific character. Florence, of course, owes much to the 15C, during which it grew in size and many new buildings were erected. Pienza *(qv)* was the setting for the first modern town planning project (1459) designed by Bernardo Rossellino (1409-1464), who worked with Alberti on the Palazzo Rucellai in Florence; the central square was flanked by the cathedral, the bishop's palace, the patron's palace, the

Medici Villa, Poggio a Caiano.

People's Palace and a huge well. In Montepulciano the town was renovated and given a Renaissance character by Michelozzo, Antonio da Sangallo and Vignola. The finest buildings in the main street of Monte San Savino are the work of Sansovino, a brilliant architect who was born in the town, as his pseudonym suggests.

Sculpture and Painting – An impressive number of artists working in these two fields came from Florence *(see Firenze)* but in the 15C the whole Tuscan region became involved in the Renaissance movement. Although Siena followed its own course until the 16C, it was the birthplace of **Jacopo della Quercia** (1374-1438), the inventive sculptor who created, among other works, the tomb of Ilaria del Carretto in Lucca and the Fonte Gaia in Piazza del Campo in Siena. **Francesco di Giorgio Martini** (1439-1502), painter, sculptor and architect, was born in Siena, although his main architectural works are in Urbino and in Pesaro in the Marches; **Baldassare Peruzzi** (1481-1536), who spent most of his career in Rome, was also a native of Siena.

R. Leslie

Tomb of Ilaria del Carretto by Jacopo della Quercia in Lucca Cathedral.

Arezzo and Cortona were the birthplaces of two very great painters – **Piero della Francesca** (1416-1492), who worked on the fresco cycle in the church of San Francesco *(see Arezzo)* and one of his pupils, **Signorelli** (1450-1523), whose drawing techniques were powerful and incisive and who created most of the decoration in the cloisters in Monte Oliveto Maggiore *(qv)*. Filippino Lippi was born in Prato where his father, Fra Filippo Lippi, had painted the frescoes in the cathedral. Lucca was the birthplace of **Matteo Civitali** (1436-1501), sculptor and architect who worked on St Voult's Chapel in Lucca Cathedral, in the manner of Alberti.

MODERN TIMES

In the 15C a few Florentine artists left the city and began to work elsewhere in Tuscany; Benozzo Gozzoli worked on the cathedral in San Gimignano and on the Camposanto in Pisa; others including Donatello, Verrocchio and Alberti even moved to neighbouring regions such as Umbria, the Marches, Lombardy and Venetia. In the 16C the movement away from the city gathered pace. Because Florence had lost its political importance, the entire region suffered as artists moved to the new artistic centres of the day. Raphael, Michelangelo, Filippino Lippi, Giuliano and Antonio da Sangallo, Peruzzi, Cellini and others went to Rome, Leonardo da Vinci to Lombardy initially, Sangallo the Younger and Sansovino to Venetia and Leonardo da Vinci, Cellini and Rosso Fiorentino to France.

In the centuries that followed, Tuscany seemed to be exhausted and provided very little in the way of new talent or artistic trends. The end of the 19C was, however, marked by the Florentine Verist movement of the **Macchiaioli** *(qv)*, who can be compared with the French Impressionists, and the 20C produced **Amedeo Modigliani**, a native of Livorno, who was famous for his involvement in the Paris School, and **Marino Marini** *(qv)*, the Florentine painter and sculptor.

In the 19C the golden age of Tuscany was rediscovered and its spontaneity, freshness and search for an ideal were promoted by the German **Nazareans**, a group whose Bohemian lifestyle caused the Florentines to give them their nickname, who wandered aimlessly in and around Florence, poorly-dressed and sleeping rough. There were also the English **Pre-Raphaelites** – such as Rossetti or Burne-Jones – who showed a marked preference for the Italian Primitives dating from the period before Raphael, hence their name. They looked on these early artists as great masters whose style was to be imitated in order to breathe new life into the world of painting.

Tuscan Villas

The villas, set in the middle of gardens, date mainly from the Renaissance period and were once aristocratic residences. They were purchased or built by the members of such prestigious families as the Medici, Rospigliosi, Chigi or Ricasoli, and provided a retreat during the hot summer days from the stifling heat of the cities – Florence, Pistoia, Lucca, Siena – where the families spent the rest of the year. Most of them are fairly simply and rigorously designed and all had huge gardens, some of them magnificently laid out. They regained popularity in the 17C when many were extended or given lavish interior decoration in the form of frescoes, at least in the reception rooms. The plainest villas are to be found in the countryside round Florence where some still have their medieval structure. Around Lucca, on the other hand, in the 17C the façades were embellished with loggias and wide bays, sculptures and balustrades. In the Siena district, in addition to the medieval castles, there are villas that blend into the countryside, underlining their simple design by the use of natural materials such as undressed brick and stone.

★ **Villa d'Artimino** – One of the Medici villas. *See Artimino.*

★★ **Brolio Castle** – *See Chianti – Tour no 3.*

★ **Villa de Castello** – One of the Medici villas. *See Castello.*

★ **Villa de Cafaggiolo** – *Not open to the public.* One of the Medici villas. *See Mugello.*

★ **Villa de Cerreto Guidi** – One of the Medici villas. *See Cerreto Guidi.*

★ **Villa de Cetinale** ⊘ – *West of Siena, not far from Sovicille, among the houses in the small town.* Built in the late 17C by Carlo Fontana for Cardinal Flavio Chigi. From the rear, there is a long view up to a small hermitage perched on the hilltop.

★ **Villa Chigi de Castelnuovo Berardenga** – *See Chianti – Tour no 3.*

Villa Contri di Mezzaratta – *See Settignano.*

Villa Demidoff (or Villa de Pratolino) – Former Medici villa and **Park★**. *See Firenze – Excursions.*

★★ **Villa Garzoni** – *See Collodi.*

Villa Gamberaia – Gardens★ *(see Settignano).*

Villa Mansi – *See Lucca – Excursions.*

★ **Meleto Castle** – *See Chianti – Tour no 3.*

★ **Villa de la Petraia** – One of the Medici villas. *See Castello.*

★★ **Villa de Poggio a Caiano** – One of the Medici villas. *See Poggio a Caiano.*

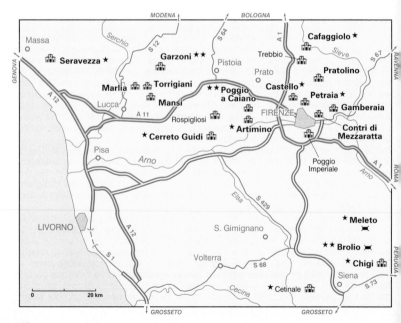

Villa de Poggio Imperiale ⊙ – *Near the Pitti Palace on the south side of Florence*. One of the Medici villas. 15C fortified house with extensive alterations and extensions dating from the days of the Medici and the Dukes of Lorraine. Neo-Classical façade. 17C frescoes.

Villa de Pratolino – See Demidoff *(above)*.

Villa Reale de Marlia – *See Lucca - Excursions*.

Villa Rospigliosi in Lamporecchio ⊙ – *South of Pistoia on Monte Albano*. 15C villa rebuilt in the 17C to plans by Bernini at the request of Pope Clement IX Rospigliosi. Ovoid reception room with trompe-l'oeil paintings.

★ **Villa de Seravezza** – *See Versilia - Tour no 2*.

Villa Torrigiani – *See Lucca - Excursions*.

Villa del Trebbio ⊙ – One of the Medici villas. Former 14C castle turned into a villa in the 15C by Michelozzo at the request of Cosimo the Elder. It has retained its 15C character.

In Italian the following terms are used for the centuries between the 13C and the 20C

Duecento	*1200s*	*13C*
Trecento	*1300s*	*14C*
Quattrocento	*1400s*	*15C*
Cinquecento	*1500s*	*16C*
Seicento	*1600s*	*17C*
Settecento	*1700s*	*18C*
Ottocento	*1800s*	*19C*
Novecento	*1900s*	*20C*

Artistic and architectural terms

(Duomo: words in blue print are Italian)

Altarpiece: a large painting adorning an altar.
Ambo: small pulpit at the entrance to the chancel from which the Gospel or Epistle were read.
Ambulatory: extension of the aisles around the chancel for processional purposes.
Apse: semicircular or polygonal end of a church, behind the altar; the outer section is known as the chevet.
Apsidal chapel: small chapel projecting from the apse.
Archivolt: arch moulding over an arcade or upper section of a doorway.
Barrel vaulting: a vault produced by a continuous semi-circular arch.
Bay: the area between two supporting columns or pillars.
Bond: size and arrangement of brickwork used in the construction of a building.
Bucchero: Etruscan pottery, black and shiny in colour.
Cappella: chapel.
Ciborium: a baldaquin over an altar.
Corinthian: *see Order*.
Cornice: projecting section along the top of a wall.
Cortile: interior courtyard of a palace.
Diaphragm arch: transversal arch used to relieve side walls.
Diptych: *see Polyptych*.
Doric: *see Order*.
Duomo = cathedral.
Ecce Homo: an illustration of Jesus wearing the crown of thorns from the Latin for "Behold the Man" (John 19, 5).
Entablature: in certain buildings, the section over the top of a colonnade consisting of three parts: the architrave (flat section resting on the abaci of the capitals of a colonnade), the frieze (decorated with carvings) and the cornice (projecting top section).
Fresco: mural painting applied over a fresh undercoat of plaster.
Gable: triangular part of an end wall carrying a sloping roof; the term is also applied to the steeply-pitched ornamental pediments of Gothic architecture.
Greek cross: a cross with four arms of equal length (in contrast to the **Latin cross** which has one arm longer than the other three).
Ionic: *see Order*.
Jambs: pillars flanking a doorway and supporting the arch above.

Lesena: *see Lombard bands.*

Lintel: horizontal cross-beam above a window or door supporting the weight of the wall.

Lombard bands: decorative band of pilasters joined at the top by an arched frieze.

Low relief: bas-relief, carved figures slightly projecting from their background.

Maestà: Madonna in majesty, generally seated on a throne holding the Infant Jesus in her arms.

Mascaron: a medallion carved in the form of a human head.

Merlon: part of a crowning parapet between two crenellations.

Modillion: small console supporting a cornice.

Narthex: interior vestibule of a church.

Nave: the area between the entrance and chancel of a church, with or without aisles.

Oculus: round window.

Order: system in Classical architecture ensuring a unity of style characterised by its columns (base, shaft, capital) and entablature. The orders used in Tuscany are: Doric (capitals with mouldings – the Tuscan Doric order is a simplified version of this), Ionic (capitals with volutes), Corinthian (capitals with acanthus leaves) and the Composite, derived from the Corinthian but more complex.

Overhang: overhanging or corbelled upper storey.

Pala: Italian term for altarpiece or reredos.

Palazzo: a town house usually belonging to the head of a noble family; the word derives from the Palatine Hill in Rome where the Ceasars had their residences and came to mean the official residence of a person in authority.

Pediment: ornament in Classical architecture (usually triangular or semi-circular) above a door or window.

Piano nobile: the principal floor of a palazzo raised one storey above ground level.

Pietà: Lamenting Virgin with the dead Christ.

Pietra serena: blue-grey stone from the quarries north of Florence.

Pieve: Romanesque parish church.

Pilaster: engaged rectangular column.

Pinnacle: vertical top section of a buttress adding to its weight.

Polyptych: a painted or carved work consisting of more than three folding leaves or panels (diptych: 2 panels; triptych: 3 panels).

Portico: covered gallery with vaulting supported by columns.

Predella: base of an altarpiece, divided into small panels.

Presbiterio: the chancel or sanctuary of a church.

Pulpit: an elevated dais from which sermons were preached in the nave of a church. It is often carved and surmounted by a sounding board.

Pulpitum: front section of the stage in an antique theatre.

Rustication: deliberately rough texture of dressed stone.

Scroll: *see Volute.*

Sfumato: atmospheric impression of perspective (invented by Leonardo da Vinci), in which outlines and backgrounds are blurred in a light haze.

Sinopia: underdrawing, *see Pisa, Museo della Sinopia.*

Squinch: the projecting part of a vault supporting the vertical thrust of an overhanging section in each corner of a square tower: the four corner squinches allow for the transition from square to octagon.

Stele: a Greek word *(stela* in Latin) meaning an upright block (1.50m – 5ft high) of marble or stone used as a tombstone and carved in low relief.

Tempera: a painting technique in which pigments are ground down and bound usually by means of an egg-based preparation. The technique was replaced by oil.

Transept crossing: area at the intersection of the transept and nave.

Transverse arch: arch perpendicular to the aisles.

Triptych: *see polyptych.*

Tunnel vaulting: *see barrel vaulting.*

Tympanum: the section above a door (or window) between the lintel and archivolt.

Volute: architectural ornament in the form of a spiral scroll.

From Philosophy To Writing

Early writing – Tuscany has made a vital contribution to the Italian language and literature. In the Middle Ages Latin was the only written language and there was no literature in the vernacular. The appearance of poetry written in the Tuscan dialect was the first, and earliest, example of an attempt to preserve one of the many dialects spoken in the Italian peninsula and was the first step which ensured that it became the language of Italy as a whole.

From the 13C onwards various literary trends co-existed side by side. There was the allegorical, didactic style influenced by the *Roman de la Rose* and followed by Dante's teacher, **Brunetto Latini** (*c*1220-1295). There were burlesque chronicles like those produced by **Cecco Angiolieri** (*c*1260-c1312) from Siena whose sonnets are a celebration of wine, gaming, women and money. There was also lyric verse inspired by the poetry of Sicily and Provence of which the greatest exponent was **Guittone d'Arezzo** (*c*1235-1294).

The most famous of all the schools of poetry during the 13C was the one that used what Dante called the **gentle new style** *(dolce stil nuovo)*. The main poets in this movement, who opposed the earlier tradition by singing of platonic and spiritual love in verse, were **Guinizzelli** (*c*1235-1276), **Cavalcanti** (*c*1255-1300), who was a Guelf and was immortalised in the *Inferno* in the *Divine Comedy* (Song X, 52 et seq.), and Dante himself.

Three Great Writers – In *De vulgari eloquentia*, which was written in Latin, **Dante Alighieri** (1265-1321) proposed the theory of literature written in the vernacular for the first time. He also used his writings to express his political convictions *(De Monarchia)* and his philosophical ideas *(Il Convivio)*. Much of his poetry was inspired by Beatrice Portinari whom he met when she was ten years old and for whom he proclaimed his platonic love, even after her death at the age of 24. She was the inspiration for *Vita Nova,* through which he linked himself to the *Dolce Stil Nuovo* and in which he described womankind as the repository of all virtue and a sort of intermediary between Man and God. His masterpiece, the *Divine Comedy,* is an allegorical poem describing his journey beyond the grave. Guided by Virgil in Hell, which is a huge abyss created by the expulsion of Lucifer from Heaven for all eternity, and in Purgatory, a mountain created while the pit of hell was being dug, and by Beatrice in Paradise, which consists of nine concentric spheres controlled by God. Dante meets many dead people, some damned and some among the chosen. Their sufferings or joys are proportionate to their behaviour during their time on Earth. It is a racy review of human nature, based on medieval imagery, and also an interesting source of historical detail. Dante, a supporter of the White Guelf faction *(qv),* played an active part in the politics of Florence and was appointed prior in 1300. In 1302 he was forced into exile by his opponents, the Black Guelfs, and spent the remainder of his life travelling throughout Italy until he died in Ravenna.

The two other great writers, who with Dante were instrumental in laying the foundations of the Italian language, were **Boccaccio** (1313-1375), who was born in

Dante reciting the Divine Comedy to the city of Florence (Florence Cathedral).

Certaldo *(qv)*, the amazing storyteller of the **Decameron** whose style is sometimes almost modern, and his friend **Petrarch** (Francesco Petrarca, 1304-1374), who was born in Arezzo, the herald of Humanism and the greatest of Italian lyric poets. During his youth, spent at the papal Court in Avignon, he met Laura, traditionally said to have been Laura de Noves, the ideal subject of his love whom he was to immortalise in his melancholic sonnets, published collectively as **Canzoniere** ; they reveal a deep introspection described with virtuosity, stylistic elegance and refinement. Petrarch was a diplomat and a traveller, employed in turn by the Pope and the great noblemen of Italy. He was crowned Prince of Poets on the Capitol in Rome.

The *Libro dell'arte,* produced during the 14C, though not great literature, is extremely important in the history of art as it is a manual for painters on the techniques of the period, particularly frescoes, and has been used by many generations of artists. The author was **Cennino Cennini**, a painter, but none of his paintings has survived.

The Renaissance – The 15C was a period overflowing with new ideas. In Italy it was marked by renewed interest in Greek and Latin culture and by the birth of Humanism which exalted the human spirit. Florence played a leading role through the patronage of **Lorenzo the Magnificent** who occasionally wrote poetry and surrounded himself with philosophers such as Giovanni Pico della Mirandola and poets such as **Poliziano** who was born in Montepulciano. Artists also turned their talents to writing; **Alberti** and **Leonardo da Vinci** both wrote treatises and composed poetry. The 15C was also marked by the preaching of **St Bernard of Siena** (1380-1444) and **Savonarola** (1452-1498).

The early 16C, a time of political upheaval, inspired **Niccolò Machiavelli** (1469-1527), a statesman and pioneer of Italian unity, to write *Il Principe (The Prince)*, an essay on politics and the exercise of power dedicated to Lorenzo II, grandson of Lorenzo the Magnificent, but strongly inspired by the character of Caesar Borgia. His realism, which has given rise to the term Macchiavellian , wrongly used as a synonym for cunning and deceitful, was echoed by **Francesco Guicciardini** (1483-1540), a Florentine diplomat, who expressed his ideas in measured and carefully objective terms in his political and historical works. A different type of treatise, the *Galateo* by **Giovanni della Casa** (1503-1556) laid down the etiquette then observed in every court in Europe.

In poetry **Michelangelo** (1475-1564) expressed, with the same vigour that characterises his sculptures and paintings, his torments as a man and an artist, his neo-platonistic stirrings of the heart and his later search for God. **Benvenuto Cellini** (1500-1571), the goldsmith and sculptor who was also attracted to writing, was the first to publish an autobiography describing his life as an artist and a passionate and bellicose adventurer. **Giorgio Vasari** *(see Arezzo)* was the forerunner of art historians through his valuable work entitled the *The Lives of the Most Eminent Italian Painters, Architects and Sculptors*. Pietro Aretino (1492-1556), on the other hand, who was born in Arezzo, was an unscrupulous, much-feared storyteller who wrote biting but elegantly-formulated satire.

Comedy, a *genre* lost since the days of the Ancient Greeks and Romans, was relaunched in the 16C by Cardinal Bernardo Dovizi, also known as **Bibbiena** the town of his birth, with his work *Calandria* (1513), inspired by the writing of the Latin writer, Plautus. Machiavelli continued in the same comic vein with his *Mandragore,* followed by Pietro **Aretino** who wrote five comedies. In the space of just over 30 years, through this small number of Tuscan works, comic theatre gained a reputation for excellence and became very popular throughout Europe.

The 16C also saw the founding of the **Accademia della Crusca** *(qv)* which began work on a dictionary of the Italian language in 1591.

The last of the great figures in the most intense period of creativity and inventiveness in the artistic and intellectual history of Tuscany was **Galileo** (1564-1642), who was born in Pisa; by referring to Archimedes rather than Aristotle, he made a distinction between the scientific approach to matter and the theological or philosophical approach.

From the Renaissance to the 20C – In the 19C few names stand out in the literary field. Carlo Lorenzini (1826-1890) achieved worldwide fame with **Pinocchio** which he wrote under the name of Collodi, his birthplace. The first Italian to be awarded the Nobel prize, **Giosué Carducci** (1835-1907), spent his youth in Tuscany, he was a fervent detractor of the Romantic Movement, prone to melancholia; in his *Odi Barbare* he attempted to recreate the metre of the ancient poetry which he preferred. **Curzio Malaparte** was the pen-name of Kurt Suckert (1898-1957) from Prato, author of *The Skin* and a writer and journalist, who described Italian society, particularly in the post-war years, in the crudest of terms. One of the neo-realists, **Vasco Pratolini** (1913-1991) described everyday life in Florence, his birthplace, depicting the wealthy middle classes and people of more modest means involved in great historic events and in their own private love affairs. The Tuscan countryside often served as the backdrop to the novels of **Carlo Cassola** (1917-1987); *Timber Cutting* and *Bubo's Girl* are the best-known. **Indro Montanelli**, who was born in Fucecchio in 1909, worked as a journalist on *Il Corriere della Sera*, the great national daily, before becoming founder and managing director of *Il Giornale* (until 1994) and later of *La Voce*.

Tuscan Table

Tuscan cooking is typified by its simplicity, which gives pride of place to the fine quality of the abundant regional produce.

It was Catherine de Médicis, who introduced the pleasures of the table to France after her marriage to Henri II. This marked the beginning of modern European cookery and gastronomic culture. She also introduced the fork and table napkin into court life, so that the behaviour of the guests would be as refined and elegant as the dishes they ate.

Like the landscape and the many works of art fashioned by the hand of man, the specialities of the Tuscan table exhibit a serene sense of harmony. The chance to taste them *in situ*, accompanied by Tuscan wines, is an experience that cannot be reproduced elsewhere, even though the dishes are prepared in exactly the same way.

The first taste of true Tuscan fare is often quite simply the **bruschetta**, a slice of toast, sometimes rubbed with a clove of garlic, sprinkled with oil and salt, or, even better, its regional variation the *fett'unta*, literally "anointed slice". Thus visitors may taste two of the culinary staples of Tuscany – the excellent bread which smells.

Olives and Olive Oil

One of the main features of the countryside in Tuscany is the olive trees. The oil they yield is always in abundant supply, available on the table at meals and of excellent quality.

According to custom the olive harvest, known locally as the *brucatura*, takes place on the day of the dead at the beginning of November. The first olives, which are picked from the tree by hand, are for the table. The fruit picked up off the ground in nets is pressed using millstones. Only the oil obtained from this type of pressing, which does not include the addition of chemicals and complies with the statutory manufacturing regulations, can be classed as extra-virgin *(extra vergine)*. Tuscan olive oil is green. In most cases it is unfiltered and should be used within 18 months of harvesting. Its characteristic piquant flavour, which is sometimes erroneously considered a defect, is in fact proof of the freshness and strength of the oil.

For more information about Italian food and wine, consult the Practical Information at the end of the guide, which explains the composition of an Italian meal and drinking in restaurants, describes the most common pasta dishes, the many different ways of drinking coffee and the cornucopia of Italian ice-cream. Buon appetito!

PRIMA PRESS

Cacciucco alla livornese.

delicious and is unusual in that it rarely contains salt, and the famous olive oil.

In Tuscany, the production of oil is conducted with almost religious fervour, an ancient activity involving equally ancient skills.

By local tradition, people waiting to be served in a Tuscan restaurant begin by tasting savoury *crostini*, crusty slices of bread topped with large white haricot beans, cooked *al fiasco* (in a bottle) or, more commonly, spread with poultry liver paté or one of the numerous local variations made from game or mushrooms.

There is an abundance of wild mushrooms in Tuscany, of many different species and all of excellent quality. As to vegetables, there are so many that there is a wide range of interesting dishes such as fried artichokes vegetable flans and soups (*minestrone* and *aquacotta*). Nature is generous but man has learnt to make good use of the produce. Pork products include the strongly-flavoured uncooked Parma ham, which is traditionally sliced by hand with a knife, and **finocchiona**, a cooked sausage flavoured with wild fennel seeds. Among the cheeses are **pecorino** (sometimes also known as *cacio*) which is made solely from the milk of a ewe *(pecora* in Italian). It is eaten at various stages of maturity but never before it has ripened for at least eight months.

Ribollita.

The best-known of all the traditional hot hors d'oeuvres *(primi)* are **pappa al pomodoro** and **ribollita**. The former consists of croutons cooked in herb-flavoured stock to which are added sieved tomatoes; the croutons are left to cook until the bread becomes soft, hence the name *pappa*. The latter is a bean and cabbage stew which derives its name from the fact that it used to be reboiled and served on several successive days.

Other hot hors d'oeuvres are cheap fish soups, such as the famous Livorno-style **cacciucco**, which have spread throughout the region from the coast. In Tuscany, as elsewhere in Italy, pasta is cooked in a variety of ways and makes a good start to a meal; the most unusual pasta dish is *pappardelle* with hare sauce.

The queen of regional fare is Florentine-style steak *(bistecca all Fiorentina)* better-known quite simply as **La Fiorentina**, which consists of a thick slice of tender beef cut from the sirloin and fillet (about 400g per person) and usually grilled. Among typical Tuscan main

Cantucci.

courses (secondi) are Tuscan **tripe** and **fried lamb**, **chicken** and **eel**.

The choice of cakes provides a fitting end to a meal – from simple **cantucci**, almond-flavoured biscuits that are traditionally accompanied by Vin Santo, to the **castagnaccio**, a cake made with chestnut flour, and **brigidini** from Pistoia, small waffles cooked in moulds heated over a flame. The famous **panforte** of Siena used to be eaten only at Christmas. It is made from a recipe faithfully handed down since the 13C, which consists of a blend of cocoa, walnuts,

hazelnuts, almonds, spices and crystallised fruit which form a fairly stiff paste.

WINE

Within the very wide range of wine production in Italy, Tuscany holds pride of place.

A whole set of factors such as the terrain of gently-rolling hills, the long hours of sunshine and a temperate climate have created ideal conditions for the production of excellent wine-producing vines.

It is known from documents and works of art that wine has been made in Tuscany for many centuries; it was the Etruscans who introduced wine into Gaul. Throughout the region the seasons of the year are marked by the activities and rituals involved in wine production.

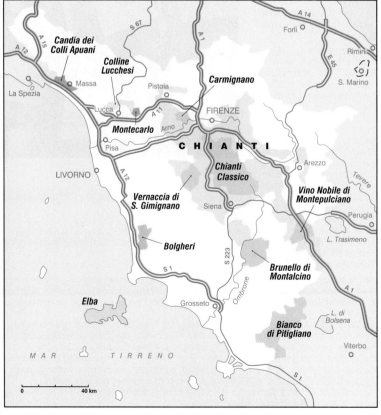

It was in Tuscany that the first attempts were made to standardise the criteria for granting a title to good quality wine produced in a specific region *(denominazione di origine controllata)*. Edicts promulgated in the 18C expressed the intention of controlling production in the Chianti and Carmignano areas. Almost one-half of the region is now covered in vineyards whose names appear in the registers of the various regions; the map, which names the main *denominazione di origine*, shows that Tuscany boasts dozens of fine wines.

Chianti – This is one of those well-known wines whose names immediately call to mind their region of origin. Chianti is a red wine produced in the districts around Arezzo, Florence, Pisa, Pistoia and Siena, and the Chianti vineyard is the largest in Tuscany as regards acreage and production. The characteristics of the soil and other conditions vary considerably from one sector to another and the wine produced in them is equally different.

The blends of grapes are however the same – *Sangiovese, Canaiolo Nero, Trebbiano Toscano* and *Malvasia del Chianti* – and they produce a deep ruby red wine with a heady bouquet, the ideal accompaniment for Tuscan cooking.

The word *classico* is reserved for wine produced in the district straddling the provinces of Florence and Siena. This is the region famous in the Middle Ages for the Chianti League *(qv)*. The **Chianti Classico** consortium, which was set up in 1924 to control production, took over the League's emblem, the black cockerel *(gallo nero)* and began to reproduce it on the wine bottles. Gradually the emblem became synonymous with *classico* wines.

A second consortium was then founded in opposition to Chianti, under the general name of **Chianti Putto** and the emblem of a cherub, to act as an umbrella organisation for the other *denominazione* – Montalbano, Rufina, Colli Fiorentini, Colli Senesi, Colli Aretini and Colline Pisane; the title is granted only to wines produced with grapes harvested and made into wine within the respective areas.

Heady reds – Another prestigious wine is **Brunello de Montalcino** which cannot be sold under this name unless it has aged for four years or, in the case of the *riserva,* for five years. Brunello, like Chianti, is a DOCG *(denominazione di origine controllata e garantita)*. Its alcohol content

Chianti Rufina.

usually exceeds 12° and it is an excellent accompaniment to roast meat and game.

The famous **Nobile di Montepulciano** is said to have acquired its name not only because of its sophistication but also because it was produced directly by local noble families. Like Brunello, it requires a great deal of care during production and the wine itself should be left to age for a long time.

Tignanello and **Sassicaia** are good table wines.

White wines – Although most Tuscan wines are red there are also some white wines that provide a pleasant surprise. Among them is **Vernaccia de San Gimignano** which has a characteristically dry taste and was one of the first wines to be classified as a fine wine.

Vin Santo is an excellent dessert wine produced from semi-crushed grapes left for several months on wooden slats until over-ripe so that the juice has evaporated and the sugar content is concentrated. The grapes are then crushed and the wine is aged for at least three years in sealed casks. It is traditionally drunk with biscuits called *Cantucci* which are dipped in the wine. It is usually made from white grapes – *Malvasia* and *Trebbiano* – but there is also a little-known red Vin Santo.

According to Cardinal Bessarion attending the Council of Florence, it resembled the wine of Xantos in Greece, hence its name.

Sightseeing

ABBADIA SAN SALVATORE✷

Population 7 324
Michelin Map 988 south of fold 15 or 430 N 17

The small town of Abbadia San Salvatore is a summer and winter holiday resort at the foot of Monte Amiata. It has a large **medieval quarter**, a labyrinth of arched streets and alleyways and a fortress. It takes its name from an abbey which was once the wealthiest monastery in Tuscany.

> **Chiesa abbaziale** – The abbey church is all that remains of the monastery founded in 743 AD by Rachis, a Lombard king converted to Christianity. Building work on the church was completed in the 11C; slight alterations were made in the 16C. The austere façade contains a large bay with colonnettes; the tall belltower is crenellated. The interior has a nave but no aisles. The chancel, raised above the level of the nave, has rounded arches painted with Renaissance friezes. The transept was decorated with frescoes in the late 17C and early 18C. A large 12C painted wooden Crucifix adorns the south wall of the nave.
> Beneath the chancel is the **crypt★** (8C) of the original church. It was built in the shape of a Cross (one of the arms has been reconstructed) and is supported by a profusion of columns with decorated capitals. Beside the church are the traces of the cloisters.

ABETONE✷

Population 758
Michelin Map 988 fold 14 or 430 J 13-14
Alt 1 388m – 4 511ft

Abetone is a large winter sports and summer holiday resort in the Tuscan Apennines, built on the mountain slopes flanking the pass of the same name. It lies in an attractive setting above two valleys (superb scenery). This is the most famous winter resort in central and southern Italy where Puccini himself used to stay. The numerous interlinked pistes make it possible to ski in several valleys – Sestaione, Lima, Scoltenna and Luce. Cross-country skiing and ice skating are also available.

The resort is strung out along the edge of a majestic forest (3 700ha – 9 143 acres) and takes its name from one of the gigantic pines (*abetone* is the superlative form of *abete* meaning pine tree), which was chopped down in the 18C to make way for the Ximenes-Giardini road.

The mountain pass itself is indicated by two pyramid-shaped stones that serve as a reminder of the old border between the Grand Duchies of Tuscany and Modena.

EXCURSIONS

★ **Cutigliano** – Alt 670m – 2 178ft. *14km – 9 miles south-east.* Cutigliano, a delightful village built in terraces up the northern slopes of the deep Lima Valley in the midst of dense woodland, has become one of Tuscany's main winter sports resorts, owing to the **Doganaccia cablecar**. The village is also popular in summer because of its climate.

The older buildings include the **Palazzo Pretorio** which was built in the 14C by the seven largest towns in the Pistoia mountains. Its façade is decorated with the coats of arms of the Captains of the Mountain who, between the 14C and 18C, held legal and administrative authority over Cutigliano and the neighbouring hamlets. The church, known as the **Madonna di Piazza** (Our Lady on the Square) contains a superb altarfront by Andrea della Robbia. An avenue of pine trees leads to the **parish church**.

★ **San Marcello Pistoiese** – Alt 650m – 2 112ft. *20km – 12 miles southeast.* This, the largest town in the mountains of the Pistoia district, is set in the middle of beautiful scenery. The district includes the town itself and also some hamlets of outstanding interest to tourists, such as Maresca and **Gavinana**. It was in Gavinana, on 3 August 1530, that the militiamen of the Republic of Florence, under the command of Francesco Ferrucci whose equestrian statue stands on the main square, valiantly resisted the troops of the Emperor Charles V. Ferrucci was fatally wounded by a man named Maramaldo, to whom he said, as he died, "You are killing a dead man". The battle is recalled in the nearby **Ferrucciano Museum** ⊙.

Take the fast road (SS66) from San Marcello to Mammiano.

Mammiano – The rickety **suspension bridge**, now restored, was built in 1922 to link the Mammiano metalworks with the villages on the opposite bank of the Lima river.

Monte AMIATA★

Michelin Map 988 south of fold 15 or 430 N 16

This old volcano, the highest mountain (1 738m – 5 649ft) in Tuscany south of the Arno, is the source of several rivers and springs which supply water to Siena and Grosseto. The mountain also has numerous deposits of mercury and antimony, which were already well known in the days of the Etruscans and Romans. Nowadays, this is a pleasant place for winter sports.

The lower slopes are covered in vines and olive trees, while the summit is clothed with a fine forest of chestnuts, beech trees and pines, criss-crossed between the rocks by many waymarked footpaths.

A winding road (13km – 8 miles) runs round the mountain (recommended access from Abbadia San Salvatore, brown signs for "Vetta Amiata"), providing a number of impressive views. From the south side, the most attractive of all, the road runs up to the summit marked by an iron cross (22m – 72ft high) at the top of a paved path (15min Return on foot) flanked by a chair-lift and ski-lifts. From the observation platform on the summit, there is an interesting view★ of the peaks and valleys, and the towns and villages to the southwest.

ANGHIARI

Population 5 867
Michelin Map 988 fold 15 or 430 L 18

This small town, built of brick and terracotta, huddles **picturesquely**★ on the top of a hill; its narrow, winding, irregular streets running up and down the hillside, preserve their medieval charm. From the 16C to the 19C, the town was famous for the production of firearms.

In 1440 a battle between the troops of Florence and Milan was fought on the wide Tiber Plain between Anghiari and Sansepolcro. As the latter were beaten, the town surrendered to Florence. The **Battle of Anghiari** has been remembered because it was chosen as the theme for the decoration of the Hall of the Five Hundred in the Palazzo Vecchio (City Hall) in Florence and the work was commissioned from Leonardo da Vinci who painted it between 1503 and 1506. Only a few drawings have survived as da Vinci tried out an innovatory technique in fresco-painting and the paint ran down the wall as it dried.

Park in the town centre in the great Piazza Baldoccio at the top of Via Matteotti. Turn right opposite this road into the labyrinth of narrow streets.

★★ **Museo statale di Palazzo Taglieschi** ⊙ – *Halfway along Via Garibaldi in a tiny triangular square.* The **museum** housed in the 15C Taglieschi Palazzo contains mainly works of art and exhibits relating to popular traditions in the Upper Tiber Valley connected with aspects of domestic or religious life and farm work. There are pieces of Romanesque and Gothic architecture, fragments of frescoes, furniture, 15C and 16C paintings, and Renaissance sculptures including a superb painted *Madonna* by Jacopo della Quercia and a *Nativity* by the Della Robbia school.

A few yards further along Via Garibaldi, turn right and then left.

In the square stands the **Town Hall**, easily recognisable by its many shields.

Take the narrow street opposite leading to another small square.

Chiesa di Badia – This **church** dates from the Romanesque period but has been much altered. Its interior layout is unusual and asymmetrical. The decorative elements on one of the altars (second to the left), a fine example of Renaissance *pietra serena*, are said to be the work of Desiderio da Settignano.

ARCIPELAGO TOSCANO★★

Michelin Map 988 folds 14, 24 and 25
or 430 L-M 11 and N-O-P 12-13-14

The Tuscan Archipelago is a string of seven islands, of which Elba is the largest. The other six islands – **Giglio** (21.21 km – 8 sq miles), **Capraia** (19.50 km – 7.5sq miles), **Montecristo** (10.39 km – 4 sq miles), **Pianosa** (10.25 km – 4 sq miles) **Giannutri** (2.62 km – 1 sq mile) and **Gorgona** (2.23km – 0.75sq mile) – are also mountainous, with a rich unspoiled natural environment that is seen at its best during the seasons when the climate is mild and the coastline free from crowds of tourists.

★★ **Isola d'Elba (Island of Elba)** – *See Elba.*

★ **Isola del Giglio** ⊙ – The mountainous island of Giglio (Lily Island) lies just off Monte Argentario; there are only three villages – **Giglio Porto** where the boats from the mainland dock, **Giglio Castello**, the medieval village encircled by the walls of its fortress, and **Campese**, a village, offering accommodation for visitors, overlooking a delightful bay fringed with a sandy beach.

Baia di Campese, Isola del Giglio.

The sheer, rugged coast carpeted with scrub blends harmoniously with the natural beauty of the wild and emotive environment which is the product of the very dry climate. Vines adapt particularly well to these conditions; the local wine is *Ansonico*.

The range of sports which can be enjoyed here includes sub-aqua, windsurfing, walking, riding and tennis.

★ **Isola di Giannutri** ⊙ – Giannutri, which lies southeast of Giglio, is privately-owned but open to visitors for a few hours every day *(no camping or picnics)*. There are traces of a 1C Roman villa which may have belonged to Domitian Enobarbus.

Capraia ⊙ – Capraia lies nearer the northern tip of Corsica than Italy. The western side is mountainous; the eastern side is gentler and more hospitable. The natural environment is rugged and the only parts of the island that are inhabited are the centre and the harbour. It is this untamed nature that makes the island a paradise for walkers, who come to admire the tiny lake *(laghetto)* in an old volcanic crater, and for sailors, who like to view the island from the sea and admire the gulls' nests and the deep colours of the Cala Rossa (Red Creek). The coastline is particularly suitable for sub-aqua and windsurfing.

Gorgona, Pianosa and Montecristo – *Not open to visitors*. There are prisons on **Gorgona**, which lies offshore from Livorno (Leghorn), and on **Pianosa**, which is south of Elba.

Montecristo, south of Pianosa, is a granite island dominated by Monte Fortezza (645m – 2096ft), classified as an uninhabited nature conservancy zone. The island is famous as the setting chosen by Alexandre Dumas (1844) for his novel in which the fabulous treasure of Monte-Cristo enabled Edmond Dantès, later Count of Monte Cristo, to pursue his vendetta against his enemies.

AREZZO★★

Population 91 578
Michelin Map 988 fold 15 or 430 L 17
Town plan in the current Michelin Red Guide

The old town of Arezzo is built in terraces on a hill crowned by a citadel, surrounded by a fertile basin planted with cereal crops, fruit trees and vines. From the parapet walk of the citadel, there are a number of delightful views of the town and the surrounding countryside.

Arezzo was a free town by the end of the 11C; as a supporter of the Ghibelline *(qv)* faction, it was involved in a long struggle against Florence, which was pro-Guelf, before being merged with the latter larger town in 1384. During those days of conflict were built a large number of tower-houses, which now contribute to the picturesque aspect of the town.

A long artistic tradition – After a period as one of the centres of Etruscan civilisation (it was in Arezzo that the splendid, and famous, chimera was discovered which can now be seen in the archeological museum in Florence), Arretium became a prosperous Roman town famous for its production of "Aretine" vases.

This type of pottery was made of very fine, reddish-brown, glazed clay. It was smooth but carried a raised monochrome decorative pattern. It was invented by a man from Arezzo named Marcus Perennius who specialised in the reproduction of Greek metalware. The major period of prosperity for this "industry" seems to have lasted for more than a century, between 30 BC and AD 40. Production spread from Arezzo to other towns in the peninsula and was exported throughout the Roman world from Gaul to Syria.

It is likely that **Maecenas** (69-8 BC), the legendary patron of artists and writers (Virgil, Horace, Propertius etc) and himself a poet, was born in Arezzo. He was also a friend and minister to Caesar Augustus.

Long after the Roman period, the town was the birthplace of a number of major figures in the field of the arts – the Benedictine monk, **Guido of Arezzo** (*c*990-*c*1050), who was recognised as the inventor of a system of musical notation; the poet **Petrarch** *(qv)*, who was born in 1304; the writer, Pietro Aretino, also known as **The Aretine** *(qv)*, who was born in 1492; the painter and art historian, **Giorgio Vasari** *(qv)*, who was born in 1511. The town owes it greatest claim to fame to **Piero della Francesca** *(see below)*, who was born in Sansepolcro *(qv)*.

The painter and glassmaker, **Guillaume de Marcillat** (1467-1529), a master craftsman from the Berry region of France, who was also known as **Gughelmo** and had worked in Rome in the Vatican beside Raphael and Michelangelo at the invitation of Pope Julius II, later settled in Arezzo, where he designed a number of stained-glass windows; the designs were harmonious and the subject matter proof of his consummate knowledge of perspective and anatomy. His works were described by Vasari as "not stained-glass windows but marvels, dropped from heaven to give consolation to Man".

SAN FRANCESCO (ABY) *30min*

This is a vast church, designed for the preaching of sermons and built in the Gothic style in the 14C for the Franciscan Order. It was altered in the 17C and 18C but restoration work has now returned it to its original austerity. The Franciscan monks, as keepers of the Holy Places, showed particular devotion to the Holy Cross. They commissioned Piero della Francesca to decorate the chancel of the church.

★★★ **Frescoes by Piero della Francesca** – The frescoes were painted on the walls of the apse between 1452 and 1466 and are considered as one of the most outstanding examples of Renaissance painting in Tuscany. They illustrate the **Legend of the Holy Cross**, a common theme in Franciscan churches and friaries in the Middle Ages. This is an admirable set of paintings, a masterpiece of nobility, balance and power that has retained a sense of tenderness.

The artist did not intend to follow the chronological order of the tale in any strict fashion. Instead, the work "reads" as follows –

Piero della Francesca (*c*1416-1492)

This artist, who divided his time mainly between his birthplace, Sansepolcro *(qv)*, the courts in Ferrara and Urbino, and Arezzo where he painted his masterpiece, was one of the most unusual and most outstanding representatives of the 15C, because of the austerity and powerful sincerity of his work. He was initially influenced by the painters of the Sienese School and it was they who gave him his taste for harmonious colours and accurate drawing. In his portraits especially, this gives his subject matter a heightened reality. As a young man, he worked in Florence for more than five years with a Venetian named Domenico Veneziano who taught him how to produce a soft, unreal light and use pale, light colours. During this period Masaccio taught him about perspective and its links with a rigorous form of geometry; Uccello gave him a feeling for volume in his paintings. It may have been his admiration for Flemish painting that led to his use of light and *chiaroscuro*, which give some of the details in his frescoes a strong resemblance to oil painting.

His statuesque, impassive figures have all the robustness and solidity of slow-moving peasant stock. His compositions are strongly-structured and comply with geometric rules. When taken with his preference for soft colours, some of them slightly muted (ash greys, dull blues, and faded browns), these characteristics produce an impression of balance and solemnity in his work. He spent almost all the last 20 years of his life writing two treatises, one on pictorial perspective (this was the first time the notion had been set down in a structured manner) and the other on the geometry of "pure forms".

I The tympanum shows the death of Adam *(right)* and his burial *(left)*. Three seeds, from which will grow the Tree of the Cross, are being placed in his mouth by his son, Seth.

II The Queen of Sheba, having received a divine revelation, prostrates herself in front of the bridge made from the tree that has grown from Adam's tomb *(left)*. After travelling to Jerusalem, she explains her vision to Solomon *(right)*.

III The sacred bridge, which Solomon has decided to bury, is taken to a new place.

IV The angel tells the Blessed Virgin Mary of her Son's Crucifixion (the angel is holding the martyrs' palm and not the lily of virginity). This scene forms a central point in the story of the wood of the True Cross (before and after the Crucifixion) without depicting the central episode in the story.

V On the eve of his battle with Maxentius who is disputing his claim to the Imperial crown, Constantine (later to be the first Christian emperor) is advised by an angel in a dream to fight under the sign of the Cross. This is the first example of the use of *chiaroscuro* in Italian art.

VI Constantine, brandishing the Cross, has defeated Maxentius at the Milvian Bridge (AD 312).

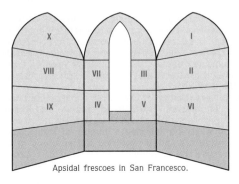

Apsidal frescoes in San Francesco.

VII The torture of the Jew. St. Helena, Constantine's mother, while trying to trace the wood from the True Cross in Jerusalem, was told that only one Jew knew where the relic had been buried. As the man refused to speak, Helena had him dropped down a well where he remained for six days before agreeing to her request.

VIII Empress Helena discovers the three Crosses from Calvary. The resurrection of a dead man shows her which one was the Cross of Christ.

IX Three hundred years later, Heraclius defeated the Persian King, Khosrow, who had stolen the Cross to decorate his throne.

X Heraclius returns the True Cross to Jerusalem.

The Story of the True Cross by Piero della Francesca (detail showing the Queen of Sheba).

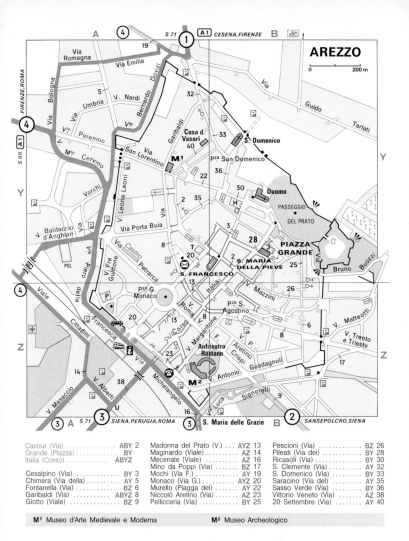

AREZZO

0 ___ 200 m

★ **Other works of art** – Ancient frescoes decorate the other walls – *(south aisle)* an *Annunciation* by Spinello Aretino (early 15C); *(left of the entrance)* a superb 16C *Madonna and Child*; *(south apsidal chapel)* the *Assumption Triptych* painted by Nicolo di Pietro Gerini in the early 15C; *(centre of the south side of the nave)* a huge Crucifix painted on wood, dating from the late 13C.

The oculus *(west wall)* is filled with a superb stained-glass window, bearing the coat of arms of the Berry region with its fleur-de-lis, in which the artist, Guillaume de Marcillat, depicted St Francis giving roses to Pope Honorius III, in the middle of the month of January.

★**PIAZZA GRANDE** (BY) *30min*

The main square is surrounded by medieval houses, some with crenellated towers, the Romanesque galleried apse of Santa Maria della Pieve (parish church), the late 18C Law Courts, the part-Gothic part-Renaissance Palazzo della Fraternita, and the 16C galleries *(Loggie)*, designed by Vasari, from which the lower social classes used to be excluded.

The main square is the setting for the **Saracen Joust** *(Giostra del Saracino)* in which the best horsemen in Arezzo tilt with lances at a representation of a Saracen, accompanied by a huge procession of people dressed in 14C and 15C costume *(last Sunday in August and first Sunday in September)*.

★ **Santa Maria della Pieve** – This superb Romanesque parish **church** is crowned by a haughty campanile, which, owing to its numerous double bays (there are 40 of them in all), is called the "One Hundred Holes". Construction of the church began in the mid-12C and was completed in the 14C. In the 16C alterations were made, notably under the direction of Vasari. The **façade★★**, which was inspired by the Romanesque style used in Pisa *(qv)*, is very ornate with three tiers of arcades supported by colonnettes, decorated with a variety of motifs; the distance between the colonnettes decreases towards the top. The upper coving of the central doorway is decorated with witty representations of the symbols of the 12 months of the year.

The interior includes a half-rounded apse and a raised chancel in which the pillars are decorated with capitals carved with large human heads. Among the works of art are two marble low-reliefs – *(rear of the façade) Epiphany*, of Byzantine origin; *(wall in the north aisle) Nativity*, dating from the 13C.

The High Altar includes a superb polyptych (1320-1324) by Pietro Lorenzetti from Siena.

Via dei Pileati (28) – This **street,** which runs along the façade of Santa Maria della Pieve (parish church), is a strange sight with its palaces, Gothic towers, and old houses. On one corner overlooking a crossroads is the Palazzo Pretorio (14C-15C) covered with coats of arms of the governor *(podestà)*.

ADDITIONAL SIGHTS

Duomo (BY) – The **cathedral** was built from 1278 to 1511 but the façade is neo-Gothic. On the south side is an attractive Romanesque-Gothic portal dating from the first half of the 14C. The cathedral contains some fine **works of art**★ including *(middle of the south aisle)* stained-glass windows by Marcillat *(The Moneylenders Being Chased from the Temple)*; *(north aisle)* the tomb of Bishop Guido Tarlati and *(near the vestry)* the fresco by Piero della Francesca depicting *Mary Magdalen*, an admirable example of "the nobility of the peasantry"; *(centre of the cathedral)* two 16C marble pulpits and *(behind the High Altar)* 13C tomb of St Donatus.

San Domenico (BY) – This **church**, built in the Gothic style in the 13C but since restored, has an asymmetrical façade. It contains frescoes by the Duccio School, and by Spinello Aretino and his school. On the High Altar, there is an admirable **Crucifix**★★ by Cimabue; in this youthful work, still dominated by the Byzantine tradition, the artist – described by Vasari as a precursor of the rebirth of Italian painting – already gives some indication of a hitherto-unknown sense of the dramatic and feeling for projection.

Casa del Vasari (Vasari's House) – (AY) ◷ – The residence was luxuriously decorated in 1540 by Vasari – painter, sculptor, architect and writer – whose multiplicity of talents made him a typical Renaissance Man. The house contains works by Tuscan Mannerist painters and a terracotta by Andrea Sansovino *(portrait of Galba,* who succeeded Nero).

★ **Museo d'arte medievale e moderna (Museum of medieval and modern art)** (AY **M¹**) ◷ – The fully-furnished Palazzo Bruni-Ciocchi contains sculptures, gold and silverware and numerous paintings dating from the Middle Ages to the 19C. Early works are by Margaritone of Arezzo, Guido da Siena, Parri di Spinello, Bartolomeo della Gatta, Luca Signorelli, Andrea della Robbia, Cigoli, Vasari, Salvator Rosa, and Gaspart Dughet. The 19C is represented by some of the main *Macchiaioli (qv)* artists such as Fattori and Signorini. The extensive range of exhibits also includes an outstanding collection of Renaissance **majolicaware**★ from Umbria, 17C and 18C ceramics, glassware, weaponry, ivories and a large collection of coins.

Museo archeologico (Archeological Museum) (AZ **M²**) ◷ – The museum stands adjacent to the oval **Roman amphitheatre** which dates from the 1C and 2C. It contains interesting collections of Etruscan and Roman bronze statuettes (from 6C BC to 3C AD), Greek vases (Euphronios' crater), Aretine vases, and ceramics dating from the Hellenistic and Roman periods.

Santa Maria delle Grazie (AZ) – *1km – 0.5 mile south by Viale Mecenate* – This mid-15C **church** is preceded by a graceful, ethereal **portico**★ designed by Benedetto da Maiano (15C) from Florence. Inside, behind the High Altar, is a delightful marble **reredos**★ by Andrea della Robbia framing a painting by Parri di Spinello *(Virgin Mary of Pity)*.

Michelin Green Guides for North America:
    California
    Canada
    Chicago
    Mexico
    New England
    New York
    Quebec
    Washington

Promontorio dell'ARGENTARIO★

The **Argentario Promontory**. formerly an island, is linked to the mainland by ancient sandspits, **Tombolo di Feniglia** and **Tombolo di Giannella**; it consists of the small limestone range known as **Monte Argentario** (635m – 2 064ft high). The headland is approached by three causeways and served by a coastal road which offers a series of picturesque views. Argentario was once called Promontorio Cosano (after the neighbouring Etruscan town of Cosa); it is said to owe its present name to the shiny, silvery appearance of its rocks – although its name may be an allusion to the activities of its former owners who were bankers *(argentarii)*. It had an eventful history both in the Middle Ages when it belonged to the Aldobrandeschi and Orsini families and in the 16C when it passed out of the hands of the Republic of Siena and became a Spanish fortress. In the 18C it passed to the Austrians, then to the Bourbons and later to the Grand Duchy of Tuscany before being annexed to the Kingdom of Italy in 1860.

ROUND TOUR STARTING FROM ORBETELLO
43km – 27 miles – about 2 hours

Orbetello – The town lies on the middle causeway which crosses the lagoon and carries the main access road to the peninsula (SS 440). In the past the town was known by the Latin name of *Urbis Tellus* (literally territory of the City i.e. of Rome), perhaps because in 805 AD it was given by Charlemagne to the Abbey of the Three Fountains in Rome. The fortifications date from the days of Sienese then Spanish occupation, when Orbetello was the capital of the Garrison State *(see above)*. The **cathedral** stands on the site of an ancient Etruscan-Roman temple. According to an inscription on the architrave on the central portal, the late Gothic façade was altered in 1376 under the direction of Nicolo Orsini. The two aisles date from the days of the Spanish occupation. The Lombard-style chancel rail is decorated with entwined vine shoots.

Between the edge of the lagoon and Porto Santo Stefano, the road (S440) runs uphill along the north coast of the peninsula between hedgerows, villas and hotels, finally providing a view of the Talamone headland on the mainland and Porto Santo Stefano on the island.

Porto Santo Stefano – This is the main town on the peninsula and the embarkation point for boat trips to the neighbouring island of Giglio *(qv)*. The houses are built on the hillside, flanking the 17C Aragonese fortress *(Rocca)* from which there is a superb **view**★ north over the harbour and Talamone Bay.

From Porto Santo Stefano take the scenic route (Strada Panoramica) north.

Beyond the headland at Lividonia, there is a succession of views over the west coast and the island of Giglio offshore. The corniche road descends between cypress trees, passing above Cala Grande Bay, distinguished by the tiny island of Argentarola, and the small seaside resort of Cala Piccola and its bay, sheltered to the south by Uomo Cape. Further south the island of Giannutri is visible offshore.

Stato dei Presidi (Garrison State)

In 1555 the Republic of Siena was conquered by the troops of the Emperor, Charles V, who delegated power to his son, Philip II. In 1157, in gratitude for the assistance given to Spain by the Medicis, Philip granted the territory to Cosimo I but retained power over the garrisons *(presidi)* that controlled the shores of the Tyrrhenian Sea, an area that had been designated as a State in 1555. The State contained five garrisons and covered the entire Argentario promontory, including Orbetello (the capital), Porto Ercole, Porto Santo Stefano, the Maremma district, on the mainland, which extended from the shores of Lake Burano (southeast of Cosa) north to the Monti dell'Uccellina and Talamone, and the southeastern horn of the Island of Elba, around Porto Azzurro (formerly Porto Longone).

These towns strengthened the Spanish hold on the entire western section of the Mediterranean and were integrated into a vast system of military bases already established on the Balearic Islands, on Sardinia, in Tunisia, on Malta and Sicily. The State was recognised and left to Philip II under the Treaty of Cateau-Cambrésis between France and Spain but in 1646, during the Thirty Years' War, it was annexed to France. In 1713, together with the Kingdom of Naples, it was handed over to the Austrians, from whom it passed to the Bourbons in 1738. After a further period of French occupation between 1801 and 1815, it was finally annexed to the Grand Duchy of Tuscany.

Porto Ercole.

Beyond the junction with a road running across country to Porto Santo Stefano, the road continues to twist and turn as it runs downhill; there is no retaining wall.

At high altitude, there are several **views★** of the rocky creeks along the southwest coast, the island of Rossa (consisting of reddish rocks) and *(inland)* of the terraced fields and peaks of Monte Argentario. One part of the road *(unmetalled for 3km - 2 miles)* looks down on the rugged headland of Torre Ciana (crowned by a tower), the south coast and then of the island of Isolotto and Fort Stella. The road then passes Rocca Spagnola, a 16C bastioned citadel, before reaching Porto Ercole.

⌂⌂ **Porto Ercole** – The seaside resort stands at the foot of the Rocca Spagnola, to which it is linked by two parallel walls capped with battlements. A medieval gate with hoarding and machicolations leads into the old town. Piazza Santa Barbara is flanked by the arcades of the former Governor's Palace (16C); from the square there is a view of the yachting marina, the bay and the two old Spanish fortresses, opposite on Monte Filippo.

The road completes the round tour by skirting the eastern slopes of the Argentario promontory where it soon runs at water level between the headland and the Levante lagoon before joining (right) the road (SS440) to Orbetello.

ARTIMINO

Michelin Map 430 K 15

The area around the high Artimino hill was inhabited in the Paleolithic era. In the 7C BC an Etruscan town was built on the site and gained prosperity rather more, it would appear, from control of the natural trade routes along the River Arno and River Ombrone than from the exploitation of the local agricultural resources. The acropolis probably stood on the hill now occupied by the Villa Ferdinanda. Opposite the villa is the **village,** which still has some of its medieval walls. The church stands further down the hill.

Pieve di San Leonardo – This Romanesque parish **church,** said to have been commissioned by Countess Matilda of Canossa in 1107, is unusual in that it was partly built with materials from the Etruscan graveyard, including urns (some of them carved). The interior has a nave and two aisles with ogival vaulting.

★ Villa La Ferdinanda – *The interior is not open to the public*. This vast building was commissioned towards the end of the 16C from Buontalenti by one of the Medici, Grand Duke Ferdinando I, whose memory lives on in the villa's nickname. It stands in a dominant position in the middle of a terrace (views south over the Arno Valley to Florence and north over Prato and Pistoia); the lawn is dotted with amusing metal statues. The first noticeable feature about the villa is the profusion and variety of chimneys projecting above the roof. In front of the villa are double-spiral steps extending into a ramp leading straight to the colonnaded balcony on the first floor.

Museo archeologico etrusco (Etruscan Archeology Museum) ⊘ – *In the basement of the villa; entrance behind the grand staircase*. The museum contains all the items uncovered during a dig in the area of the ancient Etruscan town *(see above)*, including imported Greek vases, Etruscan buccheroware, coins, sculptures and some interesting exhibits from the graveyard. There are also exhibits from a few large tombs in the surrounding area *(see below)* – a rare buccheroware perfume-burner dating from the 7C BC. There is a 20-minute film (Italian commentary only).

EXCURSIONS

★ Etruscan graves in Comeana – *4km – 2.5 miles northeast*. These graves date from the 7C BC. The best-preserved of them is the **Tomba di Montefortini★ (Montefortini Grave)** ⊘ *(43 Via di Montefortini)*. It lies beneath a huge barrow, now covered in trees, and consists of a passage *(dromos)* (13m – 43ft long), a vestibule that used to be closed off by a stone slab (still visible) and a rectangular burial chamber. The grave has a corbelled roof composed of horizontal stones set one above the other in staggered rows up to the very top. The unusual feature of the grave is the continuous bracket running along the top of the walls, which was used as a shelf for funeral articles. This grave stands next to an older one containing a circular burial chamber *(closed to the public)*. The collapse of the earlier chamber explains why the second grave was built beneath the same barrow. The **Boschetti Grave** *(near the cemetery, to the left of the Poggio-Caiano road)* is smaller and only parts of its walls now remain.

Carmignano – *6km – 4 miles north*. This small town is surrounded by vines and olive trees. All that remains of its medieval castle is a single tower. The most important building, however, is the **Church of San Michele**; the portico and cloisters date from the 16C. Inside *(second altar on the right)* is a splendid **Visitation★★** by Pontormo ((c1530) in which the profound mutual love and respect of the Blessed Virgin Mary and St Elizabeth are indicated by the depth of feeling contained in their expressions.

ASCIANO

Population 10 197
Michelin Map 988 fold 15 or 430 M 16

Asciano is separated from Siena by a line of hills. It is an old medieval fortified town on a rise overlooking the Ombrone river. The Corso Matteotti runs through it from one end to the other.

Basilica di Sant'Agata (St Agatha's Basilica) – This 12C Romanesque church, built entirely of travertine marble, has a Gothic façade approached by a wide flight of steps. The nave, with its bare rafters, is separated by an arch from the transept crossing which is capped by a fine dome on squinches. Three apsidal chapels with half-domes open into the chancel and the transept. On the south wall of the nave is a wonderful fresco of the *Madonna and Child* attributed to Girolamo del Pacchia.

Museo di Arte Sacra (Museum of Sacred Art) ⊘ – *Left of the basilica*. The museum houses a collection of paintings and sculptures by the Sienese School, dating from the 14C and 15C, including an *Annunciation* by Taddeo di Bartolo, a *Birth of the Virgin Mary* by Sassetta and a polyptych by Ambrogio Lorenzetti with *St Michael Slaying the Dragon* on the central panel.

Museo Archeologico (Archeological Museum) ⊘ – *Corso Matteotti*. The museum is housed in the tiny Church of San Bernardino. It contains exhibits (ceramics, urns) dating from the 5C to 1C BC from the neighbouring Etruscan cemetery in Poggio Pinci.

Museo Cassioli (Cassioli Museum) ⊘ – The museum is devoted to the works of Amos Cassioli (1832-1892), who was famous in his day for his portraits and historical paintings, and of Guiseppe Cassioli (1865-1942), his son.

BARGA

Population 10 197
Michelin Map 988 fold 14 or 430 J 13

The town stands amid trees and vineyards in a delightful setting on a plateau on the northern slopes of the Serchio Valley over which it had control during the Middle Ages. Its "castle" *(castello)* consists, in fact, of the upper town, a medieval district of winding, steep and narrow streets behind the remains of the town walls. High above the upper town is an elegant cathedral.

Duomo (Cathedral) – This is a superb Romanesque church built of white limestone. The lintel on the portal in its wide, austere façade is carved with scenes of the grape harvest. The portal is flanked by two engaged columns, each crowned by a lion in the Lombard Romanesque style. The powerful belltower capped by merlons has bays with colonnettes. From the terrace in front of the church there is a pleasant view over the rooftops of the upper town to the mountains on the horizon.

Inside the cathedral, in front of the presbytery, which is closed off with coloured marble screens, is a superb 12C marble **ambo★** decorated with low relief carvings (scenes from the Life of Mary and the Life of Christ). It rests on four columns (two of them are supported by lions slaying their prey and one by a man in a squatting position). Other outstanding features of the cathedral include the eagle-lectern, the stoop decorated with carved heads, the 12C statue and the 18C painting of St Christopher carrying the Child Jesus.

EXCURSIONS

Castelvecchio Pascoli – *4km – 2.5 miles northwest*. The village is invariably linked in the Italian mind with the *Songs of Castelvecchio* composed by **Giovanni Pascoli**, a pupil of Carducci, and contains **Casa Giovanni Pascoli** ⊙ which stands in the middle of a quiet, rural landscape, was maintained for 40 years by the poet's sister and still has its original furniture. Pascoli used to say jokingly that he had bought the house "with the assistance of Horace and Virgil" because it was partly paid for as a result of the five gold medals he won at the Latin poetry competition held in Amsterdam. Brother and sister are buried in the same grave in the chapel.

Grotta del Vento (Windy Cave) ⊙ – *14km – 9 miles southwest (in Fornovolasco)*. The cave lies on a winding road bristling with sheer rocky cliffs and providing a breathtaking view down over the Calomini hermitage set in a wall of rock at an altitude of more than 100m – 325ft.

The cave gets its name from the perceptible draught that can be felt at its mouth caused by the difference in level between two natural ventilation holes. Inside the cave, the

Giovanni Pascoli (1855-1912)

This poet, who came from Romagna, was marked very early in life by the painful experience of death and grief as his father was murdered and he lost a sister, his mother and two brothers in succession. Indeed, he was convinced of a tragic destiny closely linked to the lot of the human race. He looked back nostalgically at the age of innocence and its wonderment and defined his poetry in *Le Petit Enfant*. He was a prolific poet. Among his many works was the collection entitled *Tamarisks* and the Latin poems entitled *Carmina*. This was a genre in which Pascoli excelled, as is obvious from his many successes in the Latin poetry competition held in Amsterdam.

temperature is a steady 10.7 ºC. The "wind" is therefore sucked into the cave during the winter when the temperature outside is lower and, in summer, the phenomenon is reversed. Until the First World War, the cave had almost one sole purpose – it was used as a natural icebox. Potholers, though, began to explore it at the turn of the century. It contains interesting stalactites and stalagmites which are particularly bright because they are constantly covered in a film of water.

The chapter on art and architecture in this guide gives an outline of artistic achievement in the region, providing the context of the buildings and works of art described in the Sights section

This chapter may also provide ideas for touring

It is advisable to read it at leisure

BIBBIENA

Population 10 000
Michelin Map 988 fold 15 or 430 K 17

Bibbiena used to extend no further than a hilltop; today it stretches down to the valley floor, making it the largest town in the Casentino area.

Cardinal **Bernardo Dovizi**, better known as **Bibbiena** (1470-1520) was born here. He was secretary to Leo X and a friend of Raphael; he was also the author of *La Calandria* (1513), the first comedy in the history of Italian theatre, a genre which was to be reborn in Italy in the 16C. There had been no other examples of this type of theatre since the days of Ancient Rome but from then on it was to enjoy success throughout Europe.

OLD TOWN

The old town, perched right on the top of the hill in a position that guarantees a panoramic view, has sloping narrow streets and is steeped in the discreet charm typical of rugged, mountainous areas like this where ostentation is totally out of place.
The first entrance is at the top of a long climb, to the left of a major crossroads. The town centre is signed. Turn into Via Dovizi.

★ **Palazzo Dovizi** – *26-28 Via Dovizi.* This is the residence commissioned by Bibbiena early in the 16C. It is a fairly austere building with plain brick facing yet it has a certain air of elegance. The regular layout of the windows on the first two floors highlights the central doorway surmounted by a coat of arms, and the loggia above the building adds a touch of ethereal originality.

San Lorenzo – This **church**, standing opposite the palace, was built in the 15C. Its natural stone frontage, austere like the façade of the palace, conceals an interior with nave and two aisles laid out in a uniform Renaissance style in alternating greys and whites. The aisles are decorated with two glazed **terracotta sculptures**★★ by the Della Robbias. On the third altar to the right is *The Adoration of the Shepherds*; on the third to the left *The Deposition*.
Via Dovizi leads to Piazza Roma.

Palazzo Comunale – *On the opposite side of the square, at the end and to the right of a narrow street.* The Town Hall dates from the 16C.
Turn left off the square and climb up to Piazza Tarlati.

Piazza Tarlati – The square was named after the Tarlati family, one of whose members, Pier Saccone, had one of the four towers of the fortress *(cassero)* built on this very spot. Very little of any significance remains today except the crenellated **Clock Tower** on the right of the palace which has an attractive five-arched porticoed entrance. To the rear of the square is the sole vestige of the fortress – a wall linking the clock tower to a lower tower.
Opposite it is the **Church of Santi Ippolito e Donato,** built in the early 12C as a private chapel for the Tarlati castle. It is built in the Romanesque style and has an unusually wide transept crossing flanked by very short arms. The walls are covered with numerous frescoes dating from the 14C to 16C. On the south side just inside the door is a *Crucifixion* painted by the Master of San Polo in Rosso (13C) followed by a sculpture of the *Madonna and Child* (14C Tuscan School). In the north transept is a *Crucifixion* by the School of Giotto (second half of the 14C). The apse contains a triptych of the *Madonna and Child with Saints* by Bicci di Lorenzo (1435). In the south arm of the transept is a rare painting by Arcangelo di Cola da Camerino, **The Madonna and Child with Angels**★.
To the left of Piazza Tarlati is a terrace from which there is a superb **view**★.

BUONCONVENTO

Population 3 098
Michelin Map 988 fold 15 or 430 M 16

Buonconvento stands at the confluence of the Arbia and Ombrone rivers, on the Via Cassia, the Roman road between Siena and Rome. The town, which houses a small farming community, is built entirely of brick and enclosed within 14C town walls. Emperor Henry VII, in whom Dante placed his hopes of a unified, pacified Italy, died here in 1313.
On the north side of the fortifications stands the great **Porta Senese** (Siena Gate), topped with small relieving arches and battlements, from which Via Soccini traverses the town. In a small square to the left is the **Church of SS Pietro e Paolo** (St Peter and St Paul) which has a Jesuit façade; further on is the **Palazzo Pretorio** surmounted by an elegant tower designed to resemble the one in Siena.

★ **Museo d'arte sacra della Val d'Arbia (Sacred Art Museum)** ⊘ – *17 Via Soccini.* This small museum presents 14C to 17C paintings by the Sienese School, as well as church plate, liturgical vestments, reliquaries and decorated bier ends from the Buonconvento area and the Arbia Valley.

CAMALDOLI★★

Michelin Map 988 fold 15 or 430 K 17
Alt 816m – 2 652ft

The mother house of the Camaldolese religious order, which was established in the 11C by St Romuald, was built among the mountains in the depths of the vast Casentino Forest, an appropriate location for the austerity of the Rule which combines the minimum of community life with the life of a hermit.

The winding **road★★** from Poppi *(18km – 11 miles)* provides views over the town, the castle and the Arno Valley before climbing the slopes of a small valley and passing through the forest.

★ **Convento** – The **monastery** is impressively sited at the end of a dark valley flanked by slopes covered with pine trees.

Within the section that has been converted into an inn, one may see an 11C portico in the courtyard and small 15C cloisters leading to a number of rooms and chapels.

The lefthand entrance in the façade opens into the 16C church. The Baroque interior includes several paintings by Vasari including a *Deposition* above the high altar.

The monks' monastery is on the upper floor.

Round to the left of the building is the 15C **pharmacy★★**. Its origins can be traced to the 11C when the monks, having built a hospital, began to care for and treat the sick free of charge. Their hospital continued to function until the beginning of the last century.

The road climbs steeply through the forest beside the stream until it reaches the hermitage, in an austere and lonely setting (2.5km – 1 mile).

★★ **Eremo (Hermitage)** ⊙ – Alt 1 027m – 3 338ft. The **Hermitage** is a veritable monastic village, consisting of some 20 small houses built between the 13C and 17C and enclosed by a wall. In front of the Hermitage are a few buildings open to the public.

On the right of the inner courtyard is the superb 18C **church** which has two belltowers and a façade decorated with statues. At the entrance is a fine low relief by Mino da Fiesole. The interior is decorated in the Neapolitan Baroque style, with a mixture of stuccowork, gold leaf, marble, paintings, wood carvings and statues, together with a number of older works. In St Anthony's Chapel *(left of the entrance to the rear)* there is a glazed earthenware figure (15C) by Andrea della Robbia. The apse is flanked by two marble **tabernacles★★** (15C) by Desiderio da Settignano; the *Crucifixion* is attributed to Bronzino.

Opposite the church is the tiny garden and St Romuald's cell, a small apartment with dark wainscoting laid out like the other monks' lodgings with a living room where the monk lived, slept and worked, a private chapel, a woodshed, a washing area and a store-room leading off a single corridor.

Camaldoli Hermitage.

CAMPIGLIA MARITTIMA

Population 12 509
Michelin Map 988 fold 14 or 430 M 13

Campiglia developed on a hilltop (210m – 682ft above sea level) in what was once the Pisan section of the Maremma district. The village consists of a strange collection of stone-built houses surrounded by walls that were once impregnable. The village must be very old as a document dating from 1004 states that Count Gherardo II della Gherardesca granted ownership of the town to a monastery near Chiusdino. From 1259 onwards the community was governed by a captain from Pisa, a judge and a lawyer, and this form of local government continued even after 1406 when Pisa was conquered by Florence. In the 16C it declined in military power and from then on it was ruled by influential families.

Palazzo Pretorio – *In a street running uphill from the Piazza della Repubblica in the town centre*. The building is decorated with the coats of arms of the captains who lived here until 1406. The column to the left was used as the base of the cage in which wrongdoers were exposed to public ridicule.

Porta Florentina (Florentine Gate) – *At the end of Via Cavour*. The four coats of arms on the gate recall the rulers of Campiglia – the Cross of Pisa, the lily of Florence, the greyhound of Campiglia and the star of the Gherardesca family.

Rocca – Overlooking the Porta Florentina are the remains of the **fortress**, built in the 12C-13C, probably on the site of an earlier 8C fortress. The remains include a delightful twin bay.
Via Roma leads to **Porta a Mare** and Piazza della Vittoria from which there is an extensive **view** of the coast.

Pieve di San Giovanni – *In the cemetery*. This parish **church** was built in the 12C in the shape of the Greek letter 'tau' (T) and has two particularly interesting features. Beneath the side portal is a low relief depicting *The Boar Hunt in Meleagre*; beneath the roof of the side chapel is an inscription of the mysterious **magic square** which dates from the beginning of the Christian era if not from earlier times. The five words are set out in a square of five lines which read the same both backwards and forwards and up and down –

```
S A T O R
A R E P O
T E N E T
O P E R A
R O T A S
```

It is apparently a Latin pun but the meaning remains obscure. It is well known throughout the Mediterranean world from Spain to Turkey and seems to have been used as a magic spell to ward off evil spirits.
The country round Campiglia is part of the belt of mineral-bearing hills. There are **archeological excavations** ⊙ on the slopes of Monte Calvi not far from the Rocca San Silvestro (10C), which reveal mining actitivity in the Middle Ages.

CAPALBIO

Population 4 015
Michelin Map 988 fold 25 or 430 O 16

Capalbio occupies a favourable position on a hilltop (209m – 679ft above sea level), overlooking a varied and fertile landscape of undulating hills not far from the sea. Its medieval appearance, dominated by a crenellated tower, is visible from all directions.

Historical notes – The first document to mention Capalbio dates from 1161.
In the 14C the Aldobrandeschi family gave the village to the Republic of Siena and thereafter the destinies of the two places were linked. In 1555 Capalbio, like Orbetello, was invaded by the Spaniards (allies of the Medici). In the 18C and 19C the town suffered from the neglect of the surrounding farmland which had been allowed to return to marsh, causing malaria and the general impoverishment of the whole area. Not until the 20C did Capalbio see an increase in its population, due to a revival of farming.

Historic town centre – There are two gates – Porta Senese (Siena Gate) and Porticine (Little Gate) – into the walled medieval village. Within stands the Romanesque **Church of San Nicola** which contains 14C frescoes *(chapels on north side)* and 15C frescoes *(chapels on south side)*. The belltower, pierced by twin bays, dates from the 12C. Nearby is the Aldobrandeschi fortress *(Rocca)*.
Outside the walls, in Piazza Provvidenza, the **Oratorio della Provvidenza** is decorated with a 15C fresco based on works by Peruggio and Pinturicchio.

Giardino dei Tarocchi by Niki de Saint-Phalle.

EXCURSIONS

Giardino dei Tarocchi (Tarot Gardens) ⊘ – *In Garavicchio, 8km – 5 miles southeast of Capalbio*. These unusual gardens laid out by Niki de Saint Phalle against a background of olive and cypress trees, provide the setting for sculptures made of reinforced cement and polyester covered with mirrors and coloured ceramics so that they sparkle in the sunshine. The colossal sculptures represent the 22 Greater Arcana of a pack of tarot cards.

The artist was the wife of Tinguely (d 1991) and she considered the gardens to be her life's work. The sculptures are characteristic of her art, combining forms, colours and materials in a way that goes beyond the imaginary to border on the unreasonable. Her inspiration was a simple pack of tarot cards given to her by a friend, which led her to study the ancient origins of this mysterious art of fortune telling and then to illustrate it on a hillside above one of the loneliest landscapes in Tuscany. The resultant effect is almost surreal.

CAPRESE MICHELANGELO

Population 1 698
Michelin Map 430 L 17

The controversy as to whether Chiusi della Verna or Caprese could claim the honour of being the birthplace of Michelangelo on 6 March 1475 was settled in 1875 by the discovery of a copy of the artist's birth certificate – the original had been lost. It was mere chance that Michelangelo was born in Caprese, where his father, a governor *(podestà)* employed by Florence, had been posted. After his birth, Michelangelo was placed with a wet-nurse in Settignano, not far from Florence.

Park at the top of the village. A cobbled street (pedestrians only) leads to the castle.

Casa di Michelangelo (Michelangelo's House) – The 14C castle contains **Casa del Podestà**, the governor's house, where Michelangelo's family lived. Coats of arms adorn the façade but the architectural style is modest. The house is now the **Museo Michelangiolesco** (Michelangelo Museum) ⊘. On the ground floor are a few plaster casts and photographs showing the artist's sculptures and paintings. On the upper floor are reproductions of paintings illustrating his life. Michelangelo was probably born in the small room at the end of the corridor. In the garden to the left are a number of statues by contemporary artists.

At the foot of the castle is the 13C Church of St John the Baptist (San Giovanni Battista), a small, modest building with bare stone walls, where Michelangelo is said to have been christened.

CARRARA

Population 67 092
Michelin Map 988 fold 14 or 430 J 12

Carrara lies in a delightful valley on the edge of a ruggedly spectacular limestone mountain range – the Apuan Alps – which are so white that they seem to be covered in snow. The name comes from the Ligurian root "kar" meaning "stone" and the town is world-famous for its fine-grained white marble, which is exceptionally pure and has been quarried since Roman times. Michelangelo used to come to Carrara to choose blocks of stone for his masterpieces.

In 1769 Maria Teresa Cybo Malaspina (the last of the aristocratic family which controlled events in Massa and Carrara for many centuries) set up an Academy of Fine Arts, which still provides teaching in techniques and artistic skills.

The town is fairly modern and has, from time immemorial, been the home of quarry workers and artists working in marble. Every year in July during the *Simposio*, which is held in a square in the heart of the old town, 20 or 30 Italian and foreign sculptors work in the open air, turning the square into a vast workshop where passers-by can see the craft being practised.

Duomo – The **cathedral** was built (11C-14C) in the Romanesque-Gothic style with a façade in the Pisan style, pierced by a rose window, decorated with superb marble tracery, and flanked by an elegant 13C belltower. The interior contains a number of interesting statues including a wooden *Crucifix* and a marble *Annunciation*, both dating from the 14C.

Beside the cathedral is a huge 16C fountain decorated with a statue by Baccio Bandinelli (1493-1560).

★ **Museo del Marmo** (Marble Museum) ⊙ – *1km – 0.5 mile from town centre, on the right in the avenue linking the town to Marina di Carrara*. Marble and the uses to which it has been put from Antiquity to the present day, is presented in five different sections. The first explains how marble was quarried during the days of the Ancient Romans, information that has been obtained from archeological excavations. The second section, the **Marmoteca★**, is a "library" including more than 300 samples of marble and granite from the largest seams in the world. The third section deals with quarrying techniques from the 18C to the early 20C. The fourth concerns various aspects of the use of marble and the final section consists of a collection of modern sculptures.

EXCURSIONS

★ **Cave di marmo** (Marble quarries) – The untamed scenery, the white scree slopes and the gigantic scale of the work undertaken by man are an amazing sight. Beside the road stand small platforms which provide a view *(during working hours)* of the machinery in operation.

To extract the marble, the quarrymen use a "diamond wire", a steel wire containing small cylinders covered with diamond dust which acts as a highpower

---

Carrara Marble

The marble seams in the Apuan Alps extend over several square miles but the largest of all is in Carrara. It is famous for its translucent whiteness and fine grain, both qualities which are highly prized in statues, hence its title – *statuario*. Once polished, it acquires the pearly sparkle that is its characteristic quality. Carrara also produces veined or coloured marbles (dark red, green, grey-blue, orange). The colours result from the presence of mineral salts (or other elements) in the original limestone which, after crystallising for several million years, has turned into marble.

On this side of the Apuan Alps, quarrying has been in progress for some 2 000 years, removing the top layer of rock from the wooded slopes, cutting into the hillsides and revealing areas of white rock that sparkle in the sunshine. Quarrying is now concentrated in three valleys – Colonnata, Fantiscritti, and Ravaccione *(qv)*. Over the centuries, quarrying has undergone constant expansion and the industry now produces 800 000 tonnes of marble a year. This has been made possible, since the 19C century, by new techniques and the opening, in 1876, of a railway linking the quarries to the sea, thereby facilitating the transport of the stone. From the reign of Caesar Augustus until the 5C, imperial Rome, which made extensive use of marble, obtained three-quarters of its building stone from Carrara. Thereafter, Carrara marble was used for such prestigious works as the main staircase in the Hermitage in St Petersburg or the outer cladding of the Arche de la Défense in Paris. Since the Renaissance many sculptors – Michelangelo, Giambologna, Bernini, Canova and Henry Moore – have come to the quarries in the vicinity to choose the stone for their work.

LARA PESSINA

abrasive. The blocks of stone are then taken down to the plain where they are divided in stone-cutting plants; after being processed in marble works, the stone is exported from the harbour in Marina di Carrara *(qv)*.

★★ **Fantiscritti Quarries** – *4 or 5km – 2.5 or 3 miles northeast beyond Miseglia*. This is the most impressive of all the quarry sites because of its ruggedness, terracing and particularly steep road up to the various levels. The site is reached by a road, which crosses three viaducts known as the *Ponti di Vara*; they were built in the 19C for the mining train and have been converted into road bridges.

★ **Colonnata Quarries** – *8km – 5 miles east via Bedizzano or Carrara along the valley floor*. These quarries are more easily accessible than the others; the road mounts from one level to the next, passing several stone-cutting plants. The setting is less grandiose but more attractive owing to the surrounding greenery.

★ **Campo Cecina Road** – *20km – 12 miles north of Carrara by the Fosdinovo road (S446ᵈ) to the viewing point*. The road climbs unendingly upwards above a wooded valley and passes through Gragnana and Castelpoggio. The first view *(left)* is over the final outcrops of the Apuan Alps dotted with hilltop villages and down to the sea that is visible between the beach at Marina di Carrara and the headland at Montemarcello.

Turn right into the winding Campo Cecina road which is used by the large trucks transporting the marble from the quarries.

The road runs along the south-facing, pine-clad slopes of Monte Pizza. There are more views *(right)* over the Carrara area, each one more extensive than the last. A picturesque trip along a road cut into the bare marble hillsides of Monte Uccelliera, interspersed with forest sections, leads to **Piazzale dell'Uccelliera**, a vast roundabout from which there is a magnificent **view**★ – over the amazing Torano quarries, the beaches at Marina di Massa and Montignoso, the islands in the Tuscan Archipelago and the peaks in the Southern Alps.

Help us in our constant task of keeping up-to-date
Please send us your comments and suggestions

Michelin Tyre PLC Tourism Department
Edward Hyde Building
38 Clarendon Road WATFORD
Herts WD1 1SX

Tel : 01923 415166 – Fax : 01923 415250

CASCIANA TERME✝

Population 3 233
Michelin Map 988 fold 14 or 430 L 13

Casciana Terme is surrounded by hills planted with vines and peach and olive trees. It enjoys a mild climate and is an ideally quiet yet varied holiday venue where visitors can alternate between taking the waters and visiting nearby towns of artistic and architectural interest.

Taking the waters – The springs in Casciana had already been discovered in the days of Caesar Augustus and they have been famous since the 11C. One episode in their history is tantamount to legend. From the window of her castle in Casciana, Matilda of Canossa (1046-1115), Marchioness of Tuscany, is said to have seen a blackbird come back day after day to bathe its swollen foot in a stream until, finally, it ceased to limp and flew away.

The springs are strongly recommended for the treatment of circulatory disorders, hypertension, arthritis, rheumatism, asthma and bronchitis.

The treatment takes the form of baths, mud baths, inhalations or drinks of water.

CASCINA

Population 36 312
Michelin Map 988 fold 14 or 430 K 13

The town specialises in the small-scale and mass production of furniture, hence its size. At first it was controlled by Pisa but came under Florence in 1364 after the **Battle of Cascina**. The battle remained famous because Michelangelo chose it as the subject of a major fresco that was never painted but which later generations knew about because of its magnificent cartoon. It was designed for the Hall of Five Hundred in the Palazzo Vecchio *(qv)* in Florence where it would have appeared opposite the fresco painted by Leonardo da Vinci of the Battle of Anghiari *(qv)*. The artist, who was fascinated by the anatomy of the human body, chose to illustrate this episode which allowed him to depict Florentine soldiers bathing naked in the Arno when they were subjected to a surprise attack by Pisan troops.

TOUR

The old town centre, laid out in a grid pattern, is traversed by Corso Matteotti, a street lined with arcades. At one end, there is a clock tower containing a small bell; this is all that remains of the walls which encircled the town in the Middle Ages. At the other end of Corso Matteotti is the Oratory of San Giovanni (late 14C) which has a *Crucifixion* by Martino di Bartolomeo (1398) above the altar, including *(top right)* the beginning of a cycle of frescoes telling the story of Genesis.

Santa Maria – This 12C church, which is set back from the Corso Matteotti and flanked by two other churches, has a typically Pisan façade★ built of local stone *(verrucano)* and encrusted with white marble motifs.

CASTAGNETO CARDUCCI

Population 8 244
Michelin Map 430 M 13

The town, attractively situated on a hilltop in a landscape of olive trees, used to belong to the Counts della Gherardesca. All that remains of their castle are the ruins of one tower *(torre di Donoratico, 3.5km – 2 miles south)* where the infamous Ugolino della Gherardesca *(qv)*, having been accused of treachery by Pisa after the Battle of Meloria (1284), is said to have found temporary refuge before suffering the terrible punishment of starving to death with his children in 1289. Castagneto had belonged to Pisa since the 12C but it came under Florentine jurisdiction in 1406. The village, however, has a claim to fame that is rather more literary than historic. It is named after the Italian poet Giosuè Carducci (born in 1835 in Valdicastello *(qv)*; died in 1907 in Bologna), who stayed in the village during his youth and wrote poetry in honour of the beautiful Tuscan countryside. His life and work is recalled in the **museo archivio** (museum) ⊘ in the Palazzo municipale (Town Hall).

EXCURSION

Bolgheri – *7km – 4 miles to the north*. This is the village in which Carducci lived from 1838 to 1848. The long avenue lined with large cypress trees leading to the village from San Guido *(west)* was described by the poet in his elegiac work, *In Front of San Guido,* a work well known to Italians.

CASTELFIORENTINO

Population 17 139
Michelin Map 988 fold 14 or 430 L 14

The name, which means Florentine Castle dates from 1149 and the area became
the property of the Bishop of Florence in the 12C. It was here that the peace treaty
was signed by Siena and Florence after the Battle of Montaperti *(qv)* in 1260.

From **Piazza Gramsci,** a large square, the Siena road leads to the brick-fronted **Church
of San Francesco** and then to the **Church of Santa Verdiana,** one of the most significant
examples of early 18C architecture in Tuscany, standing at the end of a superb
esplanade of trees.

In the centre of the village is the **Raccolta Comunale d'Arte** ⊙ *(no 41 Via Tilli)*, a small
art collection containing **frescoes** and underdrawings for frescoes *(sinopie)* by
Benozzo Gozzoli★ (1420-1497) which have been removed from their original setting
(two tabernacles) and restored. The painter's style is remarkably well represented both in the frescoes of the Madonna della Tosse Tabernacle, which depict
the *Virgin Mary, St John and Two Saints,* the *Funeral of the Blessed Virgin Mary*
and the *Assumption,* and in the frescoes from the Visitation Tabernacle, which
also depict scenes from the life of the Virgin Mary.

CASTELLO★

5km – 3 miles north of Florence
See plan of Florence in Michelin Map 430, the Europe or Italy road atlas or
the Michelin Red Guide to Italy

This village, which is on the outskirts of Florence, is known for two villas that once
belonged to the Medici.

★★ **Villa di Castello** ⊙ – *Northwest in Castello (signed). Large semi-circular car park
in front of the villa. The gardens, the only part open to the public, are at the
rear.*
The villa was purchased by the Medici in 1477 and embellished by Lorenzo the
Magnificent. As it was ransacked in 1527, Duke Cosimo I commissioned Tribolo
to refurbish it and lay out the gardens. Since 1974, the villa has housed the
Accademia della Crusca, the body set up to maintain and protect the Italian language.
The gardens include a large Italian-style flowerbed set out with an exquisite
feeling for proportion so that it sets off the beautiful central fountain designed
by Tribolo. The fountain is decorated with a bronze statue, *Hercules and Antaeus,*
by Ammannati *(restoration in progress)*. Further along the same axis is a grotto
with three niches containing animal statues (the bronze animals sculpted by
Giovanni da Bologna are in the Bargello Museum in Florence).

★ **Villa della Petraia** ⊙ – *Northeast in Castello at the end of Via della Petraia
(signed)*. In 1576 Cardinal Ferdinand Medici commissioned the architect
Buontalenti to turn what was then a fortresss into a villa and lay out the gardens.
In the 19C the villa became the summer residence of King Victor-Emmanuel II
and the interior was refurbished. The ground floor, including the State
apartments, the courtyard and the Renaissance portico were all glassed in so
that they could be used as a ballroom. The **gardens** (16C) consist of flowerbeds
in front of the villa and a wooded park at the rear. A superb fountain designed
by Tribolo, which originally stood in the grounds of the Villa de Castello *(see
above)*, was re-sited on the righthand side of the villa *(the basin and statue have
been removed for restoration)*. The admirable statue of Venus by Giovanni da
Bologna can, however, be seen on the first floor of the villa.

CASTIGLION FIORENTINO

Population 11 419
Michelin Map 988 fold 15 or 430 L 17

The town is set on a slope, once the site of an Etruscan settlement, above the Chio,
a short tributary of the Chiana. The first stronghold, built on the hilltop during the
Barbarian invasions in the 5C, was replaced in the 11C-12C by a citadel *(cassero)*
dominated by a slender square tower.
The busy centre of the town is Piazza del Municipio; the side facing the valley and
the 16C Town Hall is lined by the arcade of a 16C portico, known as the **Logge del
Vasari** because of its style and not because of a connection with Vasari, the artist;
the back wall is covered with coats of arms and pierced by three bays; beyond is
a pleasant **view** of the Collegiate Church of San Giuliano *(downhill to the right)* and
the countryside through which the Chio flows.

70

SIGHTS

★ **Pinacoteca** ⊘ – *Take the street to the right that climbs up behind the Town Hall.* The art gallery, which is housed in the Chapel of Sant'Angelo next to the citadel, contains a number of valuable paintings including two Umbrian Crucifixion scenes painted on wood and dating from the 13C and 14C, a painting of *St Francis of Assisi* by Margaritone of Arezzo (13C), a *Virgin Mary in Majesty* (14C) by Taddeo Gaddi and two reredos panels by Giovanni di Paolo (15C). There are also some superb pieces of church plate including a bust-reliquary of St Ursula (14C Rhenish School), a Crucifix-reliquary from the Moselle (late 12C), and a French Crucifix dating from the second half of the 13C.

From the top room *(saletta della Torre)*, there is a wonderful view of the Church of San Giuliano, the countryside and the mountains.

Collegiata di San Giuliano (Collegiate Church) – This church, which was rebuilt in the 19C, is capped by a dome and preceded by a portico. It contains a 17C carved wooden presbytery and a number of interesting works of art – *(south aisle)* *St Anthony the Abbot,* a painted earthenware figure from the Della Robbia workshop, a *Virgin Mary in Majesty* by Bartolomeo Della Gatta and *Mary and Joseph Adoring the Infant Jesus* by Lorenzo di Credi (15C); *(south transept)* an *Annunciation* from the Della Robbia workshop; *(north transept)* a *Virgin Mary in Majesty* by Segna di Bonaventura (14C).

Immediately adjacent and also preceded by a portico, is the 16C **Chiesa del Gesù** (Church of Jesus) ⊘, which has an ornate Baroque interior.

Chiostro di San Francesco (Cloisters) – These small cloisters, next to the uninspiring 13C Church of St Francis, were rebuilt in the 17C with an upper storey that forms a balcony with colonnettes. The cloisters are decorated with a series of frescoes *(in poor condition)* depicting the life of St Francis of Assisi.

EXCURSION

★ **Montecchio Castle** – *3.5km – 2 miles south by S71*. The castle stands on a rise on the east side of the road between Castiglion Fiorentino and Cortona. It is interesting for the size of its crenellated outer wall reinforced by eight small towers and for its keep (30m – 97ft) which contained the main apartments. Originally Montecchio shared the lot of Castiglion but was later raised to borough status in its own right, its walls enclosing several houses, a church and a town hall, all of which have since disappeared. This was the largest fortress in the Chiana Valley and it retained its military importance until the 17C.

CECINA

Population 24 638
Michelin Map 988 fold 14 or 430 M 13

Cecina is a farming and industrial town (brickworks) which was founded in the mid 19C following local land improvement. It is set at the heart of a wide strip of land, known as the Etruscan Riviera, which stretches from Livorno (Leghorn) south to Piombino; it extends to the coast as **Marina di Cecina**≙, a seaside resort sheltered by a wonderful pine wood that still contains numerous Etruscan remains which are studied by archeologists.

The **Museo archeologico** (Archeological Museum) ⊘ contains Etruscan buccheroware, Greek vases decorated with painted figures dating from the Classical and Hellenistic Periods, urns dating from the 6C BC and funeral items from the days of imperial Rome.

ETRUSCAN RIVIERA

≙ **Castiglioncello** – *14km – 9 miles north*. This is an elegant seaside resort on the Etruscan Riviera, well known for its delightful beaches sheltering in creeks in the shade of pine woods. The resort has an excellent climate owing to its ideal situation, protected by a headland and by hills descending to the water's edge.

Rosignano Marittimo – *15km – 9 miles north*. The remains of the medieval centre are in the upper part of the village. The **Museo Archeologico** (Archeological Museum) ⊘ in the castle provides an insight into local history from the Etruscan period to the Middle Ages.

Nearer the coast is **Rosignano Solvay**, an industrial town, named after a Belgian chemist who developed a method of mass-producing soda.

Marina di Castagneto-Donoratico – *18km – 11 miles south*. This is a seaside resort with a long sandy beach sheltered by attractive pine woods.

≙ **San Vincenzo** – *26km – 16 miles south*. This is a seaside resort with many amenities. It is famous for its sandy beach *(5km – 3 miles)* dotted with rocks.

CERRETO GUIDI*

Population 8 939
Michelin Map 430 K 14

This village, which stands on a hill among the delightful uplands southwest of Monte Albano, grew up around the castle that once belonged to the Counts Guidi. Their connection with the village is remembered in its name, now the only trace of the old estate which passed into the hands of the Medici family. The residence was then totally rebuilt by Cosimo I c1560, to look as it does now. The villa was surrounded by vast vineyards and extensive hunting grounds reserved for the Grand Dukes; it was used as a hunting lodge for the Medici and their courtiers and its cellars as a wine warehouse. It fell into decline, however, after the tragic death of Cosimo I's favourite daughter, Isabella Orsini, Duchess of Bracciano; her husband, Paolo Giordano Orsini, who himself spent very little time in her company, had her strangled after learning that she had become the mistress of the man to whom she had entrusted the protection of her honour.

★ **Villa medicea** ⊙ – This austere villa, which stands at the top of the village, was designed by Buontalenti. The approach is embellished by two majestic, monumental flights of brick steps, known as the *Ponti*. From the terrace there is a wonderful view of the Arno Valley hills and *(left)* of San Miniato and its high tower.

The entrance hall is hung with portraits *(right)* of Isabella Orsini and her husband and *(left)* of Bianco Cappello *(qv)*, wife of Francesco I Medici, a woman with an equally unfortunate destiny. On the first floor is the Medici portrait gallery. From the balcony *(loggia)*, there is a delightful view of the garden and its pergola.

Flanking the villa *(left)* is the Church of San Leonardo.

The Pratical Information section at the end of the guide lists :
- *information on travel, motoring, accommodation, recreation*
- *local or national organisations providing additional information*
- *calendar of events*
- *admission times and charges for the sights described in the guide*

CERTALDO

Population 15 945
Michelin Map 988 fold 14 or 430 L 15

The town of Certaldo, built of pink brick and set in the attractive Elsa Valley, may have been the birthplace of Giovanni Boccaccio. It was certainly the place in which he spent the last few years before his death.

An Incomparable Storyteller (1313-1375)

Boccaccio wrote commentaries on Dante's work and was a close friend of Petrarch with whom he corresponded regularly for more than 20 years. He was a precursor of Humanism and is recognised as the third "major figure" in medieval Italian literature. He was born to a Frenchwoman of high birth who had a love affair with a merchant named Boccaccino di Chellino de Certaldo. While still an adolescent, he was sent to Naples as his father had decided that his son should follow him into business.

For 12 years he frequented the brilliant, cultured Court of Robert of Anjou and fell in love with the good king's illegitimate daughter, the blond Maria of Aquino who has gone down in history under the charming nickname of *Fiametta* (little flame). The poet was a tender-hearted man but he made light of everything and was typical of the 14C Italian bourgeoisie, loving the Arts and pleasure. Boccaccio became a canon of the church but he was cynical as well as gracious. In Florence he wrote his masterpiece the *Decameron (Ten Days)* in a clear and fast-moving style. The collection of 100 novelle was presented as the work of three youths and seven young girls who, during the outbreak of plague in Florence in 1348, sought refuge far from the town and decided to pass the time by telling each other a new story every day for ten days. *Decameron* is a spirited and sometimes satirical work describing the charms of the Tuscan countryside and the cultured life that accompanied the development of Humanism. Several of the tales were re-worked by La Fontaine; some were adapted for the screen by Pasolini.

Palazzo Pretorio in Certaldo bearing the coats of arms of the local governors.

The **Casa-museo del Boccacio** (Boccacio Museum) ⊙ in the upper walled town has been rebuilt, having been almost totally destroyed during the war.
Higher up is the 13C Church of San Jacopo (St James); the cenotaph *(north wall)* was set up as a memorial to Boccacio in 1503; the spot where he was buried was marked by a tombstone in 1954.
Nearby is the **Palazzo Pretorio** ⊙, which was rebuilt in the 16C. Its frontage is decorated with earthenware and marble coats of arms and it has an arcaded courtyard. The palace contains frescoes by Pier Francesco Fiorentino (15C).

CETONA

Population 3 026
Michelin Map 430 N 17

The Etruscan origins of this town explain its picturesque setting on a small hill, which was crowned in the Middle Ages by a fortress. At that period Cetona lay on the border between the Republic of Siena and the Papal States and was fiercely possessed or angrily coveted by both parties.
The village has been extensively restored since becoming fashionable with the Italian jet set (a number of actors, industrialists and dress designers have holiday homes in Cetona).

Collegiata - This collegiate **church** dates from the 13C and contains a fresco of the *Assumption* attributed to Pinturicchio (15C).

Museo civico per la preistoria del Monte Cetona ⊙ - The **museum**, which is housed in the Town Hall, has exhibits illustrating the geology of Monte Cetona *(see below)*, particularly items proving the existence of prehistoric settlements from the Paleolithic era to the end of the Bronze Age - bones, pottery, stone implements, and dioramas depicting everyday life at that time.

EXCURSIONS

Monte Cetona - *5.5km - 3.5 miles southwest of Cetona by car; 500m - 547yds on foot to the summit.*
The summit of the bare rocky mountain (1148m - 3731ft) provides a superb **panoramic view**. Since the Paleolithic era (*c*50 000 years ago) the many natural caves in the slopes attracted human settlement, especially by Neanderthal Man, who gained a livelihood from hunting and herding. The major period of population growth took place in the middle of the second millennium BC. The place was then abandoned as the people moved from a pastoral to an agriculturally-based way of life.
Around **Belverde** *(signs)* some of the **caves** ⊙ have been made accessible and electricity has been installed.

CETONA

Sarteano – *6.5km – 4 miles northwest. Facilities*. This is a holiday resort with three swimming pools filled with water which has a high mineral content and a temperature of 24°C; the water comes from a thermal spring which was known to the Ancient Romans. The village is dominated by a wooded hill crowned by an 11C fortress which was altered in the 15C by the Sienese; its walls and mighty square tower with machicolations are well preserved.

The **Church of San Martino** has a single nave and contains a number of interesting paintings – *(left)* a large **Annunciation**★★ by Beccafumi and a *Madonna and Child between St Roch and St Sebastian* by Andrea di Niccolò; *(right)* a *Visitation* by Vanni and two works by Giacomo di Mino del Pellicciaio – a *Madonna and Child* signed and dated 1342 and a triptych.

CHIANCIANO TERME⚕⚕

Population 7 447
Michelin Map 988 fold 15 or 430 M 17

Chianciano Terme is a large, elegant spa town delightfully situated overlooking attractive rolling scenery at the foot of the old hilltop village of Chianciano Vecchia. The mineral water here has a high sulphate and calcium content; it was already known to the Etruscans and Romans and was mentioned by Horace. There are four separate thermal establishments, treating liver and biliary complaints (Acqua Santa, Acqua Fucoli and Acqua Sillene) and disorders of the kidneys, urinary tract, metabolism and digestive tract (Acqua Sant'Elena). The resort has ultra-modern hotels and treatment centres and a number of beautiful, shady parks. The main street, **Viale Roma**, is the most elegant in the resort.

EXCURSION

Chianciano Vecchia – *2km – 1 mile northeast*. The entrance to the old town from the spa town is the Rivellini Gate. The first part of the main street is dominated by the clock tower, decorated with the coat of arms of the Medici. Further on, there is a superb view *(left)* over the Chiana Valley before reaching a square flanked by the Palazzo del Podestà, decorated with a few coats of arms, and *(opposite)* the Palazzo dell'Arcipretura. The small **Museo di arte sacra** (Museum of Sacred Art) ⊙, which is housed in the latter building, contains mainly Sienese paintings and gold or silverware from the 13C to 19C, including a **Virgin Mary of Humility**★ by Lorenzo di Niccolò.

Further along the main street stands the **Collegiate Church**, which has an austere travertine façade decorated with a delicate Romanesque portal.

From Via della Croce *(turn right)* there is a fine view of the surrounding countryside.

Slightly further on *(left)* is the Porta del Sole leading to the late-16C **Church of La Madonna della Rosa**, built entirely of brick and stone. From the Porta del Sole, Via Garibaldi skirts the town walls and returns to the entrance.

MICHELIN GUIDES

The Red Guides (hotels and restaurants)
Benelux – Deutschland – España Portugal – Main Cities Europe – France – Great Britain and Ireland – Italia – Suisse

The Green Guides (fine art, historical monuments, scenic routes)
Austria – California – Canada– England : the West Country – France – Germany – Great Britain – Greece – Ireland – Italy – London – Mexico – Netherlands – New England – New York – Paris – Portugal – Quebec – Rome – Scotland – Spain – Switzerland – Washington

... and the collection of regional guides for France

IL CHIANTI★★

Michelin Map 988 folds 14-15 or 430 L 15-16

The Chianti region is famous for its excellent wine; the vineyards which produce it extend well beyond the boundaries of the geographical region, which lies between Florence and Siena; it is bordered to the east by the Chianti Hills with the Arno at their foot and extends west and south to the river valleys of the Greve, Pesa, Elsa and Arbia.

The territory which produces Chianti, a wine of guaranteed and controlled designation of origin (D.O.C.G.), also includes Monte Albano south of Pistoia, the hills in the southern part of the province of Pisa, the Mugello district, the Pratomagno slopes beside the Arno, the neighbourhood of Arezzo, the west side of the Chiana Valley and the neighbourhood of Montepulciano, the south of the Siena district around Montalcino, the Montagnola district west of Siena and the neighbourhood of San Gimignano *(qv)*.

The central area, which produces Chianti Classico (including the towns which set up the Chianti League in the 13C), coincides almost exactly with the geographical region from which the wine takes its name. It is bisected from north to south by the **Via Chiantigiana** (S 222). The landscape shows that the soil has been tilled for many centuries. Among the forests of chestnut, oak, pine and larch which grow on the slopes that are least easy to cultivate, there are rows of vines and silvery-green olive trees carpeting the gently-rolling hillsides which are also dotted with cypress trees. Small villages and a few superb estates around a castle, villa or abbey blend harmoniously into a natural environment partially tamed by the hand of man.

EXCURSIONS IN THE CHIANTI DISTRICT

The three excursions described below all follow **Via Chiantigiana** (S 222) for some distance. Visitors doing a rapid tour of Tuscany, including Florence and Siena, are advised to travel from one city to the other along this road, which provides wonderful views of the local forests and vineyards. The motorway-type road *(superstrada)* between Florence and Siena, known as the *Raccordo,* which runs along the west side of the Chianti region, is particularly attractive in the Pesa and Staggia Valleys.

☐ **From Florence**
the Pesa and the Greve Valleys *about 100km - 62 miles*

★★★ **Florence** *– See Firenze.*

Leave Florence by Via Senese going to Galluzzo (see the map of the Florence area in the Michelin Europe Atlas or the Michelin Italy Atlas or on Michelin Map 430).

★★ **Galluzzo Charterhouse** *– See Galluzzo.*

Take S2 to Siena rather than the Superstrada or the Raccordo autostradale Firenze-Siena. South of Tavarnuzze, pass under the motorway. After about 1.5km – 1 mile turn right to Sant'Andrea in Percussina, crossing the River Greve (the road has flowed the course of the river since Tavarnuzze).

The first few miles are through forest but the road gradually runs out from the trees and gives the first glimpses of the vines. In the hamlet of **Sant'Andrea in Percussina** *(left)* is the Albergaccio di Machiavelli, now a restaurant, where **Machiavelli** lived after being banished from Florence on the return of the Medici because he had served the Republic from 1498 to 1512. It was here that he wrote *The Prince* in 1513. He was not allowed to return to Florence until 1526, one year before his death.

San Casciano in Val di Pesa – The town is set on a hilltop, between the valleys of the Greve and the Pesa, and still has some of its 14C and 16C town walls. From the tiny central square known as the Orazio Pierozzi *(junction of Via Roma and Via 4 Novembre)*, Via Morrocchesi leads to **Chiesa della Misericordia**, a Romanesque-Gothic church *(later restoration)*, which contains some interesting works by 14C and 15C Tuscan artists. Santa Maria del Gesù *(Via Roma)* contains a **Museo di Arte Sacra** (Museum of Sacred Art) ⊘ – Tuscan paintings and sculptures, church plate and altarpieces. Further on is the large public park, Piazza della Repubblica, flanked by the remainder of earlier fortifications including a 14C tower. From the terrace, there is a fine view over the Pesa Valley.

The road (S2) descends into the Pesa Valley and follows the course of the river for some distance. Before reaching Sambuca, turn left towards Badia a Passignano.

★★ **Badia a Passignano** ⊘ – This splendid **abbey**, a daughter house of Vallombrosa *(qv)*, stands on the top of a gentle rise planted with vines and cypress trees. Passignano was founded in 1049 by Giovanni Gualberto who died there in 1073 and is buried in the abbey. From a distance, the combination of the village houses nestling up against the crenellated walls and towers of the abbey resembles a

75

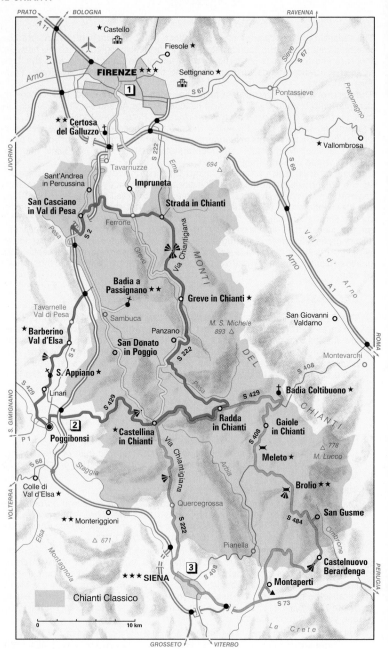

PRATO · BOLOGNA · RAVENNA
★ Castello
Fiesole ★
FIRENZE ★★★
1
Settignano ★
Pontassieve
★ Vallombrosa
★★ Certosa del Galluzzo
Sant'Andrea in Percussina
Tavarnuzze
Impruneta
San Casciano in Val di Pesa
Strada in Chianti
Ferrone
Badia a Passignano ★★
Greve in Chianti ★
San Giovanni Valdarno
Tavarnelle Val di Pesa
Sambuca
Panzano
M. S. Michele 893 △
Montevarchi
★ Barberino Val d'Elsa
San Donato in Poggio
★ S. Appiano ★
Linari
† Badia Coltibuono ★
2
Poggibonsi
★ Castellina in Chianti
Radda in Chianti
Gaiole in Chianti
△ 778 M. Lucco
Meleto ★
Colle di Val d'Elsa ★
Brolio ★★
Quercegrossa
San Gusme
★★ Monteriggioni
△ 671
Pianella
3
Castelnuovo Berardenga
★★★ SIENA
▲ Montaperti
Chianti Classico
Le Crete
0   10 km
GROSSETO · VITERBO

fortified town. *Park at the rear of the abbey.* A flight of steps lined with cypress trees leads up to the entrance to the church. The façade is surmounted by a 13C marble statue of St Michael the Archangel, to whom the church is dedicated. The interior is decorated with 16C paintings by Domenico Cresti, who is known as Il Passignano in memory of his birthplace.

The road back towards the Pesa Valley crosses a landscape of coppices, olive groves, vineyards and fields of cereal crops. In the valley bottom the road skirts the old village of Sambuca before returning to the hilltops, where the scenery is wild and wooded again.

San Donato in Poggio – This medieval hilltop village, which is partly fortified, was once part of an old castle. In the central square is the Palazzo Malaspina (fine rusticated window mouldings) and a Renaissance water tank. Below the houses stands the **Parish Church of San Donato,** which dates from the second half of the 12C;

its regular, meticulous bonding emphasises the elegant austerity of Romanesque architecture. The original basilica-like layout has survived; it comprises the nave, with pitched roof, and aisles ending in three apsidal chapels, with semicircular roofs. The crenellations of the belltower betray its original defensive purpose; the dark stone used for the upper section contrasts sharply with the rest which is built of white limestone.

The road to Castellina continues to cross vast stretches of countryside consisting of largely unfelled forest, where the views are interrupted by thickets and broom. From a bare hilltop *(7km – 4 miles from San Donato)* there is an extensive **view**★ *(right)* over the Elsa Valley and beyond.

★ **Castellina in Chianti** – *See below – Tour 2.*

The road twists and turns as it descends into the Pesa Valley; over the river and nearer to Panzano the countryside is less heavily-wooded and less austere.

Panzano *(left)* is visible from some considerable distance because its church and belltower stand on a rise; the modern portal frames a bronze door and is surmounted by a tympanum decorated with a stucco representation of the Assumption of the Blessed Virgin Mary.

The next stretch of the Via Chiantigiana passes through a delightful succession of olive groves, vineyards, thickets and rows of cypress trees.

★ **Greve in Chianti** – The village, which is situated on the floor of the valley of the River Greve, centres on an attractive square, Piazza Matteotti, shaped like a huge funnel; it is bordered by irregularly-shaped porticoes supporting flower-decked terraces. At the narrow end of the square stands the tiny church of Santa Croce, rebuilt in the 19C, also preceded by a portico. The interior of the church is in the Renaissance style. In the apsidal chapel beside the chancel *(north side)* there is a triptych *(left)* of the *Madonna and Child with Saints* and *(right)* a small *Annunciation of the Virgin Mary* by Bicci di Lorenzo.

The road continues north beside the Greve, through fairly wild countryside. In Le Bolle bear left to Ferrone (the major road (S 222) bears off right to Florence). North of Ferrone the road climbs up to Impruneta *(for some 500m – 540yds it becomes a dirt track)* lined with many trees – cypress, pine and oak.

Impruneta – *See Impruneta.*

Return to Florence.

② From Poggibonsi (or San Gimignano) the Heart of the Chianti League *about 100km – 62 miles*

Poggibonsi – A dynamic, modern town that owes its expansion to its industries. The old town is set slightly above the valley. In Piazza Cavour stands the small **Palazzo Pretorio**, decorated with coats of arms, dominated by a crenellated Gothic tower and surrounded by more recent buildings. Beside the palazzo is a collegiate church which was rebuilt in the 19C in the neo-Classical style; its crenellated belltower may be part of an old castle.

Pass through the industrial estate to reach the hills on the other side of the valley.

As the road gradually climbs the Chianti uplands, the slope becomes steeper and the hills become less rounded but vineyards are still very much in evidence. The bends in the road increase in frequency as the road reaches the crest, where it runs through stretches of woodland; there are a few magnificent views of the hills below, particularly in the last stretch before Castellina.

★ **Castellina in Chianti** – At the end of the 13C the town was on the border between the territories of Florence and Siena and it often changed hands because of its strategic position between the river valleys of the Elsa, Pesa and Arbia.

At the entrance to the town, opposite the neo-Romanesque Church of San Salvatore, is the start of an unusual street, **Via delle Volte**★, that is vaulted along almost its entire length. It skirts the interior of the town walls and, in the past,

Chianti League

At the beginning of the 13C, Florence set up the **Chianti League**, a military alliance to counter the territorial expansionist policies of Siena. The League, which included the towns of Castellina, Gaiole, and Radda, took as its emblem a black rooster *(gallo nero)*, which is now used by the wine consortium producing Chianti Classico. Each of the three territories *(terzieri)* forming the League, was administered by a governor *(podestà)*, originally based in Castellina. In 1415 his offices were moved to Radda. In the middle of the 16C, when the Republic of Siena was annexed to the Grand Duchy of Tuscany, the League ceased to have any purpose.

Grocery shop, Radda in Chianti.

riders could go right round the fortress on horseback. From the 16C onwards, when Tuscany was unified and became the Grand Duchy of the Medici, openings were made to give views of the wooded hillsides in the Chianti area.

At the end of the vaulted street, turn back along Via Ferruccio.

The impressive **Palazzo Ugolino** *(no 26)* has wine cellars dating from the Renaissance period. Opposite this palazzo, a narrow street climbs to the **Rocca**, the crenellated 15C castle *(restored)*; on the ground floor are two glass cabinets containing artefacts discovered in Poggino, the Etruscan graveyard in Fonterutoli (6C BC). From the second storey there is a panoramic view.

As the road approaches Radda, the countryside becomes more open and the woods on the hillsides gradually give way to a variety of crops and rows of vines.

Radda in Chianti – This medieval village, composed of a long line of houses, used to be one of the three territories *(terzieri)*, with Castellina and Gaiole, in the Chianti League *(see above)*; Radda became the main town in the League in 1415. It has retained one side of its town walls and its 15C Town Hall, which is decorated inside the double-arched porch with a fresco painted by the Florentine School.

West of Radda turn left into a minor road beside the Pesa to join S222 going north.

From Panzano to Greve – *See above* – *Tour 1.*

From Greve continue north on S222.

The area between Greve and Strada contains some of the most attractive scenery in the Chianti region. The magnificent road follows the crest of the hills in several places, providing an extensive **panoramic view★★** of the vineyards.

Strada in Chianti – In the past travellers between Florence and the Chianti district would have had to pass through this village, hence its name *(strada* means road). All that the modern village has retained of its past is the Romanesque church of San Cristoforo; the façade is decorated with a rose window. In front of the church is a porch with three arches supported on two elegant columns.

Take the road west via Ferrone.

San Casciano in Val di Pesa – *See above* – *Tour 1.*

Take the expressway (superstrada) south towards Siena.

As the road runs downhill, there is a fine view over the Pesa Valley flanked by hills.

Turn right off the expressway at the Tavarnelle exit.

South of Tavarnelle there is a view *(right)* over the Colli Fiorentini and *(left)* of the Pesa Valley.

★ **Barberino Val d'Elsa** – Barberino has now extended beyond the limits of the fortified hilltop village, which has been restored. The Porta Senese, the only gate in the 13C and 14C fortifications, leads into the main street, Via Francesco da Barberino, which contains *(left)* a superb corbelled house. Further on is Piazza

Barberini, flanked *(right)* by the Palazzo Pretorio; its wonderful Renaissance façade is decorated with coats of arms. Beside it rises the flat east end of the church. From the church door there is an admirable **view** of the Pesa Valley.

On the outskirts of Barberino turn right off S1 to Sant' Appiano.

The road to this hamlet provides some outstanding **views★★** of the Colli Fiorentini clothed in vineyards and olive groves.

★ **Sant'Appiano** – This pre-Romanesque church (10C-11C) has retained its original apse and part of the north aisle, neither of which were damaged when the belltower collapsed in 1171. The remainder of the church was rebuilt in the late 12C. In front of the façade are four sandstone pillars, the remains of a separate octagonal baptistery similar to the one in Florence (it was demolished by an earthquake in the early 19C). The fasciculated pillars and the pilaster-strips decorating the east end are indicative of Lombard influence.

Beside the church *(right)* is a set of buildings enclosing picturesque little cloisters which are reached via the **Antiquarium** ⊙ at the rear of the building.

After winding its way through woodland, the road provides a view of a promontory *(right)*, crowned by the village of **Linari** *(steep hill 25 % – 1: 4)*. Near the church is a small castle which has been restored.

Take to S429 to return to Poggibonsi.

③ **From Siena to the Chianti Hills** *about 100km – 62 miles*

★ **Siena** – *See Siena.*

Between Siena and Castellina, the road (S222) passes through woods of young oak and pine trees which leave very little room for vineyards. South of Quercegrossa, the slopes are not steep and the road follows the contours of the land; then it climbs slowly, providing some magnificent **views★★** *(left)* over the Staggia Valley.

★ **Castellina in Chianti** – *See above – tour 2.*

Radda in Chianti – *See above – tour 2.*

East of Radda, neat vineyards alternate with a succession of dark wooded hills – a well-tended landscape.

At the junction of five roads turn left into a hairpin bend leading to Badia Coltibuono (900m – 0.5 mile).

★ **Badia Coltibuono** – This prosperous abbey, a daughter house of Vallombrosa *(qv)*, was built in the 11C and extended in the 15C and 18C. It was, however, vacated by its monks in 1810, under an edict signed by Napoleon, and turned into a farm. The Romanesque church, devoid of aisles and surmounted by a crenellated belltower, as well as the neighbouring buildings, give some idea of past grandeur. From the east end of the church there is a view over the middle reaches of the Arno to the wooded uplands of Pratomagno.

The road to Gaiole *(5km – 3 miles)* is full of bends and is flanked by dense woodland.

Gaiole in Chianti – This village is a mainly modern holiday resort in a small valley surrounded by vine-clad hillsides.

Take S408 south; after 2km – 1 mile turn left towards Meleto; after 400m – 433yds turn right into a dirt track (700m – 758yds).

★ **Meleto Castle** – *Private property.* This is a fine example of a quadrangular medieval castle with round towers at the corners, a reminder that its primary purpose was defensive. It was built in the 12C and badly damaged during the numerous attacks to which it was subjected over the centuries before being restored and turned into a stately residence in the 18C.

Continue south and east by S408 and S484.

The Brolio district abounds in vines and olive trees.

★ **Brolio** ⊙ – *1km – 0.5 mile from the entrance to the castle door.*

This huge crenellated **castle** has belonged to the Ricasoli family since the 11C; Bettino Ricasoli, the famous Italian politician, who was born in Florence in 1809, died here in 1880.

The castle was dismantled in 1478 and rebuilt in 1484 by the Florentines. Its pentagonal fortifications, which include the first bastions ever built in Italy, were probably designed by Giuliano da Sangallo in his youth.

From within the castle walls there is access to the gardens and the parapet walk. The castle, which is still inhabited, underwent extensive restoration in the 19C using brick. Beside it stands the Chapel of Saint Jacopo; the Ricasoli family tomb is in the crypt.

From the top of the walls *(south side)* there is a magnificent **view★★★** over the Arbia Valley. In the distance beyond the towers of Siena is the high peak of Monte Amiata; to the west, downhill, are the buildings where the castle wine is produced.

Return by car to the valley following a dirt track (4km – 2.5 miles) that loops through the Brolio vineyards with the castle on the right.

Brolio Castle and vineyard.

There are some fine views downhill over the castle.

Beyond the estate farm buildings, turn right into S484 which returns past the entrance to the estate.

Between Brolio and San Gusme *(7km – 4 miles)* the country is still fairly wooded, except near San Gusme where it becomes more open.

Turn left off S484 into a narrow road (700m – 758yds to the village).

San Gusme – This stone-built farming village, which lies near the source of the Ombrone, has retained its medieval character with outer walls, gateways and narrow streets, some of which are arched.

From the village, there is an attractive view over the southern part of the province of Siena with Monte Amiata in the background, the fortress of Radicofani, standing on a flat-topped hill, and the succession of bare peaks in the Siena Hills.

The same view can be enjoyed from Castelnuovo Berardenga *(see below)*.

Castelnuovo Berardenga – This, the most southerly village in the Chianti region, stands on a hilltop above the upper reaches of the River Ombrone. The road which skirts the village turns south into the axis of majestic **Villa Chigi★**, which was built in the early 19C on medieval foundations. It is surrounded by a beautiful park full of very old trees which can first be seen from the San Gusme road.

Next to a well-proportioned square with a central fountain is the Church of Santi Giusto e Clemente. Its main features are its neo-Classical portico and a small belltower to one side. It contains a *Madonna and Child with Angels* by Giovanni di Paolo (1426).

On the outskirts of Castelnuovo, there is a breathtaking **view★★** over the gently-rolling, bare hills of the Sienese countryside.

After 1.5km – 1 mile turn right to Pianella (not left to Montaperti as this road is unsurfaced). At the next junction (beyond a stud farm) turn left into the road to Siena.

Montaperti (also **Monteaperti**) – It was near this village on 4 September 1260 that the famous battle took place in which the Ghibellines of Siena defeated the Guelfs of Florence. A memorial to the battle, a small pyramid flanked by cypress trees, stands on an eminence *(on the outskirts of the village opposite the war memorial turn left into a narrow dirt track [1.5km – 1 mile]).*

Take S73 west to return to Siena.

CHIUSI★

Population 9 089
Michelin Map 988 fold 15 or 430 M 17

Chiusi, now a quiet, friendly little town, was built on an easily-defended hilltop as it was once one of the 12 sovereign towns of the Etruscan confederation. It derived its prosperity not only from the farmland in the surrounding fertile plain but also from its control of the Chiana, then a tributary of the Tiber, which therefore linked the town to Rome and to the sea.

Two towns with entwined destinies – In 507 BC **Porsenna**, the powerful King of Chiusi (according to some he was King of Etruria), attempted – and seems to have succeeded at least for a time – to reimpose on Rome, the capital of Latium, the domination which had endured for over a century under three Etruscan kings, before the Romans set themselves free by instituting a republic. Once Rome regained its freedom, it gradually gained in power and finally seduced Chiusi which rallied to Rome in the 4C BC and began a period of Romanisation. These links also explain why, in the early days of Christianity, so many of the people of Chiusi were converted to the new religion.

Mustiola, patron saint of Chiusi – The Roman Emperor, Aurelian, fell in love with a young aristocratic Roman girl called Mustiola and wanted to marry her. She, however, being a devout Christian, refused his offer of marriage and fled with a priest named Felice and a deacon named Irenaeus to Chiusi where her family owned land. The Emperor immediately flew into a rage and ordered the persecution of the Christians. Felice was killed and Irenaeus died a martyr's death in Chiusi at the hands of the imperial deputy, Turcio. In her grief Mustiola rebelled against Turcio who condemned her to be whipped to death with a lead-studded rope in July 274 AD. Her body was recovered by the bishop and buried near the town in the catacombs that were later named after her.

SIGHTS

★ **Museo archeologico (Archeological Museum)** ⊘ – The museum contains numerous artefacts excavated in local graveyards and presented in a display illustrating Etruscan art and civilisation as it existed in the Chiusi region.

The earthenware **funeral urns** are bi-conical in shape and date from the Villanovan period. The anthropomorphic urns, also known as canopic jars, which were first used in the 7C BC, were replaced in the 6C BC by carved busts (the head serving as the lid) made of rottenstone, a local limestone that gets its name from the unpleasant odour it gives off when being carved. At the end of the century gravestones *(cippa)* began to become commonplace, as did urns with dual-sloping lids; there were a few sarcophagi. The decorative features became increasingly Hellenistic and consisted mainly of processions, family occasions (marriages, funerals), dancing and hunting scenes. In the late 5C BC, the deceased was depicted lying on the urn or sarcophagus. Over the centuries various materials (alabaster, rottenstone, travertine, clay) were

SCALA

Etruscan canopic jars
(Museo archeologico, Chiusi).

81

chosen and the representation of the deceased and the decoration of the sides changed but the overall structure remained the same. Among the decorative features were scenes from Greek mythology; certain episodes – the fratricide committed by Oedipus' sons – were mass produced for the less wealthy classes. From the 2C onwards Chiusi became famous for its high output of clay urns with moulded decoration. Realist art forms and Etruscan fantasy were also expressed in architectural terracotta ornaments for temples and mansions, in bronze sculptures and utensils (mirrors, jugs, tripods), gold jewellery, lamps, glassware, clay votive offerings, and decorated tableware. Chiusi was a major producer of buccheroware, the glazed black pottery which in the 6C was decorated with low-relief motifs and from the 5C was produced without any decoration. The museum also contains Attic black-figure and later red-figure vases, which were initially imported but later made locally by Greek artists who settled in Etruria. At the same time imitation ceramics of inferior quality began to be produced. Painting, an art form that was rare in the north of Etruria, is represented here by the reconstitution of a tomb *(tomba delle Tassinaie)*, which dates from after the mid-2C BC and is thought to have been decorated by artists from Tarquinia.

A museum warden will accompany visitors who have a car to see a few of the surviving tombs along the Lake Chiusi road (3km – 1.5 miles).

Visitors are usually shown two tombs – the **tomba del Leone,** which was originally painted and in which the burial chambers (including benches) are set out in the shape of a Cross around a central area, and the **tomba della Pellegrina** at the end of a corridor *(dromos)* and containing 3C and 2C urns and sarcophagi decorated with reliefs drawn from Greek mythology or, on later artefacts, the war between the Galatians and the Romans.

Cattedrale di San Secondiano – The earliest building on this site, a 4C-5C paleo-Christian basilica, was destroyed by the Goths and rebuilt in the 6C by Bishop Fiorentino. After being destroyed again during the Barbarian invasions, the church was rebuilt to an identical design in the 12C. The twisted columns in the baptistery *(right of the entrance)* were once part of the 6C basilica. The nave and aisles are separated by 18 ancient but dissimilar columns, revealing the re-use of Roman material from various sources. A false mosaic (1887-1894) painted by Viligiardi from Siena, imitates in its upper part the decoration of a Roman church. In the 17C the body of St Mustiola was interred in the south transept.

Campanile – The belltower *(campanile)* was built in the 12C as part of the town's system of defence. The upper section was converted into a belltower in the 16C. The interior contains a water tank dating from the 1C BC.

Museo della Cattedrale ⊘ – On the ground floor are Etruscan, Roman and Paleo-Christian remains discovered beneath the cathedral. From the gardens, there is a view of part of the Etruscan wall dating from the 3C BC. On the first floor, the museum displays a collection of furniture, religious ornaments and reliquaries, including two magnificent 15C chests (from the Embriachi workshops) covered with marquetry and decorated with illustrated ivory disks. There is a valuable collection of illuminated antiphonaries, psalters and graduals dating from the 15C and 16C; they were brought here from the Abbey of Monte Oliveto Maggiore *(qv)*. There are also some fine pieces of gold and silverware (mainly Sienese) from the 14C to 18C, and a few paintings by the Sienese and Florentine Schools.

EXCURSIONS

Etruscan tombs – *See above under Museo archeologico*.

Catacombe di Santa Mustiola e di Santa Caterina ⊘ – *On the lake road*. These **catacombs** were discovered in 1634 and 1848 respectively; they are the only ones known to exist in Tuscany and prove the vitality of Christianity locally. They were built in the 3C and were still in use as burial places in the 5C. The earliest catacombs, where St Mustiola was buried, consist of an extensive network of galleries bearing a large number of inscriptions; the second catacombs are smaller and owe their name to the tiny chapel dedicated to St Catherine of Alexandria which was built above them.

Torri Beccati Questo e Beccati Quello (Take this and Take that Towers) – *3km – 2 miles east*. Although they are only a few yards apart, the first tower stands in Umbria and the second in Tuscany, recalling the former rivalry between the two provinces. The Tuscan tower, octagonal and furnished with machicolations, is dominated by the Umbrian tower which is square and slightly taller.

Lago di Chiusi – *5km – 3 miles north*. As the approch road ends at the **lake,** this is a quiet spot offering boating, rowing and angling. Fish from the lake is used in the traditional dishes of Chiusi including pike *(brustico)* cooked directly on reeds from the lake and served off the bone with oil and lemon, and a kind of fish stew *(tegamaccio)* consisting of a range of lake fish cooked in tomato sauce and served on slices of toast rubbed with garlic.

COLLE DI VAL D'ELSA*

Population 15 659
Michelin Map 988 fold 14 or 430 L 15

The town has three districts *(terzieri)* divided into two distinct urban districts – **Colle Bassa** (terziere di Piano) which is in the valley beside the river Elsa, and **Colle Alta** (terzieri di Castello e Borgo) which clings to the hillside and has retained its 16C bastioned walls and fortified gate.

COLLE ALTA

From Porta Vecchia *(north)* the road up to the castle *(castello)* runs south through the upper part of the town *(borgo)* beneath one of the arches of the Palazzo Campana, a 16C mansion, and along the main street, Via del Castello, which is paved and bordered by 16C mansions *(palazzi)* and medieval tower-houses with truncated towers.

Piazza del Duomo (Cathedral Square) – The 17C cathedral has a neo-Classical façade, a robust quadrangular belltower and interior furnishings in the Baroque style *(restored in 1992)*.
Opposite the cathedral stands the Bishop's Palace, flanked by *(right)* the Palazzo Renieri and the former Town Hall (13C).
Beside the belltower *(left)* stands the 14C Palazzo Pretorio, decorated with coats of arms; it now houses the **Museo archeologico R Bianchi Bandinelli** ⊘ (Archeological Museum) which displays some interesting Etruscan collections. Next is the Palazzo Giusti, the Old Seminary (17C).
From the southwest corner of the square a strange 14C and 15C street, Via delle Volte, leads down under the houses; it is arched-over for its entire length (110m – 120 yds).

Via del Castello – *Access from Piazza del Duomo*. This street contains several interesting buildings – the **Palazzo dei Priori** (15C), now the **museo civico** (municipal museum) ⊘, which displays 16C and 17C paintings by the Florentine and Sienese Schools); the 18C Teatro dei Varii which is housed in the 13C Hospital of the Holy Spirit; the house that belonged to Lorenzo Lippi, 15C poet and humanist; the tower-house (the last one in the street) that is said to be the birthplace of Arnolfo di Cambio *(c*1245-1302), the architect and sculptor who designed Florence Cathedral.
From the nearest bastion, there is an extensive view over Colle Bassa, the Sienese hills, the Chianti region and the surrounding countryside.

COLLINE METALLIFERE*

Michelin Map 988 fold 14 or 430 M 14

The **Metalliferous Hills,** which owe their name to the presence of iron, copper and pyrite mines, are particularly interesting near Larderello because of the strange appearance of the countryside.

Valle di Diavolo (Devil's Valley) – Once the road from the coast *(SS329 between Donoratico and Larderello)* has passed the turning to Canneto, the scenery gradually changes and becomes particularly unusual. The gently-rolling hills and peaceful fields form a stark contrast to the fantastic scenery of smoking chimneys from which enormous shiny steel tubes radiate across the landscape, snaking their way over the hills and following or crossing the roads in disturbing configurations. This was once a desolate area where the puffs of smoke that rose into the air, accompanied by a persistent smell of sulphur, were sufficient to explain the sinister name of **Devil's Valley**.
The spontaneous jets of steam are emitted from the bowels of the earth at very high pressure and at a very high temperature (230°C). They have a very high content of boric acid, a valuable substance which used to be extracted for use as an antiseptic, and also contain sulphur-bearing hydrogen, anhydrous carbon, methane, ammoniate, and a few rare gases. At present, however, the steam is used to produce electricity.
The surrealistic effect of this power plant is particularly noticeable in **Larderello**, a town which owes its name to Francesco de Larderel who in 1818 began to extract boric acid from the "lagoons" of Montecerboli, stretches of muddy, boiling water *(north of Larderello)*.
North of Larderello the panoramic road *(SS439 between Massa Marittima and Volterra)*, gradually leaves the silvery spider's web in Devil's Valley and enters the heart of the Metalliferous Mountains, passing through **Pomarance**, the birthplace of two painters, Cristoforo Roncalli (1552-1626) and Niccolò Circignani *(c*1530-1592), each of whom is known as Pomarancio.

Everything in this town, set amid rural hillsides, relates to the famous string puppet, Pinocchio, a storybook character created by Carlo Lorenzini (1826-1890) who took as his *nom de plume* the name of the village where his mother was born.

Villa Garzoni gardens.

★★ **Villa Garzoni** ⊘ – The 17C **gardens★★★**, which complement a villa erected on the foundations of a medieval building, are a typical example of exuberant Italian Baroque landscaping. The entrance opens on to a highly formal design with fountains, waterfalls, terraced flowerbeds flanking flights of steps decorated with balustrades and vases or statues. The reverse perspective is equally attractive, viewed from the hilltop which is crowned by a gigantic statue of Fame. From each step there is a view of some part of these gardens, which used to be famous throughout Europe – huge round lily ponds, yew trees pruned into shapes reminiscent of architecture or imaginary animals, flowerbeds set against green shrubs and cypress trees, Rococo "grottoes" at the foot of each flight of steps, mythological or allegorical statues.

Pinocchio, the little wooden puppet

Since the 19C the story with its apparently simple theme has achieved international recognition, due in particular to the numerous film versions, of which the best known is undoubtedly the Walt Disney cartoon produced in 1940. The story goes that an old carpenter named Geppetto carved a wooden puppet, dreaming that one day the puppet, which he called Pinocchio, would become a real little boy. When night fell, the Blue Fairy granted him his wish and the puppet came to life. Thereafter, Pinocchio, who always acted with the best of intentions but who was whimsical and disobedient, suffered a number of unfortunate adventures under the discreet but watchful eye of the Blue Fairy. The most famous of all the lessons that she tried to teach him was to tell the truth. Every time the puppet told a lie, his nose grew longer. The story ends when Pinocchio, wiser as a result of all the mishaps that have befallen him, passes from dream to reality and becomes a real little boy.

The book, which is generally considered the most outstanding classic of Italian children's literature, is much more than a mere story. It depicts life among Italian provincial poor, imbued with resignation and pessimism, and demonstrates that the values upheld by the peasantry are vulnerable to greater guile.

From the top of the steps to the castle *(left)* and from the castle to the exit from the park, visitors pass through a series of enchanting features – the "camellia wood", the "natural maze" and the exotic "bamboo grove".

The **castello,** built in the 18C by the marquesses of Garzoni who were lords of Collodi, has a wide façade with coats of arms above the entrance and mythological terracotta statues on the roof. On the first floor are the gallery which is decorated with *trompe-l'oeil* frescoes, and the music and ballroom (18C); the ground floor contains the kitchens, where Collodi, the chef's nephew, began writing Pinocchio, and also the chapel.

★ **Parco di Pinocchio** ⊘ – *Signed.* This park was laid out in the form of a winding trail in memory of the author of the famous story. It is situated in a pine wood on the banks of the tumbling Pescia near the Villa Garzoni. The route, which is clearly signed, is illustrated at intervals by bronze sculptures and other creations, mostly designed by Emilio Greco and Venturino Venture, inspired by the story of Pinocchio, which was written in 1883, and accompanied by a commentary in the form of information panels recounting certain episodes from the puppet's adventures. The path enters the jaws of the enormous shark that swallowed Geppetto. The trail, which unfolds quietly and artistically in a beautiful natural setting, ends in the Laboratory of Speech and Figures, which is devoted to temporary exhibitions of works and illustrations evoking the adventures of Pinocchio.

CORTONA★★

Population 22 591
Michelin Map 988 fold 15 or 430 M 17

Cortona occupies a **remarkable site★★** planted with olive trees on the steep slope of a hill overlooking the Chiana Valley not far from Lake Trasimene.

It used to belong to the League of Twelve Etruscan Towns before coming under the control of Rome. It has retained its medieval town walls, commanded by a huge citadel *(fortezza)* which replaced the Etruscan precinct.

The town, which was annexed to Florence in 1411, has barely changed since the Renaissance period, which produced some fine mansions *(palazzi)*, narrow, paved streets, mostly very steep, leading to irregularly-shaped squares lined with arcades and public buildings.

Art – Cortona began to attract artists in the 14C and it was the Sienese School which predominated, until the arrival of Fra Angelico. The town's main claim to fame, however, is that it was the birthplace of a number of famous old masters.

Luca Signorelli (1450-1523) was a painter who, through his dramatic temperament and sculpture-like forms, was a precursor of Michelangelo. He died by falling from the scaffolding as he painted frescoes in the Villa Passerini *(east of Cortona).*

Among architects the most famous name is that of Domenico Bernabei (1508-1549), known as **Boccador** (literally "Mouth of Gold"), who worked principally in France; at the age of 25 he was invited by King François I to Paris where he worked from 1533 to 1549 on the design of the City Hall.

Pietro da Cortona (1596-1669), painter and architect, was one of the great masters of the Roman Baroque style. He had a prodigious imagination and was a genius in interior decoration. In Rome with his friends, Poussin, Claude Lorrain and the sculptor Duquesnoy, he used to admire Titian's *Bacchanalian Scenes* in the Casa Aldobrandini. His main works include the decoration of the Pitti Palace in Florence and the Barberini Palace in Rome and the façade of the Church of Santa Maria della Pace in Rome.

Before taking a more Classical view of Art, the painter **Severini** (1883-1966) was one of the best representatives of Futurism, the great Italian avant-garde movement created in Paris at the turn of the 19C.

Religion – The people of Cortona have a very special regard for St Francis, who set up a hermitage at Celle *(see below)* for St Margaret, a 13C Magdalen, and for Brother Elias, St Francis' first friend and follower, who supervised the construction of the basilica in Assisi and is buried in Cortona, beneath the chancel in San Francesco, the church which he had started to build in the upper part of the town.

SIGHTS *Tour – about 2 hours*

Piazza Garibaldi – From the square there is a **view★★** *(south)* to Lake Trasimene and *(southwest)* over the Chiana Valley to Montepulciano.

Via Nazionale (6) – This pleasant shopping street, the only really level street in Cortona, is lined with picturesque alleys, most of them consisting of flights of steps to match the incline. From **Vicolo Vagnucci** there is a delightful view of the countryside below.

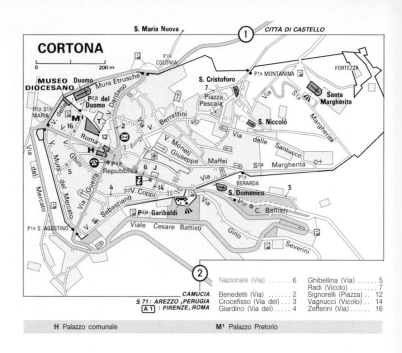

H Palazzo comunale   M¹ Palazzo Pretorio

Palazzo comunale (Town Hall) (H) – The building dates from the 13C but was completed in the 16C by a belltower and a huge flight of steps leading up from Piazza della Repubblica. The **Sala del Consiglio★** (Council Chamber) ⊘ overlooks Piazza Signorelli, the site of the original façade of the Town Hall. The fireplace is 16C but the medieval character of the building is evident in the richly-painted ceiling subdivided by wooden beams, and the stone walls, one of which is decorated with a huge fresco.

★ Palazzo Pretorio (M¹) – The building is also known as Palazzo Casali in memory of its former owners who were the lords of the town. It dates from the 13C but was altered at a later date. The frontage facing Piazza Signorelli dates from the early 17C but the righthand wall decorated with the coats of arms of governors *(podeste)* is Gothic in origin.

★ Museo dell'Accademia etrusca ⊘ – The **museum** is at the top of a flight of steps leading from the courtyard which also contains coats of arms. The main central hall contains the most important exhibits. Among the Etruscan items are an amazing bronze **oil lamp★★** (second half of the 4C BC) composed of a Gorgon's head, which forms the base, surrounded by 16 figures of Sileni and goddesses holding 16 lights. There is also a collection of bronze Etruscan and Roman statuettes, ceramics, and 15C Italian ivories. Among the paintings are works by Signorelli and his followers, a superb *Miracle of St Benedict* by Andrea Commodi (17C), a *Madonna* by Pinturicchio and a huge *Virgin and Child with Saints* by Pietro da Cortona (17C). The smaller rooms display an Egyptian collection, 14C paintings, a lapidary collection dating from Antiquity and funeral urns. The Severini Room contains the works donated to the town by this artist, including *The Gypsy Woman* (1905) and **Motherhood★** (1906).

Piazza del Duomo – The square abutting the town walls provides an attractive view of the valley and the cemetery. The **cathedral** was originally built in the Romanesque period but it was altered during the Renaissance period; the furnishings are interesting and there are numerous 16C and 18C paintings.

★★ Museo Diocesano (Diocesan Museum) ⊘ – The museum and its valuable collections are housed opposite the cathedral in the Chiesa del Gesù (Church of Jesus), which has a superb carved ceiling dating from 1536.
Fra Angelico is represented by two of his best works – an **Annunciation** which is very delicate, where the attention is drawn to the exchange of looks between the angel, conveying the will of God, and the Virgin Mary, exhibiting total submission; a **Madonna** surrounded by the saints which is more interesting for the tenderness on Mary's face than for the liveliness of the scenes from the life of St Dominic on the predella.
There are a number of superb paintings by the Sienese School – a *Madonna* by Duccio, a *Madonna with the Angels* and a huge *Crucifixion,* in which Christ's skin is particularly livid, by Pietro Lorenzetti (late 14C) and a triptych of the *Madonna and Child* (1434) *(restored)* by Sassetta.

The museum also houses a carefully-selected collection of paintings by Signorelli, of which the best are the *Communion of the Apostles* and *The Deposition* in which the horror is heightened by the gentle background landscape. Among the sculptures is a fine 2C Roman sarcophagus with low reliefs (Lapiths and Centaurs). The former vestry displays church plate, including the Vagnucci reliquary made by Giusto da Firenze (1458).

The small lower church is covered in 16C frescoes based on designs by Vasari; it also contains an expressive painted terracotta *Pietà* dating from the same period.

San Cristoforo – This small, elongated church, which is said to date from the late 12C, is surmounted by a bellcote. The sacristy serves as the entrance. Inside there is a 14C fresco of the Crucifixion, the Annunciation and the Ascension.

San Niccolò – An elegant porch extends across the façade and down one side of the 15C church. The Baroque interior includes two works by Luca Signorelli – *(left of the entrance)* a fresco *The Virgin Mary surrounded by the Saints* and *(on the High Altar)* **The Entombment**★ steeped in a sense of deep devotion.

Santuario di Santa Margherita – The church, which stands above the town, was built in the 19C but the belltower dates from the 17C. The interior contains *(left of the chancel)* the Gothic **tomb**★ of the saint (1362), an unusual design ornamented with two pinnacles flanking a gable; the saint's body lies on view at the High Altar; *(right of the chancel)* a moving representation of *The Crucifixion* (13C).

From the esplanade there are some attractive **views**★ of the town, the valley below and Lake Trasimene.

To the right of the terrace in front of the church is Via Santa Margharita decorated by Severini with mosaics representing the **Stations of the Cross** (Via Crucis).

San Domenico ⊙ – This early 15C Gothic church contains *(south apsidal chapel)* a *Madonna with Angels and Saints* by Luca Signorelli; *(sanctuary)* a triptych of the *Coronation of the Virgin Mary* (1402) by Lorenzo di Niccolo Gerini; *(near the north apsidal chapel)* an *Assumption* by Bartolomeo della Gatta (1480-1485) surmounted by a fresco by Fra Angelico of *The Madonna and Child between two Dominican Friars*.

From the promenade opposite the church there are delightful views of Lake Trasimene.

Santa Maria Nuova – This 16C church, which stands proudly outside the Porta Colonia, was built to a square design, the ideal layout according to Renaissance thought, and slightly later capped by a dome designed by Vasari. The interior is decorated with numerous paintings including *(altar on the right of the entrance) The Birth of the Virgin Mary* by Allori.

EXCURSIONS

★ **Santa Maria del Calcinaio** – *3km – 2 miles south of Cortona by exit (2)*. The Church of Santa Maria was built between 1485 and 1513 in the style of Brunelleschi, to designs by Francesco di Giorgio Martini *(qv)* from Siena. It is built of a dark-coloured stone and, despite its poor condition, it is admirable for the elegance and coherence of its overall design and its well-balanced proportions.

The light and elegant interior, laid out in the form of a Latin Cross, is capped by a dome. The oculus in the façade contains an outstanding stained-glass window (1516) by Guillaume de Marcillat *(qv)* depicting the *Madonna of Mercy*, who is also honoured in a separate small 15C fresco *(above the High Altar)*.

R. Meazza/LAURA RONCHI

Santa Maria Nuova.

Tanella di Pitagora – *3km – 2 miles south of Cortona by exit (2); at the lefthand hairpin bend, continue straight on towards Arezzo*. The tomb stands in a delightful setting surrounded by cypress trees and is a circular Etruscan mausoleum dating from the 4C BC. It is called the tomb of Pythagoras because of an age-old confusion between Cortona and Crotona; Pythagoras the mathematician lived in Crotona.

Le Celle ⊘ – *3.5km – 2 miles east of Cortona by exit (1); after 1.5km – 1 mile, at a righthand bend, turn left into a narrow road*. All along the road, there are wonderful views of the Chiana Valley.

On his return from Rome, after the Pope had officially recognised the Franciscan Order (1210), St Francis, il Poverello, set out on an apostolic mission. After stopping in Cortona, he withdrew to Le Celle where he founded his first community. He chose this spot for its natural silence and austerity (characteristics which are still very evident).

The monastery, consisting of houses of varying heights clinging to the hillside, is occupied by Capuchins and retains the original chapel used by St Francis' first companions. Behind the altar is the tiny cell used by St Francis himself, to which he returned after receiving the stigmata in La Verna *(qv)*.

Abbazia di Farneta ⊘ – *15.5km – 12.5 miles southwest of Cortona by exit (2)*. This austere T-shaped church was built by the Benedictines on the site of a Roman temple. In the 18C the 12C belltower and the first part (14 metres – 15yds) of the nave were demolished. The interior contains *(north transept)* a 15C tabernacle and *(south wall)* a fresco depicting *The Madonna of Loreta with St Roch and St Sebastian* (1527). The most interesting feature is the **crypt** (9C-10C), which has ribbed barrel vaulting and three multifoiled apsidal chapels supported by Roman columns from a variety of sources.

Adjacent to the church is a small **Museo-Antiquarium** (Archeological and Paleontological Museum) containing a number of finds discovered in Farneta and the surrounding area.

Rovine di COSA★

Michelin Map 988 fold 25 or 430 O 15

North of **Ansedonia**≙ stand the ruins of Cosa on the top of a promontory overlooking the Laguna di Orbetello and the Argentario peninsula *(qv)*. Crickets sing here among the wild herbs and olive trees. There is a **Museo-Antiquarium** ⊘ in Ansedonia.

Excavations ⊘ – The town, a Roman colony from the 3C BC until the 4C AD, was built beside the Via Aurelia.

The areas that have been excavated represent two distinct centres of interest, even though they are only a few hundred yards apart. On the top of the promontory is the acropolis, its outer walls consisting of huge blocks of stone enclosing the surviving walls and columns of the capitol, a temple and other smaller buildings. Further north is the town itself – paved streets intersecting at right angles, foundations of the buildings within the forum (basilica, temples, curia, shops), numerous water tanks and houses. The north gate (Porta Romana) is still standing, a massive structure built of square blocks of stone.

Every year
the Michelin Red Guide Italia
revises its selection of hotels and restaurants which
– are pleasant, quiet, secluded
– offer an exceptional, interesting or extensive view
– have a tennis court, swimming pool or private beach
– have a private garden...

It is well worth buying the current edition

Isola d'ELBA★★

Pop 28 495
Michelin Map 988 fold 24 or 430 N 12-13

Elba, island of seahorses, is the largest island in the **Tuscan Archipelago★★** *(qv)*. It is popular with tourists for its solitary beauty, its silence, its dry, mild climate, its untamed nature and its varied landscapes.

The two main towns are Portoferraio and Porto Azzurro.

Elba is more of a holiday resort than a place for a day excursion but it is possible to tour the island in one day, either in one's own car or in a hire car available in Portoferraio.

• Access •

By ferry – There are numerous ferries to Elba.

From **Piombino** there are at least 10 sailings a day and more in the peak season to Portoferraio on the north coast – about one hour by car ferry (single hull or catamaran); 40 minutes by hydrofoil *(aliscafo)* (pedestrians only). Some ferries sail direct to Porto Azzurro and Rio Marina on the east coast.

From **Livorno** (Leghorn) there is one ferry per week.

Information and reservations – In summer it is advisable to book a crossing on the car ferries. Contact the following companies at their offices in Piombino –
> Navarma, piazzale Premuda 13, Tel 0565-221212
> Elba Ferries, piazzale Premuda, Tel 0565-220956, Fax 0565-220996
> Toremar, piazzale Premuda 13-14, Tel 0565-31100, Fax 0565-35294

By train to Piombino – From Campiglia Marittima on the Genoa-Rome west-coast main line there is a train direct to Piombino harbour *(14km – 9 miles)*.

By car to Piombino – Turn off the Livorno (Leghorn)-Grosseto expressway at San Vincenzo or Venturina.

• •

HISTORICAL AND GEOGRAPHICAL NOTES

During the Primary era, the Island of Elba was part of the Tyrrhenian continent which was partially submerged beneath the sea in the Quaternary era, leaving behind the islands of Corsica, Sardinia, the Balearics, Elba and two mountain ranges on the French Riviera (Les Maures and L'Estérel).

Elba is a mountainous island; its highest peak, Monte Capanne (1018m – 3308ft), overlooks a granite mountain range where stone-quarrying is carried out. The jagged coastline consists of natural, well-sheltered coves with small beaches. Underwater fishing is common all along the sheer rocky shores of the west coast which is riddled with sea caves. Professional fishermen catch tunny fish and anchovies.

The Mediterranean-type vegetation consists of palm trees, eucalyptus, cedars, bamboos, magnolias and, most of all, olive trees, corn and vines. There are two varieties of grape grown locally which produce powerful wines with a heady bouquet – white Moscato and red Aleatico.

The island is particularly superb in June when the broom is in flower.

Iron ore mines – The seams were first discovered in the 6C BC by the Etruscans who exploited them to the full in open-cast mines in the eastern part of the island, at Cape Calamita, and between Rio nell'Elba and Cavo. The iron was then taken by barge, pulled by tugs, to the blast furnaces in Piombino. These mines, formerly one of the best-known features of Elba, now lie idle.

Napoleon, sovereign of the Island of Elba – After signing the Act of Abdication in Fontainebleau, the deposed French Emperor lived on Elba from 4 May 1814 to 26 February 1815.

Napoleon had with him a small court governed by Bertrand, the Grand Marshal of the Palace. He also commanded about 1 000 soldiers, of whom 300 had accompanied him at the outset, together with 100 grenadiers and infantrymen from his Imperial Guard, and 600 more came to join him, including Polish lancers under the orders of Drouot and Cambronne. He also had his own navy consisting of one brig, *L'Inconstant*.

During his short stay he used to dream as he looked across at Corsica or travelled round his kingdom on board his brig. He had roads built by Cambronne's men and the Polish lancers, made improvements to the farming methods, developed the mines and modernised the road network in Portoferraio.

★ WESTERN TOUR

66km – 41 miles anticlockwise from Portoferraio following the route indicated on the map

⚓ **Portoferraio** – This is the capital of the island; it lies on the shores of a beautiful bay, protected by the remains of outer walls and two fortresses. In the upper part of the town overlooking the sea *(north)* stands **Villa dei Mulini** (Mill Villa) ⊙, a simple house with a patio and garden, where Napoleon lived during his brief period of sovereignty. His personal library and a collection of memorabilia are on view.

The **road**★ from Portoferraio to Marciana Marina is particularly recommended for the views it provides down to Procchio and over Procchio Bay.

Biodola – Vast, beautiful sandy beach.

⌂⌂ **Marciana Marina** – This is a harbour protected by two jetties, one of which bears the ruins of the Medici Tower *(torre Medicea)*.

West of Marciana Marina and the sea front, the road climbs through the woods on the northern slopes of Monte Capanne.

Poggio – Small resort perched on a spur of rock.

The road continues to climb through the trees. To the left, on the outskirts of Marciana, is the lower station for the cable car to the summit of Monte Capanne.

★★ **Monte Capanne** – *15min by cable car* ◷. From the rocky summit *(15min on foot from the top station)*, there is a superb **panoramic view**★★ over the entire island of Elba, *(east)* to the coast of Tuscany and *(west)* to the east coast of Corsica.

Marciana – The village lies at the foot of its ruined castle on the eastern slopes of Monte Giove, providing a wonderful **view**★ of Poggio, Marciana Marina and Procchio Bay. The small **museo archeologico** (archeological museum) ◷ has exhibits dating from the Iron and Bronze Ages and a collection of Greek pottery.

Madonna del Monte – Alt 627m – 2 037ft. *45min Return on foot from the road to the castle above Marciana*. A rocky path runs through the trees at the beginning of the walk but later provides panoramic views as it climbs to the 16C chapel built on the north slope of Monte Giove. Near the chapel is a strange semi-circular fountain dating from 1698 and the "hermitage" where Napoleon lived with Maria Walewska for a few days in the summer of 1814.

From the adjacent rocks the **view**★ embraces the creeks on the north coast, Marciana Marina and Procchio Bay, and the villages of Marciana and Poggio.

Return to Poggio and turn right into the forest road leading up Monte Perone.

After a delightful stretch through the woods and a few wonderful views over the north coast of the island, the road descends to San Piero in Campo, providing a succession of **views**★ over the south coast and its villages, Marina di Campo and its bay.

Marina di Campo – Marina di Campo lies on the edge of a plain dotted with olive trees and vineyards, at the head of a picturesque bay, and is popular for its superb beach. Fishermen make the delightful little harbour a bustling place.

Take the road that runs up the Galea Valley, bordered to the right by the wild, uninhabited Lacona region, to return to Procchio. From Procchio take the road towards Portoferraio; in San Martino turn right to Villa Napoleone.

★ **Villa Napoleone di San Martino** ◷ – The silent hillsides planted with oak trees and terraced rows of vines have not changed since Napoleon's day; nor has the view, except for the neo-Classical palace built by Prince Demidorff, King Jerome's son-in-law. Above it stands the modest house used by the Emperor Napoleon as his summer residence; the interior decoration has been restored to what it was during Napoleon's occupation. From the terrace, there is a pleasant view of Portoferraio Bay. Superb trees provide the gardens with shade.

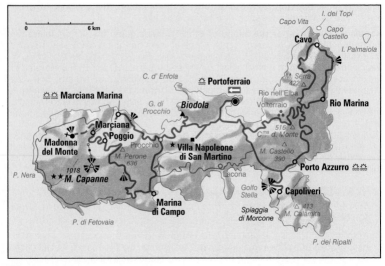

Stella Bay.

★EASTERN TOUR

68km - 42 miles - about 3 hours - clockwise from Portoferraio following the route indicated on the map

⌂ **Portoferraio** - *See above.*

Take the road south; after 3km - 2 miles turn left towards Porto Azzurro.

The road skirts Portoferraio harbour before bearing south across the plain, the narrowest part of the island. It then crosses the Monte Calamita peninsula (iron mines).

Turn right to Capoliveri.

Capoliveri - On the western outskirts of this small town is the point known as **Three Seas Panorama★★**, from which three bays are visible - Portoferraio Bay *(north)*, Stella Bay *(west)* and Porto Azzurro Bay *(east)*; below *(south)* is the beach at Morcone. Out to sea *(southwest)* are the islands of Pianosa and Montecristo.

Return to the road to Porto Azzurro.

⌂⌂ **Porto Azzurro** - The town, which was called Porto Longone during the existence of the Garrison State *(qv)*, faces a delightful harbour commanded by a fortress that is now a prison. The vegetation consists mainly of cacti and agaves.
The road then winds north across the eastern slopes of Monte Castello and Cima del Monte.

Before reaching Rio nell'Elba turn right to Rio Marina.

Rio Marina - This is a delightful village and mining harbour protected by a small tower with merlons.
The **coast road★** to Cavo provides a number of attractive views of the tiny rocky islands of Cerboli and Palmaiola in the Piombino Strait and of Follonica Bay and the mainland.

Cavo - This is a pretty little harbour, the nearest to the mainland, protected by Cape Castello.

Take the road via Rio nell'Elba towards Porto Azzurro. At the crossroads, turn left and then first right.

The **Volterraio road★★** runs high above the sea, providing a number of breathtaking views of the ruins at Volterraio and Portoferraio Bay.

Use the Index to find more information about a subject mentioned in the guide - towns, places of interest, isolated sites, historical events or natural features...

EMPOLI

Pop 43 534
Michelin Map 988 fold 14 or 430 K 14

Empoli lies in the fertile plain of the lower Arno Valley and the town has experienced massive development since the Second World War, initially in glass making, the craft for which it was famous, and more recently in the clothing industry. The region, which was once mainly agricultural, has now been largely taken over by the industrial suburbs that provide most of the employment.

Reprieve for Florence in Empoli – After the defeat of Florence at Montaperti in 1260, a Ghibelline parliament was set up in Empoli to decide on the future of the Guelf capital. The Ghibellines were in favour of razing Florence to the ground in order to emphasise their enemy's defeat but a passionate plea that the city should be spared was made by Farinata degli Uberti, the Ghibelline leader of Florence, who had been banished from Florence by the Guelfs in 1258 and was so delighted to return home that he could not countenance his city's destruction. He died four years later and when the Guelfs defeated the Ghibellines in 1266 and returned to power in Florence, they took their revenge by demolishing the Uberti houses and banishing the Uberti descendants.

> **Ferruccio Busoni (1866-1924)**
>
> Empoli was the birthplace of the great virtuoso pianist, Ferruccio Busoni, who was famous for his piano transcriptions of Bach and his research as a composer into harmonics, in which respect, he was a precursor of Schönberg. Busoni's memory is honoured each year during the autumn and winter by a season of concerts called **Giornate Busoniane** (Busonian Days) organised in Empoli.

SIGHTS

★ **Piazza Farinata degli Uberti** – This place is one of the few surviving parts of the old town and its name commemorates the man, Farinata degli Uberti *(see above)*, who persuaded the Ghibelline parliament assembled in Empoli in 1260 to spare Florence from destruction. The square is surrounded by a regularly-designed portico and decorated with a large central fountain erected in the 19C. Opposite the collegiate church is the **Palazzo Ghibellini** (since altered) where the famous "parliament" met.

Collegiata Sant'Andrea – Its delightful Romanesque **façade**★ built of white and green marble marks the westernmost limit of the use of the Florentine style. Only the lower arches are original; the upper section was built to the same design in the 18C when the interior was also totally remodelled.

★ **Museo della Collegiata** ⊙ – *At the end of the tiny square, to the right of the church.* The museum contains a superb collection of 14C-17C paintings and sculptures. There is a **fresco**★ representing a *Pietà* by Masolino da Panicale, works by Filippo Lippi and Lorenzo Monaco, sculptures by Bernardo and Antonio Rossellino, and painted terracotta pieces by Andrea della Robbia *(upper floor in the cloisters)*.

The visit continues with a guided tour of the **Church of Santo Stefano,** built by the Austin Friars in the 14C in the Gothic style and reconstructed after the Second World War.

It contains a reredos *(1st chapel in the north aisle)* by Bicci di Lorenzo of *St Nicholas de Tolentino protecting Empoli from the Black Death*; an emotive fresco *(tympanum of the door into the sacristy)* by Masolino of *the Madonna and Child*; an *Annunciation (Mercy Chapel near the sacristy)* by Bernardo Rossellino; traces of other frescoes by Masolino *(1st chapel in the south aisle)*.

EXCURSIONS

Montelupo Fiorentino – *7.5km – 4.5 miles east.* The modern-looking village has a **museo archeologico e della ceramica**★ (archeological museum) ⊙ housing archeological exhibits from Prehistory to the Middle Ages and a fine set of ceramics produced in Montelupo between the 14C and the end of the 18C. The collection, in which majolicaware predominates, demonstrates the importance of the Montelupo workshops, especially during the Renaissance period.

Pontorme – *1km – 0.5 miles east.* Take the narrow street to the left of the Firenze (Florence) road. This village was the birthplace of the painter Jacopo Carrucci, better known as Il **Pontormo**. The tiny brick-built Church of San Michele contains *(south transept)* two *Saints* painted by the artist, which hang each side of the altar.

FIESOLE★

Population 15 077
Michelin Map 988 folds 14-15 or 430 K 15
For access see general map of Florence on Michelin Map 430,
in the Michelin Road Atlas Europe or Italy or the Michelin Red Guide Italia

Anybody who has driven from Florence along the road that winds between fields of olive trees, lavish gardens and long lines of cypress trees, up to the top of the hill at Fiesole, will never forget the sense of amazement and wonder aroused by this **incomparable landscape**★★★ glimpsed in many a painting by an Italian Renaissance master, as elegant and contained as Florentine Art itself.

Fiesole, an Etruscan and Roman town – Fiesole was founded by the Etruscans in the 7C or 6C BC and was the largest town in northern Etruria. The site had been chosen for its position on a rise commanding the routes which passed over the barrier of the Apennines *(north)* into the Arno Plain and continued south to Rome. This was, moreover, a healthier spot than the plain which in those days consisted largely of swamps.

For several centuries Fiesole within its mighty walls was a town of greater power and importance than Florence. Sulla set up a colony of Veterans here c80 BC. In 63 BC the town rallied in support of Catiline who sought refuge here before the battle of Pistoia, where he was fatally wounded. From then on the destiny of Fiesole was linked to that of Rome. New buildings were erected on the ruins of the Etruscan structures and the Roman town, known as Faesulae, with its temples, theatre, and baths, became the main centre of the region. From the 1C AD onwards it began to fall into a decline and was overtaken by Florence, its rival and neighbour. In 1125 Faesulae was finally conquered by Florence and almost razed to the ground.

SIGHTS

Piazza Mino da Fiesole – All roads to Fiesole lead to the vast, sloping square, which occupies the site of the old Roman Forum. On the north side stand an oratory, Santa Maria Primerana with a late-16C portico, and the small 14C and 15C **Palazzo Pretorio** (H) bearing the coats of arms of the governors *(podeste)* whose residence it used to be.
Opposite the cathedral entrance *(southwest corner)* a narrow and steep street, Via S Francesco, leads up to one of the heights, where the Acropolis of Faesulae stood in the Roman era.

★★ **View of Florence** – *Half way up Via S Francesco*. To admire the view, one of the high points of a visit to Florence, walk out into the small public park *(left)* which projects like a balcony, overlooking the Arno Basin spread out below, suffused in a subtly opalescent light.

Basilica di Sant'Alessandro – *Via S Francesco*. The basilica (c9C) was built on the site of a Roman temple that had been converted into a church by Theodoric (6C). The neo-Classical façade, added in 1815, is not inviting but the austere interior has a certain nobility; its nave and aisles are separated by superb Roman columns reused from other, earlier buildings.

★ **Convento di San Francesco** ⊙ – *Via S Francesco*. This very modest friary, which is admirably located on the highest part of the hill, has been occupied by Franciscans since the early 15C. The tiny 14C cloisters *(entrance to the right of the church)* are visible through a wrought-iron grille. On the first floor *(steps to the left of the grille)* are several of the tiny cells, furnished with plank bed, chest, desk and chair, where the friars used to live. One of them was occupied by St Bernard of Siena *(qv)* who was Prior here for a few years.
The adjacent **church,** built in the mid-14C but with major alterations from subsequent periods, still has its original early 15C Gothic façade decorated with

a small multifoiled canopy of simple design that is utterly charming. The church contains a number of interesting **paintings**★. On the south wall is an *Immaculate Conception* by Piero di Cosimo and, opposite it, an *Annunciation* by Raffaellino del Garbo.
The **museo missionario** (Franciscan Missions Museum – *access through the church)* contains a large collection of exhibits from the Orient

93

(sculptures, paintings, clothing, porcelain etc.) and a small archeology section (artefacts excavated near the friary, Egyptian objects and a mummy found by missionaries in Egypt).

★ **Duomo (Cathedral)** – *Piazza Mino da Fiesole*. This is a Romanesque building, started in the 11C and extended in the 13C and 14C. Between 1878 and 1883, it was subjected to a massive restoration programme during which the façade was rebuilt. It is surmounted by a belltower erected in 1213 which was altered in the 18C by the addition of merlons and machicolations to look like a belfry. The stark **interior**★ is laid out like a basilica with a chancel raised above the crypt, as in San Miniato in Florence. The crypt is supported on columns, most of the capitals date from ancient times.

Above the west door is a polychrome glazed terracotta niche by Giovanni della Robbia containing a statue of St Romulus, Bishop of Fiesole, to whom the cathedral was dedicated. The Salutati chapel *(right of the chancel)* is decorated with frescoes by Cosimo Rosselli (15C) and contains two delightful **works**★ by Mino da Fiesole – the tomb of Leonardo Salutati (including a bust of the bishop) and a carved reredos full of grace and elegance representing the Virgin Mary in adoration with the young St John and other saints.

Archeology Zone ⊘ – In an enchanting **setting**★ on a hillside clothed in cypress trees are the remains of several Etruscan and Roman buildings. The archeological items found on the site have been placed in a small museum to the right of the entrance.

Excavations – The **Roman theatre**★ (1) dates from 80 BC. It was buried for several centuries and was not excavated until the end of the 18C. Its 23 tiers of seats are well-preserved; the central portion is set into the hillside and the first four rows were reserved for VIPs. At the foot of the tiers of seats is the semicircular orchestra, once paved with multicoloured marble. Behind the orchestra, on a slightly higher level, was the stage. The front curved inwards in the centre and was decorated with a frieze of carved marble reliefs, now in the museum. Behind the stage, in the base of the wall forming the backdrop, were the openings by which the actors made their entrances and exits.

To the left beyond the theatre was a small **Etruscan temple** (2) built towards the end of the 4C BC. It was partly destroyed by fire; the remains were then integrated into a new building constructed during the days of Sulla. The rectangular layout of the building is still apparent, as are the steps leading up to it.

To the right are a few fragments of the **Etruscan walls**.

Opposite the temple and to the right of the theatre, were the **baths** (3) built by the Romans in the 1C AD. Three arches have been reconstructed. The baths were composed of an open-air section, consisting of two large rectangular swimming

Roman Theatre, Fiesole.

pools, the second of which had two basins, and at the rear, under cover, the hot baths *(caldarium)* where the floor was supported on small brick pillars around which hot air circulated *(hypocaust)*.

★ **Museo archeologico** (Archeological Museum) (4) – Most of the exhibits are laid out according to their place of origin so that objects from very different periods are presented together.

Room I contains the items found during the restoration of the town walls. In the second room are funeral items excavated from the graves in an Etruscan necropolis, which was used in later years by the Romans and lay beside one of the main roads leading into the town; displayed alone in a small glass case is a cylindrical lead urn★ *(cista)*, thought to date from the 3C or 4C AD, which when it was discovered, contained burnt bones and ashes but originally would have been used to carry hot water for Roman baths or banquets; its final use may be attributable to its having become too worn for its original purpose.

The third room contains objects from the Archeology Zone, among which are antefixes (sort of gargoyle) in the shape of female figures and tiny bronze votive offerings, some of which are shaped like feet or legs; they date from the period prior to Roman colonisation. Against the wall at the end of the room is a row of fragments of the carved marble frieze which once decorated the stage in the theatre (games in honour of Dionysius).

The rooms on the first floor house exhibits relating to the Later Roman Empire and the Middle Ages. The first room displays objects excavated in tombs found on the site of the main square and in the Archeology Zone – bottles, iron belt ornaments dating from the 7C-8C (case 28), gold threads found on the arms and chest of a dead man (case 38), pearls from a necklace (case 39), and silver hairpins found beneath the skull of a dead woman (case 40). In the next two rooms the most outstanding exhibits are a tombstone of a type specific to the Fiesole region (5C BC) decorated with an illustration of a funeral meal, a dance and an animal combat, several pieces of black Etruscan buccheroware *(qv)* dating from the 6C BC (cases 43, 46 etc); and vases from Apulia in Southern Italy with refined decoration dating from the 4C BC (cases 51-52).

Antiquarium Costantini ⊘ (5) – Ground floor – superb collections, made in the 19C, of red and black figure Greek vases and Etruscan buccheroware. Basement – presentation of the excavations conducted on the site now occupied by the museum (partial remains of murals dating from Roman times).

Museo Bandini ⊘ – On the first floor – paintings from the 14C and 15C Tuscan School – Petrarch's *Triumphs,* a work by the Florentine School at the end of the 15C; *(left) The Triumph of Love and Chastity* and *(right) The Triumph of Time and Religion*.

EXCURSIONS

Badia Fiesolana – *3km – 2 miles southwest of Fiesole. Almost halfway down between Fiesole and Florence, turn right into the narrow Via Badia dei Roccettini.* The Badia Fiesolana (Fiesole Abbey), which now hosts the European University Institute, was originally a Benedictine convent. In the 15C it was partly rebuilt in the elegant style of Brunelleschi at the expense of Cosimo the Elder, who was a frequent visitor.

The highly ornate decoration of the original Romanesque **façade**★, composed of geometric motifs in green and white marble, in a similar style to San Miniato in Florence, has been rather strangely integrated into the new façade which was left unfinished on the death of Cosimo the Elder.

San Domenico di Fiesole – *2.5km – 1 mile to the southwest, beside the Florence road (left), just after the junction with Via Badia dei Roccettini.*
The church of San Domenico was built in the 15C and altered in the 17C; the arcaded porch and belltower date from the latter period.

Fra Angelico *(qv)* took his vows here, *c*1420, and spent several years in the adjacent monastery *(private)*. The church contains *(1st chapel on the left)* a delicate but vividly-coloured **painting**★ representing the Virgin Mary in Majesty surrounded by angels and saints, which he painted *c*1430; it was originally painted on a gold background and designed as a triptych but the various parts were brought together in 1501 by Lorenzo di Credi; *(second chapel on the right) The Baptism of Christ* by Lorenzo di Credi.

Firenze

97

FIRENZE★★★

(Florence)

Population 402 211

Michelin maps 988 folds 14-15 and 430 K 15

Florence is not only a prestigious city of art, generally acknowledged to be one of the finest in Italy; it is also, and principally, a source of genius. It was the birthplace of Dante and the cradle of the Italian language and is still a centre of civilisation, where the first flames of Humanism and the Renaissance were fanned into life in the first half of the 15C; these two movements were closely linked and their spread was a vital factor in the development of the arts and philosophy throughout the Western world.

The city occupies an **admirable setting**★★ which has inspired countless artists and writers, on the banks of the Arno, against a wonderful backdrop of hills suffused by an ethereal amber light.

Its austere beauty and narrow streets are ill-suited to dense traffic but those who succeed in forgetting the hustle and bustle which penetrates even to the historic centre, will find a rich offering of museums, churches, mansions filled with countless masterpieces and wonderful shops, in which elegance is elevated to refinement. The unique charm of the famous **countryside**★★★ is the most contrived, noble and subtle landscape anywhere, part the gift of nature, part man-made; Anatole France said that the god who created it could not have been other than an artist – and a Florentine.

•••••••••••••••• **PRACTICAL INFORMATION** ••••••••••••••••

Telephone dialling code for Florence – 055.

Travelling to Florence

By plane – Owing to its small size, Florence – Amerigo Vespucci Airport (4km – 2.5 miles northwest in Peretola) is used mainly for internal flights but also for a few international flights from 11 European cities. There is a direct coach link (20min) to the city centre, departure every hour; tickets on sale at the airport bar.

Most international flights arrive at Galileo Galilei Airport in Pisa; there is a direct link (about one hour) to the centre of Florence by Alitalia coach or by train; direct access to the railway station from the airport.

By train – Santa Maria Novella Railway Station is on the west side of the city centre and is linked to the urban districts by regular bus services or by taxi.

By car – There is an excellent network of roads converging on the city including the A1 Milan-Naples motorway via Bologna, the A11 Florence-Pisa motorway and the Florence-Pisa-Livorno (FI-PI-LI) expressway.

Visiting Florence

Best time of year – To take full advantage of all that the city has to offer, it is best to avoid the summer months when the heat is stifling and when the city loses some of its character, as many of the locals are away on holiday in high summer. The best times of year to visit Florence are spring and autumn but it is advisable to book accommodation one or two months in advance.

What to see – Obviously the less time one has to spend in Florence, the more one has to juggle with the opening times of museums, historic buildings and churches, and limit oneself to the main sights described in the first 15 sections of this chapter. The chapter entitled **Old Streets and Houses** gives a guide to the sombre, austere façades of the old mansions and a closer view of the history of the city.

The **Multivisione (Experience of Tuscany)** provides an excellent introduction to the region, when Florence is the first stop in a tour of Tuscany. It is a slide show (approximately 30min) describing various aspects of the region – landscape, coastline, towns and works of art – and is located in the Church of Gesù Pellegrino, Via S Gallo, at the junction with Via XXVII Aprile, on the corner opposite Santa Apollonia *(show at 1000, 1100, 1200, 1300, 1500, 1600, 1700 (also at 1800 in the high season; and Saturdays and Sundays at 2030 and 2130. Tel 055 48 09 14)*.

Travelling in Florence – Florence is such a rich city that it takes at least four days just to see the main sights. The principal buildings and museums are nearly all in the city centre and fairly close to one another. As traffic is dense and difficult for visitors, it is advisable to walk rather than drive.

Taxis – Tel 47 98 or 43 90 (Central Booking Office).

Buses – A bus map, which can be seen at the railway station, is published by the bus company (ATAF). Tickets can be purchased at the railway station, in shops displaying the ATAF sticker and in tobacconist's shops (indicated by a rectangular black sign bearing a white "T").
Leaflets showing only the bus routes which are useful to tourists are available from the tourist office (APT *address below*).

no 13 follows the Hill Road on the South Bank via Piazzale Michelangiolo;
no 7 runs from the Railway Station to Fiesole
no 10 runs from the Railway Station to Settignano
no 17B runs from the Railway Station to the youth hostel.

A ticket, valid for 1 hour, costs L1 400 (1995); there is also a day ticket, valid for 24 hours, which costs L5 000.

Open carriages – For hire daily, 0900 to 1830; L40 000 or L50 000, capacity 4 adults or 4 adults and 1 child. Standard circular tour (20 min) from Piazza Duomo or Piazza della Signoria passing the Cathedral, Museo dell'Opera del Duomo, Orsanmichele, Piazza della Signoria, San Carlo, Casa di Dante, Piazza della Repubblica, Mercato della Paglia.

Car – In the city centre traffic is strictly controlled; no vehicle is permitted to enter between 0730 and 1830 without a pass; the restricted times are shown on the relevant signs.

Parking – Some hotels have parking spaces in private car parks for which a fee is charged and which may be some distance from the hotel. The larger public car parks are at Fortezza da Basso *(open 24 hours a day)* and beside Santa Maria Novella Railway Station *(open 0530 to 2200)*. On the edge of the restricted city centre there are a number of small supervised car parks, which are often full *(from L2 000 to L3 000 per hour; only whole hours are counted)*.

Car hire – Hire cars are available at the airport or in the city from:
AVIS, Borgo Ognissanti 128r; ☎ 055/21 36 29 or 23 98 826
BUDGET, Borgo Ognissanti 134r; ☎ 055/20 30 31
EUROPCAR, Borgo Ognissanti 53-59; ☎ 055/23 60 072
HERTZ, Central Booking Office; ☎ 1678/22 099

Accommodation

Hotels – The Michelin Red Guide Italy provides a selection of hotels in and around the city.

Youth Hostels (Ostelli della Gioventù) – Villa Camerata, Viale Righi 2-4, ☎ 055/60 14 51, is part of the International Youth Hostel Association (only card-holding members are admitted). There is also the Santa Monica youth hostel, Via S Monica 6, ☎ 055/26 83 38 (privately-managed).

Campsites – There are several sites on the outskirts of the city or in nearby country districts. Detailed information can be obtained from the tourist office (APT *address below*).

Additional Information

House numbers – House numbers are supposed to start from the banks of the Arno in streets lying perpendicular to the river and to run in the same direction as the flow of the river for streets lying parallel to the river. In some places, however, the numbering seems to be (and is) somewhat confused and illogical, as the system retains elements of the earlier layout. When a road is displaced or a part of it changes its name, the old numbers do not change, thus causing complications in some districts.

MICHELIN

The difference between red and blue street numbers is much simpler; red numbers apply to commercial premises; blue numbers to residential property (houses and hotels). To add to the confusion, some of the numbers are accompanied by letters (A, B or C), which have the same meaning as in Britain. The letter "r" however signifies "red".

Tourist Offices – The central tourist office, Azienda di Promozione Turistica (APT), is in Via Manzoni 16 (☎ 23320) on the east side of the city; a city plan and the opening times of museums are, however, available in the city centre (Chiasso de' Baroncelli 17r or Via Cavour 1 near Piazza della Signoria – signs).

Post Office and Telephones – Letters sent *poste restante* can be claimed from the main post office near Piazza della Repubblica (Via Pelliceria 3). The city has a large number of phonecard telephones; an operator service is also available until midnight.

Lost property – Via Circondaria 19. Open daily except Sundays, 0900 to 1200. ☎ 055/36 79 43.

Medical – 24 hour pharmacists/chemists
    Pharmacy at Santa Maria Novella Railway Station; ☎ 055/21 67 61
    All'insegna del Moro, Piazza S Giovanni; ☎ 055/21 23 43
    Molteni, Via Calzaiuoli 7; ☎ 055/21 54 72

Emergency phone numbers – For absolute emergencies only
    112 – Police *(Carabinieri)*
    113 – Paramedics (Red Cross)

Consulates
    UK – Lungarno Corsini 2; ☎ 055/21 25 94, 28 74 49, 28 41 33
    USA – Lungarno Vespucci 38; ☎ 055/239 82 76, 21 76 05, 28 02 61, 28 40 88

Piazza della Signoria.

Life In Florence

Newspapers – The daily newspaper in Florence is *La Nazione* which prints the programmes and times of special events and shows being staged in the city. The major national dailies, such as *Il Corriere della Sera* and *La Repubblica*, include sections dealing specifically with Florence.
Firenze avvenimenti is a monthly leaflet, which gives the main events scheduled for the current month with a street plan of Florence on the reverse side (available from the tourist office, Via Cavour 1).

Eating out – Tourists who want to enjoy typical Tuscan cuisine *(qv)* in a real Florentine atmosphere should eat in one of the basement restaurants (called *buca* meaning cellar). The entrance is usually a low door opening onto a flight of steps descending from street level. Few restaurants serve meals before 1930 in the evenning.
Fresh food for picnics can be bought in the **covered market** (near San Lorenzo) which offers a good range of produce.

Theatre outings – Florence is a city of the arts even in the evenings when shows and concerts fill the theatres. The programmes are printed in *La Nazione* and in the Florence pages of the main national daily newspapers. Information is also available at the theatres themselves –

Teatro della Pergola, Via Pergola 12-32; ☎ 055/24 79 651
Teatro Verdi, Via Ghibellina 101; ☎ 055/21 23 20
Teatro di Cestello, Piazza di Cestello 4; ☎ 055/29 46 09
Lyceum di Firenze, Via degli Alfani 48; ☎ 055/24 78 264
Teatro Niccolini, Viale Ricasoli 3; ☎ 055/23 96 653
Teatro Comunale, Corso Italia 12; ☎ 055/27 791

In the summer months there are numerous outdoor shows in the gardens and cloisters of the city.

Strolling through Florence

Shopping, arts and crafts – Craftwork can be found in abundance in Florence; it varies from one district to another but is always based on the ancient traditions that have brought prosperity to the city since the Middle Ages.

The streets around Santa Croce are famous for their leatherwork (clothing, leather goods, leather-bound items). Some of the buildings in the Santa Croce monastery house a leatherwork school (Scuola del Cuoio) where the creation of new items or the restoration of old is commissioned by some of the world's most famous people.

The Borgo Ognissanti is a delightful place for a stroll, as it boasts a succession of embroidery and antique shops. More antique shops are to be found in Via de' Fossi, Via de' Serragli and Via Maggio. The finest goldsmiths' shops are in Via de' Tornabuoni and on the Ponte Vecchio where the shop windows are so small that the jewellers (some of whom can be seen at work inside) have to lay out their wares in serried rows.

Paper is another speciality in Florence, especially designs produced by the stippling technique. The decoration is produced by dripping paint, in suspension, over a tank. The drops are then stretched with a comb to produce beautiful marbled effects. The attractiveness of this art also depends on the harmony of the colours used. When a sheet of paper is gently laid on the paint, the design is printed on it. As the technique is particularly difficult to use, the finest motifs are edited using a process of photo-engraving and then reproduced on a wide range of cardboard office supplies. Mass-produced goods are on sale all over the city. The finest papers and by-products (some of them made to order) are to be found in Piazza della Signoria, Via de' Tornabuoni and Piazza Pitti.

Florence has a long-standing reputation for articles made of silk, wool and other fibres, which are on sale in the luxury boutiques in the city centre. Another enjoyable place for a stroll is the street that extends beyond the Ponte Vecchio – Via Por Santa Maria, Via Calimala, and Via Roma – or along Via de' Calzaiuoli which runs parallel to it. This is an area full of fashion houses, shoe shops and leatherware shops.

Visitors may linger in the bookshops near l'Annunziata and in Via Cavour, explore the **Flea Market** in Piazza dei Ciompi or stroll in the New Market, along the arcades in Piazzale degli Uffizi and around San Lorenzo, where there are souvenir shops and stalls in abundance.

Arcades in Piazza della Repubblica, Florence.

J.P. Langeland/DIAF

Caffè Rivoire Terrace.

Famous cafés – Piazza della Repubblica contains three of the great Florentine coffeehouses. Le **Giubbe Rosse** has been a literary coffeehouse since 1890; the waiters still wear the traditional red waistcoats *(giubbe rosse)*. Opposite and side-by-side are the **Paszkowski** coffeehouse founded in 1846 by a former Polish general (there is music on the terrace in the evening) and **Gilli**, which opened in 1733 and has a superb interior décor unchanged since 1910.

Rivoire in Piazza della Signoria is famous for its unique hot chocolate – to be taken with cream *(panna)*. It has a wonderful 18C-style interior although it actually dates from 1882. **Giacosa** (87-r Via Tornabuoni), which opened in 1800, is popular with young Florentines; the display of tiny sandwiches and cakes is particularly attractive.

HOURS OF GLORY AND MOMENTS OF DESPAIR

Florence has revealed very little of its distant past and very few reminders of its early history are visible today. The Italiots are said to have settled at this point, where the Arno was particularly easy to cross, between the 10C and 8C BC. They were soon outnumbered by the Etruscans, who preferred the hilltop of Fiesole *(qv)*. Not until 59 BC did Julius Caesar found a colony on the river bank to control the Arno crossing and the passage of traffic along the Via Flaminia, the road which ran from Rome to northern Italy and thence into Gaul. The colony was set up in the spring; its name, Florentia, was reminiscent of floral games *(ludi florales)* or of fields of flowers *(arva florentia)*. The old city centre has the grid layout of a Roman *castrum*. Via Roma and Via Calimala follow the line of the main Roman north-south street *(cardo)*; Via del Corso and Via Strozzi follow the line of the main east-west street *(decumanus maximus)*; Piazza della Repubblica was created at the end of last century on the site of the Roman forum; Via de' Bentaccordi and Via Torti near Santa Croce still echo the outline of the Roman amphitheatre.

The rise of a city – Florence rose to a position of power in Tuscany fairly late in the city's history. For many years Fiesole and later Lucca were predominant. Early in the 11C Count Ugo, Marquess of Tuscany, transferred his residence from Lucca to Florence where he built an abbey *(Badia - qv)*. In the second half of the century, power was in the hands of a particularly strong-willed woman, Countess Matilda, who supported Pope Gregory VII in his struggle against Emperor Henry IV of Germany on the question of Investitures. It was in one of her strongholds, in Canossa *(see Michelin Green Guide Italy)*, that the two protagonists held a meeting at which the Emperor was humiliated.
During this period Florence began to acquire power and influence. When Matilda died in 1115 the city had already gained a degree of independence which was to increase during the 12C. It was at this time that the two Romanesque master-pieces – the Church of San Miniato al Monte and the Baptistery – were built. It was also at this time (1125) that Florence annihilated its rival, Fiesole. A more important contemporary event was the addition of a third class of citizen – the wealthy merchants who provided the city with an extraordinary level of prosperity

which endured for several centuries – to the two existing social classes which had previously governed the affairs of the city – the Aristocracy, who supported the emperor, and the Clergy.

Florin.

The power of money – As trades and crafts began to develop, their practitioners were organised into influential guilds *(arti)*, which were to form the basis of legislative power when Florence declared itself a Free Commune *(qv)* in the late 12C.

In the 13C the city enjoyed an extraordinary level of economic development, owing to its wool and, later, its silk industries. Officially it had seven "Major Guilds", five "Medium Guilds" and nine "Minor Guilds" *(see below)*. In the following century the weavers' guild *(Arte della Lana)*, whose mansion can still be seen near the Church of Orsanmichele *(qv)*, and the guild whose members finished imported cloth *(Arte di Calimala)*, employed between them approximately one-third of the city's population and exported cloth that was famous for its quality in all the major trading centres in Europe (Genoa, Venice, Paris, London, Bruges and Barcelona). Indeed, its reputation spread as far as the Muslim Orient.

In addition to the craftsmen and merchants, a third category of Florentines did much to increase the wealth of the city. Following in the footsteps of the Lombard and Jewish moneylenders, Florentine **bankers** became famous throughout Europe. In 1199 they were in contact with England. In 1269 they instigated the very first bills of exchange which were to give considerable impetus to trade in Florence and Europe as a whole. At almost the same period they minted the famous gold florin, which bore the Florentine lily on one side and the effigy of city's patron saint, John the Baptist, on the other. This coin was to become international currency until it was overtaken in the late 15C by the Venetian ducat.

The banking tradition was continued by the Bardi-Peruzzi who advanced enormous sums of money to King Edward III of England at the beginning of the Hundred Years' War. They were joined in the world of finance by the Pitti, Strozzi, Pazzi and Medici.

Internal strife – Guelfs and Ghibellines – The economic "miracle" was all the more amazing given the violent feuds that raged not only between Florence and other major towns in Tuscany but also between various Florentine factions within the city.

It was in the 13C that the Guelfs, supporters of the Pope, and the Ghibellines, supporters of the Holy Roman Emperor *(qv)*, first appeared on the scene. At first the Guelfs were victorious but the Ghibellines set up alliances with other cities that were opposed to Florence, in particular with Siena, and defeated the Guelfs at Montaperti *(qv)* in 1260. Despite their crushing defeat, the Guelfs regained their strength and in 1266 they defeated the Ghibellines

---

The "Guilds" in Florence in the late 13C

The classification of the craft guilds into three categories (major, middle and minor) took place from 1282 to 1293. Initially there was only one guild, for merchants, named after the street where they conducted their business – Calimala. Gradually various crafts set up their own guilds, each with its own coat of arms; the arms below are those of the major craft guilds.

Calimala – Leading merchants.

Arte della Lana – Wool-workers.

Arte di Por Santa Maria – Silk-workers.

Doctors and apothecaries.

Money-changers.

Furriers.

Magistrates and lawyers.

The **five middle guilds** were swordsmiths and armour-makers; locksmiths; shoemakers; harness-makers and saddlers; tanners and curriers. The **nine minor guilds** were linen-drapers and clothiers, blacksmiths, masons and carpenters, joiners, oven-men and bakers, butchers, wine merchants, oil merchants and hoteliers.

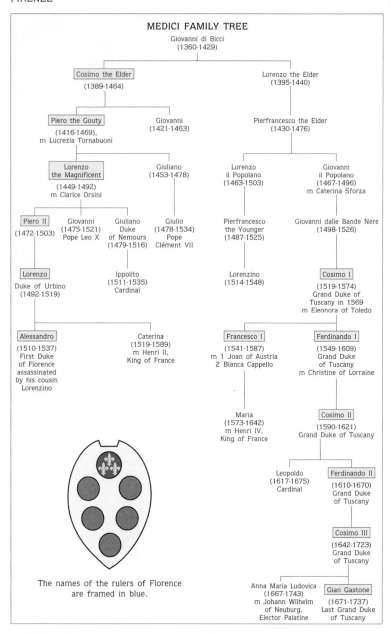

MEDICI FAMILY TREE

Giovanni di Bicci
(1360-1429)

Cosimo the Elder
(1389-1464)

Lorenzo the Elder
(1395-1440)

Piero the Gouty
(1416-1469),
m Lucrezia Tornabuoni

Giovanni
(1421-1463)

Pierfrancesco the Elder
(1430-1476)

Lorenzo
the Magnificent
(1449-1492)
m Clarice Orsini

Giuliano
(1453-1478)

Lorenzo
il Popolano
(1463-1503)

Giovanni
il Popolano
(1467-1496)
m Caterina Sforza

Piero II
(1472-1503)

Giovanni
(1475-1521)
Pope Leo X

Giuliano
Duke
of Nemours
(1479-1516)

Giulio
(1478-1534)
Pope
Clément VII

Pierfrancesco
the Younger
(1487-1525)

Giovanni dalle Bande Nere
(1498-1526)

Lorenzo
Duke of Urbino
(1492-1519)

Ippolito
(1511-1535)
Cardinal

Lorenzino
(1514-1548)

Cosimo I
(1519-1574)
Grand Duke of
Tuscany in 1569
m Eleonora of Toledo

Alessandro
(1510-1537)
First Duke
of Florence
assassinated
by his cousin
Lorenzino

Caterina
(1519-1589)
m Henri II,
King of France

Francesco I
(1541-1587)
m 1 Joan of Austria
2 Bianca Cappello

Ferdinando I
(1549-1609)
Grand Duke
of Tuscany
m Christine of Lorraine

Maria
(1573-1642)
m Henri IV,
King of France

Cosimo II
(1590-1621)
Grand Duke of Tuscany

Leopoldo
(1617-1675)
Cardinal

Ferdinando II
(1610-1670)
Grand Duke
of Tuscany

Cosimo III
(1642-1723)
Grand Duke
of Tuscany

Anna Maria Ludovica
(1667-1743)
m Johann Wilhelm
of Neuburg,
Elector Palatine

Gian Gastone
(1671-1737)
Last Grand Duke
of Tuscany

The names of the rulers of Florence
are framed in blue.

and returned to Florence; they made considerable changes in the city centre since they systematically demolished the many tower-houses built by the Ghibelline noblemen *(see below – Old Streets and Mansions)*.

Under the Guelfs the city became a republic with a democratic constitution ruled from the Palazzo Vecchio *(see below)* by a government mainly composed of representatives *(Priori)* of the guilds.

Divisions then began to appear between Black and White Guelfs; the latter broke away from the Papacy. Owing to this tragic development, Dante, a member of the White Guelf faction, was banished for life from his native city in January 1302. In 1348 the Black Death killed more than one-half of the population of Florence and put an end to internal strife.

The Medici – This family came from an obscure land-owning background. In the 14C several members of the family were to be found in Florence, all of them little-known merchants and modest money-changers, yet for three centuries the family was to give the city its leaders, unofficially at first, officially in later years.

Some of them played a vital part in shaping the city's destiny. Several of them were influential in the world of literature, the arts and the sciences. Almost all of them made extensive art collections.

The Century of the Medici – Giovanni di Bicci, founder of the dynasty, was a circumspect, prudent man who was the head of a prosperous bank and had become a leading citizen in his home town by the time he died in 1429.

His son, **Cosimo the Elder**, the "Great Merchant of Florence", was then aged 40. Like his father, he was a self-effacing man with an extraordinary feeling for business; he turned the family enterprise into the largest of its kind in Florence, gave the wool and silk industries an "international" dimension and conducted the bank's activities on a European scale. When he came to power, the prosperity of Florence had enabled the city to gain control of several towns in Tuscany and, with the surrender of Pisa in 1406, Florence became a maritime power. This was a golden era for Florence. Cosimo led an austere life and, although he never held any official position, he acted like a statesman and virtually ruled the city for 30 years. By placing his own men in key positions and by forcing into exile and thus ruining the great families who were hostile to him (he himself had been banished from the city for a year in 1433), he exercised a firm but prudent foreign policy through intermediaries (curtailing the expansionist intentions of Venice) by maintaining a peaceful hegemony in Florence and skillfully combining his own interests with those of the city.

His greatest merit, however, remains his active participation in the arts. He was a major patron and, although he himself was not a cultured man, he encouraged the spread of Humanism by attracting to his circle the very best of Florentine intellectuals and artists – Marsilio Ficino (philosopher), Poliziano (poet), Brunelleschi, Donatello, the della Robbias, Paolo Uccello, Filippo Lippi, Andrea del Castagno, Benozzo Gozzoli, Fra Angelico. He set up the Platonic Academy and a number of libraries including the famous Laurenziana Library *(qv)*. He had a great love of building; he commissioned numerous major constructions or improvements and counted Michelozzo, the architect, among his friends. When he died in 1464, the Florentines had the inscription *Pater Patriae* (Father of his Country) engraved on his tomb.

His son, Piero I, also known as **Peter the Gouty**, was a sickly man who had inherited neither his father's political skills nor his business acumen and he survived him for only five years. His marriage to Lucrezia Tornabuoni allied the Medici dynasty to one of the greatest families in Florence.

The Medici were not known for their looks but his younger son, **Giuliano**, who was assassinated in 1478 at the age of 25 during the Pazzi conspiracy *(qv)*, has gone down in history as a handsome young man, owing to the work of artists such as Botticelli. The woman with whom he fell in love, Simonetta Vespucci, who also died at a very young age, was probably the model for the famous *Venus (qv)* by Botticelli and her portrait was also painted by Piero di Cosimo *(now in the museum in Chantilly, France)*.

Giuliano's elder brother, **Lorenzo the Magnificent** (1449-1492), was quite different. He was a highly-intelligent but not a handsome man, the most famous of all the Medici. Although he was only 20 when his father died, he began to direct the affairs of Florence but covertly, in accordance with the family tradition. He was less discreet than his predecessors, ruling like a prince and exercising personal power. He was outstanding for his skilful diplomacy and, like his grandfather, he succeeded in maintaining the dominant position of Florence in Italy and the balance of power between the Papacy and the various States; he was likened to the pointer on a set of scales *(ago della bilancia)*. On the other hand, he proved to be less than able in managing the commercial and banking business bequeathed to him by his father, and this led to the ruin of the financial empire of the Medici. He was less generous than his father and grandfather; following the **Pazzi conspiracy** *(qv)*, which had been mounted in the name of lost freedoms and supported by the Pope, he instigated a cruel and merciless repression against the Pazzis. He was a fascinating character, a combination of hedonism and political realism, cold calculation and intransigence, yet a man with enormous artistic and humanistic sensitivity, a supreme example of Renaissance man. He was a lover of the arts and a talented writer of verse; his friends – the painters, philosophers and poets who made up his court – were on familiar terms with him and called him Lauro (laurel bush).

The two brothers gave the Christian world two popes – Leo X, Lorenzo's younger son, and Clement VII, Giuliano's illegitimate son.

The death of Lorenzo the Magnificent in 1492 – the news spread throughout Europe – marked the end of the "century of the Medici" but also the beginning of a new era of discovery.

SCALA

Lorenzo the Magnificent.

Savonarola.

SCALA

Savonarola

Savonarola – Savonarola (1452-1498), a Dominican monk from Ferrara who became prior of St Mark's monastery, was to cause the downfall of the Medici by taking advantage of a difficult period when the people of Florence were faced with crumbling republican institutions and France and Spain were at war, each struggling for control of Europe as a whole. The fanatical, ascetic monk was the complete antithesis of ordinary Florentines who had a deep love of the arts and life in general. Yet they submitted to his power in 1493, when he preached a terrifying and powerful sermon from the pulpit of the cathedral, denouncing the pleasures of the senses and love of the arts. He banished Peter II (Piero il Fatuo), Lorenzo's son, whose grand-daughter, Catherine, became Queen of France, accusing him of cowardice in the face of the French. Yet he unreservedly welcomed Charles VIII to Florence in 1494.

In these increasingly troubled times, Machiavelli, then Secretary to the Chancery, was worried by the city's inability to resist rebellion by towns such as Pisa, Arezzo or Pistoia, and the threat posed by the European powers. In 1497 Savonarola organised a "bonfire of vanities" in Piazza della Signoria. Masks, wigs, musical instruments, books of poetry and works of art perished in the flames. The following year, on the same spot, Savonarola himself was burnt at the stake.

The return of the Medici – After several popular uprisings and several short-lived attempts to govern, the Medici returned to power in Florence officially in 1530, supported by Charles V, the Holy Roman Emperor.

Alessandro, Lorenzo's grandson, took the title of Duke of Florence but he was murdered in 1537 by his cousin Lorenzino, a member of the cadet branch of the Medici family.

It was this branch of the family, descended from Giovanni de' Bicci, that was to take control of the situation.

Cosimo I (1519-1574) was the son of the military leader *(condottiere)*, Giovanni of the Black Bands (who was the grandson of Cosimo the Elder's brother). When he took power, he was only 18 years old but his statesmanlike qualities soon became apparent. He was strong-willed, resolute, well-organised and endowed with a well-developed political sense and he soon imposed himself on others by his unwavering firmness, competence and wisdom. His was an authoritarian regime both in terms of administration and policy. Yet he gave Florence back the sparkle that it had lost and brought it renewed prosperity. He created a Tuscan state, keeping the reigns of government firmly in his own hands.

In 1555 he overpowered Siena, thus achieving (except for Lucca) the unification of Tuscany, which became a Grand Duchy in 1569. He also sought to protect his State from external predators such as Charles V, Philip II of Spain and the Papacy. Following in the tradition set by the senior branch of the family, he became a patron of the arts and he extended his protection to sculptors such as Giovanni da Bologna and Benvenuto Cellini and to the painter Bronzino. In 1539 he married the daughter of the Viceroy of Naples, **Eleonora of Toledo**, an intelligent and beautiful woman, whose portrait was painted, in a stilted style, by Vasari and Bronzino.

The first of their 11 children to reign was **Francesco I** (1541-1587) who was more enthusiastic about science and alchemy than political power but he showed extreme firmness in the face of opposition. He married Joan of Austria, daughter of Emperor Maximilian, and they had one daughter, Marie, the future Queen of France. His greatest claim to fame, however, was his love affair with Bianca Cappello from Venice, which began as an illegitimate liaison. He married her after the death of his first wife but the couple died a tragic death, in his villa in Poggio a Caiano *(qv)*.

His younger brother, **Ferdinando I** (1549-1609), was the last enterprising member of the Medici family. He was a courteous and active man who ensured the prosperity of the State and married a French princess, Christine of Lorraine, but his descendants – Cosimo II, Ferdinando II, Cosimo III and the last of the male line Gian Gastone, a disillusioned libertine – caused the decline of the Grand Duchy of Tuscany.

The last in the female line of this extraordinary family was Anna Maria Ludovica, Gian Gastone's sister, who married the Elector Palatine and died in 1743, expressly bequeathing to Florence all the priceless treasures that had been collected over the years by her ancestors.

The post-Medici period – The Grand Duchy then passed to the princes of Lorraine, who continued in possession until the arrival of Napoleon in 1799. He renamed Tuscany the Kingdom of Etruria and made Florence its capital (1801-1807) before

Maestà by Cimabue (Uffizi).

Death of St Francis
by Giotto (Santa Croce).

The Church Militant by Andrea da Firenze
(Spanish Chapel in Santa Maria Novella).

Giovanni Acuto
by Paolo Uccello
(Santa Maria del Fiore).

Hercules and the Hydra of Lerna by
Antonio Pollaiolo (Uffizi).

FIRENZE

turning the city into the main town in the French *département* of Arno (1807-1809).
Finally he restored the Grand Duchy and placed his sister, Elsa, at its head. She
was forced to flee Florence in 1814.
Lorraine then regained possession and the Prince of Lorraine remained Grand Duke
of Tuscany until 1859.
In 1860 Florence was defeated by the House of Savoy and integrated into the
Kingdom of Italy, of which it was the capital from 1865 to 1870.

THE WORKSHOP ON THE ARNO

From the 13C to the 16C, from Byzantine conventionalism to decadent Mannerism,
Florence saw an extraordinary development of the visual arts which reached its
apotheosis during the century of the Medici.

Florentine Painting

The characteristics of the Florentine School are the search for beauty of form, a
preoccupation with evoking an idealised natural environment, a preference for
balanced composition and the importance of perspective.

The first glimmerings of the Renaissance – The first painter to point Florentine
and Tuscan art in this direction was **Cimabue** (1240-1302). Although he remained
loyal to the Byzantine School, retaining its linear forms, its draped garments and
its lack of of any three-dimensional background, he gave his paintings greater
humanity through the facial expressions of his figures and by modelling their bodies
to give an impression of volume. His pupil and successor, **Giotto** (1266-1337), freed
himself of the traditional constraints by seeking to suggest the plastic reality of
his figures. His aim was to represent volume in real space, to paint whole scenes
(rather than a *Maestà* or a *Crucifixion*) and he thereby brought to his paintings the
sense of movement and expression that was necessary if they were to be understood
and convey figurative truth *(see the frescoes narrating the life of St Francis in Santa
Croce)*. Nevertheless, he made no attempt to translate reality in the proper sense
of the term (volume, space, expression); he wanted simply to make the subject
matter more comprehensible. The means he employed were decidedly limited – a
tree and a rock suggested a landscape; figures were draped with grand garments
to create a solid mass; gesture and visual expression were intended to emphasise
the central point in a composition. Constituent parts of a work were not painted
to depict individual accuracy but in order to underline the truth of the work as a
whole. Among his successors were **Taddeo Gaddi, Maso di Banco** (also known as Giottino) and
Bernardo Daddi, who were unable to retain the heroic spirit of their master; by
producing more vividly-coloured works containing a welter of detail, they failed to
match his style.

A return to older values – In the second half of the 14C, Florentine (and Tuscan)
painting went into a decline. Every level of society was affected by the period of
crisis which followed the ravages of the Black Death in 1348. When **Andrea da Firenze**
painted the frescoes in the Spanish Chapel (in the cloisters of Santa Maria Novella)
*c*1365, he opted for a style of composition that was no longer realistic and narrative
but dogmatic and extremely animated, typical of the 13C. **Orcagna** worked from
1344 to 1368 (very few of his paintings have survived) using the same basic
concepts (Santa Croce Museum and reredos in Santa Maria Novella). In the late 14C
the narrative style returned, embellished with the beauty of the international Gothic
movement, that was so popular in Siena, and which the great wealth of that city
enabled it to spread throughout Tuscany. **Agnolo Gaddi** (*c*1345-1396), Taddeo's son,
and **Lorenzo Monaco** (*c*1370-post 1422) worked in the same style. Monaco, who was
a Camaldolite monk in Florence, began by illuminating manuscripts before painting
altarpieces in which he expressed a blandness that was typical of the Gothic period.
Masolino da Panicale (1383-1447), Masaccio's master, who was faithful to the
decorative techniques of the Sienese School, gave greater importance to the
representation of volume and space.

Perspective, volume and structure, a revolution in design – A precursor in the
technique of foreshortening, **Masaccio** (1401-1428) undertook a study of space and
the play of light across volume. Assisted by his friend, Brunelleschi, he was the first
person to define a rigorous, scientific form of architectural perspective, thereby
including painting among the disciplines that were influenced by the spirit of the
Renaissance. In the simplicity of his work and the firm line of his figures, Masaccio,
like his predecessor Giotto, painted an objective reality that was tranquil and
self-assured.
This determination to express the structure of volume reached its height with **Paolo
Uccello** (1397-1475) and **Andrea del Castagno** (1423-1457). Uccello reduced form to
it purest expression, drowning it in light until he achieved an almost abstract use
of colour – his frescoes in the Chiostro Verde in Santa Maria Novella and his reredos
depicting the *Battle of San Romano* in the Uffizi Gallery; the latter expressed the

Madonna of the goldfinch
by Raphael
(Uffizi).

Lucrezia Panciatichi
by Bronzino
(Uffizi).

The Deposition
by Rosso Fiorentino
(Volterra Art Gallery).

The Annunciation by Leonardo da Vinci (Uffizi).

SCALA

power of volume with such tension that his figures seem to be made of stone *(Last Supper in Sant'Apollonia)*. These two artists, who both possessed drawing skills bordering on the unreal, created *trompe-l'oeil* sculptures *(see Santa Maria del Fiore and the Uffizi Gallery)* where their somewhat stilted finish acquires a true reality.

The painters of light and colour – In contrast to these artistic ideals, some painters who adopted the technique of spatial construction – introduced by Masaccio – continued to make use of pastel shades, detailed ornamentation or dense composition. The arrival of **Domenico Veneziano** *(c*1400-1461) from Venice *c*1435 helped them to find a middle course between the stolid drawings of the Early Renaissance and the Gothic-style mannerisms of the heirs of the 14C. He showed the artists of Florence (who had already mastered frescoes and *a tempera* painting) how to use oils and how to organise space, making it lighter through the luminosity, lightness and fluidity of his colours. In this way he reinforced the style of those painters who inclined towards more gentle representations, such as the Dominican monk Fra Angelico (1387-1455), a pupil of Lorenzo Monaco *(see San Marco)*. Fra Angelico respected perspective and used the new architectural vocabulary based on Antiquity while retaining a very fresh, new approach to aesthetics, embellished with gold, brocade and pearls. **Alessio Baldovinetti** *(c*1425-1499), a pupil of Domenico Veneziano, combined his clear, careful drawing techniques with a liking for wide landscapes and delicate colours.

Narrative artists – The quietly graceful, descriptive trend led a number of artists to explore the field of narrative painting and some of them even developed an anecdotal style. From his teacher, Fra Angelico, **Benozzo Gozzoli** (1420-1497) inherited a taste for luminous colours and exquisite detail but his works have their own charm which derives from a Gothic-style exuberance which brought so much life to his strong compositions that they are almost buzzing with activity. Then came **Domenico Ghirlandaio** (1449-1494) who excelled in the descriptive style and became a chronicler of Florentine society during the last quarter of the 15C. His tranquil drawing techniques were combined with clarity of composition to depict costume and details of domestic life and to depict landscapes with long perspectives in the style of the Flemish artists. The arrival in Florence in 1482 of the Portinari triptych by Hugo Van der Goes *(Uffizi Gallery)* had a profound effect on other artists of the day. Apart from the technique of oil painting, of which they had until then seen very few examples, the most outstanding feature of the work was the realism of the figures and the background.

Among those who made even less use of colour than Ghirlandaio were **Antonio Pollaiolo** (1431-1498) and his brother, **Piero** (1443-1496), who followed in his footsteps. Antonio who had a vigorous drawing technique learnt from Castagno. Unlike other painters of his day who were concerned to depict humanity as wise, serene and even stolid, Antonio was interested in conveying a sense of movement and illustrating physical and spiritual contortions. Even the backgrounds of his paintings were filled with sinuous movement, so that his compositions give an impression of great dynamism.

The painters of grace – The last artistic trend in the 15C was one of suave, ethereal beauty filled with a sense of purity, innocence and delicacy. Strangely, the artist who was the precursor of this trend was **Filippo Lippi** (1406-1469) *(see Prato)*, an unfrocked monk and pupil of Masaccio, who completed his master's cycle of frescoes in the Brancacci Chapel in Santa Maria del Carmine. His portraits of the Virgin Mary dressed in transparent veils are precursors of works by his pupil, Sandro Botticelli, who taught Lippi's son, **Filippino Lippi** (1459-1504). The apogee (and also the decline) of the Early Renaissance was marked by Botticelli (1444-1510 – *qv*). The main feature of his work is its sensuality but the artistic experience of the century in which he lived is also evident in his fine, incisive drawing, his sense of background and landscape, the studied poses of his figures draped in flimsy garments and with veils fluttering in a gentle breeze.

His paintings mark the end of an epoch and the distress he suffered after the death of Lorenzo the Magnificent and the remorse he experienced for supporting Savonarola's theories, marked the end of the serene humanism of this period.

The masters of the High Renaissance – Although the High Renaissance reached maturity in Rome, it was in Florence that it first took root, in the studios of the artists of the 15C. **Leonardo da Vinci** (1452-1519) began learning his craft in the studio of the painter and bronze sculptor Verrocchio *(see below)*, Michelangelo (1475-1564) was one of Ghirlandaio's pupils, and Raphael (1483-1520) came from Urbino while very young to follow his master, Perugino, to the city of the Medici. In Florence Perugino created a large number of works characterised by a lascivious gracefulness *(Crucifixion* in the Convent of La Maddalena dei Pazzi – *qv)*.

Leonardo, who came from Vinci *(qv)*, was particularly successful in synthesising the art forms developed by his predecessors while enriching the art of painting with his knowledge of various scientific disciplines. His paintings *(Uffizi Gallery, Room 15)* are designed to express perfect beauty devoid of any of Nature's imperfections

Madonna and Child
by Luca della Robbia
(Bargello).

David by Donatello (Bargello).

Cosimo I
by Cellino (Bargello).

Tomb of Lorenzo, Duke of Nemours by Michelangelo in the New Sacristy in San Lorenzo.

and rendered through technical mastery. There is perfection in the landscape, the composition, the balance of colours and the architectural and atmospheric perspective (through the use of *sfumato*, which blurs outlines and suffuses backgrounds in a bluish light). In his fresco of the Battle of Anghiari *(qv)* designed for the Palazzo Vecchio in Anghiari, which unfortunately no longer exists, he proved his ability to organise a highly complex composition and provide a skilful representation of human anatomy. Only Michelangelo could rival him *(see Cascina)*, although he was convinced that the supreme art form – the one that could best represent perfection in nature – was sculpture rather than painting. Raphael followed the example of these masters and sought consummate beauty, first in the manner of Perugino using softness and balance, then through the use of da Vinci's *sfumato* technique and finally by acquiring Michelangelo's knowledge of anatomy and vigorous creative skills.

Classicism and Mannerism – Although overshadowed by Leonardo da Vinci and Raphael, **Fra Bartolomeo** (1475-1517), a Dominican and follower of Savonarola, and **Andrea del Sarto** (1486-1531) represented Florentine Classicism, the final expression of the real Renaissance, in search of the very essence of Beauty. Del Sarto was a brilliant colourist and, like Fra Bartolomeo, very fond of *sfumato*. He paved the way for Mannerism by showing an interest, in some of his works, in the expression of feelings (*The Last Supper* in San Salvi). The torments of the soul became more important than the ideal of beauty and the corresponding impression of timelessness.

His pupil, **Pontormo** (1494-1556), gave full vent to his natural anxiety in tormented works, sinous attitudes and faded colours that have a profound effect on the viewer (*The Deposition of Christ* in Santa Felicità and *The Annunciation* in Carmignano). This generation of artists was enormously affected by the paintings of Michelangelo, who painted the ceiling of the Sistine Chapel between 1508 and 1512. The power of his human figures, their sculpture-like positions, often based on a twisting of the trunk, and his vivid colours were all imitated. The result depended on the sensitivity of the artist.

Rosso Fiorentino (1494-1540) revealed his morbid anxiety in tortured works, elongated figures and strident colours. He was invited to France by François I and finished his career at Fontainebleau.

The second generation of mannerists moved away from this uncontrolled sensitivity steeped in pathos and, on the contrary, restricted itself to a solemnity that was almost painful. **Bronzino** (1503-1572), who was trained by Pontormo, was official portrait painter to the Grand Duchy after 1539. He was concerned to represent the psychological truth of his models and the beauty of their costume (Uffizi Gallery, *Cosimo I, Eleonora of Toledo,* and *Lucrezia Panciatichi*). His vigorous, rather cold drawings and vivid colours show the continuing influence of the great artistic figure of the day – Michelangelo.

Vasari, who was born in Arezzo *(qv)*, the great historian of Italian art from Cimabue to his own time, was also Court painter to the Medici; he created all the grand décors in the Palazzo Vecchio, including the allegories and the historical and mythological paintings which, unfortunately, ensnared Florentine art in the academic style.

Architecture and Sculpture

The architects of the day created a style based on restrained grandeur. The proportions were harmonious and the décor in religious buildings consisted of geometric motifs picked out in coloured marble while the mansions were decorated with rustication and projecting cornices (*for vernacular architecture see also Florence - Old Streets and Houses*).

The Middle Ages – The two magnificent buildings known as the Baptistery and the Church of San Miniato al Monte date from the Romanesque period. Their simple volumes – a centred layout for the Baptistery and a basilica-like layout based on a square and a cube for San Miniato – and harmonious geometric décor of coloured marble made them reference works for the movement known as the Pre-Renaissance. They were the direct precursors of the west front of Santa Maria Novella by Alberti and showed a determination to achieve rational constructions in terms of space by the use of pure volume based on straight lines and semicircular arches, a feature common to all ancient Roman designs.

The appearance of the city as it is today owes something to the Gothic style. The blossoming of new religious orders led to buildings in this style – Santa Maria Novella for the Dominicans, Santa Croce for the Franciscans, Santa Annunziata for the Servites, Ognissanti for the Humiliati, Santo Spirito for the Austin Friars, Holy Trinity for the Vallombrosians and Santa Maria del Carmine for the Carmelites (some of these buildings were substantially altered in later centuries). There were two main architectural designers in the Gothic period. **Arnolfo di Cambio** (*c*1250-1302) created the initial plans for the Cathedral and, according to Vasari, for Santa Croce;

he was also director of works at the Palazzo Vecchio between 1299 and 1302. **Giotto** built the belltower (from 1334 onwards). **Orcagna** (1308-1368), a pupil of Arnolfo di Cambio and Giotto, was the designer of the Tabernacle in Orsanmichele, a building on which work began in 1336 and which marked the beginnings of an architectural style in which prestige and decoration took precedence over utility. The Loggia della Signoria with its extremely wide arches is a fine example of this style.

The Blossoming of the Renaissance – The beginning of this new era in Florence can for the sake of convenience be dated to 1401. This was the year in which Lorenzo Ghiberti (1378-1455) and Filippo Brunelleschi among others took part in the competition to choose the designer of the second doorway to the baptistery, the first one having been designed by Andrea Pisano (1336). When Ghiberti was chosen, Brunelleschi felt constrained to give up sculpture, although he had trained as a goldsmith. Ghiberti was later chosen to design the third doorway, which Michelangelo called the Gate of Paradise because of its great beauty; he also created some of the monumental bronzes in Orsanmichele.

Following his failure to secure the commission **Brunelleschi** (1377-1446) left for Rome and returned there several times in the following years. He became an enthusiast for Classical architecture, for the ruins of Ancient Rome and for their gigantic scale. He was the first person to understand these structures and to adapt his findings to the needs of his day. The work that revealed his talent and the extent of his knowledge was the dome of Florence Cathedral. Nobody else at the beginning of the 15C would have been capable of erecting such a dome (42m – 136ft wide and 60m – 195ft above ground level) without the support of flying buttresses. Owing to the force of the lateral thrust he was obliged to produce an ogival form rather than the perfect hemisphere so beloved of the ancient Romans. The first building designed by **Brunelleschi** in accordance with his own Classical ideal was the Foundling Hospital. The portico is composed of semicircular arches supported on columns and surmounted by a horizontal entablature; the entire structure is emphasised by the use of *pietra serena* (the grey-blue stone quarried in the vicinity of Florence) which stands out against the white wall of the main building. He used the same procedure in San Lorenzo, Santo Spirito and the Pazzi Chapel in Santa Croce. In each of these buildings the volumes are composed of simple forms which are used as modules and their repetition produces the overall sense of harmony. His building technique was rational and based on calculation and mathematical perspective. He was the founder of modern architecture, who based his designs on plans and not merely on his experience as a master-mason.

Leon Battista Alberti (1404-1472) was the other great architect of the early 15C. He was a scholar and a humanist who wrote a number of treatises on painting, sculpture and architecture as well as on subjects such as the family or grammar. He was born in Genoa and travelled to Florence in 1428 when his family, which had been banished, was allowed to return to the city. As an intellectual he was not interested in the pragmatism of ancient architecture; he was interested only in its aestheticism. He was more of a designer than a builder but he shared with Brunelleschi a love of simple geometric forms, as is evident in his design for the west front of Santa Maria Novella. It is inscribed within a square and its details are structured around this motif. The Rucellai Palace in Florence is also his work.

He was a friend of both Alberti and Brunelleschi but was closer to the latter with whom he travelled to Rome. Their opposite number in sculpture was **Donatello** (1386-1466). He observed the architecture and art of the Ancient Romans and learnt to emphasise the reality and energy of his figures. He revolutionised Gothic art by refusing the easy, contemporary stereotypes of draped clothing, gentle movement and serene expressions, as is obvious in his determined figure of St George in Orsanmichele *(original in the Bargello)*. Throughout his life he created a great variety of characters – the prophets on the Belltower *(now in the Museo dell'Opera del Duomo)*, the young David *(in the Bargello)*, Judith and Holofernes *(Palazzo Vecchio)* and Mary Magdalen *(Museo dell'Opera del Duomo)*; they are a magnificent embodiment of the grandeur of their actions, their purpose in life and their own particular characters. Donatello did not seek to invent a model of sublime beauty; each of his sculptures reveals expressive intensity and a truth that is sometimes crude but always real.

The Golden Age of the Florentine Renaissance – The second half of the century saw the development and blossoming of the forms which had originally been created by Brunelleschi, Alberti and Donatello. In architecture, **Michelozzo** (1396-1472) was the man who made popular in vernacular buildings the forms used by his master, Brunelleschi, in public buildings such as churches and chapels. He was appointed architect to the Medici and built their mansion in Florence, including the inner courtyard, which resembled cloisters. He also refurbished their feudal residences in Cafaggiolo and Trebbio in the Mugello district. He inspired **Benedetto da Maiano**, another sculptor, who built the Strozzi Palace, and **Giuliano da Sangallo** (1445-1516), who designed the Gondi Palace and the sacristy in Santo Spirito.

The way forward inaugurated by Donatello was followed by his contemporaries and the next generation. **Luca della Robbia** (1400-1482) also sought realism in his human figures, their attitudes and their expressions but he tended to idealise them, preferring greater flexibility and modesty to the sharpness of his rival. This difference is obvious in the two *cantorie,* which were made during the same period - one by Donatello, the other by Luca *(now in the Museo dell'Opera del Duomo).* The popularity of high reliefs by Luca della Robbia - in azure blue and white glazed earthenware dotted with yellow and green - provided a livelihood for his workshop and his descendants, Andrea (1436-1524) and Giovanni (1446-1527).

Many artists working in or around the middle of the century in emulation of Donatello showed little interest in monumental sculpture. **Desiderio da Settignano** (1428-1464) created some magnificent low reliefs, revealing a taste for more tenderness and inner sentiment, a feeling for feminine gentleness. He died young, leaving the way open for **Mino da Fiesole** *(c*1430-1484), whose style was more graceful, and **Benedetto da Maiano** (1422-1497), who created the pulpit in Santa Croce; both were famous for their work in marble.

In contrast to this trend in which flexibility was all-important, **Antonio Pollaiolo** and **Verrocchio** (both of them painters and sculptors) and their pupils were attracted by vigour, energy, and muscular strength, which they expressed in bronze.

SCALA

Entrance Hall of the Laurenziana Library by Michelangelo.

Michelangelo - At the end of the century, owing to the political upheavals following the death of Lorenzo the Magnificent, Florence entered a period of uncertainty which was perfectly translated by the passionate personality of Michelangelo, who combined pride and agony in his work. In his sculptures, as in his paintings, he achieved great realism; he surpassed the best of his predecessors, who produced merely probable personalised figures. Michelangelo's creations seem to be throbbing with inner life; the weight of their limbs and the strength of their muscles seem to be those of real people captured at a precise moment in time rather than set against the gentle timelessness of the perfect beauty favoured during the Renaissance. Examples of his genius include his proud *David (original in the Galleria dell'Accademia),* his drunken *Bacchus (in the Bargello),* his gentle *Virgin Mary and Staircase (in the Casa Buonarroti)* or his *Pietà (in the Museo dell'Opera del Duomo).* In architecture also, he breathed life into space by revolutionising the formalism of the Classical repertory - he divided up pediments and included empty niches in the new sacristy in San Lorenzo. In the entrance hall to the Laurenziana Library, he set columns into the walls, supporting them on fluted brackets, treated the internal walls as if they were external and designed the staircase in three parts so that it occupied almost all the floor space. He appropriated Brunelleschi's techniques – highlighting structural elements with *pietra serena,* a taste for centred designs, unification of volume – but used them only to give greater freedom to the dynamics of space, in which the old vocabulary is only a tool rather than a rigid means of achieving harmony.

Florentine Mannerism – Michelangelo had such a strong personality that most artists were influenced by him. The most interesting was Ammannati (1511-1592) who worked for Cosimo I from 1555 onwards. He designed the courtyard *(cortile)* and the rear of the Pitti Palace; he also designed the Santa Trinità Bridge with its elegant, flattened arches and sculpted the Neptune Fountain in Piazza della Signoria. He often worked with Vasari (1511-1574), the architect and painter *(qv)* who supervised work on the Uffizi.

The best of all the late-16C Florentine architects was **Bernardo Buontalenti** (1536-1608) who succeeded Vasari at the Uffizi, designed the west front of Santa Trinità and drew up the project for the Belvedere Fort.

Among the sculptors, **Baccio Bandinelli** (1488-1560) carried over into the 16C a taste for well-balanced, ordered, Classical statues that were, nevertheless, lacking in warmth. His *Hercules and Cacus* stands opposite Michelangelo's *David* in Piazza della Signoria.

Benvenuto Cellini (1500-1571), who produced a dazzling autobiography describing his life as an adventurer, was a fervent admirer of Michelangelo. Although principally a goldsmith, he also created bronzes of great impact, despite over-elaborate ornamentation, in which he managed to combine the many facets of his talent *(Perseus* in the Loggia della Signoria, and a *Bust of Cosimo I* in the Bargello).

Giovanni da Bologna (1529-1608), who was born in Douai in France, arrived in Florence from Rome in 1555. His refined talents combined incisive gracefulness with a disciplined academic approach.

From this time on, however, Florence began to lose its artists. In the 16C the new beacon was Rome and it was this city which attracted the finest talents of the day. Over the next few centuries, the Medici city lived in the reflection of its past glories but never again succeeding in bringing together the miraculous combination of rapid economic expansion, financial power as a banking centre, aristocratic patrons and a wealth of talented artists, intent on mutual emulation, unequalled since the days of Athens' greatness.

Literature

Florence played a particularly important role in the literary development of Tuscany *(see the Introduction – Tuscan Literature)*.

TRADITIONAL EVENTS

Scoppio del Carro – This event – the Exploding of the Cart – is held on Easter Sunday in Piazza del Duomo. It dates from 1101, the year in which a crusader returned from Jerusalem with three stones from Christ's tomb. In each year that followed on Easter Sunday the stones produced sparks that were used to re-light the lamps extinguished on Good Friday. From the 16C onwards the sparks began to light larger and larger "lamps" until the event acquired its present form. A wooden cart (6m – 20ft high), known as *Il Brindellone,* is drawn through the streets to the square in front of the cathedral by four oxen with gilded horns and hooves. The chariot is accompanied by a procession of people dressed in Renaissance costume, comprising a standard-bearer, representatives of the four districts of the city and the teams participating in the historic football match *(calcio storico – see below)*. Once the procession arrives in the square in front of the cathedral, the cart is unhitched and set on fire by a dove which "flies" along a wire from the high altar in the cathedral to the cart, where it sets off a cascade of fireworks. Then a young child draws lots to determine the order of play for the semi-finals of the football *(calcio)*.

Calcio storico fiorentino – *Calcio* is the name given to a sort of football played in 16C costume – the first match is on the Feast of St John the Baptist (June 24) and the two others on the following days. The matches are played by teams from the four districts of the city and consist of two semi-finals and one final. The Greens represent San Giovanni (the Baptistery), the Reds Santa Maria Novella, the Blues Santa Croce and the Whites Santo Spirito *(Oltr'Arno* on the south bank). The game has no precise rules and is a combination of Association and Rugby football and wrestling. It is descended from the ball games played by the Romans in *Florentia,* in which the objective was to carry the ball into the goal of the opposing team. The tradition was perpetuated into the Middle Ages when the town council was obliged to impose restrictions on the unruly players and their fans who invaded the streets and squares, disturbing the other citizens well into the night. The present game commemorates a match played on 17 February 1530 when the city, which was under siege by the Holy Roman Emperor, Charles V, dared to demonstrate its

Traditional Florentine Football.

defiance despite its privations, celebrating Carnival with much noise and clamour. Charles V was eventually victorious but the match went down in history. At the end of the 18C the game went out of fashion but, on the occasion of the fourth centenary in 1930, the festivities were revived and the tradition has continued unbroken except during the Second World War.

The event begins with a huge procession of 530 players dressed in period costume, representing every sector of 16C Florentine society. To the sound of trumpets and drums and with standards flying in the wind, the procession sets off from Santa Maria Novella to the square in front of Santa Croce, which is covered with sand for the occasion of the match. The kick-off is given by a blast on a culverin, which is also sounded each time a goal is scored. Play lasts for 50 minutes. The teams have 27 players each – four goalkeepers, three backs, five half-backs

Procession preceding the Florentine Football Match.

and 15 forwards. The winning team receives a white calf which used to be cut up on the spot for the ensuing banquet. Nowadays the calf is sold but the banquet still takes place.

Rificolona – This festival takes place on the evening of 7 September, the eve of the Feast of the Birth of the Blessed Virgin Mary. The tradition probably dates from the days when peasants from outlying country and mountain districts used to travel to Florence for the festival, hoping to sell their produce at the fair which was held at that time. The long distances travelled by some of these visitors meant they spent several days on the road and had to carry lanterns when it was dark. The Florentines may have been thinking of these old-fashioned lights when they created the first paper lanterns *(rificolone)*, which were originally in the shape of dolls recalling the peasants who came down from the mountains to take part in the festivities. The lights consisted of a candle shaded by the doll's skirt, carried high in the air on the top of a long pole. Later the shape of the lanterns changed and people began to hang them in the windows of their houses.

OTHER TOURIST EVENTS

During the May Music Festival **(Maggio Musicale)** there are concerts, operas and ballets in the Teatro Comunale and the programme often spills over into June.
In May there is also a standard or pennant competition known as the **Trofeo Marzocco** when groups perform in Piazza Santa Croce.
For the Feast of St Lawrence on 10 August the district of the same name stages a number of special events.
From November to January the city hosts the Festival of Old Toys **(Festival del giocattolo d'epoca)**.

As these events in Florence take place during the tourist season, the city is likely to be very crowded on these dates and it is advisable to make hotel reservations well in advance so as to avoid disappointment.

★★★ BUILDINGS OF THE PIAZZA DEL DUOMO (Y) *Tour – half a day*

At the centre of the city stands a remarkable group of buildings in white, green and pink marble – cathedral, belltower and baptistery – which mark the transition from medieval Florentine architecture to the Renaissance period.
On the south side of the Piazza on the corner of Via dei Calzaiuoli stands the **Loggia del Bigallo (A)**, which was built in the mid 14C with two perpendicular semicircular arcades surmounted by double windows. Lost or abandoned children used to be displayed beneath the loggia.

★★ Duomo (Cathedral) ⓥ

The cathedral is a symbol of the wealth and power of Florence in the 13C and 14C. It is one of the largest buildings in the Christian world (155m – 504ft long [St Peter's in Rome 186m – 605ft long, St Paul's in London 152m – 494ft long, Notre-Dame in Paris 130m – 423ft long]; 90m -293ft wide from one end of the transept to the other; 107m – 348ft high from the floor to the top of the lantern). Its dedication to Santa Maria del Fiore recalls the flower, a golden rose, presented by Pope Eugenius IV when the cathedral was consecrated.
The cathedral was built on the site of the Romanesque cathedral of Santa Reparata, which was deemed too modest a building for such an important city as medieval Florence. Its construction mobilised the resources of the city for almost 150 years. The commission was given to the renowned architect, Arnolfo di Cambio, and, although work began in 1296, the cathedral was not consecrated until 1436. During this time considerable modifications to the initial plans were made by Arnolfo's successors, Giotto, Andrea Pisano and particularly Francesco Talenti.
The building, which is mainly Gothic, is a striking example of the original character of this particular style in Florence – large volumes and horizontal lines in preference to carved surfaces. A marquetry design of multi-coloured marble in typical Florentine style forms the geometrical decoration of the stone courses. The west front designed by Arnolfo di Cambia was demolished in 1588 without ever being completed. It was replaced in the late 19C by the existing front, a complex imitation of the Gothic style.
The huge **dome★★★**, an integral part of the Florentine landscape, is the most beautiful part of the building. It is the work of Filippo Brunelleschi, described by Vasari as "an architectural genius sent down by heaven to bring new form to an architecture that had gone astray"; in 1420 he solved the problem of how to roof the vast sanctuary. In order to reduce the massive thrust towards the

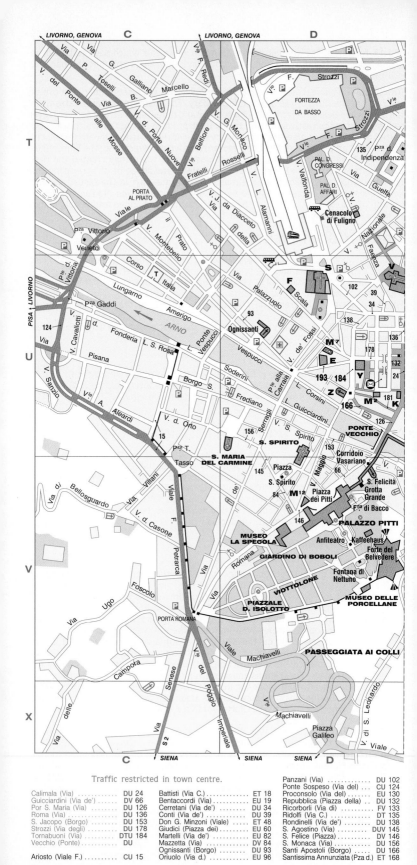

Traffic restricted in town centre.

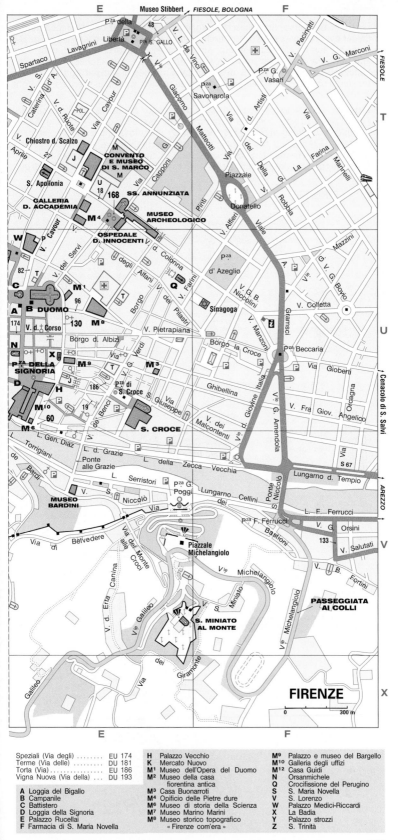

Museo Stibbert / FIESOLE, BOLOGNA

119

centre of the dome, Brunelleschi designed a roof made of two flattened domes linked by a complex network of arches and buttresses. The construction of the gigantic dome, erected without any apparent support, aroused enormous admiration and enthusiasm in Florence at the time. For almost 15 years the building site, with its hoists designed by Brunelleschi himself and capable of moving blocks of stone weighing over three tonnes, was an unprecedented sight for the Florentine people.

Exterior – *Starting on the south side, walk round the cathedral anticlockwise.* From the south side there is a striking view of the building; the amazing marble marquetry cladding accentuates the already grandiose appearance created by the lack of relief and the regular repetition of the various elements. The **east end**★★★ is remarkably extensive consisting of three polygonal apses radiating from the transept crossing; together with the dome, which rests on a high drum,

A	Loggia del Bigallo
B	Campanile
C	Battistero
D	Loggia della Signoria
E	Loggia di S. Paolo
G	Loggia dei Rucellai
H	Palazzo Vecchio
K	Mercato Nuovo
L	Palazzo di Parte Guelfa
M¹	Museo dell'Opera del Duomo
M²	Museo della casa fiorentina antica
M⁶	Museo di Storia della Scienza
M⁷	Museo Marino Marini
N	Orsanmichele
R	Torre della Castagna

Traffic restricted in town centre.

it forms a complex yet superbly well-balanced composition. Originally a gallery was to run round the base of the dome but its construction was apparently discontinued when Michelangelo remarked that it resembled a "cage for crickets".

On the north side of the building is the **Mandorla Door**, surmounted by a mandorla containing a carving of *the Virgin Mary of the Assumption* by Nanni di Banco in the early 15C. The mosaic work on the tympanum (1490) depicting *the Annunciation* is the work of Domenico Ghirlandaio.

Nave – After the lavish ornamentation of the exterior the nave is disconcertingly plain. The small difference in height between nave and aisles, the four widely-spaced arches in the nave (80m – 260ft long) and a cornice at the base of the vaulting break the verticality of the nave and seem to reduce the overall proportions of the building.

The stained-glass windows of the west end, especially the central rose window depicting *the Assumption of the Virgin Mary,* were based on drawings by Lorenzo Ghiberti; their composition uses a remarkable shade of green. The tomb of Bishop Antonio d'Orso who died in 1321, was carved by the Sienese sculptor, Tino di Camaino, who produced a number of famous monumental tombs during the Gothic period. A fragment of the original work (1) *(left of the centre door)* shows the deceased asleep and seated, above a sarcophagus.

In the first bay of the south aisle, just above the place where his tomb was discovered in the crypt *(see below)* in 1972, is a portrait of Brunelleschi (2) carved in a medallion by one of his pupils.

In the north aisle are two frescoes containing fictitious equestrian sculptures in honour of two military men *(condottieri)* who hired their services to Florence; the first one (3) is by Andrea del Castagno (1456) and the second one (4) by Paolo Uccello (1436). Another fresco (5), painted in 1465, depicts Dante explaining his *Divine Comedy* to the city of Florence, which is represented by its cathedral as it was in the 15C; the fresco illustrates the "geography" of the other world as imagined by the poet – the pit of Hell, the mountain of Purgatory and the heavenly ranks of Paradise.

The aisles are lit by remarkable 14C stained-glass windows.

★★ **Sanctuary** – It is here that the true grandeur of the building can best be appreciated. The huge octagonal sanctuary is enclosed by an elegant marble screen erected in the mid 16C; from it radiate three vast apses forming a trefoil, each one containing five chapels. Above rises the breathtaking **dome★★★** *(c*50m –

162ft in diameter at its base and 91m – 296ft high), which is decorated with a huge fresco depicting *the Last Judgement*; it was begun by Vasari who worked on it for two years from 1572 to 1574 but it required a further five years' work by Federico Zuccari before it was finished in 1579.

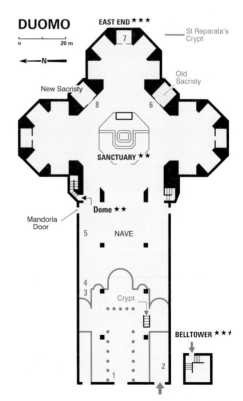

The tympanum above the righthand door of the Old Sacristy (*Sacrestia Vecchia*) (6) is decorated with a terracotta *Ascension* by Luca della Robbia.

Beneath the altar (7) in the axial chapel lies the tomb of St Zanobi, the first Bishop of Florence. This remarkable work consists of bronze reliefs depicting scenes from the saint's life; it was made by Lorenzo Ghiberti. On either side of the altar are two delightful white glazed terracotta angel candle-bearers by Luca della Robbia. Their faces recall those of the adolescents in the famous "*Cantoria*" by the same artist now in the museum *(see below)*.

The door of the New Sanctuary *(Sacrestia Nuova)*, symmetrically opposite the Old Sacristy, is also surmounted by a typanum decorated by Luca della Robbia (8) depicting the **Resurrection**★ in light shades of blue. It was in the New Sacristy that Lorenzo the Magnificent took refuge when attacked by two monks involved in the Pazzi Conspiracy. The Pazzi, who were rivals of the Medici, attempted to assassinate Lorenzo on Sunday April 26 1478, during the Elevation at the Easter Mass. He was only wounded but his brother, Giuliano, was killed.

Skillful lighting shows off *(through a partition)* the **marquetry cabinets**★ which reach half-way up the walls of the room and were produced in the second half of the 15C, mainly by Benedetto and Giuliano da Maiano. The splendid bronze door panels depicting figures of the Evangelists and Prophets are also worthy of note.

★★ **Dome** ⊙ – *Access via the north or south aisle (10). Tour – 45min.*
The ascent to the dome (463 steps) is difficult but impressive.

The narrow gallery overlooking the chancel provides a breathtaking **view**★★ down into the cathedral and also a close-up view of the remarkable **stained-glass windows**★ in the oculi of the drum; they were produced in the first half of the 15C and are based on sketches made by the leading figures of the time – Ghiberti, Donatello, Paolo Uccello and Andrea del Sarto.

From the staircase leading to the top of the dome, which is constructed between the two vaults, there is an interesting view of the structural features; the final section, which is very steep and close against the wall, is the most spectacular. It leads to the exterior at the foot of the lantern turret which was Brunelleschi's last work and not set in place until after his death. From here there is a magnificent **panoramic view**★★ of Florence – *(northwest)* the dome of San Lorenzo backed by Santa Maria Novella standing out against the green of Cascine Park; *(left of the belltower)* the arch of Piazza della Repubblica and cube-shaped Orsanmichele church, backed *(south bank)* by the huge and impressive Pitti Palace and *(left)* the Boboli Gardens laid out on the hill. In the foreground *(south)* is the Loggia della Signoria and the Palazzo Vecchio in front of the long building of the Uffizi, flanked *(left)* by the slender belltower of the Badia standing out against the massive outline of the Bargello. The light speck in the background is San Miniato near Piazzale Michelangiolo. Slightly nearer *(southeast)* is the white marble façade of Santa Croce. In the far distance *(north)* rises Fiesole Hill.

Santa Reparata's Crypt – *Staircase by the first pillar on the south side of the nave.*

The crypt is in fact all that remains of an earlier Romanesque church (13C-14C), which was discovered during excavation work in 1966. It had itself been created through the conversion of a paleo-Christian basilica (5C-6C) and was demolished during the construction of the present cathedral.

The place where Brunelleschi's tomb was discovered can be seen through an iron grille in an opening overlooking the uncovered section to the left of the staircase.

The structural features so far uncovered have made it possible to reconstitute the layout of the original cathedral (a nave and two aisles and a raised chancel above a crypt). Ground level was then significantly lower than at present. A drawing *(in a showcase)* shows the relevant periods of construction of the different architectural features and the large fragments of mosaic flooring; most of them date from the paleo-Christian era. Other display cases contain miscellaneous objects discovered during the excavations – spurs and a sword found in the tomb of one of the Medici buried in Santa Reparata in 1351 – the tombstone is displayed on a pedestal.

★★★ **Campanile** (Belltower) **(B)** ⊙

The belltower by Giotto is no less famous than Brunelleschi's dome. It is a slim, slender tower (82m – 267ft high), its straight lines forming a harmonious contrast with the curved structure of the dome.

The importance placed on horizontal lines and the geometrical ornamentation again illustrate the unusual character of the Gothic style in Florence. The light colours of the marble cladding and the distribution of the bays which increase in number towards the top of the tower, create an impression of lightness.

St Reparata, patron saint of their first cathedral, was long cherished by the Florentine people, even after the construction of the new church dedicated to Santa Maria del Fiore. The young martyr was beheaded in Palestine at the age of 12. The delightful legend that a dove flew out of her neck up to heaven, forms the background to the festival (Scoppio del Carro) held on Easter Sunday, when a steel dove swoops down in front of the cathedral and sets light to an explosive charge on a cart.

The plans for and decoration of the belltower were the work of Giotto, who was appointed to supervise work on the cathedral. Construction began in 1334 but only the decorated section of carved panels had been built by the time he died in 1337. His successors, Andrea Pisano and Francesco Talenti, who completed the building work between 1349 and 1360 and designed the traceried section of the bays, both made a number of modifications to the original plans.

Copies have replaced the original low reliefs in the bottom section of the building. The decoration was based on an overall design by Giotto. The first register was carved by Andrea Pisano and Luca della Robbia; the second by pupils of Andrea Pisano, including Alberto Arnoldi. The originals, together with the statues of Prophets and Sibyls, which once occupied the niches on the second floor, are in the Museo dell'Opera del Duomo *(see below)*.

Staircase to the top – *30min Return (414 steps)*. From the upper terrace there is a fine **panoramic view**★★ of the cathedral and the city of Florence.

★★★ Battistero (Baptistery) (C) ⊙

"My beautiful St John's" is how Dante described the baptistery which is dedicated to John the Baptist, patron saint of Florence, whose effigy appeared on the famous gold florin in the Middle Ages. This elegant octagonal building, clad in white and dark-coloured marble, is highly representative of Florentine architecture where proportion and harmony are all-important; it conveys an exceptional impression of precision and delicate purity.

The Baptistery is a Romanesque building, probably dating from the 11C, which nonetheless contains a number of Renaissance features (pilasters, capitals, triangular pediments, etc) typical of Florentine architecture, which had always drawn on Antiquity for inspiration.

The strict geometry of the exterior décor becomes increasingly less rigid, as it passes from the windowless base, through a level pierced by small windows within large arches, up to the top level which is lighter in colour and contains more detailed decorative motifs.

★★★ **Baptistery Doors** – The bronze doors decorated with magnificent carved panels are famous throughout the world.

Facing away from the cathedral, walk round the building starting on the left.

The **South Door** *(now the entrance)* is the oldest. Work was begun in 1330 by Andrea Pisano and is distinctly Gothic in style because of the quatrefoils containing a number of different scenes. The 20 upper panels depict episodes from the life of John the Baptist. In the eight lower panels, the sculptor represented the Theological and Cardinal Virtues, carved with remarkable freedom and ease – *(left to right and top to bottom) (left door)* Hope, Faith, Fortitude and Temperance; *(right door)* Charity, Humility, Justice and Prudence.

The Renaissance border, skilfully decorated with foliage, birds and cherubs, was the work of Vittorio Ghiberti, the son of the artist who produced the other two sets of doors. The bronze group depicting *the Beheading of John the Baptist* at the top of the doors was made by Vincenzo Danti (c1570).

The commission for the **North Door** (1403-1424) was given to Lorenzo Ghiberti, aged only 25, after a competition in which the city's greatest artists, including Brunelleschi, took part. Although he was working almost 100 years later, Ghiberti achieved a harmony with Andrea Pisano's doors, by retaining the quatrefoil composition of Gothic tradition for the medallions. The eight lower panels depict the Evangelists and the Doctors of the Church. Above are scenes from the Life and Passion of Christ *(from bottom to top)* depicted with remarkable austerity, nobility and harmony of composition. Above the doorway is *John the Baptist Preaching* (early 16C) by Rustici.

In the square a few yards from the North Door, stands St Zanobi's Column, which dates from 1384; it is capped by an unusual crown of leaves, recalling the legend of the dead elm tree which began to sprout leaves on the day in January 429 when the Saint's relics were transferred from San Lorenzo to Santa Reparata.

The **East Door** *(facing the cathedral)* is the most famous of all, the one which Michelangelo thought worthy to be called the Gate of Paradise.

Between 1425 and 1452 Ghiberti, then at the peak of his talent, produced a masterpiece of sculpture and metalwork. The ten panels contain highly complex compositions illustrating episodes from the Old Testament executed with an abundance of characters in scenes that are remarkably lively, elegant and poetic.

From top to bottom, each register including the left and right doors.

Register 1 – Creation of Adam and Eve, Original Sin. Adam and Eve expelled from Paradise.

Cain and Abel – Cain the labourer; Abel the shepherd; sacrifices made to God by the two brothers; Abel slain by Cain; the divine curse.

Register 2 – Story of Noah – his family and the animals saved from the Flood; the rainbow sent as a sign of God's covenant with Noah; the drunkenness of Noah.

Register 3 – Esau and his brother Jacob – Esau sent hunting by Isaac; Esau gives up his birthright to Jacob; Rebecca advises Jacob; God speaks to Rebecca; Jacob receives Isaac's blessing instead of Esau.

Joseph's life – *(top right)* Joseph sold by his brothers; *(bottom left)* discovery of the cup in Benjamin's sack; storing the corn after Joseph interprets Pharaoh's dream and predicts seven years of famine; Joseph seated on a throne is recognised by his family.

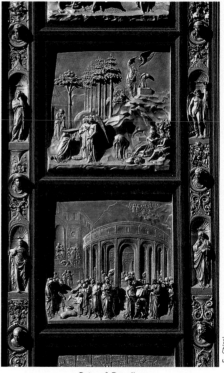

Gate of Paradise
(self-portrait of Ghiberti – bottom left).

Register 4 – Moses receives the Tables of the Law; in his absence the Hebrews at the foot of Mount Sinai fall into despair.

Joshua and the Fall of Jericho; *(below)* the people cross the dry River Jordan and pick up the stones of memory.

Register 5 – Saul and David – the battle against the Philistines led by Saul standing in a chariot; *(below)* David beheads Goliath.

Meeting of King Solomon and the Queen of Sheba.

The surround is decorated with carved heads set in medallions and full-length figures of the Prophets and Sibyls in the niches; on the left door approximately at mid-height towards the centre, Ghiberti has depicted himself as a bald and roguish-looking man. *The Baptism of Christ* above the door *(removed for restoration)* is by Sansovino.

Interior – The inside of the baptistery (25m – 106ft in diameter) is a dazzling sight. The marble-clad walls, two orders of granite pilasters and columns, with gilded Corinthian capitals, create an extraordinary impression of grandeur and harmony.

The most striking feature, however, is the dome covered in sparkling **mosaics★★★**. It seems that during the first half of the 13C mosaic workers from Venice were called in to carry out the work; this would explain the clearly Byzantine style of certain scenes. Florentine artists, including Cimabue, also

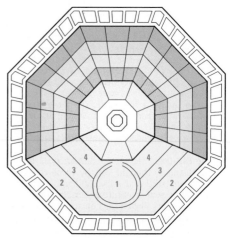

Mosaics in the dome of the Baptistery.

worked on the dome. The mosaics, set on a gold background, are laid out in concentric registers covering the eight sections of the dome. They depict the following scenes, often in a wonderfully fresh manner.

– The Last Judgement *(in yellow on the plan)*. The large Christ in Majesty (1) is flanked on both sides by the Resurrection of the Dead with Heaven and Hell (2), the Virgin Mary with the Saints and Apostles (3) and the Angels of the Resurrection (4).
– Genesis *(pale pink)*.
– Various choirs of angels or celestial hierarchies *(darker pink)*.
– The Life of Joseph *(blue)*.
– The Life of the Virgin Mary and Jesus *(light green)*.
– The Life of St John the Baptist *(darker green)*.

Fine marble mosaics, some with motifs borrowed from oriental designs, form the pavement leading to the Gate of Paradise, which was originally the main entrance to the baptistery, opposite the altar and the large Christ depicted on the dome.

To the right of the small apse *(scarsella)* is the tomb of the Antipope John XXIII, friend of Giovanni di Bicci (the father of Cosimo the Elder). It is a remarkable work produced in 1427 by Donatello assisted by Michelozzo.

It may come as something of a surprise to learn that the Baptistery in Florence contains the tomb of Pope Alexander V's successor, John XXIII, who died in 1419. He was elected pope by the cardinals but his serious political blunders and flight from Rome caused him to be deposed in favour of Martin V. It was not until the 20C that a new pope took the name of John and, having occupied the throne of St Peter with dignity, went down in history as the 23rd pope of this name (the ordinal was deemed not to have been previously attributed).

★★ Museo dell'Opera del Duomo (Cathedral Museum) (M¹) ⊘ - *9 Piazza del Duomo*

A tour of the cathedral, belltower and baptistery would not be complete without a visit to the museum which houses numerous sculptures and artefacts from the three buildings.

Ground floor – The great hall situated behind the entrance is devoted to the west front of the cathedral, shown in a 16C drawing as it appeared shortly before it was demolished. The drawing is the work of Arnolfo di Cambio, who produced most of the sculptures decorating the cathedral in a well-balanced, majestic style reminiscent of Classical statuary. Against the wall opposite the entrance is an impressive *Madonna and Child*; beside it is a remarkable *St Reparata* bearing a vase, which for many years was thought to date from the days of Antiquity. Other sculptors carved the monumental statues of the Evangelists *(against the entrance wall)*, the most remarkable of which is *St Luke* by Nanni di Banco. At the far end of the hall *(left)* there is a series of small rooms. The first contains some of the equipment used by Brunelleschi during the construction of the dome – square, compass, pulleys, brick moulds, iron tensioners used to set the blocks of stone accurately in place, a wooden winch used to hoist materials and a small cart used to transport tools. The second room contains scale models of the dome and its lantern, in addition to the death mask of the great architect. The first of the two rooms on the other side of the great hall contains various scale models proposed for the west front of the cathedral – by Buontalenti, Giovanni da Bologna and Giovanni de' Medici – as well as a collection of liturgical chants dating from the 16C. The second room contains part of the cathedral treasure.

Mezzanine floor – Here is the famous Pietà★★ sculpted by Michelangelo at the age of 80. He intended it for his own tomb but left it unfinished because he was dissatisfied with the quality of the marble. He is supposed to have depicted himself as Nicodemus supporting the Virgin Mary and Christ. The figure of Mary Magdalen, added by one of Michelangelo's pupils, attempts to hold up the body as it sinks to the ground but, as she does not appear to participate with the same intense effort as the other two, she detracts from the unity of the whole work.

First floor – The great hall houses the famous cantorie★★, choir galleries that once surmounted the doors of the sacristies in the cathedral. The more famous of the two *(left of the entrance)* is the one by Luca della Robbia (1431-1438); the separate panels *(at the bottom of the wall)* are the originals; the gallery above is a reconstruction made from moulds. These exquisitely-charming carved reliefs are the first known works by the artist. He took his inspiration from Classical metopes but gave his groups of singing children, musicians and dancers a delicate, serene and natural quality that are all his own. The gallery (1433-1439) by Donatello *(opposite)* was also based on Classical low reliefs and, although it is less graceful, it nevertheless conveys a remarkable impression of movement and liveliness.

Above the galleries is the famous statue of **Mary Magdalen**★ repenting, a late work (1455) by Donatello carved in wood, which is striking for its expressiveness and dramatic force.

In the same room is a group of statues that once adorned the belltower. They include three more works by Donatello. Against the wall to the right of the entrance is a prophet whose remarkably lifelike expression would suggest that the work is a portrait. Along the opposite wall are the prophets Jeremiah, whose twisted robes emphasise inner tension, and Habakkuk, nicknamed *Zuccone* (marrow) because of the shape of his bald head. Both of them are depicted in an astonishingly lifelike fashion.

Detail of the cantoria by Luca della Robbia.

The room *(left of the Cantoria room)* displays the admirable **low reliefs**★★ that once decorated the belltower. The hexagonal ones, depicting various trades and activities, a number of characters from Antiquity and scenes from the Book of Genesis, were produced by Andrea Pisano and Luca della Robbia; they show wonderful vigour and often great lyricism. The other diamond-shaped works, carved by pupils of Andrea Pisano, represent the Liberal Arts, the Virtues, the Planets and the Sacraments.

The room *(right of the Cantoria room)* contains the magnificent **silver altar**★★ from the baptistery, a splendid example of Florentine gold and silversmithing from the 14C-15C, which combines Gothic and Renaissance style features and took over a century to produce. The story of John the Baptist was depicted on it by numerous artists, including Michelozzo, Antonio Pollaiolo and Verrocchio, who had the largest workshops in Florence.

Above it stands the cross which stood on the Baptistery altar, also made of silver and produced in the mid 15C by Betto di Francesco, Antonio Pollaiolo and Bernardo Cellini. The display cases on either side of the room contain the panels of the altar **frontal**★ from the Baptistery, a splendid silk and filigree embroidery worked with great skill and artistry, which depicts episodes from the life of John the Baptist and Jesus. Seven artists of French, Flemish and Florentine origin worked on the piece over approximately 20 years.

In the centre of the room are four original low reliefs from the Gate of Paradise in the Baptistery *(see above)* depicting the Creation, Cain and Abel, David and Goliath and the Story of Joseph.

★★ PIAZZA DELLA SIGNORIA (z)

This was, and still is, the political centre of Florence set against the backcloth of the magnificent Palazzo Vecchio, the Loggia della Signoria and, in the wings, the Uffizi Gallery. It was created in the 13C when the victorious Guelfs razed to the ground the tower-houses belonging to the Ghibellines in the city centre. The numerous statues along the outside of the Palazzo Vecchio and the loggia make this a veritable open-air museum.

In the middle of the square is an equestrian statue of Cosimo I, made in 1594 by Giovanni da Bologna.

The Neptune Fountain at the corner of the Palazzo Vecchio is more impressive for its maritime gods, its elongated Mannerist-style nymphs and its bronze fawns, whose sensuality is both provocative and joyful, than for its enormous marble statue of Neptune, the sea god, whose local nickname is *Il Biancone* (The White Roly-Poly). The fountain was made by Bartolomeo Ammannati, assisted by Giovanni da Bologna, for the wedding in 1565 of Cosimo I's elder son with Joan of Austria. It was to some extent a challenge to the rigorous morality preached by the Dominican friar, Savonarola, who had constantly criticised the Medici style of government, as it was erected on the very spot where he was burnt at the stake on 23 May 1498 having first been hanged. In front of the fountain is a round slab marking the place of execution; Savonarola's death is commemorated every year in a ceremony known as the *Fiorita*.

Beside the steps up to the building *(left)* is the *Marzocco*, the lion of Florence resting on a lily, executed by Donatello *(original in the Bargello)*. Beside it is an admirable copy of the famous group by the same artist representing **Judith and Holofernes★** *(original in the Palazzo Vecchio)*. Near the entrance is a huge marble statue of David, a copy of Michelangelo's famous work *(original in the Galleria dell'Accademia)*.

★★ Loggia della Signoria (D)

The loggia was constructed at the end of the 14C to accommodate the members of the *Signoria (see below)* during official ceremonies. When later it was

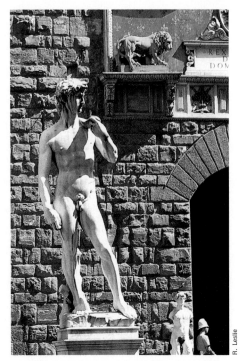

David by Michelangelo in Piazza della Signoria.

R. Leslie

used as a guard room by Cosimo I's lancers (16C), it became known as the Loggia dei Lanzi. Although Gothic in design, it has wide semicircular arches built in the Florentine tradition, opening onto the square. An elegant decoration is provided by four shields representing the cardinal virtues, a band decorated with seven coats of arms which have been damaged, a graceful frieze of small trefoiled arches and a slender roof balustrade *(terrace accessible from the Uffizi during the high season only)*.

Statues dating from the days of the ancient Romans *(restored)* and the Renaissance have been placed in the loggia. The admirable statue of **Perseus★★★** brandishing the head of the Medusa *(front left - restoration in progress)* was made between 1545 and 1553 by Benvenuto Cellini. By this time the artist had reached his mature period and the work demonstrates his extraordinary skill both as goldsmith and sculptor. The detailed study of anatomy and the powerful modelling of the statue, together with the subtle refinement of the details on the base, make this bronze a masterpiece of Renaissance sculpture. The low relief depicting *Perseus Delivering Andromeda* is a copy *(original in the Bargello)*. *The Kidnap of a Sabine Woman (right)* dates from 1583; *Hercules Slaying the Centaur, Nessus (behind)* (1599) is by Giovanni da Bologna.

★★★ Palazzo Vecchio (also Palazzo della Signoria) (Z H) ⊙
Tour - 2 hours 30min

The impressive mass of the mansion, surmounted by an elegant belfry (94m - 306ft high), dominates the square.

At the end of the 13C Florence decided to build a City Hall worthy of its importance, a decision similar to the one taken about the cathedral, and it was probably Arnolfo di Cambio, the cathedral architect, who drew the design for the new City Hall.

It is in an austere Gothic style with an almost total absence of doors or windows on the lower level; on the upper storeys there are twin windows with trefoiled arches, machicolations, parapet walkways and crenellations; the merlons on the mansion are Guelf and those on the tower are Ghibelline.

The building was designed to house the city government **(la Signoria)** composed of six representatives of the guilds **(priori delle Arti)**, which held great power in Florence at that time, and an official *(Gonfaloniere di Giustizia)* whose post combined juridical and military authority. These officials were elected for only two months and, during their period of office, lived almost like recluses within the *palazzo*, where they worked and ate and slept; they were permitted to leave only for exceptional reasons. Dante lived there in 1300 as a member of the magistrature.

In the 16C Cosimo I made the building his residence and also adapted it to suit the lavish lifestyle of the grand-ducal court, by enlarging it and making radical alterations to the interior. The work was supervised by Giorgio Vasari who, for almost 20 years, from 1555 until his death, was employed there as architect, painter and decorator. When Cosimo I left the building to his son Francesco I and his wife, Joan of Austria, and moved to the Pitti Palace, it became known as Palazzo Vecchio (Old Palace) instead of Palazzo della Signoria.

The luxurious, elegant Renaissance interior forms a striking contrast to the exterior. The **courtyard★** (**C**) with its tall portico was almost totally redesigned in the 15C by Michelozzo and was elegantly decorated a century later by Vasari who added stuccowork on a gold background to the columns and painted grotesque figures on the vaulting. In the centre is a graceful fountain with a porphyry basin, surmounted by a small winged genius, a copy of a bronze by Verrocchio, which can be seen on the Juno Terrace inside the building.

Access to the various parts of the palazzo depends on the number of visitors. The text given below describes the most usual tour; if the order in which the rooms are visited is changed, the text will still be valid provided it is used in conjunction with the plans below.

First Floor

Visitors usually reach the first floor by the superb double staircase built by Vasari *(right at the end of the courtyard)*.

Hall of the Five Hundred - The Hall *(Salone dei Cinquecento)* is a gigantic chamber (1 200m² - 12 912 sq ft in area, 18m - 59ft high), built in 1495 during the days of the Republic instituted by Savonarola. It was designed to accommodate the Grand Council which had so many members (1500) that only one-third of their number could participate in the government of the city at any one time. Here Savonarola spoke in 1496, during his brief reign as master of Florence, and here he was condemned to death two years later.

When the Medici returned to power, they used the hall as their audience chamber, sitting on the raised dais, and also for receptions, including the one given to celebrate the marriage of Francesco and Joan of Austria.

The walls and sumptuous coffered ceiling were decorated by Vasari and his assistants with allegories and scenes in honour of Florence and Cosimo I. He is depicted like a god in the central coffer, amidst a circle of cherubs and coats of arms representing the city's various guilds. Battle scenes cover the walls along the entire length of the chamber, in honour of the victories won by Florence, mainly over its two great rivals, Pisa and Siena.

Most of the sculptures placed along the walls were already in the chamber in the 16C. Among them *(left of the door opposite the entrance)* is *La Vittoria*, an admirable group representing Genius slaying Might; it was made by Michelangelo for the tomb of Julius II but, as it was never finished, it was given to Cosimo I by Michelangelo's nephew.

★★ **Studiolo** - *Access to the right of the entrance. Visible from the door. No admission to the room itself.*

The exquisite but disturbing room was the study *(studiolo)* of Francesco I. Originally it could only be reached from his bedchamber via a small concealed door *(behind the bare panel to the right at the end of the room)*. It has no external source of light, reflecting the solitary character of the prince and his taste for secrets.

It was Vasari who designed this tiny but elegant room. For its decoration, he sought inspiration from the personality of this member of the Medici family who was so fond of the arts and sciences. The base of the walls contain cupboards. The walls themselves are covered in panels painted by several of the Florentine Mannerist painters. Using a symbolism that is often difficult to comprehend, they illustrated the myth of Prometheus (decoration on the ceiling) or the four elements - Water, Air, Earth and Fire - or human enterprise, scientific discoveries and the mysteries of alchemy. The two portraits placed opposite each other at the ends of the room depict Francesco's parents, Cosimo I and Eleonora of Toledo. Both were painted by Bronzino's studio.

Leo X's Apartments - *Access from the Hall of the Five Hundred by the door opposite the Studiolo. Most of the rooms are not open to the public as they house the offices of the current mayor.*

This wing of the mansion was added in the 16C by Cosimo I. The rooms in Leo X's apartments were designed as reception rooms for the guests of the grand-ducal court. Their decoration glorified the merits of the Medici, each feature being dedicated to one illustrious member of the family. Owing to the desire for verisimilitude that fired Vasari and his pupils when painting the scenes that cover the walls and ceilings, the decoration comprises not only a series of historical documents but also a veritable portrait gallery.

Leo X's Chamber – The largest chamber in Leo X's Apartments bears his name and is dedicated to the son of Lorenzo the Magnificent who re-established the family's authority in Florence in 1512 and was elected pope in 1513. He is depicted arriving in Piazza della Signoria during his visit to his birthplace two years later *(on the wall opposite the fireplace)*.

Access to the second floor from this room.

Second Floor

This floor contains three suites of rooms *(quartieri)* – the Elements Apartments, Eleonora of Toledo's Apartments, and the Priors' Apartments.

Elements Apartments – These rooms, which are situated above Leo X's Apartments, were built at the same time and to an identical layout. The decoration, based on ancient mythology, was designed by Vasari using complex symbolism with the aim of exalting the virtues of Cosimo I.

Elements Chamber (1) – The chamber is named after the allegorical scenes in its decoration and the name was then transferred to the entire suite of rooms. On the walls are illustrations of Water (the Birth of Venus), Fire (Vulcan's smithy), and Earth (Saturn receiving fruit). On the ceiling, in the rectangular coffer above the allegorical representation of Earth is Air (Apollo's chariot).

Ops and Cybele Chamber (2) – This chamber is dedicated to Ops, the Roman goddess of Abundance and Fertility, who is often assimilated to the Greek goddess, Cybele, mother of all the gods. It has retained its remarkable terracotta pavement dating from 1556. The geometric decoration on the floor is reflected on the ceiling. The two superb secretaires inlaid with tortoiseshell belonged to Cosimo I.

Ceres Chamber (3) – *Currently closed*. At the centre of the coffered ceiling is Ceres, the goddess of harvests, searching for her daughter Proserpina (Persephone in Greek).

Jupiter Chamber (4) – On the central coffer in the ceiling, Vasari and his pupils described the mythical childhood of Jupiter. He was removed by his mother, Ops, from the cruel grasp of his father, Saturn, who ate his own male children, and brought up by the nymphs on Mount Ida where he was suckled by a she-goat. The chamber contains a superb cabinet incrusted with hard stones.

Juno Terrace (5) – The ante-chamber contains the small statue by Verrocchio of a Winged Cupid holding a dolphin. It was designed to be placed in the entrance courtyard. From the terrace the view extends to the south bank of the Arno, and the peaceful hillsides of Belvedere and San Miniato al Monte, dotted with cypress trees.

Hercules Chamber (6) – On the ceiling are paintings of the Twelve Labours of Hercules. The central coffer shows Hercules as a child with his parents, Jupiter and Alcmene; he is strangling the serpents sent to kill him by Juno, Alcmene's rival.

Saturn Terrace (7) – *Open to the public during the summer months*. The terrace looks out onto one of the most attractive stretches of countryside in the Florence district – *(from right to left)* the Belvedere Fort, San Miniato and Piazzale Michelangiolo.

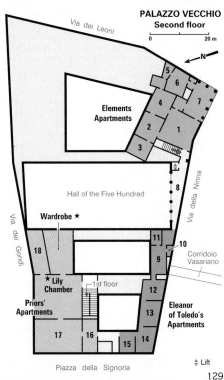

PALAZZO VECCHIO
Second floor
0   20 m

Via dei Leoni

Elements Apartments

Via della Ninna

Hall of the Five Hundred

Via dei Gondi

Wardrobe ★

★ Lily Chamber

1st floor

Priors' Apartments

Corridoio Vasariano

Eleanor of Toledo's Apartments

Piazza della Signoria

⇕ Lift

In the centre of the ceiling is a painting of Saturn devouring his sons; the four triangular coffers contain representations of the Four Ages of Man; the 12 rectangular coffers round the edge are decorated with illustrations of the 12 hours of the day.

Gallery (8) – The Elements Apartment is linked to Eleonora of Toledo's Apartments by this tiny balcony, which overlooks the Hall of the Five Hundred and gives a good idea of the exceptional height of the hall. Through the windows opposite there is a view of the drum supporting the cathedral dome and the Tuscan hills in the distance.

Eleonora of Toledo's Apartments – When Cosimo I came to live in the Palazzo della Signoria with his 18-year-old wife, he commissioned his court architect, Battista del Tasso, to refurbish for her use some of the austere apartments, once occupied by the guild representatives *(priori)*. A few years later Vasari and a Flemish artist, Jan Van der Straet, better-known as Lo Stradano, gave these chambers a less severe look by decorating the ceilings with scenes constituting a sort of hymn to femininity.

Green Chamber (9) – This chamber, the only one on which Vasari did not work, was Eleonora's bedchamber. On the vaulting is a shield bearing the coats of arms of the Medici and the House of Toledo. The ducal crown and two-headed imperial eagle are also represented.

This room opens into a tiny cabinet **(10)** with a small window, used by the duchess as her office *(scrittoio)*. It also opens into her private chapel **(11)**, which was decorated from 1541 to 1545 with scenes from the story of Moses by the portrait painter, Bronzino; the artist is said to have taken Cosimo and Eleonora's eldest daughter as his model for the Virgin Mary in *The Annunciation* which hangs on the back wall next *(right)* to *the Deposition from the Cross*.

Sabine Chamber (12) – This chamber was used by Eleonora's ladies-in-waiting. On the ceiling is a painting of the Sabine women standing between their fathers and their Roman husbands to prevent the men fighting.

Esther Chamber (13) – This chamber was used as the dining room. It contains an attractive 15C marble wash basin, introduced in the 19C. Almost the entire ceiling is covered with a large coffer decorated with an illustration of Courage and Determination in the person of Esther, the Hebrew woman who succeeded in saving her people; in this scene she is being crowned by Ahasuerus.

Penelope Chamber (14) – In the great central medallion is an exaltation of faithfulness symbolised by the wife of Ulysses dressed in 16C Florentine costume. In several places the Medici shield with its five roundels appears together with the chequerboard shield of the House of Toledo as well as *(on the window side of the great medallion)* the emblem of Cosimo I, which is the tortoise, a symbol of prudence, and a veil, which evokes a sense of opportunity.

La Gualdrada Chamber (15) – This chamber is dedicated to Virtue, embodied in the young Florentine girl who gained fame in the 13C by refusing a kiss from Emperor Otto. The frieze below the ceiling contains a number of buildings in Florence which are easily recognisable although they are depicted as they were in the 16C.

Priors' Apartments – These apartments were laid out a century earlier than the remainder of the mansion, which was altered by Cosimo I.

Priors' Chapel (16) – The officials *(Priori)* gathered here to pray before taking decisions of a legal nature, as is evident from the quotations from the Old and New Testaments contained in the series of panels round the walls. In the late 15C the chapel was decorated by Rodolfo Ghirlandaio against a background of fake mosaics.

Audience Chamber (17) – This chamber, which was decorated in the second half of the 15C, has a sumptuous coffered ceiling in shades of blue and gold, made by Giuliano da Maiano; with the assistance of his brother Benedetto, he also carved the delightful marble doorway opening into the adjacent room; above it in the niche is a statuette by Benedetto representing Justice.

★ **Lily Chamber** – This is one of the most beautiful chambers in the mansion. It owes its name to the golden fleurs de lys on a blue background decorating its walls. This is not the Florentine lily, which is red, but the emblem of the King of France with whom the Republic of Florence was on friendly terms. The superb gold and blue coffered ceiling was made, like the ceiling in the previous chamber, by Giuliano da Maiano (1478) whose brother was responsible for the delicate marble doorway surmounted by a statue of St John the Baptist. The marquetry doors are decorated with portraits of Dante and Petrarch. The admirable sculpture entitled *Judith and Holofernes* by Donatello is displayed in this chamber.

Cancelleria (18) – Machiavelli worked in this small room for his last 15 years in office as Secretary to the Chancery, leading Florentine diplomacy, until he was forced into exile following the return of the Medici in 1512. The room contains two portraits of Machiavelli – one a terracotta bust and the other a posthumous painting by Santi di Tito.

★ **Wardrobe** – In this chamber, designed by Vasari for Cosimo I, the Medici kept their state dress and their valuables. The decoration on the cupboards round the walls was completed in the second half of the 16C. It consists of a collection of maps of outstanding interest since all the areas of the world known at that time are shown. The enormous terrestrial globe in the centre of the room dates from the same period.

★★★ GALLERIA DEGLI UFFIZI (UFFIZI GALLERY) (Z) ⊘
Tour – 2 hours 30min for all rooms

The "Uffizi" – In 1560 Cosimo I commissioned a building to house the offices *(uffizi)* of the Medici administration. Vasari designed this unusual building in late-Renaissance style on the site of a Romanesque church. It consists of two long parallel wings joined at one end in a curve to form a kind of enclosed square like a courtyard, and extends from Piazza della Signoria to the Arno.

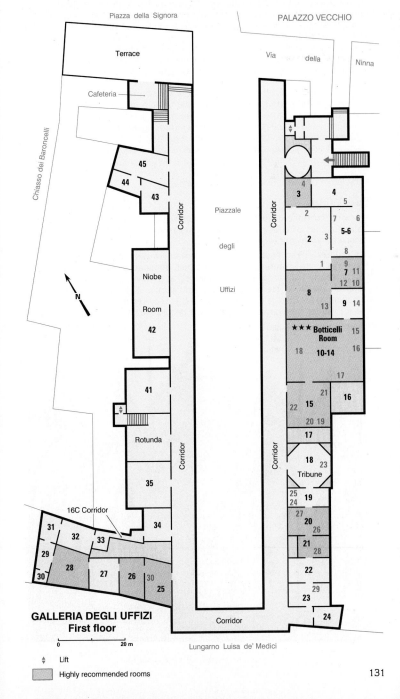

GALLERIA DEGLI UFFIZI
First floor

0   20 m

Lungarno Luisa de' Medici

⇕ Lift

Highly recommended rooms

A suspended corridor, which is still visible and now glazed, once linked the Palazzo Vecchio to the gallery and formed the top floor of the latter building. In 1581 the east section of the gallery was laid out by Francesco I to house the works of art acquired by earlier generations and was opened to the public ten years later. The Medici collections represent a large part of the works of art which now make the Uffizi one of the world's leading art galleries.

The **ground floor** displays relics from the Romanesque church of San Pier Scheraggio, the former occupant of the site. There are a number of fresco portraits of famous men by Andrea del Castagno and a fine representation of the *Battle of San Martino,* which took place on the same day and in the same area as the Battle of Solferino, painted in oils in 1936 by Corrado Cagli in the style of the famous *Battle of San Romano* by Paolo Uccello *(see Room 7).*

In the entrance to the gallery *(right)* hangs a large portrait of Anna Maria Ludovica, the last of the Medici who, on her death in 1743, bequeathed to the City of Florence the extraordinary treasures acquired by her ancestors.

The monumental staircase built by Vasari leads to the top floor of the building. The lifts *(far right of the foyer)* are reserved for those with special needs.

The collection in the Drawings and Prints Room situated on the first floor is not open to visitors. A selection of these works is, however, on view to the public in the temporary exhibition room (unrestricted admission).

The car bomb attack on 27th June 1993, which occurred close to the West Wing, completely destroyed three works and damaged a number of others (paintings and sculptures). It also led to the closure of the rooms in this wing. Each day a sign is placed at the museum entrance indicating which rooms are closed. The refurbishment of the premises and the restoration of the works of art proceed from day-to-day and the damaged rooms are gradually being re-opened in accordance with the original layout. The description given below of rooms 26 to 45 (closed at the time of publication of this guide book) is based on our knowledge of the museum before the attack.

East Wing

The long corridor displays Classical sculptures – sarcophagi, statues (mainly Roman copies of Greek works) and busts from the Imperial era. The ceiling is decorated with grotesque figures.

Art Gallery – The first four rooms contain works by the Tuscan Primitives. The three large Madonnas in Majesty which dominate **Room 2** illustrate the main 13C and early 14C trends in Italian painting as it moved away from the Byzantine tradition which is visible in the earlier works. The painting *(far right)* by Cimabue (1) *(c*1280) is a composition in the early vertical and symmetrical style but it includes innovative features – the decorative curved lines, the movement

The Annunciation by Simone Martini.

Battle of San Romano by Paolo Uccello.

and a sense of humanity in the figure of the Virgin Mary and the expression on the faces of the prophets below the throne. The *Madonna Rucellai (left)* (2) (1285) by the Sienese artist Duccio, a painter close to Cimabue in his use of traditional Byzantine-style techniques but inspired by a sensitivity that was already a feature of Gothic art, displays a lightness, grace and affectation characteristic of the Sienese School. In the Centre is Giotto's *Madonna* (3) (c1310), a precursor of the Renaissance with its sense of perspective, the vigour in which the characters are treated and its expression of humanity.

Room 3, which is devoted to the Sienese School of the 14C, contains Simone Martini's exquisite *Annunciation* (4) (1333), resplendent with its many shades of gold. The main features of this triptych, which is a masterpiece of Gothic painting, are its austere decoration, extremely graceful movement and delicate colours. Martini was the first to illustrate this Biblical scene, which was depicted so often over the following centuries, and his arrangement became a model – angel on the left and the Virgin Mary on the right – which was to be followed throughout history.

Room 4 contains 14C Florentine paintings, mainly by Giotto's pupils (Bernardo Daddi and Giottino, whose *Deposition* (5) shows less dramatic effect than the works by his teacher, Taddeo Gaddi).

Rooms 5 to 6 house a collection of "International Gothic" works (late 14C – early 15C), a late exaggeration of the Gothic style which strives to reproduce nature in painstaking detail. The large number of figures, blazing colours, golden backgrounds, abundance of ornamentation, love of decorative lines and expressions of tenderness are the distinctive features of this art form. It seems to have no other purpose than to please the eye. The most brilliant representatives of this style, associated with the art of miniature and originating in the affectation that was characteristic of Sienese painting, were Lorenzo Monaco, whose style influenced Fra Angelico, and Gentile da Fabriano. Works by the first artist include the *Adoration of the Magi* (6) and a vivid *Coronation of the Virgin Mary* (7). The second of the two painters developed this artform to the ultimate in his sumptuous, dazzling *Adoration of the Magi* (8).

The following rooms are devoted to the Renaissance.

Room 7 (the early years – 15C) is dominated by Paolo Uccello's famous *Battle of San Romano* (9), one panel of a huge triptych. The other sections are in the Louvre Museum in Paris and the National Gallery in London. The painter laid the battle out like a geometrical composition and structured the space with a view to achieving a sense of perspective, one of the main concerns of Renaissance artists. By making daring use of foreshortening and reducing certain features (soldiers) to mere volume through the unusual use of colour (red horses), he set himself apart from his contemporaries and gave his work a modern, abstract character which has often led him to be considered as a distant precursor of Cubism.

During the Early Renaissance, there were two other painters who focused their attention on conveying a sense of volume. The first of them was Masaccio, represented by a *Madonna and Child with St Anne* (10) painted in collaboration with Masolino, who worked on the Brancacci Chapel *(see below)*; the second was Piero della Francesca, who was born near Arezzo *(qv)*. The powerful portrait (1465) of the Duke of Urbino, Federico da Montefeltro (11) and his wife, Battista Sforza, can be seen on an easel by a window. Their impassive figures are highlighted by a strong line against a deep background of hills suffused in a gentle and somewhat unreal light. On the back of the work is a painting of the two nuptial chariots bringing the couple together.

During this same period another movement was being formed by artists who felt greater affinity with their Gothic training and were more concerned with beauty of line and soft colours. They included Domenico Veneziano - *Madonna surrounded by Saints* (12) - and Fra Angelico - *Coronation of the Virgin (right of the entrance door) (see below under San Marco)*.

Room 8 contains a number of Filippo Lippi's works. They are among the most captivating of all Italian paintings and they provided inspiration for Botticelli, who also made use of the dark outlines round his subjects, the gossamer veils worn by angels or Madonnas, and depicted a somewhat affected grace that envelops the figures while their calmness expresses a profound silence. On the wall between Rooms 8 and 9 is a delicate *Madonna and Child* (13) (1465), a masterpiece of elegant charm and subtle sensuality in which the Virgin Mary appears as a graceful young woman seated at her window; the model was Lucrezia Buti *(qv)*, the attractive nun with whom the painter was in love. The painting hangs between two exquisite works depicting the Adoration of the Child.

Antonio Pollaiolo was the elder and more prominent of the two brothers (second half of the 15C); Room 9 contains one of his famous female portraits *(left by the window)*. The style is characteristic of this artist. The elegant profile is encompassed within heavy, flowing outlines, the clothing is finely detailed and the background is a plain vitreous blue. The large figures representing the theological and cardinal virtues were painted by Piero.

The painting of Fortitude *(by the entrance to the next room)* is by Botticelli. The display case (14) contains four very small pictures painted in meticulous detail - *The Labours of Hercules* by Antonio Pollaiolo and *the Story of Judith* by Botticelli.

The **Botticelli Room**★★★ (10-14) is the gallery's crowning glory. Apart from a series of world-famous pictures by the Renaissance master, it also contains splendid works indicating the reciprocal influence of Florentine painters and Flemish Primitives that accompanied the commercial exchanges of the 15C. Botticelli's

Botticelli (1444-1510)

Botticelli was a pupil of Filippo Lippi and later Verrocchio; he was also an admirer of Pollaiolo. All three artists had a great influence on Botticelli who retained the linearity and contour of Lippi, while showing, in his work, the energy characteristic of the other two. He remained indifferent, however, to the introduction of atmosphere into painting that Verrocchio had begun to explore. By the end of the 15C he was the greatest painter in Florence - he was among the artists called to Rome to paint the walls of the Sistine Chapel - and he mixed with the circle of neo-Platonist scholars, philosophers and writers at the court of Lorenzo the Magnificent, a great admirer of this artist. He revived the themes of Antiquity and painted mythological subjects - Venus, Pallas and the Centaur, Primavera (Spring) - bringing to them a tender lyricism that gave them an allegorical quality. He also painted numerous Madonnas and he excelled in introducing a sense of movement and rhythm to fabrics, veils, hair and limbs. The faces of his subjects are tilted rather systematically to one side in a somewhat Mannerist style.

The death of Lorenzo the Magnificent, the preaching of Savonarola and the future of his artistic style, which through its exaggerated curves bordered on an affectation of the Gothic style, all conspired to push the artist from a state of extreme sensitivity to open doubt, as is shown in his *Calumny of Apelles*, a work drawn in such an incisive way that it arouses a feeling of distress. Although he embodies all that was best during the finest years of the century of the Medici, Botticelli failed to influence other artists because his originality was difficult to emulate.

major works *(from left to right)* include **the Madonna of the Magnificat** (15), a roundel including remarkable intricacy of detail and extraordinary harmony. From the peak of the artist's career comes the allegorical **Birth of Venus** (16) and *(next wall)* **Primavera** (17), undoubtedly the most representative examples of Botticelli's poetic lyricism and the idealism that characterised the Humanist culture favoured at the court of Lorenzo the Magnificent. The artist, who sought "with the movements of the body, to convey the movements of the soul", carries to perfection the features that constitute the charm of an artform steeped in spirituality, with its curving lines, heavy precise outlines, meticulous detail, lightly-shaded tones, graceful movement and pained, melancholic facial expressions. In the *Birth of Venus*, a young woman expressing a melancholy and fragile grace emerges from a background of sea and sky painted in remarkably transparent cold tones; the artist is said to have represented the features of Simonetta Vespucci, mistress of Giuliano, the brother of Lorenzo the Magnificent. The undulating outlines of the fabrics, the loose flowing hair and the slightly-bent figure of Venus give the scene a graceful dance-like quality. In *Primavera,* the characters move nimbly against a dark background depicting a countryside dotted with flowers and fruit in a style akin to a tapestry. Zephyr *(right)* pursues Flora, while Spring approaches, gossamer-like in her floral dress (this character, the only smiling figure in Botticelli's work, has been likened to

Simonetta); Venus *(centre)* is flanked *(left)* by the Three Graces and Mercury. Between these two works hang Botticelli's **Pallas and the Centaur** depicting bestiality tamed by Thought, and his admirable **Madonna of the Pomegranate**, another roundel in which the artist displays a skill acquired from his contact with goldsmiths. The small picture next to it is the famous **Calumny,** a late work, which shows the development of the artist's skill. His last years were deeply marked by the mysticism of Savonarola *(qv)*. Next to *Primavera* is *the Adoration of the Magi* depicting several members of the Medici family; Cosimo the Elder kneels at the feet of the Virgin Mary, Lorenzo *(left)* is resting on his sword and in the group *(right)* is his brother Guiliano, dressed in sombre clothing, recognisable by his dark hair. The character in yellow *(far right)* is said to be Botticelli.

The **Portinari Triptych** (18), opposite the *Birth of Venus,* is a masterpiece by Hugo Van der Goes; it was painted *c*1478 for the Bruges representative of the Medici bank. The centre panel depicts *the Adoration of the Shepherds*; the donors and their children are shown kneeling on the left and right. This skilfully structured work, painted in deep colours, reflects an Italian influence in the taste for huge compositions and life-size characters. Its realism –

Primavera Botticelli (detail).

SCALA

135

the roughness of the shepherds whose faces are lit up in naive curiosity and joy – had a great effect on Florentine artists, as did the meticulous attention to detail and the masterly techniques used to depict landscapes, where the series of successive planes created remarkable depth.

This technique, borrowed from the Flemish masters, can also be seen in *The Adoration of the Magi*, a medallion painted in 1487 by Domenico Ghirlandaio *(left of the Portinari Triptych)*.

The **Leonardo da Vinci Room (15)** contains two of Leonardo's most famous paintings. **The Annunciation (19)**, painted during the artist's youth *(c*1475), is traditional as regards its composition yet it exudes a sweetness and lyricism seldom seen in other works. Although the background is lost in a subtle haze, the famous *sfumato* technique that was characteristic of the artist's style was not used in the foreground, where the details are treated with meticulous care and the characters outlined with precision. As to the unfinished **Adoration of the Magi (20)** (1481), its triangular composition and the expressive faces of the figures make this a very unusual work for the late 15C.

It is almost certain that Leonardo also painted the angel which can be seen in profile in the remarkable *Baptism of Christ* painted *c*1470 by his master, Verrocchio.

In Perugino's works, the peaceful and almost languid grace of the characters and their inherent sweetness hint at the influence that the artist was to have in later years on his pupil, Raphael. Note the *Christ on the Mount of Olives* **(21)** and, opposite, *the Madonna and Child between John the Baptist and St Sebastian* **(22)** in which the symmetry of the composition and the gentle lighting are characteristic of the artist's style.

Return to the corridor (Rooms 16 and 17 are closed).

The **Tribune** (Room 18) is an octagonal room with red hangings and a marble marquetry floor and is covered by a dome decorated in mother-of-pearl. It was built by Buontalenti for Francesco I who wanted it to contain the most valuable items in his collections. *(Only 30 people are allowed into this room at any one time because of its size and the fragility of the works).*

Among the Roman sculptures, which are copies of Greek works from the 3C-4C BC, visitors can see the famous **Medici Venus (23)** inspired by Praxiteles. Numerous portraits are hung around the room including several of the Medici family – *(from left to right)* Alessandro Allori's beautiful and intriguing Bianca Cappello *(qv)*; Lorenzo the Magnificent by Vasari and Cosimo the Elder by Pontormo; Bronzino's haughty Lucrezia Panciatichi and her husband (this powerful family from Pistoia formed an alliance with the Medici in the 15C); on either side of the niche containing the Venus, two of Cosimo I and Eleonora of Toledo's children; the delightful portrait by Bronzino of Bia, the other daughter of Cosimo and Eleonora, shows less diffidence than most of his portraits; the large portrait of Eleonora with one of her sons (of astonishing realism) and the painting of Cosimo I in armour, again by Bronzino, the official painter of the Medici court.

In **Room 19** Umbrian Renaissance painting is mainly represented by Perugino, whose harmonious, serene style so attracted his pupil, Raphael. Note the portrait of the Florentine craftsman, Francesco delle Opere **(24)** and an indescribably melancholic portrait of an adolescent boy **(25)**. The room also contains works by Signorelli, whose style is characterised by incisive and realistic lines, and a highly detailed painting by Piero di Cosimo, who was greatly influenced by Signorelli. It depicts *Perseus Delivering Andromeda (left of the door to the next room).*

Room 20 is devoted to the German Renaissance, represented here by its greatest masters. Dürer (1471-1528) made several visits to Venice where he was deeply influenced by the painting of Mantegna and Giovanni Bellini, as shown in his **Adoration of the Magi (26)** with its brilliant colours and skilfully composed perspective set against a background of ruined buildings. The famous **Adam and Eve (27)** by Cranach (1472-1553) is painted in a style that achieves extreme elegance through the elongated lines; the exaggerated curves and pale nudity hint at a certain sensuality. The artist also painted very understated portraits of his friend and intellectual guide, Luther, and his wife, Catherine Bore *(left of the doorway).*

Venetian painting from the 15C and very early 16C is represented in **Room 21** by Giovanni Bellini (1435-1516) and his pupil Giorgione (1477-1510). The famous **Sacred Allegory (28)** by Bellini is an arcane composition in which the well-balanced landscape, harmony of colours and dreamlike quality of the water and light convey a contemplative vision, and combine to create a remarkably serene atmosphere. In the two early works by Giorgione – *the Trial by Fire of the Young Moses before Pharaoh* and *the Judgement of Solomon (left of the door)* – the composition seems to be structured around the light; the landscape blurring into a soft haze *(sfumato)* in a style reminiscent of da Vinci becomes the essential feature of the painting.

Room 22 displays works by other leading German painters and a number of Flemish masters – Albrecht Altdorfer (1480-1536), founder of the Danube School and one of the forefathers of landscape painting, with two brightly painted scenes from the life of St Florian *(wall opposite the entrance – right)* in which the characters, treated with popular realism, are depicted against an imaginary landscape shot with phantasmagorical light; Hans Holbein the Younger (1497-1543), who at about the age of 40 became official court painter to Henry VIII of England, represented here by a self-portrait and an excellent portrait of the Ambassador, Sir Richard Southwell *(on either side of the corridor to Room 23)*; the Flemish painters Joos van Cleve (c1485-1540) and Van Orley (c1490-1540), each with a portrait of an unknown man and a portrait of their wives *(left of the corridor to Room 23)*.

Room 23 is devoted to Correggio, whose painting, described as "sweet and tender" by the French writer Stendhal, makes unusually sensitive use of Leonardo da Vinci's *sfumato* technique. His Adoration of the Infant Jesus **(29)**, which is bathed in an abstract golden half-light, conveys a lively charm and a languid, somewhat affected, grace that heralded the beginnings of Mannerism.

Room 24, decorated during the 17C to house the Medici jewellery, contains a collection of medallions and miniature portraits.

From the corridor linking the two wings of the building, there is a fine **view** of the Ponte Vecchio *(foreground)* and across the River Arno to San Miniato on the hill.

West Wing

During the era of the grand dukes, this wing housed the Medici workshops, where craftsmen worked, producing *pietra dura* artefacts, miniatures and even perfumes, medicines, poisons and antidotes, of which the merits were vaunted to distinguished guests.

Art Gallery (continued) – Room 25 provides an introduction to the High Renaissance (16C) through work by Michelangelo and the Florentine School. The famous **Tondo Doni (30)** painted by Michelangelo in 1503, depicts the Holy Family against a background of young nudes. The artist's talents as a sculptor are obvious in the powerful rendering of his figures, while the perfection of the glaze where not one brushstroke is visible is evidence of mastery acquired only by painters. The complexity of the composition, in which the Virgin Mary seems to be frozen in such a position that it is impossible to tell whether she is taking the child from Joseph or offering the infant to him, expresses Michelangelo's own tormented character. The contortion of the bodies paves the way for Mannerism and can be seen again in later works, especially in many of the figures within the Sistine Chapel.

Room 26 displays a number of works by Raphael. The famous **Madonna of the Goldfinch** *(left opposite the door)*, painted c1506, is one of his most harmonious and most serene compositions. The gently-curved lines, the warm tones

Tondo Doni by Michelangelo.

SCALA

Madonna delle arpie by Andrea del Sarto.

sublimated by a golden light and the gracefulness of the postures and expressions are softened still further by the use of *sfumato*, producing a gentle half-light that blurs the outlines. In the sumptuous portrait of his patron, Pope Leo X, Raphael shows exceptional skill in the art of representing the texture of fabrics by using the effects of colour. Self-portrait of the artist *(right of the window)*.

The large **Madonna delle arpie** *(entrance wall)*, who is named after the **Harpies** which decorate the pedestal on which the Virgin Mary is standing, is a majestic, somewhat academic work (1517) by Andrea del Sarto, the artist most representative of Florentine classicism.

In a reaction against this art form, Pontormo (1494-1556) sought inspiration in the works and style of Michelangelo and was a leading figure in the Tuscan Mannerist movement. His *Supper in Emmaus* in **Room 27** *(righthand wall)* reflects a restless melancholy.

Room 28 contains 16C Venetian paintings and displays a number of works by Titian including the **Venus of Urbino** *(righthand wall)*, one of the artist's late masterpieces (1538). The intimist nature of the scene, the languid attitude of the character and the dazzling nude placed obliquely across the painting and contrasting with the sombre tones of the background, show a sensuality and warmth far removed from the severity that characterised Florentine art at this time. The **Flora** painted *c*1515, is remarkable for the intensity and richness of the shading and its white and gold tones.

The following two rooms are dedicated to the 16C Emilian School. Parmigianino gave **Mannerism** a stylisation which originated in an extreme refinement and an even greater elongation of forms. **Room 29** displays the **Madonna with the Long Neck**, a sophisticated work in cold colours, with a vertical composition – long legs of the character on the left, elongated figure of the Virgin Mary and tapered column – that is counter-balanced by the horizontal lines of the Infant's body.

The Ferrara-born artist Dosso Dossi *(c*1490-1542) constituted a link between the Emilian School and the Venetian School that had a profound influence on him (**Room 31**).

Room 32 contains works by the Venetians, including *the Death of Adonis* by Sebastiano del Piombo *(c*1485-1547). His apprenticeship with Giorgione is evident in the languid figures and dim lighting but the numerous female nudes (set against a backdrop of Venice) reveal the influence Michelangelo had on him in Rome.

The tiny "Cinquecento Corridor" leads to **Room 34** which contains a number of works by the Venetian painter Veronese (1528-1588), who was influenced during his early career by the elegance and subtlety of the Emilian Mannerists.

Flora by Titian.

His *Holy Family with St Barbara (left of the door)* is a superb work for the impression of serenity it conveys and the magnificent texturing of the fabrics.

Room 35 contains a number of portraits by Tintoretto (1518-1595), in particular his **Leda and the Swan**. The body is set diagonally, giving an impression of movement to the composition, and is depicted in bright colours making it stand out dramatically against a background of brown drapes.

The next section covers **17C Italian and European** works.

The Flemish School is represented in **Room 41** through portraits by Sustermans and Van Dyck and, in particular, a number of works by Rubens. He, more than any other Flemish painter, had extensive contacts with Italian artists (especially the Venetians). Ruben's works include an admirable portrait of his first wife, Isabella Brandt, painted with a deep-felt force and extraordinary warmth.

The following large room, known as the **Niobe Room**, was refurbished and decorated with stuccowork in the 18C in order to house Roman copies of a group statue representing Niobe and her children, carved in 4BC by the Greek sculptor Scopas. Legend has it that Niobe mocked Leto who had had only two children, Apollo and Artemis, by her husband, Zeus. In order to avenge their mother, the two sons killed Niobe's seven sons and seven daughters with their arrows. Niobe was so grief-stricken that Zeus granted her wish to be changed into a rock.

Room 43 is dedicated to **Caravaggio** (1573-1610).

The artist was only 20 when he painted the famous **Adolescent Bacchus**, a bright, vivid oil painting as yet devoid of the brutal contrasts of light and shade that were to characterise most of his work. The young god depicted as a popular character is a clear indication of the naturalistic style which was to have such considerable impact on 17C-18C European art. His painting of *the Sacrifice of Isaac,* where the sudden arrival of the angel seems to be taken from true life, is also a very early work yet it already expresses forcefully the quest for reality at the expense of beauty, a sense of dramatisation and a taste for the dazzling interplay of light and dark. The striking head of Medusa, painted on a shield *(on an easel),* has a certain Baroque quality in the dramatically exaggerated expression.

Also displayed in the room *(righthand wall)* is a splendid **Seascape** by Claude Lorrain (1600-1682); the familiar scenes of harbour life are acted out against a backdrop of solemn buildings and hazy ships, which take on a ghostly quality in the resplendent golden light coming from the sea.

Room 44 displays 17C Flemish and Dutch painting, including works by Rembrandt (1606-1669) whose treatment of light and shade reveals the combined influences of Caravaggio and the Venetian masters. On the end wall, there is a remarkable portrait of an old man and two self-portraits.

Room 45 contains 18C works from Spain, with two portraits by Goya *(left of the door),* and from France with portraits by Nattier *(right)* and works by Chardier – *Small Girl Playing Badminton* and *Small Boy Playing Cards,* both of them delightfully spontaneous works *(next to the Goyas)*. There are also *(wall opposite the door)* Venetian views of Venice. The first two, executed with photographic accuracy, are by Canaletto (1697-1768) – *the Doges' Palace* and *The Grand Canal at the Rialto Bridge*. The second two are by Francesco Guardi (1712-1793) and have an almost impressionistic feel, with their light brushstrokes and delicate nuances of light.

Terrace – From the cafeteria terrace, which is situated at the far end of the gallery overlooking the Loggia della Signoria, there is a superb view of the upper storeys of the Palazzo Vecchio. The terrace area used to be a garden with a fountain, where the Medici would come to listen to the musicians playing in the square.

The **rotunda** in front of the staircase contains a marble statue of a boar (Hellenistic art dating from the 3C BC) given to Cosimo I by Pope Paul IV; a bronze copy of the work adorns the fountain in the Mercato Nuovo *(qv)*.

Ponte Vecchio.

★PONTE VECCHIO (Z)

The unusual outline of this bridge is one of the most famous features of Florence. The Ponte Vecchio is the city's oldest bridge, built at the narrowest point on the course of the Arno, near where a Roman bridge once spanned the river carrying the road linking Rome to northern Italy. Over the centuries the bridge was destroyed on a number of occasions; the current structure dates only from 1345.

In 1944 it was the only bridge in Florence to be spared by the Germans who, in order to block the advance of American troops approaching from the south, razed the surrounding old districts almost entirely to the ground (one medieval tower standing on the north bank slightly upstream of the entrance to the bridge survived). The Ponte Vecchio did, however, suffer extensive damage during the 1966 floods.

The arcades that initially lined the bridge housed the tanners' workshops and, later, the stalls of butchers for whom the river provided a handy "sewer". In the 16C, on the orders of Grand Duke Ferdinando II, the butchers were forced to make way for craftsmen whose activities were of a less insanitary and more decorative nature – jewellers and gold and silversmiths who built most of the tiny corbelled shops above the Arno still occupied by craftsmen today. The shops attract a continuous flow of visitors, who come to buy or just to look and who throng the bridge during the summer season until late in the evening.

The esplanade in the middle of the bridge contains a bronze bust of the most famous goldsmith of all, Benvenuto Cellini, placed there in the 19C. From here, there is a fine **view** of the banks of the Arno and the succession of bridges that span it.

The top storey of the buildings on the Ponte Vecchio consists of a gallery (1 km – 0.5 mile long), the **Corridoio Vasariano** (Vasari Corridor), built in the 16C by Vasari. It links the gallery of the Uffizi, via a passage above the arcades along the quaysides (Lungarno Archibusieri), to the Pitti Palace on the south bank and was used by Cosimo I to go from the Palazzo Vecchio to the Pitti Palace without having to mingle with the crowds.

Where the gallery passes above the porch of the church of Santa Felicità (DV), it provides access to a sumptuous internal balcony, like a theatre box, above the entrance, where the grand dukes could attend Mass discreetly. The church was rebuilt in the 18C except for the chapel *(immediately to the right of the entrance)* which was built in the early 15C by Brunelleschi, and contains the famous **Deposition**★★ by Pontormo, painted in clear sharp tones with undulating, elongated forms in a style characteristic of Tuscan Mannerism.

★★ PALAZZO PITTI (PITTI PALACE) (DV) ⊘ *Tour – half a day*

This huge Renaissance palace stands on three sides of a sloping square overlooked by the building's long, severe façade. Only the shading of the heavy rustication work softens the imposing architectural style and breaks up a unity verging on the monotonous.

Work began on the palace in 1458. It was designed for the Pitti, a family of influential merchants and bankers who were initially friends but later great rivals of the Medici. The building then consisted of no more than the section comprising the seven central bays. Several years later the Pitti family was financially ruined and the residence designed to outshine their rivals was left unfinished.

The palace was bought in 1549 by Eleonora of Toledo, wife of Cosimo I, and she turned it into a princely residence to which Cosimo I transferred his court *c*1560. The work of conversion was entrusted to the architect and sculptor, Ammannati. The hillside was laid out as a magnificent garden but it was not until the 17C that the front of the building attained its current length (over 200m – 650ft). The two projecting wings were added in the 18C.

It provided the inspiration for the Palais du Luxembourg in Paris that was built by Marie de Médicis who had lived in the Pitti Palace in her youth.

The Pitti Palace is a remarkably rich repository of works of art, furniture and priceless objects.

The solemn austere courtyard designed by Ammannati is enclosed by high arcading and three storeys of heavily-rusticated engaged columns and thick cornices. On the far side is a terrace, level with the first floor, which overlooks the gardens.

★★★ Galleria Palatina (Palatine Gallery) – *First floor*

The entrance to the gallery is in the corner of the courtyard to the right of the entrance up the staircase designed by Ammannati.

This art gallery takes its name from the title of the last of the Medici, Anna Maria Ludovica (1667-1743), who was married to the Elector Palatine. The luxurious interior houses an outstanding collection of 16C, 17C and 18C works including a series of **paintings★★★ by Raphael and Titian** which make the Pitti Palace one of the richest art galleries in the world. The works were collected from the 17C onwards by the Grand Dukes of the Medici family and later by the Grand Dukes of Lorraine; they are exhibited regardless of didactic or chronological order, as was the fashion of the great stately collections of the time.

E. Baret

Palazzo Pitti from the gardens.

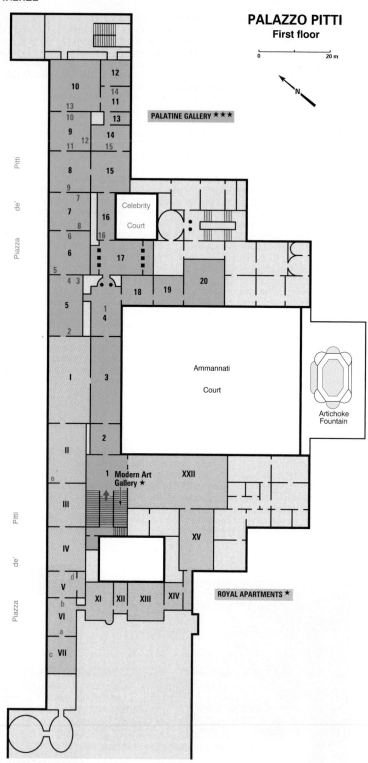

PALAZZO PITTI
First floor

0   20 m

N

PALATINE GALLERY ★★★

Celebrity Court

Ammannati Court

Artichoke Fountain

Modern Art Gallery ★

ROYAL APARTMENTS ★

Room 3 (Statue Gallery), decorated with 2C-3C Roman sculptures from the Villa Medici in Rome, leads into **Room 4** (Castagnoli Room) which contains the remarkable **Table of the "Muses"** (1), with some splendid inlaid work in *pietra dura* and semi-precious stones on a lapis lazuli background, executed during the first half of the 19C by the Florence Pietra Dura Workshop (in the centre is Apollo's chariot surrounded by the symbols of the nine Muses). Note also a large oil painting by Sodoma depicting the martyrdom of St Sebastian.

The rooms on the left side of the palace are named after the subjects of the mainly mythological scenes with which they are decorated.

The **decoration**★★ of the first five, formerly used by the Medici as reception rooms, includes sumptuous stuccowork, gold leaf and *trompe-l'oeil* paintings. It was designed in the 17C by the decorative artist, Pietro da Cortona.

Room 5 (Venus Room) is hung with two large Seascapes *(on opposite sides of the room)* by the Neapolitan artist, Salvator Rosa (1615-1673), who worked at the Medici court for almost ten years. The resplendent golden light which sets sky and sea aglow, touches the hilltops, ships and figures giving them a wonderful luminous quality. More importantly however, the room contains some of Titian's finest oil paintings. **The Concert** (2) is an early work painted under the influence of Giorgione, to whom it was long attributed, in which the artist expresses with admirable sensitivity the inner tension driving the central character. On the opposite wall hangs a powerful portrait of **Pietro Aretino** (3), writer and friend of Cosimo I, painted in 1545 using small brushstrokes in warm gold and brown shades. The elegant female portrait known as **La Bella** (4) was painted *c*1536 for the Duke of Urbino; the woman's golden complexion contrasts sharply with the clothing rendered in sumptuous tones of brown and blue-green (the mysterious model may perhaps have been the same woman who sat for the Venus of Urbino exhibited in the Uffizi Gallery). In the centre of the room is the **Italic Venus** (Pauline Borghese), an outstanding example of neo-Classical sculpture completed in 1811 by Antonio Canova, who was commissioned to undertake the work by Napoleon.

Room 6 (Apollo Room) contains Van Dyke's portrait of **Charles I of England** and his wife, **Henrietta of France** (5), daughter of Henri IV and Marie de Médicis. The artist admirably conveys the aristocratic elegance of the figures through his subtle depiction of the King's profoundly melancholy character and the gentle irony of his consort, and through the extraordinary attention paid to details of their clothing. The room also contains other paintings by Titian, including a *Mary Magdalen (opposite corner)*, a work in which the artist skilfully plays upon the alternating brown and gold tints reflected in her wonderful hair. Among his better-known works is the fascinating **Portrait of a Gentleman** (6) familiarly known as "The Man with Grey Eyes" painted *c*1540. The man's lightly-shaded face with eyes of indefinable colour, emerging from the dark background on which the deep black of his clothing is only just visible, is extremely eye-catching.

Room 7 (Mars Room) contains two examples of a *Madonna and Child* by Murillo, in which the artist uses delicate blends of colour. The paintings hang either side of the **Four Philosophers** (7), one of Ruben's last canvasses. The painter can be seen standing on the left and seated beside him is his brother. The large portrait of **Cardinal Bentivoglio** (8) is a splendid work by Van Dyke. All the aristocratic dignity of the figure who was Ambassador of the Holy See in Flanders and France is expressed in the lavish texturing of the heavy red robe, depicted with an extraordinary richness of colour that contrasts with the splashes of light colouring forming the extremely pale face, long delicate hands and the extraordinary fine texture of the surplice.

Room 8 (Jupiter Room) houses the famous **Veiled Lady** (La Velata) (9) by Raphael. In this portrait he displays his skill as a brilliant colourist using a range of shades based almost exclusively on browns, golds and whites. The flowing outlines, the solid harmony created by the opulent forms and abundance of rounded contours, and the sheer extravagance of the shimmering iridescent fabric, make this work a masterpiece. The model may have been the famous Fornarina, the artist's beloved. *The Holy Family with Basket (righthand corner)* by Rubens is a painting of an intimist rather than sacred nature. The splashes of colour in Fra Bartolomeo's moving *Deposition (opposite wall)* are combined with a certain simplicity. The painting, left unfinished on the artist-monk's death, gives an impression of balance reminiscent of the works of Perugino, whose *Adoration of the Child*, also known as the "Madonna with Pouch" *(same wall by the window)*, is a fine symmetrical composition set against a background of an intensely bright sky (this was characteristic of his style) in which religious feeling and poetic sensitivity combine in gentle harmony.

Room 9 (Saturn Room) contains eight oil paintings by Raphael, including two world-famous Madonnas. **The Madonna of the Grand Duke** (10), of which Grand Duke Ferdinand III of Lorraine was so enamoured that he refused to be separated from it, was painted *c*1505 in Florence. At that time Raphael was influenced by both Michelangelo and Leonardo, borrowing from the latter the technique of vague contours better known as *sfumato*. The shining pale golden shades of the Virgin Mary's serene, tender face, and the gentleness which exudes from the painting are reminiscent of Perugino, who was Raphael's teacher. The **Madonna della Seggiola** (11) was painted a few years later and the artist, at the peak of his talent, uses a more subtle and varied palette. The gentle serenity of the faces, graceful positions and mysticism so characteristic of religious scenes, is combined with a force generated by the forms and pictorial structure (emphasised by the round composition that suggests circular movement, a reminder of Michelangelo's influence). Note, too, several portraits by Raphael (Maddalena and Agnolo Doni) which show remarkable psychological

Madonna della Seggiola by Raphael.

intensity. Also worthy of note is a melancholy **Mary Magdalen** (12) painted by Perugino in austere colours and very pure outlines. Her exquisitely beautiful hands and face stand out clearly against a deep brown background, an unusual feature for this artist.

Room 10 (Iliad Room) is of particular interest for its series of portraits by Joost Sustermans (b Antwerp 1597, d Florence 1681) who was official portrait painter to the Medici. One of his most successful portraits is that of the young **Prince Waldemar-Christian of Denmark** (13), a superb example of penetrating analysis and detailed description in the Flemish tradition (note the detail in the damascened breast-plate and white lace collar). Other outstanding works include an equestrian portrait of Philip IV of Spain by Velasquez *(left of the entrance)* and *(right of the door leading to the next room)* the *Woman with Child (La Gravida)* by Raphael.

Room 11 (Education of Jupiter) contains an astonishing *Sleeping Cupid* (14) painted by Caravaggio shortly before his death. It is a particularly good summary of his style with its uncompromising realism, its low-level and violently-contrasting light brutally revealing forms and expressions, and its contempt for décor. Opposite hangs an admirable *Judith* by the Florentine artist, Cristofano Allori (1577-1621). Her superb clothing is treated with an extraordinary richness of colour. The artist used himself as the model for the head of Holofernes, and Judith is said to bear the features of the woman he loved.

Room 12 (Stove Room) with its majolica flooring was formerly the bathroom in the ducal apartments. The large allegorical **scenes**★★ depicting the four Ages of Humanity were painted between 1637 and 1640 by Pietro da Cortona, who executed the work using bright colours in a light-hearted and lively style.

Room 13, the small bathroom, was fitted out in the early 19C for Napoleon's sister, Elisa Baciocchi, who became Grand Duchess of Tuscany in 1809.

Room 14 (Ulysses Room) contains another famous Madonna by Raphael, **the Madonna of the Window** (Madonna dell'Impannata) (15) remarkable for its warm tones and blends of colour.

Room 15 (Prometheus Room) contains *The Madonna and Child* by Filippo Lippi *(righthand side above the fireplace)* which is unusual in that it was set against a background depicting a familiar scene, an innovation which was followed by numerous artists in Florence, just as composition in the round *(tondo)* was adopted by Florentine artists in many 15C and 16C works. The interesting portrait *(next wall)* of a young man wearing the 15C Florentine head-dress *(mazzocchio)* was produced in Botticelli's studio.

Room 16 (Poccetti Gallery) contains a portrait by Rubens of the first Duke of Buckingham (16), one of Charles I of England's favourites, and a magnificent table inlaid with *pietra dura* and semi-precious stones depicting foliage, fruit, birds and fans, produced for Cosimo III in the Medici workshops in 1716.

Room 17 (Music Room), decorated in neo-Classical style, is embellished with eight cipolin marble columns. In the centre is a huge table with Russian malachite top and superbly finished legs, a work dating from 1819 made by the French bronzesmith, Pierre-Philippe Thomire (who also made the cradle for the King of Rome).

Rooms 18 and 19 (Allegory Room and Fine Arts Room) exhibit 16C-17C Italian paintings.

Room 20 (Hercules Room) was decorated in neo-Classical style by Giuseppe Cacialli early in the 19C. It contains a large Sèvres porcelain vase, embellished with gilt bronze by Thomire, and frescoes depicting the story of Hercules.

★ **Appartamenti Reali** (Royal Apartments)

1st floor – Access via the foyer of the Palatine Gallery

The rooms extending from the centre of the façade to the end of the right wing had always been used as state rooms or private apartments by Tuscany's three ruling families – the Medici, the Grand Dukes of Lorraine and the House of Savoy, sovereigns of Italy when Florence became the capital city (1865-1870).

Room XXII (White Room) is the former palace ballroom. It is illuminated by 11 magnificent crystal chandeliers.

Room XV (Bona Room) is the largest room in the guest apartments. Ferdinando I commissioned Poccetti to depict his great military victories here. The room is named after the fresco on the right wall, illustrating the conquest in 1607 of Bona (now Annaba in Algeria).

Rooms XIV, XIII, XII, XI – This small apartment, decorated in 19C style, consists of four rooms – an antechamber (XIV), crimson reception room (XIII), study (XII) and bedchamber (XI) in which *(right of the door)* hangs a fine *Madonna and Child with St John the Baptist* by Andrea del Sarto.

Room VI (Parrot Room) gets its name from the design on the silk-hung walls. Above the doorways, are the portraits of Henri IV of France and his wife Marie de Médicis (b) by the Flemish artist, Frans Pourbus II (1569-1622), who painted the portraits of monarchs and grand dignitaries in all the courts of Europe.

Room VII (Yellow Room) contains a splendid ebony, ivory and alabaster **cabinet** (c) dating from the early 18C, which was produced by German and Dutch craftsmen in the Medici workshops.

Room V (Chapel) contains a tender *Madonna and Child* by the Florentine artist, Carlo Dolci. The painting is displayed in a sumptuous ebony and gilt bronze **frame** (d) embellished with *pietra dura* fruits, made in the Medici workshops in 1697 for Gian Gastone, the brother of Anna Maria Ludovica.

Room IV (Blue Room) has a finely decorated white and gold stucco ceiling.

Room III (Throne Room) looks exactly as it did when Victor Emmanuel II of Savoy became the first King of Italy. Beneath the baldequin is the gilded throne on which all the kings of Italy took the oath.

Room II (Green Room) contains another superb ebony and gilt bronze **cabinet** (e) with *pietra dura* inlay made in the late 17C in the ducal workshops. Beside it hangs a portrait of the young Louis XV by Rigaud. The room also contains a number of other French paintings.

Room I (Niche Room), aristocratic and perfunctory, formerly served as a dining room. The niches around the room contain classical statues which are copies of Roman and Greek works. The large full-length portraits of various members of the Medici family were painted by Sustermans.

★ **Galleria d'Arte Moderna** (Gallery of Modern Art) – *Above the Palatine Gallery*

The neo-Classical setting created for the Grand Dukes of Lorraine by the architect Poccianti, now houses an exhibition of mainly Tuscan work, illustrating the various trends that inspired Italian painting and sculpture from the late 18C to the early decades of the 20C.

Academism – The academic art of the last years of the Grand Dukes of Lorraine was characterised between 1790 and 1860 by three movements. After the annexation of the Grand Duchy by Napoleon, Tuscany came under the influence of **neo-Classical** art, the official style of the Empire, which was characterised by its imitation of Classical models and its quest for ideal beauty. The **Purist tendency**, which came from Rome, is a reaction to neo-Classicism; it extols the virtues of nature and Renaissance works, taking them as its models. The **Romantic movement** reacted more resolutely against neo-Classicism, holding the Middle Ages in high esteem and taking its subject matter from Literature and History.

Rooms 1 to 12 – Room 2 *(left of Room 1)* contains a collection of neo-Classical and Romantic works, including paintings by the first Tuscan follower of the Romantic Movement, the Florentine Giuseppe Bezzuoli *(Self Portrait, sketch of Cain)* and one of its leading exponents, the Venetian Francesco Hayez *(Samson)*. Room 3 *(also left)* houses a collection of Romantic paintings. Their subject matter was based on literary works.

Room 4 is dedicated to the Purists, with works inspired by masters such as Verrocchio in sculpture and Raphael in painting.

In Room 7 *(access via Room 1)*, which illustrates the artistic links between France and Italy during the French Revolution and Napoleonic Empire, there are two busts by Canova who was official sculptor to the Empire – a bust of Napoleon dressed as a Roman emperor and another depicting Calliope with the idealised features of Elisa Baciocchi.

Room 8 contains a superb deep green Sèvres porcelain vase with bronze detail by Thomire, a gift from Napoleon to Ferdinand III of Lorraine.

Room 10 contains very large works, and the entire far wall is occupied by the painting that brought fame to the Romantic artist, Giuseppe Bezzuoli – *The Arrival of Charles VIII in Florence*. Note also two fine bronze sculptures *(Cain and Abel)* by the Sienese sculptor Giovanni Dupré, displaying a somewhat affected tragic realism.

The Macchiaioli – The most lively artistic expression during this period came from the "Macchiaioli", and the gallery owns an outstanding collection of their works★★, which are exhibited in various rooms. The movement, a contemporary of Impressionism, grew up in Florence in the mid-19C and breathed new life into painting, which had become entrenched in rigid academic conventions.

The Macchiaioli were enamoured of the truth and rejected subjects borrowed from mythology or the great historical paintings. Instead, they took their models directly from nature but they sought to give an impression of their subject rather than render an exact description.

They generally painted small-sized works, translating reality by means of splashes ("macchie") of colour with light playing upon them.

The Leghorn artist, **Giovanni Fattori** (1825-1908), a complex character with a nevertheless sober and vigorous style, and the more poetic **Silvestro Lega** (1826-1895) were the movement's most illustrious members, although they were relatively late in expressing their support for the group's theories (many of their works show their recognition of the value of drawing techniques).

Telemaco Signorini (1835-1901), who was also a brilliant controversial writer enjoying friendships with Degas and Manet, moved away from the group to seek an even sharper sense of realism. **Adriano Cecioni** (1836-1886), who was more of a sculptor than a painter, was the theorist and critic of the movement. **Giuseppe Abbati** (1836-1868) gave a touch of seriousness to his works and his contemplation of nature is tinged with melancholy. The Ferrara artist, **Giovanni Boldini** (1842-1931), spent only a brief time with the Macchiaioli before going on to become a fashionable portrait painter, especially in Paris. The work of **Giuseppe de Nittis** (1846-1884), who came from the Puglia region, is characterised by the use of typical Mediterranean colours. He also emigrated to Paris, where he enjoyed a career as a society painter.

Rooms 13 and 18 – These rooms are beyond the ballroom, which contains a full-length portrait (lefthand corner) of Empress Elizabeth of Austria (Sissi) by Giuseppe Sogni. This section covers the period from 1860 (the year of Italian Unification) to 1871 (when Florence ceased to be the capital of the new kingdom). The works are grouped thematically (portraits, landscapes, genre scenes and historical events relating to the Risorgimento) and most of them were painted by the "Macchiaioli" group.

Rooms 13 to 16 are temporarily closed to visitors.

Room 17 contains works depicting genre scenes – *(right of the door)* the *Visit to the Studio* by Silvestro Lega and *The Moneylender* by the Milanese painter, Domenico Induno (1815-1878), who was a pupil of the Romantic artist, Francesco Hayez; a fine landscape painting *(above the fireplace)* by Giuseppe de Nittis, who, before his arrival in Florence, painted the **Beach near Barletta**. The spit of brown land, along which stretches a line of dejected-looking buffalo, streaks across the confusion of colour evoking the immensity of sky and water. One of the few paintings by the sculptor Cecioni *(next)* is a *Portrait of his wife*.

Room 18 is dedicated to the Risorgimento and acts as a reminder that, before going on to tackle small intimist scenes, Giovanni Fattori was a painter of large military compositions.

Rooms 19 to 28 – These rooms cover the period between 1870 and the eve of the First World War and contain a large number of paintings by Macchiaioli artists, including several masterpieces which sprang from this movement.

Palmieri Rotunda by Giovanni Fattori.

Room 23 contains some of the most famous oil paintings by Telemaco Signorini and Giovanni Fattori. The most outstanding painting by Signorini is the stunning **Portoferraio Prison** *(opposite the windows)*. Works by Fattori include *(on the same wall)* a portrait of his daughter-in-law (la **Figliastra**) and the **Staffato** (Rider thrown from his horse) treated with striking economy of style and force (ground devoid of vegetation and a bare, chalky sky against which sweeping brushstrokes depict the floored man and wild horse in a series of dark patches). The famous **Rotonda di Palmieri** *(one of the central display cases)* is a very small yet remarkably suggestive work, in which the characters, sketched out in very flat colours, stand out like the silhouettes of a shadow theatre against a landscape that is also depicted in an unusually sparse manner using simple horizontal strips of colour.

Room 24 also contains an extensive collection of both Macchiaioli and post-Macchiaioli works. On the wall opposite the window hangs Giovanni Fattori's portrait of his cousin **Argia**, and by Giuseppe Abbati **The Window** which displays a remarkable quality of light.

★★ Museo degli Argenti (Silver Museum) ⊘
Ground floor and mezzanine – Access – The entrance is situated at the far left of the Ammannati courtyard

The museum's outstanding collections consist mainly of the treasures of the Medici family and House of Lorraine. Most of the exhibits were made in the workshops of Florence but others were added to the grand ducal treasure after being brought over from Germany or Austria, first on the occasion of the marriage of Anna Maria Ludovica to the Elector Palatine following the union of the houses of Lorraine and Habsburg, and secondly during the Napoleonic occupation after the period spent in exile in Austria by Ferdinand II of Lorraine.

Ground Floor – This section of the palace, designed to accommodate important guests, was also used as the grand dukes' summer apartments. The state rooms were lavishly decorated during the 17C, with mythological paintings, allegorical scenes in honour of the Medici and astonishing *trompe-l'oeil* architectural features.

Room I, **Sala di Giovanni da San Giovanni**, a former reception room, takes its name from the Tuscan painter who specialised in depicting historical subjects and who undertook its decoration in 1634 to celebrate the marriage of Ferdinando II to Vittoria della Rovere. The event is depicted in the main fresco on the ceiling. The huge scenes covering the walls refer to the patronage provided by the Medici, particularly Lorenzo the Magnificent, who can be seen in red robes and hat surrounded by artists or giving refuge to the Muses driven from Parnassus.

Room II was formerly the bedchamber of the grand duchess. Some of the 16 cups and **ancient vases** *(one of the main central display cases)* (1), from the prestigious collection belonging to Lorenzo the Magnificent, are examples of Roman art of the Later Empire and others of 14C Venetian art. Their magnificent gold and silver mounts, which bear the engraved monogram of Lorenzo – **LAVR.MED**, were produced later by the Florentine workshops.

The small 17C **chapel** leads to **Room IV** (Audience Room) with its profuse and uninspiring *trompe l'oeil* architectural features; to **Room V** (Private Audience Room) where the ceiling depicts the *Triumph of Alexander*; and to **Room VI**, another State Room. These three rooms contain some splendid pieces of ebony and *pietra dura* furniture dating from the late 16C and 17C – a cabinet *(first room)* (2) made in Augusta and a prayer stool (3) from the Medici workshops in Florence. A blue and yellow chess board *(second room)* (4) was made in the same workshops in 1619. A large round porphyry table *(last room)* (5) is placed in the centre; the cabinet *(right)* (6), which dates from 1709 and was produced by the Medici workshops, was a gift from Cosimo III to his daughter Anna Maria Ludovica, who was married to the Elector Palatine; the statuette *(central niche)* represents her husband).

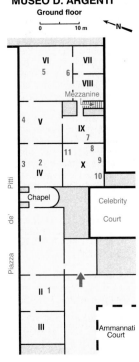

MUSEO D. ARGENTI
Ground floor

Rooms VII and VIII house a very fine collection of German and Flemish **ivories** which once belonged to the Medici; most of them date from the 17C.

Room IX, formerly the Grand Duke's bedchamber, contains a fine **table** (7) with a splendid *pietra dura* marquetry top depicting a series of small landscape scenes arranged around a remarkably detailed central landscape. It was probably made in Prague during the 17C. There is also a remarkable amber collection exhibited in three display cases (18C).

Room X, the **Crystal Room,** contains some of the museum's most valuable pieces. To the left of the door is the famous **lapis lazuli gourd** (8) with a gold mount decorated with enamel and precious stones, a priceless work produced in the late 16C for Francesco I. The no less famous **Diana of Poitiers' Cup** *(next display case against the lefthand wall)* (9) was based on a design by Buontalenti; it is made of engraved rock crystal and has an intricately-worked golden lid bearing the famous interlaced initials of King Henri II of France and his mistress (16C French). Exhibited in various display cases are a number of rock crystal and gold cups, vases and shell-shaped receptacles including an exceedingly elegant cup representing a dragon (10) (16C Milanese) and a splendid bird-shaped vase (11) bearing seven dragons' heads and encrusted with gems and pearls.

Mezzanine – *Access via the small staircase between Rooms IX and X on the plan.*

The **Medici Treasure** – **Room XI** (Cameo Room) contains a number of exhibits that are worthy of note. A large white onyx cameo *(central glass case)*, bearing effigies of Cosimo I and members of his family, is a superb piece of work dating from the 16C. A series of small gold panels on an amethyst background depicting the great Feats of Francesco I was based on designs by Giovanni da Bologna and produced in the Medici workshops during the late 16C. From the same period and origin is the *pietra dura* mosaic depicting Piazza della Signoria, in which the equestrian statue of Cosimo I is picked out in gold.

Room XII (Jewellery and Engraved Stone Room) contains the jewels of Anna Maria Ludovica, whose portrait can be seen hanging on the wall opposite the door. An illuminated glass case displays a series of engraved and sculpted gemstones. The most unusual collection in the museum is undoubtedly the late 16C and 17C Baroque jewellery and other small items made of pearl, gold and precious stones, the extraordinary work of German goldsmiths who took their inspiration from the natural shape of the pearls. In a display cabinet *(left of the door)* visitors can admire, through a magnifying glass, the work produced by a virtuoso sculptor in the 16C on a cherry stone.

Ferdinand III's Treasure – The treasure consists mainly of collections belonging to the prince-archbishops of Salzburg brought to Florence in 1814 by Ferdinand III of Lorraine.

In **Room XIII** *(against the lefthand wall)* is an engraved silver altar front eloquently depicting the Madonna and Child, around which are 16 small panels giving an account of the Life of the Virgin Mary and Christ. They are surrounded by stylised lapis lazuli roses. This splendid piece of work, which displays extraordinary finesse, was produced in Salzburg in the 16C. Note also a highly intricate mother-of-pearl and silver portable altar (18C), showing a Crucifixion and scenes from the Passion of Christ in alabaster and coral, and inset with cameos and gems.

Room XIV contains the sumptuous gold and silver-gilt tableware of the prince-archbishops. The most valuable pieces, which are displayed at the far left of the room, are the enamelled pure gold cups decorated with grotesque figures and coats of arms, with handles in the shape of Harpies (Salzburg early 17C). The central display case contains the dinner service used by Ferdinand III during his travels; it was produced in Paris in the 18C.

The **Medici Exotic Collections** – These are exhibited in the last two rooms. Room XVI contains an unusual 16C Mexican mitre made of bird feathers depicting the Passion of Christ *(left of the door)* and a series of shell-shaped vases dating from the 16C-17C *(righthand display case)*. The second room contains famille rouge and famille verte Chinese porcelain in addition to blue-and-white ware, and a brightly-coloured Chinese ceremonial dress with a strikingly modern appearance (first half of 17C).

★ **Galleria del Costume** (Costume Gallery) ⊙

Meridian Pavilion – Access by lift situated in the ticket office and staircase leading to the Palatine Gallery. Collection changed twice a year.

This gallery offers an insight into the history of fashion from the 18C to *c*1930 through its extensive collection of costumes, shoes, linen and accessories. There is a reconstruction of the burial clothes of Eleonora of Toledo and her husband, Cosimo I, based on the remnants found in their tomb.

★ GIARDINO DI BOBOLI (BOBOLI GARDENS) (DVX) ⊘

Visit – 90min. Entrance to the left of the main building of the Pitti Palace. Direct access to the amphitheatre at the far end of the courtyard.

In 1549 Cosimo I commissioned the architect, sculptor and landscape gardener, Nicolo Pericoli alias Tribolo, to convert the hill behind the Pitti Palace into a vast garden; together with Ammannati's courtyard and the terrace, it was to be the setting for the lavish pageants held by the grand dukes. When Tribolo died the following year, he had only drawn up the plans. He was succeeded in 1550 by Ammannati then in 1583 by Buontalenti, who both added a number of refinements to the original design.

The park is a fine example of an Italian terraced garden with many different perspectives, interspersed with ramps, flights of steps and terraces and dotted with statues and fountains. The entrance is situated on the far side of the inner courtyard. A flight of steps leads to the terrace which is separated from the rear of the palace by the elegant Artichoke Fountain *(Carciofo)*, built in 1641.

The 17C **amphitheatre**, where extravagant entertainments were once held, dominates the centre of the park. In 1841 the Royal House of Lorraine had a Roman granite basin and a 2C Egyptian obelisk from Thebes placed in the centre.

Walk towards the top of the hill; before reaching the first terrace, turn right into an uphill path which leads to a circle.

This part of the gardens, covering the hillside, was not laid out until the early 17C. The long and steep **Viottolone★** *(opposite)* descends majesticly between a double row of age-old pines and cypress trees to the charming circular **Piazzale dell'Isolotto★**; at the centre is a round lake adorned with statues; in the middle of the lake is an island with orange and lemon trees and the Ocean Fountain, carved by Giovanni da Bologna in 1576. The standing figure represents Neptune; the three others symbolise rivers.

On turning back towards the palace, visitors see **Neptune's Pool**, adorned with a bronze statue (16C) of the sea god and, on the following terrace, a statue of Plenty which was begun by Giovanni da Bologna and finished in 1636 by the Florentine, Pietro Tacca.

A short path (right) leads to the Porcelain Museum (see below).

The path *(left)* leads to the foot of **Fort Belvedere** *(access now resticted by a gate)*. Further down stands the **Kaffeehaus,** an extravagant and predominantly red edifice built by Zanobi del Rosse in 1776 and evidence of the 18C taste for exoticism. From the bar patio, there is a **fine view★** of Florence.

Walk back down towards the palace and turn right into the wide ramp.

At the end is a path leading to the **Grotta grande,** a fanciful creation designed mainly by Buontalenti (1587-97) and consisting of several chambers decorated with basins, statues, paintings, stalactites and a form of Rococo decoration depicting sheep, goats, shepherds, etc. The walls were once the backdrop to a multitude of waterfalls. The small **Bacchus Fountain** *(right near the exit)* includes a monstrous figure, one of Cosimo I's midgets, astride a tortoise.

Boboli Gardens looking towards the Belvedere Fort.

★ **Museo delle Porcellane** (Porcelain Museum) ⊘

A double-flight staircase leads to the delightful Cavaliere Pavilion which was built for Cosimo III in the late 17C. In front of the building is a small terraced garden overlooking the exquisite Florentine countryside.

In the first room above the fireplace is a portrait of Napoleon on Sèvres porcelain (early 19C) based on work by Gérard. The two main central display cabinets contain two dinner services belonging to Elisa Bacciocchi which were produced by the Sèvres Factory in 1810. The third display case opposite the door contains a series of small unglazed folk characters, made in Naples in the late 18C. The display cases round the walls contain exhibits which include *(from left to right starting at the door)* numerous French items (mainly Sèvres, 18C) including some amusing oyster stands; porcelain from Doccia near Florence dating from the 18C and 19C *(display cases on the left wall)*, most of it with white background and floral motifs (a set of cups bears the reproduction of several Florentine monuments); a number of late 18C pieces from Capodimonte in Naples decorated with gilded scenes from Antiquity on a black background *(front wall)*.

The second room is dedicated to Viennese porcelain from the 18C and early 19C, with pieces brought to Florence by the Royal House of Lorraine. These include a large amount of the gilt decoration, which was a speciality of the famous Augarten factory, and the miniature decorative features from the golden age of Viennese ware. The display case to the right of the door contains a deep blue dinner service covered with gilt trellis-work, which once belonged to Anna Maria Ludovica (note her interlaced initials). The display case against the righthand wall contains unglazed busts of Joseph II and Maria Theresa of Austria, a reminder that it was she who gave the Augarten works a royal appointment. The third room contains German ware – from Frankenthal and Augsburg, a superb chinoiserie-covered jug dating from the first half of the 18C *(first display case on the right)*; from Meissen, a splendid gilded dinner service with blue floral decoration *(second display case)* and *(opposite the door)* a collection of the famous figurines (singly or in intimate groups) which made Meissen porcelain so fashionable during the second half of the 18C.

★★★ PALAZZO E MUSEO NAZIONALE DEL BARGELLO (Z) ⊘
Tour – 90min

This forbidding **palazzo**★ is a fine example of medieval vernacular architecture. The oldest part of the façade, surmounted by an elegant tower with merlons, was built in the mid-13C. It originally housed the Capitano del Popolo, who represented the working classes within the Florentine government, then the Podestà, the first governor who held executive and judicial powers. The later part of the building, which is lower and less austere in appearance, was built in the Gothic style a century later.

In 1574 the building became the residence of the Chief of Police (called Bargello) and part of it was turned into a prison.

Today the building houses a museum which provides a valuable insight into Italian Renaissance sculpture and also has a section devoted to the decorative arts.

The severity of the **courtyard**★★ is softened by a porch with wide arcades and a loggia reached by a picturesque outside staircase. In fact, this is one of the finest medieval courtyards in Italy. The coats of arms of the governors *(podeste)* who lived in the palace from the 14C to 16C provide a charming decoration. Condemned prisoners were put to death beside the well.

Works by 16C Tuscan sculptors have been placed along the galleries, whose walls and vaulting are enlivened by the bright colours of the coats of arms from the city's various districts. The single statues and the impressive group standing against the wall opposite the entrance were once part of a fountain designed by Ammannati, the architect of the Pitti Palace, for the great Hall of the Five Hundred in the Palazzo Vecchio. It was subsequently placed in the courtyard of the Pitti Palace. Beneath the loggia there is a splendidly decorated canon, produced in the 17C for Ferdinando II, bearing the head of St Paul. Nearby is the small charming bronze fisherman, made by a Neapolitan sculptor, Vincenzo Gemito (1852-1929). On the other side of the courtyard is a fine wrought-iron torch-holder dating from the 16C.

Ground Floor

Scultura medievale toscana (Medieval Tuscan Sculpture Room) – *Opposite the entrance at the far end of the gallery*. This room contains the museum's few Gothic sculptures. In the small *Madonna and Child* by Tino da Camaino *(against the lefthand wall)* the Virgin Mary has the sturdy appearance of a peasant girl (14C).

Michelangelo e della scultura florentina del Cinquecento (Michelangelo and 16C Florentine Sculpture Room) – *At the foot of the outside staircase*. This is mainly devoted to the two most contrasting artistic figures of the Florentine Renaissance.

There are four splendid **Michelangelo** sculptures *(lefthand bay)*. The **Drunken Bacchus** group accompanied by a laughing satyr (1497-1499) is an early work which still bears traces of Classical influences. In the famous **Tondo Pitti**, a large roundel representing the Madonna and Child with St John, carved between 1504 and 1506 for one of the members of the Pitti family, the artist seems to have transposed the *sfumato* style of Leonardo da Vinci into sculpture by creating roughly-sketched reliefs. The powerful marble bust of **Brutus** (1540) also takes its inspiration from Roman statuary. The unfinished **David-Apollo** (c1530) *(further along)* seems to have been captured midway between motion and immobility.

At the far end of the room are miniature copies of works by Michelangelo, produced in the Mannerist style by a number of his famous contemporaries. There are also various works by Baccio Bandinelli, Sansovino and Rustici.

In contrast to the forceful artistry of Michelangelo, the work of **Benvenuto Cellini** is admired for its virtuosity and delicacy. The righthand bay contains a number of his masterpieces.

Drunken Bacchus by Michelangelo.

In the centre of the room stands the marble **Narcissus** with its slender forms and melancholy incurved lines. For many years it was one of the statues in the Boboli Gardens. Arranged in a circle half-way round the room are the bronze statuettes of Perseus, Mercury, Danae and her son Perseus, Minerva and Jupiter which once filled the niches of the pedestal supporting the famous Perseus in the Loggia della Signoria. On the wall is the original bronze plaque which decorated the base, representing **Perseus Delivering Andromeda**, a work treated with the gusto characteristic of the Mannerist style (graceful drapes, elegant slender bodies, flowing movement). The bronze bust of **Cosimo I** (1546) *(wall to the right of the door)* is an admirable portrait vigorously expressing cruelty, intelligence and energy; the decoration on the armour is worthy of a goldsmith. In the centre of the circle formed by Cellini's bronze statuettes, stands Danti's *Honour Triumphant over Falsehood*, where, through the highly tensed muscles, the artist has managed to convey the opposing forces, while making skilful use of the block of marble (Falsehood is held firm in an almost curled position).

First Floor *(plan below)*

Loggia – The Loggia houses works by Giovanni da Bologna, including the Allegory of Architecture in the centre, and remarkable bronze animals which once adorned a grotto in the gardens of the Villa di Castello *(qv)*.

Salone del Consiglio Generale (General Council Room) – *Entrance at the top of the outside staircase*. Until the last century this vast high-ceilinged room, which has the majestic appearance of the nave of a cathedral, was still divided into prisoners' cells, constructed in the late 16C.

Beneath the vaulting there is an outstanding **collection of works**★★★ by **Donatello**, whose genius dominated the Early Italian Renaissance. There is a small lively bronze Cupid (1). The marble statue of **David** (2) is one of the artist's early works (1409) showing a realistic observation far removed from the Gothic tradition. The famous **"Marzocco"** (3), the Florence lion, whose paw rests on the city's shield, stood for many years in front of the Palazzo Vecchio. The famous bronze **David** (4) is a masterpiece dating from Donatello's more mature period. The adolescent, crowned with a laurel wreath, is a symbol of hope overcoming brute strength. Standing with legs slightly apart, he strikes a pose of detached pride. The splendid body, tensed yet carved in gentle relief, is the expression of an artistry that had reached the height of perfection. The imposing **St George** (5) *(in the niche in the end wall)* originally stood outside Orsanmichele; it is an early work (1416) which still displays a certain Gothic stiffness.

The room also contains a number of other important works from the 15C. *St John the Baptist as a Child* (6) by **Desiderio da Settignano**, one of Donatello's most illustrious pupils. The delicate outline and painful inquiring expression are charged with emotion. The touching *profile* (7), also of St John the Baptist as a child, has an exceptionally gentle quality. The artist learned from his master the technique of *schiacciato* – graduated flattened sculpture with slight relief. The delicate relief of the *Madonna and Child* (8) is a charming example of this style. Another of Donatello's pupils, **Agostino di Duccio**, carved the *Madonna and Child with Angels* placed within a *pietra serena* surround (9), a composition which displays exquisite finesse and a joyful charm and in which the profusion of undulating lines creates an impression of harmonious movement. The room also contains a number of Madonnas and Child by **Luca della Robbia**, the creator of one of the two famous *Cantorie*, now in the Museo dell'Opera del Duomo *(see above)* but who achieved popularity mainly by rediscovering the technique of enamelled terracotta which he elevated to an art form by integrating it into sculpture. The *Madonna of the Rose Garden* (10) and *Madonna with Apple* (11) are among his most accomplished youthful, serene Madonnas. Carved in flowing relief and with a simple gracefulness, they stand out white on a blue background, holding in their arms an Infant Jesus depicted with unrivalled realism.

Along the wall to the right of the doorway to the next room is a painting of a St John the Baptist on the road (12) by Francesco da Sangallo, and the two quatrefoil panels of *The Sacrifice of Isaac*, produced in 1401 for the competition to find the architect of the north door of the Baptistery. These panels were made by the winner, Lorenzo Ghiberti (13), and by Brunelleschi (14).

Sala Islamica (Islamic Art Room) – This room is a testimony to Florence's trade links with the Middle East. It contains carpets, costumes and weaponry, cloth, ceramics, pewter and bronzeware, and ivories, some of which were collected by the grand dukes.

Sala del Podestà (Governor's Room) – This is where Justice was done. The room houses a large part of the extensive collection owned by Louis Carrand, who was born in Lyons, and bequeathed to Florence in the late 19C. The collection, mainly consisting of objets d'art, is also displayed in other parts of the palace. The room has a remarkable display of enamels including some

MUSEO DEL BARGELLO
First floor

from Limoges and the Rhineland dating from the 12C and 13C *(first display case on the left)*, 15C and 16C Venetian ware *(second group of display cases in the centre)* and Limoges ware dating from the 15C and 16C *(fourth display case on the left and last on the right)*. Note also the surgical instruments used in the 16C *(first display case to the right of the door)* and a collection of ironware – locks, keys, bolts and latches dating from the 15C and 16C. Two display cabinets *(left at the back of the room)* contain items of jewellery, some of which date from the Roman and Byzantine period. Other pieces of silver jewellery *(in the centre of the first display case)* once belonged to the Medici.

Prisoners sentenced to death spent their last moments in the chapel. The stalls and the central lectern (15C) were transferred from San Miniato al Monte. The sacristy contains gold and silver church plate.

Sala degli avori (Ivories Room) – This houses one of the most extensive collections of ivories in the world, with works dating from the 5C to 17C. The display case against the wall beside the door contains Italian ivories from the 14C and 15C (triptych depicting religious scenes, boxes covered in figures, convex mirror) and medieval combs mainly from France. The first glass case in the centre displays a splendid chess board made by the Burgundy School. The second display cabinet on the left side wall is dedicated to 14C French art including carved mirror backs, intricate miniature-work designed to be worn at the waist by ladies (chivalrous scenes of courtly love or tournaments). The next display case *(set away from the wall)* contains works from the Paleo-Christian era, including the famous diptych depicting the life of St Paul and, in particular, Adam in Paradise accompanied by numerous animals (late 5C).

Sala delle maioliche (Majolica Room) – This room contains some spectacular basins from Urbino (16C) with a highly elaborate combination of shapes, decorative motifs and colours *(display cases in front of the windows)*, and some large white and brown Hispano-Moorish dishes (15C and 16C) with remarkably fine detail made in metallic shades.

Second Floor

Sala delle armi (Armoury) – *To the right of the first room above the Governor's Room*. The armoury contains a fine collection of mainly 16C-17C weapons and armour, most of which belonged to the Medici family.
The display case to the right of the door contains a fine collection of remarkably well-executed oriental weapons and shields. The first display case against the lefthand wall contains a series of rifles and pistols decorated with fruit, animals and figures, all beautifully inset in ivory and mother-of-pearl. The same case also contains some magnificent carved ivory saddles. The remainder of the collection consists mainly of the state **armour of the Grand Dukes** of the Medici dynasty including a number of splendid shields.

Sala di Giovanni della Robbia (Giovanni della Robbia Room) – *Above the Ivories Room*. This room houses a collection of works by the last of the three great della Robbia sculptors, the great-nephew of Luca, who carried on the technique of glazed terracotta sculpture, extending it to larger and more complex compositions with greater variety of colour, which may arouse a certain regret for the limpid charms of Luca's Madonnas and the joyful freshness of his sculptures of the Infant Jesus. A typical example of this development can be seen *(right of the door)* in the predella depicting Christ and the saints. Its main feature is its realism, its profusion of ornamental motifs and its chromatic complexity. The same is true of the large Pietà in bold relief set against a landscape full of rocks, buildings, trees and horsemen, and the huge Nativity surrounded by two Apparitions of Jesus to Mary Magdalen *(Noli me Tangere)*.
Giovanni also created simpler and more tranquil compositions such as the tender *Madonna and Child with St John (wall opposite the door)*.

Sala di Andrea della Robbia (Andrea della Robbia Room) – *Left*. Like his successor, Andrea della Robbia, nephew of Luca and father of Giovanni, also created some delicate and graceful Madonnas. In Andrea's sculptures, however, the flowing forms and noble simplicity so characteristic of Luca's work, give way to a certain affectation and a continual striving for greater decorative effect. His Madonnas and Child are embellished with heads of cherubs, flowers and foliage and are enlivened with bright colours. No less exquisite masterpieces, if only for the harmony of their composition, are **Our Lady of Architects** *(to the right of the window)*, produced for the Guild of Masons and Carpenters whose tools are depicted in the surrounding frieze, and his **Madonna with Cushion** *(to the left of the door)*. The bust of a child in the centre of the room and the inset portrait of an unknown young man on the righthand wall both display remarkable finesse.

Sala del Verrocchio (Verrocchio Room) – *To the left*. This room contains a collection of several sculptures by the Florentine artist who, as both painter and sculptor, was one of the leading figures of the Italian Renaissance. Near the centre of the room stands the famous bronze **David**, dating from *c*1465 and sculpted for the young Lorenzo the Magnificent and his brother, Giuliano, whom Verrocchio had befriended. Like Donatello's works, whose themes Verrochio used repeatedly, the Biblical hero is depicted as a delicate yet determined adolescent, and is treated with grace and sensitivity. Against the wall opposite the windows, note the bust of a young woman holding a bunch of flowers. Her long hands are admired for their lifelike, aristocratic appearance, and there are very few rivals in the world of sculpture. The identity of the model remains a mystery (it may have been Lucrezia Donti, Lorenzo the Magnificent's mistress). Note also by the same artist, two delightful marble Madonnas and Child, which contrast sharply with the expressionism and dramatic character of works such as the polychrome terracotta *Resurrection* and *The Death of Francesca Pitti-Tornabuoni*, indicating Verrocchio's ability to adapt to his subject matter.
Among the works by other sculptors of the late 15C, the most outstanding are – *(left of the door)* Francesco Laurana's plain, unemotional bust of Battista Sforza, Duchess of Urbino, the town in which the Dalmatian artist also worked although he spent most of his time in Naples; *(right of the door)* a number of sculptures by Mino da Fiesole, including a very fine medallion of the *Madonna and Child*,

and the remarkable portrait of *Rinaldo della Luna*; an *Adoration of the Infant (against the far wall)* in the form of a *tondo* and the extremely unsightly bust of Matteo Palmieri by the Florentine Antonio Rossellino.

The two adjoining rooms *(at the far end on the left)* contain a collection of medallions. The first room contains a large bust of Cardinal Zacchia Rondanini by Algardi.

Sala dei bronzetti (Bronze Statuette Room) – This room *(opposite the Verrocchio Room)* houses a large collection of bronze statuettes from the Italian Renaissance. At the time they were highly prized items of interior decoration among fashionable society. These bronze statuettes were miniature replicas of either ancient statues *(display case to the left of the door – the Laocoon)*, contemporary works by Michelangelo and Giovanni da Bologna *(first display case on the lefthand wall)* or original creations from renowned artists' studios – Cellini, Giovanni da Bologna and Riccio of Padua *(central display cases)*. There are also items in everyday use – mortars, lamps, candlesticks etc *(display cases at the far end)*.

★★★ SAN LORENZO (ST LAWRENCE'S CHURCH) (Y) ⊘ *Tour – 2 hours*

★★ Church

The church is situated close to the Medici Palace *(now the Palazzo Medici-Riccardi)*, and was formerly the Medici family parish church (several members of the Medici family bore the name Lorenzo). For over three centuries it was also their burial place.

Construction of the church was begun *c*1420 by Brunelleschi, who was commissioned to undertake the work by Giovanni di Bicci, Cosimo the Elder's father. Subsequent generations of the Medici family added their own embellishments.

As in the case of a number of other Florentine churches, the harsh façade never received the marble cladding included in the designs. The huge dome that caps the rear of the building is part of the Princes' Chapel *(see below)*, which was added in the 17C.

For the interior Brunelleschi broke with Gothic conventions and introduced a style that became typical of the Florentine Renaissance. He adopted the traditional basilica layout – nave and two aisles – of the former building with 11C restorations, and combined its Romanesque structures – semicircular arches, for which Florence retained a certain preference – with features taken from ancient Greek and Roman architecture – Corinthian columns, fluted pilasters, cornices. San Lorenzo thus came to represent a new style of church with an austere, pure architectural design, where the sublime soaring lines and ornamentation of Gothic buildings were replaced by carefully-balanced volumes, a formal geometrical plan and a strict contrast between the grey stone *(pietra*

San Lorenzo.

SAN LORENZO

0   20 m

N →

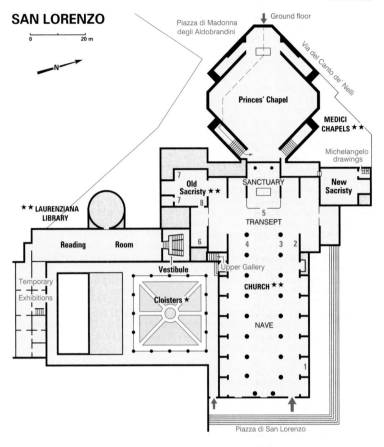

Piazza di Madonna degli Aldobrandini

Ground floor

Via del Canto de' Nelli

Princes' Chapel

MEDICI CHAPELS ★★

Michelangelo drawings

7

Old Sacristy ★★

SANCTUARY

New Sacristy

★★ **LAURENZIANA LIBRARY**

7

8

5

TRANSEPT

Reading Room

6

4 3 2

Vestibule

Upper Gallery

Temporary Exhibitions

CHURCH ★★

Cloisters ★

NAVE

1

Piazza di San Lorenzo

serena) and white rendering. The building has a coffered ceiling decorated, in the nave, with four reproductions of the Medici coat of arms. The barrel-vaulted aisles are flanked by shallow chapels surmounted by oculi.

In 1516 Pope Leo X, Lorenzo the Magnificent's son, commissioned Michelangelo to complete the east front that had been left unfinished on Brunelleschi's death in 1446. Michelangelo drew up a number of grandiose plans but only the inside was completed with a small gallery designed to display relics to the faithful.

In the *Marriage of the Virgin Mary* (1) *(second chapel on the right)* by the Mannerist painter, Rosso Fiorentino, the forms in the painting are gracefully elongated and the colours dazzlingly vivid. The delightful marble **relief★** in the shape of a small temple (2) *(end of the south aisle)* was carved by Desiderio da Settignano. The work was inspired by Donatello and it formed the basis for the many such elegantly-structured compositions with exquisite decorative effect called **tabernacles** *(tabernacoli)*, which were produced in great numbers in Florence during the 15C. The work also shows a remarkable sense of perspective, one of the main features of Renaissance art. The two **pulpits★★** (3 and 4) are faced with splendid panels produced by Donatello during the last years of his life and completed after his death by his pupils. The artist has used an unusual technique to create a three-dimensional feeling, by varying the depth of the relief.

The apparent confusion created by a crowd of characters, who are in fact arranged in a very stage-like manner, add a note of pathos to the scenes treated, most of which depict episodes from the Life of Christ. They are not set out in any particular chronological order.

North pulpit		South pulpit
Christ before Pilate	*Facing the façade*	Pentecost
Praying on the Mount of Olives	*Facing the aisle*	The Martyrdom of St Lawrence
St John the Evangelist		Saint Luke
Scourging of Christ		Mocking of Christ
The Entombment	*Facing the sanctuary*	The Women at the Tomb
The Deposition	*Facing the nave*	Descent into Hell
The Crucifixion		The Resurrection, the Ascension

In front of the chancel is a large circular slab (5) with an inlay of multicoloured marble. In the corners of the surrounding square is the Medici coat of arms. This marks the spot above the crypt where Cosimo the Elder is buried.

The **Martelli chapel** (6) contains the **Annunciation**★ painted c1440 by Filippo Lippi, a work which is remarkable for the perspective in the arches, buildings and pergolas.

★★ **Old Sacristy (Sacrestia Vecchia)** – Work on the new church of San Lorenzo began with the Old Sacristy, which is considered to be one of the most successful achievements of the Early Renaissance. It was a joint project involving Brunelleschi, who was responsible for the architecture, and Donatello, who undertook the decoration. This square chapel, with its hemispherical dome on pendentives and various architectural features highlighted by grey *pietra serena* – fluted pilasters in the corners crowned by Corinthian capitals, entablature, coving of the arches, pendentives, base and ribs of the dome – admirably conveys the well-proportioned unity of geometrical lines that are characteristic of Brunelleschi's style. It was the great architect's first attempt to express his ideal of a clear, ordered architecture on a human scale.

Donatello produced the cherubs comprising the frieze round the entablature, the polychrome medallions depicting the four Evangelists and scenes from the life of Saint John, and the remarkable **bronze doors**★ (7) containing 40 figures of holy martyrs and Apostles. He also designed the splendid traceried marble screen and the altar in the tiny domed apse. To the rear of the altar is a remarkable triptych *(Madonna and Child)* by Taddeo Gaddi.

In the centre of the room within the marble sarcophagus, which is capped by an altar table, lie Giovanni di Bicci and his wife Piccarda Bueni.

The elegant **tomb**★ *(left of the entrance)* (8) was produced in 1472 by Verrocchio, who was commissioned to undertake the work by Lorenzo the Magnificent and his brother Giuliano in honour of their father, Piero, and uncle, Giovanni. The lavish porphyry and bronze tomb is set in a bay connecting the sacristy to the adjoining chapel and is surmounted by an unusual trellis in which the mesh represents ropes.

On a cabinet to the right of the door stands the terracotta bust of Lorenzo as an adolescent, a work displaying great tenderness in the facial expression, which is attributed to Donatello.

★ **Chiostro (Cloisters)** – *Entrance via the north aisle or by the doorway on the left of the façade*. The cloisters were built in the 15C in the elegant style of Brunelleschi. A staircase from the upper gallery leads to the Laurenziana Library.

★★ **Biblioteca Medicea Laurenziana** (Laurenziana Library) ⊙
Entrance via a staircase from the upper gallery of the cloisters.

The library was founded in the 15C by Cosimo the Elder and considerably extended by Lorenzo the Magnificent, from whom it takes its name. It was not until the following century that Michelangelo was commissioned by Pope Clement VII (a member of the Medici family), to build (1523-1524) premises in the cloisters of San Lorenzo to house the library's priceless collection.

Vestibolo (Vestibule) – To decorate this exceptionally small yet disproportionately high space, the artist divided the walls into sections in an unusual way using architectural features that are normally found only on façades, while at the same time playing on the contrast between the white surfaces and grey *pietra serena* relief. The unusual use of huge twin columns, heavy cornices on brackets and window frames set flat against the wall already heralds the Baroque era. This style is further emphasised by the volutes on the consoles and the splendid monumental three-flight **staircase**★★, in which the width of the treads increases towards the bottom, creating an impression of a waterfall. Michelangelo left for Rome in 1534, where he settled permanently, and the staircase was left at the planning stage. It was completed in 1559 by the Mannerist architect, Ammannati, who used the original drawings and acted in accordance with the numerous instructions sent to him by Michelangelo from his distant retreat.

Sala di lettura (Reading Room) – Although the architectural style is more austere, it has its own charm because of the strict geometrical lines that are systematically repeated along the whole length of the room, creating a remarkable sense of perspective. The desks and lavish coffered ceiling, carved in warm-coloured wood and shown off by skilful lighting, were both designed by Michelangelo. The fine terracotta flooring from the same period is by Tribolo (the designer of the Boboli gardens), who added decorative features reflecting the design of the ceiling.

A selection of the library's 10 000 manuscripts are exhibited in rotation. They include a 5C Virgil, a Horace annotated by Petrarch, Lorenzo the Magnificent's Book of Hours, Leonardo da Vinci's notebooks, a letter from Catherine de Médicis to Michelangelo, and manuscripts by Petrarch, Ariosto, Machiavelli and Michelangelo.

★★ Capelle Medicee (Medici Chapels) ⊙
Entrance in Piazza della Madonna degli Aldobrandini

The term Medici Chapels is used to refer the Princes' Chapel and the New Sacristy.

Princes' Chapel (Cappella dei Principi) – Entrance to the chapel is by way of a huge crypt with low vaulting and heavy pillars designed by Buontalenti, in which the Medici grand dukes were buried; the stone just in front of the staircase to the right marks the tomb of Anna Maria Ludovica, the last member of the dynasty. The Princes' Chapel was designed during the lifetime of Cosimo I but was not completed until the early 17C under his younger son Ferdinando I. It was built to immortalise the grand dukes for whom it was intended as a funeral chapel. The architect, Matteo Nigetti, worked to plans drawn up by Don Giovanni, Cosimo's illegitimate son.

The most immediately striking features of the building are its overwhelming proportions and gloomy appearance. It is octagonal in design with walls and floor faced with *pietra dura* and precious marble, an impressive piece of workmanship produced in the Medici workshops *(qv)*. At the base of the walls are 16 coats of arms with lapis lazuli, coral and mother-of-pearl inlay representing the towns within the Grand Duchy of Tuscany. In this breathtaking mineral décor are the huge tombs, made of Oriental granite and green Corsican jasper, of Cosimo I *(left of the altar)* and his descendants, all of whom are buried below.

The altar is also lavishly inlaid with *pietra dura*. Behind it are two small rooms containing reliquaries, including 10C Muslim works made of rock crystal, once part of Lorenzo the Magnificent's collections *(lefthand room, left display case)*.

New Sacristy (Sacrestia Nuova) – *Outside the Princes' Chapel, entrance in a small corridor on the left*. The sacristy is in fact a funeral chapel, designed to house the tombs of the Medici family. It was commissioned in 1520 by Cardinal Giuliano, the future Pope Clement VII, from Michelangelo. It was Michelangelo's first commission as an architect; when he left Florence in 1534 the work was unfinished and it was not completed until 20 years later by Vasari and Ammannati.

It is called the New Sacristy because it is symmetrically opposite the Old Sacristy and is reminiscent of the latter's architectural design, although the style is somewhat less cold. It uses the same grey *pietra serena* decoration, which forms a stark contrast with the pale-coloured marble and white walls. In the layout of windows, arches, cornices, niches and pediments – features that are mainly borrowed from Classical architecture – Michelangelo gives the spatial layout a new rhythm that conveys a touching solemnity. The rectangular building is capped by a coffered dome on which the coffering gradually reduces in size towards the top to emphasise the feeling of height.

★★★ **Medici Tombs** – The sculptures were also produced by Michelangelo. Closely combining his work as both sculptor and architect, the brilliant artist executed the famous tombs of the two members of the elder branch of the Medici family between 1526 and 1533.

The monumental group was to be composed of four mausoleums but only two were in fact completed. On the right is the tomb of Giuliano, Duke of Nemours (son of Lorenzo the Magnificent), who died in 1516 at the age of 35; Giuliano is portrayed as a Roman emperor holding the baton of an army commander on his knees. At his feet are the famous semi-reclining allegorical figures of **Day** (unfinished), conveying a powerful energy, and **Night**, sleeping in a pose of graceful abandon. Opposite is the tomb of Lorenzo, Duke of Urbino (the grandson of Lorenzo the Magnificent and father of Catherine de Médicis), who died in 1519 at the age of 27; he is shown in meditation and at his feet lie the other two famous statues depicting **Dusk**, in the guise of a melancholy old man, and **Dawn**, portrayed as a woman rising uneasily from her slumber. Each of these marble figures conveys a tragic grandeur and remarkable vigour. It is possible that the two idealised figures were intended to represent *Action* and *Thought* triumphing over time which, through the different stages of life (symbolised by times of the day), leads man to his death.

The only work to be produced for the tomb of Lorenzo the Magnificent *(right of the entrance)* is the admirable *Madonna and Child,* a work showing a remarkably sharp sense of observation and understanding. Lorenzo, the most famous of the Medici, lies with his brother Giuliano in the plain sarcophagus below.

A small room beneath the chapel displays some mural **drawings** ⊙, attributed to Michelangelo, which were discovered in 1975. They are studies sketched in charcoal with agitated lines, depicting a confusion of nudes, faces, limbs, a horse's head and architectural features. They may have been drawn during the few months the artist spent in hiding in the monastery of San Lorenzo, while being sought by the Medici for his part in the 1527 revolt that had driven the powerful family from Florence.

★★PALAZZO MEDICI-RICCARDI (Y) (MEDICI PALACE) ⊙

Tour – 30min; as the building now houses the Prefecture, only the former chapel and one room on the first floor are open to the public.

This mansion, the Medici family residence, was begun in 1444 on the orders of Cosimo the Elder to the design of his friend, Michelozzo. Cosimo did not, however, live in the building, which he deemed too large, until 1459; he died here five years later. His grandson, Lorenzo the Magnificent, held a princely court here, frequented by his poet, philosopher and artist friends such as Poliziano, Pico della Mirandola and Botticelli. The building was also once the home of the young girl who became Catherine de Médicis, queen of France.

The mansion played host to Charles VIII of France in 1494 and to Charles V in 1536. In 1540 Cosimo I left the residence to settle in Piazza della Signoria. The mansion remained in the possession of the Medici family for another hundred years or so before being sold to the Riccardi. Cosimo the Elder wanted a residence worthy of the Medici fortune and power but the main concern of the as yet semi-official ruler of Florence was that it should not arouse envy – "a dangerous weed" – but be of sober appearance, a reflection of the discretion with which he exercised his power. The noble building, which was considered the prototype for the aristocratic residences of the Florentine Renaissance, reflects a medieval austerity with huge rusticated stonework gradually softening towards the top, elegant twin bays surmounted by semicircular arches and an overhanging cornice. The arcades of a loggia used to be visible on the ground floor, at the corner of Via Cavour and Via de' Gori, but they were walled up and later replaced by pedimented windows on high consoles designed by Michelangelo.

Breaking with medieval tradition Michelozzo structured the building around a fine courtyard with a tall portico. Twin windows are set above the semicircular arcades which are supported by elegant Ionic and Corinthian columns with capitals. On the top floor there is a loggia which has now been glazed. Between the arcades of the portico and the first floor, a stringcourse decorated with medallions carved in Donatello's workshop and depicting the Medici coat of arms or classical motifs, adds a graceful touch to the general architectural austerity. The Antique marbles – inscriptions, reliefs, busts – which adorn the courtyard galleries were collected by the Riccardi family from the 16C onwards, although they were not set up here until the early 18C. The garden, which was considerably reduced by the extensions made to the building by the Riccardi family, had originally included a fountain decorated with Donatello's *Judith (now in the Lily Chamber in the Palazzo Vecchio)*.

★★★ **Cappella (Chapel)** – *First floor.*
Entrance via the first staircase on the right in the courtyard.

Adoration of the Magi by Benozzo Gozzoli
(detail showing Lorenzo the Magnificent).

SCALA

The tiny chapel with its rich gilt coffered ceiling and splendid flooring with polychrome marble inlay was designed by Michelozzo.

The walls are decorated with **frescoes**★★★ painted in 1459 by **Benozzo Gozzoli,** Fra Angelico's pupil, who had been trained by Ghiberti in the painstaking art of gold and silver work. In a style that still echoes the influence of the international Gothic, the artist has produced a brilliant and picturesque illustration of Florentine life based on the theme of the **Procession of the Magi**. The work shows both a sharp sense of observation and a delightful imagination. It was intended to honour the refined court of the Medici and to commemorate the Council which met in Florence in 1439 and made a great contribution to the prestige of both the Medici and the city. A landscape dotted with horsemen, animals, hunting scenes, slender trees, fantastic rocks and castles bristling with towers, forms the backdrop to the procession in which, mingling in the crowd, are famous figures from Florentine society, members and friends of the Medici family, and exotic Eastern characters who came to take part in the Council; they are easily recognisable by their lavish costumes and beards, as it was then the fashion in Florence to be clean-shaven.

There are those who have claimed that the young horseman in blue with the cheetah *(lefthand wall)* in front of the Three Kings, is Giuliano, Lorenzo's brother. The Three Kings, representing the three ages of life, are portrayals of other major figures of contemporary society. At the head of the procession *(lefthand corner)* is the patriarch of Constantinople who died in Florence during the Council. Behind him, dressed in a splendid green and gold coat and Oriental head-dress, is the Byzantine Emperor John VII Palaiologos, riding a magnificently harnessed horse *(wall opposite the altar – right of the entrance)*. At the end *(righthand wall)*, clothed in a beige and gold jerkin and mounted on a palfrey (the harness bears the Medici coat of arms), is the young Lorenzo the Magnificent. Behind him on the white horse is his father Piero the Gouty. In the middle of the group behind him is a self-portrait of Benozzo; his cap bears the inscription "Opus Benotii". The three adolescent girls on horseback *(righthand corner of the wall opposite the altar)*, who are dressed in light-coloured tunics, are Giuliano and Lorenzo's sisters.

On the chancel walls is an *Adoration of the Angels,* also by Benozzo Gozzoli.

★★ **Sala di Luca Giordano** – *First floor. Entrance via the second staircase on the right in the courtyard.*

This bright and elegant gallery was built towards the end of the 17C, by which time the mansion had become the property of the Riccardi family. Its decoration is dazzling; it is panelled throughout with gilded stucco work, alternating with mirrored panels bearing remarkably graceful painted motifs depicting cherubs, foliage, flowers and birds. The elegant row of windows with embrasures embellished with rich gilded panelling overlooks the garden.

The room's crowning glory, however, is its barrel-vaulted ceiling decorated with a huge fresco painted in 1683 by the Neapolitan artist, **Luca Giordano** (1632-1705). This fine exponent of Baroque decorative art earned the nickname "Luca Fa Presto" ("Luke works quickly") because of the extraordinary speed with which he executed his works. He learnt the art of grand decorative compositions and acquired his taste for light colours from his master, Piero da Cortona (who painted the splendid Baroque ceilings in the Palatine Gallery in the Pitti Palace). With remarkably restrained exuberance and a cheerful liveliness, the artist has depicted an **Apotheosis of the Second Medici Dynasty**. Above a frieze full of scenes borrowed from mythology, swirling figures soar upwards into the clouds, while the daring use of foreshortening gives a remarkable sense of movement. The skilful arrangement of vivid splashes of colour – intense blues and deep reds – in addition to the subtle blending of colour in the pale and light shades are evidence of the artist's mastery as a colourist.

★★ CONVENTO E MUSEO DI SAN MARCO (ET) ⊙ *Tour – 1 hour*

St Mark's Convent adjoins the church of the same name and houses the museum which contains **works**★★★ **by Fra Angelico**.

The convent was built for the Dominicans on the orders of Cosimo the Elder in 1436. It was his loyal friend and favourite architect, Michelozzo, who completed this extremely simple building in about seven years. Fra Angelico and Fra Bartolomeo, another artistic monk who also lived in the monastery but over half a century later, worked on its decoration. St Antoninus (1389-1459) and Savonarola were both priors of St Mark's.

Pianterreno (Ground Floor)

The elegant Renaissance **cloisters** in the shade of a huge cedar tree contain tympani decorated with frescoes (late 16C to early 17C) recounting the life of St Antoninus.

Ospizio (Former Hospitium) – *On the right, at the entrance to the cloisters*. The room contains numerous altar paintings that rank among the Dominican's best-known works.

Although the large *Descent from the Cross (right of the entrance)* is a triptych, it is the one of all Fra Angelico's works that most reflects the spirit of the Renaissance – background of buildings and landscape, humanity in the attitudes and facial expressions.

In the famous **Last Judgement** (1425) *(next wall)* Fra Angelico combines elements inherited from the Gothic tradition – golden colouring, details treated with the delicacy of the miniaturists – with features characterising the spirit of the Renaissance – sense of perspective in the receding line of tombs and the semicircular composition, dramatic realism in the depiction of the open graves. Above all he expresses a touching mysticism in the figures that populate Paradise. The damned were painted by Fra Angelico's assistants. The admirable series of small panels *(further along)*, illustrating the Life of Christ, once covered the door of a church cabinet *(Armadio degli Argenti)*. Among the scenes depicted *(from left to right)* against the exquisite backdrop of buildings and landscapes, the most outstanding include the Flight into Egypt, the Prayer on the Mount of Olives, the Kiss of Judas and the Arrest of Jesus. The tiny *Virgin with the Star (next pillar)*, a work that is still very much part of Gothic tradition, forms a stark contrast to the moving *Lamentation over the Body of Christ (further along)*.

The famous **Linaioli Madonna** *(far wall)*, painted in 1433, was Fra Angelico's first public work, commissioned by the Linen Merchants' Guild to adorn a marble tabernacle. There is evidence of Masaccio's influence in the substance of the bodies and the feeling of space. The angel musicians depicted in the border are among the most exquisite of all the figures painted by Fra Angelico. The predella contains the Preaching of St Peter before St Mark, the Adoration of the Magi and the Martyrdom of St Mark.

One of the two tiny square panels *(towards the door against a pillar)*, is a remarkable miniature depicting a *Coronation of the Virgin Mary*. Then comes the magnificent **Annalena Madonna**, named after the monastery for which it was painted, also showing the miniaturist technique and use of gold but already typical of the Renaissance style in the rectangular format and landscape background. The small Gothic panel *(next pillar)* with two registers depicting the *Annunciation* and the *Adoration of the Magi* is also a masterpiece of miniature painting.

The **Lavabo Room** *(end of the next gallery on the right)* contains Fra Angelico's *Crucifixion between St Nicholas of Bari and St Francis*, which was extensively damaged by a flood in 1557. In the **main refectory** *(right)* the front wall is decorated with a huge fresco by Giovanni Antonio Sogliani depicting *St Dominic and his brother monks fed by the angels* (1536). Two rooms *(other side of the Lavabo Room)* contain works by Fra Bartolomeo and Alessio Baldovinetti.

Fra Angelico

Fra Giovanni da Fiesole, better known by the name of Fra Angelico, was born in the latter years of the 14C in Vicchio northeast of Florence *(30 kilometres – 19 miles)*. He entered the Dominican Order in Fiesole and later came to St Mark's in Florence where he spent about ten years covering the walls of the cells and conventual rooms with edifying scenes designed to inspire meditation.

Through his art this modest monk achieved fame within his own lifetime. He was called to Rome on several occasions by Pope Eugenius IV and Pope Nicholas V; the latter commissioned him to decorate the Papal chapel in the Vatican. Orvieto Cathedral has some admirable frescoes painted by him. He also produced numerous altarpieces.

He died in 1455 during a visit to Rome and for several centuries bore the title "Blessed" *(Beato)* until he was eventually canonised in 1983.

His paintings are characterised by their serenity, sweetness and humility. Although he was deeply attached to the Gothic tradition and therefore often worked on triptychs, creating golden backgrounds and using the precious style of the miniaturist, he was also attracted by the new Renaissance theories, as is shown by a certain number of his works in which the figures are steeped in a sense of humanity and space is structured in such a way as to hint at perspective. His altar paintings and frescoes, however, which are true acts of faith, are impressive for the simple mysticism of his vision and the purity of line and colour. In many cases he worked with his pupil, Benozzo Gozzoli, and with Filippo Lippi, and it is sometimes difficult to distinguish what was actually painted by him.

Sala Capitolare (Chapter-house) – The chapter-house leads off the gallery opposite the entrance containing a 15C bell. This bell has been an anti-Medici symbol ever since it was rung to call the people to defend Savonarola, then prior of St Mark's, when he was arrested in 1498.

The main wall of the room is covered with a huge, austere *Crucifixion* in which Fra Angelico depicted the people present at the historical event and the founder saints of the Order or saints who had links with the monastery (St Mark) and the Medici family (Cosmas and Damian).

Refettorio piccolo (Small Refectory) – *Entrance from the small corridor on the left of the chapter-house*. Domenico Ghirlandaio's **Last Supper★** preceded a variation on the same subject painted by the artist in 1480 in the refectory in Ognissanti *(qv)*. Although the composition of the landscape and attitudes of the Apostles are rather rigid, the decorative intricacy of detail shows the freshness of inspiration that was characteristic of this artist.

Another room contains architectural fragments from central Florence.

Primo piano (First Floor)

The monks' cells are all decorated with scenes portraying the Life of Christ and the Life of the Virgin Mary and the mysteries of the Christian religion. The artistic value of the works varies depending on whether they were executed by Fra Angelico or his assistants. These frescoes were intended to encourage the meditative contemplation of the monks rather than as altarpieces or tabernacles to impress the faithful. The painter's artistic expression is conveyed through a remarkably simple style and an exceptional sobriety of colour.

Overlooking the staircase is a huge **Annunciation**, one of the artist's masterpieces. The cells line three corridors under bare rafters.

Fra Angelico's finest frescoes *(left side of the corridor)* include a fresh, poetic *Appearance of Jesus to Mary Magdalen* (no 1), another admirable **Annunciation** (no 3) in which the bare décor and extreme economy of colour convey an extraordinary sense of spirituality, a *Christ on the Cross* (no 4), a *Transfiguration* (no 6), *Christ being mocked* (no 7), the *Holy Women at the Tomb* (no 8), a *Coronation of the Virgin* in which the colours seem to be absorbed by the light (no 9) and the *Presentation of Jesus in the Temple*, in which the reddish background is in fact an undercoat from which the actual colour has worn away (no 10).

The two cells *(end of the next corridor)* once occupied by Savonarola contain his missal, rosary, hair-shirt, Crucifix and *(small vestibule)* his ardent, obstinate and zealous portrait by Fra Bartolomeo whom he had converted.

Return to the staircase.

St Antoninus' cell (no 31 *immediately to the left in the righthand corridor*) contains his death mask and a number of his manuscripts.

The splendid **library★** *(before the cell on the right)* is a bright, spacious room, containing three aisles with elegant arches, and is one of Michelozzo's most accomplished works.

The Annunciation by Fra Angelico.

The plaque *(near the entrance)* marks the place where Savonarola was arrested on the night of 8 April 1498; he was executed two months later in Piazza della Signoria.

His own cell (no 33) is decorated with the Kiss of Judas by Fra Angelico. The two adjoining cells (nos 38 and 39 far right), which were used by Cosimo the Elder, the monastery's munificent benefactor, during religious retreats, are decorated with *Christ on the Cross (first)* by Fra Angelico and an *Adoration of the Magi (second)*.

★★ GALLERIA DELL'ACCADEMIA (ET) ⊘ *Tour - 30min*

The Accademia is of exceptional interest for its collection of sculptures by Michelangelo. The gallery also houses an art collection of mainly Florentine works dating from the 13C-19C.

The first room contains paintings from the late 15C and early 16C, including a fine *Deposition* by Perugino *(opposite the entrance)*; it has an almost Mannerist quality in the flowing lines formed by the strips of cloth used to bring Christ down from the cross. The terracotta group in the middle of the room is the model produced by Giovanni da Bologna for his *Rape of the Sabine Women* in the Loggia della Signoria.

★★★ **Michelangelo Gallery** - On either side of the gallery are four of the famous **Slaves** (the other two are in the Louvre Museum in Paris) made for the tomb of Pope Julius II in Rome. A number of designs were produced for this mausoleum which was originally intended to include 40 huge statues and to be erected in the centre of St Peter's in Rome; the final version is in the Church of St Peter in Chains in Rome. In their contorted movements, the unfinished figures (1513-1520) seem to be attempting to break free from the marble from which they emerge; they convey a feeling of strength and pathos.

Flanked by the two Slaves *(right)* is St Matthew, part of a series of 12 statues of the Apostles that Michelangelo was commissioned to produce for the cathedral; this statue too is only roughly carved and the others were never produced.

The so-called **Palestrina Pietà**, together with the Pietà in the Museo dell'Opera del Duomo and the *Rondanini Pietà* in Milan, represents the final apotheosis of Michelangelo's art. The overdeveloped arms and torso and roughly-carved legs, portrayed with unusual foreshortening, suggest the heaviness of Christ's dead body and illustrate the artist's remarkable knowledge of human anatomy.

At the end of the room stands the huge statue of **David**, in an apse that was specially built for the work in 1873. Michelangelo was 25 years old and already immensely famous when he carved this masterpiece (1501-1504), one of his most famous sculptures, from an enormous block of marble that was considered to be unusable. The Biblical hero who defeated the giant Goliath, symbolised the determination of the Florentine Republic to defend its freedom in the face of its enemies, however powerful they might be. In contrast to older works *(see those in the Bargello on the same theme)*, David is nervously poised for action with sling in hand, not yet experiencing the serenity and pride of victory. He stands with his body weight on his right leg to suggest – using the **"contrapposto"** technique – the tension arising immediately before movement. The artist also broke with tradition by portraying the character, not as a frail adolescent, but rather as a muscular young man whose consummate beauty makes him reminiscent of an Apollo from Antiquity. The statue was placed in front of the Palazzo Vecchio where it remained until 1873.

The walls are hung with magnificent **tapestries** made in Brussels in the 16C and based on sketches of the Creation attributed to Van Orley.

★ **Pinacoteca (Art Gallery)** - The first of the three small adjoining rooms *(right of the main gallery)* displays the front panel of the famous **Adimari Chest** *(second bay on the right)* depicting the wedding celebrations held in Florence for one of the members of this aristocratic family. The artist, an unknown 15C painter referred to as the "Master of the Adimari Chest", has captured in a fresh, lively style, one moment in the life of some of his wealthiest contemporaries, depicting in detail the costumes, head-dresses and ceremonial artefacts of the time. In the background are the Baptistery and surrounding houses. The room also contains works providing a remarkable insight into the changeover from Gothic to Renaissance art. In the first bay is the flamboyant Virgin Mary with a girdle *(Madonna della Cintola)* flanked by St Thomas and St Catherine of Alexandria, by Andrea di Giusto Manzini (first half of the 15C). It is still clearly Gothic in style with its dazzling golden background, composition in the form of a triptych, multifoil arches and expressionless characters. The fine Madonna and Child with angels and saints *(first bay opposite the entrance)*, painted in the mid-15C by Mariotto di Cristoforo, retains a Gothic feeling in the gold-coloured fabric background, executed with the intricacy of miniaturist art, but the overall layout (rectangular form) and the sketched-in landscape in the far distance are characteristic of the Renaissance style. Filippo Lippi's *Annunciation (third bay right of the door)* is a typical Florentine Renaissance work. This evolution towards Renaissance art is illustrated in the two following rooms.

There are *(third room)* two exquisite paintings by Botticelli – the famous **Madonna of the Sea** and a delightful **Madonna and Child with the young St John and Angels,** a work displaying a wonderful freshness and tender sweetness.

In the continuation of the art gallery *(after the Michelangelo gallery)* is a statue of David flanked by 16C Italian paintings. The large *Deposition from the Cross (far right)* by Bronzino depicts a descent from the cross in a range of browns and yellows in the background. Alessandro Allori's *Annunciation (left)* unusually depicts the Virgin with her back almost turned towards the Archangel Gabriel and her hands raised as if she were already aware of her son's destiny, while at her feet her book and embroidery form a fine still-life.

The **Gipsoteca** (Plasterwork Gallery) *(opposite end of the gallery)* contains works by two 19C sculptors, Bartolini and Pampaloni, professors at the Academy of Fine Arts. The plaster casts are the original models for marble sculptures. On the walls are 19C paintings, also by professors from the Academy.

The three rooms *(back towards the David gallery)* contain 13C-14C Tuscan paintings, including three eye-catching Crucifixion scenes. The first *(immediately to the left of the entrance)* depicts an exaggerated twisted pose, which was a common feature of the Sienese School's taste for contorted lines and contrasts with the two other works *(end of the two rooms on each side)*.

The first floor displays a collection of 14C-15C Tuscan paintings.

★★ SANTA MARIA NOVELLA (Y) ⊘ *Tour - 1 hour*

The church and cloisters of Santa Maria Novella stand at the north end of the irregularly-shaped **Piazza Santa Maria Novella**, which was laid out in the 14C; the south side is lined by the Renaissance arches of the long, slightly-elevated **Loggia de San Paolo (E)**.

In the Middle Ages the square was used for numerous tournaments and other pageants and from the mid-16C to the last century it hosted the Palio dei Cocchi, the chariot race held on St John's Day (24 June), which was introduced by Cosimo I and based on the two-horse chariot *(biga)* races of Ancient Rome. The grand dukes presided over the event from a canopied box set up on the steps of the loggia. The central area was divided into two tracks by a rope stretched between two wooden pyramids which were replaced in the 17C by marble obelisks designed by Giovanni da Bologna.

★★ Church

Although the Dominicans commenced work on Santa Maria Novella in 1279 in an attempt to heal the rift between the Guelfs and Ghibellines, the main part of the building was not completed until 1360.

Santa Maria Novella.

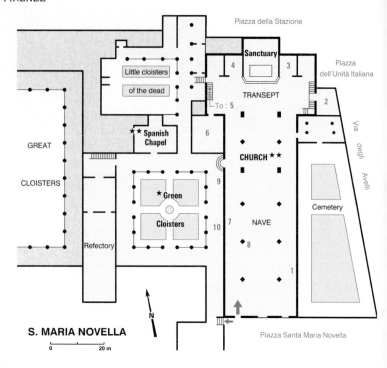

S. MARIA NOVELLA

0 _____ 20 m

Exterior – The lower part of the extremely elegant **façade** – side doors and recesses – with its light geometrical design picked out in green and white marble, dates from the mid-14C. In 1458 the work was taken over by Leon Battista Alberti, who succeeded in blending the existing Gothic features with the Renaissance style by creating an overall structure based on simple forms such as squares and circles. The central doorway, pillars and the whole of the upper section of the façade were built to his plans. The remarkable voluted consoles in coloured marble marquetry were designed to fill the space between the aisles and the higher nave. This treatment was then adopted in a great number of Renaissance churches and in Baroque façades. Funding for the work was provided by the Rucellai, a rich family of merchants, whose dedicatory inscription – IOHANES·ORICELLARIVS·PAV·F·AN·SAL·MCCCLXX – appears on the pediment. The Rucellai coat of arms, a billowing sail, is included in the middle frieze.

Above the twin recesses at each end of the façade there is a sundial *(right)* and an armillary sphere *(left)*.

The small **cemetery** *(right – closed to the public)*, where Domenico Ghirlandaio was buried, is enclosed by a screen composed of a series of Gothic recesses which like those on the façade contain the remains of Florentine families. At the base of the recesses are marble sarcophagi carved with the People's Cross and the coats of arms of the families of the deceased.

From Piazza dell'Unità Italiana and Piazza della Stazione *(at the north end of the church)*, there is a remarkable **view★** of the powerful chevet, surmounted by a slender, austere Romanesque Gothic belltower.

Interior – The interior of Santa Maria Novella was bright and vast (almost 100m – 325ft long) because it was designed for the preaching of sermons. In architectural terms, it was strongly influenced by the Cistercian Gothic style. Its layout has the form of a Latin cross with a very short transept and flat chevet. The outstanding feature of the interior is its austerity. The elegant, spacious nave is lined with arches that become narrower towards the chancel, thus accentuating the feeling of depth. There are alternating black and white archstones and the ogival vaulting in the nave and aisles is highlighted by geometrical designs, also in black and white.

East aisle – The austere elegant tomb (1) *(second bay far right)* of the blessed Villana delle Botti, a Dominican nun who died in 1361, shows her recumbent figure, carved by Bernardo Rossellino almost one century later, lying beneath a baldaquin of flowing draperies.

East transept – Above the altar *(end of the transept)* in the raised **Ruccellai Chapel** (2) is Nino Pisano's sweetly-smiling marble **Madonna and Child★**. In the pavement is a bronze gravestone bearing the effigy of a Dominican friar carved by Ghiberti.

The **Filippo Strozzi Chapel** (3) is decorated throughout with **frescoes**★ *(charge for lighting)* painted in a tormented, almost breathless style, by Filippino Lippi, who portrayed scenes from the life of St Philip and St John the Evangelist against a backdrop of exuberant architecture. The rich merchant to whom the chapel is dedicated and who commissioned one of the finest mansions in Florence, the Palazzo Strozzi *(qv)*, is buried in an ornate basalt sarcophagus, above which Benedetto da Maiano carved an inset Madonna and Child amid a graceful flight of angels.

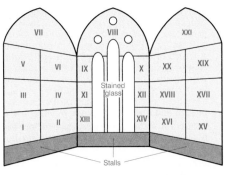

Sanctuary frescoes in S. Maria Novella.

Sanctuary – The dazzling **frescoes**★★★ with which Domenico Ghirlandaio covered the walls of the chancel in 1485 at the request of Giovanni Tornabuoni, the uncle of Lorenzo the Magnificent, are considered his finest work *(charge for lighting)*. In his illustration of the lives of the Virgin Mary *(left)* and St John the Baptist *(right)*, he modelled his figures on members of the Tornabuoni family and their friends, and painted a brilliant and detailed picture of Florentine high society, in a fresh style that showed a keen sense of observation.

Lefthand wall – (I) Joachim chased from the Temple because he has no children (the young man with the fine mop of hair to the left of the foreground is Giovanni Tornabuoni's son-in-law; the figure with hand on hip, in the group to the right, is said to be the artist himself; the Loggia de San Paolo is recognisable in the background); (II) The Birth of the Virgin Mary (the young woman in the rich white and gold dress leading the group of women is Giovanni Tornabuoni's only daughter, Ludivoca, who died in childbirth at the age of 15; (III) Mary being presented in the Temple; (IV) The marriage of the Virgin Mary; (V) The Adoration of the Magi (damaged); (VI) The Massacre of the Holy Innocents; (VII) The Death of the Virgin Mary and *(above)* the Assumption.

End wall – (VIII) The Coronation of the Virgin Mary; (IX) St Dominic committing heretical and orthodox books to the flames; (X) St Peter the Martyr; (XI) The Annunciation; (XII) St John in the wilderness; (XIII and XIV) The patrons of the work, Giovanni Tornabuoni and his wife, Francesca Pitti, at prayer.

Righthand wall – (XV) The angel appearing to Zachariah (this scene is a veritable portrait gallery; the man shown full face in the group on the left in the foreground is said to be Poliziano, the finest of all Florentine Renaissance poets, and the man on the far left is Marsilio Ficino, the city's finest Humanist, who popularised Plato's theories throughout Italy; (XVI) The Visitation; (the first of the three women on the right of the Virgin Mary and Elizabeth is said to be Giovanna degli Albizi, Giovanni Tornabuoni's daughter-in-law who also died in childbirth in

1488); (XVII) The birth of St John the Baptist; (the scene is set in a Florentine interior; the woman on the right, in front of the servant carrying a basket of fruit on her head, is Lucrezia Tornabuoni, Giovanni's sister and Lorenzo's mother); (XVIII) Zachariah, having lost the power of speech, is writing down the name to be given to his son; (XIX) St John the Baptist preaching; (XX) The Baptism of Christ; (XXI) Herod's feast.

West transept – Stark and white against a dark porphyry background in the **Gondi Chapel** (4) is the famous **Crucifix**★★ by Brunelleschi, a work that is striking for its elegance

Birth of John the Baptist by Ghirlandaio (detail on lefthand wall).

and realism. Tradition has it that Donatello was so struck by the work that he dropped the eggs he was carrying. The walls of the slightly-raised **Capella Strozzi di Mantova** (5) *(charge for lighting)* are decorated with unusually large **frescoes**★ painted by a Florentine artist, Nardo di Cione, *c*1357. Facing the entrance is a fresco of the Last Judgement; Hell *(righthand wall)*, based on the work by Dante, is depicted in dark, earthy colours which form a stark contrast to the light, golden tones of Paradise *(lefthand wall)*. Above the altar is a Flamboyant Gothic **polyptych**★ in which Andrea Orcagna, Nardo di Cione's brother, showed Christ surrounded by seraphim handing St Peter the keys to the kingdom of heaven and giving St Thomas Aquinas the Book of Wisdom.

Sacristy (6) – The sacristy contains a **Crucifixion**★ painted by Giotto. There is also a lavabo consisting of a marble basin surmounted by a glazed terracotta **niche**★ which is one of the most delightful of all Giovanni della Robbia's works.

North aisle – The famous fresco on the subject of the **Trinity**★★ (7), painted by Masaccio, is a work which is of vital importance in the history of Art. In this fresco he broke away from the attractive elegance of Gothic painting by painting God the Father in a Renaissance setting, holding the upright of the Cross and presenting the sacrifice of His crucified Son. The outline of the Holy Ghost in the form of a dove stands out on His chest. Christ is flanked by the Virgin Mary (her face and outstretched hand also show that she has accepted the sacrifice), St John and the donors, on their knees. An austere alternation of pink and blue shows the extent to which the artist emphasised the drawing rather than the colour. In this work Masaccio made use of new mathematical theories on perspective, drawn up by Brunelleschi, and so achieved one of the finest and earliest examples of architectural perspective. The faces of the figures, which are seen from below, show the determination for realism which is another of this artist's main characteristics.

The marble pulpit (8) *(against the following pillar)* has decorations in gold leaf designed by Brunelleschi. The panels recount the story of the Virgin Mary.

One of the most interesting private collections of works of art in Florence is housed in La Pietra (no 120 via Bolognese), the former home of Sir Harold Acton, historian. The beautiful garden contains topiary dating from 1904 (admission by appointment only).

★ Monumental cloisters

★ Chiostro Verde (Green Cloisters) – The cloisters were built in the mid-14C in a style that was still Romanesque, with wide semicircular arches. The name refers to the predominant colour, green, of the decorative **frescoes**, which were painted *c*1430 by Paolo Uccello and his students, depicting scenes from Genesis. The frescoes on the wall between the cloisters and the church are the work of the master alone; they are painted in sombre tones and depict *(left to right)* scenes ranging from the Creation to the story of Noah. Only two bays are still in good condition – the one (9), in which the creation of animal life, Adam and Eve and Original Sin are all clearly visible, and the one in the fourth bay (10), depicting the Flood (the storm is particularly interesting) and Noah's drunkenness.

★★ Cappellone degli Spagnoli (Spanish Chapel) – *North Gallery*. Behind the elegant Gothic twin windows with multifoiled arches and delightful twisted columns, is the chapter-house, which was built in the 14C; it is also known as the Spanish Chapel as in the 16C it was frequented by the courtiers of Eleonora of Toledo. The walls and vaulted roof are covered with highly-complex symbolical **frescoes**★★ painted in vivid colours by Andrea di Bonaiuti, also known as Andrea da Firenze, between 1365 and 1370, in honour of the Dominicans. The succession of allegorical figures and didactic scenes is representative of one of the main features of Art during the Italian 15C.

Lefthand wall – The Triumph of Divine Wisdom and the Glorification of St Thomas Aquinas. On the vaulting is a representation of Pentecost (the dove of the Holy Ghost coming down to the Apostles who are grouped round the Virgin Mary). Below them is a Dominican theologian personifying Catholic doctrine; he is sitting on a throne surrounded by the Wise Men of the Old and New Testaments above whom are the Virtues. Through Roman Catholic doctrine, the Holy Spirit brings to life the Liberal and Sacred Arts, symbolised by 14 female figures sitting in Gothic niches with figures representing these disciplines at their feet.

Righthand wall – The Triumph of the Church. Activities of the Dominincans. On the vaulting is St Peter's boat, representing the Church. At the bottom of the wall, in front of a building that is one of the projects drawn by the artist for Florence Cathedral, are the two people at the very top of the social hierarchy –

the Pope and the Holy Roman Emperor. In front of them *(left)* is a group consisting of representatives of religious orders and orders of chivalry. Among the group of Christian believers *(right)* is a standing figure, dressed in a great brown cloak, shown full face and said to be Cimabue. Beside him, depicted in profile and wearing a green hood, is Giotto. Boccaccio is further to the right, dressed in purple and holding a closed book; above him, wearing a cloak and hood of white ermine, is Petrarch. The figure beside him, shown in profile and wearing a white cap, is Dante.

On the same register the Dominicans are shown *(right)* protecting the Faithful from attack by Sin. The name "Dominicans" comes from the Latin *Domini Canes* meaning the Hounds of God; they are therefore symbolised as dogs tearing to pieces heretics depicted as wolves.

Above them, being welcomed into Heaven, are the souls of believers who succumbed to mortal sin but who were saved through their Confession received by a Dominican. Only three sins are depicted (Avarice, Lust and Pride); they are sitting next to a woman playing a viol. The Faithful are shown contemplating the Almighty who is surrounded by angels with the Virgin Mary in their midst (she is in the group on the left). At the foot of the throne is the Lamb of God and the symbols of the Evangelists.

End wall – The paintings *(left to right)* depict the climb up to Calvary, the Crucifixion and the descent into Hell. On the vaulting is the Resurrection. To the left of the tomb are the Holy Women who have come to embalm the Body of Christ; to the right, Christ appears to Mary Magdalen.

Entrance wall – This was not integrated into the overall decoration and was used to depict the first Dominican martyr – St Peter the Martyr. On the vaulting is the Ascension.

Chiostrino dei Morti (Small Cloisters of the Deceased) – *Right of the Spanish Chapel*. The pavement and walls of these irregularly-shaped cloisters and the small entrance gallery are almost entirely covered in gravestones.

Refectory – From the entrance lobby there is a view into the **Great Cloisters** (part of the Police College). The refectory and the room preceding it house the treasure of Santa Maria Novella – gold and silverware, reliquaries, frontals, vestments – and a number of frescoes that have been removed from the church walls, including the ones by Orcagna (35 busts of figures from the Old Testament) which used to decorate the chancel before it was painted by Ghirlandaio. They were found during restoration work.

In the southwest corner Piazza di Santa Maria Novella turn right into Via della Scala.

Farmacia di Santa Maria Novella (Pharmacy of Santa Maria Novella) (DUF) – *16 Via della Scala (blue); 100m – 108yds from the square, on the righthand side*. The pharmacy was founded in 1221 when the Dominicans first came to Florence. It has also sold spices since the 16C and their scents waft out into the street. The large shop is set out in an old chapel with ogival vaulting which was dedicated to St Nicholas. It was built in 1332 and redecorated in the neo-Gothic style in 1848. A *Directoire*-style room adjacent to the gardens is also open to the public, as is the old apothecary's shop with its stucco-work vaulting and 17C furnishings including display cabinets containing real stills. The frescoes in St Nicholas' sacristy depict *Christ's Passion*.

★★ SANTA CROCE (ST CROSS CHURCH) (EU) ⊘ *Tour – 90min*

The white marble façade of Santa Croce fills the east side of a vast square, **Piazza Santa Croce**, one of the oldest and most grandiose squares in the city. It still has several of its old houses – *(no 1 opposite the church)* Serristori Palazzo, built in the 15C; *(nos 21 and 22)* the early 17C Palazzo Antella decorated with frescoes and flanked *(left)* by an old similarly-corbelled house. In the Middle Ages the people of Florence used to gather in this square. It was the site chosen by all the great Franciscan preachers including St Bernard of Siena in the 15C. One of the tournaments held here, in which Giuliano, the brother of Lorenzo the Magnificent, was the winner, was immortalised by Poliziano in one of his poems. From the 16C onwards one of major events in Florence was staged in the square – the form of football *(calcio) (qv)* played in period costume. The game was discontinued at the end of the 18C but came back into fashion from 1930 onwards. Since 1986 the event has again been staged in the square *(see Calendar of Events in the Practical Information at the end of the guide)*.

This was one of the worst-affected districts during the 1966 floods and Santa Croce was one of the historic buildings of Florence which suffered most from the mud that reached a height of three metres inside the church and up to five metres in the cloisters.

★★ Church

Building began in 1394 and was completed in the second half of the 14C, except for the present belltower (the original belltower collapsed in the 16C) and the neo-Gothic west front which dates only from the 19C. This is the Franciscan Order's church in Florence. It is a huge building (140m – 455ft long and 40m – 130ft wide) because it was designed for preaching. It was built in a T-shape. The Florentine Gothic interior is remarkably elegant. The austerity of the architecture, the size of the nave compared to the aisles, the width of the arches separating one from the other, and the elongated lines of the apse in which the narrow stained-glass windows reach almost from floor to roof produce an impression of lightness and add to the overall sense of space within the building as a whole. The nave is roofed with fine painted rafters.

Because of the 276 gravestones set in the pavement and the lavish tombs contained in the church (most of them the tombs of famous men), Santa Croce has been nicknamed the "Italian Pantheon".

The west front includes a fine stained-glass window designed by Lorenzo Ghiberti.

Navata destra (South Aisle) – The highly decorative *Madonna and Child*, set in a mandorla surrounded by cherubim (1) *(against the first pillar)*, was carved in a flowing style by Antonio Rossellino in 1478 and surmounts the tomb of a famous person who was killed during the Pazzi Conspiracy *(qv)*. The tomb of Michelangelo (2) *(opposite)* who died in 1564 (Rome also laid claim to his body) was designed in 1570 by Vasari (the three female statues represent Painting, Sculpture and Architecture), who also designed the great *Climb to Calvary* (3) above the following altar. The memorial to Dante (4), who died in 1321 and is buried in Ravenna, dates from the 19C (on the left is an allegorical statue of Italy; on the right is Poetry).

The superb marble **pulpit★** was carved with scenes from the life of St Francis in 1476 by Benedetto da Maiano who depicted the Virtues beneath the narrative panels, in the form of very slender statuettes of women seated in niches separated by delightful, traceried brackets.

Beyond the pulpit is a monument (6) to Machiavelli (d 1572) dating from the late 18C. The allegorical figure representing Diplomacy, seated on the top of the sarcophagus and holding the portrait of the writer-statesman, is a reminder of his diplomatic missions.

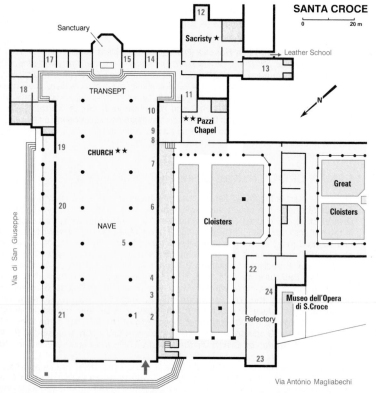

The famous **Annunciation**★★ (7) created by Donatello *c*1430 in *pietra serena* touched with gold
is one of the most harmonious examples of this
type of low relief, set in a frame in the shape of
a small classical temple. Such works *(tabernacoli*
in Italian) were first created in Florence during
the Renaissance period.

For the **tomb of Leonardo Bruni**★★ (8), a humanist
and chancellor of the Florentine Republic who
died in 1444, Bernardo Rossellino created a new
style of funereal architecture in the mid-15C and
it was then copied for a large number of tombs
during the Italian Renaissance. It consists of a
niche set hard up against the wall and formed
by two grooved pilasters linked by a rounded
arch, a Classical sarcophagus, bearing a sculpture
of the recumbent figure of the deceased, and a
tympanum decorated with a *Madonna and Child*
set in a medallion, cherubs carrying coats of
arms, and decorative foliage.

Annunciation by Donatello,
Santa Croce, Florence.

Beside it is Rossini's tomb (9) (he died in 1868)
and the tomb of Ugo Foscolo (1778-1827), one of the great poets of modern
Italy (10).

Transetto destro (South Transept) – The frescoes★ decorating the **Baroncelli Chapel** (11) were painted from 1332 to 1338 by Taddeo Gaddi, Giotto's main
follower. The Life of the Virgin Mary is depicted with amazing attention to
picturesque detail and unusual skill in the use of lighting effects (in particular
in the night-time scene when the shepherds are told of Christ's Birth) – *(top
to bottom and left to right)* Joachim being chased from the temple and the
angel's announcement to Joachim *(left wall)*; the meeting of Joachim and Anne
and the birth of the Virgin Mary *(below)*; Mary's presentation in the temple and
her wedding *(below)*; the Annunciation and the Visitation *(top of the end wall)*
with the angels appearing to the shepherds and the Nativity *(middle)* and *(lower
level)* the Magi being told of Christ's Birth and the Adoration of the Magi. On
the altar is a fine **polyptych**★ representing the Coronation of the Virgin Mary
painted in a rich palette of colours in Giotto's workshop.

★ **Sacrestia (Sacristy)** – A Renaissance doorway created by Michelozzo leads into
the sacristy, a fine 14C chamber which still has its painted rafters and one wall
covered with frescoes from the same period. A *Crucifixion* painted by Taddeo
Gaddi is flanked by a *Climb up to Calvary*, attributed to Spinello Aretino, and
by a *Resurrection* by Niccolo di Pietro Gerini.

Inside one of the inlaid cupboards (15C-16C) is a reliquary containing the habit
and belt of St Francis of Assisi.

The **Rinuccini Chapel** (12) *(opposite the door)* is closed off by a wrought-iron grille
and decorated with **frescoes**★ recounting the Life of the Virgin Mary *(left)* and
the life of Mary Magdalen *(right)*. The scenes were delicately drawn by Giovanni
da Milano, one of Lombardy's main artists in the 14C who became a citizen of
Florence. He sought to combine the solemnity of the medieval style with reality
as he saw it. Behind the altar is a superb Gothic polyptych.

Beyond the sacristy is a narrow passageway leading to the Leatherwork School.

Cappella dei Medici (Medici Chapel) (13) – *Closed but visible through a window
in the door*. This delightful chapel built by Michelozzo in 1434 contains a graceful
terracotta **reredos**★ glazed by Andrea della Robbia. It represents the Madonna
and Child with the saints, flanked by pilasters finely decorated with foliage and
surmounted by a cornice adorned with cherubim.

Cappella maggiore e cappelle adiacenti (Sanctuary and adjacent chapels) – The
chancel is flanked by ten small chapels. The Giugni Chapel (14) contains the tomb
of Julie Clary, Joseph Bonaparte's wife *(right)* and the tomb of their daughter
Charlotte Napoleon Bonaparte *(left)*. The **Bardi Chapel** (15) is decorated with the
admirable **Frescoes of the Life of St Francis**★★ (restored) which were painted *c*1320
by Giotto. He used subjects that had already been touched upon in his famous
frescoes in the basilica in Assisi; in some places his style was particularly
emotive – *(right)* the Trial by Fire in the presence of the Sultan *(upper section)*
and the visions of Brother Augustine and Bishop Guido of Assisi *(lower section)*,
and *(left)* the saint's appearance to St Anthony in the church in Arles *(upper
section)* and St Francis' death *(lower section)*, the scene which shows the most
tenderness and self-containment; *(on the altar)* a rollicking 13C painting on wood
depicting the saint surrounded by small pictures of episodes from his life.

The **sanctuary** (16) is decorated with **frescoes**★ telling the legend of the True Cross
in a lively and vivid manner. They were painted in 1380 in a late-Gothic style
by Agnolo Gaddi and were based on the Golden Legend.

The frescoes in the Pulci Chapel (17) were painted c1330 by Bernardo Daddi and his pupils - Martyrdom of St Lawrence *(right)* and Condemnation and Martyrdom of St Stephen *(left)*. The glazed terracotta statue *(above the altar)* of the *Madonna and Child between Mary Magdalen and St John the Evangelist*, is an ornate and very colourful piece of work that is typical of Giovanni della Robbia's style.

Transetto sinistro (North Transept) - The **Bardi Chapel** (18) contains the famous wooden **Crucifix**★★ by Donatello, a work so realistic that it shocked some of the artist's contemporaries. Brunelleschi wanted to surpass this work when he created his statue in Santa Maria Novella.

Navata sinistra (North Aisle) - The **Tomb of Carlo Marsuppini**★ (19), humanist and secretary to the Florentine Republic who died in 1453, brought fame to its sculptor, Desiderio da Settignano after he had carved it in 1455 using the style first developed for Leonardo Bruni's tomb by Bernardo Rossellino. Da Settignano's work, however, shows more sophistication and less rigour.

Lorenzo Ghiberti (d 1455) and his son, Vittorio, are buried opposite the fourth pillar (20).

Galileo's tomb (d 1642) was built in the 18C.

Chiostro (Cloisters)

These delightful 14C cloisters lead to the Pazzi Chapel *(at the end)* and the Santa Croce Museum *(to the right)*. The closed gallery *(left)*, which runs the entire length of the church, contains a large and varied number of gravestones and tombs.

★★Capella dei Pazzi (Pazzi Chapel)

This small chapel, one of the most exquisite of all Brunelleschi's designs, was built for the Pazzis *(qv)*, who were the main rivals of the Medici. The artist worked on the chapel until 1445, the year before his death, but it was not completed until c1460.

The portico is reminiscent of Classical triumphal arches because of its raised central arch, its Corinthian columns, and its entablature decorated with a frieze of medallions and divided off into sections with slim grooved pilasters. Above the door is a dome decorated with glazed terracotta by Luca della Robbia.

The interior is a masterpiece of Florentine Renaissance architecture owing to its unusual design, majestic proportions, purity of line and harmonious decoration. In this chapel Brunelleschi raised to perfection the architectural ideal that he had already expressed in the old sacristy in San Lorenzo *(qv)*. The layout is designed around a square with a ribbed central dome over pendentives. The rectangular apse is capped by a small circular dome. All the architectural features - pilasters, cornice, coving round the arches, pendentives, base and ribs on the dome - are emphasised by the grey of the *pietra serena* which stands out against the white pebble-dash in a manner that is strict yet elegant. A frieze of cherubim and mystic Lambs, and glazed terracotta medallions by Luca della Robbia representing the Apostles *(on the walls)* and the Evangelists *(in the pendentives)* add a note of colour to the otherwise austere, but harmonious, interior.

Chiostro Grande
(Great Cloisters)

A superb Renaissance doorway opens into the cloisters. The vast and elegantly-proportioned construction was designed by Brunelleschi shortly before his death and completed in 1453.

Medallions, which were probably created by Bernardo Rossellino, decorate the squinches on the light arcades below a wide, open gallery including slender columns.

Pazzi Chapel.

Museo dell'Opera di Santa Croce (Santa Croce Museum)

The old **refectory**, an elegant chamber with lancet windows and rafters, displays Cimabue's famous **Crucifixion**★ (22), which has been restored with exemplary care after the considerable damage it suffered during the floods in 1966. Although large parts of the work have been irremediably lost, it still radiates an intense dramatic power through the way in which the body bends and sags.

The end wall is covered by a huge fresco representing the Last Supper; above is the Tree of the Cross (23), painted in the 14C by Taddeo Gaddi. Among the other remarkable exhibits are a gilded bronze statue of St Louis of Toulouse (24) by Donatello *(left)* and small fragments of frescoes by Orcagna found on the wall of the church but which had been concealed by restoration work carried out in the 16C by Vasari – *(left)* are fragments of *Hell*; *(right panel 3)* is a group of beggars that was once part of the *Triumph of Death*; the beggars are calling on Death to relieve them of their suffering.

The rooms between the two cloisters contain underdrawings for frescoes *(sinopie)* and frescoes from the church, dating from the 14C and 15C. There are also a number of sculptures, including Tino da Camaino's tomb.

★★SANTA MARIA DEL CARMINE: FRESCOES IN THE BRANCACCI CHAPEL (BUV) ⊘

Tour – 15min; if the church is closed, the Brancacci Chapel can be reached from the cloisters to the right of the church.

What makes this church, which was ravaged by fire in the 18C, so interesting is the extraordinary series of **frescoes** decorating the walls of the Brancacci Chapel at the end of the south transept, one of the few parts of the building to have escaped fire damage. They were painted by three different artists and describe original sin and the life of St Peter; the latter subject was probably chosen because Florence had political links with the papacy.

Affreschi di Masolino da Panicale (frescoes) – Masolino was the first artist to be commissioned, in 1424, to undertake the decoration of the chapel built for the Brancacci, a family of silk merchants. Although the spirit of his work is still noticeably Gothic, as is obvious from his kindly, serene treatment of the subject matter, there is already an attempt to render perspective and volume. He was probably influenced in this respect by his pupil, Masaccio. On the upper section, he depicted the *Temptation of Adam and Eve* (VII), *St Peter raising Tabitha from the Dead* (VI), and *St Peter Preaching* (III).

Affreschi di Masaccio (frescoes) – This chapel is a fine example of the innovatory genius of this artist, who pointed the way forward to the Renaissance through his feeling for relief and expression. In 1427, when he was no more than 25 years old, shortly before his death in 1428, he created this set of frescoes that are now considered as one of the most consummate examples of Italian painting in existence.

In his famous painting of **Adam and Eve being expelled from Paradise** (I), symmetrically opposite the *Temptation* painted by Masolino, he totally excluded idealism in order to express, with poignant intensity, the shame and despair of the figures. The light projected onto the scene and the splashes of shadow that conceal certain parts of the bodies and faces add to the dramatic effect and accentuate the impression of relief, giving the figures a striking reality.

The **Payment of the Tax** (II) depicts the Apostles as vigorous figures radiating supreme gravity. The fresco includes three episodes, reduced to their main elements. They show

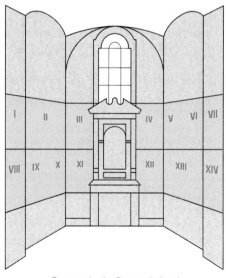

Frescoes in the Brancacci chapel in Santa Maria del Carmine.

St Peter curing a sick man by Masaccio
(the two figures on the right are by Masolino).

the tax-collector *(rear view)* at the Capernaum Gate, demanding payment of the toll from Jesus who is showing Peter the water in which he will find the fish with the silver coin in its mouth *(central scene)*. The Apostle takes hold of the fish *(left)*, then hands the coin over to the tax-collector *(right)*.

Another fresco depicts *St Peter baptising the newcomers* (IV) and *St Peter curing a sick man* (V). This scene was painted with Masolino whose regular, more anecdotal style is obvious in the two elegant figures crossing the square.

The subjects treated by Masaccio *(on the lower register)* are *St Peter and St John giving alms* (XII), *St Peter curing the sick by the sole power of his shadow* (XI); *St Peter on the episcopal throne*.

Affreschi di Filippino Lippi (frescoes) – The decoration of the chapel was still incomplete by the time Masaccio left for Rome (he died in 1428). It was completed in 1481 by Filippino Lippi who painted the following scenes in an elegant style *(on the lower section of the wall)*: *St Paul visiting St Peter in prison in Antioch* (VIII); *St Peter raising the Son of Theophilus, Prefect of Antioch, from the dead* (IX), a fresco which had been started by Masaccio; *St Peter set free by an Angel during his second term of imprisonment in Jerusalem* (XIV) and *St Peter being brought before Agrippa* and *The Crucifixion of St Peter* (XIII).

★★PASSEGGIATA AI COLLI (SOUTH BANK HILLSIDE ROUTE)

This trip (about 1 hour) is best done by car or bus ⊘, preferably in the morning, starting from Piazza F Ferrucci (FV) and returning via Porta Romana (CV) – see plan of Florence above.

The splendid hillside route (Viale dei Colli), which is sub-divided into Viale Michelangiolo (at the east end), Viale Galileo (in the middle) and Viale Machiavelli (at the west end), overlooks Florence from the south bank. It was built between 1865 and 1870 and its superb route was selected by the architect Giuseppe Poggi who was in charge of urban improvement during the brief spell when Florence was the capital of the Kingdom of Italy. The road, which is lined with luxurious mansions, wends its way in wide curves across the hillside between two majestic rows of pines and cypresses.

Piazzale Michelangiolo (EFV)

See the Practical Information at the beginning of this chapter.

From this vast esplanade overlooking the city, there is a magnificent **panoramic view**★★★ – *(right to left)* Santa Croce in the foreground; further left and set slightly further back, the dome of the cathedral and the belltower; in front of them the belltower of the Badia and the tower on the Bargello; on the river bank the Palazzo Vecchio and Ponte Vecchio; spread out like a backdrop behind the city are the Apennine Mountains.

The memorial to Michelangelo, erected in 1875 in the centre of the square, is decorated with copies of some of the artist's most famous statues.

★★ San Miniato al Monte
(EFV)

From Piazzale Michelangiolo continue uphill away from the city along Via Galileo (part of Viale dei Colli); a steep flight of steps leads up to the church (left).

The church of San Miniato was built in an outstandingly beautiful **setting**★★ overlooking Florence, at the top of a wide flight of

---

Masaccio (1401-1428) or the introduction of volume in painting

Masaccio died prematurely at the age of 27 after travelling to Rome with Donatello and Brunelleschi. He was to painting what his two friends were to sculpture and architecture. From the former, he acquired a taste for powerful figures, realistic expressions and heavy draped clothing; from the latter, he learned about perspective which he then applied not only to illustrations of buildings but also to human figures as in his frescoes in S Maria Novella *(qv)*. He discovered that light contained sculptural resources and concentrated on giving volume to his figures and improving his spatial layout, leaving aside the grace, ornamentation and excessive detail of the Gothic style. He paved the way for the Renaissance style in painting and his works had a huge impact on successive generations because of their lifelike realism.

---

steps commissioned by Poggi. It is flanked by a delightful graveyard from which there is a view of the countryside laid out like a picture – *(left)* the Boboli Gardens laid out on the hill below the Belvedere Fort which is distinguished by its 14C fortifications.

A Benedictine monastery was founded here in the 11C and its church is one of the finest examples of Florentine Romanesque architecture. It was built in memory of **St Minias** who fell victim to the persecutions ordered in 250 AD by the Roman Emperor Decius. Minias, probably a Tuscan of humble origins who, according to popular belief, was a king from Armenia, had already miraculously

San Miniato al Monte.

SCALA

173

escaped a number of executions. When he had finally been beheaded, he crossed the River Arno holding his head in his hands, returning to die on the hillside where he had lived as a hermit (then known as Mons Florentinus).

Exterior – The 12C **west front** is exceptionally elegant and is reminiscent of the Baptistery. It is decorated with geometric motifs picked out in green and white marble, semicircular arcarding, and a small window beneath a triangular pediment; it has the same Classical features, the same grace and the same balance, which are typical of the Florentine Romanesque style. The upper section is decorated with a 13C mosaic (Christ between the Virgin Mary and St Minias) which has been restored. At the tip of the triangle is an eagle perched on a bale of wool, the emblem of the guild of linen-drapers who were responsible for the administration of the church for many years.

On the left is the belltower, designed in the 16C by Baccio d'Agnolo but never finished. Michelangelo, who was commissioned to add fortifications to the hillside, decided to use the tower as a base for artillery when Florence was besieged in 1530 by the troops of Charles V in an attempt to re-establish the Medici who had been ousted from power. This is why the tower became the target of enemy cannon fire and was encased in a thick layer of wool for protection. The Bishop's Palace *(right)* dates from the end of the 13C.

Interior – Like the west front, the interior is remarkable for the pleasing geometric combination of green and white marble. It is laid out like a basilica (rectangle ending in a semi-circle, nave rising higher than the aisles and lit from the clerestory, no transept); the chancel is raised above a vast crypt. The nave is covered by wooden rafters, which were painted in the 14C and have undergone extensive restoration since. It is divided by huge transversal arches supported by green marble pillars. The other columns separating the nave from the aisles were given fake marble cladding in the late 19C. The superb pavement (1207), inset with white and black marble, is like a piece of lace.

The tiny **Crucifix Chapel** shaped like a tabernacle stands at the chancel step and was built in 1447 on the orders of Pietro I to designs by Michelozzo. Its purpose was to house a miraculous Crucifix. The glazed terracotta coffering decorating the roof is by Luca della Robbia. Agnolo Gaddi painted the panels above the altar in the late 14C. In the centre, dressed in red, is St Minias.

The **Chapel of the Cardinal of Portugal★** which was built in the 15C opens off the north aisle and is a fine example of Renaissance architecture, designed by one of Brunelleschi's pupils. It houses the tomb of James of Lusitania, Archbishop of Lisbon and nephew of the King of Portugal, who died in Florence in 1459. The work is graceful if rather stiff and was created in 1461 by the sculptor Antonio Rossellino. In the niche opposite the sculpture is a delicate *Annunciation* (restored) painted by Alesso Baldovinetti. The painting on the altar is a copy of a work by the Pollaiolo brothers, now kept in the Uffizi. The vaulting in the chapel is covered with glazed terracotta by Luca della Robbia and depicts the dove of the Holy Ghost and the cardinal virtues in a remarkable toning palette of blues.

The **pulpit,** and the **choir screen** against which it stands, form a superb **set of furnishings★★** including some magnificent craftwork with inlays of white, green and pink marble dating from the early 13C.

Above the **apse** is a huge late 13C mosaic representing Christ giving His Benediction. He is flanked by the Virgin Mary and St Minias.

In the **sacristy,** Spinello Aretino painted **frescoes★** (restored) in 1387 in a style reminiscent of that of Giotto; they illustrate the *Legend of St Benedict*. The **crypt** includes seven aisles separated by a multitude of wonderful, slender columns crowned by Classical capitals. The altar contains the remains of St Minias.

The drive along the hillside on the south bank then continues through a series of sweeping curves to the Porta Romana.

Forte del Belvedere ⊘

Some 2km – 1 mile from the Piazzale Michelangiolo turn right into a narrow one-way road which eventually descends to Lungarno Torrigiani quay. Pedestrians wishing to climb up to the Fort on foot should start from this quay.

The fortress, and the elegant villa above it, were built in the late 16C to plans by Buontalenti for the Medici who wanted to ensure that their mansions were defended and that they had a retreat in case of unrest. The splendid **panoramic view★★** from the glacis provided many painters with inspiration. To the north is the city. To the south the scenery is steeped in harmony and typical of the famous Tuscan countryside. There are hills capped with a tower, a villa or a mansion with merlons, and vast fields of olive trees where the subtle silvery shades seem to soften outlines which are sometimes emphasised by the dark clear-cut rows of cypress trees.

175

OLD STREETS AND HOUSES

Limited museum opening times (often mornings only) or a desire simply to take a stroll and drink in the charms of a Renaissance city left unscathed by the building projects of subsequent centuries, often lead tourists to wander through the streets in search of vistas that have remained almost unchanged since they were first created. For those wishing to put architectural details into their historical context, the following summary provides a few basic principles which will help them to appreciate the true value of famous historic landmarks and can also give them an insight into the importance of the many otherwise anonymous façades which create the picturesque harmony of Florence.

The 13C : a forgotten period – The economic boom that began in the 13C led to numerous wooden structures being replaced with stone buildings, although **medieval Florentine houses** were still designed to meet the same requirements – the ground floor constituted the workplace (workshop or shop) and the family lived on the upper storeys, which could be increased if and when more space was needed. The nobility, who began arriving in the city from their estates in the 11C, habitually commissioned the building of **towers** based, in the early days at least, on the design of their castle keeps. Common interests then brought these nobles and members of the wealthy middle classes from the same district together in "tower communities" which strongly defended each other if they came under attack or fell into dispute with a rival clan. Their towers (up to 70m – 230ft high) were interconnected by external wooden galleries. The political upheavals of the 13C led to the destruction of a number of these towers, first those of the Guelfs from 1260 onwards and then, after the victorious return of the Guelfs *(qv)* in 1266, those of their enemy the Ghibellines *(qv)* (there were said to have been 150 in Florence). Very few towers have survived to the present day (apart from their bases which were often used as the foundations for new buildings) particularly as their height was gradually subject to legislation. From the 14C onwards, the noblemen abandoned their towers in favour of more elegant mansions.

The 14C or Late Middle Ages – The **traditional 14C palazzo** was still capped with battlements and consisted of four main buildings surrounding a courtyard *(cortile)* from which an outside staircase led to the upper storeys. On the street front the upper floors were separated by a narrow cornice which, for aesthetic purposes, was set on a level with the window ledges rather than the floors as this gave greater emphasis to the windows. No particular attention, however, was paid to the regularity and symmetry of the façades – Palazzo Vecchio *(qv)* and Palazzo Davanzati *(qv)* – nor was any attempt made to conceal the bonding and this gave the residences a fortress-like appearance.

As in previous centuries, some of the buildings retained a corbelled upper section supported by a row of semicircular arches.

The ground floor or one corner of the mansion was often used for the family's business activities and was therefore built with a **loggia**. Many of the loggias were walled up during the following century. Sometimes a loggia was sited nearby rather than incorporated into the walls of the palazzo.

The 15C : pride in harmony – The leading families of the 15C took advantage of their recently-amassed fortunes and a period of greater peace to build themselves new residences to match their reputation; for the sake of pride, however, they purposely avoided ostentatious façades. Their **mansions** usually consisted of three storeys, still divided by narrow cornices. The ground floor contained small square windows and one or more large doorways, whereas the two upper floors were built with majestic arched windows divided by mullions or colonnettes. As in the previous century, the windows were supported by intermediate cornices. Classical features were introduced, including super-imposed pilasters (Palazzo Rucellai) or imposing terminal cornices (Palazzo Medici and Palazzo Strozzi).

Some buildings retained the traditional heavily-rusticated stonework throughout the façade (Strozzi and Pitti Palaces); on others, it was restricted to the ground floor, with the masonry becoming gradually smoother on the upper storeys (Palazzo Medici and Palazzo Gondi). As in previous centuries, windows were faced with stone.

Just as the street fronts complied with rules of symmetry and well-balanced proportions, so emphasis was placed on the harmony of the inner courtyard. The staircase was located inside one of the main buildings, which meant that all four sides of the courtyard could be embellished with regular colonnades in the style of cloisters. Some of the mansions began to have their own gardens.

A time of limited change – In the 16C, when the Roman Renaissance style was fashionable, windows became rectangular and were surmounted by rounded or triangular pediments *(Palazzo Larderel in Via Tornabuoni)*, the rusticated

The Florentine Palazzo

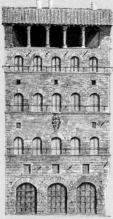

Palazzo Davanzati (14C).

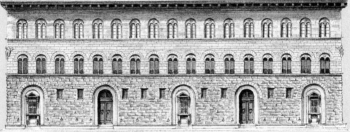

Palazzo Medici-Riccardi (1444-1459).

Palazzo Rucellai (1446-1451).

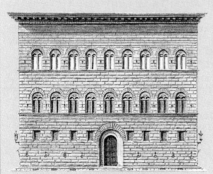

Palazzo Strozzi (1489-1504).

Palazzo Bartolini-Salimbeni
(1517-1520).

stonework gave way to smooth walls (at least for the upper storeys) and stretches of wall without doors or windows were decorated with niches *(Palazzo Bartolini Salimbeni in Piazza S Trinità),* engaged columns or pilasters *(Palazzo Uguccioni in Piazza della Signoria).*

Over the next few centuries, owing to a decline in the influence of Florence, the city centre at least was saved from new building projects and the old architectural heritage was preserved.

As it would take too long to describe the many façades worthy of interest in detail, we have listed a few streets which contain varied examples of Florentine residences.

Piazza della Signoria (Z) : **Palazzo Vecchio★★★**, late 13C.

Piazza Santa Trinità (Z 163) : **Palazzo Bartolini-Salimbeni** (1517-1520) *(on the corner of Via delle Terme)* designed by Baccio d'Agnolo with fine mullioned windows.

Via Tornabuoni (Z) :

no 2, **Palazzo Spini-Ferroni★** *(on the corner of the quay)* crenellated 13C

no 3, **Palazzo Tornabuoni-Beacci** *(almost on Piazza Santa Trinità),* fine 14C mansion

no 7, **Palazzo Strozzi★★**, 15C *(see below)*

no 7, **Palazzo dello Strozzino** *(past Piazza Strozzi)* apparently a smaller replica (hence its name) of its prestigious neighbour, although it is an earlier building (begun in 1458 by Michelozzo, first storey by Giuliano da Maiano completed during the early 1460s

no 19 (blue), **Palazzo Larderel**, built by Dosio in 1580, windows capped with pediments.

Piazza degli Antinori *(north end of Via Tornabuoni)* (Y 10) : no 3, **Palazzo Antinori** (1461-1466) attributed to Giuliano da Sangallo and demonstrating the survival of certain 14C features well into 15C.

Via della Vigna Nuova (Z 193) : no 16, **Palazzo Rucellai★★**, mid-15C *(see below).*

Borgo Santi Apostoli (Z) :

no 10, **Acciaiuoli Houses**, 15C

no 8, **Palazzo Acciaiuoli★** (formerly **Buondelmonti**) dating from 14C with an adjacent 13C tower

no 17-19, **Palazzo Usimbardi**, 16C

no 9, **Palazzo Buondelmonti**, 14C-15C with restorations.

Via delle Terme (Z 181) : old tower-houses.

Via del Fiordaliso (Z 52) *(leading to the Borgo SS Apostoli)* : some interesting corbelled houses.

Via Porta Rossa (Z) :

Palazzo Torrigiani (Porta Rossa House) (14C), a rare example of a mansion with corbelled upper storeys.

Palazzo Davanzati★, 14C *(see Museo della casa fiorentina antica below).*

Piazza Davanzati (Z 43) : a fine truncated tower-house.

Piazza di Parte Guelfa (Z 106) : **Palazzo di Parte Guelfa**, 14C *(see description below under Mercato Nuovo).*

Piazza dei Giudici (Z) : **Palazzo Castellani**, 14C *(see description below under Science History Museum).*

Via dei Gondi (Z 61) : **Palazzo Gondi★** *(corner of Piazza S Firenze),* major work by Giuliano da Sangallo (1490).

Via della Condotta (Z) : old tower-houses.

Via del Proconsolo (Z) :

Palazzo del Bargello★, second half of 13C *(see above)*

no 10 *(corner of Borgo degli Albizzi)* **Palazzo Pazzi★** (late 15C) with twin windows.

Via del Corso (Z) : no 6, **Palazzo Portinari** (named after the family of the young Beatrice, Dante's sweetheart; it is now the head office of the Banca Toscana), 16C **interior courtyard★** (refurbished).

Via Cavour (Y) : **Palazzo Medici-Riccardi★★**, 15C *(see below).*

Via dei Servi (Y) : no 15, **Palazzo Niccolini★**, built *c*1550 to plans by Baccio d'Agnolo.

Piazza dei Pitti (DV 117) : **Palazzo Pitti★★**, central section dating from 15C *(see above).*

Via Maggio (Z) : no 26, **Palazzo di Bianca Cappello★** *(qv),* built during the second half of the 16C by Buontalenti; the inscription on the façade is by Poccetti.

Piazza Santo Spirito (DV 159) *(south-east corner)* : **Palazzo Guadagni★** surmounted by a splendid loggia (1503) and attributed to Baccio d'Agnolo or Simone del Pollaiolo known as *Il Cronaca.*

★ Museo della Casa fiorentina antica (Old Florentine House Museum) (Z M²) ⊙ : The museum is housed on the three floors of the **Davanzati Palace★**, a narrow, towering residence built in the 14C for a rich wool merchant and purchased in the 16C

SCALA

Dining Room, Palazzo Davanzati.

by the historian and man of letters, Bernardo Davanzati. It was at this time that the typical loggia at the top of the building was added beneath the overhanging roof.

The building was superbly restored at the turn of the century and it contains a splendid collection of furniture (mainly Florentine or Tuscan from the 14C, 15C and 16C), tapestries, paintings, sculptures, ceramics, everyday objects and fabrics most of which originate from the Bargello. The museum, part of which still dates from medieval times, provides a vivid insight into what a rich Florentine residence would have looked like during the Renaissance period – with its narrow, majestic courtyard flanked on either side by vaulted galleries, its steep flights of stairs closed off by doors, the well supplying water to every floor, and the painted decoration of the rooms imitating tapestries or familiar scenes against backgrounds of arcades and orchards.

The museum also has a collection of lace, mainly from northern Europe, exhibited in two rooms on the first floor.

The first and second floors each comprise a dining room, bed chamber, lavatory and great hall – the hall on the first floor was used for family gatherings such as weddings, funerals etc, while the room on the second floor was reserved for the mistress of the house and contains a large Davanzati family tree. Most of the objects in the kitchen on the third floor date from the 16C. The furniture is 17C – a cereal-hulling machine *(left of the first window)*; a loom *(far end of the room)* that was used to weave swaddling clothes for new-born babies and a 17C broom *(corner opposite the entrance)* from the Monastery of San Marco.

★★ **Palazzo Rucellai** (Z) – *18 Via della Vigna Nuova*. The mansion, built between 1446 and 1451 by Bernardo Rossellino to plans by Leon Battista Alberti, was constructed for Giovanni Rucellai, a member of a leading Florentine family. The Rucellai were related to the Strozzi and Medici and owed their name and fortune to imports from the Orient of a lichen, Rocella *(oricella)*, used to produce red dye. Their family emblem, a sail billowing in the wind, is depicted on a frieze on the first floor, on the loggia opposite and in Santa Maria Novella.

The mansion is the first example since Antiquity of a **façade** articulated by three orders superimposed. A rigorous sense of uniformity is created vertically by the alignment of pilasters and horizontally by the cornices that run along the top of each storey. The windows are set within these grid-like divisions against a background of slightly-rusticated stonework which contrasts greatly with the heavy rustication on the ground floor of the Palazzo Medici and throughout the façade of the Palazzo Strozzi which dates from a later period.

One section of the ground floor houses the **Museo di storia della fotografia Fratelli Alinari** (History of Photography Museum) ⊙ which specialises in temporary exhibitions. Opposite stands the **loggia (G)** that accompanied every notable family's residence. It is also attributed to Leon Battista Alberti. Although the bays are walled up, they have retained a certain elegance.

★★ **Palazzo Strozzi** (Z) – This was the last of the great private mansions to be built during the Florentine Renaissance and it represents one of the period's finest achievements in terms of vernacular architecture.

A rich merchant named Filippo Strozzi commissioned Benedetto da Maiano, architect and sculptor, to design the building. By the time the patron symbolically laid the first stone of his residence on the 6 August 1489, the mansion of his rivals, the Medici – from which the Palazzo Strozzi draws much of its inspiration – had already been in existence for 30 years. In 1490, the year before he died, when building work had only just started, Filippo Strozzi commissioned another Florentine, Giuliano da Sangallo, to produce a scale model of his future residence. It was, however, a third architect, Simone di Pollaiolo, otherwise known as *Il Cronaca,* who eventually took charge of the work.

Cronaca is responsible for the splendid stone cornice at the very top of the building; its huge overhang and weight made it a feat of considerable technical prowess. Only part of the cornice, however, was completed, along the two sides of the building that overlook Piazza degli Strozzi and Via degli Strozzi.

The building was finished in 1504 and remained in the Strozzi family until 1937. It then underwent major restoration before becoming the headquarters of various cultural institutes; it is now also the venue for the Biennial International Antiques Fair *(qv)*.

In contrast to the Palazzo Medici, where the typical rusticated stonework gives way to a gradually smoother surface on the upper storeys, here it covers the whole of the façade. Each storey includes a row of austere twin windows beneath curved pediments.

The stately, elegant **courtyard** *(entrance in Piazza degli Strozzi)*, surrounded by a high portico and overlooked by an open loggia on the upper floor in the Florentine tradition, is the work of Cronaca.

★ **Mercato Nuovo (New Market Loggia)** (Z K) – In the 16C Cosimo I ordered the construction of this loggia with elegant Renaissance arcades in a district that had been occupied by traders and merchants since the Middle Ages. Its name, Mercato Nuovo (New Market), distinguished it from the old medieval market-place which once stood nearby but was demolished in the late 19C during the construction of Piazza della Repubblica *(qv)*. The loggia now houses a market selling Florentine craftwork including souvenirs, embroidery, lace, leather goods, *pietra dura* ware and gilded and painted wooden items.

At the edge of the building, on the side facing the Arno, stands the Porcellino ("piglet") Fountain. It was so named by the people of Florence on account of the bronze boar produced in the early 17C by Pietro Tacca and inspired by the Classical marble sculpture exhibited in the Uffizi *(qv)*. The bottom of the basin is strewn with coins that tourists traditionally throw into the fountain while making the wish that they may one day return to Florence.

Standing with its back to the Porcellino on the opposite righthand corner is the **Palazzo di Parte Guelfa** (Palace of the Guelf Party Captains) (L). Its façade overlooking Piazza di Parte Guelfa dates from the 14C and is adorned with a picturesque covered outdoor staircase. The extension to the rear was built in the 15C to plans by Brunelleschi.

RELIGIOUS BUILDINGS

★ **Santissima Annunziata (Annunciation)** (ET) – This is the name of one of the prettiest squares in Florence and of one of the Florentine people's most beloved churches.

★ **The Square** – Renaissance arcades run along three sides of this elegant square. At the far end *(approaching from the south)* stands the tall church porch and *(right)* the famous elevated portico of the Foundling Hospital. The portico of the Order of the Servants of Mary *(left)* was built to the same design by Antonio da Sangallo the Elder and Baccio d'Agnolo in the early 16C.

In the middle of the square stands a bronze equestrian statue of Ferdinando I, the last work to be produced by Giovanni da Bologna. The square is also adorned with two delightful Baroque fountains made in 1629 by Pietro Tacca, who also worked on the completion of the equestrian statue that his master had left unfinished when he died suddenly in 1608.

Church ⊘ – The church was built in 1250 for the Order of the Servants of Mary, founded in the 13C by St Filippo Benizzi, who was also a founder of the Convent of Monte Senario *(qv)* north of Florence. It was rebuilt in the 15C in the Renaissance style by Michelozzo.

It is preceded by cloisters *(Chiostrino dei Voti)*, surrounded by a portico and covered with a glass roof, which was built between 1447 and 1452; its decoration was begun in 1460 and continued sporadically over some 50 years. The **frescoes★** had suffered from the passage of time but have now been restored. The cycle *(right of the entrance)* relates to the Virgin Mary *(beginning with her death)* –

The Assumption by Rosso Fiorentino and *The Visitation* by Pontormo; *The Marriage of the Virgin Mary (on the following wall)* by Franciabigio in which the Virgin Mary's face is said to have been destroyed by the artist himself; a small marble Madonna and Child *(next)* carved by Michelozzo and *The Birth of the Virgin Mary* by Andrea del Sarto, a splendid painting treated as an intimist scene but conveying a deep sense of nobility; *The Arrival of the Magi (flanking the door leading into the church)* also by del Sarto and *The Nativity* by Alessio Baldovinetti, set against a large, simple background. The life of St Filippo Benizzi *(last two walls)* is a cycle painted mainly by Andrea del Sarto.

The inside of the church has a more Roman than Florentine feel and was lavishly renovated in the Baroque style during the 17C; the sumptuous coffered ceiling dates from this period.

The marble chapel *(left after entering the church)* in the form of a small temple *(tempietto)* was built to plans by Michelozzo and designed to house the miraculous picture of the *Virgin of the Annunciation* which was said to have been completed by an angel after its artist fell asleep.

The choir in the form of a rotunda with nine radiating chapels is capped by a dome of impressive proportions compared to the building *(to reach the dome follow the signs in the north transept to Sagrestia and Confessioni)*. The Lady chapel, which was altered by Giovanni da Bologna to receive his own tomb, contains a bronze Crucifix of his own design. The large *Resurrection (next chapel on the left)* was painted *c*1550 by Bronzino.

The two separate frescoes *(last two chapels in the north aisle)* are by Andrea del Castagno – the *Trinity (first)*, a strikingly realistic work and *St Julian and the Saviour (second)*.

The **Cloisters of the Deceased** *(entrance in the north transept or by the doorway in the front of the church on the lefthand side beneath the porch)* are in the Renaissance style. The door *(at the end of the gallery opposite the street)* is surmounted by a famous fresco by Andrea del Sarto *(under glass)*, the *Rest during the Flight into Egypt* (1525), known more familiarly as **The Virgin of the Sack**★ because of the magnificent sack on which St Joseph is leaning. The chapel of the Brotherhood of St Luke *(further along in the next gallery)*, which belonged to an association founded in the 14C by Florentine artists, is the burial place of Benvenuto Cellini, Pontormo and Franciabigio among others.

★ **Ospedale degli Innocenti** (Foundling Hospital) (ETU) – The Foundling Hospital, one of the city's most popular institutions, was built in the early 15C to designs by Brunelleschi. The buildings are slightly elevated above the square and in front of them stands an elegant **portico**★★ consisting of nine semicircular arches set on very slender columns. This work was the first attempt to demonstrate the new theories formulated by Brunelleschi, and it marked the beginning of the era of great architectural achievements created during the Italian Renaissance. In 1463 Andrea della Robbia decorated the arches with a frieze of touchingly fresh **medallions**★★ depicting infants in swaddling clothes. The tiny window *(left beneath the portico)*, which is now walled up and surrounded by a large door frame, recalls the wheel where, for four centuries until 1875, children were abandoned anonymously.

Foundling Hospital by Brunelleschi.

R. Mazin/TOP

The clear, harmonious geometry of the small inner courtyard was also the work of Brunelleschi. The door at the end of the gallery on the left of the entrance is surmounted by Andrea della Robbia's graceful, flowing **Annunciation★**, a statue made of blue and white glazed terracotta.

The **art gallery** ⊙ *(second floor)* specialises mainly in 14C-17C religious paintings. In the great hall *(right of the entrance)* are **The Coronation of the Virgin Mary**, a fine composition in warm tones (15C) by Neri di Bicci, and *The Madonna and Child* by Filippo Lippi. In the small adjoining room *(end wall)* hangs a huge **Adoration of the Magi** (1488) by Domenico Ghirlandaio; the background is bristling with detail, including splendid landscapes and a Massacre of the Innocents echoed in the foreground by two small victims praying to the Virgin Mary. The fine *Virgin Mary with Saints (right wall)* painted in brilliant colours is by Piero di Cosimo; beside it is an enamelled terracotta *Madonna and Child* by Luca della Robbia.

★ **Orsanmichele (Z N)** ⊙ – This unusually-shaped church occupies a building that was initially a loggia used as a grain store. The loggia was partly destroyed by fire in 1304 and was rebuilt in 1337 in a delicate and elaborate transitional Gothic-Renaissance style. In the late 14C the arcades were walled up and the height of the building was raised so that it could be used as a chapel. The upper storey, however, continued to be used until the 16C for the storage of food in case of famine. In 1569 Cosimo I set up the Deeds Office on the first floor. He also commissioned Buontalenti, the architect, to construct an arched passage above street level between the rear of the building and the mansion of the Linen Merchants' Guild *(Arte della Lana)*, in order to provide an access without having to pass through the chapel.

Orsanmichele takes its name from a much older church dedicated to St Michael which stood on this site near vegetable gardens *(orti)* in the 8C.

The **external** niches round the building are occupied by statues of the patron saints of the various guilds *(Arti)*, which form a veritable museum of 14C-16C Florentine sculpture. On the side in Via de' Calzaiuoli *(from left to right)* are a bronze statue of *St John the Baptist* cast in 1416 by Lorenzo Ghiberti for the Drapers' Guild, a bronze group for which Verrocchio was commissioned in 1484 by the Merchant's Court depicting the *Disbelief of St Thomas (missing)* and a bronze figure of *St Luke* made in 1562 by Giovanni da Bologna for the Guild of Judges and Notaries. On the side in Via Orsanmichele were *St Peter (missing)* carved in marble by Donatello in 1413 for the Butchers' Guild, *St Philip* (1410, *missing*) made for the Shoemakers, a group of four saints (1408) produced by Nanni di Banco for the Master Stoneworkers and Woodworkers and a copy of the famous St George by Donatello *(original in the Bargello)* created in 1416 for the Armour Merchants and Sword Cutlers. On the side in Via dell'Arte della Lana are the bronze statues of *St Matthew* and *St Stephen* produced by Ghiberti, the first in 1422 for the Money Changers and the second for the Wool Merchants in 1426, and *St Eligius* (1416, *missing*) by Nanni di Banco for the Blacksmiths. On the side in Via dei Lamberti are *St Mark* (1411-1413) by Donatello, *St James (missing)* carved in marble for the Furriers' Guild, a Madonna and Child known as the *Madonna of the Rose* (1399) made for the Physicians and Apothecaries and a bronze figure of *St John the Evangelist* cast by Baccio da Montelupo for the Silk Merchants in 1515.

The **interior** is a simple rectangular hall divided into two aisles of three bays by square pillars supporting semicircular arches. It contains a splendid Gothic **tabernacle★★** (a kind of ciborium), begun in 1349 by **Andrea Orcagna**, architect, painter, sculptor and goldsmith, one of the leading figures of 14C Tuscan art. On its base, which is decorated with polychrome marble, mosaics, bronze and gold, and round the edges are eight delightful low reliefs depicting the Life of the Virgin Mary *(lighting to the right in front of the tabernacle)*. In the centre of the vaulting are rings which date from the days when the building was used as a corn store.

★ **Chiesa di Santo Spirito (DUV)** – This Renaissance church designed by Brunelleschi is situated at the end of a peaceful, shady square off the main tourist track. Building began in 1444 and had not progressed very far when the great man died two years later. Construction work continued until 1487 using the original plans, although a number of changes were made.

The modest façade covered with light rendering and the south side with its three tiers of structural features do not figure in Brunelleschi's plans, but are nevertheless fairly harmonious constructions.

The solemnity of the interior forms a stark contrast with the simplicity of the exterior and is in many respects reminiscent of the church of San Lorenzo – same contrasting colours created by the use of "pietra serena" emphasising the architectural lines against the light rendering, same full semicircular arches, same purity of lines, same geometrical ordering of space. In this church, however, the arcades separating the nave from the aisles extend in an unbroken line around the transept and flat chevet, accentuating the effect of unity and creating numerous perspectives. Supporting the arches are magnificent mono-lithic columns with Corinthian capitals surmounted by a high entablature. The building includes 38 small semicircular chapels which, according to Brunelleschi's plans, were doubtless intended to be visible from the outside. The chapels open into the aisles through arches of the same height as those in the nave and it is this that gives the church its remarkably spacious character.

Santo Spirito contains numerous **works of art★** – *(third chapel in the south transept)* a naïve *Madonna of Succour* barring the path of a glowing red, cloven-hoofed devil, by an unknown 15C Florentine painter; *(fifth chapel in the south transept)* a delightful painting by Filippino Lippi depicting, against a picturesque landscape background, a **Madonna and Child** and the young St John between St Catherine of Alexandria and St Martin presenting the donor and his wife; *(first chapel in the apse)* a *Virgin surrounded by Saints* by Lorenzo di Credi; *(second chapel in the apse)* a polyptych by Maso di Banco (an early 14C Florentine painter, who studied under Giotto) portraying the Madonna and Child between four saints; *(fifth chapel in the apse)* an elegant painting by Alessandro Allori depicting the episode of the *Adulteress*; *(penultimate chapel in the apse)* a delicate *Annunciation* by an anonymous 15C Florentine artist; *(at the far end of the north transept)* the **Corbinelli Chapel** containing an ornate carved marble reredos dating from the early 16C by Andrea Sansovino.

The splendid **sacristy★** *(entrance in north aisle by the door next to the second chapel)* is a monumental construction designed in 1489 by Giuliano da Sangallo in the spirit of Brunelleschi's designs. It is preceded by an impressive columned vestibule roofed with a deep barrel vault with carved panelling that was completed in 1495 by Cronaca, the architect of the Palazzo Strozzi.

Cenacolo (Old Refectory) ⊘ – *Left of the church – no 29*. The fine Gothic hall with bare rafters is the former refectory of the Augustinian friary adjoining the church. One of its walls is covered by a large *Crucifixion*, a fresco painted *c*1360, and the remains of the *Last Supper (above)*, which are attributed to Andrea Orcagna and Nardo di Cione.

The refectory also displays sculptures dating from the pre-Romanesque to the Baroque periods – two 13C sea-lions *(beneath the main fresco)*; a polychrome relief of the *Madonna and Child* by a pupil of Jacopo Della Quercia *(opposite the entrance)*; a 15C surround of a well *(centre of the room)*; a marble basin supported by a tortoise made by Ammannati (16C) *(against the wall opposite the well)*; and *The Adoring Angel* by Tino di Camaino, a high relief dating from *c*1320, and a quadrangular basin with Cross (6C); a low relief *(end wall)* of *St Maximus* by Donatello.

One of the cafés in the square (lefthand side) *in front of the church has a large constantly-changing exhibition of photographs illustrating the façade of Santo Spirito from every imaginable aspect – from the eccentric to the highly colourful and exciting.*

Santa Trinità (Holy Trinity Church) (Z) – The church was built in the second half of the 14C. The Baroque façade by Buontalenti was added in the late 16C.

The extremely austere, slender interior is a fine example of the beginnings of Gothic architecture in Florence. The façade of the Romanesque church built in the 11C can be seen incorporated into the current façade. It was revealed by restoration work carried out at the end of the last century.

The chapels contain some interesting works of art. The *Madonna in Majesty with Saints (third chapel in the south aisle)* is a 15C altarpiece by Neri di Bicci. The **Chapel of the Annunciation★** *(fourth chapel)*, enclosed by a fine 15C screen and decorated with Lorenzo Monaco's frescoes recounting the Life of the Virgin Mary, contains a fine Gothic altarpiece by the same artist depicting the Annunciation; the predella includes the Visitation, the Nativity, the Adoration of the Magi and the Flight into Egypt. The fifth chapel has an early 16C marble altar set in a splendid carved *"tempietto"* surround.

The main feature of interest in this church is, however, the decoration in the **Sassetti Chapel★★** *(second chapel on the right in the south transept)* undertaken by Domenico Ghirlandaio in 1483. Using a technique he was later to employ in the chancel of Santa Maria Novella, the artist created a colourful portrait gallery of his contemporaries to depict episodes from the life of St Francis of Assisi. The *Renunciation of Worldly Goods (lefthand wall at the top)* and *(below) St Francis receiving the Stigmata* showing La Verna *(qv)* on the rock. The *Approval of the Franciscan Rule (end wall at the top)* shows in the background the Palazzo Vecchio and Loggia della Signoria, in the group standing *(right)* Lorenzo the Magnificent and the donor and his son *(left)* and in the immediate foreground emerging from the staircase, Poliziano with Lorenzo's three sons. The *Saint raising a child from the dead (below)* takes place in front of the Romanesque Santa Trinità Church. The *Trial by Fire before the Sultan (righthand wall at the* *top)* is above *the Death of St Francis*. The vaulting is decorated with four splendid female figures representing sibyls. The donors, Francesco Sassetti and his wife, are depicted kneeling. They both lie in the magnificent tombs with basalt sarcophagi - probably the work of Giuliano da Sangallo - on each side of the altar. Above is an *Adoration of the Shepherds,* another famous work by Domenico Ghirlandaio (1485) in which certain critics have observed the influence of the Portinari Triptych by Van der Goes *(now in the Uffizi)*.

The chapel, which balances the Sassetti chapel on the other side of the main altar, contains the marble tomb of Bishop Federighi, inset with a bright garland of foliage made of glazed polychrome terracotta by Luca della Robbia.

The north aisle contains – *(first chapel)* a wooden statue of Mary Magdalen begun by Desiderio da Settignano and completed by Benedetto da Maiano; *(second chapel)* St John Gualbert, founder of the monastery in Vallombrosa *(qv)*, surrounded by saints and monks by Neri di Bicci, who also produced the *Annunciation (above the altar in the next chapel)*; *St Jerome Repenting (fourth chapel)* and an *Annunciation,* both painted in 1503 by Ridolfo del Ghirlandaio.

The crypt was part of the original Romanesque church.

Domenico Ghirlandaio (1449-1494)

Ghirlandaio painted a large number of frescoes including the cycles in Santa Maria Novella and Santa Trinità, and the Last Supper scenes in the refectories of San Marco and Ognissanti. He ran a leading studio in which Michelangelo was a pupil. The main characteristics of his style are his sense of decoration, his taste for detail and his love of line and colour. His works depict the finery of the wealthy bourgeois society from whom most of his clients came. The portraits, costumes, head-dresses, buildings and furniture are all excellent descriptions of contemporary life in Florence.

Badia (Z) – *Opposite the Bargello, entrance in Via del Proconsolo or Via Dante.* This was the church of an ancient and very influential Benedictine abbey *(badia)*, founded shortly before the year 1000 by Countess Willa, Marchioness of Tuscany. It was a centre of intense spiritual and intellectual activity throughout the Middle Ages.

It is believed that the building was extensively renovated in the late 13C by Arnolfo di Cambio. The hexagonal **belltower★**, an elegant, slender structure with lower levels built in Romanesque style and a Gothic upper section capped by a spire, was rebuilt between 1310 and 1330. It is one of the finest belltowers in Florence and can be fully admired only from a distance.

The church underwent further restoration in 1627 and the present interior dates from this period. It is designed in the form of a Greek cross in an austere Baroque style and has a splendid carved wooden coffered **ceiling★★**.

The church contains a number of interesting Renaissance works – *(left of the entrance)* a painting depicting the **Apparition of the Virgin to St Bernard★** by Filippo Lippi, in which the artist is said to have used his mistress and children as models for the Virgin Mary and angels; *(opposite)* an exquisite carved marble **relief★★** by Mino da Fiesole, in which the youth and beauty of the characters – Madonna and Child, St Leonard and St Lawrence – are extremely moving. The church also has two elegant **tombs★** carved by Mino da Fiesole in the style of Renaissance tombs as first introduced by Bernardo Rossellino in his work for Leonardo Bruni in Santa Croce. The two tombs are those of Bernardo Giugni *(south transept)* – an eminent figure of the Florentine Republic – and Count Ugo *(north transept)*, Marquess of Tuscany, who was a great benefactor of the church and the son of the founder of the abbey.

Cenacolo di Sant'Apollonia (St Apollonia's Refectory) (ET) ⊘ – The large hall, once used as a refectory for the nuns of this Camaldolese convent, is preceded by a small room containing a number of 15C Florentine paintings, including a *Madonna and Child surrounded by Saints* by Neri di Bicci, in which the Child is rather unusually depicted placing his hand inside his mother's bodice. The huge **Last Supper★** covering one of the refectory walls is a masterpiece by Andrea del Castagno. The artist painted it towards the end of his very short life *(c1450)*, at the same time as the other frescoes. It conveys great dramatic force because of the well-structured framework, the abundance of mineral decoration, the relief achieved in the representation of the characters and the degree of realism. The depiction of the Passion of Christ *(above)*, which shows the Crucifixion *(centre)*, the Entombment *(right)* and the Resurrection *(left)*, is painted in a freer style against a single landscape background.

Ognissanti (All Saints' Church) (DU) ⊘ – This church, which dates from the 13C, was completely rebuilt during the 17C, with the exception of the belltower (13C-14C) standing on the south side. The Baroque façade was designed by

The Last Supper by Andrea del Castagno (Cenacolo di S Apollonia).

Matteo Nigetti and is decorated with a glazed terracotta *Coronation of the Virgin Mary* produced in della Robbia's workshops *(lunette above the doorway)* and Florence's coat of arms characterised by its lily *(centre of the pediment)*.

The interior contains two frescoes by Domenico Ghirlandaio *(behind the second altar on the right)* depicting a *Descent from the Cross* and a *Virgin Mary of Mercy* protecting the members of the family of Amerigo Vespucci, the Florentine navigator, whose tombstone can be seen at the foot of the altar *(left)*. It is interesting to compare Botticelli's fresco of *St Augustin (between the third and fourth altars)*, with Ghirlandaio's fresco on the north wall of the nave opposite, portraying another Father and Doctor of the Church, *St Jerome*; both were painted in 1480. Botticelli is buried in the south transept *(chapel on the right towards the entrance)* beneath a circular marble slab bearing the name Filipepi. The habit worn by St Francis of Assisi when he received the stigmata in September 1224 has been kept in the second chapel of the north transept since 1503.

Cenacolo (Old Refectory) ⊙ - *Off the cloisters on the south side of the church: access from the transept of the church or no 42 Borgo Ognissanti*. The former refectory was decorated by Domenico Ghirlandaio in 1480 with a huge fresco of the **Last Supper★**, painted after the version in the Monastery of San Marco also by Ghirlandaio *(qv)*. These two works have numerous similarities - the same general layout and décor (Judas separated from the Twelve by a U-shaped table covered with an embroidered cloth, the room opening onto a luxurious garden with fruit trees standing out against a sky filled with birds in flight, the righthand window decorated with a peacock). Compared to the fresco in San Marco the Last Supper in Ognissanti conveys a greater sense of serenity and is more natural owing to the slightly more austere décor and the very varied poses of the Apostles.

Cenacolo di Foligno (Foligno Refectory) (DT) ⊙ - *42 Via Faenza*. This is the refectory of the former convent of Franciscan Tertiaries in Foligno. Its fresco of the **Last Supper★** is attributed to Perugino and is said to date from slightly after 1491, the year in which Neri di Bicci died. It was di Bicci who had received the original commission for the work from the nuns. The scene depicts the moment

The Last Supper by Domenico Ghirlandaio (Cenacolo di Ognisssanti).

when Jesus is about to speak so that the painter could present a serene, dispassionate, rather gentle gathering in a style characteristic of his work. Judas is alone in the foreground in the conventional manner, clutching his traitor's purse, and only Jesus and three Apostles are looking at him; John is still asleep. The names of all the Apostles are indicated on the dais at their feet. A certain theatrical effect is created by the splendid backdrop of a receding portico, in the centre of which the artist depicts Jesus praying on the Mount of Olives, suffused in soft lighting.

The other frescoes are by Bicci di Lorenzo.

★ **Cenacolo di San Salvi (St Salvi's Refectory)** ⊘ - *16 Via San Salvi, to the east of the city. From Piazza Beccaria (FU), take Via Vincenzo Gioberti and Via Aretina, its continuation on the other side of Piazza L B Alberti; turn left into Via San Salvi. By bus take no 3 (Ponte Vecchio), no 6 (Duomo) and no 20 (San Marco); alight at Viale E De Amicis after the large bridge over the railway; after the bridge turn right into Via Tito Speri and right again into Via San Salvi.*

The refectory of the former Monastery of San Salvi is preceded by a long gallery and two halls, containing altar paintings (16C Florentine School) and works stylistically related to Andrea del Sarto. It was he who in *c*1520 painted the refectory's splendid fresco of the **Last Supper**★★ inspired by the work of Leonardo da Vinci the in Milan. The main characteristics of this masterpiece are its serenity and nobility yet it also highlights the inherent drama of the event. It is an admirable example of the restrained sensitivity of this master of Florentine Classicism, and his taste for blending warm colours which he doubtless inherited from Raphael. The enclosed space, devoid of distracting details, is simply lit by an open loggia looking out onto the sky where two characters secretly watch the scene. The composition concentrates on the Apostles and Christ, who has just announced that one of the 12 will betray Him thereby provoking all possible reactions from wild stupefaction to disbelief, sadness to repressed anger and petrified surprise to deep thought. The scene has a greater dynamic force than earlier works on the same subject, and the artist also broke with Florentine tradition by placing Judas to the right of Jesus, rather than setting him opposite, apart from the rest.

The refectory also contains a *Noli me Tangere* by the same artist.

The Last Supper, a favourite theme of monastery refectories

Monastery refectories *(cenacoli* in Italian) take their name from the Latin *(cenaculum)* meaning an eating room or more specifically the upper room where the Last Supper was held. It was usual for them to contain an illustration of this biblical scene as it was an important subject of meditation during meals.

The Last Supper by Leonardo da Vinci (Cenacolo di S Maria delle Grazie, Milan).

Numerous works on this theme were produced in Florence. The 12 Apostles are usually portrayed seated in a row at a long table covered with a cloth, with Jesus in the centre and John by his side, bending towards him or leaning against his breast. Judas, without a halo, is almost always depicted alone in the foreground facing the others. Leonardo da Vinci was the first to interpret the scene with the 13 companions seated on the same side of the table (1495-1497 - in the refectory of Santa Maria delle Grazie in Milan). There are two different representations of the event - either immediately after the announcement of the betrayal, "Verily I say unto you, that one of you shall betray me" (St Matthew 26, v 21), or less frequently, when Judas reveals himself as the traitor (St Matthew 26, v 25) or accepting the sop that Jesus offers to him (St John 14, v 26).

The Last Supper by Andrea del Sarto (Cenacolo di S Salvi).

★ **Crocifissione del Perugino (Crucifixion by Perugino)** (**EU Q**) ⊙ – *58 Borgo Pinti; access via the church sacristy (far right) and an underground passage.* Perugino painted this fresco in the chapter-house of the Benedictine convent of Santa Maria Maddalena dei Pazzi between 1493 and 1496. The composition is divided like a triptych into three pictures set within the arcades, and depicts *(left to right)* St Bernard and the Virgin Mary, Mary Magdalen at the foot of the cross and St John and St Benedict. The whole work is given a unity through the admirable Umbrian landscape portrayed with great depth and bathed in a gentle morning light.

Chiostro dello Scalzo (Scalzo Cloisters) (**ET**) ⊙ – *69 Via Cavour.* These small and intimate cloisters contain a cycle of frescoes by Andrea del Sarto, painted in a warm shade of yellow ochre. Two of the 12 scenes depicting the life of St John the Baptist, the patron saint of the cloisters, were completed by Franciabigio. Andrea del Sarto worked in the cloisters between 1512 to 1524 but only sporadically. Interruptions in the work included a visit to the court of François I of France. The cycle is a fine example of his drawing skills and his gentle expressiveness.

Sinagoga (Sinagogue) (**EU**) ⊙ – *4 Via Farini.* The Florence Synagogue was built between 1874 and 1882 and was based on the Byzantine Agia Sophia in Constantinople. It is designed in the shape of a Greek cross surmounted by a bronze dome. The interior has a rich Moorish decoration including frescoes and mosaics, in addition to a superfluous pulpit in the Christian tradition. Part of the furniture originates from the two synagogues of the **old ghetto** which was located near Piazza della Repubblica. The Jews of Florence lived in a ghetto between 1571 (with authorisation from Cosimo I) and 1848, the year in which the restrictions were abolished. It was gradually demolished in the late 19C.

OTHER MUSEUMS

★★ **Museo Archeologico (Archeological Museum)** (**ET**) ⊙ – *38 Via della Colonna.* The museum contains numerous objects and works of art from most of the Etruscan settlement sites and graveyards, as well as extensive collections of items from Ancient Egypt, Greece and Rome. On the landing of the first floor is a huge painting representing the Franco-Tuscan expedition to Egypt showing Ippolito Roselinni, the father of Italian Egyptology *(standing left)* and Jean-François Champollion *(seated in the central group).*

Most of the exhibits in the Egyptian collections *(stele* with numerous low reliefs, vases, Canopic jars, parchments, sarcophagi, mummies...) come from Thebes (18th and 19th dynasties) and Saqqarah (26th to 30th dynasties).

Among the Etruscan funereal sculptures are cinerary urns, used only in the north of Etruria around Volterra, Chiusi and Perugia; they contained the ashes of the deceased who was depicted on the lids in a seated or standing position (6C) or lying down at a banquet (from the 5C onwards). Men were depicted holding a chalice or horn and women holding a mirror, fan or pomegranate. Among the sarcophagi, the Sarcophagus of the Amazons is outstanding for its interesting painted decoration.

The large collection of bronzes includes devotional items, vases, lamps, weights and measures, weaponry and a few large high-quality sculptures. The **Chimera**★★ dating from the first half of the 4C BC was discovered in 1553 in Arezzo and is thought to have been made by an Etruscan workshop in the Chiusi or Arezzo region. The mythical monster in the form of a lion with two extra heads – of a goat and a snake – bears a votive inscription on its front right paw; its wound and its defensive attitude suggest that it may originally have been part of a group including Bellerophontes, who rode Pegasus and killed the monster. Another Etruscan statue called the *Arringatore*, an orator demanding silence, is thought to date from 100 to 80 BC because of its aristocratic Roman garb. The *Minerva* found in Arezzo in 1541 is said to be a Roman copy (1C BC) of a Greek variation on an original statue carved by

The Chimera of Arezzo.

Praxiteles (340 – 330 BC) of which more than 20 copies are known to date. Among the extensive collection of ancient ceramics in the museum (Greek, Roman and Etruscan) the most outstanding exhibit is the famous **François Vase**★ named after the Florentine archeologist who found its pieces in 1844 – 1845 scattered in an Etruscan grave near Chiusi. The vase indicates the popularity of Attic ceramics among the Etruscans; it is a superb example dating from 570 BC and is painted using the so-called "black figure" technique in which details are obtained by cutting into or touching up lighter-coloured paint. Its decoration includes hunting scenes, festivities and combats taken from Greek mythology, all showing remarkably skilful artwork.

★ **Casa Buonarroti (Buonarroti House) (EU M³)** ⏱ – *70 Via Ghibellina*. In March 1508 Michelangelo purchased a group of houses at the corner of Via Ghibellina and the alleyway at right angles to it. It is thought that he lived in one of them. When he moved to Rome in 1534, he sold the houses to his nephew, Leonardo, and left him the plans for alterations designed to convert the units into the present residence, in which Michelangelo never lived.

The building was sold to Florence City Council in 1858 by the last surviving member of the Buonarroti family. It contains a large collection of memorabilia relating to the family and also the collections built up by the great-nephew of Michelangelo, also called Michelangelo, the one Buonarroti who was most interested in art and most devoted to the great master. He bought back numerous drawings by Michelangelo and obtained from Cosimo II the return of works that had been given by his father to Grand Duke Cosimo I.

The ground floor houses the collections of ancient Roman and Etruscan sculptures built up by the Buonarroti family. In the first room *(right of the hall)* are portraits of Michelangelo and a bronze sculpture of the artist, cast in two parts. The head is said to have been sculpted by Daniele da Volterra; the bust by Giovanni da Bologna.

On the first floor are works by Michelangelo. The first room to the left of the staircase contains small sculptures that show the development of his art form. Among his earliest works are the unfinished marble relief *(right of the door)* depicting the **Battle of the Centaurs** (before 1492), inspired by ancient sarcophagi, and the famous **Virgin Mary and Staircase** (1490-1492), another relief which he made when, aged only 15, he was the guest of Lorenzo the Magnificent. The small wooden Crucifix *(display cabinet to the left of the door)*, which represents his style at the end of his life, dates from just over one year before he died. In the next room on the left are a large model (clay, wool and wood) of a statue of the river god which was intended to decorate one of the two Medici tombs in San Lorenzo *(qv)* and a wooden scale model made by the artist of the west front of the church.

The room behind the staircase contains rotating exhibitions of works by the artist. There are several rooms *(right)* containing the wooden Crucifix carved by Michelangelo at the age of 17 for the Church of Santo Spirito and *(further room)* two *Noli me tangere* by Battista Franco and Bronzino which are copies of the originals. The remainder of this floor consists of a suite of rooms magnificently refurbished by the younger Michelangelo Buonarroti in honour of his great-uncle – *(first room)* canvases depicting outstanding episodes from his life and *(ceiling)* the apotheosis of his life. Beyond is the Day and Night Chamber (named after the scene painted on the ceiling), the chapel and the library containing *trompe-l'oeil* paintings which include every famous artist, writer, scholar or humanist from 17C Florence.

★ **Opificio delle Pietre dure** (Pietra Dura Workshop) (ET M⁴) ⊘ – *78 Via degli Alfani*. This workshop upholds one of the grand traditions of Florentine craftwork. The art of working hard stone *(pietra dura)* which had been fairly popular during the days of Ancient Rome and Greece, was brought back into fashion in the 15C by the Medici family. Lorenzo the Magnificent's liking for ancient objects made of semi-precious stones stimulated skills in restoration and reproduction which his successors maintained and diversified with similar enthusiasm. In the 16C Cosimo I and his son, Francesco I, brought artists to their court from all over Italy and other European countries. They included cameo carvers, rock crystal engravers, stone cutting specialists, goldsmiths such as Jacques Bilivert and they were joined by the Florentine architect, Bernardo Buontalenti. In Florence this period marked the beginning of the assembly *(commesso)* of hard stones, a form of mosaic in which the main feature is the juxtaposition of stones carved with such precision that the joins are invisible to the naked eye. To create contrasts of light and shade, the technique exploited the variations in colour of the stones themselves. The most commonly-used stones were granite, porphyry, quartz, onyx and jasper, sometimes in conjunction with softer stones such as marble and alabaster.

In the early 17C the workshops, which had been installed in the Uffizi by Francesco I and given the status of an official institution (1588) by his brother, Ferdinando I, were involved in the decoration of the Princes' Chapel in San Lorenzo. Their innovations included the production of the superb pieces of furniture known as cabinets *(stipi)* made of precious woods and decorated with rare stones. There are several examples in the Pitti Palace. During the second half of the century, the sculptor Foggini assisted in a range of work. In the 18C, with the help of Giuseppe Zocchi, painter and engraver, output changed and the workshop produced veritable pictures – landscapes, genre scenes, sights of Florence, Roman buildings.

The workshop was transferred to its present premises at the end of the 18C and is now almost exclusively concerned with restoration work. Its small museum is open to the public.

Detail of Tuscan landscape in *pietra dura* by Cigoli (1559-1613).

★ **Museo di Storia della Scienza** (Science History Museum) (Z M¹) ⊘ – The museum is housed in the austere medieval **Palazzo Castellani**. It displays a vast collection of ancient scientific instruments. Many of the exhibits come from the collections built up by the Medici family and the Grand Dukes of Lorraine who were passionately interested in the sciences from the Renaissance period onwards because of their humanist taste for all fields of knowledge.

First floor – Rooms 1 to 3 contain 16C and 17C mathematical instruments from Florence, Tuscany and foreign countries. They include instruments representing the heavens – globes, armillary spheres and instruments to measure the sky and earth – astrolabe, quadrants, sundials, compasses. The fourth room is one of the most important because it contains memorabilia relating to **Galileo** (1564-1642), physicist and astronomer from Pisa – the lens, now broken but set in an ivory mount, which he used in 1609 to discover Jupiter's satellites (to which he gave the name of "the Medicean Stars"), his two telescopes, the compass that he made himself, a few instruments used for scientific experiments and one of his fingers (in a reliquary).

Rooms 5 and 6 deal with optics, a science that made huge progress in the 17C. The origins and development of the telescope, a prism, used for the study of light, and optical games are on display. Cosmography – the representation of the canopy of heavens – is illustrated in Room 7 by splendid terrestrial and celestial globes and armillary spheres including the particularly grand and lavish centrepiece, made between 1588 and 1593, on which the earth, the centre of the universe in Ptolomey's system, is surrounded by a large number of circles representing the movement of the stars.

Rooms 8 to 11 house a collection of observation and research instruments beginning with a microscope, invented in the 17C, which paved the way for enormous progress in the fields of biological and environmental observation. There is also a magnificent set of scientific instruments made of glass, numerous meteorological instruments (17C-18C) and astronomical instruments (18C-19C), all of them Florentine in origin.

Second floor – Room 12 is devoted to clock mechanisms, which first appeared in the Western world in the 13C, and to clockwork figures which were very fashionable in the 18C and in which the mechanisms are very similar to the ones used in clocks.

Room 13 contains mathematical instruments and measuring devices which were perfected throughout the 18C and 19C, thereby paving the way for the extraordinary development of the precision instrument industry, especially in Britain, Germany and France.

In Room 14 are 18C devices used to demonstrate electrical and magnetic phenomena, which were fairly recent discoveries at that time.

Room 15 describes the success of pneumatics and hydrostatics from the mid-17C to the end of the 18C through numerous pieces of equipment used for experiments and demonstrations.

Rooms 16 and 17 trace how mechanics also aroused a great deal of enthusiasm and consequently made huge strides forward throughout the 17C from Descartes to Newton whose principles became widely accepted in the 18C. There is a large collection of teaching aids to demonstrate mechanical phenomena in a fairly spectacular fashion (centrifugal force), hoists, pulleys etc.

Rooms 18, 19 and 20 all contain exhibits relating to the medical fields. Room 18 deals with surgery and contains numerous surgical instruments and a very extensive collection of wax and terracotta teaching aids used in obstetrics (some of them are life-sized, or almost). Room 19 covers the history of pharmacy and Room 20 the origins of modern chemistry.

The last room contains weights, measures and balances.

★ **Museo Marino Marini** (Z M') ⊘ – The Church of San Pancrazio now provides the setting for works by Marino Marini (1901-1980), sculptor and painter, and has thereby cleverly regained the sense of space it lost when occupied by a succession of official departments after its deconsecration in 1808. The huge equestrian group *Aja* in the chancel is brilliantly lit through the glass construction replacing the apse which was destroyed. Sculptures, paintings, drawings and engravings show the artist's marked interest in the austere, static plastic art of ancient statuary onto which he grafted an anxiety typical of his day. The main themes represented are Woman, the Horseman and the Warrior.

★ **Museo Bardini** (EV) ⊘ – *1 Piazza de' Mazzi*. The collections of this museum are displayed in the delightful setting of a 19C mansion – sculptures, stucco work, paintings, small bronzes and medals, Persian rugs (16C-17C), tapestries made in the 18C in Florence workshops, ceramics and old musical instruments – all bequeathed to the city in 1922 by Stefano Bardini, a famous antique dealer, and all indicative of his eclectic taste. In the construction of his residence, Bardini made use of sections or features from older buildings – altar fronts as window frames, Renaissance door frames, painted rafters, coffered ceilings.

The ground floor, apart from rooms 2 to 4 which are used solely for restoration work, is devoted exclusively to sculptures, most of them ancient or dating from the Renaissance period. Room 7 *(opposite the entrance)* contains a group representing *Charity* by Tino di Camaino. Room 10 *(at the top of a few steps)* houses a graceful relief of the *Madonna and Child* by a 15C Sienese artist and another *Madonna and Child* set within a mandorla with angels and cherubs. The latter is a glazed terracotta reredos made in the workshop of Andrea della Robbia.

The first floor presents collections of paintings and woodcarving – an exquisite polychrome terracotta relief *(Room 14)* of the *Madonna and Child* by Donatello, a fine 15C inlaid ceiling *(Room 16)* on which the coffers are decorated with silver foliage against a blue background, the work of a 15C Sienese artist and *(above the fireplace) St Michael the Archangel* painted on canvas by Antonio Pollaiolo.

★ **Museo La Specola** (DV) ⊙ – *17 Via Romana; at the top of the flight of steps on the left at the end of the street*. This natural history museum, which was founded in 1775 by Grand Duke Leopold, is named after the astronomical and meteorological observatory (*specola* in Italian) which was installed at the request of the Grand Duke. Rooms I to XXIV now house an extensive zoological collection - vertebrates and invertebrates. Rooms XXV to XXXII present over 600 amazingly lifelike **anatomical waxworks**, many of which were made by Clemente Susini. They reproduce to scale all the anatomical organs and functions; some are shown individually; others are part of entire bodies whose contorted attitudes are reminiscent of Michelangelo's nudes.

★ **Museo Stibbert** ⊙ – *Via Federico Stibbert; take bus no 1 (Piazza dell'Unità d'Italia) or no 4 (Piazza della Stazione behind the chancel of Santa Maria Novella)*. The Stibbert Villa (19C) stands at the entrance to a small park filled with trees. It now houses the huge art collections built up during last century by Federico Stibbert, the Anglo-Italian Garibaldian hero - arms and armour, sculptures, paintings, furniture, faïence, tapestries, embroidery, knick-knacks, and costumes of varying origins and periods of history (Renaissance to the 19C).

The 57 rooms display a profusion of items; the most outstanding are - a malachite and gilded bronze table in the hall made by Thomire for King Jerome; the coronation robes worn by Napoleon when he was crowned King of Italy, Murat's sabre and other Napoleonic memorabilia; 16C and 17C Flemish tapestries; a *Madonna and Child (Room 32)* for many years attributed to Botticelli; Venetian costumes from the 18C.

Special mention must be made of the hundreds of pieces of **old armour**★★ worn by Tuscans, Turks, Moors, Spaniards, Indians, Japanese etc. Many of them are mounted on models of men and horses lined up in impressive processions *(mainly on the ground floor and the top storey)*.

★ **Museo storico topografico "Firenze com'era"** (Florence Historical Topographical Museum) (EU M⁸) ⊙ – *4 Via Oriuolo*. Paintings, engravings and old maps trace urban development in Florence and describe the history of its various districts from the Renaissance to the 19C. There is a fine series of lunettes representing the Medici villas created by Giusto Utens in Tuscany in 1599.

★ **Casa di Dante** (Z) ⊙ – *1 Via S Margherita (corner of Via Dante Alighieri*. It was in this urban district that the Alighieri family had its houses although it is not known which one was Dante's birthplace. The museum retraces the life of the

16C armour (Sala della Cavalcata, Museo Stibbert).

poet from the origins of his family, members of the ancient Florentine aristocracy, to his official positions within the city and his years in exile. It also records Italian history and the position of Florence during Dante's lifetime, which were closely linked to his political preoccupations, as well as his major work, the *Divine Comedy*, and his platonic love for Beatrice Portinari, whose family lived in the same district and who was buried in the Church of Santa Margherita *(further up the street)*.

In Via Dante (corner of Piazza S Martino) stand the remains of the 12C **torre della Castagna (R)**, where the representatives *(priori)* of the Guilds *(qv)* met before the construction of the Palazzo della Signoria *(qv)*.

Casa Guidi (VD M12) ⊙ – *8 Via Maggio*. The 15C house contains the first floor rented flat where Robert and Elizabeth Barrett Browning lived from their marriage in 1846 until her death in 1861. It contains some mementoes of them and is now owned by the Browning Institute.

TOURS NORTH OF FLORENCE

See general map of Florence on the Michelin Map 430, in Michelin Road Atlas Italia or Europe, or in the Michelin Red Guide Italia.

★ **Scenic route through the Colli Alti** – *26km* – *16 miles from Florence (exit ①* *on the map), by S 65 (Bologna road). Beyond Montorsoli turn left into the Monte Morello road*. The road climbs sharply at first and then winds across the southern slopes of Mount Morello, alternately running through woods of pines and fir trees or in the open flanked by gorse bushes, providing views *(south)* over Fiesole and Florence and the Arno Basin. The most extensive **view**★ extends over a considerable distance (3km – 2 miles) from Piazzale Leonardo da Vinci (6km – 3.5 miles beyond Montorsoli – alt 595m – 1934ft – *restaurant)*; the view embraces Florence and the Arno Valley; in the background are the Chianti Hills *(south)* and the Prato plain *(west)*.

Beyond the Gualdo Refuge (alt 428m – 1391ft) the road narrows and runs down a steep hillside (22 %) in a series of bends with views through the pines of Prato and Sesto Fiorentino.

In Colonnata take the road to Sesto Fiorentino. In Quinto Alto turn left into Via Fratelli Rosselli, a long road.

★ **Tomba etrusca della Montagnola** ⊙ – *Enquire at no 95*. The Etruscan tomb dates from the 7C or 6C BC and is interesting for its remarkable roofing systems concealed beneath an earth tumulus. In the corridor leading to the burial chamber are enormous monolithic stones which meet at the top to form a sort of pointed roof, In the circular chamber itself there is a dome (over 5m – 16ft in diameter) supported by a central pillar. The vaulting consists of concentric circles of stone laid one above the other.

Sesto Fiorentino – *See Sesto Fiorentino.*

★ **Monte Senario Tour** – *38km – 24 miles north; from Florence to Montorsoli the tour follows the same route as the previous tour.*

From the Trespiano hill there are views *(right)* over Florence in the valley below, to Fiesole, followed by a few rare glimpses of the Mugnone Valley.

800m – 867yds beyond the junction with the winding road (left) to Monte Morello turn right into the entrance to the villa which is indicated by traffic lights and a huge gate surmounted by two lions.

★ **Demidoff Villa Park** ⊙ – This park is a masterpiece of Tuscan mannerism. Within it used to stand the most luxurious of all the Medici villas, then known as the **Pratolino Villa**, built in the 16C by Buontalenti but later abandoned by the House of Lorraine and finally demolished in the 19C when Ferdinando III ordered alterations to convert the grounds into a romantic park. Its present name is that of the prince who purchased the property in 1872.

Among the surviving traces of its past splendour is the huge statue of the **Appennino**★ by Giovanni da Bologna (1579-1580) containing grottoes decorated with frescoes and fountains. Behind it is a 17C winged dragon.

To the right of the avenue is the chapel by Buontalenti, a hexagonal building with a loggia designed to enable the servants to follow the service from outside. Two other remaining features are the Mugnone Fountain by Giovanni da Bologna, which was part of the grottoes set out at the foot of the Medici villa destroyed during the alterations made by Ferdinando III of Lorraine, and the Mask fish pond *(beside the path running downhill from the bar)*, a statue with a disturbing facial expression.

In Pratolino turn right off S65 into the road to Bivigliano. At the following junction, where the road divides on a bend (before the junction with the road to Olmo, turn into the road up to Monte Senario. After 2.5km – 1.5 miles turn right; drive to the top of the hill (car park). A short private drive leads to the monastery.

Appennino by Giovanni da Bologna (Parco di Villa Demidoff).

From the hilltop approach road there are some delightful views of the surrounding hills and the monastery glimpsed among the fir trees.

Convento del Monte Senario ⊘ – Alt 817m – 2655ft. The **monastery** lies in a superb **setting**★★ on the edge of a wooded promontory high above the Sieve Valley. It was founded in the 13C by seven Florentine aristocrats, the seven founding saints of the Order of the Servants of Mary. The monastery has been rebuilt or restored on numerous occasions and the present building dates from the 17C and 18C. Its tiny **church** has an elegant Baroque interior with a few works of art including a 15C terracotta *Pietà* in the Chapel of the Apparition *(on the altar)*. The monastery's private drive leads to St Alexis' Cave and St Filippo Benizzi's Fountain, named after two of the founding saints.

On returning down the hill, turn right at the road junction towards Bivigliano (signed).

Bivigliano – This pleasant shady residential village is near a fine pine wood. From the village the road runs along a delightful road built on terraces above the Carza Valley north of Pratolino.

Take S65 to return to Florence.

OTHER TOURS AROUND FLORENCE

From Florence it is easy to make interesting excursions into the surrounding countryside.
- to view the Medici villas in **Castello**★, **Poggio a Caiano**★★, **Artiminio**★ and **Cerreto Guidi**★
- to visit the cathedral and historic centre of **Prato**★★ *(17 km – 10 miles northwest)*
- to experience the peace of the **Galluzzo Charterhouse**★★ *(6 km – 4 miles south)*
- to see the Etruscan and Roman ruins in **Fiesole**★ *(8 km – 5 miles north)*
- to see **Vinci**★ where the genius Leonardo was born *(33 km – 20 miles west)*
- to walk in the hills aroud **Settignano**★ *(6 km – 4 miles east)*
- to tour the villages and vineyards of the Chianti region *(southeast)*
- to explore the country to the north of the city where the Medici family originated.

Bernard Berenson (1865-1959), art historian and collector, lived for many years near Settignano in Villa I Tatti (entrance in Via Vincigliata) set in an Italianate garden. In his Will he bequeathed the property to Harvard University as a Center of Italian Renaissance Studies. His library is open to post-doctorate scholars and his collection of Italian paintings is shown by appointment to scholars with a letter of introduction.

Certosa del GALLUZZO★★

Michelin Map 430 K 15 – 6 km – 4 miles south of Florence
on the west side of the road to Siena
See plan of the Florence area on Map 430, in the Michelin Road Atlas
Europe or Italia, or the Michelin Red Guide Italia

The **Galluzzo Charterhouse** ⊘, also known as the **Florence Charterhouse**, was founded in the 14C by the great Florentine banker, Niccolò Acciaiuoli, and underwent numerous alterations until the 17C. The Carthusian monks occupied the premises until 1957 and were succeeded a year later by a Cistercian community.

A monumental staircase leads to the monastery buildings and to the Palazzo Acciaiuoli which now houses an art gallery – frescoes by Pontormo (1523-25) depicting scenes from the Passion of Christ, originally in the cloisters.
The church, in front of which is a large 16C square, was divided into two distinct sections to separate the lay brothers from the Carthusian monks. Only the monks' church dates from the 14C, although its decorative features and choirstalls date from the 16C. The Gothic Chapel of S Maria *(right)* leads to the underground chapels in which the members of the Acciaiuoli family are buried. The parlour *(left of the church)*, where the monks were allowed one hour of recreation a week, leads into small cloisters and from there to the chapter-house which contains the magnificent **tomb of Leonardo Buonafé** (1550) by Francesco di Giuliano da Sangallo and an intricately-carved door (16C). Round the great Renaissance **cloisters**, adorned with medallions by the Della Robbias, are the 18 monastic cells *(one is open to the public)*. The visit continues via the refectory, lay cloisters and guesthouse.

Grand Cloisters of the Galluzzo Charterhouse.

Chiesa di GROPINA★

Michelin Map 430 L 16 – 1.8km – 1mile southeast of Loro Ciuffenna
(sign – S Giustino Valdarno); after 1.2km – 1 mile turn right

The Romanesque Church of San Pietro in Gropina with its even sandstone bonding dates from the first half of the 12C. It stands on the lower slopes of the Pratomagno, slightly above the Arno Valley, on a site formerly occupied by a Roman construction and two religious buildings, one dating from the paleo-Christian era and the other from the 8C. The aisles of the present church were extended during the second half of the 12C and the belltower was completed in 1233.

The interior has roof rafters except in the last bay of the aisles, which has rib vaulting. The semicircular central apse has an external gallery with colonnettes; the central colonnettes are interconnected. The richly **carved decoration**★ inside the church is unequalled anywhere else in Casentino. The capitals and ambo in the south aisle (the first to be completed) date from the second half of the 12C and are carved in an early Romanesque style still using flattened sculpture. The capitals in the north aisle are more highly sophisticated and are thought to be the work of Emilian workshops; until 1191 Gropina was dependent on Nonantola Abbey not far from Modena. The most interesting designs are – *(south side, starting from the entrance pillar)* the sow, a symbol of the Church, suckling her litter; the knights-in-arms fighting the demon; the highly-stylised vine stocks; the eagles crowning the ambo which is carved both in flattened relief and in the round; *(north side, third column)* the figures of Christ, St Peter and St Paul, Samson killing the lion, and St Ambrose presenting the new Law; *(fourth column)* the punishment of lust – a man being dragged by his beard and three women whose breasts are being bitten by dragons.

GROSSETO

Population 71 329
Michelin Map 988 folds 24-25 or 430 N 15

Grosseto is a modern provincial capital situated in the fertile Ombrone plain near the sea *(13km – 8 miles)*. The old centre is enclosed within huge hexagonal brick ramparts fortified with bastions, built by the Medici in the late 16C. The heart of the old town is the area around Piazza Dante Alighieri, flanked by the cathedral and the provincial palace, a Gothic-Renaissance pastiche.

SIGHTS

Museo diocesano ⊘ – *Second floor of the Archeology Museum*. The most noteworthy paintings include the *Universal Judgement* by the Sienese School (13C), the *Madonna of the Cherries*, a masterpiece by Sassetta *(c*1400-1450) and the *Madonna of Grosseto* by Casolani (1552-1606). Note also the 17C polychrome statues and medieval ivories, bronzes, antiphonaries and altarware.

Chiesa di San Francesco – The interior of this 13C conventual church with its double-sloping Gothic façade, has a number of small frescoes by the Sienese School (14C-15C) and *(above the main altar)* a fine Crucifix painted in the 13C and attributed to Duccio di Buoninsegna. In the adjoining cloisters *(rebuilt)* is a portico-covered well dating from the days of the Medici (1590), which is known as the buffalo well because a number of animals from the Maremma, including buffalo, came to drink there. There is another older well (1465) outside *(right of the church)*.

IMPRUNETA

Population 15 006
Michel Map 988 fold 15 or 430 K 15

Impruneta is a pretty little town situated in the Chianti wine-growing region and is traditionally renowned for the manufacture of high-quality bricks, tiles and decorative terracotta ware. It is a commonly-held belief that Brunelleschi ordered Impruneta tiles for the roof of Florence Cathedral.

Double link with St Luke – Since the Middle Ages the village has been famous for a **Portrait of the Virgin Mary** *(in the church)* said to have been painted by St Luke the Evangelist. According to tradition the ancient portrait was brought to Tuscany by St Romulus but persecution forced him to bury the painting. Many years later, when the villagers were attempting to build a church, they found that the walls built during the day collapsed at night. Eventually they left it to the oxen carrying the stone for the building to indicate God's will about the site for the church. The oxen knelt down on the spot where the church now stands and when the villagers dug the foundations, they discovered the portrait of the Virgin Mary. The picture was thereafter the subject of deep veneration; pilgrimages were organised and the painting was also carried to Florence at the head of a procession when major disasters befell the area (plague, war, floods etc).

The **Fiera di San Luca**, organised each year around the Feast Day of St Luke (18 October), is an ancient tradition that has been famous for many centuries. In the past, its horse, donkey and mule fair attracted buyers from all over Europe and was depicted by Jacques Callot, the engraver, in 1629. Today the event consists of a horse race and an exhibition of agricultural machinery.

SIGHTS

★ **Basilica di Santa Maria dell'Impruneta** – The five arches of the Renaissance portico open into the huge main square. Little has survived from the Romanesque period except the 13C belltower. Inside is a nave and on either side of the choir are two **private chapels★★** designed by Michelozzo to resemble the one in Santissima Annunziata in Florence (1456). The south chapel is decorated with glazed ceramics by the Della Robbias; the north chapel contains the famous portrait of the Virgin *(see above)* which is thought to date from the 13C. The building was bombed in 1944 *(photographs in the baptistery to the left of the entrance)* and was reconstructed using sections that were not destroyed.

Museo del Tesoro (Treasury) ⊘ – The basilica's treasure is the result of many centuries of devotion to the Virgin Mary of Impruneta and the generosity of eminent Florentine families including the Medici – gold and silver ware, reliquaries, church plate, numerous ex-votos dating from the 14C-19C and a fine collection of illuminated liturgical works (14C-16C).

LIVORNO
(Leghorn)

Population 167 087
Michelin Map 988 fold 14 or 430 L 12
Town plan in the Michelin Red Guide Italia

A jetty was built here in 1571 by Cosimo I and in 1573 he ordered a canal to be dug to link Livorno to Pisa. In the early 17C the town was protected by a bastioned wall, still visible today and in 1620, during the reign of Cosimo II, building work was completed on the port *(Porto mediceo)*.

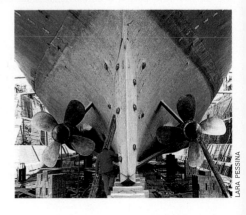

LARA PESSINA

The commercial harbour is now the largest in Tuscany and one of the main ports on the Mediterranean, shipping mainly wood, Florentine craftwork, marble, rough-cut or crafted alabaster and cars. There are a number of heavy industries nearby.

The local fishing trade has given rise to two culinary specialities – fish soup *(cacciucco)* and red mullet *(triglie)* Livorno style.

Leghorn is famous as the **birthplace** of two painters – Giovanni Fattori and Amadeo Modigliani (1884-1920) – and the composer Pietro Mascagni.

SIGHTS

The hub of city life in Livorno centres on Via Grande lined with arcaded buildings, Via Cairoli and Via Ricasoli. This elegant district lies next to the grounds of the Villa Fabbricotti.

In the northwest of the town near the harbour, between the Old Fortress *(Fortezza Vecchia)* and the New Fortress *(Fortezza Nuova)*, lies the **New Venice** district *(Venezia Nuova)*, founded in 1629 by the Medici. Its main features are its canals, bridges and narrow lanes. In the past it was connected to the harbour by its warehouses; nearby are the **Oil Pits** *(Bottini dell'Olio)* ⊘, warehouses dating from 1705-1731 in which oil used to be stored. In Piazza Guerrazzi near the New Fortress stands the small tank **(cisternino)** built in 1837 by Poccianti. It never fulfilled its original function as a water tank and in the 1950s it was converted into an Arts Centre which now hosts figurative art exhibitions.

In the post-war years one of Livorno's best-known sights, despite its name, is its **American Market** *(mercatino americano)* in Piazza XX Settembre. It was originally set up to sell American army surplus clothing and camping equipment but has since diversified to include other goods.

★ **I Quattro Mori** – This **monument** dedicated to Ferdinando I in memory of a victory over the Moors by the knights of St Stephen *(qv)* was built in Piazza Micheli from which there is view of the 16C Old Fortress (Fortezza Vecchia). The bronze statues of the Four Moors were produced in 1624.

Viale Italia – This avenue runs south from the town centre to the district of Ardenza, providing sea views and passing close to the **Aquarium** *(Acquario Diacinto Cestoni)* ⊘ (Mediterranean fish) and the **Accademia Navale** (Italian Naval Academy).

Museo civico G Fattori (Fattori Museum) ⊘ – The museum displays paintings by Giovanni Fattori (1825-1908), leading exponent of the Macchiaioli movement, and by his Macchiaioli colleagues.

Museo Pietro Mascagni (Mascagni Museum) ⊘ The museum houses a collection of the scores, instruments and memorabilia of this composer (1863-1945) who is best-remembered for his opera *Cavalleria Rusticana*.

EXCURSIONS

Montenero ⊘ – *9km – 5 1/2 miles south of Livorno by S1 (signs after Ardenza)*. A cable railway runs alongside the road on the last uphill stretch. Around the square are the chapels making up the temple of fame *(famedio)* designed for the tombs of famous Livorno townspeople. The **sanctuary** itself (1721) is a place of pilgrimage dedicated to Our Lady of the Graces, the patron Saint of Tuscany. It is richly decorated in the Baroque style. The rooms adjacent to the church are hung with unusual ex-votos, most of them connected with the sea.

LUCCA★★★

Population 86 966
Michelin Map 988 fold 14 or 430 K 13

Pink brick town ramparts surmounted by trees and grass, narrow streets lined with the tall façades of old houses, numerous churches, some of which are among the finest achievements of Pisan Romanesque architecture *(qv)*... these are some of the memorable images left by this city, which was once a minor capital. It has remained surprisingly lively and, sheltered behind its ramparts, untouched by 20C town planning.

Its location in the heart of a fertile plain has traditionally linked it with farming. Haricot beans *(fagioli bianchi)* from Lucca are one of Tuscany's culinary specialities and its olive oil ranks among the best in Italy.

Tourists are unfailingly struck by the numerous jeweller's shops, their windows displaying a vast range of good quality items at reasonable prices.

The many cultural events include the **Sagra Musicale Lucchese** which offers a programme of classical and religious music concerts from April to the end of the summer. The concerts are staged in the main churches, thereby continuing the musical tradition of the city where Puccini was born in 1858.

Legend of the True Cross – The city of Lucca is synonymous with the Holy Face *(Volto Santo)*, the miraculous Crucifix worshipped in the Cathedral city of San Martino. According to various traditions it was carved from memory by Nicodemus after the Entombment or his hand was guided by angels as he worked; that is why Christ's face is such a good likeness.

The *Volto Santo* is said to have been washed up on the shores of Luni, north of Viareggio, in the 8C. The story as to how it arrived there differs; some say it was cast into the sea by Nicodemus himself, in obedience to an order from on high, while others believe that it was found by an Italian bishop on a pilgrimage to the Holy Land and that he left it to float with the tide. When the devout Christians of Luni and Lucca began to argue about ownership of the holy image, the Bishop of Lucca settled the matter by placing it on an ox cart and leaving the animals to decide on its destination; they headed towards Lucca.

In the Middle Ages the *Volto Santo* was famous far beyond Lucca. Its story was told by merchants from Lucca and soon spread to northern Europe. In France in the 13C-14C the worship of "St Voult" was so popular that the kings themselves took an oath by "St Vaudeluc" (*"Santo Volto di Lucca"*).

The **Luminara di Santa Croce** (evening of 13 September) commemorates the mysterious arrival of the *Volto Santo*. The whole town joins with various religious orders from the region and representatives from other Tuscan towns, to take part in a huge procession that makes its way through the streets. On the day of the festival, the holy Crucifix is decorated with velvet and gold.

Aerial view of Piazza dell'Anfiteatro and San Frediano.

PUBBLI AER FOTO

FROM CAESAR TO ÉLISA BONAPARTE

The origins of the town of Lucca are remembered in its name, which comes from a Celto-Ligurian word, *"Luk"*, meaning "marshy place". It was colonised by Rome in the early 2C BC and still has the layout of a Roman military encampment, with streets intersecting at right angles along each side of two main perpendicular thoroughfares. It was already a large town when Caesar, Pompey and Crassus met there to form the First Triumvirate.

In the Middle Ages a network of narrow winding alleys and uneven squares was constructed within the Roman chequerboard plan; the amphitheatre was obliterated but the site reappeared with the construction of Piazza dell'Anfiteatro *(qv)*.

Prosperous merchants – In the 12C-13C, after becoming a free town, Lucca continued to enjoy economic growth owing to the manufacture of and trade in silk. It experienced its period of greatest prosperity under the leadership of the great *condottiere*, **Castruccio Castracani** in the early 14C. It was at that time, when Lucca's merchants exported their famous silks throughout Europe and even to the countries of the Orient, that most of the churches were rebuilt and the splendid façades were constructed in a style borrowed from Pisan architects, although in Lucca the decoration was given an extra touch of fantasy and refinement. A number of imposing Gothic residences, some of which still have their towers, have also survived from this period.

Another major figure in local history was **Paolo Guinigi,** who came from a wealthy merchant family and was lord of the town in 1400. Under his rule Lucca enjoyed an artistic revival. He left to posterity a mansion and a villa bearing his name; his wife is immortalised by a recumbent statue in the cathedral.

Renaissance and agriculture – During the second half of the 16C Lucca abandoned its declining trade and industry and turned instead to farming. Its economic recovery was accompanied by intense architectural activity. Numerous "villas" *(qv)* were built in the country districts. Construction began on the town walls but almost a century passed before they were complete. Inside the town most of the houses were rebuilt or extensively altered; stone replaced the brick used in medieval buildings. This period saw the construction of the many Renaissance façades which give the town its character today.

A short-lived principality – For a very short period in the early 19C life in Lucca was dominated by one woman, **Élisa Bonaparte,** who was crowned Princess of Lucca and Piombino by her brother, Napoleon, after his conquest of Italy. From 1805 to 1813, aided by her husband Félix Baciocchi, she ruled decisively and wisely over her principality and showed a remarkable talent for managing affairs.

MAIN CHURCHES *Tour – 3 hours*

Lucca owes its fame to three churches – Duomo San Martino, San Michele in Foro and San Frediano.

★★ **Duomo San Martino** (C) – Lucca Cathedral, which is dedicated to St Martin, was first rebuilt in the 11C and later its outside and interior were almost completely redesigned in the 13C and 14C-15C respectively.

The splendid alternating white and green marble **façade**★★ – the work of the architect Guidetto da Como – gives a remarkable impression of balance, despite the asymmetry caused by the belltower and lack of pediment. The upper section contains three storeys of open arcades supported by colonnettes. This was the first example of Pisan Romanesque architecture in Lucca although the style was altogether more ethereal and

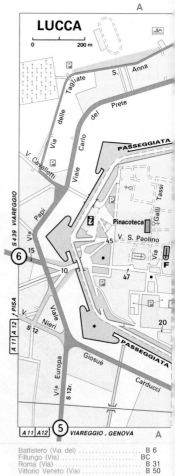

carefree, owing to the greater width of the arcade arches, the remarkably elaborate columns and the introduction of a marble marquetry frieze of geometrical, floral and animal motifs above each register of arcades.

The **belltower★** *(campanile)*, which dates from the 13C, displays a distinctive and impressive elegance; the feeling of lightness derives from the combination of various architectural features – the contrast between the ochre and white colours of the materials, the arcades which increase in number (1 to 4) from the base to the top of the building, the window arches and the small blind arcades outlined on each register with white festoons.

The **decorative features★** in the portico include pillars with colonnettes and naïve sculptures, blind arcades picked out in red marble, a marble marquetry frieze, narrative carvings – *(north door)* a *Descent from the Cross* and an *Adoration of the Magi* by Nicola Pisano, and *(two other doors)* the *Ascension* and the *Martyrdom of Regulus,* a saint from Lucca who was beheaded, by 13C Lombard masters, *(between the doors)* episodes from the life of St Martin and *(below)* the Labours of the Months.

Interior – The interior is Gothic in style. An elegant triforium with graceful columns dominates the nave and forms a pleasing contrast to the semi-circular arches supported by sturdy pillars. The inside wall of the façade contains a freely-carved Romanesque sculpture (1) depicting the famous scene of St Martin sharing his cloak. Above the second altar in the north aisle is a *Presentation of the Virgin Mary at the Temple* by Bronzino (2).

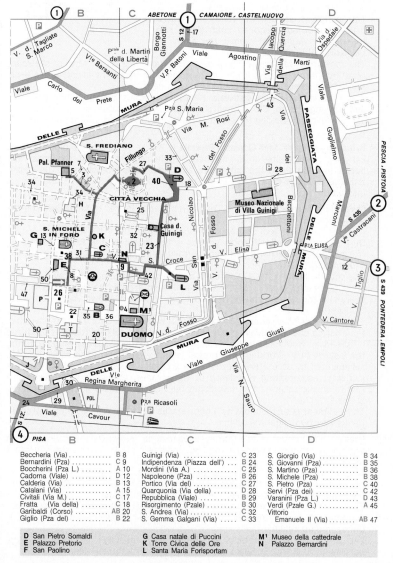

A little higher up stands a small private chapel in the form of an elegant temple *(tempietto)* built in 1484, during the Renaissance period, by **Matteo Civitali** (1436-1501), the local sculptor and architect, to house the **Volto Santo**. The **Large Crucifix★**, carved in wood blackened through age and bearing the figure of Jesus stiffly portrayed in a long tunic, dates from the late 11C. It is said to be a copy of an older work, perhaps the very one that gave rise to the legend.

The north transept contains one of the purest examples of Italian funerary sculpture, produced in 1406 by the Sienese artist Jacopo d ella Quercia. It is the white marble **tomb★★** of **Ilaria del Carretto**, Paolo Guinigi's wife, who died in 1405. The young woman is portrayed in a recumbent position, clothed in a long unusually-soft flowing robe, with a dog (the symbol of faithfulness) at her feet.

In the Sanctuary chapel is a *Madonna and Child flanked by St Stephen and St John the Baptist* (3), painted in 1509 by the Florentine artist Fra Bartolomeo in a poised, sweet style reminiscent of his contemporary Perugino.

The sacristy *(south aisle)* contains a delightful brightly-coloured *Madonna and Child surrounded by Saints* (4) *(above the altar)* by Domenico Ghirlandaio.

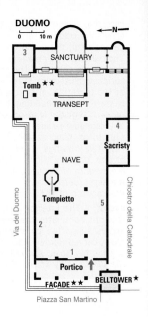

DUOMO

Piazza San Martino

The spectacular **Last Supper★** (5) *(above the altar in the third chapel of the south aisle)* by Tintoretto, is a lively composition onto which the artist, in his usual style, has succeeded in projecting a superb light.

The nearby **Museo della cattedrale** (**C M'**) ⊙ contains church plate, paintings and carvings from the cathedral, including the statue of an apostle by Jacopo della Quercia and the ceremonial vestments used during the Volto Santo festival.

★ **Battistero e chiesa dei Santi Giovanni e Reparata** (**B B**) ⊙ – Archeological digs spanning 20 years have resulted in the discovery of the remains of a Roman house and baths, in addition to the initial site and successive extensions of the **original cathedral** and **baptistery**. The façade of the 10C church is surprising for its inscription.

★★ **Chiesa di San Michele in Foro** (**B**) – The church stands in Piazza **San Michele**, on the site of the old Roman forum.

It is surrounded by old houses, some dating from the 13C-14C.

On the corner of Via Vittorio Veneto is the loggia of the **Palazzo Pretorio** (**E**) (formerly the Governor's mansion) formed by the Renaissance arcades on the ground floor.

The church, built in the 12C-14C, is a huge white building with rows of blind arcading on the exterior of the nave and open arcades on the west front. It overlooks the square and is flanked by a massive belltower built above the transept.

The 13C **façade★★** is remarkably tall, since it was designed for a higher nave than the existing one. It displays the most exuberant and delicate features produced by the Pisan Romanesque style, despite major restorations undertaken during the last century. Working to a typical layout – several rows of open arcades surmounted by decorative friezes – the architect produced a work of extreme intricacy, accentuating the depth of the arcades, multiplying the decorative motifs on the columns and developing the marble marquetry friezes depicting animals.

The pediment is surmounted by a huge statue of St Michael slaying the dragon, flanked by two angel musicians.

Interior – The interior is also Romanesque in style, except for the vaulting which replaced the timbered ceiling in the 16C, and its simplicity forms a stark contrast to the exterior.

The chancel arch rises the full height of the nave.

Above the first altar in the south aisle is a white glazed terracotta **Madonna★** with a delightfully youthful expression by Andrea della Robbia.

The painted Crucifix hanging above the chancel is attributed to a local artist from the first half of the 12C, who, unusually, has depicted the bust and clothing of Christ in light relief.

The south transept contains a splendid vivid **painting★** by Filippino Lippi portraying St Roch, St Sebastian and St Jerome with St Helena.

★ **Chiesa di San Frediano** (B) – This Romanesque church is one of the largest in the town. It was built in the 12C on the site of a basilica constructed in the 6C by St Frediano, Bishop of Lucca, to whom the miracle of the damming of the River Serchio is attributed. It is unusual in that its apse faces west, contrary to the tradition whereby Christians look towards Jerusalem and their churches therefore face east.

The **façade**, which differs significantly from the fronts of the churches of Santi Martino and Michele, dates from the 13C, when the building and in particular the nave were considerably heightened. It is built of bare white stone that was originally used in the Roman amphitheatre *(qv)*. The very high central section is dominated by a huge Byzantine-style mosaic of the Ascension, produced by local artists in the 13C.

A fine crenellated belltower rises above the building.

Interior – Like the façade, the Romanesque basilica-shaped interior has a simplicity that gives it a sense of nobility. The nave, which is extremely tall compared to the aisles, is lined with Classical columns crowned with splendid capitals, probably from the amphitheatre. The chapels added in the aisles in the 14C-15C broke up the overall harmony.

To the right of the entrance is an admirable 12C Romanesque **baptismal font**★ decorated with carved panels giving a lively account of episodes from the life of Moses – the Crossing of the Red Sea with Pharaoh's soldiers dressed as medieval knights and the Good Shepherd surrounded by prophets. Behind the font is a fine door surround with an extremely graceful glazed terracotta **Annunciation** by Andrea della Robbia.

The Trenta chapel *(first chapel coming back along the north aisle)* contains a Gothic marble **polyptych**★ portraying the Madonna and Child surrounded by saints, intricately carved by Jacopo Della Quercia in a lively, flowing style.

The chapel of Sant'Agostino *(third chapel)* is covered with early-16C frescoes by Amico Aspertini, a painter of the Ferrara School – *(lefthand wall in the foreground)* the famous episode of the Volto Santo being taken from Luni to Lucca and *(righthand wall)* an *Adoration of the Shepherds* and an illustration of the miracle worked by St Frediano.

★ **CITTA VECCHIA** (Old Town) *about 1 hour*
Start in Piazza Napoleone and follow the route indicated on the plan

The streets and squares of old Lucca *(città vecchia)* have lost nothing of their former distinctive character and harmonious medley of Gothic and Renaissance styles. They are steeped in charm through their palaces, noblemen's towers, old shops, traceried entrances, carved coats of arms and elegant wrought-iron railings and balconies.

Piazza Napoleone (B 26) – Along the west side of the square, which is shaded with plane trees, is the austere façade of the Palazzo Provinciale, which was begun in the 16C under the direction of the Florentine architect, Bartolomeo Ammannati.

Via Fillungo (BC) – *Take Via Beccheria and turn right into Via Roma*. Via Fillungo is an elegant shopping street, among the most picturesque in Lucca. The Romanesque church of **San Cristoforo** (BC) *(righthand side)*, now deconsecrated, has a delightful entrance surmounted by a lintel carved with floral motifs and a fine rose window set in the alternating dark and light marble-clad façade. The interior is suffused in a pink light, conveying a sense of noble austerity. Engraved into the stone walls are the names of Lucca's citizens killed in action. Also in the same street is the 13C **Torre Civica delle Ore** (BK) (Civic Tower of Hours). In Via degli Asili is the 17C **Palazzo Pfanner** (B) *(not open to the public but the gardens can be seen from the ramparts)*. Its former splendour can be detected in the monumental external flight of steps with arcades and balustrades and in the gardens laid out in the 18C against the backdrop of the rampart walk.

The final section of Via Cesare Battisti is overlooked by the robust belltower of San Frediano.

Piazza dell'Anfiteatro (C 2) – *Access through a vaulted alleyway from Via Fillungo.* Passages beneath the houses lead into this unusual enclosed oval space, which occupies the site of an amphitheatre built by the Romans in the 2C. The amphitheatre fell into ruin during the Barbarian invasions and provided a large part of the building materials used during the Middle Ages to reconstruct the town's churches, particularly the marble used for the façades. The site was later covered by houses. It was not until 1830 that this space was laid out within the medieval quarter.

Close to the Piazza dell'Anfiteatro is the **Piazza San Pietro** (C 40), a small, irregularly-shaped square surrounded by stately 16C façades. It is overlooked by the two-tone belltower (stone for the base and brick for the upper section) of the 12C Romanesque church of **San Pietro Somaldi**. Its façade was completed in the 14C by two registers of arcades in the Pisan tradition. The lintel above the central doorway depicts *Jesus handing St Peter the Keys of Heaven*.

Via Guinigi (C 23) – This is one of the most picturesque streets in Lucca. **Guinigi House** (Casa dei Guinigi – No 29) is built of bricks and, rising above it, is its famous tree-topped **tower** ⓥ *(visible from the corner of Via S Andrea and Via delle Chiavi d'Oro)*. The exterior of the impressive building is ornamented by two, three and four-bay Gothic windows covering a remarkable area. The two large brick-built houses *(nos 20 and 22 opposite)* also belonged to the Guinigi family.

Chiesa di Santa Maria Forisportam (C L) – The name of the church indicates that it was originally outside the Roman walls. It dates from the early

Guinigi Tower.

13C. The marble façade (unfinished) was built in the typical design of Pisan churches, with two registers of arcades on the facade and south side and three doors with architraves beautifully carved with floral and animal motifs; the lunette above the central doorway contains a *Coronation of the Virgin Mary* carved in light relief.

The interior is Romanesque in style, with the exception of the vaulting and the small dome which were added in the 16C. A paleo-Christian marble sarcophagus decorated with S-shaped carvings *(niche to the right of the entrance)* is used as a font. There are two works by Guercino – *St Lucy (last altar in the south aisle)* and *The Virgin Mary, St Francis and St Alexander (north transept)*.

Via Santa Croce, Piazza dei Servi and Piazza dei Bernardini, overlooked by the austere façade of the **Palazzo dei Bernardini (16C)** (C N), lead to Piazza San Michele.

ADDITIONAL SIGHTS

Passeggiata delle Mura (Rampart Walk) – The ramparts that give Lucca its characteristic appearance run right round the town (4km – 2.5 miles). They took the whole of the 16C and the first half of the 17C to complete and include 11 forward-projecting bastions *(baluardi)* connected by curtain walls (30m – 100ft wide at the base). The walls originally included four gateways but in 1804 Élisa Baciocchi had a fifth opened on the east side, known as Élisa's Gate. The ramparts were planted with two rows of trees in the 19C and now form an unusual public park reserved for pedestrians and cyclists.

Pinacoteca (A) ⓥ – The picture gallery housed in the Palazzo Mansi (17C) displays large compositions by Italian painters including Veronese, Giordano, Domenichino, Salvator Rosa, Bronzino, Pontormo *(Portrait of a Young Man)*, Tintoretto and Ventura Salimbeni *(St Catherine of Alexandria)*; portraits including *Young Della Rovere* by Federico Barocci; and small paintings from Italy (**Christ carrying the Cross** attributed to Il Sodoma) and from abroad, particularly by the Flemish School.

Apartments – A number of rooms display remarkable 17C-18C **decorative features**★. They include morning rooms in which the ceilings are painted with frescoes depicting mythological subjects and the walls hung with sumptuous 17C Flemish tapestries recounting the story of the Emperor Aurelian and Queen Zenobia, and the 18C-style "Conjugal Chamber" with its canopied bed beneath a fresco of Eros and Psyche.

Chiesa di San Paolino (A F) – The church, dedicated to the town's patron saint, was built between 1522 and 1536. It contains the 19C organ sometimes played by Puccini, a parishioner of San Paolino.

Casa natale di Puccini (B G) ⊘ – This tiny museum, housed in Puccini's birthplace, has collections of letters from the composer, his piano, illustrations depicting the stage set for some of his operas, portraits and postcards and other exhibits such as scented calendars inspired by his works.

Museo Nazionale di Villa Guinigi (D) ⊘ – This impressive Romanesque and Gothic brick building was once the country seat of Paolo Guinigi, who had it built in 1418 just outside the medieval walls. After extensive renovation work, the building, if not the garden, has been restored to its original appearance.

The museum displays archeological finds from the region, offers a retrospective exhibition of local sculpture and houses a collection of paintings mainly by artists from the Lucca area.

Note, in particular, the bronze jewellery from Ligurian graves (2C-3C BC), a splendid Attic crater (3C BC) decorated with a mythological scene, and some remarkably well-preserved Etruscan gold jewellery (5C BC).

Romanesque sculpture is represented by the panel depicting **Samson** sitting astride a lion (early 13C), while the Renaissance is present in a fine low relief of the **Annunciation** and an **Ecce Homo** (head of Christ bearing the crown of the thorns) by Matteo Civitali, who carved the *Tempietto* in the cathedral.

Marquetry panels show the importance of woodcarving in Lucca during the Renaissance (Views of old Lucca, executed in remarkably fine detail).

Notable examples of late 15C-16C local painting include a fine wooden *Dormition of the Virgin Mary* carved and painted by the Sienese artist Vecchietta, and two well-balanced compositions by the Florentine painter, Fra Bartolomeo, including a somewhat dramatic *Virgin of Mercy*. 18C works include a skilfully-drawn *Ecstasy of St Catherine* in pleasing shades by the local artist, Pompeo Batoni. There are some splendid gold-embroidered **vestments** made of silk or silver thread in Lucca between the 15C and the 18C.

EXCURSIONS

Villa Reale di Marlia ⊘ – *8km – 5 miles north of Lucca (exit ① on the plan) by S12; after 6km – 4 miles turn right towards Marlia (signed) and cross the railway line.*
The Villa Reale is surrounded by magnificent 17C **gardens★★** with alterations by Élisa Bonaparte. Visitors can stroll through the flower garden, lemon grove, grotto and parkland with its statues, niches, terraces and topiaried yew trees.

Villa Torrigiani ⊘ – *12km – 7.5 miles northeast of Lucca (exit ② on the plan) by the Pescia road (Pesciatina); in Zone turn left to Camigliano.*
This 16C villa was transformed into a luxurious summer residence in the 17C by Marquess Nicolao Santini, Ambassador of the Republic of Lucca to the Papal Court and to the Court of Louis XIV of France. The gardens designed by Le Nôtre are decorated with fountains, caves and grottoes. The residence with its amusing "Rococo" façade stands at the end of a long tree-lined avenue.

Devil's Bridge, Borgo a Mozzano.

The villa has played host to a number of famous guests including Maria Malibran in the 19C, the princes of Savoy-Aosta in the early 20C and the French President, Georges Pompidou, in 1972.

Villa Mansi, Segromigno ⊙ – *11km – 7 miles northeast of Lucca by the same route as above for Villa Torrigiani; from Segromigno follow the signs.* This superb 16C building has numerous statues on its façade. It stands in the middle of a huge **park★** (the west section was designed by Juvara in the 18C) which was partly laid out as landscape gardens dotted with magnificent trees and partly as Italianate gardens containing a walk lined with statues leading to a large lake.

Borgo a Mozzano – *23km – 14 miles northeast of Lucca by S12 to Abetone.* The village attracts attention because of its peculiar 12C **Magdalen Bridge** *(Ponte della Maddalena)* across the River Serchio. Its name derives from a statue of Mary Magdalen now conserved in the parish church. The bridge is also known as the **Devil's Bridge** *(Ponte del diavolo)* because legend has it that the builder requested Satan's help in order to complete it. In exchange the devil accepted the soul of the first body to cross over. The builder cunningly avoided sending a human being to hell by sending a dog over the bridge.

LUCIGNANO

Population 3 352
Michelin Map 430 M 17

Lucignano is a peaceful village in the Val di Chiana. It has an unusual elongated shape as the main street rises in spirals before entering a picturesque maze of medieval streets.

The remains of the 14C **castle** *(cassero)* backing onto the town walls stand opposite the **collegiate church of San Michele** built in the late 16C. In front of the church is a beautifully-designed staircase (in a poor state of repair). It is concave then convex in shape and set around an oval stairhead. Inside the church, the barrel vaulting is highlighted by the *pietra serena* of the pillars and arches. The monumental Baroque altar was designed by Andrea Pozzo.

The street running along the left side of the church leads to Piazza del Tribunale; at one end stands the small **palazzo comunale** decorated with coats of arms. The **museum** ⊙ presents a number of Sienese paintings (13C-15C) and *(ground floor)* a remarkable gold gem-incrusted reliquary, which owing to its shape, is known as the **Tree of St Francis★★**. It is a masterpiece produced in Sienese goldsmiths' shops during the 14C-15C.

Church of San Francesco *(right of the palazzzo comunale)* is a simple building with a harmonious Romanesque façade of alternating black and white stone. The lintel of the carved doorway is eye-catching because it consists not of the usual single horizontal block but of several upright pointed stones.

LUNIGIANA★

Michelin Map 988 folds 13-14 or 430 I-J 11-12

This historical and geographical region runs along the River Magra on the borders of Tuscany, Liguria and Emilia. Although it combines a number of different cultures, it still retains a strongly discernible character of its own.

Lunigiana was first inhabited in paleolithic times. Later there were Etruscan settlements in the area and the Romans founded a 2000-strong colony in the town of Luni (now in Liguria) from which the name Lunigiana is derived. During the Middle Ages the region was still a single entity, under the authority of the bishop.

The backdrop consists of castles – Aulla, Malgrate, Fivizzano, Fosdinovo and Pontremoli – and of Romanesque parish churches *(pievi)* – Sorano and Codiponte. The region is now famous for culinary specialities – **testaroli**, wheatflour pastry cooked in dishes *(testi)*, cut into diamond shapes, plunged into boiling water and seasoned with olive oil, basil and sheep's cheese *(pecorino)*; seasonal vegetable pies **(torta di erbe)** of which the best known is made from leeks, onions, borage and nettle tips; **focaccette**, made of wheat and corn; various traditional cakes.

① From Aulla to Casola in Lunigiana
35km – 22 miles – about half a day

Aulla – The town is overlooked by the **fortezza della Brunella** (fortress), a name most probably derived from the brown-coloured rock. This quadrangular construction dates from the early 16C and is believed to have been built by Giovanni dalle Bande Nere *(qv)*. It now houses the **Natural History Museum** ⊙, which contains a reconstruction of the natural environments of the Lunigiana region, ranging from the caves to the Mediterranean scrub *(macchia)*.

Take S63 east; beyond Rometta turn right into S445; on the outskirts of Gragnola follow the signs to Equi (south).

Equi Terme – This spa resort with its sulphur-rich springs provides treatment for respiratory and skin disorders and bone and joint diseases. In addition to its therapeutic virtues, the locality is also of special archeological and speleological interest.

The karst **caves** ⊙ are open to the public and contain a wealth of stalactites and stalagmites. In some of their deep, rugged cavities, remains have been found showing evidence of human settlements in the Paleolithic and Neolithic Ages. There are also traces of the passage of cave bears.

Return to S445. Continue east towards Codiponte and Casola in Lunigiana (Aulella Valley).

Codiponte – Its main attraction is the Romanesque parish church with Lombard-Carolingian decorative motifs. It has retained its old font.

Casola in Lunigiana – A stroll through the old village with its typical 15C-16C buildings is highly recommended.

☐ **From Aulla to Pontremoli** *22km – 13.5 miles – about half a day*

Aulla – *See above.*

Take S62 north towards Pontremoli.

Villafranca in Lunigiana – This small town is best known for its **Ethnography Museum★** ⊙, which is housed in a splendidly-restored 14C mill. It provides a clear illustration of the cultural identity of Lunigiana's rural civilisation through numerous theme-based displays and audio-visual presentations. Exhibits include weights from the Roman era, graceful wooden ex-voto statuettes, utensils for peeling chestnuts, looms, hods, cheese moulds, butter churns, etc.
Continue north on S62.

Filattiera – Beside road stands the **pieve di Sorano**, the parish church, built in the Tuscan and Lombard style. The finest example of this architectural style can be seen in the splendid apse.

Continue north on S62 to Pontremoli.

> **"La pieve"**
>
> The Italian word *pieve* is derived from the Latin *plebs*, meaning the common people, and is used to indicate the local place of worship – the parish church, Romanesque church or chapel. These churches are often rich in symbolic carvings depicting sin and redemption.

Pontremoli – Pontremoli lies at the confluence of the Rivers Magra and Verde. In 1953 the town created the Bancarella literary prize, an initiative launched by its traditional itinerant booksellers. **Piagnaro Castle**, begun in the 10C, bears witness to the town's cultural history. It gets its name from the slate slabs *(piagne)* used to roof buildings in the Lunigiana region. The castle houses the interesting **Lunigiana Museum of Statues and Steles** ⊙, a collection of female anthropomorphic sculptures representing the Mediterranean mother goddess and symbol of fertility, and male sculptures whose weapons may be intended to indicate deified heroes or tribal chiefs. The statues are arranged in three groups in typological order and span a long period dating from the second millennium BC to the 5C BC.

The large belltower *(campanone)*, situated between Piazza della Repubblica and Piazza del Duomo, is the symbol of the town. It was once part of the wall known as the war-guard *(Cacciaguerra)*, built in the 14C on the orders of Castruccio Castracani to separate the Guelf and Ghibelline districts of the town.

MAGLIANO IN TOSCANA

Population 4 071
Michelin Map 988 fold 25 or 430 ○ 15

Magliano stands at the top of a hill covered with olive trees and is half concealed by its 14C and Renaissance walls. The main street – Via di Mezzo meaning Central Street – contains two churches, San Giovanni Battista which has a Renaissance façade and San Martino which dates from the Romanesque period.

Originally there was an Etruscan town nearby; its **necropolis** ⊙ is still visible. The town later became a Roman colony under the name of **Heba**.

★ **Ruins of San Bruzio** – *Southeast in the Marsiliana direction.* Just beyond the village beside the road *(left)* are the remains of a 12C church standing solitary in the middle of a vast field. The peaceful beauty of the Romanesque ruins blends harmoniously into the changing, soft, water-colour hues of the surrounding countryside.

The MAREMMA★

The **Maremma** is a huge geographical sector usually divided into three areas – the Pisan Maremma covering the area from the southern foot-hills of the Livorno region to San Vincenzo; the Grossetan Maremma corresponding to the Grosseto province; the Latin Maremma stretching from Tarquinia to Cerveteri. The Maremma is, however, more than a coastal strip; it also reaches inland as far as the western flanks of the Metalliferous Mountains.

Although the territory is geologically very old, it is mistakenly classed as a marshy area formed during the Quaternary era. Certain sectors in fact date from the Primary, as proved by animal fossils, Secondary and Tertiary eras, and include a range of hills (Monti dell'Uccellina). This belies the image of a huge, regular alluvial plain with marshes, lakes and coastal dunes *(tomboli)* acting as natural dams.

Over 2000 years of history – The history of the Maremma could be summed up in the words "Etruscans, Romans and land reclamation." The Etruscans, who founded Populonia, Roselle and Vetulonia, were the first to attempt to drain the area, but the first major hydraulic work was undertaken during the Pax Romana. After the decline of the Roman Empire, the communication routes fell into disuse. The region returned to its natural state and the land reclaimed as a result of these first drainage projects was lost. Malaria became rife in the wild marshland areas.

Pirate raids along the coast and Barbarian invasions had particularly dramatic consequences during the Dark Ages but, from the 10C onwards, during the Lombard period and until the reign of the Aldobrandeschi, the Maremma enjoyed relative peace. Although it was still an unhealthy region, it was under the control of the Sienese and then the Medici. Dante described it on several occasions as hell on earth. In 1826 the Dukes of Lorraine, especially Leopold II, resumed land reclamation and the work continued during the period of Italian Unification and under the Fascist regime. The territory was finally drained and agriculture is now its main source of income.

Fauna – **Boars,** the symbol of the Maremma, roam wild here. Boar hunts *(cacciarella)* are a traditional event bringing together hunters, hounds and whippers-in.

Other animals typical of the region are the **Maremma ox,** a huge beast with lyre-shaped horns, and the **Maremma horse,** a small and very sturdy animal, probably descended from the Berber horse. Herdsmen **(buttero),** similar to the cowherds of the Camargue region in southern France, carry out their ancient and taxing task on horseback. The highlight of the year is the branding of the cattle *(merca)* which takes place on 1 May in Alberese.

The **fallow deer** is another common inhabitant of the region; its hide is reddish-brown dotted with white in the summer and grey-brown in the winter.

The woods are also home to **roe-deer, porcupine** and **badgers.** Indeed, porcupine and badgers often share the same set. As for the **fox,** it is the undisputed lord of Maremma, at home in all types of natural environment, whether fields of crops, pastureland, woods, rocky areas, pine forests, marshes or dunes. The area also boasts **wildcats, stone martens, weasels** and other mammals, as well as a multitude of beautifully-coloured birds including **falcons, buzzards, owls, shoveller ducks, seagulls, hoopoes, herons, cormorants and kingfishers,** which are of great interest to bird-watchers.

Plantlife – Like the fauna, the plantlife varies depending on the environment. **Juniper** and **lentiscus** can be found growing between the **marine lilies** of the coastal dunes and the pine forest. The rocks are covered with **thyme** and **red valerian,** while the hills are overrun by scrub and **heather.** Among the many other species native to the region are the **dwarf fan-palm, rosemary, asphodel, broom, yellow poppies** and **orchids.**

① Countryside, Pine Forests and Sea *135km – 84 miles – 1 day*

The Grosseto province is generally considered the area most typical of the Maremma region. It consists of a plain which rises from below sea-level along the coast to rolling countryside further inland. The hills are planted with olive trees and vines and interspersed with farmland. Near the sea the colours can be intense and vary with the changing seasons. Along the coast the fine sandy beaches are fringed with pine forests.

Grosseto – *See Grosseto.*

A quiet country road with very little traffic leads to the archeological site at Roselle.

Rovine di Roselle – *See Rovine di Roselle.*

After crossing S1 (Via Aurelia), continue towards Buriano.

The road crosses the plain south of Vetulonia on the hillside and climbs along a series of terraces to the burial ground and the site of an archeological excavation before reaching the village.

★ **Necropoli di Vetulonia** – *See Necropoli di Vetulonia.*

To reach Follonica either take the road through Gavorrano or take S1 (superstrada).

Kingfisher

Hoopoe

Grey Heron

Mallard duck

Wild boar

Porcupine

Badger

Dessins : Maël Dewyter

207

The MAREMMA

⌂ **Follonica** – This seaside resort is popular for its mild climate, fresh pine forests and proximity to places of artistic interest. It faces west across Fallonica Bay to the island of Elba.

⌂⌂⌂ **Punta Ala** – This modern and luxurious residential resort is set in a picturesque pine forest on the southern promontory of Follonica Bay. The superb sheltered beach is complemented by a large yachting marina, sports facilities – water sports, riding and polo – and a golf course which hosts international tournaments.

⌂⌂ **Castiglione della Pescaia** – The fishing harbour and seaside resort of Castiglione was built as a canal port at the foot of a hill. On the slope is a walled medieval town with steep paved streets, houses with barred windows, covered passageways and fortified gates.

From the summit, capped by a small castle with large rectangular towers, there is an interesting view of the canal port and the fine sandy beaches skirting the headland.

South of Castiglione the road skirts the Pineta del Tombolo, a long stand of umbrella pines.

⌂ **Principina a Mare** – This peaceful seaside town lies in the heart of the pine forest that stretches south along the coast from Follonica. There are some splendid walks beneath the pine trees or along the long beach of fine sand.

Return to Grosseto.

② From the Uccellina Hills to Argentario
160km - 100 miles - 1 day

Grosseto - *See Grosseto.*

Take S1 (Via Aurelia) to the Alberese exit.

As the landscape south of Grosseto becomes gradually more varied, the typical features of the Maremma region become more apparent.

In Alberese park in front of the visitor centre (centro-visito) which sells admission tickets to the park and is also the departure point for coach tours.

★ **Parco Naturale della Maremma** ⊘ – The **park** consists almost entirely of the Monti dell'Uccellina (almost 4 000 hectares – 9 884 acres), an area of

forest, Mediterranean scrub, running parallel to the coastline between Principina a Mare and Talamone.

The many species of local flora and fauna are influenced by the varied climate that includes features typical of continental, Mediterranean and, in certain cases, sub-desert conditions.

There is much evidence of the first human settlements from the Paleolithic era through the Bronze Age up to the days of the Romans. Man has been able to hunt here since ancient times owing to the great mammals which have always been a characteristic feature of the Maremma region. In the past, however, the coastal areas were infested with mosquitoes carrying malaria and it was impossible for people to settle there permanently.

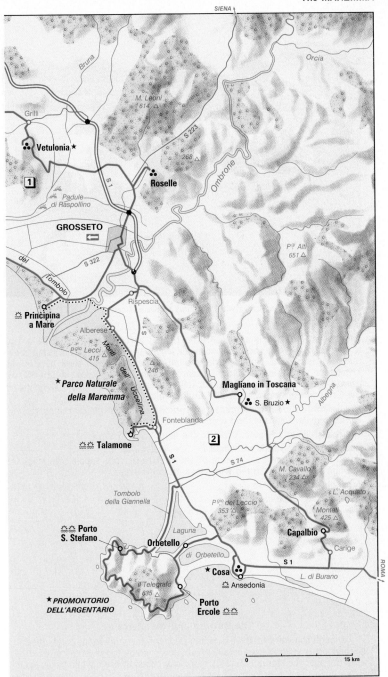

There are guided tours or self-guided tours along the theme-based itineraries designed to include the various different aspects of the park – forest, wildlife and panoramic views.

Also available are the "Parkland" itineraries *(guided tours in summer; self-guided tours along the paths in winter)* of San Rabano *(5 hours – one departure per day)* and delle Torri *(tour of the Towers – 3 hours – two departures per day)* or a tour of the outlying area around Alberese concentrating on the flora and fauna.

Continue south to rejoin S1.

Fonteblanda – *At the junction with the road to Talamone.* The town is famous for its spa, Terme dell'Osa.

E. Sailler/GLMR

Herdsmen with Maremma horses and cattle.

♨♨ **Talamone** – Talamone is a typical little fishing harbour, overlooked by a 15C fortress. The town has both Etruscan and legendary origins. The hill rising above the town is said to be the burial mound of Telamon who took part in the Argonauts' expedition to Colchis in search of the Golden Fleece. In 225 BC two Roman consuls, Emilius Papus and Attilius Regolus, won a major victory over the Gauls in the nearby plain of Campo Regio.

The best way to tour the Argentario promontory is to begin on the north side, Tombolo della Giannella, and visit Orbetello at the end.

The road follows the pine forest to the lagoon.

★ **Promontorio dell'Argentario and Orbetello** – *See Argentario.*

North of Carige the final section of the tour runs from Capalbio to Magliano through rolling hills planted with vines and olive trees.

★ **Rovine di Cosa** – *See Cosa.*

Capalbio – *See Capalbio.*

Magliano in Toscana – *See Magliano in Toscana.*

The Buttero and the Merca

Although the work of the herdsman *(buttero)* has undergone fundamental changes, it still requires a daily effort governed by the rhythms of nature. In the past the Maremma herdsman's day began at dawn when he selected his horse, and was followed by a range of different tasks, including the supervision and sorting of the cattle and pens and helping any cow having difficulty giving birth. While still inside the cow the calf was hitched to the horse and then pulled out. The high point of the herdsman's working year is the **merca,** a ceremony rather than a practice, in which cattle are branded to indicate ownership. To facilitate the branding and ensure more rapid healing, the job is done in spring when the animals have lost their winter hide. This exhausting and hazardous work used also to be seen as a form of entertainment. As the saying goes: "Anyone whose heart has not been seared by the *merca* could not really have been there". The cowherds were not the only people involved in the day's events. The glorious finale was entrusted to the women of the farm, who spent several days preparing pasta, meat and cakes, and served up a meal fit for a king.

MASSA

Population 66 680
Michelin Map 988 fold 14 or 430 J 12

Massa lies in the plains at the foot of the Apuan Alps, a short distance *(4km – 2.5 miles)* inland from the Versilia Riviera. This provincial capital is a modern town with several historic buildings. The squares are adorned with large fountains and marble sculptures and there are also numerous white marble façades owing to the proximity of Carrara.

Historic buildings – From the 15C-18C the town belonged to the powerful Malaspina family. Their 15C-16C Renaissance **castle**, Castello Malaspina, is incorporated in the half-ruined medieval fortress *(Rocca)* on the stony hillside overlooking the town, and their 16C-17C family residence, **Palazzo Cybo Malaspina**, now houses the Prefettura *(Piazza Aranci in the town centre)*.

From Piazza Aranci take Via Dante Alighieri.

The **cathedral** *(duomo)* has a modern marble façade, is constructed throughout of marble and contains a number of interesting works of art – the font, a *Madonna* by Pinturicchio *(above the altar)*, a 16C crib, 13C Crucifix and *(in an underground chapel)* the tombs of the Malaspina family.

The modern church of **San Sebastiano** is decorated with figurative murals by Dino Cellini (1978).

MASSA MARITTIMA★★

Population 9 498
Michelin Map 988 fold 14 or 430 M 14

The name Massa Marittima is believed by some to indicate that the territory formerly extended as far as the sea; others think it refers to the nearby Maremma region. This old medieval town stands on the last foot-hills of the Metalliferous Mountains in rolling countryside and blends harmoniously with the various activities – mining, farming and craftwork – on which its prosperity has been based since the very beginning.

Twice a year *(May and August)* Massa recalls the Middle Ages during the historic pageant *(Balestro del Girifalco)* when pennant-throwers in 14C costume give spectacular demonstrations accompanied by drum rolls and trumpet fanfares. *(See the Calendar of Events at the end of the guide.)*

SIGHTS

★★ **Piazza Garibaldi** – The square has a strong medieval atmosphere and is surrounded by three Romanesque buildings – the Palazzo del Podestà with double window bays, the town hall capped with merlons, and the cathedral.

★★ **Duomo (Cathedral)** – This majestic Pisan Romanesque building surrounded by blind arcades probably dates from the early 11C. It was extended by Giovanni Pisano in 1287 and its façade was completed with a triple-pointed pediment. Its fine **belltower★**, which was formerly crenellated, now has four bellcotes and contains window bays increasing in number from ground floor to top. On the façade note the roaring lions, delicately undercut capitals and the lintel above the central doorway depicting the life of St Cerbone, Bishop of Populonia and patron saint of the town, to whom the church is dedicated.

The interior is laid out in the style of a basilica. Note the varied capitals in the nave and *(inside wall of the façade)* the remains of 14C frescoes and fragments of Byzantine-style low reliefs (10C). Near the entrance is a marble low relief originating from a 3C Roman sarcophagus; above it is a late-13C fresco of the *Madonna and Child*.

The unusual font consists of a monolithic Romanesque basin, decorated with low reliefs depicting episodes from the Old and New Testaments.

The chapel *(north side of the chancel)* contains a *Virgin of the Graces* attributed to **Duccio di Buoninsegna** *(c*1255 – *c*1318) and fragments of the *Presentation of Jesus in the Temple*, a work by Sano di Pietro (1406-1481) in a very poor state of repair.

The chancel houses St Cerbone's marble sarcophagus *(arca)*, carved by Goro di Gregorio in 1324.

The chapel *(south side of the chancel)* contains a *Crucifixion* by Segna di Bonaventura (early 14C).

Palazzo del Podestà – This building dates from 1225-1230 and was formerly the residence of the most eminent governor *(podestà)* and holder of executive powers. The façade is decorated with the coats of arms of the various governors who lived here. The building now houses the **Museo archeologico** (Archeology Museum) ⊘ which contains an interesting *stele* from Vado all'Arancio, the only example found in Etruria of a style typical of northwest Tuscany and southern France, and Etruscan collections from the burial ground at Accesa Lake.

The art gallery has a fine *Virgin in Majesty* by Ambrogio Lorenzetti (1285-*c*1348).

★ **Fortezza dei senesi e Torre del Candeliere** (Sienese Fortress and Tower) ⊘ - Massa is surrounded by walls dating from the 13C, which were partly destroyed by the Sienese in 1337 and rebuilt by them during the 14C.

The fortress, with its five towers, was built in 1335 and divides the town into two sections joined by the Porta alle Silici. It is connected to the tower (Torre del Candeliere) by an arch (22m - 72ft wide). The tower was reduced to a third of its height by the Sienese and is all that remains of an earlier fortress built in 1228.

Museo di storia e arte delle miniere (History and Art of Mining Museum) ⊘ - The museum is close to the Sienese Fortress and contains collections of tools, some of them dating from the Middle Ages, minerals, scale models of main mine shafts and an interesting display of documents illustrating the town's ancient mining industry.

Antico frantoio (Old Press) ⊘ - Fine 18C wooden press.

Sant'Agostino - This early 14C church has a large unadorned Romanesque façade, a fine Gothic apse and a crenellated belltower added in the 17C. On the left of the tower are the remains of two wings of the original Romanesque cloisters. Note the deep red and blue stained-glass windows in the apse within the timber-vaulted interior.

San Francesco ⊘ - This Gothic church has recently undergone extensive restoration work, which has modified the original structure, and is part of the monastery, now a seminary, said to have been founded by St Francis *c*1220. Although little has remained intact except the apse, the building nevertheless still has the simple charm that is so characteristic of Franciscan churches. The modern stained-glass windows in beautiful shades of green depict episodes in the lives of St Francis, St Cerbone and St Bernard.

Museo della Miniera (Mining Museum) ⊘ - *Near Piazza Garibaldi*. The museum gives an insight into the mining of iron ore in the region, with a long gallery (700m - 2300ft) containing reconstructions of the various kinds of pit props - wood, iron, concrete - which were used in turn and the recesses contain the trucks, machinery and tools used in mining. There is also a display of mineral samples.

EXCURSION

★★ **San Galgano Abbey** - *32km - 20 miles northeast. See San Galgano.*

MONTALCINO★

Population 5 077
Michelin Map 988 fold 15 or 430 M 16

The hillside town of Montalcino still has part of its 13C walls and its fortress *(rocca)* built in 1361. It was ruled by Siena for several centuries and served as a refuge for the members of the government of the Republic of Siena when their town was captured by Charles V in 1555. Each autumn during the **Thrush Festival** *(Sagra del Tordo - see Calendar of Events at the end of the guide)*, the four districts of the medieval town recall the past with a procession in period costume. They also compete against each other in an archery contest.

Montalcino is known throughout Italy for its excellent red wine, **Brunello**, a very high-quality vintage from a restricted wine-growing area.

SIGHTS

★★ **Rocca** ⊘ - This fine example of a 14C fortress has been remarkably well-preserved despite the fact that the development of artillery in the following century made this type of defensive system vulnerable to attack. The high walls, complete with a parapet walk and machicolations, form a huge pentagon in which the population could seek refuge. The angles of the structure are marked by five polygonal towers, one of which has been partly destroyed.

In the interior *(left of the entrance)* are the remains of a basilica and *(far right)* the keep *(mastio)* designed to house officials and noblemen in times of siege; there is wine-tasting *(ground floor)* and the standard of the Republic of Siena painted by Il Sodoma *(second floor)*. From the **parapet walk** there is a vast panoramic **view** over the town and surrounding countryside.

★ **Palazzo Comunale** – The building overlooking Piazza del Popolo was built in the 13C. It is flanked by a 14C-15C arcaded loggia and surmounted by a tall belfry.

Sant'Egidio – *Piazza Garibaldi, behind the town hall*. The church has a nave with wooden rafters and is divided by three arches. Near the entrance is a large gilded wooden tabernacle dating from the 16C.

Museo Civico e Diocesano (Civic and Diocesan Museum) ⊙ – *Via Ricasoli*. In addition to a number of prehistoric and Etruscan remains and a collection of ceramic ware from Montalcino (13C-18C), the museum contains paintings and polychrome wooden statues by the Sienese School (14C-15C) and a two-volume Bible and a Crucifix, both dating from the 12C, from the nearby abbey of Sant'Antimo.

Sant'Agostino – *Near the museum, where Via Ricasoli widens into a small square*. This 14C Romanesque-Gothic church includes a west front decorated with a rose window and an elegant marble doorway. Inside are 14C frescoes by the Sienese School including a *Scourging of Christ (right of the side entrance)* and *Scenes from the Passion of Christ and the Life of the Abbot St Antony (righthand wall)* by unknown artists.

EXCURSION

★★ **Abbey of Sant'Antimo** ⊙ – *10km – 6 miles south. See Sant'Antimo.*

MONTECATINI TERME✚✚✚

Population 20 671
Michelin Map 988 fold 14 or 430 K 14
Town plan in the current Michelin Red Guide Italia

Montecatini has a large number of hotels and is one of the most elegant and popular spa resorts in Italy. The spa season is particularly long here and the town provides the ideal setting for an enjoyable break – parks, wide variety of entertainments, race-course.

Its spring water has been famous for its medicinal properties for centuries. It is used to treat metabolic disorders, liver, stomach and intestinal complaints and rheumatism. Numerous different therapies are used, including mud baths and balneotherapy, but the commonest form of treatment is drinking the water straight from the spring.

Museo dell'Accademia d'Arte ⊙ – *Viale Diaz*. This modern art gallery contains sculptures by Dupré, a dramatic colourful fresco by Pietro Annigoni *(Life)*, personal souvenirs of Verdi and Puccini and works by Guttuso, Primo Conti, Galileo Chini, Gentilini and Messina.

LARA PESSINA

Montecatini Terme.

EXCURSIONS

Montecatini Alto - *5km - 3 miles northeast*. This is a small but elegant hillside village overlooking the Nievole Valley. In 1315 it was the site of the meeting between Uguccione della Faggiuola, a member of the Ghibelline faction from Lucca, and Castruccio Castracani, a Ghibelline from Pisa; together they defeated the Guelfs of Florence.

Piazza Giusti is made particularly attractive by the medieval tower known as Casa di Ugolino (Hugolin's House), the town houses decorated with coats of arms and the attractive cafe terraces.

✚ **Monsummano Terme** - *4km - 2 1/2 miles southeast*. The resort of Monsummano is best known for providing therapy in its caves for the treatment of gout, arthritis, diseases of the circulation and disorders of the respiratory system.

It was also the birthplace of the Italian poet, **Giuseppe Giusti** (1809-1850), who is commemmorated by the memorial in the square and the nearby **Casa Giusti** national museum ⊙.

Abbazia di MONTE OLIVETO MAGGIORE★★

Michelin Map 430 M 16

The tour (about 1 hour) ⊙ includes the church and the main cloisters; the refectory is occasionally open to view. 5min on foot from car park to the abbey.

The huge pink brick buildings of this famous abbey nestle among the cypress trees in a landscape of eroded hills. Monte Oliveto is the mother-house of the Olivetians, a congregation of Benedictine monks founded in 1313 by Blessed Bernard Tolomei of Siena.

A fortified tower with terracotta decorations by the Luca Della Robbia School leads into the monastery grounds.

Main Cloisters – The cloisters were decorated with a superb series of 36 **frescoes★★** recounting the life of St Benedict. They were painted by Luca Signorelli *(qv)* from 1498 onwards and by Sodoma *(qv)* between 1505 and 1508.

The cycle *(left to right)* begins near the church door with the main arch on which are paintings of *Christ at the Pillar* and *Christ carrying His Cross*, both of them masterpieces by Sodoma. Like the frescoes on the north side, the first 19 scenes, starting with *St Benedict leaving his Father's House*, are by the same painter. They are followed by a fresco by Riccio and then eight frescoes by Signorelli.

Sodoma, who is portrayed in the third fresco facing the viewer with his hair tumbling about his shoulders, was a man of refinement and a genius, who was influenced by Leonardo da Vinci and Perugino. He was not particularly pious and was mainly attracted by the aesthetic portrayal of human types, landscapes and picturesque detail, as shown in the 4th fresco in which St Benedict receives the hermit's habit, the 12th fresco *(first on the south side)*, where the saint welcomes two young men in the midst of a crowd of characters in varying poses, and the 19th fresco *(last on the south side)*, in which lascivious courtesans are sent to tempt the monks; it shows splendid architectural details opening out onto a deep-set landscape.

The work of Signorelli *(qv)* is distinguishable by the sculpture-like power of his figures and the dramatic settings in which the landscapes are reduced to a mere suggestion of space. This is evident in the 24th fresco where St Benedict restores to life a monk who has fallen from the top of a wall.

The cloisters give access to the 15C refectory which is decorated with frescoes dating from the same period *(Last Supper)*.

Abbey Church – The interior has been refurbished in 18C Baroque style but the stained-glass windows are of modern design.

The chapel *(left of the entrance from the exterior)* contains a wooden Crucifix brought to the abbey by its founder in 1313. The nave is lined by magnificent **choirstalls★★** (1505) by Fra Giovanni da Verona; they include marquetry inlays of birds, architectural vistas, tabernacles and musical instruments etc. A staircase to the right of the chancel leads to the crib.

Admission times and charges for the sights described are listed at the end of the guide

Every sight for which there are times and charges is identified by the clockface symbol ⊙ in the Sights section of the guide

Population 13 846
Michelin Map 988 fold 15 or 430 M 17

Montepulciano is an attractive little town typical of the Renaissance period. It occupies a remarkably picturesque **setting**★★ on the top of a tufa hill separating two valleys.

The town was founded in the 6C by people from Chiusi fleeing the Barbarian invasions. They named it Mons Politianus, which explains why people from the town are known as Poliziani.

Poets have long sung the praises of its ruby-red wine *(vino nobile)*.

Antonio da Sangallo the Elder, one of the two senior members of the famous family of Renaissance sculptors and architects, bequeathed some of his most famous works to Montepulciano.

Poliziano

Poliziano (b 1454 Montepulciano, d 1494 Florence) was one of the most eloquent poets of the Renaissance. He became a friend of Lorenzo the Magnificent whom he nicknamed *Lauro* which means laurel bush. They met and conversed in Fiesole where Poliziano had a villa, a gift from Lorenzo because Poliziano had saved him from the assassins of his brother Giuliano during the Pazzi Conspiracy *(qv)*. The *Stanze*, Poliziano's masterpiece, describe a kind of Garden of Delights haunted by touching female figures. His poetry corresponds in style to the painting of his friend, Botticelli.

★OLD TOWN
Tour – 90min

Within Porta al Prato, a fortified gate bearing the Tuscan coat of arms, and beyond the Florentine lion *(Marzocco)*, the main street lined with numerous interesting **mansions**★ and churches climbs uphill. At the end of the first section *(Via Roma)* the street divides in two to enclose the main historic landmarks. The splendid Palazzo Avignonesi *(no 91 Via Roma)* dates from the late Renaissance period (16C) and is attributed to Vignola. The mansion *(no 73)*, which belonged to the antique dealer Bucelli, is decorated with engraved Etruscan and Roman stones. Further along *(right)* is the church of Sant'Agostino (restored) with its Renaissance **façade**★ designed by Michelozzo of Florence in the 15C. The Jack-o'-the-clock on the tower *(opposite)* is none other than Mr Punch.

Turn left at the Logge del Mercato (Corn Exchange) into Via di Voltaia nel Corso.

The Palazzo Cervini *(no 21)* was designed by Antonio da Sangallo the Elder and is a fine example of the Florentine Renaissance style, with its rustication and rounded and triangular pediments.

Continue along Via dell'Opio nel Corso and Via Poliziano.

Poliziano was born at no 1.

★★ **Piazza Grande** – The Main Square at the top of the town is the central landmark. Its irregular layout and the different styles of façade avoid architectural monotony and combine to give an overall sense of harmony.

★ **Palazzo comunale** – *West side.* The Gothic town hall includes 15C alterations by Michelozzo. It is reminiscent of the Palazzo Vecchio in Florence with its machicolations, battlements and picturesque square tower.

From the top of the **tower** ⊙ there is an extensive **panoramic view**★★★ of the town and its outskirts including the Church of the Madonna di San Biagio *(west)* and the Tuscan countryside embracing Mount Amiata *(southwest)*, Pienza *(west)*, Siena *(northwest)*, Cortona *(northeast)* and Lake Trasimene *(east)*.

On the other side of the square stands Palazzo Contucci, which was begun in 1519 by Sangallo the Elder but was not completed until the 18C.

★ **Palazzo Nobili-Tarugi** – *North side.* This majestic Renaissance palace opposite the cathedral is attributed to Sangallo the Elder. It features a portico and huge doorway with semicircular arches. Six Ionic columns set on a very high base support the pilasters of the first floor. The loggia *(left)* used to be open but has been walled up.

The bay windows with their rounded pediments are set on small consoles. On the left above the central doorway, note the window from which the occupants of the palace could watch visitors arriving.

Next to Palazzo Tarugi is the Palazzo del Capitano *(north side)*.

★ **Well** – This picturesque well is made especially charming by the two lions supporting the Medici coat of arms.

Duomo - *South side*. The **cathedral** was built in the 16C-17C, though the façade never received its marble cladding. The interior, consisting of nave and two aisles, is austere and stylistically pure. Beside the central doorway *(left)* is the recumbent statue of Bartolomeo Aragazzi, Secretary to Pope Martin V; the statue was formerly part of Aragazzi's tomb, designed by Michelozzo (15C) and dismantled in the 17C. The two elegant statues flanking the high altar and the low-relief sculptures on the first two pillars were also originally part of the tomb. The 14C baptistery is surmounted by a fine piece of terracotta by Andrea Della Robbia. One of the pillars in the north aisle bears a portrait of the Madonna painted by Sano di Pietro in the 15C. Behind the high altar is a monumental **reredos**★ painted in 1401 by Taddeo di Bartolo, the Sienese artist, depicting the *Assumption*, the *Annunciation* and the *Coronation of the Virgin Mary*.

Museo Civico ⊘ - *Via Ricci*. The museum displays a superb collection of glazed terracotta ware by Andrea Della Robbia, Luca's nephew. There are also Etruscan exhibits and 13C-18C paintings.

Continue north down the main street.

Piazza San Francesco - The square provides a fine view of the surrounding countryside and the church of San Biagio below.

Continue down Via del Poggiolo; turn right into Via dell'Erbe to return to the Logge del Mercato (Corn Exchange).

ADDITIONAL SIGHTS

★★ **Chiesa della Madonna di San Biagio** - *Below the town (west); off S146 to Pienza*. An avenue of cypress tress leads to this magnificent church built of pale golden stone which stands in a delightful setting in the middle of a grassy stretch of flat land high above the valley. It is the masterpiece of Antonio da Sangallo the Elder and was inaugurated in 1529 by Pope Clement VII, a member of the Medici family. As Sangallo's building was strongly influenced by Bramante's plan for the reconstruction of St Peter's in Rome which, owing to the artist's death, was not carried out as planned, it is a valuable reminder of the designs drawn by the architect for the Pope. Although somewhat simplified, San Biagio copies the notion of the central plan in the form of a Greek cross with domed roof, the main façade being given greater emphasis by two belltowers set in the recesses of the cross. One is incomplete; the other includes the three orders – Doric, Ionic and Corinthian. The south arm extends into a semicircular sacristy. The harmonious lines and skilful design of the architectural motifs enhancing the structural features convey a sense of majestic solemnity, which continues into the interior. Note *(left of the entrance)* an *Annunciation*, painted in the 14C, and the impressive marble high altar (1584).

The elegant building with a portico *(opposite)* is the canon's residence *(Canonica)*.

San Biagio.

MONTERIGGIONI★★

Michelin Map 988 fold 15 or 430 L 15

> *Traffic is restricted within the walls to residents and hotel guests only. Car park beside the approach road 5min on foot from the entrance. As the approach road beyond the car park is steep, it is not advisable to drive up to the village with a trailer or caravan in tow.*

Monteriggioni stands peacefully on top of one of the graceful hills north of Siena. It owes its picturesque beauty to the clear-cut outline of its enclosing wall and 14 square towers. The fortress was formerly a Ghibelline outpost, built by the Sienese in the early 13C, and was described by Dante in his *Divine Comedy*.

The village, which is totally contained within its walls, consists of a long main street running from south to north between the two gates and passing along one side of the square which is flanked *(east)* by a small Romanesque-Gothic church. The few houses are in a narrow lane leading off the northwest corner of the square.

MONTE SAN SAVINO

Population 7 838
Michelin Map 988 fold 15 or 430 M 17

This medieval town was the birthplace of the sculptor and architect, Andrea Contucci, otherwise known as Sansovino (1470-1529) a deformation of San Savino. A thoroughfare lined with some fine historic buildings runs right through the town linking the two gates set within the partly-preserved walls of the old stronghold *(cassero)*.

Piazza G F Gamurrini – The square lies near the Porta Fiorentina and is marked by an obelisk erected in 1644. Next to the old stronghold, built by the Sienese in 1383, stands the humble 17C church of **Santa Chiara**. It contains two examples of terracotta ware by Sansovino – a group depicting *St Sebastian, St Lawrence and St Roch* and a *Madonna and Child between four saints*, glazed by Giovanni Della Robbia.

★ **Loggia dei Mercanti** – The lines of this majestic loggia, attributed to Sansovino (1518-1520), are emphasised by the use of *pietra serena*. Its Corinthian capitals display remarkable finesse.

Palazzo Comunale – The palace stands opposite the loggia and was built for the Del Monte family by Sangallo the Elder between 1515 and 1517. It consists of a ground floor built in heavily rusticated stonework, supporting a well-structured *piano nobile*, including windows surmounted by alternating rounded and triangular pediments. The corner of the building is decorated with a fine coat of arms of the Del Monte family. The typical Renaissance courtyard contains two wells; the upper storey has mullioned windows.

Chiesa della Misericordia – This Romanesque church consists of a nave with wooden rafters. It was redecorated throughout in the Baroque style during the 17C-18C. The tomb immediately to the left of the main entrance was an early work by Sansovino (1498).

Palazzo Pretorio – This 14C building, formerly the residence of the Florentine magistrate *(podestà)*, is decorated with the coats of arms of those who held the office.

Sant'Agostino – This 14C church (extended in the 16C-17C) is decorated with a fine Gothic doorway and a rose window with stained glass designed by Guillaume de Marcillat. Inside are a number of early 15C frescoes.
To the left of the church is the entrance to small cloisters with semicircular arcades built to plans by Sansovino. Beyond them is the baptistery of San Giovanni, which has a splendid door designed by the same artist.

EXCURSION

Santuario di Santa Maria delle Vertighe – *2km – 1 mile east*. A stand of chestnut trees flanks this 16C building, which was formerly a Marian church dating from the 11C. The nave and aisles, roofed with wooden rafters, incorporate the Romanesque chevet of the original chapel which was the subject of popular devotion. This ensured that the two successive portraits of the Virgin could be kept in their original setting. They consist of a fresco of the *Assumption* (partly preserved) which adorns the small oven-vaulted apse, and the **Virgin altarpiece★** by Margarito of Arezzo (13C), which became the subject of worship after being placed on a lower level in the 15C.

IL MUGELLO*

Michelin Map 988 folds 14 and 15 or 430 J/K 15/16

This delightful valley north of Florence, through which flows the River Sieve, was popular with the Florentine aristocracy and wealthy middle classes as a summer resort as early as the 14C. Its attraction over the centuries has been due to its mild climate, the beautiful rolling hills, the well-stocked forests and the abundant water supply which means the countryside never loses its lushness. The region was the birthplace of the Medici family and was particularly popular with Cosimo the Elder, who had the fortresses of Cafaggiolo *(qv)* and Trebbio *(private estate)* built nearby and also organised alterations to the Franciscan friary of Bosco ai Frati.

Unfortunately the Mugello region suffered extensive damage during the 1919 earthquake.

BY HILL AND DALE

100km - 62 miles - about 5 hours

Borgo San Lorenzo – Although badly damaged during the 1919 earthquake, Borgo San Lorenzo is nonetheless still the main town in the Mugello area. The Palazzo Pretorio in Piazza Garibaldi was reconstructed exactly as it had been, so too was the west front of the church of San Lorenzo, visible from the square.

The church dates from the 12C but its unusual hexagonal belltower dates from the 13C. The extremely bare interior contains a number of fine works by the Florentine School including – *(4th altar on the south aisle)* a *Madonna and Child* attributed to Taddeo Gaddi (15C), *(right of the chancel)* a fragment of a reredos depicting the face of the Virgin Mary, attributed to Giotto, and *(apse)* a *Crucifix* dating from the second half of the 14C.

From Piazza Garibaldi the route to Piazza Cavour passes beneath the clock tower in Corso Matteotti. Just before **Porta Fiorentina** (14C) *(second street on the right)* there is a lane *(right)* which runs beside the old rounded town walls to Piazza Cavour.

Take S302 towards Faenza; after 2.8km - 1 3/4 miles turn left into the lane leading to the church (400m - 433yds).

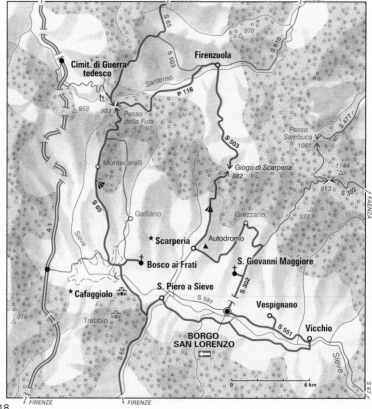

Chiesa di San Giovanni Maggiore – This pretty little country **church** set behind an elegant arched portico and flanked by a graceful octagonal belltower, contains a marble pulpit with symbolic inset motifs (vases) in black stone on all four sides.

Return to S302; continue towards Faenza; then turn left towards Grezzano and Scarperia.

Autodromo Internazionale del Mugello (Mugello Motor Racing Track) – *1km – 1/2 mile east of Scarperia*. The race track hosts Formula 2 races and motor cycle world championships.

★ **Scarperia** – This is a small well-maintained town with a thriving and traditional cutlery trade. It still has its splendid crenellated **Palazzo Pretorio**★★, built in the small central square in the early 14C to serve as a residence for the deputies of the Mugello region. A large number of stone and glazed ceramic coats of arms adorn the façade and courtyard, while the interior is decorated with numerous 14C-15C frescoes – religious scenes and painted coats of arms.

Opposite the Palazzo Pretorio stands the **church** which contains *(high altar)* two extremely delicate marble sculptures, the first a tabernacle by Mino da Fiesole and the second a tondo of the *Madonna and Child* by Benedetto da Maiano. Just outside the church on the left side of the square is a small **oratory** known as the **Madonna di Piazza**. Inside is a Gothic shrine with wreathed columns containing a *Madonna and Child* by Jacopo del Casentino, which is held in great veneration by local people.

Take S503 north.

The road climbs sharply up the range of hills on the north side of the Sieve Valley. The steep and winding road provides fine views south over the Mugello region before entering a wooded area. Further on, the road crosses the pass, Giogo di Scarperia, before heading down to Firenzuola, which is visible in the distance.

Firenzuola – Although Firenzuola was badly damaged during the last war, it has nevertheless retained its grid layout bisected by a picturesque thoroughfare lined with porticoes. At the southern end of the street is the Porta Fiorentina, surmounted by a pinnacle turret, and at the north end the Porta Bolognese. The crenellated Palazzo del Populo *(Piazza Agnolo Firenzuola)*, surmounted by a tower, is a faithful reconstruction of the 14C building.

From Porta Bolognese turn left into S503; after approximately 1.5km – 1 mile bear left into SP116 towards Passo della Futa. At the junction with S65 turn right and continue for approximately 100m – 108yds.

Cimitero di guerra tedesco (German Military Cemetery) – Beside the road *(left)* stands a huge, towering building erected in memory of the 30 653 German soldiers who were killed in this area during the Second World War.

Take S65 south towards Florence.

The road soon crosses the pass (Passo della Futa) and then descends into the Sieve Valley through pine and beech trees. South of Montecarelli the view widens out to embrace the scenic Mugello Valley, bounded by gently-rolling hills.

8km – 5 miles south of Montecarelli, at the crossroads after the righthand turn to Barberino di Mugello (about 250m – 270yds) turn left towards Galliano. After another 150m – 162yds turn right to Bosco ai Frati.

Bosco ai Frati – This Franciscan friary lies off the beaten track and retains the ideal of solitude, one of the basic tenets of the Franciscan Order when it was founded in the 13C. Cosimo the Elder *(see above)* commissioned Michelozzo to rebuild it between 1420 and 1428. In front of the church is a small porch with two columns crowned by capitals bearing the Medici coat of arms, which also appears on the tall façade. The church has a nave but no aisles. The chancel contains a huge gilded wooden reredos carved in the Florentine Mannerist style against which stands a statue of St Francis.

Return to S65 and drive south.

★ **Villa de Cafaggiolo** – *Not open to the public*. On the righthand side of the road just before a bend stands the old Florentine fortress that Cosimo the Elder had converted into a country manor by Michelozzo in 1451, so that he could stay in the region of his ancestors in reasonable comfort. The grounds and outbuildings were also designed by Michelozzo. The villa has retained the proud appearance conveyed by its central tower, fairly massive size and crown of battlements, which are now slightly obscured by the roofs erected over the old parapet walks. Lorenzo the Magnificent and his brother Giuliano spent part of their childhood here and Lorenzino (Musset's Lorenzaccio) sought refuge in the fortress after murdering his cousin, Duke Alessandro.

The small town of Cafaggiolo was also famous in the 15C-16C for its majolica ware.

On the south side of Cafaggiolo turn left at the second junction from the hamlet.

San Piero a Sieve – San Piero is a small, relatively modern village overlooked to the west by **San Martino Fortress** , which was built on a high wooded hilltop by Buontalenti in the late 16C; it can be glimpsed *(left)* on entering the village *(access 800m – 865yds beyond the village via a narrow dirt track)*. From the high brick walls of the pentagonal fortress, there is a panoramic view of the Mugello Valley. The parish church in the village *(main street)* contains a magnificent glazed ceramic baptismal **font★** *(left of the entrance)*.

Take the road along the south bank of the Sieve.

The road passes through superb scenery in the heart of the lush green Mugello Valley, bounded by wooded hillsides.

Vicchio – A public park is laid out in the centre of the main square facing the loggia of the town hall (municipio).

Take Via Garibaldi on the left side of the building; in Piazza Giotto turn right into Corso del Popolo.

Benvenuto Cellini's house is where the famous sculptor spent the last 12 years of his life.

A raised terrace nearby offers a fine view over the rolling hillsides of the Mugello region.

The **Museo Beato Angelico** ⊙ *(Piazzetta Don Milani)* is named after the Dominican artist who was born in Vicchio; it contains a collection of works of art from churches and religious buildings throughout the Mugello region, including a bust of St John the Baptist by Andrea Della Robbia.

From the main square opposite the town hall take the Gattaia road.

On the outskirts of the village the road skirts a splendid man-made **lake** which is particularly popular with anglers.

Take S551 west; after 3.5km – 2 miles turn right to Casa di Giotto (1km – 1/2 miles).

Vespignano (district of Vicchio) – Tradition has it that Giotto, the artist who was the precursor of Florentine art, was born here *c*1266. **Casa di Giotto** ⊙, his birthplace, displays a number of documents relating to his life and works. There is a wonderful view of the Mugello Valley from the church overlooking the house.

Take S551 west to return to Borgo San Lorenzo.

MURLO★

Population 1 787
Michelin Map 430 M 16

The tiny medieval village of Murlo consists of several buildings in a single row of houses backing onto the town walls. From the 11C to the 18C it belonged to the Bishops of Siena. Today it is famous for the Etruscan archeological discoveries made in Poggio Civitate, not far from Vescovado (north of Murlo).

★★ **Antiquarium di Poggio Civitate** ⊙ – The museum is housed in the former bishop's palace *(palazzone)* and contains the remains of a patrician residence (7C-6C BC) discovered in Poggio Civitate. This early Etruscan quadrangula villa formerly had a central porticoed courtyard. It gives a rare insight into domestic architecture, including the roofing structure which has remained almost intact.

The reconstructed roof and its rich terracotta decoration demonstrate the importance of this architectural feature, which was a reflection of the family's social status. The ridge is adorned with a series of statues (over 1.50m – 5ft high), consisting of some 20 animal and human figures, including a man wearing a wide-brimmed hat and boasting a Pharaonic beard. The roof was further emphasised by a border of antifixae representing Gorgon heads and a large frieze decorated in the Greek style with banqueting and horse-racing scenes. In addition to this exhibit, there are also some fine ceramic vases imported from Greece and locally-produced *bucchero* ware *(qv)*, crockery used in the kitchen or by servants, and ivory and bronze decorative objects and jewellery, giving an insight into the life of an aristocratic Etruscan family from the mid-7C to the late 6C BC.

The man with the broad-brimmed hat from Poggio Civitate.

PESCIA

Population 18 109
Michelin Map 988 fold 14 or 430 K 14

Pescia is historically the main town in the Nievole Valley and was the object of dispute between Lucca, Pisa and Florence for many years. The town was founded in the 12C to link up the routes across the Apennines.

Pescia has retained traces of its past in a number of buildings of architectural interest, although it is better known throughout Europe for its horticulture. In keeping with this tradition, the town hosts a biennial flower show, a huge exhibition of cut flowers and ornamental plants.

Porta Fiorentina – For visitors arriving from Pistoia, this is the starting point for a tour of the town. The gate was built in 1732 in honour of Gian Gastone de' Medici and is surmounted by the Medici coat of arms.

Duomo – This old parish church, built in 857 AD, has been the seat of the bishop since 1726. The belltower is a massive structure. Despite its early origins, there is very little evidence of the existence of the cathedral before 1693 when it was completely refurbished. The west front dates from 1892. Opposite the building is the **church of Santa Maria Maddalena**.

Sant'Antonio Abate – The church stands near the cathedral and contains a 13C wooden carving depicting the *Deposition from the Cross*. The frescoes in the apse are attributed to Bicci di Lorenzo (1373-1452).

San Francesco – *Past the hospital in Piazza San Francesco.* The huge interior comprising a single nave, transept and three apsidal chapels, contains an altarpiece depicting St Francis of Assisi, who visited Pescia in 1211, and six illustrations of episodes from his life by Bonaventura Berlinghieri dating from 1235. Also worthy of note is the *St Anne Triptych,* the *Martyrdom of St Dorothy* and Brunelleschi's Cardini chapel dating from the 15C.

Beside the church are the monastery buildings, now used as the law courts. Opposite is the 18C **Affiliati Theatre**.

Palazzo dei Vicari – *On the opposite side of the river.* This 12C building is now the town hall. It stands on the corner of Piazza Mazzini and is particularly attractive with its façade decorated with coats of arms. The council chambers are open to the public and contain the banner of Pescia surmounted by a dolphin, the municipal symbol.

On the other side of the square stands the **Oratory of Santi Pietro e Paolo**, also called the **Cappella della Madonna di Piè di Piazza**, built in 1447. The gilded wooden ceiling painted with a fresco of the Virgin dates from the 15C.

Continue towards Piazza Obizzi.

San Stefano e San Niccolao – Records show that the church was in existence in 1068. A fine double staircase leds up to the entrance.

Nearby stands the building once occupied by the governor (Palazzo del Podestà, also called Palagio). It now houses the **Gipsoteca Libero Andreotti** ⊙, a collection of 230 works by Andreotti, the local sculptor.

Castello church stands on the hillside nearby.

PIENZA★★

Population 2 325
Michelin Map 988 fold 15 or 430 M 17

Pienza displays a remarkable unity of style, especially in its main square, and is a perfect example of Renaissance town planning as requested by Pope Pius II, a scholarly man who wanted to build the ideal town.

Lovers' Lanes – At the end of the 19C Pienza changed some of its street names, particularly in the district east of the main square. To harmonise with the concept of the ideal city, the new names were inspired by love rather than war. The streets on the right of the main thoroughfare are named after Fortune (Via della Fortuna), Love (dell'Amore), the Kiss (del Bacio), Darkness (Via Buia) and there is also a Blind Lane (Vicolo Cieco); these streets lead to a panoramic walk on the town walls.

The humanist pope, Aeneas Sylvius Piccolomini (1405-1464)

Aeneas undertook numerous diplomatic missions before becoming Pope under the name of Pius II in 1458. He was famous for his knowledge and writings and in 1442 Emperor Frederick III appointed him poet laureate. As he was also an art lover, he released Filippo Lippi *(qv)* and Lucrezia Buti from their vows. Shortly after his election as Pope, he commissioned **Bernardo Rossellino**, the Florentine architect and pupil of Alberti, to undertake the rebuilding of his native village, Corsignano. It was later renamed Pienza in memory of the papal name of its most famous citizen.

★★ PIAZZA PIO II (PIUS II SQUARE) *Tour – 1 1/4 hours*

This tiny square is the earliest example of a real town planning policy and it is flanked by the main monumental buildings constructed by Rossellino. It was designed so as to reflect the balance between the civil and religious authorities through architectural harmony.

On the south side stands the cathedral; opposite is the Palazzo Comunale with an open loggia on the ground floor; on the east side is the bishop's palace, with simple 15C restorations; on the west is an aristocractic mansion, surmounted by an architrave bearing the Piccolomini coat of arms. In front of it is a charming Renaissance well.

A walk round the outside of the cathedral gives an opportunity to enjoy a picturesque **view**★ of the Orcia Valley.

★ **Duomo** – The cathedral, completed in 1462, has a simple yet grand Renaissance façade. The restored interior is Gothic in style and consists of a nave and two side-aisles of equal height and an apse with five radiating chapels. It contains some major 15C works by the Sienese School, including altarpieces (south aisle) by Giovanni di Paolo and (south transept) by Matteo di Giovanni. The most remarkable works, however, are the *Madonna and Saints* by Sano di Pietro (north transept) and **Vecchietta's** masterpiece (north apse) depicting the **Assumption**★★ of the Virgin Mary between St Agatha, who bears a cup containing her breasts which had been cut off by her torturer, Popes Pius I and Calixtus and St Catherine of Siena. Note the golden backgrounds, the impression of relief, the delightful use of colour and the accuracy of the drawing. The chancel contains a wooden Gothic lectern and stalls bearing the Piccolomini coats of arms.

Museo del duomo (M) ⊘ – The top floor of the cathedral museum contains 14C-15C paintings by the Sienese School, 15C-16C Flemish tapestries, a 14C panel with 48 painted compartments depicting scenes from the Life of Christ, and an extraordinary 14C cope decorated with narrative embroidery given to Pius II by an Eastern prince.

★ **Palazzo Piccolomini** ⊘ – *Guided tour of 1st floor*. This building, Rossellino's most accomplished work, was much inspired by the Palazzo Rucellai *(qv)* in Florence. The three façades overlooking the town are identical in appearance. Their most characteristic feature is the well-ordered harmony created by the vertical pilasters and the horizontal entablatures. The courtyard owes its elegance to the slender Corinthian columns. The interior contains an armoury, early printed books in the library and a Baroque bed in the papal chamber.

This was the first mansion purposely designed to look out over a wide expanse of countryside and it enjoys a view over the Orcia Valley from its three-storey loggia and hanging gardens on the south side.

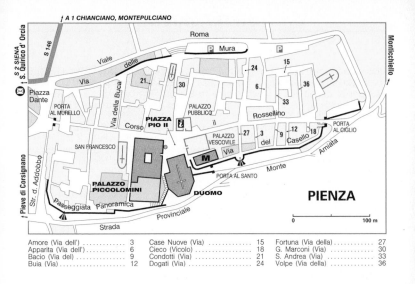

Amore (Via dell') 3
Apparita (Via dell') 6
Bacio (Via del) 9
Buia (Via) 12
Case Nuove (Via) 15
Cieco (Vicolo) 18
Condotti (Via) 21
Dogati (Via) 24
Fortuna (Via della) 27
G. Marconi (Via) 30
S. Andrea (Via) 33
Volpe (Via della) 36

EXCURSIONS

Pieve di Corsignano – *1km – 1/2 mile west along the south side of Pienza past the town walls.* This was the old village church before Pienza was built. It is an 11C-12C Romanesque building standing alone at the foot of the town. The façade is built of pale golden stone and is decorated with a carved doorway and a window with a column in the form of a statue. Beside it is a short cylindrical belltower set with semicircular bays.

Monticchiello – *10km – 6 miles east.* This medieval hillside village, surrounded by walls dotted with crenellated towers, is riddled with lanes and little squares steeped in charm. The village church has a pentagonal staircase leading up to its austere Gothic doorway. From the car park at the entrance to the town, there is a superb **view**★ of the Orcia Valley. On the right is Pienza with a foreground of arid hilltops, a characteristic feature of the landscape south of Siena, and (left) the summit of Mount Amiata.

★ **San Quirico d'Orcia** – *10km – 6 miles southwest. See San Quirico d'Orcia.*

Pienza and the country of the Orcia Valley.

The towns and sights described in this guide
are indicated in black lettering on the local maps and town plans

PIETRASANTA

Population 24 756
Michelin Map 430 K 12

Pietrasanta stretches out at the foot of its fortress, the **Rocca di Sala** (13C). Like its neighbour Camaiore *(qv)*, it was built in 1255 as an outpost for Lucca, in an attempt to define and protect a route to the sea. The town also kept watch over the Via Aurelia which, in this region, more or less coincided with the Via Francigena leading to France.

Like all free towns founded between the 11C and the 13C Pietrasanta had a mainly military function and its original rectangular layout, which is still perfectly visible today, had the rigorous grid appearance of a Roman encampment, with four rows of houses separated by three roads intersected in the centre by a large square.

The town walls were built in the early 14C and were connected to the fortress by two crenellated curtain walls, of which a few stretches have survived.

Historically, Pietrasanta is the main town in Versilia and is also a major artistic centre. Since the 1960s it has attracted painters and sculptors from all over the world – Adam, César, Ipousteguy, Lipchitz, Mitoraj, Miró and Moore to name but a few – because of the marble of both Versilia and the Carrara basin and above all, because of the local craftsmen who are famous for their skilful working of stone and, perhaps more surprisingly, of bronze.

The 100 or more local workshops also produce copies and undertake the restoration of works of art.

Piazza del Duomo – The main historic buildings are located in this large rectangular square. The cathedral, **Duomo di San Martino** *(restored)*, has a white tripartite marble façade. In the centre is a huge rose window surmounted by the coats of arms of the Medici and the Papacy (Pietrasanta came under Florentine rule in the 16C).

To the left of the cathedral are a large brick **belltower**, the Renaissance **Palazzo Moroni** at the top of a double flight of steps and, in the corner, the church of **Sant'Agostino**. At this end of the square stand a monument to Grand Duke Leopold II and the Marzocco column bearing the Florentine lion, erected in 1513.

To the right of the cathedral, beyond the 14C **Palazzo Pretorio** and the **clock tower** dating from 1560, the square is closed by the limited remains of the **Rocchetta Arighina** (also Porta Pisa) decorated with small overhanging arches.

Museo archeologico ⊙ – *Ground floor of the Palazzo Moroni.* The museum provides an insight into life in Upper Versilia from prehistoric times to the period when the area was under the control of Genoa, Lucca, Pisa or Florence, from the Middle Ages to the 18C.

Botero, the adopted son

Born in Columbia in 1932, the painter and sculptor, Fernando Botero, combines a knowledge of pre-Columbian art and the South American Baroque with his passion for the Italian Renaissance. This led him to settle in Pietrasanta where he now works. His paintings display vivid, cheerful colours and intricate detail reminiscent of his original culture; Italy has taught him the skill of drawing and the traditional techniques of marble sculpture, bronze casting and oil and fresco painting. A master of round voluptuous forms, he brings grace and lightness to obesity, artificial naiveté to sensuality and humour to solidity. His imagination often conveys a sense of sometimes rather wry satisfaction that is seldom found in contemporary art.

★ **Frescoes in the church of San Biagio e Sant'Antonio** (also della Misericordia) ⊙ – *Via Mazzini.* Two frescoes (opposite sides of the nave) by Fernando Botero depict the **Gateway to Paradise** and the **Gateway to Hell**. The influence of the Renaissance masters is apparent in the choice of technique, subject matter and composition, such as the cherubs, landscape or the moulding on the frame, but the whole work is enhanced by the imagination of an artist confronted with the modern world and his country's history. This has led him to include numerous details such as Mother Teresa, Hitler, the Italian flag and a conquistador. Perhaps by way of a signature, a modest self-portrait can be seen at the bottom of Hell, where he can be recognised by his goatee beard.

Piazza Matteotti – *North entrance of the town.* Opposite the town hall *(Municipio)* stands Botero's bronze statue of a naked, armed **Warrior**★ in the Classical style but displaying the roundness that is characteristic of the artist.

PIOMBINO

Population 36 750
Michelin Map 988 fold 24 or 430 N 13

Piombino lies midway down the coast of ancient Etruria and was built on a promontory which has been the site of three successive harbours since Antiquity – the Etruscan port of **Baratti**, the port of **Marina** which operated between the 12C and the early 20C, and the old Falesia harbour, now known as **Portovecchio**.
Little is known of Piombino's historical and artistic aspects. The town is best known for its harbour which is Italy's leading passenger ferry port and is also used by commercial traffic. There has also been a development in industrial activity, notably in the iron and steel sector.

Piazza Verdi – This is the starting point for walks through the town centre. The buildings in the square include the **Rivellino** (1447), Piombino's old main gate, and the **Torrione**, a massive tower built in 1212.

Palazzo Comunale – *Corso Vittorio Emanuele*. The town hall, built in 1444, was comprehensively restored in 1935. The Sala Consiliare (Council chamber) contains a Sienese Gothic wooden statue of the *Madonna and Child* (14C). There is a copy of it in the tower.
The 13C **Casa delle Bifore** (nearby in Via Ferruccio), a house with double bay windows, contains the municipal archives.

Piazza Bovio – *Far end of Corso Vittorio Emanuele.* The square, which is shaped like a ship's prow, provides a fine **view**★ of the Tuscan Archipelago (Arcipelago Toscana – *qv*).

Fonti dei Canali (Canal Fountains) – *From Piazza Bovio, turn right down towards the tiny port of Marina.* These 13C public marble fountains are attributed to Nicola Pisano and have provided the local water supply for almost seven centuries.

Citadel – It was built between 1465 and 1470 on the orders of Jacopo II Appiani and is remarkable for its marble **reservoir** opposite the Renaissance family chapel designed by Andrea di Francesco Guardi.

Fortifications – A walk towards Via Leonardo da Vinci brings into view the bastions of the town walls. East of Piazza Verdi *(Piazza del Castello)* there is the 13C-16C castle *(cassero)* and the fortress *(fortezza)* built in 1552 on the orders of Cosimo I.

For information about ferries from Piombino to the Isle of Elba see the chapter about the Isle of Elba.

Every year
the Michelin Red Guide Italia
revises its selection of starred restaurants
which also recommends culinary specialities and local wines

It also includes a selection of simpler restaurants
offering carefully prepared dishes which are often regional specialities...
at a reasonable price

It is well worth buying the current edition

The Leaning Tower of Pisa and the Cathedral.

S. Chirol

PISA★★★

Galileo Galilei Airport

The international airport *(3km – 2 miles from the town)* has flights to all the major European cities (☎ 050/28088 or 48219). There is a rail link between the airport and the city centre (10min). Hire cars are also available. The airport has a small duty-free shop selling a range of goods including some fresh produce.

Traffic and Parking

Driving is difficult because of the pedestrian precincts and one-way streets designed to take traffic away from the city centre. The larger car parks are near Piazza dei Miracoli outside the town walls and there are numerous small car parks or parking spaces in the streets or along the banks of the Arno in the centre near the main sights. In all cases, wait for the attendant to come and issue a ticket and, on returning to the car, pay the attendant the appropriate sum – between L1 500 and L2 000 per hour.

Pisa has the atmosphere of a minor capital city which has lost some of its hustle and bustle. Its superb buildings reflect past splendours.

The city is more spacious than Florence and less austere thanks to its yellow, pink or yellow-ochre house fronts but, as in Florence, the River Arno, which forms one of its most majestic meanders at this point, flows through the middle of the city. Pisa also owes its charm to its somewhat aristocratic air, the genteel lifestyle that this seems to encourage, and the special quality of the light, probably owing to the proximity of the sea.

The city is almost totally encircled by walls and is traversed from north to south by a main street lined with shops, which on the south bank is the Corso Italia and on the north bank is a narrow street flanked by arcades, **Borgo Stretto**. The winding street, **Via Santa Maria**, linking Piazza del Duomo to the Arno, is one of the most characteristic streets in Pisa with its noble yet cheerful appearance. These two streets on the north bank flank the busiest district in the city, full of shops and restaurants.

HISTORY OF A PORT

Maritime splendour – When it was founded *c*7C BC, Pisa was on the coast but the shoreline soon receded some distance from the city because of the accumulation of alluvium at the mouth of the Arno; this development can be seen in the plain extending westwards from the city and in the flat seabed. The city was occupied by the Etruscans and was an ally of Rome for many years. From 180BC onwards it was colonised by the Romans who took advantage of its geographical location on the banks of the Arno only a few miles from the sea and turned it into a naval base free from the risk of attack by pirates. Pisa continued to fulfil the role of a naval base until the fall of the Roman Empire in the Western world 476 AD.

In 888 AD the city became an independent republic but not until the Middle Ages did it begin to take advantage of its geographical location to encourage economic development. Like Genoa and Venice, the city was one of the powerful maritime republics which resisted the Muslim domination; its "merchant-warriors" fought stubbornly throughout the Mediterranean Basin. Pisa took possession of Sardinia in 1015 and later of Corsica, over which it exercised absolute control in the last quarter of the 11C. In 1114 it captured the Balearic Islands. It expanded its conquests into Tunisia and began to set up trading posts in the eastern part of the Mediterranean, which extended as far as Syria.

Pisa developed into a very active port in the 11C and reached the peak of its prosperity in the 12C and first half of the 13C. Its ships plied the Mediterranean carrying arms, wool, furs, leather and timber from the Apennines to the Orient, together with iron mined on the island of Elba. They returned with spices, silk, cotton etc. This period was marked by the construction of the finest buildings and the founding of the University, which still enjoys a reputation for excellence.

Decline – When a major quarrel, the Investiture Controversy *(qv)*, broke out between the Papacy and the Empire, Pisa, a resolutely Ghibelline city, rallied to the Emperor's camp. At sea it successfully resisted the threat of Genoa, its main maritime rival for commercial supremacy in the Mediterranean. On land it withstood its two Guelf rivals, Lucca and Florence.

When, however, Pisa was deprived of the support of Emperor Frederick II (d 1250) and of King Manfred, his son who was killed in 1266, the city began to fall into decline. In August 1284 at the great **Battle of Meloria** (a small island off Livorno), the Pisan fleet was wiped out by Genoese ships. The city was forced to transfer all its rights in Corsica to Genoa and to give up Sardinia. It was unable to prevent the collapse of its commercial empire in the East as it was cut off from its trading posts by the loss of its fleet. The city was also undermined by internal strife and was eventually taken over by Florence in 1406.

The Medici dynasty was particularly interested in Pisa. Lorenzo the Magnificent reorganised its university and began to build a new one. In the 16C Pisa was incorporated into the Grand Duchy of Tuscany and Cosimo I founded the Order of the Knights of St Stephen *(qv)* in the city. During this period the city enjoyed a renewal of its influence, mainly in the sciences.

Galileo

Galileo Galilei was born in 1564 into a well-educated family in Pisa. He abandoned his medical studies in favour of physics and astronomy. He was only 19 when, warching a swinging lamp in the cathedral in his native town, he realised that the oscillations always took the same amount of time whatever their range. From this observation he developed the principle of the pendulum and decided to apply the measurement of its movement to the measurement of time. He used the Leaning Tower of Pisa to study the laws of falling bodies and uniformly-accelerated motion. In the field of optics he built one of the very earliest microscopes.

He invented the telescope that now bears his name and began to study the stars, measuring the height of relief on the moon's surface, discovering Saturn's ring and Jupiter's satellites, and observing sun spots.

In 1610 Grand Duke Cosimo II of Tuscany appointed him Court philosopher and heaped honours on him.

He was a strong supporter of Copernicus' theory of the movement of the planets around their own axes and around the sun, in particular the theory of the double rotation of the Earth. This led to problems with traditionalist scholars who had him summoned before the Inquisition in 1633. After a trial lasting 20 days, sentence was passed and he was forced to recant on his knees. According to tradition, as he rose to his feet, he added in desperation a sentence that has remained famous to this day – *Eppur si muove*! (Yet it does turn!). He was 70 years old at the time.

He retired to a villa near Florence where he spent the last years of his life under the watchful eye of the Inquisition, under a form of house arrest. He died, blind, in 1642.

PISAN ARCHITECTURE

Between the 11C and the 13C, while the city was increasing in economic prosperity and political power, an innovatory art form was developing that had a marked effect on architecture and sculpture.

Religious architecture – This type of architecture, which was different from the other styles present in Italy during the Romanesque period, reached its heyday in the 13C and spread throughout Tuscany, to towns such as Lucca, Pistoia and Arezzo. It also left its mark on churches in Sardinia and Corsica, both then Pisan possessions.

The style was known as Pisan Romanesque and it brought together a pleasing combination of several influences, most markedly the architecture of Lombardy. To it was added a wealth of decoration inspired by the shapes and motifs of articles brought back from the Orient or the Islamic world by the Pisan fleet. This trend led to buildings of outstanding elegance and unity of which the cathedral in Pisa is the most rigorous and solemn example. The west front, side walls and apse are all skilfully faced with green and white marble, a costly building material that was as popular in Pisa as it was in other Tuscan towns, in particular Florence. Whereas the architects of Florence emphasised the geometric divisions on the façades of churches by framing them in marble, the craftsmen of Pisa made extensive use of relief – tall but shallow blind arcading running all round the building and galleries with colonnettes, a feature that is discreetly present in Lombard architecture but used in Pisa with great exuberance, marking off the upper section of the gable and dappling it with light and shade. Rose windows, diamond shapes and other small motifs picked out in marble marquetry show Oriental inspiration in their use of colour.

In the second half of the 11C and early 12C the architects whose names are inextricably linked with the great buildings of Pisa were **Buscheto**, **Rainaldo** his direct successor who was a contemporary of **Diotisalvi**, and **Bonanno Pisano**, architect and sculptor. **Giovanni di Simone** was the main architect working in the second half of the 13C.

Pisan sculpture in the 13C and 14C – Medieval Pisan sculpture has pride of place in the history of Italian art.

Local artists such as **Bonanno Pisano** and **Fra' Guglielmo**, or Lombards such as Guido da Como, worked on the decoration of the Romanesque churches of Pisa in the 12C and early 13C. It was, however, Nicola Pisano, a sculptor thought to have come from Apulia, who is credited with paving the way for a whole succession of artists in the second half of the 13C. In their eyes Pisa was the birthplace of Italian Romanesque and especially of Gothic sculpture. These sculptors, who were also architects and interior decorators, were responsible for the creation of huge and unusual pulpits, veritable masterpieces owing to their harmonious structure, their intricate decoration and the aesthetic beauty of their carvings.

Nicola Pisano (born c1220, died shortly after 1280) had studied classical sculpture. He assimilated its majesty and

The pulpit by Nicola Pisano in the Baptistery, Pisa.

power and added to it the sense of humanity and the realism seen in the paintings of his contemporary, Giotto. His main works are the pulpit in the baptistery in Pisa and in the cathedral in Siena. With the assistance of his son, Giovanni, who worked with him in Siena, he also built the Fontana Maggiore in Perugia. One of his pupils was Arnolfo di Cambio, the architect of the cathedral in Florence.

Giovanni Pisano (born c1250, died c1315-1320) was undoubtedly the greatest of all the sculptors. He had a more flexible technique and was more concerned to express dramatic intensity. He worked with his father until the latter's death. His art form developed towards the creation of compositions that were increasingly complex with figures that were more and more tormented, although they were also filled with an outstanding intensity, which gave them a wonderful lifelike quality. It was his genius that created the splendid pulpit in the Siena cathedral and in Sant'Andrea in Pistoia. He was also the first person to direct work on Siena cathedral, which he wanted to cover with huge statues like the Gothic cathedrals in France which he had visited c1270. Giovanni was the last member of the first Pisano dynasty and his death marked the end of the great period of powerful and monumental Gothic sculptures in Tuscany. His most able pupil was Tino di Camaino, from Siena.

Andrea da Pontedera, named after a town near Pisa and also known as **Andrea Pisano**, was born at the end of the 13C and worked mainly in Florence where one of his major works was the first bronze door for the baptistery. His elegant and refined style, which he developed while training as a goldsmith, and his attractively-drawn scenes were not inspired by his Pisan predecessors. He also sculpted some powerful high reliefs used to decorate the belltower by Giotto in Florence *(qv)*.

Andrea's son, **Nino Pisano**, who died c1365-1370, preferred to work in the round. He was a past master in the art of relief and he created graceful Madonnas including a famous *Madonna del Latte* (in the San Matteo National Museum – *see below*). This second Pisano dynasty, which also included Tommaso, Nino's brother, enjoyed a reputation in the late 14C that made their workshop an obligatory training ground for a number of great Sienese and Florentine sculptors in the early 15C including Lorenzo Ghiberti and Jacopo della Quercia.

FESTIVALS IN PISA

All the city's traditional festivals take place in June.

Historical Regatta of the Maritime Republics (May/June) – Since 1956 the Regatta of the Four Maritime Republics (Amalfi, Genoa, Venice and Pisa) has been held in each city in turn. The festivities begin with a costumed pageant. The procession of pages, damsels, captains and men-at-arms, all dressed in period costume, makes its way through the city, together with historical figures whose costumes are designed from old documents – Kinzica de' Sismondi, dressed all in pink, the heroine whose courage saved Pisa when it was besieged by the Saracens; the Duke of Amalfi in a gold lamé costume; Guglielmo Embriaco from Genoa, also known as Testa di Maglio; the Doge of Venice accompanied by Caterina Cornaro. The regatta itself is a boat race in which the old rival republics compete.

The "Luminara" di San Ranieri (16 June) – On the banks of the Arno on the evening before the Feast Day of St Rainier, the patron saint of the city, the Lungarno Mediceo and Lungarno Galilei quays are lit with hundreds of tiny lanterns outlining the windows, architectural lines of mansions, parapets along the quays and the architecture of Santa Maria della Spina. The lanterns are reflected in the Arno where other tiny lights float on the water. This festival of light is best seen at sunset when the sky too turns red. After nightfall there is a spectacular firework display.

Historic Regatta in honour of St Ranieri (17 June) – In the afternoon a regatta is held on the Arno, using historic boats. Four of the city's historical districts *(Rioni)* compete against each other in a race (2km – 1 mile) against the current; the rowers are dressed in traditional costume.

Il Gioco del Ponte (last Sunday in June) – Based on the game of *mazzascudo* played at least as far back as the 12C, the *Gioco del Ponte* is said to have been played for the first time on 22 February 1569. The Pisans have always been very proud of their game and they would not permit it to be copied in any of the territories they conquered, as shown in a decree dated 1318 concerning Sardinia. The various districts of the town are organised in two groups reflecting the two parts of the city which is divided by the Arno – the north bank *(Tramontana)* and the south bank *(Mezzogiorno)*. They compete on the Middle Bridge *(Ponte di Mezzo)*, which is divided into two equal sections where the teams take up their positions. The aim is to gain control of the entire bridge. Over the centuries the rules have remained unchanged but the game has been altered to make it less violent. The *Mazzascudo*, literally a bludgeon-shield, had one narrow end designed for attack and one broad end for defence. For the game *(Gioco del Ponte)* it was replaced by a limewood or poplar shield *(targone)*, which had more or less the same shape, that of a small oar, but was less dangerous despite its length (1m – 3 1/4 ft) and its weight (2.5kg – 5.5lbs). Nevertheless the hand-to-hand struggles between men in armour remained violent and so, since the Second World War, the competition has consisted of pushing the other team backwards across the bridge using a 7-tonne cart mounted on a central rail. A flag drops automatically as soon as the entire cart has crossed into the other camp. The six districts in each of the two halves of the city compete against each other in groups of two. The overall winner is the team which has obtained at least four victories in the quarter- and semi-finals.

Before the game the two "armies", each bearing their local colours, parade along the quaysides in two processions of more than 300 people dressed in ornate 16C costumes and armour. The procession of magistrates, which has some 60 participants, is separate and neutral. On the following Sunday the pennant *(palio)* is formally handed over to the winning team in the Palazzo Comunale. Festivities are then held in the victorious districts.

Piazza dei Mircoli, Pisa.

PUBBLI AER FOTO

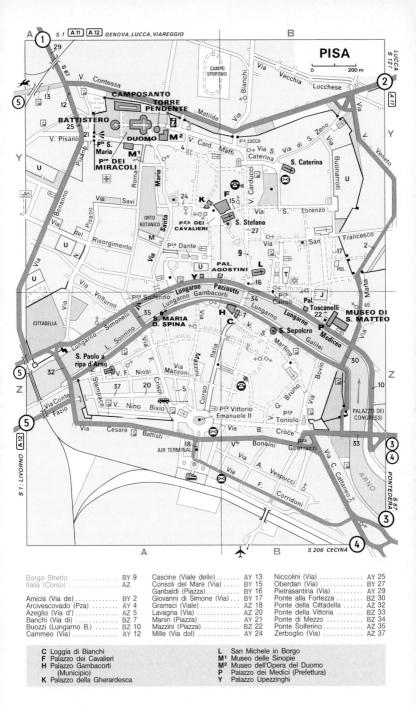

PISA

0 200 m

| Borgo Stretto | BY 9 |
| Italia (Corso) | AZ |

Cascine (Viale delle)	AY 13
Consoli del Mare (Via)	BY 15
Garibaldi (Piazza)	BY 16
Giovanni di Simone (Via)	BY 17
Gramsci (Viale)	AZ 18
Lavagna (Via)	AZ 20
Manin (Piazza)	AY 21
Mazzini (Piazza)	BZ 22
Mille (Via del)	AY 24

Amicis (Via de)	BY 2
Arcivescovado (Pza)	AY 4
Azeglio (Via d')	AZ 5
Banchi (Via di)	BZ 7
Buozzi (Lungarno B.)	BZ 10
Cammeo (Via)	AY 12

Niccolini (Via)	AY 25
Oberdan (Via)	BY 27
Pietrasantina (Via)	AY 29
Ponte alla Fortezza	BZ 30
Ponte della Cittadella	BZ 32
Ponte della Vittoria	BZ 33
Ponte di Mezzo	BZ 34
Ponte Solferino	AZ 35
Zerboglio (Via)	AZ 37

C	Loggia di Bianchi	L	San Michele in Borgo
F	Palazzo dei Cavalieri	M¹	Museo delle Sinopie
H	Palazzo Gambacorti	M²	Museo dell'Opera del Duomo
	(Municipio)	P	Palazzo dei Medici (Prefettura)
K	Palazzo della Gherardesca	Y	Palazzo Upezzinghi

★ PIAZZA DEI MIRACOLI (SQUARE OF MIRACLES) (AY) *Tour 3 hours*

This prestigious square, which is also known as **Piazza del Duomo**, contains four buildings which constitute an exceptionally beautiful sight – one of the most famous in the world.

It resembles a vast enclosure, lined on two sides by a slim wall of red brick to which crenellations were added in the mid-12C. Within are the dazzling white marble mass of the Baptistery and the cathedral with its famous belltower, known as the Leaning Tower of Pisa. In the background is the cemetery *(Camposanto)* with its long row of blind arcading, also made of white marble.

This succession of buildings is best seen from **Porta Santa Maria** and it is also from this point that the angle of the Leaning Tower is most spectacular.

31

PISA

★★★ **Torre Pendente** ⊙ – The **leaning tower of Pisa**, the belltower (58m – 189ft high) of the cathedral, is the symbol of the city.

Its famous angle (it approximately 5m -16ft off the vertical) has made it one of the most popular tourist attractions in the world. There is now no doubt that the architect did not intend the tower to lean. Its angle is caused by the alluvial soil, which is not compact enough to bear the weight of the building.

The building work was begun by Bonanno Pisano in 1173 and had reached the first floor when the first subsidence occurred. The architect, however, ignored it and another two storeys were built. When the second subsidence occurred, work stopped and did not start again until a century later when another architect, Giovanni di Simone, tried to correct the angle of slope by ensuring that the side which was sinking into the ground carried less weight. He died at the Battle of Meloria before his work was completed. The top of the belltower was added in 1350.

The peculiarity of the tower cannot conceal the beauty of its architecture. It was built as a cylinder, like the towers in Byzantium, and has six floors of galleries which seem, because of the angle of incline, to be unwinding in an ethereal spiral. On the lower level, in the purest of Pisan Romanesque styles, is the circle of blind arcading decorated with diamond-shaped motifs.

Attempts to save the building

Since 1178, when the tower was first observed to lean, 8000 projects have been drawn up to remedy the problem, with varying degrees of success. The tower leans by an average of 1 to 2 mm – 0.07 inch per year and it is thought that it will collapse altogether in 2040. From 1550 to 1817, however, the movement was arrested when Vasari shored up the base. Unfortunately in the 19C hydraulic engineers changed the soil structure by pumping out the underground water and lowering the water table.

Since 7 January 1990 the tower has been closed to the public because of the inherent danger of collapse and it is now the subject of constant care. Two stainless steels rings were quickly placed around the first floor.

In 1991 the tower was attached to the ground by 18 steel cables.

In 1993 the foundations were strengthened with a reinforced concrete sheath containing 670 bars of lead (1m – $3\frac{1}{4}$ ft in length) in order to counterbalance the angle of incline (from an aesthetic point of view, this has not changed the appearance of the square).

Early in 1994 it was noted that the tower had moved back towards the vertical by 9mm – $\frac{1}{3}$ inch but the work was then stopped owing to a lack of funds.

The tower is scheduled to re-open at the end of 1995 but it will remain closed unless the experts succeed in bringing it back towards the vertical by 20cm – 50in. People will then be allowed to climb the 294 steps again and experience the feeling that they are being pulled towards the sloping side of the tower. From the top there is a superb **view**★ of the square and the city spread out below. In fine weather the view extends across the countryside to the coast. In this prestigious university town, however, it is worth recalling the age-old curse that is so wellknown to Italians – "Any student hoping to graduate should never risk the climb to the top."

★★ **Cathedral** ⊙ – The cathedral's architects were Buscheto, who began the building work in 1063, and Rainaldo, who completed it towards the middle of the 12C after enlarging the transept and extending the nave towards the west front which he also designed.

It was the fabulous booty brought back to the city after major victories over the Saracens in Sicily that provided the funds required for the construction of this lavish building.

Pisa Cathedral is a vast building in the shape of a Latin Cross and it gives an impression of being wonderfully well-balanced with its long nave, huge transept and boldly-projecting apse. To counterbalance this solemnity, a light touch is created by the rows of galleries on the west front, the blind arcading, the three rows of windows flanked by pilasters round the building and the bonding with alternating light and dark marble string-courses. All these features formed the major characteristics of the Pisan Romanesque style.

Set in the **west front**★★★ decorated with elegant geometric motifs picked out in marquetry and mosaics of marble and multi-coloured glazed terracotta is the tomb of Buscheto (first arch on the left).

Bronze **doors**★ cast in 1602 to designs by Giambologna replaced the original doors which were destroyed by fire in the late 16C. They depict the Life of the Virgin Mary (centre) and the Life of Christ (sides).

The most famous of the doors is the one named San Ranieri, after opening into the south transept opposite the Leaning Tower. Its admirable Romanesque bronze **panels**★★ were cast in the late 12C and designed by Bonanno Pisano. Using a rigorous economy of figures but showing prodigious inventiveness, he depicted the Life of Christ in 20 small tableaux in a manner that was highly stylised and gracefully naive *(it is difficult to see the work because of the constant flow of visitors)*. Panels laid out like friezes from top to bottom of each door and a frame consisting of twisted columns and small roses create a superb decorative effect.

Interior – The interior of the building (best seen from the end of the nave) is less uniform than the exterior. It is a very impressive sight with its nave (100m – 325ft long), four aisles, deep apse, triple-bay transept and slightly oval dome. The 68 columns, each carved out of a single block of stone, provide an amazing variety of perspectives.

The overall effect of lightness created by the upper galleries for women opening onto the nave and transept and by the alternating light and dark bands of colour along the upper section of the building is somewhat muted by the gilded wooden coffering that has replaced the original coffered ceiling, which was destroyed by fire. The painted decoration on the arches in the chancel has the same muting effect.

The mosaic of Christ Pantocrator on the vaulting above the apse dates from the early 14C.

The splendid **pulpit**★★★ on which Giovanni Pisano worked for almost ten years (1302-1311) is a masterpiece of strength and delicacy. The pulpit itself is supported by porphyry columns, two of which stand on lions, a motif taken from the Lombard tradition, and by five pillars decorated with statues. The female figures on the central pillar symbolise the theological virtues – Faith, Hope and Charity. The pillar stands on a base decorated with small figures representing the Liberal Arts. On the pillars round the edge of the pulpit *(from left to right starting on the side facing the chancel)* the carvings represent St Michael, the Evangelists carrying Christ, the cardinal virtues – Fortitude, Justice, Prudence and Temperance – supporting a woman with a baby at her breast, an allegorical representation of the Church being nourished by the Old and New Testaments, and Hercules. The pulpit is almost circular owing to the eight slightly-convex carved panels. In a set of tumultuous carvings filled with human figures Giovanni Pisano gave full vent to his talent for expressiveness and his sense of the dramatic. The first panel *(from left to right starting at the entrance to the pulpit)* depicts the Annunciation and the Visitation of the Virgin Mary, followed by the Nativity, the Adoration of the Magi, the Presentation in the Temple and the Flight into Egypt, the Massacre of the Holy Innocents, Christ's Passion, the Crucifixion and the Last Judgement *(two panels)*.

Near the pulpit is the bronze lamp, known as Galileo's Lamp. According to tradition it was while watching the lamp swing as it was lit by the sexton that Galileo was inspired to develop his famous theory. In fact Galileo had already made his discovery a few years before the lamp was placed in the cathedral.

The Crucifix above the high altar was made by Giambologna who also created the two bronze angel candlesticks at the corners of the choir screen. Two 16C paintings face each other on pillars on each side of the chancel – *(right) St Agnes* by Andrea del Sarto and *(left)* a *Madonna and Child* by Antonio Sogliani.

★★★ **Battistero (Baptistery)** ⊙ – This is a majestic, circular building (almost 110m – 358ft in circumference and just under 55m – 179ft high) almost equal to the height of the Leaning Tower. It took 250 years to build. Work began in 1153, almost a century after building commenced on the cathedral, and lasted, with a break of 50 years in the 13C, until 1400. The project and the early work were directed by Diotisalvi. Nicola and Giovanni Pisano also worked on the baptistery, producing many of the carvings and sculptures.

Like the blind arcading and colonnaded galleries in the belltower, the external decoration of the baptistery was designed to reflect the ornamentation on the cathedral. Although the first two levels were designed in the Pisan Romanesque style, there is a decidedly Gothic flavour about the second floor and the gables and pinnacles above the arches on the first floor. At the very top of the building is a strange dome rising to a small, truncated pyramid and a statue of St John the Baptist.

The doors are among the most decorative features in the building. The one opposite the cathedral, the most ornate of the four, is flanked by columns carved with foliage in the 13C. On the lintel, carved in a Byzantine style, are episodes from the Life of St John the Baptist; above is a representation of Jesus between the Virgin Mary and St John with the four Evangelists on either side, alternating with angels. On the jambs are illustrations of the work of the 12 months of the year *(left)* and carvings of the apostles (right).

Interior – The interior (35m – 114ft in diameter) is impressive for its tall rows of arching, its deep dome, its striking majesty and the amount of light that floods into it. A remarkable echo can be heard in the baptistery *(in summer visitors enter the building in small groups every 10 minutes for a demonstration by one of the attendants)*.

The alternating strips of light and dark marble create an austere form of decoration. Elegant monolithic columns with attractively-carved capitals alternate with huge pillars to form a uniform peristyle on the lower level with a wide gallery above which is open to visitors *(staircase left of the entrance)*. The effect of the near-perfect spatial layout can be seen at its best from the gallery. The circular building, articulated by the ring of columns and pillars, converges on the superb octagonal **font★**, austere in its design, which is repeated in the pavement. It was designed in 1246 by Guido Bigarelli, an artist from Como and was used for christenings by total immersion. Against the interior wall are small cylindrical basins in which newborn babies were immersed. The tank is slightly raised and decorated with square marble panels containing roses carved with acanthus leaves and animal heads. There are also insets of small multi-coloured geometric motifs of Oriental design. The altar panels, which were made in the same style in the previous century, originally formed the chancel screen in the cathedral.

The baptistery also has an admirable **pulpit★★**, carved by Nicola Pisano who completed it in 1260. It is more austere than the one produced for the cathedral by his son, Giovanni, and it stands on plain columns. Semicircular arches, in which the trefoil design nevertheless points to the imminence of the Gothic style, support the pulpit which consists of five framed panels and groups of red marble columns. On one of the corners is a lectern shaped like an eagle, the emblem of St John. In retracing the Life of Christ, the artist sought inspiration in the classical sculptures seen on the Roman sarcophagi in the Camposanto. This influence is particularly strong in the first two panels *(starting at the entrance to the pulpit and going from left to right)* representing the Nativity and the Adoration of the Magi in which the Virgin Mary resembles a Roman matron. The following panels depict the Presentation in the Temple, the Crucifixion and the Last Judgement; the face of Lucifer *(bottom righthand corner)* is reminiscent of the masks used in Classical theatre).

★★ Camposanto ⊘ – The cemetery is almost as famous as the other buildings in Piazza del Duomo. Building began in 1277 under the direction of Giovanni di Simone, the second architect to work on the belltower, but was interrupted by the war against Genoa which ended in the Battle of Meloria (1284); the cemetery was not finished until the 15C. One of the gates opening in the Romanesque blind arcading along the south wall is surmounted by a charming little Gothic construction with tracery which was added in the 14C. Inside is a statue of the *Madonna and Child* carved in the workshops of Giovanni Pisano.

Originally designed like an unroofed cathedral nave, this huge graveyard now resembles vast cloisters, as the tall Romanesque arches were converted in the 15C into wonderfully light four-bay Gothic windows. In the middle is the Sacred Field *(Camposanto)* which is said to have been laid out using earth brought back from Golgotha in the early 13C by the Crusaders. The earth was said to have the power to reduce dead bodies to skeletons in a few days. The galleries are paved with 600 tombstones and contain several superb Greco-Roman sarcophagi, most of them re-used in the Middle Ages for the burials of Pisan noblemen. The walls used to be covered with admirable **frescoes** painted in the second half of the 14C and in the following century by artists such as Benozzo Gozzoli, Taddeo Gaddi, Andrea di Buonaiuto and Antonio Veneziano. In July 1944 artillery caused a fire which melted the lead roof, destroying or badly damaging most of the frescoes. Some of them, however, including the famous fresco depicting the *Triumph of Death,* were saved and restored.

Walk round the Camposanto anticlockwise.

North Gallery – This gallery, now totally bare like the South Gallery, is lined by a number of rooms containing the most remarkable of the frescoes.

Beyond a small chapel, containing the St Rainier Altar carved by Tino di Camaino, is a room containing a photographic reconstruction of the frescoes as they were originally. In the centre of the room is a very fine Attic marble urn (2C BC) carved with Dionysian scenes in light relief.

Fresco Room – The great chamber beyond contains the frescoes which have been removed from the walls in the galleries. Among them *(left wall)* is the **Triumph of Death★★★** (1360-1380), one of the most interesting examples of 14C Italian painting considered to be the work of an unknown artist referred to as the *Maestro del Trionfo della Morte*. It is an edifying work, probably painted shortly after the plague epidemic of 1348, and it illustrates themes that were very popular in western Europe at that time – the vanity of earthly pleasures and the shortness of life. The work displays remarkable originality owing to the lifelike figures, which are in fact lively portraits of the artist's contemporaries, the combination of poetic freshness and harsh realism used to depict life and death and the taste for narrative and the sense of movement. One part of the painting is taken from the story of the *Three Living and Three Dead Men*. St Macaire is depicted *(left)* holding an unrolled scroll and pointing to the decomposed bodies of three kings, while he explains to a group of noblemen on their way to a hunt that the only reality is death, the inevitable. Above are Anchorite monks calmly preparing for death as they go about their daily business. Death *(right)* is ignoring a group of beggars pleading for his attention *(in the centre)* and preparing instead to swoop down triumphantly on a party of carefree young people in a delightful orchard. The two magnificent frescoes covering the end wall of the room and part of the next wall represent the **Last Judgement**★★ and **Hell**★. They were originally part of the same cycle as the previous fresco and were painted by the same artist. So too was the *Story of the Anchorites in the Thebaid (beyond)* which depicts various details of the hard, lonely and ascetic life led by the early Christians who sought refuge in Egypt from persecution. On the last wall *(right of the entrance)* is the *Patience of Job* by Taddeo Gaddi.

Sinopia

Although frescoes *(qv)* can withstand the passage of time and the effects of the elements, they must be painted on a fresh base. They therefore have two main disadvantages – they have to be completed quickly and, once dry, cannot be touched up. In order to overcome these disadvantages, artists used to draw a sketch called an underdrawing *(sinopia)* on the wall, after the initial base had been prepared. This type of sketch got its name from a town, Sinope, on the shores of the Black Sea which provided the reddish-brown pigment usually used to draw them. Once the scene had been roughly sketched in, the artist could take his time to produce the final work, preparing the base only for the area he wanted to paint on a particular day. Many of these underdrawings have come to light over the past few decades as frescoes have been removed from walls for restoration.

West Gallery – Against the wall are the chains that used to close off the entrance to the harbour. This gallery was the first one to be filled with the lavish tombs of Pisan noblemen from the 16C onwards. Each tomb was placed symmetrically in relation to the others. The East Gallery was organised in the same way. In the 18C the custom became so popular that the tombs began to spread into the longer North and South Galleries. In 1807 Carlo Lasinio was appointed Curator and he introduced the ancient sarcophagi which had lain along the sides of the cathedral and in the many monasteries and churches in Pisa.

★ **Museo delle Sinopie (M¹)** ⊘ – This museum, formerly a hospice built in the 13C and 14C, contains the underdrawings of the Camposanto frescoes.

Ground floor – Most of the underdrawings displayed here were sketched in the 15C and are very rough since it was customary for artists to work at their studies on paper and only the main lines of the work were sketched on the wall.

During the restoration work on the frescoes which had been damaged in 1944 the underdrawings were also removed and restored. They are now skillfully displayed in a high-ceilinged chamber covering two floors.

The Triumph of Death
(detail of an underdrawing for a fresco)

SCALA

235

Upper floor – A series of platforms *(staircase at the end of the room)* gives a panoramic view of the gigantic underdrawings created before the completion of the most famous frescoes in the Camposanto. At the end of the room is the underdrawing for the *Crucifixion*, the first fresco to be painted *c*1320-1330 by Francesco Traini who was the most important artist in Pisa in the 14C. The grandiose compositions used for the *Triumph of Death*, the *Last Judgement* and *Hell* (the last two were sketched in a single session using wide sweeping lines) and the *Story of the Anchorites in the Thebaid* show the remarkable drawing talents, especially in the facial expressions, of the unknown artist who is nevertheless the most famous artist in the Camposanto.

Two higher galleries provide different views of the works.

★★ **Museo dell'Opera del Duomo (M²)** ⊘ – The works in the museum come from the buildings in Piazza dei Miracoli. Room 1 gives visitors a view of the buildings, in the form of 19C models, before seeing the sculptures and furnishings.

Ground Floor – The first pulpit produced (1158 to 1162) for the cathedral *(Room 2)* was carved by **Guglielmo,** the architect and sculptor, who was in charge of the building work; it was his greatest masterpiece. In 1310 it was replaced by the pulpit carved by Giovanni Pisano and given to Cagliari Cathedral in Sardinia. Copies of the pulpit are shown here and its structure was such that it became a prototype for future creations throughout Tuscany.

The foreign works *(Room 3)* are part of the cathedral's furnishings and the shapes imported from distant lands enrich the early, mainly classical, Romanesque architecture. Most of the additions were from the Islamic world with which the Pisans were well acquainted owing to their maritime trading links. New geometric and iconographic motifs were introduced, with a taste for polychrome marble marquetry, a craft form which was already known through Byzantine art and architecture. Sculptures from Provence – a head of David – and Burgundy – a wooden statue of Christ – prove that there were links with French Romanesque artists.

The other buildings on the square – the tower *(Room 4)* and the baptistery *(Rooms 5 and 6)* – are celebrated together with their glorious Pisan sculptures. The nine busts *(in the cloister gallery)*, which adorned the top of the baptistery loggia, were the work (1269-1279) **of Nicola Pisano** and his son, **Giovanni Pisano**. The latter also created (1302-1310) the second pulpit *(Room 5)* and some other works *(Room 7)* – the *Madonna of Henry VII*, a French-inspired composition showing the Virgin Mary seated with the Child Jesus standing on her lap, and *Pisa Kneeling,* which was part of the same work completed in 1312 in honour of the emperor. The bust of the *Madonna and Child* is a markedly Gothic work but the mute expressiveness of the eyes is typical of Giovanni's style.

The Sienese sculptor **Tino di Camaino** *(Room 8)*, who worked in Pisa for many years, was one of the most famous sculptors of funeral monuments in the 14C. The statues of the emperor, four of his advisers, an Annunciation and two angels (1315) come from his mausoleum for Henry VII of Luxembourg who died in 1313 *(See Buonconvento)*.

Nino Pisano *(Room 9)* also created a number of the tombs in the cathedral in the second half of the 14C. The tomb of Archbishop Giovanni Scherlatti so delighted Archbishop Francesco Moricotti that he asked Nino to create an identical one for him; this explains why the face on the recumbent statue is so young despite the fact that he died 27 years after the sculptor.

The main figure in the 15C art world was the Florentine, **Andrea di Francesco Guardi** *(Room 10)*, a pupil in Donatello's workshop. His main piece of work was Archbishop Pietro Ricci's tomb *(end wall)*.

The cathedral **treasury** *(Room 11)* displays some of the oldest and most precious items – an 11C ivory chest decorated with *putti* and animals, a small 12C silver gilt Crucifix known as the "Pisans' Cross" (the pedestal mount dates from the 14C), two Limoges reliquaries (13C), and six fragments of the cathedral girdle *(cintola)* dating from the 13C and 14C. It was made of red damask decorated with narrative metal plaques and precious stones and, before it mysteriously disappeared, it used to be laid right round the cathedral on major feast days. There is the charming little *Madonna and Child* by Giovanni Pisano (1299) in which the curvature of the Virgin Mary's spine follows the natural curve in the elephant tusk used to carve it. The display cabinets *(Room 12)* contain pieces of silver plate made for the cathedral from the 16C to 19C – reliquaries, Crucifixes, monstrances, and chalices.

First Floor – The 16C-18C paintings and sculptures *(Rooms 13-14)* are followed by *(Room 15)* the marquetry decorating the choir stalls in the cathedral. This art form was very fashionable in the late 15C and 16C and it reveals the artists' talent in producing a sense of perspective. The three panels depicting *Faith, Hope* and *Charity* were made by Baccio and Piero Pontelli to drawings by Botticelli. The panels by Guido da Seravallino show views of the quays in Pisa in the 15C.

Among the illuminated manuscripts and antiphonies *(Room 16)* are two *"Exultet"* - one made in Benevento in the 12C, the other in Tuscany in the 13C. On one side of these rolls was a transcript of the liturgical chant sung by a deacon on Easter Saturday while on the other were the paintings seen by the congregation, representing scenes from the mystery of the Resurrection.

The vestments *(Rooms 17 to 20)* provide an opportunity to admire fabrics and embroideries dating from the 15C to 19C. The display also includes Flemish lace.

The final part of the museum deals with archeology - Egyptian, Etruscan and Roman remains collected from the various churches and monasteries in Pisa in the 19C by Carlo Lasinio, the curator of the Camposanto. With his son, he also produced a series of etchings based on the Camposanto frescoes *(see above)*.

ADDITIONAL SIGHTS

★★ **Museo Nazionale di San Matteo** (BZ) ⊘ - The rooms in this museum, which are set out around the cloisters in the former St Matthew's Monastery (15C), contain an extraordinary collection of sculptures and paintings, from Pisan churches and monasteries, by local artists, all showing the extent to which the city was a major centre of artistic creativity from the 13C to 15C.

Ground Floor - *Turn right into the cloisters*. At the end of the first gallery are the rooms *(left)* dealing with medieval sculpture *(in preparation)*.

The collections of **ceramics** *(other side of the cloisters)* are of varied provenance. Pisa acquired a large quantity of Islamic ceramics and was also famous in the 13C-17C for its original work; from the 14C onwards production was exported throughout the Mediterranean basin from Spain to Turkey, including Provence, Corsica and Greece. It was used locally as an unusual feature in the architectural decoration of churches *(see San Piero a Grado below)*. From the mid-13C Pisan workshops, which were among the largest in Tuscany, succeeded in making their ceramics waterproof by coating them in pewter-based vitreous enamels. The main feature of this "early majolica" is its brown and green painted decoration. From the 15C onwards the designs were etched into the ceramics and usually highlighted by a brown ochre tint. The item itself could be left white or uniformly painted in pale yellow, yellow ochre or green. These incisions *(a stecca)* later developed into the decorative style known as "peacock's feather eye". The following rooms contain ceramics imported from Liguria, southern Italy, Islamic countries or the Middle East. The collection of 10C-13C Islamic items is especially extensive.

First Floor - The upper gallery in the cloisters *(at the top of the staircase)* contains pieces of 12C-13C architectural sculpture.

The tour of **Pisan painting** begins in the room *(left at the top of the staircase)* with works dating from the 12C-13C. The huge Crucifixes are characteristic of this period, which was still strongly influenced by Greek and Byzantine works. Christ is shown variously - triumphant with a calm and serene expression or suffering with his head to one side and eyes shut. Giunta di Capitinio (died mid-13C), one of the artists influenced by ancient Greek works, often accentuated the human aspect of divine suffering whereas Ranieri di Ugolino was representative of an innovatory style based on the research carried out by Cimabue.

14C works *(right of the staircase)* show the extent to which Pisa was open to new artistic trends. Simone Martini, a painter from Siena, produced a magnificent polyptych for the Church of Santa Caterina *c*1320 *(on the end wall)* representing a *Madonna and Child* with *(left to right)* Mary Magdalen, St Dominic, St John the Evangelist, St John the Baptist, St Peter the Martyr and St Catherine. This work is attractive for the compassion in the facial expressions but it is steeped in a gentle melancholy. Francesco di Traino, who was equally influenced by Simone Martini and Giotto, developed a style that was both mannered yet vigourous as is evident in his large polyptych in honour of *St Dominic* (1344) *(set at right angles to the room near the door)*, his *Madonna and Child with Saints* and a *St Catherine of Alexandria* resplendent in a rich cloak *(righthand wall)*.

The room at the end on the right is filled with examples of **Pisan sculptures** from the 14C, a period that was dominated by the workshop of Andrea Pisano and his sons, Nino (the best-known) and Tommaso *(qv)*. Note the delightful marble *Madonna and Child* by Nino Pisano and, more particularly, the **Madonna del latte** on which the Virgin Mary is depicted gracefully leaning over with a delicious smile on her face. The work was carved jointly by Nino and his father. As to the life-size polychrome and gilded woodcarvings, most of them were by Francesco di Valdambrino who learnt his craft from the Pisanos. His mainly female figures used to decorate the monasteries and convents of Pisa.

The tour of the world of painting continues in the room opposite *(and in the cloister gallery at right angles to it)*. Although the outbreak of plague in 1348 interrupted the flow of commissions and caused a break in the choice of subject matter, Pisa remained a major centre of creativity even after that date. Two of Francesco di Traino's pupils stood out from the other members of the Pisan School. They were Francesco Neri da Volterra and Cecco di Pietro. The former painted the *Madonna and Child surrounded by Saints (to the right of the door)* and the latter a *Pietà* and a very ornate polyptych representing the *Crucifixion between the Saints,* whose lives are depicted on the predella. The frescoes being painted in the Camposanto also gave painters who had learnt their craft in Florence an opportunity to work in Pisa. Among them were Spinello Aretino *(Coronation of the Virgin Mary, Three Saints)*, Agnolo Gaddi (four saints), Taddeo di Bartolo (five charming little panels depicting the life of St Galgan) and Antonio Veneziano whose small processional pennant bears a *Crucifixion* on one side including a host of figures filled with life and vigour and, on the other, a representation of St Rainier and the Flagellants.

The following room *(in the corner of the cloisters)* has works by Turino Vanni (d 1444) and artists influenced by him. In the centre is one of the artist's last works, a *Crucifixion* showing the donor kneeling *(lefthand side)* with the walls of Pisa behind him and the tower, already leaning *(left)*.

The other rooms reveal the level of artistic activity in Pisa in the 15C. After coming under Florentine control in 1406, Pisa saw an influx of prestigious artists from the Tuscan capital. In the corner of the cloister gallery, there is a *Virgin Mary of Humility* by Gentile da Fabriano and, in the first room in this same gallery, a **St Paul** who is stupefyingly lifelike. This was once part of a polyptych painted in 1426 by Masaccio, on a golden background in the Gothic tradition but in a style that was totally innovatory. There is also a *Madonna and Child* (stucco low relief) by Michelozzo, a delightful *Madonna and Child* in rather muted tones attributed to Fra Angelico and a gilded bronze bust of St Lussorio by Donatello. The following room contains a number of works by Benozzo Gozzoli and *(in the cloister gallery right)*, a *Madonna and Child with Saints* by Ghirlandaio.

The works dating from the 16C-19C are being kept in store while refurbishment work continues.

★ **Piazza dei Cavalieri** (AY) – This spacious, tranquil square lies in the heart of the medieval town and is now frequented by students. It has remained one of the most majestic and best-preserved areas in Pisa and it was here, in 1406, that the end of the Pisan Republic was proclaimed.

The square was totally transformed when Cosimo I de' Medici commissioned his architect, Vasari, to erect the buildings designed for the **Knights of St Stephen (Cavalieri di Santo Stefano)**. This holy, military Order, which was subject to the Rule of St Benedict, was founded in 1562 to lead the fight against the Infidel, its main task being to capture the Muslim pirates who infested the Mediterranean. The Brotherhood died out in 1860.

The square is lined by 16C and 17C buildings and dominated by the **palazzo dei Cavalieri (ABYF)** on which the long, unusual, slightly-curving **façade**★ is decorated with grotesque figures and foliage. The upper storeys are separated by a frieze of niches containing the busts of the six members of the Medici dynasty who were Grand Dukes of Tuscany. Their coat of arms – six balls – is visible in several places, as is the Cross of the Knights who were given instruction here. The building is currently the seat of a university founded during the days of Napoleon Bonaparte. In front is a statue of Cosimo I made in 1596 by Francavilla, a sculptor from Florence.

The Church of **Santo Stefano (BY)** dates from 1569 but its white, green and pink marble west front, including the Medici coat of arms and the Cross of St Stephen combined with a decoration of columns, pilasters and draperies, was built some 40 years later.

The **Palazzo dell'Orologio** (Clock House), also known as the **Gherardesca (AYK)**, was reconstructed by Vasari in 1607 on the site of two older buildings. He incorporated the remains of a tower (Torre della Fame) in which, following the defeat of Pisa in 1284 at the Battle of Meloria, Count **Ugolino della Gherardesca**, the commander-in-chief of the Pisan fleet, was accused of treason and sentenced to death by starvation with his children. Dante described this episode in his *Inferno (Divine Comedy,* Song XXXIII*)*.

★★ **Santa Maria della Spina** (AZ) – Standing alone, white and ethereal on the banks of the Arno, this tiny marble Romanesque-Gothic church looks like a reliquary with its spires, gables, pinnacles, niches and rose windows. For many years, it contained one of the thorns from Christ's Crown, hence its name.

It was built in the early 14C on a level with the river but was demolished in 1871 because of the damage caused by the proximity of the water. It was then rebuilt, stone by stone, on the spot where it stands today and underwent major restoration, in particular on its sculptures. Several of the statues that decorated the exterior, created by the Pisano School, have been replaced by copies. The west front includes two Romanesque doors flanked by particularly attractive delicate pink marble panels. The right side is the most ornate. It has Gothic

Santa Maria della Spina during the Luminara.

windows, with triple or quadruple bays inserted in surbased Romanesque arches, and two doors which are also framed with coffered jambs in a style popular in the city. At the top of this wall is a row of niches containing the Redeemer and the Apostles.

The plain rectangular room forming the nave and chancel is lit, on the side facing the Arno, by an almost unbroken row of Gothic double windows beneath a Romanesque arch. The church contains a graceful **Madonna and Child** by Nino Pisano.

San Paolo a ripa d'Arno (AZ) – As its name suggests, this 11C and 12C **church** stands on the bank of the Arno. Its attractive **façade★** with three rows of columns, its alternating rows of black and white marble and the blind arcading decorating the sides are all typical of the Pisan Romanesque style and are reminiscent of the cathedral, on a less grandiose scale.

The **cappella Sant'Agata** behind the apse is a strange little octagonal brick chapel with a pyramid-shaped roof. It dates from the 12C and, because of its resemblance to the Church of San Sepolcro, it is usually attributed to Diotisalvi.

San Michele in Borgo (BY L) – The **façade★** of the church is a remarkable example of the transition between the Romanesque and Gothic periods in Pisan architecture. It has three rows of galleries with trefoiled pointed arches and colonnades crowned by masks, which contrast sharply with the more robust lower section where, unlike most of the churches in Pisa, there is no blind arcading.

Santa Caterina (BY) – This church has a light **façade★** built of white marble discreetly marked with lines of darker marble. It consists of a harmonious combination of austere, wide Romanesque blind arches on the lower level and two successive rows of graceful Gothic columns and multifoiled arches on the upper sections. The interior is typical of Dominican churches, having a raftered nave but no aisles, and contains two white marble tombs facing one another – one *(left)* was sculpted by Nino Pisano in the mid 14C; the other *(right)* dates from the early 15C. The chancel is flanked by two sculptures of the *Annunciation* by Nino Pisano.

San Sepolcro (BZ) – Like the Holy Sepulchre in Jerusalem, this church of the same name is built to a similar layout. Its octagonal design with pyramid-shaped roof was created in the 12C by Diotisalvi. The **interior★** consists of an ambulatory and majestic central chancel around which very tall, mighty pillars support high arches surmounted by a deep dome surrounded by brick bonding.

At the foot of the altar is the tomb of **Maria Mancini** who was removed from the French Court by her uncle, Cardinal Mazarin, because she had aroused a fierce passion in Louis XIV; she was married to Prince Colonna from whom she was later separated and who had her imprisoned. She fled to Antwerp and later to France. On being widowed she returned to Italy to spend the last few years of an unhappy life in Pisa where she died in 1715.

Lungarno Pacinotti (ABY) – From Piazza Solferino and the bridge of the same name, there is a view east along the quays of a bend in the Arno, with Monte Pisano in the background. To the west is the tall brick tower of the old citadel. The slender, white church of Santa Maria della Spina stands out on the south bank. The **Palazzo Upezzinghi** (AY Y no 43) was built in the early 17C and is now part of the University. Its façade flanks a large gateway, surmounted by a window opening onto a balcony, above which is a huge coat of arms decorated with a lion. The 15C **Palazzo Agostini★** (ABY nos 28 to 25) has a decorative façade built entirely of brick including two rows of Gothic windows. The frontage is covered in terracotta medallions, shields and garlands. On the ground floor is the famous **Caffé dell'Ussero** (Hussars' Cafe) established in 1794 and frequented by the writers of the Risorgimento. On the other side of the bridge (*Ponte di Mezzo*), in close proximity to each other, are the 17C **loggia di Banchi** (BZ C) that used to house the linen market and the austere **Palazzo Gambacorti** (BZ H), the late-14C town hall built of grey-green stone decorated with a few rows of pink stone. Its three storeys (extensively restored) include double windows set in semicircular arches.

Lungarno Mediceo (BZ) – The superb **Palazzo Toscanelli** (BZ no 17) has a majestic Renaissance façade of pale stone and a roof projecting beyond a coffered cornice carved with roses. Byron wrote part of his *Don Juan* there between the autumn of 1821 and the summer of 1822. The **Palazzo Medici** (BZ P) (now the Prefettura) dates from the 13C-14C but has undergone much alteration since that time. Its most famous guest was Lorenzo the Magnificent of Florence.

EXCURSIONS

San Piero a Grado and the beaches – *30km – 19 miles southwest of Pisa (exit ⑤ on the town plan) by taking the south bank of the Arno and following signs for Mare and Marina di Pisa and then for San Piero.*
The 11C Romanesque **basilica★** of San Piera a Grado (St Peter's on the Quay) is built of fine pale golden stone and is said to stand on the old quayside in the Roman port of Pisa where St Peter is believed to have landed. It has two apses, the one at the east end being flanked by two apsidal chapels. The Lombardy arcading is decorated with alternating diamonds and circles while a frieze of ceramic bowls, a form of decoration specific to the Pisa area, runs along the top of the north wall (*see above – Museo Nazionale di San Matteo*).
The 14C frescoes in the interior depicting scenes from the life of St Peter are said to be copies of the ones which decorated the original basilica of St Peter's in Rome.

Tirrenia (SB) (*second turn to the right after the basilica*) is an elegant resort famous for its extensive pine woods, its white sandy beach and its film studios.

Marina di Pisa is a popular beach at the mouth of the Arno where, in spring, people fish for elvers with vast fine-mesh nets. There is a view of Livorno (south). Nearby is the vast pine wood on the **San Rossore** estate which belonged to the Medici family and then to the House of Savoy. It is now the property of the President of the Republic and part of the Migliarino-San Rossore-Massaciuccoli country park (*see Versilia - tour 3*).
Take the road along the banks of the Arno to return to Pisa.

Monte Pisano – *60km – 38 miles east of Pisa – about 2 1/2 hours.*
This small mountain range, an outcrop of the Apuan Alps, lying between Pisa and Lucca and separating the two cities, rises to a peak in Monte Serra (917m – 2980ft).
From Pisa (exit ② on the town plan) take SS12 (blue signs to Lucca) and A11 (green signs to Firenze).
The rugged, sheer slopes of Monte Pisano, some of which contain stone quarries, soon come into view. The narrow road lined with plane trees moves nearer to the mountain but remains in the plain, as if about to collide with the mountain.

San Giuliano Terme – This small spa town was once frequented by such famous people as Montaigne and Alfieri, and then, in the 19C, by Byron, Shelley, Louis Bonaparte and Pauline Borghese. In the distance is a large yellow ochre portico with five arches, which marks the entrance to the pump rooms and stands out against a background of pine trees.
Turn left before a small bridge to return to the village (no signs). The road runs beside a stream before crossing the first bridge on the right.
The pump rooms stand in a small square where Shelley once had lodgings. The two hot springs produce water at temperatures of 38° and 41°. The waters of San Giuliano have been famous since Roman times and are used to treat respiratory and digestive disorders as well as arthritis and rheumatism.
Turn right opposite the pump rooms to rejoin SS12. Turn right to return to the original crossroads and turn left into the road to Calci.

At first the road runs across the arid slopes of Monte Pisano but soon the mountain becomes greener and pleasantly wooded. There are a few olive groves *(left)* and the aquaduct *(night)* which used to supply Pisa with spring water. At the junction where the left turn leads Agnano, Monte Pisano comes into view in the distance, sloping gently down towards the plain. The small, aptly-named "Verruca" hill, the final promontory before the descent, used to be the site of a 13C Pisan fortress which now lies in ruins. Lower down, at the foot of one of the tower outposts of the fortress, there is a sudden break in the outline of the mountain created by the Caprona quarry which reaches right to the very edge of the fort's defences.

8km – 5 miles from S Giuliano, beyond a petrol station (right), turn left to Calci and Montemagno. After 1km – 1/2 mile of hairpin bends the road leads straight to Calci church.

Calci – The 11C **Pieve** (parish church) has a fine Pisan Romanesque west front. The interior underwent alterations in the 19C but has retained a monolithic font *(first chapel on the left)* used for christenings by total immersion, which dates from the second half of the 12C.

Continue along the same street. At the traffic lights go straight on to the charterhouse (700m – 758yds).

★ **Certosa di Pisa (Pisa Charterhouse)** Ⓥ – The charterhouse, a Carthusian monastery, consists of a fine set of 17C-18C buildings in which the Baroque church stands out in the centre of a vast façade. The monastery was designed for 15 monks and 60 lay brothers. Buildings open to the public include the church, the monks' chapels, and large Classical **cloisters**★ decorated with an amusing fountain. The monk-hermits' tiny houses open into the cloisters. The small cloisters designed for the lay brothers give access to the chapter-house and then to the refectory, the hostelry used by visiting noblemen, and the prior's cloisters (15C).

The monastery houses a **natural history museum** Ⓥ containing the oldest items from the extensive collection begun by Ferdinand I of Florence in 1591. Among the most outstanding exhibits are 19C stuffed animals "immortalised" in hunting scenes that impressed romantic writers such as Byron and Shelley. There are also invertebrates made of glass and a gallery of cetaceans.

The view extends over a ring of mountains and the ruins of the fortress on Verruca Hill.

Return to the crossroads in Calci and turn right at the traffic lights to Monte Serra.

The road starts to climb then forms a series of narrow, hairpin bends as it mounts the slopes of Monte Pisano. After the last few houses, which are more rural in style, the road quickly enters a forest of pines and deciduous trees, alternating with stretches of heather and broom. The Arno Plain is visible *(right)* with the river winding majestically through the countryside at the foot of the mountain range. There is a superb **view**★ from a lay-by *(5.3km – 3 miles from the crossroads in Calci).* At the Y-junction the road *(left)* continues to climb Monte Serra, which bristles with TV masts; the other road *(right)* going down to Buti soon crosses to the opposite side of the range where the scenery becomes less rugged.

In Buti take the direction Pontedera, Lucca and Pisa; at the T-junction, opposite the river that flows through the village, turn right towards the centre. Take the first on the left and cross the bridge. Bear left; at the fork, turn left uphill. The road soon narrows and descends through a series of bends (gradient 10 % – 1:10) to Vicopisano (not signed).

At the end of the road Vicopisano and its keep come into view on the hill.

Vicopisano – The Pisan Romanesque church (12C-13C) contains a rare woodcarving of the **Deposition from the Cross**★ (11C). The old village still has some picturesque traces of its medieval walls, including three towers – the Clock Tower, the Four Gates Tower (four pointed arches at its base) and the Brunelleschi Tower, which is connected to the keep by a machicolated wall. At the top of the hill stands the crenellated keep, next to the Palazzo Pretorio, which is decorated with a large number of coats of arms.

Tke the road along the north bank of the Arno to return to Pisa.

Near Uliveto Terme the road skirts the rugged, rocky slopes of Monte Pisano; as it approaches Caprona, the outpost of the fortress on Verruca (visible in the distance at the start of the tour) comes into view high above a quarry which produces the yellow-ochre veined stone known as *verrucano*.

Follow the signs and take S67 to return directly to Pisa.

Leonardo Fibonacci, otherwise known as Leonardo of Pisa (c1175-after 1240), is less well-known than Leonardo da Vinci but it is nevertheless to him that we owe a practice that makes our everyday life much easier. He was the person who introduced Arabic numerals into Europe, thereby simplifying arithmetic calculations.

PISTOIA★★

Population 87 697
Michelin Map 988 fold 14 or 430 K14

Pistoia is a very industrial town but visitors may be surprised by the small old centre, a network of narrow streets and alleyways clustered round a medieval square that is one of the most delightful in Italy. In the old streets the tiny shopfronts are filled to overflowing with a wide range of goods, making this a picturesque shopping area.

The town is particularly proud of its 12C religious buildings, dating from the days when it was a free borough and enjoyed its greatest period of prosperity, the product of the work of its merchants and bankers.

When Lucca and Florence began to show interest in the town in the 13C and 14C, a wall was built but the town was gradually demolished and brought under the control of the larger cities until, in 1530, it was annexed by the Medici of Florence.

★★ PIAZZA DEL DUOMO (B) *Tour – 2 hours*

This vast square is attractive for its size and the delightful layout of its main buildings, which are the largest religious and civil buildings in the city. The cathedral *(south side)* is preceded by its baptistery and flanked by the bell-tower and the old **Bishop's Palace** *(Palazzo dei Vescovi)* which has been extensively restored. Facing each other across the square are the town hall *(east)* linked to the cathedral by an arch-way and the Palazzo Preto-rio *(west)*. Set slightly back from the main line of buildings is a medieval tower, called the **Cataline Tower**; its name recalls the fact that the famous Ro-man conspirator was de-feated and killed in 62 BC beneath the walls of Pis-toia, then a Roman for-tress.

Each year in July the square is the setting for the **Bear Joust** *(Giostra dell'Orso)*. The competi-tors are dressed in 14C costume and the best horsemen from the four urban districts *(rioni)* of medieval Pistoia ride at full speed at the target, held by a dummy shaped like a bear, and tilt at it with lances.

In the adjacent square *(Pi-azza della Sala)* is the graceful **pozzo del Leoncino**, a 15C well crowned by a lion cub *(leoncino)* resting its front left paw on the shield of Pistoia.

Piazza del Duomo, Pistoia.

★ **Duomo (B)** ⊘ – The Cathedral of San Zeno was destroyed by fire in 1108 and rebuilt in the 12C-13C but it continued to undergo major alterations until the 17C.

The marble-clad **west front**★ is a delightful combination of the very austere Pisan Romanesque style – rows of galleries in the upper section – and the Florentine Renaissance style – porch with slender columns added in the 14C. The strange **belltower** (almost 70m – 227ft high) also consists of a combination of several different styles. The base consists of a massive lookout tower built of pale golden stone with very few doors or windows, which already existed in the days of Lombard domination. In the 13C a lighter upper section was added with three rows of Pisan galleries decorated with strips of light and dark-coloured marble and surmounted by two crenellated platforms built of brick. The small pyramidal roof and bellturret date from the 16C.

Glazed terracotta work by Andrea della Robbia decorates the tympanum above the main entrance *(Madonna and Child between two Angels)* and the barrel vaulting on the central arch in the porch.

Interior – The Baroque chancel with its heavy gilding, which replaced the original chancel in the 17C, forms a surprising contrast with the Romanesque nave and two aisles which are almost devoid of decoration. The fine painted rafters used to be concealed behind vaulting.

Against the wall *(near the entrance to the church in the south aisle)* is the tomb of **Cino da Pistoia,** a writer who was a contemporary of Dante and Petrarch. A 14C Sienese sculptor depicted the master teaching his followers on the sarcophagus itself and above it in the Gothic niche.

Further on is a *Crucifixion* by Coppo di Marcovaldo.

The chapel nearby contains the famous **St James Altar**★★★ *(dossale di San Jacopo)* ⓥ, an outstanding example of the silversmith's craft, part of which was created in the late 13C but which was altered and extended over the following two centuries *(ask at the sacristy (further on and right) for the screen to be opened and for the altar to be lit)*. The altar, made of *repoussé* and embossed silver, includes 628 figures. The motifs on the altarpiece are set out around two large figures, one of whom represents St James sitting on a throne, wearing the traditional hat and carrying the traditional purse and pilgrim's stick, flanked by the Apostles and saints on the predella and in the Gothic niches; this is the oldest section of the altar. Above is a Christ in Glory surrounded by cherubim and a choir of angels. The altar itself is also covered with scenes from the Bible. On the front are two episodes from the Life of Jesus and three scenes relating to St James. The nine small panels *(right)* show episodes from the Old Testament but the depiction of the life of St James *(left)* is the most outstanding part of the work. *Read each section of the altar from left to right and bottom to top.*

Left Side

St James and his brother, St John the Evangelist, answer the call	His arrest
	Trial and conviction of the saint
Their mother, Mary Salome, recommends them to Jesus	St James baptises his accuser, who has been converted to Christianity
St James' apostolic mission	
St James preaching	Martyrdom of St James
	His followers take his body to Spain

Altar Front

Annunciation and Visitation of the Virgin Mary	The Women at the tomb
	Christ appears to St Thomas
Christ in Glory, between the Virgin Mary and St James	Ascension
	Presentation of Jesus in the Temple
Procession of the Three Kings	St James preaching
Adoration of the Magi	Conviction of St James
Massacre of the Holy Innocents	Martyrdom of St James
Judas' kiss	*On the sides – the Prophets*
Crucifixion	

Right Side

Creation of Adam and Eve	on Mount Sinai and gives the Law to the Hebrews
Original sin: Adam and Eve being expelled from the Garden of Eden	
	David receives the divine blessing and is crowned king
Cain's crime and punishment	
Construction of Noah's Ark	Birth and presentation of the Virgin Mary in the Temple
Noah and his family receiving the divine blessing. Sacrifice of Isaac.	
	Marriage of the Virgin Mary.
Moses receives the Tables of the Law	

The chapel *(left of the chancel)* contains a very fine **Virgin Mary in Majesty**★ between St John the Baptist and St Donat. This is a tranquil piece of work in a subtle range of colours by Lorenzo di Credi *(c*1480), a pupil in Verrocchio's workshop. The master's hand can probably be detected in the rigorous composition and the attempt to create lighting effects.

Against the wall *(west end of the north aisle)* is the highly-ornate but generally harmonious tomb of Cardinal Forteguerri created jointly by Verrocchio and a number of his pupils; several additions were made at a later date. At the rear of the façade is the marble font shaped like a small Renaissance temple and attractively carved in 1499 by Andrea da Fiesole from drawings by Benedetto da Maiano of scenes from the life of St John the Baptist.

★ **Battistero di San Giovanni in Corte (B)** ⓥ – This is a Gothic building (14C) designed by Andrea Pisano. It is octagonal in shape and clad in alternating strips of white and green marble. It is crowned with elegant blind arcading.

The main entrance, to the right of which is a delightful little pulpit, has a tympanum decorated with a *Madonna and Child between St John the Baptist and St Peter*; the statues are attributed to Andrea Pisano's two sons, Nino and

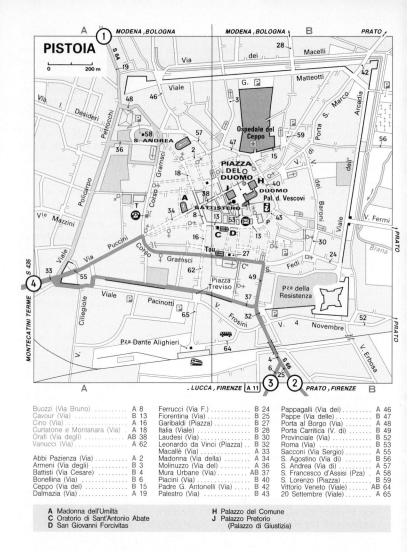

PISTOIA

0 — 200 m

A Madonna dell'Umiltà	**H** Palazzo del Comune
C Oratorio di Sant'Antonio Abate	**J** Palazzo Pretorio
D San Giovanni Forcivitas	(Palazzo di Giustizia)

Tommaso. Below are small low reliefs depicting the martyrdom of St John the Baptist – *(left to right)* St John the Baptist brought before Herod, Salome's dance, **Salome presenting the saint's head on a platter**, the burial of St John.
The interior, which is suffused in pink light because of the bricks, is almost entirely devoid of decoration on the walls and the deep octagonal dome. The elegant font *(centre)* is faced with polychrome marble panels that are finely carved and decorated with inlay; it was made in 1226 by Lanfranco da Como.

Palazzo Pretorio (**BJ**) – This was formerly the Palazzo del Podestà but has been altered from the 14C to the 19C. The only traces that remain of the original building are the entrance, the Gothic double windows on the first floor and the staircase leading to the upper floor *(in the courtyard)*. On one side of the courtyard there is a portico painted in the 19C with grotesque motifs on the vaulting; on another is a rare example of a stone seat on which the judges sat; the accused sat on the bench at the side.

Pallazo del Comune (Town Hall) (BH) – This Gothic building, constructed between 1294 and 1385, has a massive façade★ over arcades facing the square. The pale colour of the stone, the elegance and regular layout of the Gothic windows – double bays on the first floor and triple bays beneath the roof – and the small central balcony with delicate wrought-ironwork add a touch of warmth and grace to an otherwise austere building. In the centre of the façade and at the corners of the building is the Medici coat of arms with its six balls.
The building was not linked to the cathedral by an archway until 1637. It is now used as the Town Hall and it also houses the **municipal museum** *(see below – Additional Sights)*. In the centre of the courtyard is a huge sculpture (1953) from the *Miracoli* series, one of Marino Marini's most famous works. The bronze group illustrates one of his favourite themes, a horseman falling off his horse.

★ **Palazzo dei Vescovi (B)** ⊙ - *Guided tour (about 1 hour)*. The **Bishop's Palace** was built in the 11C. The tour consists of an informative archeological trail which gives an insight into the history of the palace and of the land on which it was built. The exhibits were excavated during the restoration of the palace - interesting remains of Roman town walls, remains from the Via Cassia, Etruscan funerary urns, Lombard vases.

The tour includes a visit to the **Cathedral Museum** which has an extensive collection of church plate and vestments linked to the history of the cathedral. Also worth a visit is the **sacristy** from which the treasure was stolen in the 13C by Vanni Fucci, as told by Dante in Song XXIV of his *Inferno*. Beyond it is the **room**★ containing works by Boldini (frescoes painted by the Macchiaolo painter from Ferrare) and the **Cappella San Niccolo** (13C) decorated with frescoes and bearing inscriptions scratched on the walls by prisoners held there after the 15C when the chapel was deconsecrated and turned into a gaol.

ADDITIONAL SIGHTS

Ospedale del Ceppo (B) - The hospital was founded in 1277. Its name means the hollow tree trunk *(ceppo)* which was used to receive offerings. The elegant Renaissance portico in front of the façade, which is reminiscent of the one on the Foundling Hospital in Florence, dates from 1514.

The admirable glazed terracotta **frieze**★★ decorating the portico is one of the main sights of Pistoia. The work was created shortly before 1530 in the workshop of Giovanni, the last of the Della Robbia family. Its characteristics are the harmonious composition, the freshness of the colours and the expressiveness of the figures. The seven panels, including one decorating the lefthand side,

S. Chirol

Detail of the frieze by Giovanni Della Robbia, Ospedale del Ceppo.

illustrate the *Seven Works of Mercy* - *(left to right)* clothing the naked *(on the side)*, welcoming pilgrims, visiting the sick, visiting prisoners, burying the dead, giving food to the hungry and drink to the thirsty. Between the panels are graceful female figures representing the Virtues - *(left to right)* Prudence, Faith, Charity, Hope and Justice. Medallions surrounded by garlands of leaves, fruit and flowers, in the Florentine tradition, decorate the squinches between the arches. On the righthand side is the Medici coat of arms with the emblem of Pistoia and its checkered motif beside it.

★ **Chiesa di Sant'Andrea (A)** - The church was built in the 8C but extensively altered four centuries later. It has a very attractive west front, although the upper section was never completed, in the Pisan Romanesque style with five blind arcades including slender capitals and a green and white marble decoration. The lintel above the central doorway is decorated with three scenes carved in the Byzantine style - *(left to right)* the *Travels of the Three Kings, Herod being told of the birth of the Saviour*, and the *Adoration of the Magi*. The artist signed his work, in Latin, at the bottom.

The very plain **interior**★★ is admirably pure in architectural terms. The very tall and narrow nave is separated from the aisles by low arches with a narrow span. The columns are crowned by capitals with varied types of decoration.

A 15C marble niche carved with slender foliage *(beyond the first altar on the right)* contains a gilded wooden **Crucifix**★ by Giovanni Pisano.

The most outstanding feature in the church is the famous **pulpit**★★ made between 1298 and 1301 by the same artist, in his dramatic and rather complex but very vivid style. It was designed to resemble the pulpits in the baptistery in Pisa and the cathedral in Siena made by Nicola, Giovanni's father and teacher. It is hexagonal in shape, and elegantly supported on seven red porphyry columns supporting light trefoiled Gothic arches. The pulpit itself is covered with five marble panels, each exquisitely carved – *(starting with the panel facing the wall and going from left to right)* the *Annunciation (furthest to the left)* and the *Nativity (on the same panel)*, the *Adoration of the Magi*, the *Massacre of the Holy Innocents*, the *Crucifixion*, and the *Last Judgement*.

★ **Basilica della Madonna dell'Umiltà** (Basilica of Our Lady of Humility) **(B A)** – The huge dome of this octagonal basilica is reminiscent of the one designed by Brunelleschi for the cathedral in Florence. The Renaissance basilica was built to house the miraculous picture of the Virgin Mary of Humility, the patron saint of Pistoia.

Chiesa di San Giovanni Forcivitas (B D) – The church of St John Outside the Walls was built between the 12C and 14C and has been subject to restoration on several occasions since then. The **north wall**★, a long and spectacular striped construction overlooking Via Cavour, acts as its façade. The white and green marble bonding, tall blind arches on the lower level surmounted by two rows of galleries with colonnades, and the diamond-shaped decorative motifs are all characteristic of the Pisan Romanesque style.

The gloomy interior is laid out in the form of a basilica, without aisles or apse. The fine water stoop was partly the work of Giovanni Pisano. The small marble basin decorated with female heads, representing the cardinal virtues, is supported on a pillar consisting of three statues representing the theological virtues.

A niche *(left)* contains an all-white glazed terracotta sculpture of the **Visitation**★★ by Luca Della Robbia. From this strict, limpid piece of work, which shows outstanding craftsmanship, emanates a feeling of pent-up emotion, harmony and nobility, which make it one of the artist's finest creations.

The **pulpit**★ *(righthand wall)* is a refined, severely beautiful piece of work made in 1270 by Fra Guglielmo of Pisa, one of Nicola Pisano's pupils. Its white marble panels depict the Life of Jesus and the Virgin Mary. In the centre are the symbols of the Evangelists; there is a group of three Prophets in each corner.

Against the wall *(left of the altar)* is a polyptych by Taddeo Gaddi (14C) of great gentleness. It shows the Virgin Mary surrounded by saints.

Oratorio di Sant'Antonio Abate (Chapel of St Anthony the Abbot) **(B C)** – The lower section of this small building near the church is an old private chapel built in the 14C. It was once connected to San Giovanni Forcivitas by an archway.

Chiesa del Tau (B) ⊘ – This small 14C church, which has been restored but is now deconsecrated, is famous for its Gothic **frescoes**★ painted by local artists. The expression "Tau" refers to the blue enamelled letter "T" that the monks of the Order of Hospitallers of St Anthony, who lived here in the 14C, used to wear on their tunics and cloaks.

Palazzo del Tau (B) ⊘ – This building, the former monastery of the Order of the Hospitallers of St Anthony *(see above)* now houses the Marino Marini Centre, which was established owing to a bequest to the city made by the artist himself (1901-1980). The Centre contains a collection of his sculptures, drawings, prints and etchings. His work, honed down almost to its bare bones, is based on a few recurring themes – people dancing, horses, riders – which were exploited with striking power, a sense of movement and a dramatic tension.

Among the drawings of nudes is the *Riposo (Rest, 1927)*. Also displayed is a series of portraits of famous people including a silver portrait of Stravinsky (1950), the famous *Fondale (Background, 1978)* full of angular and rather disturbing silhouettes, and also *Incontro (Meeting, 1964)* which is a huge work in muted tones of red and brown.

Museo Civico (Municipal Museum) **(B)** ⊘ – The museum is housed in the Town Hall (**H**) and includes a collection of paintings and sculptures dating from the 13C to the 19C.

On the first floor are a *St Francis* (1) surrounded by scenes illustrating his life and posthumous miracles, a *Pietà* (4) and a polyptych representing the *Madonna and Child surrounded by saints* (5), all illustrative of the work of artists from Lucca, Umbria and Florence, who came to Pistoia at the end of the 13C and the beginning of the 14C. Note the delicate *Madonna* (17), a relief by an unknown 15C sculptor, and four large Renaissance altarpieces illustrating the theme of the Holy Conversation. Two of them are by Florentine artists, Lorenzo di Credi (20) who worked in Pistoia in a style reminiscent of Perugino, his contemporary in Verrocchio's studio, and Ridolfo del Ghirlandaio (21). The other two (22 and 23) were by a local artist, Gerino Gerini, who was also influenced by Perugino in his early days. The following room has works mainly by local artists from the 15C-16C.

On the third floor, in the main reception room, are canvases dating mainly from the 17C-18C including a *Vision of St Jerome* (61) painted by Piero Paolini who was strongly influenced by the luminous qualities of Caravaggio's work.

The corridor round the courtyard contains a triptych by the Master of Frankfurt (16C) depicting the *Virgin Mary in Majesty* (104) and a painting by Mattia Preti (1613-1699), a follower of Caravaggio, representing *Susan and the Elders* (120). In the last room all the works date from the 19C; the neo-Classical and Romantic movements are represented by artists such as Luigi Sabatelli and Giuseppe Bezzuoli.

PITIGLIANO*

Population 4 329
Michelin Map 988 fold 25 or 430 O 16/17

Pitigliano stands in an impressive and picturesque setting on a massive spur of volcanic tufa high above the confluence of two rivers, the Lente and the Meleta. There is an outstandingly impressive **view**★ from the southwest (S74), particularly from the church of the Madonna delle Grazie on the southern outskirts.

The town was an Etruscan settlement before being colonised by the Romans. From the 13C to the early 17C, it belonged to the Aldobrandeschi family and later to the Orsini family of Roman Counts, before being annexed to the Grand Duchy of Tuscany. Until the 19C it had a large Jewish population, hence the synagogue in Via Zuccarelli.

SIGHTS

The foundations of the town wall are Etruscan; south of the town are the remains of the **aqueduct** – two 16C arches. From Piazza della Repubblica there is a fine view of the valley below.

Medieval town – The town is traversed by cobbled streets lit by old lanterns; the streets are linked to each other by covered alleyways or flights of steps. At the lower end of the town stands the small **Church of San Rocco** (12C) which has a Renaissance west front and a belltower decorated with arcading and tracery. The left wall incorporates an 11C low relief depicting a man with his hands in the mouths of two dragons.

Pitigliano.

PISTOIA

Palazzo Orsini – This vast square building retains its 14C appearance with crenellations, machicolations and an austere loggia with two arches of unequal size. In the 16C alterations were made at the rear, including a courtyard with a well bearing a coat of arms. Along one side of the courtyard is a wing with arcades supported by Ionic columns. The other wing has a delicately-carved Renaissance entrance.

Duomo (Cathedral) – The 18C Baroque façade forms a sharp contrast with the fortified belltower, the old medieval belfry. Nearby is a travertine column (1490) carved with coats of arms and surmounted by a bear, the emblem of the Orsini family.

EXCURSIONS

★ **Sovana** – *8km – 5 miles north. See Sovana.*

★ **Sorano** – *9km – 5.5 miles northeast. See Sorano.*

Villa di POGGIO A CAIANO★★

Michelin Map 430 K 15

Tour – 30min excluding the grounds. Park beside the church.

The villa of **Poggio a Caiano** ⊙ stands in the middle of pleasant gardens. It was built in 1485 by Giuliano da Sangallo for Lorenzo the Magnificent and was the first example of a real Tuscan villa rather than a refurbished fortress as had been more commonplace until then. It was decorated with a pediment and clock in the 18C and its double flight of steps was converted in the 19C into a horseshoe-shaped staircase. The loggia on the façade has been decorated in the manner of the Della Robbias.

Francesco I and his second wife, **Bianca Cappello** *(qv)*, died here in 1587, probably of poison. The young Venetian woman eloped from her family with her first lover whom she married in Florence. The Grand Duke, Francesco I, who was married to Joan of Austria, fell in love with Bianca at first sight and she became his mistress. He settled her and her husband in the fine Palazzo Oltrarno in Florence but he had to wait for the death of Bianca's husband, who was in fact murdered, and of his own wife before he could marry his mistress.

In the magnificent drawing room on the first floor commissioned by Pope Leo X (son of Lorenzo the Magnificent), there is a strange coffered ceiling. Among the frescoes, painted from 1521 onwards by Andrea del Sarto, Franciabigio and Pontormo, the one by Pontormo depicts Pomona and her husband, Vortumnus (the God of Spring). Several of the rooms were refurbished in the 19C for King Victor-Emmanuel II.

POPPI★

Population 5 592
Michelin Map 988 fold 15 or 430 K 17

The Arno Valley spreads out below the walls of the proud and picturesque town of Poppi, formerly the main town in the Casentino district. The streets are lined with arcades and dominated by the proud castle that once belonged to the Counts Guidi.

The end of Ghibelline hopes – As Florence was determined to expand, she allied herself to other Guelf towns in Tuscany and the Romagna. Taking advantage of the reinforcements sent by the House of Anjou, which was allied to the Pope, Florence engaged in battle with Ghibelline troops from Arezzo on 11 June 1289. The very bloody **Battle of Campaldino** was fought in the centre of the plain northwest of Poppi, at the fork in the road (S70 and S310). Despite their superior numbers, the Ghibellines suffered a terrible defeat, which marked the beginning of Florentine hegemony in Tuscany.

SIGHTS

Upper town – A long climb leads up to the entrance to the town, a gateway set among the houses. Overlooking the tiny Piazza Amerighi decorated with a central marble fountain is the Church of **Madonna del Morbo** (17C) capped by a dome and flanked by porticoes on three sides. **Via Cavour** *(opposite)*, also lined with shady porticoes, leads to the righthand side of the **Church of San Fedele**, built in the 13C by the monks of Vallombrosa. The interior consists of a nave with rafters; in the chancel is a painted *Crucifixion* dating from the second half of the 14C.

Poppi Castle.

★ **Castello** ⓥ – At the top of the upper town beyond a tree-lined esplanade stands a 13C Gothic castle with trefoiled window bays, merlons, a barbican and keep. It was built for the *priori (qv)* and is now used as the Town Hall. In the strange **courtyard**, which is decorated with coats of arms, at the rear stands a stone table from which justice used to be dispensed. Two rows of roofed wooden balconies and an outside staircase add to the impression of height. The rooms open to the public include the library *(first floor)*, containing 20 000 books, some of which date from the 13C and 14C, and the great hall in which the ceiling beams still have their original painted decoration. At the end of the chamber is a *tondo* representing a *Madonna and Child* by the Botticelli School and *(right of the door)* a glazed terracotta in the style of the della Robbias. The corner drawing room *(second floor)* has a wonderful fireplace (1512) bearing the coat of arms of the Marquess Gondi. The adjoining chapel is decorated with frescoes attributed to Taddeo Gaddi.

From the windows of the drawing room there is a delightful view of the valley and the mountains north towards Camaldoli and east to La Verna.

Zoo *(0.5km – 1/4 mile)* ⓥ – This pleasant zoo, devoted to European wild life, is traversed by a tree-lined path round a central lake.

POPULONIA★

Michelin Map 430 N 13

The **necropolis** ⓥ of the Etruscan town of *Pupluna* stands below the acropolis overlooking the sea. It dates from the Iron Age (9C-8C BC), when Baratti Bay was the site of all the great burial grounds. Economic activity was probably based on the mineral mines on the Island of Elba and in the hills around Campiglia (northeast).

From the 4C BC, when people began to mine iron on the island, the burial grounds were gradually covered with scoria and waste from the kilns. They remained concealed until the beginning of this century.

Different types of graves were excavated – pits, ditches and chambers (being the oldest) and oriental-style barrows. Among the tumuli with cylindrical bases are the **Tomb with Funeral Beds** *(letti funebri)* and the **Tomb with the Pear-Shaped Urn** *(a small Grecian urn)*. The **Funnel Tomb** *(dei colatoi)* has a tall barrow; the **Fan Tomb** *(dei flabelli)* and **Goldware Tomb** *(delle oreficerie)* are the only tumuli to have remained intact; the **Small Bronze Offering Tomb** is of a tomb with aedicule and was named after the bronze fans found among other funeral items.

The **Museo Gasparri** ⓥ, in the village of Populonia, displays funeral urns, fibulae, wine jars and other Etruscan objects found in the locality.

PRATO★★

Population 165 735
Michelin Map 988 fold 14 or 430 K 15

Despite the peaceful atmosphere and provincial air of the central districts flanked to the east by the River Bisenzio, Prato is the fourth largest city in central Italy after Rome, Florence and Livorno. It is also one of the busiest and most highly-industrialised. Its traditional wool industry was already producing cloth famous throughout Europe in the 13C; it now also specialises in manmade fibres and fabrics. Since the end of the 19C the town has specialised in the processing of "recycled" wools.

Prato, which means meadow, was originally the name of one of the districts which grew up outside the walls around a vast expanse of land used for markets. In the 11C this district finally took precedence over the others. The town belonged to the Alberti, who were named Counts of Prato by the Holy Roman Emperor and who later possessed land throughout northern Tuscany. In the middle of the 12C the town became a free, democratically-governed borough. In 1351, after many years of internal dissension and opposition to Florence in the rivalry between the Guelfs and Ghibellines, Prato came under Florentine rule and followed the fortunes of the larger city until the end of the 18C.

Prato was also a major centre of artistic activity, attracting several famous architects, sculptors and painters, who left a heritage of fine buildings and numerous works of art. Prato was the birthplace of **Filippino Lippi** (1457/8-1504), the son of Filippo *(see below)* and, more recently, of the writer, Curzio Malaparte *(qv)*.

Legend of the Holy Girdle (Il Sacro Cingolo) – Thomas the Apostle, who had doubted the Resurrection of Jesus, was also unwilling to believe in the Assumption of the Virgin Mary since he had not witnessed it for himself. When he asked for the grave of the Mother of God to be opened, he found it was full of lilies and roses. He then looked up to heaven and saw the Virgin Mary in Glory, loosening her girdle to give it to him.

In the 12C a man from Prato took a wife in Jerusalem and was said to have received the miraculous girdle as part of her dowry. His wife died during the journey home to his native town and he jealously kept the relic for himself. At night he hid it beneath the mattress but the angels punished him by throwing him out of bed while he slept. Before he died, he did reveal his secret and the relic was then taken with great pomp to the cathedral where it has been kept ever since.

The Holy Girdle is exhibited several times a year – on Easter Sunday, 1 May, 15 August, 8 September (the Feast Day of the Virgin Mary when there is a large historical pageant), and Christmas Day.

SIGHTS

The main sights all lie within the fortified town walls built in the 14C, beyond which the town did not extend until the beginning of this century.

★ **Duomo** (B) – Prato Cathedral, which was built mainly in the 12C and 13C but which was considerably extended in the 14C and the 15C, is a pleasing combination of Romanesque and Gothic styles and it gives a remarkable impression of uniformity.

An artistic, and dissolute, monk

It was in Prato, where he was painting the frescoes in the cathedral, that **Fra Filippo Lippi** (1406-1469), then aged 50, made the acquaintance of the delicious Lucrezia Buti, a nun in the convent to which he was chaplain.

He had entered Holy Orders at the age of 15 but later left his monastery. He was captured by Barbary pirates and sold in Africa where his talents as an artist so amazed the Moors that they granted him his freedom. He returned to the monastic life until he fell in love with Lucrezia. Filippino was born the following year. Despite the scandal, Cosimo the Elder obtained the Pope's permission for Lippi to be released from his vows. Filippo married Lucrezia whose smooth, triangular face and delicate blond hair he used time and again in his paintings of the Madonna and Salome. He was an unrepentant sinner and he is said to have died as a result of being poisoned by a jealous husband.

Filippo Lippi was a pupil of Lorenzo Monaco and was also strongly influenced by Masaccio. His paintings express grace and freshness and the main characteristics of this artist, who never painted anything but religious subjects, were his sincere inspiration, his natural, simple view, his pure lines and his subtle use of colours.

In his early works Filippino used his father's style but his painting shows greater melancholy.

The elegant Gothic west front, which has an unusually tall central section, is partly clad in green marble and white stone. Originally it was decorated with friezes of light carved stone medallions and quatrefoil motifs in the nave and aisles. At the righthand corner of the building is the famous circular **pulpit** with its fan-shaped canopy which was probably designed by Michelozzo in the early 15C so that the Holy Girdle could be shown to the congregation. Donatello, in whose studio Michelozzo was then employed, carved some remarkable decorative panels for the pulpit – *The Children's Dance (now in the Museo dell'Opera del Duomo).* The present panels are copies of the originals. A glazed terracotta *Madonna and Child* by Andrea Della Robbia (1489) surmounts the entrance. The south wall, which contains two delightful doorways, is decorated with a row of blind arcading in the Pisan Romanesque style, designed by Guidetto da Como. The upper part of the Romanesque **belltower** is in the Gothic style.

Interior – The interior is laid out in an austere style of harmonious proportions, with massive green marble columns supporting Romanesque arches emphasised by alternating strips of light and dark stone. The rafters were covered with vaulting in the 17C.

Holy Girdle Chapel (1) *(first chapel to the left)* was built in the late 14C to house the precious relic. The two very elegant bronze **screens**★ are decorated with roses, cherubim and animals. Between 1392 and 1395 Agnolo Gaddi and his pupils covered the walls of the chapel with frescoes. On the altar is the exquisite, tiny marble statue of the **Madonna and Child**★ known as the *Madonna della Cintola* carved by Giovanni Pisano towards the end of his life in 1317.

The marble **pulpit**★ (2) *(lefthand side),* unusually shaped like a chalice, was made by Mino da Fiesole and Antonio Rossellino (1473); its panels, carved in flowing lines, depict the lives of St John the Baptist *(Herod's Feast* and the *Beheading),* the Virgin Mary *(Assumption)* and St Stephen, to whom the church is dedicated, *(Stoning* and *Burial).*

The touching **Virgin Mary with the Olive**★ (Madonna dell'Ulivo) (3) *(end on the righthand side),* set in a niche, is a terracotta statue made by Benedetto da Maiano (1480) who used flowing lines and elegance in the Virgin Mary's clothing while giving the figure itself a solidity, emphasised by the pyramid shape of the composition as a whole, and a freshness that is decidedly rustic.

The **frescoes**★★ (4) are one of Filippo Lippi's most accomplished pieces of work (1452-1465). He used his mature talent to portray the lives of St Stephen and St John the Baptist with all the skill at his disposal in his search for light *(Herod's Feast)* and perspective *(St Stephen's Burial).* The composition is a nice balance of rigour, subtle colours and narrative spontaneity. The most famous scene depicts **Herod's Feast**★★★, and includes **Salome's Dance** with the same undulating lines, melancholic gentleness and ethereal grace that can be seen in the finest female figures painted by Botticelli, Filippo's famous pupil.

Outdoor pulpit by Michelozzo, Prato Cathedral.

The Bocchineri Chapel (5) *(first chapel on the right of the altar)* is decorated with **frescoes★**, which date from the first half of the 15C. It was Paolo Uccello who began the work *c*1436 but it was completed by Andrea di Giusto, another Florentine and contemporary of the artist – *(righthand wall)* scenes from the life of the Virgin Mary and *(lefthand wall)* scenes from the life of St Stephen.

Museo dell'Opera del Duomo (Cathedral Museum) (B) ⊙ – *Entrance via a recess to the left of the cathedral.* The few rooms in the museum are set out around a courtyard flanked on one side by the **arches★** of delightful little Romanesque cloisters where the white marble of Carrare and the green marble of Prato combine to form charming geometric motifs above graceful white columns crowned by attractively-carved capitals.

A room opening directly off the courtyard contains the seven original **panels★** from the outdoor pulpit. They were carved between 1428 and 1438 by Donatello, with the assistance of a few pupils, and depict an exquisite circle of children dancing. Also in this room are the admirable coffer in the shape of a temple decorated with cherubim, a superb piece of Renaissance goldsmith's work designed to hold the Holy Girdle, and a charming painting of St Lucy, a pleasantly-coloured composition painted by Filippino Lippi in his youth.

The next room contains *The Guardian Angel* by Carlo Dolci, a 17C Florentine painter, whose lighting effects are similar to those produced by Caravaggio. On the other side of the corridor is the door to the crypt which contains architectural and decorative fragments.

★ **Palazzo Pretorio** (A) – During the Middle Ages this was the residence of the Captain of the People *(Capitano del Populo)* who held executive power. Part of the architecture is Romanesque – the side built in brick – and part of it is Gothic – the side with the twin trefoiled windows. It is a tall rugged building resembling a fortress, standing in **Piazza del Comune,** a small square decorated with a graceful bronze fountain surmounted by a statue of Bacchus as a Child *(original in the Palazzo Pretorio)* by Ferdinando Tacca (1659).

Galleria comunale ⊙ – The gallery displays *(first floor)* a reconstruction of the small tabernacle known as the **Madonna del Mercatale** erected in 1498 by Filippino Lippi near the front door of the house of his mother, Lucrezia, who returned to live in Prato after the death of Filippo. It has frescoes and a vaulted roof decorated with grotesque figures. The house, which was in Piazza Mercatale opposite St Margaret's Convent where Lucrezia had once been a nun, was destroyed in a bombing raid in 1944, as were all the other houses in the square. The fresco, depicting the Madonna and Child with saints, was miraculously spared.

On the second floor, in the centre of the huge chamber with the fine ceiling of painted rafters used for banquets, is the collection of 14C-15C Tuscan **polyptychs★**. The most outstanding exhibits are two works by Bernardo Daddi, who sought inspiration in Giotto's style – the predella (1337) of the reredos which used to stand above the high altar in the cathedral and consisted of seven scenes telling the story *(left to right)* of the Holy Girdle, and a *Madonna and Child with St Francis, St Bartholomew, St Barnaby and St Catherine*.

Giovanni de Milano, the Lombard artist who also worked in Florence, produced the great polyptych in the late-Gothic style (1354) representing the *Virgin Mary in Majesty accompanied by St Catherine of Alexandria, St Bernard, St Bartholomew and St Barnaby,* each of the figures being depicted in the upper section of the double predella by one episode from his or her life. There is another *Madonna and Child with Angels and Saints* on a triptych attributed to Lorenzo Monaco, one of the most brilliant representatives of the "international Gothic" style *(qv)*. The *Madonna del Ceppo* (1453) is by Filippo Lippi; in it he used the golden background so popular with supporters of the late-Gothic style, including Lorenzo Monaco, his teacher.

In the small room beyond this chamber is an admirable painting by a Neapolitan artist, Caracciolo (1570-1637), one of the painters most authentically influenced by Caravaggio, as is obvious from the dramatic attitudes of the figures and the sharp contrasts between light and shade in the *Noli me tangere*. Christ is depicted wearing a hat, an allusion to Mary Magdalen's error after the Resurrection when she thought Jesus was the gardener.

The third room contains a series of small landscape paintings with ruins (views of the Roman countryside), some of which are attributed to the Dutch artist, Van Wittel, the father of Luigi Van Vitelli, the Neapolitan architect.

Castello dell'Imperatore (Imperial Castle) (B) ⊙ – Frederick II von Hohenstaufen had this mighty fortress built *c*1248 in order to strengthen the position of the Ghibelline faction *(qv)*. This castle, which is an anomaly in central and northern Italy, was probably one of the fortifications, like the others in Germany, Alsace and southern Italy, built to defend Frederick's territory in the German Empire and the Kingdom of Sicily. The Italian castles, most of which were built by the same architects and for which it is thought that Frederick II himself drew up

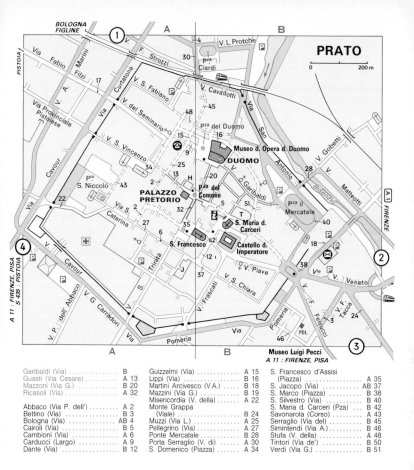

the plans, are all very similar, with a rigorous geometrical type of architecture, a square layout around a central courtyard, and cyclopean walls almost devoid of doors or windows but dotted with enormous, regularly-spaced towers projecting markedly beyond the line of the walls. The building is capped with Ghibelline fishtail merlons.

The castle underwent extensive alterations in the 18C and a number of restorations in the 20C.

Chiesa di Santa Maria delle Carceri (B) – The church gets its name from a miraculous painting on the wall of the prison *(carcere)* that stood on the site before the church was built.

This is an early Renaissance building and the exterior has never been completed. It was erected in the last few years of the 15C by Giuliano da Sangallo, architect to Lorenzo the Magnificent *(qv)*. The layout, in the shape of a Greek Cross with a central dome, was copied by several Renaissance architects.

The main characteristics of the **interior** are its austerity, geometric rigour and majestic proportions. *"Pietra serena"* has been used to emphasise the architectural lines, contrasting with the light colours of the walls in a style reminiscent of the chapels built in Florence by Brunelleschi. Above the grooved pilasters is a graceful frieze of glazed white-and-blue terracotta by Andrea Della Robbia who also produced the four medallions of the Evangelists decorating the squinches between the arches. The church has delightful late-15C stained-glass windows.

San Francesco (AB) ⓥ – Building began on this church in the late 13C. The tall façade striated with green marble was built in the early 14C but the triangular Renaissance pediment was added at the end of the following century. The interior has been extensively restored.

The chapter house, which is also known as the **Migliorati Chapel** *(access at the end of the nave to the right of the altar)* is lit by a Gothic window opening into the small 15C cloisters. It is decorated with **frescoes**★ by Nicolò di Pietro Gerini, a Florentine artist who was influenced by Giotto's work. On the wall opposite the door is a painting of the life of St Matthew. At the top in the centre with the taxpayers is Levi the publican, who was a tax gatherer, before his conversion, when he adopted the name Matthew. On the left is an illustration of Levi receiving

253

the call to follow Jesus. At the bottom *(left)* is St Matthew preaching the Gospel in Ethiopia and raising the king's daughter from the dead; *(right)* is the death of St Matthew. The Evangelists are depicted on the vaulting.

Museo d'Arte Contemporanea Luigi Pecci (Museum of Contemporary Art) ⊙ – *Viale della Repubblica 277. Bus 7 or 8. By car by ③ on the street plan and follow the signs*. This building, which has an interesting futuristic structure, houses works of contemporary art. It has temporary exhibitions, an educational service and a library.

RADICOFANI*

Population 1 295
Michelin Map 430 N 17

Fort Radicofani is perched on a natural promontory (over 800m – 2600ft high). It dominates the whole of the surrounding countryside and is easily recognisable for its mighty tower standing out proudly against the skyline.

Ghino di Tacco, an outlaw who stood up to both the Pope and the Republic of Siena and who was condemned by Dante and praised by Boccaccio, settled here at the end of the 13C and beginning of the 14C, doing good or causing terror from Pienza to Chiusi and throughout the Orcia Valley. He had sworn to avenge his father and elder brother, both of whom had been murdered before his eyes by the Governor *(podestà)* of Siena and, after killing the man who was responsible for their murder, he went into hiding. Legend also has it that he imprisoned the Abbot of Cluny who had come to seek relief for his stomach disorder at San Casciano in Bagni. He kept the abbot in a dungeon where he visited him every day and fed him on a restricted diet, pretending to be a mere servant. He began to feel pity and friendship for his prisoner and eventually cured him. He then set him free. The prelate was very grateful to him and successfully pleaded his case to the Pope.

Tour – The village of Radicofani, built in the same dark brown stone as the fortress above it, has medieval houses and steep streets nestling up against the fortress walls. To the left of the main street is a tiny square in which stand two churches, opposite one another. From the adjacent public park, there is a fine **view★** of Monte Amiata and the surrounding countryside dotted, here and there, with the sharp bare peaks of the **Orcia Hills,** which are similar to the Sienese Hills *(qv)*. The main street then leads to the 16C Palazzo Pretorio decorated with coats of arms and to the **fortress★** itself *(car park nearby)*. The fortress was built in the 13C, altered in the 16C and destroyed by an explosion in the 18C. Its majestic ruins were shored up early in the 1990's.

N. Bosques/MICHELIN

Radicofani Castle.

The annual Michelin Red Guide Italia offers an up-to-date selection of hotels and restaurants serving carefully prepared meals at reasonable prices

ROMENA*

Romena is a tiny hamlet in the upper Casentino Valley and lies within the administrative district of **Pratovecchio** *(2km – 1 mile north)*, the neighbouring village that was the birthplace of **Paolo Uccello**, the artist who specialised in portraying volume and almost abstract compositions.

★ **Pieve** ⊙ – The road from Pratovecchio provides a view of the delightful **chevet** of the church and its two rows of decorative arcading. This is a particularly fine example of early-12C Romanesque architecture.
The church lost its first two bays and its original façade in the 17C as the result of a landslide. The interior consists of a nave and aisles with rafters supported on columns carved out of single blocks of stone and crowned with attractive carved capitals. The nave and aisles rise slightly towards the east end of the church. The central apse has attractive half-barrel vaulting.
A few yards to the left on the road back to Pratovecchio is a tarred path leading to the castle.

★ **Castello** ⊙ – The impressive ruins of Romena Castle stand on a hilltop overlooking the Casentino countryside and are therefore visible from afar. In front of them is a magnificent avenue of cypress trees. The castle, which was built for Count Guidi and his descendents in the 11C, now has only three of the original 14 towers – the keep, postern and prison.
This was the setting for an episode narrated by Dante in his *Inferno* (Song XXX, verses 46-90). A man named Master Adam minted counterfeit florins here (21 carats instead of 24) at the request of the Guidi. His crime was discovered and he was arrested and burnt at the stake in Florence in 1281, the statutory punishment for all counterfeiters.
There is a magnificent **view**★★ of the picturesque ruins of the castle and its avenue of cypress trees from a point several hundred yards along the Poppi to Consuma road (S70).

Rovine di ROSELLE

The ruins of one of the most illustrious towns in northern Etruria lie to the north of Roselle, on the top of a hill. It was separated from Vetulonia *(qv) (west)* by a lake, *Lacus Prilius*, which was drained even in the days of the ancient Etruscans and was, in fact, no more than a vast lagoon, where the cultivated land of the Padule di Raspollino is now. According to Livy, the Etruscan town of Russel (*Russelae* in Latin) was colonised by the Romans in 294 BC. It fell into decline after the fall of the Roman Empire and was almost abandoned after 1138 when it ceased to be a bishopric.

Archeological Excavations (Scavi) ⊙ – The excavations, begun in 1942 and still in progress, have revealed a wall (over 3km – 2 miles long and up to 2m – 6 1/2ft high) built of polygonal blocks of stone. In front of the wall was an outer line of fortifications built of rough bricks, probably dating from the 7C BC. The wall itself was built to the north in the 6C and to the west in the 2C BC. Only three huge gateways have been discovered but it is likely that there were more roads leading into the town.
The archeologists have also uncovered various Roman buildings – amphitheatre, imperial forum, cobbled streets and a villa dating from the days of the empire with a mosaic floor – and a residential district with houses and craft workshops dating from the late 6C.

Abbazia di SAN GALGANO★★

Not far from the main road southwest of Siena to Massa Marittima stand the ruins of the abbey; above on the hill is the hermitage.

Abbey – *2min on foot from car park; restoration in progress*. The majestic and impressive unroofed church is flanked by one range of the cloister buildings – the chapter house and the scriptorium.
The Romanesque-Gothic abbey was built in honour of **St Galgan** (1148-1181) between 1224 and 1288 by Cistercian monks from Casamari *(qv)* and contained the earliest Gothic church in Tuscany which provided the inspiration for Siena Cathedral *(qv)*. A tour of the buildings reveals the traditional features of Cistercian architecture.

Abbazia di SAN GALGANO

R. Mezza/LAURA RONCHI

San Galgano Abbey.

Eremo – *Separate approach road and parking.* The hermitage, which stands on the hill (200m – 217yds from the abbey), is a strange 12C Romanesque rotunda with an amazing **dome** (1181-1185) devoid of ribs. Its design was inspired by Etruscan and Roman tombs and it should be seen as an ideal link between Classicism and the Renaissance. Its main feature is the 24 red-and-white brick and stone circles. The number is a multiple of 12, which has sacred connotations – the 12 Apostles and the 12 tribes of Israel. The church was built to house the body of Galgano Guidotti and the rock in which in 1180 he planted his sword, henceforth considered not as a weapon but as a symbol of the Cross.

Galgano Guidotti

Galgano was born into a high-ranking Sienese family from the nearby town of Chiusdino. He felt the call to take holy orders after having a vision of the Archangel Michael, which caused him to give up his aimless life and join the Cistercians. He ended his days as a hermit, in a small chapel he himself built on the site of the abbey.

SAN GIMIGNANO★★★

Population 6 945
Michelin map 988 fold 14 or 430 L 15

Tour – half a day; public car parks available on the outskirts of the town; parking in the town centre is restricted to residents and certain hotel guests.

San Gimignano is surrounded by gently-rolling countryside dotted with vines and olive trees. Its 14 grey stone towers set on a hilltop are enclosed within an outer wall including five gates. It has all the charm of a small medieval town, built mainly of brick, and has been amazingly well preserved. Little is known about the origins of San Gimignano, a bishop who lived in Modena in the 4C, and the reasons that led the town to take his name are steeped in legend.

It became a free borough in the mid 12C and continued to prosper for 200 years, although it did not escape the rivalry between the Guelf and Ghibelline factions *(qv)*, which were represented in the town by the Ardinghelli and Salvucci families respectively. The town supported the Pope and rallied to the side of Florence in her wars with Pisa, Siena, Pistoia, Arezzo, Volterra etc. In 1353 the town took an oath of allegiance binding it to Florence.

A number of great painters from Siena and, later, Florence, worked in San Gimignano where they produced great masterpieces.

Casa torre (Tower-house) – It was in the 12C, when it was a free borough, that the main buildings in the town were constructed including the outer walls, which still stand, and the famous **tower-houses** that caused the town to be called "San Gimignano dalle belle torri" (San Gimignano of the fine towers) and for which it is still famous.

In the Middle Ages there were 70 towers but the number had dropped to 25 by the end of the 16C and only 13 have survived to the present day. These feudal towers, designed like castle keeps, were built in many Italian towns by the great families during the struggle for supremacy between the Guelfs and Ghibellines and, later, between local tyrants. For reasons of prestige the nobility built as tall as they could. The holes that can still be seen in their walls are said to have been used in those days as supports for a network of footbridges linking the houses of allied families who could gather together quickly in one place in times of danger.

A more prosaic explanation is that the towers are a legacy of the period when San Gimignano was a major textile centre and held the secret of saffron yellow dye, which is

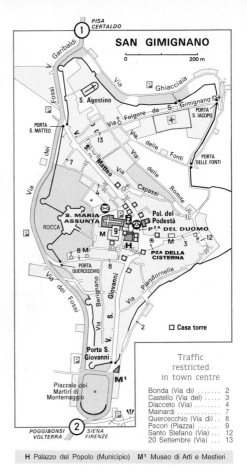

Traffic restricted in town centre

Bonda (Via di) 2
Castello (Via del) 3
Diacceto (Via) 4
Mainardi 7
Quercecchio (Via di) .. 8
Pecori (Piazza) 9
Santo Stefano (Via) ... 12
20 Settembre (Via) ... 13

H Palazzo del Popolo (Municipio)   M¹ Museo di Arti e Mestieri

produced from a particular variety of crocus. In order to fix the colour, the cloth had to be kept away from dust and sunshine and, as a higher price could be asked for the longer pieces of cloth, the rich cloth-producers are said to have been forced to build tall towers since the lack of space in the town prevented them from building horizontally. The holes in the walls would have been used to support the staircases attached to the exterior to avoid using up space in the interior.

★★ PIAZZA DELLA CISTERNA

From the massive 13C **San Giovanni Gate** *(south side of the town)* with its barbican and Sienese arch, the picturesque street (Via San Giovanni) leads up past medieval houses and the remains of a Pisan Romanesque church front *(right)* dating from the 13C, to the central square.

Piazza della Cisterna is an irregularly-shaped area paved, in medieval style, with bricks laid in heading bond forming a herringbone pattern. The square takes its name from the **well** *(cisterna)* which has occupied the centre of the space since the 13C. Around it are austere buildings dating from the 13C-14C, some of them with towers. The 13C **Savestrini House** *(south side)* is now a hotel. At the entrance to Via del Castello *(east)* is the 14C **Palazzo Tortoli** which has two rows of Gothic twin windows. Almost opposite is the **Devil's Tower** *(Torre del Diavolo)*. The north-west corner of the square, which leads to Piazza del Duomo, is dominated by the two **Ardinghelli Towers** named after the most influential Guelf family in the town.

★★ PIAZZA DEL DUOMO

The austere collegiate church, very old mansions *(palazzi)* and seven towers provide a majestic setting.

★ **Collegiata di Santa Maria Assunta** – The collegiate church or cathedral of St Mary of the Assumption is a 12C Romanesque building which was extended in the 15C by Giuliano da Maiano, the architect and sculptor, who was also responsible for alterations to the chancel. In the 19C the west front underwent major restoration. The interior is covered in frescoes.

Rear of the Façade – *Coin box for lighting near the second pillar on the right*. On the lower section of the wall, the Florentine artist Benozzo Gozzoli has depicted the *Martyrdom of St Sebastian* (1465) flanked by two painted wooden statues representing the *Virgin Mary* and the *Angel of the Annunciation* carved *c*1420 by the Sienese sculptor Jacopo Della Quercia. Above them another Sienese artist, Taddeo di Bartolo, painted a *Last Judgement* (1393) which extends on each side into the first bay of the nave. To the right is *Hell*; to the left, *Paradise*.

North Aisle – In the second half of the 14C, this aisle was covered with a cycle of **frescoes★** illustrating the Old Testament by the Sienese artist, Bartolo di Fredi. With a rather naïve liveliness and brilliant colours, the artist, who was influenced by Simone Martini and the Lorenzetti brothers *(qv)*, illustrated the following scenes: **top,** the Creation of the World, the Creation of Man, Adam in the Garden of Eden, the Creation of Eve and the Forbidden Fruit. **On the**

Towers of San Gimignano.

middle level, after two scenes which are no longer visible (Adam and Eve being chased out of Paradise and Cain killing Abel), there is the Building of Noah's Ark, the Animals entering the Ark, the Departure of the Ark, Noah's Drunkenness, the Departure of Abraham and Lot, Lot taking Leave of Abraham, Joseph's Dream and Joseph being lowered down into a Tank. **At the bottom,** again beyond the first bay where the painting is now illegible (Joseph having his Brothers Arrested, and Joseph Recognised by his Brothers), there is Moses and the Brazen Serpent, Pharaoh's Army being swept away by the Red Sea, the Jews Crossing the Red Sea, Moses on Mount Sinai, Satan receiving God's permission to tempt Job, the Murder of Job's Servants and the Stealing of his Animals, the Collapse of the House of Job, Job giving Thanks to God, and Job, in his illness, being comforted by his Friends.

South Aisle – The Life of Christ is illustrated in a series of **frescoes★★** painted *c*1335-1340, ie before the frescoes produced by Bartolo di Fredi, by one Barna da Siena who worked in Simone Martini's studio. If Vasari is to be believed, the artist died falling from scaffolding shortly before this work was completed. This cycle remains an essential part of the history of Italian Gothic painting, because of its sheer size.

In the scenes which are painted on three levels, the artist has combined the elegant drawing techniques and delicate colours that were the characteristic features of the Sienese Gothic style (Duccio, Simone Martini) with a humanity, a vigorous illustration of character and a dramatic concentration that are all indicative of Giotto's influence. The paintings depict *(starting at the lunettes, top right)* the Annunciation, the Nativity, the Adoration of the Magi, the Circumcision, the Massacre of the Holy Innocents and the Flight into Egypt; *(middle, from left to right)* starting at the great Crucifixion, they represent Jesus and the Doctors of the Church, Christ's Baptism, St Peter's Call, the Marriage in Cana, the Transfiguration, Lazarus being Raised from the Dead, and Christ's Entry into Jerusalem *(two panels); (lower level, from right to left)* the Last Supper, Judas receiving the Thirty Pieces of Silver, the Prayer on the Mount of Olives, Judas' Kiss, Jesus being brought before Caiaphas the High Priest, the Scourging, the Crown of Thorns and the Road up to Calvary, ending with the Crucifixion. On the left of this great panel are *(below)* the Entombment *(almost entirely missing)*, Christ Descending into Hell *(badly damaged)*, and *(above)* the Resurrection *(partly damaged)* and Pentecost.

Cappella di Santa Fina ⊘ – *At the end of the south aisle*. This **chapel** is dedicated to the local saint, Serafina di Ciardi, a paralysed girl who died in 1254 at the age of 15. On the day of her death, all the bells began ringing and her bed was covered with flowers, as were the tops of the towers in the town. In 1468 the

S. Chirol

townspeople commissioned Giuliano da Maiano to build this chapel in her honour. He produced this elegant chapel in which the harmonious marble and alabaster **altar**★ with its fine carvings and gold ornamentation was made by Giuliano's nephew, Benedetto. In 1475, Domenico Ghirlandaio painted some remarkable **frescoes**★ depicting the life of the saint in his usual precise, descriptive style but with a certain naïvety and a less refined elegance than is evident in his masterpiece in Santa Maria Novella in Florence, which he painted a few years later.

Piazza Luigi Pecori – *Access via a vaulted passageway to the left of the collegiate church*. One side of this charming little square is lined by a portico, also known as the **Baptistery loggia**, which is all that remains of the 14C cloisters at the end of which Domenico Ghirlandaio painted a harmonious fresco of the *Annunciation* in 1482.

To the left of the vaulted passageway is a 13C palace housing two small museums. In the **Museo d'Arte sacra** (Museum of Sacred Art) ⊘ *(first floor)* the prize exhibits are a very expressive marble bust of Onofrio di Pietro by Benedetto da Maiano (*c*1493) *(first room)* and a wooden *Crucifix* by Guiliano da Maiano *(second room, in a glass case)* and the *Madonna and the Rose* set against a golden background by Bartolomeo di Fredi. The single-roomed **Museo Etrusco** (Etruscan Museum) ⊘ *(right of the staircase)* contains mainly funeral urns and pottery.

★ **Palazzo del Popolo (H)** – This building, which is called the People's Palace and also the Magistrate's Palace, dates from the 13C-14C and is surmounted by a tower (54m-176ft) (Torre Grossa). There is a small inner courtyard on two levels, flanked by a portico, with an octagonal well in the south-west corner.

The **Museo civico**★ ⊘ *(access by the external staircase in the courtyard)* occupies the upper floors. The Grand Council Chamber, where Dante made a speech in 1300 and which overlooks Piazza del Duomo, is decorated with frescoes by the 14C Sienese School representing hunting scenes and Charles of Anjou, King of Naples. In 1317 Lippo Memmi, the Sienese primitive, painted a masterpiece entitled **Maestà**★ there, which was restored *c*1467 by Benozzo Gozzoli.

From the top of the **Torre Grossa** *(access by the staircase – 200 steps – to the right between the first and second floor)* there is an unusual **view**★★ of the towers and rooftops and the surrounding countryside.

On the second floor, a small room *(left)* is decorated with frescoes depicting married life. The other rooms *(right)* are hung with collections of paintings; most of them were the work of the 12C-15C Florentine and Sienese Schools – *(first room)* a *Crucifixion* with scenes from the Passion by Coppo di Marcovaldo and,

259

the museum's finest exhibit, an **Annunciation** by Filippino Lippi in the form of two *tondi (qv); (second room)* two paintings of the *Madonna and Child with Saints* by Benozzo Gozzoli; *(third room)* a large painting of the *Virgin Mary in Majesty* by the Umbrian painter Pinturicchio (1512) and two polyptychs by Taddeo di Bartolo *(Madonna and Child* and *Scenes from the Life of St Gimignano)*.

Palazzo del Podestà – The building on the east side of Piazza del Duomo dates from the 13C. It opens onto the square through a huge porch *(loggia)* with stone benches along each side, under a wide arch. It is surmounted by the mighty **Rognosa Tower** (51m – 166ft high). To the left of the tower is the 13C Chigi Palace, which has its own tower beside it.

ADDITIONAL SIGHTS

Via San Matteo – This is a steep picturesque shopping street, lined with mansions and tower-houses, which descends to the north gate (Porta San Matteo).

Chiese di Sant'Agostino – At the northern end of the town stands this Romanesque-Gothic church, which dates from the 13C. It has the same austere appearance as all churches with a nave but no aisles built for the mendicant orders. Its chancel nevertheless includes 17 **frescoes★★**, painted in 1464 and 1465 by Benozzo Gozzoli, one of the masters of the 15C in Florence. With his usual fresh colours, sense of perspective, and taste for intimate, personal details, the artist has depicted the life of St Augustine, the famous theologian. The most outstanding scenes are *(bottom of the lefthand wall)* Augustine being taken to school by St Monica, his mother; *(bottom of the righthand wall)* Augustine teaching philosophy in Rome and his Departure for Milan; *(lunette on the same wall)* his Funeral.
To the left of the current entrance is San Bartolo's Chapel behind a wrought-iron screen. It contains an exquisite marble altar made in 1494 by Benedetto da Maiano. The huge altar was built around the tomb of St Bartolo and is surmounted by statues of the three theological virtues.
To the left of the church *(access from the sacristy)* are graceful little Renaissance cloisters.

Museo di Arti e Mestieri (**M¹**) ⊘ – The Museum of Crafts and Trades stands outside the town walls near the San Giovanni Gate *(south)*. It has some 15 rooms dealing with life in the past, with objects and furniture from traditional Tuscan houses and tools used for old crafts in town and country – saddlery, bakery, blacksmithing, clog-making, weaving. All the exhibits date from before the 19C and many of them are medieval.

EXCURSIONS

Certaldo – *13km – 8 miles north. See Certaldo.*

★ **San Vivaldo** – *17km – 11 miles north-west. See San Vivaldo.*

The key on p 2 explains the symbols used on town plans

SAN GIOVANNI VALDARNO

Population 17 702
Michelin map 988 fold 15 or 430 L 16

San Giovanni is one of the main industrial towns in the Arno Valley and is particularly famous for its steel works and the huge lignite mines in the vicinity. The first painter of the Florentine Renaissance, Masaccio (d 1428), was born here in 1401.

★ **Palazzo Pretorio** – This building, which stands in the centre of the town, is emblazoned with the coats of arms of former magistrates *(podestà)*. It has a vaulted portico on all four sides and a loggia with rafters on the upper floor opening onto the two squares that flank the building. The building, which is said to have been designed by Arnolfo di Cambio, dates from the 13C and was altered during the Renaissance.

Chiesa di San Giovanni Battista – This early 14C church in Piazza Cavour stands opposite the main façade of the Palazzo Pretorio. It resembles its neighbour with its elegant portico decorated with glazed *tondi* in the style of the della Robbias.

Basilica di Santa Maria delle Grazie – Behind the Palazzo Pretorio stands this 15C basilica with a 19C neo-Renaissance façade facing Piazza Masaccio. Beneath the porch is an *Assumption of the Virgin Mary,* a superb, vividly-coloured glazed ceramic by Giovanni Della Robbia.

Inside the basilica, the high altar is decorated with the fresco of *Our Lady of Grace* (14C), from which the church takes its name, and *(south aisle)* a *Madonna and Child, four Saints and two Angels* on a golden background, an anonymous work dating from the 15C.

Behind the chancel is a small **museum** ⊙ containing works by the Florentine School, mainly from the 15C-16C, including a superb **Annunciation**★★ by Fra Angelico.

Oratorio di San Lorenzo – *To the right on leaving the basilica*. The chapel, which is set behind a modest brick and stone façade, contains numerous 14C-15C frescoes and a reredos depicting the *Coronation of the Virgin Mary* by Giotto's School *(behind the high altar)*.

EXCURSION

Montevarchi – *5km – 3 miles south-east*. This village is famous throughout Tuscany for its market selling Arno Valley chickens and wine from the hillsides of Aretino. The streets in the historic old town form parallel arcs on each side of Via Roma.

The 18C **Church of San Lorenzo** in Piazza Varchi *(in the middle of Via Roma)* contains an ampoule of breast milk from the Virgin Mary, kept in the tabernacle on the high altar. Above it is a theatrical illustration of the *Virgin Mary in Glory* carved by Giovanni Baratta.

SAN MINIATO★

Population 25 326
Michelin map 988 fold 14 or 430 K 14

The charming town of San Miniato, which has retained its old appearance, stretches out along a hilltop forming an amphitheatre. Its name used to be followed by the words *al Tedesco* (of the German) because, from the 10C onwards, it was the official residence in Tuscany of the Holy Roman Emperors and the seat of Imperial Vicars. Its proud outline is visible from some distance, broken up at the very top by the tower on the fortress and supported on the north-east side by the huge brick buttresses of the San Francesco Monastery, which was built on the site of the 8C San Miniato Church. A few tower-houses and aristocratic mansions dating from the 15C, 16C and 17C also bear witness to a prosperous past.

Two brothers with a love of cinema – San Miniato is the home of **Paolo and Vittorio Taviani** (b 1929 and 1931 respectively). The brothers were inseparable and they filmed part of their work in Apulia and Sicily. They returned to their native Tuscany to film *Le Pré* (1979), shot partly in San Gimignano, *Good Morning, Babylonia* (1982) which begins in Pisa, and *La Nuit de San Lorenzo* (1982) which is a reminder of a painful episode in the history of San Miniato during the Second World War.

Special Events – A number of ancient traditions have survived to the present day such as the bonfires lit for the Feast of St John (24 June), the shortest night of the year, when corn cobs and cloves of garlic are burnt on the hillsides around the town to ward off evil spirits. White truffles grow in these hills and they are picked during the autumn; this expensive fungus is the main item for sale at a large fair held during the last three weekends in November.

Since 1947 San Miniato has been the centre of the Popular Drama Institute which stages an original dramatic work of a sacred or spiritual nature every year in July during the Theatre Festival. The authors of works performed in previous years have included T S Eliot, Julien Green, Thomas Mann, Elie Wiesel and Karol Wojtyla.

See also Calendar of Events at the end of the guide for other events held in San Miniato.

SIGHTS

Prato del Duomo – This name covers a number of historic buildings.

The **cathedral**, which dates from the 12C, incorporates an older machicolated belltower, which was the defensive tower of the old castle. The cathedral was altered in the 15C and refurbished in the 18C and 19C. It has a Romanesque façade studded with a number of 13C ceramic bowls in the Pisan tradition, a style which can also be seen at San Piero a Grado *(qv)* near Pisa. The three doors date from the 15C.

The **Museo diocesano d'Arte sacra** ⊘ *(left of the cathedral)* contains paintings and sculptures from the 15C-19C by Filippo Lippi, Neri di Bicci, Cigoli and Verrocchio, as well as items of sacred art – old religious books.

Opposite the cathedral is the **Bishop's Palace** built in the 12C and initially used as the residence of the Captain of the citadel's militia. Later it was the residence of the *Signori Dodici* (the 12 governors of the town) and then of the Captain of the People. Since 1622 it has been the bishop's residence.

The **Palazzo dei Vicari dell'Imperatore** (formerly the residence of the imperial vicars but now a hotel) is surmounted by a tower. It dates from the 12C and tradition has it that Countess Matilda of Tuscany was born there in 1046.

A narrow street between these two buildings leads to a tiny terrace from which there is a view of the rooftops of San Miniato and the Tuscan countryside. Below in **Piazza della Repubblica** is the **Palazzo del Seminario★**, a building with a concave façade decorated early in the 18C with frescoes and Latin aphorisms by the Fathers of the Church along the upper section; the lower part contains medieval shop fronts which have been partially preserved.

★ **Castle Esplanade** – From the terrace to the left of the cathedral, a steep street and flight of steps *(15min return on foot)* leads to the flattened hilltop. The brick tower was rebuilt so that it was identical to the original, part of Frederick II's castle *(Rocca)* which was destroyed during the last war. It is said that Pierre des Vignes, Frederick II's Chancellor, who had been accused of treason, committed suicide in the tower after his eyes had been put out (Dante, *Inferno,* Song XIII).

From the esplanade there is a superb **panoramic view★★** of San Miniato, the Arno Valley, the hills round Pisa, Pistoia and Florence, and the Appenine Mountains.

Santuario del Crocifisso – Behind the cathedral is the 17C Crucifix Chapel capped by a circular drum. The chapel contains a 10C Ottonian wooden Crucifix. A rather dramatic flight of steps leads to Via delle Vittime del Duomo.

Palazzo Comunale – *Via delle Vittime del Duomo*. The palace contains frescoes by Giotto's School, including a *Madonna and Child between the Theological Virtues* attributed to Cenni di Francesco di Ser Cenni, and a small church, **Chiesa del Lorentino,** which has a precious altar made of marquetry with gilding and painting, a tabernacle painted by Lanfranco and 16C frescoes depicting the Life of Jesus.

Chiesa di San Domenico – *Piazza del Popolo*. This church dates from 1194 but it was altered on several occasions and its façade was never completed. One of the chapels *(on the right at the end of the nave)* contains the admirable tomb of Giovanni Chellini, the humanist doctor, attributed to Bernardo Rossellino (15C).

SAN QUIRICO D'ORCIA★

Population 2 385
Michelin map 988 fold 15 or 430 M 16

This old town set on a small rise still has its 12C walls and its huge gates. Very early in the Middle Ages, San Quirico gained importance because it straddled Via Francigena, which passed through the Orcia Valley linking Rome and the north of Italy. In 1154 Frederick I of Swabia, better known as Frederick Barbarossa, received ambassadors from Pope Adrian IV here. Every year the town commemorates the event in the *"Festa del Barbarossa" (third Sunday in June).*

★★ **Collegiate Church** – This admirable Romanesque-Gothic collegiate church was built in the 12C-13C. On the elegant but simple façade, beneath a row of arcading, is a fine carved rose window, emphasising the richness of the majestic **Romanesque portal★**. Its columns and its lintel,

Romanesque door of the Collegiate Church in San Quirico.

S. Chirol

which is carved with monsters in confrontation, are set in a great arch supported by entwined columns resting on lions' backs. On the righthand side of the church are **two Gothic portals,** the wider of the two flanked by statue-columns supported by lions and of a more complex design than the Romanesque portal on the west front. Note also the kneeling, smiling Telamones supporting the division in the double bay to the right.

The most notable features of the interior are *(between the last two pillars to the left of the nave)* the recumbent statue of Count Henry of Nassau, who died in San Quirico in February 1451 when returning from a jubilee in Rome, *(chancel)* the early-16C carved woodpanelling with marquetry inlays and *(north transept)*, most outstanding of all, a **reredos★** painted by Sano di Pietro (15C), consisting of a triptych depicting the Virgin Mary, the Child Jesus and four saints against a golden background; in the lunette is the Resurrection and Descent into Hell; the predella is decorated with scenes from the Life of the Virgin Mary.

Palazzo Chigi – One side of Piazza della Collegiata is filled by this 17C mansion. Despite its poor state of repair, its past majesty is apparent in the regular disposition of the doors and windows and the magnificent coat of arms which include the six hummocks of the Chigi family and the crown of oak leaves of the Della Rovere family.

Porta ai Cappuccini – Along the right side of the Palazzo Chigi is Via Poliziano, a narrow, medieval street leading to Porta ai Cappuccini, a 13C gate which from the outside looks like a polygonal tower.

★ EXCURSIONS

Tour – 90min without visiting Rocca di Tintinnano – about 10km – 6 miles from San Quirico to Castiglione and Rocca d'Orcia.

From San Quirico take the road south *(S2, Via Cassia towards Rome)* which descends gently into the Orcia Valley between undulating hillsides outlined with rows of trees and thickets or dotted here and there with single cypress trees. In the spring, poppies and wild flowers in shades of yellow or pink add a touch of gaiety to the scenery.
On the nearest hill is the mighty Rocca d'Orcia (fortress); in the distance is Monte Amiata and the fortress at Radicofani.

Before crossing the River Orcia, turn right towards Bagno Vignoni.

The road climbs steeply along the sheer-sided river valley, giving a fine view of the nearby fortress.

Bagno Vignoni – This hamlet is popular for its spring water which was reputed for its effectiveness in the treatment of arthritis and rheumatism as far back as Roman times.
The houses cluster round an old swimming pool flanked, on one side, by St Catherine's Portico, a reminder that the saint is said to have come here at the end of her life.
Opposite the large neighbouring car park is the Rocca d'Orcia, set high above part of the Orcia Gorge, which in the Middle Ages provided a means of communication with the Maremma region.

Return to the bridge and cross the River Orcia. After 350m – 380yds turn right into the Castiglione road.

Castiglione d'Orcia – Castiglione used to belong to the Aldobrandeschi family but in the early 14C it passed to Siena. A few years later Siena sold the village and other property in the Orcia Valley, including the fortress at Tintinnano, to the rich Sienese Salimbeni family in order to earn some money. In 1419 the Republic recovered all the land when Cocco Salimbeni was forced to capitulate in a struggle against his native town.
The main square, **Piazza Vecchietta**, of this rural medieval town, was named after Lorenzo di Petro, also known as the Vecchietta, who was said to have been born in Castiglione c1412. It is triangular in shape and its sloping surface is paved with large pebbles and bricks. In the centre is a 17C travertine well.
Little remains of the fortress, **Rocca Aldobrandeschi**, above the village. From the esplanade above the outer wall *(access by a flight of steps)* there is a view of the castle ruins and a panoramic view of Monte Amiata and the Orcia Valley.

Follow the signs to Rocca di Tintinnano; car park below the fortress.

★ **Rocca di Tintinnano** ⊘ – The promontory overlooking Via Francigena and the Orcia Valley, is said to have been occupied and built on in the 9C. The fortress was designed by one Tignoso di Tintinnano and it remained in the hands of the Tignosi until the middle of the 13C when the Republic of Siena took possession of it, attracted by its strategic position. The huge tower dates from this period. The fortress was badly damaged by the passage of time and restored in the 1970's when the missing sections were replaced by brick.

The **tour** of the fortress not only provides splendid views of the Orcia Valley and Monte Amiata but also reveals the medieval system of defence. The pentagonal fortifications enclose a military parade ground and a huge polygonal tower which contains a large water tank and an oven; the various floors are linked by staircases and narrow corridors.

Rocca d'Orcia – *Accessible on foot from the fortress*. This medieval town was built up against the walls of the Rocca di Tintinnano on which it was dependent, hence its name. The narrow streets, which are still partly cobbled, meet around a huge polygonal water tank capped by a well.

SANSEPOLCRO★

Population 15 670
Michelin map 988 fold 15 or 430 L 18

This small industrial town, once the property of the Buitoni family, is located in the centre of the Upper Tiber Valley. It is still enclosed within its walls and has numerous old houses dating from the Middle Ages to the 18C, an indication of its early and long-lasting prosperity.

Its name recalls that in the 10C two pilgrims returning from the Holy Land brought with them relics of the Holy Sepulchre *(santo sepolcro)* and a chapel was built to contain them. A village then grew up around the chapel and was quite naturally given the name Borgo San Sepolcro, which, over the years, was simplified to Sansepolcro.

This town was the birthplace of **Piero della Francesca**, who was born between 1415 and 1420, the son of a shoemaker. Although his name is connected with Arezzo *(qv)*, it was here that he spent part of his life and where he died in 1492.

The town holds a **crossbow competition** *(second Sunday in September)* at which the competitors and all their companions are dressed in Renaissance costume.

SIGHTS

★ **Patrician streets** – In the heart of the old town is a vast square, **Piazza Torre di Berta,** a popular meeting place. A medieval tower of the same name used to stand in the centre but it was destroyed by a German shell during the Second World War. Facing each other across the square are another 13C tower and a mansion with windows outlined with rusticated stonework.

Between the square and the very wide street, Via Matteotti, runs **Via XX Settembre** which is almost entirely flanked by Gothic, Renaissance and Mannerist mansions *(palazzi)*; it also contains a few truncated medieval towers. The section of road *(right)* contains some particularly fine examples (nos 127 and 131). In the intervening narrow alleyway, known as **Via Del Buon Umore,** the buildings are held apart by five brick arches. The other section of Via XX Settembre contains some attractive shops and leads *(turn left into Via Luca Pacioli)* to the **Church of San Lorenzo** where there is a superb **Deposition from the Cross★** by the Mannerist artist, Rosso Fiorentino.

Duomo (Cathedral) – *Via Matteotti*. The Cathedral of St John the Baptist dates from the early 11C but has both Romanesque features – plain interior with nave and two aisles, and rafters in the centre – and Gothic elements – polygonal chancel. Its austere façade has three coffered doorways and an alabaster rose window. The square pointed belltower was rebuilt in the 14C in the Franciscan style and is similar to the one belonging to the nearby Church of San Francesco. **Palazzo dell Laudi** *(left of the cathedral),* now the Town Hall, has, like **Palazzo Aggiunti** *(opposite),* a Mannerist design (late 16C-early 17C).

From Via Matteotti pass through Porta della Pesa into Piazza San Francesco.

★★ **Museo civico** ⊙ – *Via Aggiunti 65; left of the Porta della Pesa*. Its main attractions are some admirable **paintings★★★** by **Piero della Francesca** – *(Sala della Resurezzione)* a *Resurrection,* an impressive example of art reaching maturity, the superb triptych of the *Virgin Mary of Misericord* and two fragments of frescoes *(St Julian* and *St Ludovic)*. The museum also houses works by artists born in Sansepolcro – Santi di Tito, Raffaellino dal Colle – and by Bassano, Signorelli, and the Della Robbia School. It has engravings and a few liturgical items including the ones used to decorate Sansepolcro's *Volto Santo,* a copy of the one in Lucca *(qv)*.

The first floor – good view of Via Matteotti – displays fragments of frescoes and underdrawings *(qv)* dating from the 14C.

The basement contains sculptures and architectural ornamentation from the 13C to 18C including a beautiful Romanesque frieze of impressive proportions.

Piazza San Francesco – The **Church of San Francesco** (12C-18C) with its pointed belltower stands opposite the **Church of Santa Maria delle Grazie**, which is flanked by a small loggia with two arches; the two tall coffers above the door are decorated with skeletons and the brackets on the tympanum are supported by two skulls.

In the street running along the righthand side of San Francesco is the **casa di Piero della Francesca** *(no 71)*. This was the artist's home (15C).

On the outskirts of the town, in the direction of Perugia, are the remains of the Medici fortress.

EXCURSIONS

Monterchi – *17km – 11 miles south*. The **chapel in the cemetery** ⊘ contains an unusual work by Piero della Francesca, the **Virgin Mary giving Birth**★ *(Madonna del Parto)*. This fresco, which stands alone above the altar, was painted at more or less the same time as the *Legend of the True Cross* cycle in Arezzo and its majesty is reminiscent of the other work. Encircled in gold, the browns and greens complement each other around the luminous patch of blue formed by the great dress of the Virgin Mary, in a harmony and balance that is quite outstanding.

Anghiari – *8km – 5 miles south-west. See Anghiari.*

Abbazia di SANT'ANTIMO★★

Michelin Map 430 M 16

Sant'Antimo Abbey ⊘ lies at the foot of the village of **Castelnuovo dell'Abate** and has preserved its solitude in the depths of the delightful **landscape**★ composed of hills planted with olive and cypress trees.

The abbey, which was founded in the 9C, reached the peak of its prosperity and influence in the 12C.

The church (12C) is a particularly fine example of Romanesque Cistercian architecture. The Burgundian style is evident in the ambulatory with radiating chapels; on the other hand the porch and pilaster strips decorating the belltower and various walls are typically Lombard. The interior is spacious and austere. The raftered nave is separated from the rib-vaulted aisles by columns crowned with superb alabaster capitals. Note the graceful proportions of the ambulatory, the light apse with its double window, and the frescoes dating from the 14C-17C.

Only some of the monastery buildings have survived.

Sant'Antimo Abbey.

SAN VIVALDO★

Michelin Map 430 L 14

It was to this woodland *c*1300 that Vivaldo Stricchi, a Franciscan lay brother from San Gimignano, withdrew to live the life of a hermit. He was found dead on 1 May 1320 beneath a chestnut tree. In 1500 the Franciscans established a community in the woods to guard the saint's body.

Church – Immediately after Vivaldo's death a small chapel was built; a church was constructed beside it in the 15C. The place where St Vivaldo's body was found is commemorated in the first chapel on the right. Above the altar is a gentle *Nativity* by Giovanni Della Robbia.

Sacro Monte ⓥ – Between *c*1500 and 1520, as the lie of the land around the monastery was suitable, the Franciscans built 33 chapels of which only 17 are still standing. The chapels are miniature reproductions of the holy places in Jerusalem and all contain superb painted terracotta pieces, almost life size, depicting events from the New Testament which occurred between the Passion and Pentecost. The artists used the traditional techniques of the Della Robbias.

MICHELIN GREEN GUIDES

Art and Architecture
History
Geography
Ancient monuments
Scenic routes
Touring programmes
Plans of towns and buildings

*A selection of guides for holidays
at home and abroad*

SATURNIA

Michelin Map 430 O 16

Saturnia, a popular spa town, is famous for its Etruscan and Roman remains. It is the worthy successor of *Aurinia,* an Etruscan settlement, one of the oldest towns in Italy, which was built on a travertine rock. Its present name derives from Saturn, the Roman god of sowing and growing vines.

The castle *(cassero),* built in the days of Sienese control (15C), has been reduced to a few remains *(left of the church).* A few yards from the church, in Piazzale Bagno Secco along Via Italia, are the remains of the Roman baths, now without water, hence the name *bagno secco.* Beyond them is the Porta Romana.

A number of burial grounds have been excavated in the vicinity, including the **necropoli del Puntone** *(signed)* which dates from the 7C BC.

The town is now popular with people taking the waters in **Terme di Saturnia,** where the sulphur-rich water rises from the spring at a temperature of 37°. It is particularly effective in the treatment of skin diseases and respiratory disorders. There is also an institute practising thermal cosmetic treatments and cosmetic therapy.

SESTO FIORENTINO

Population 47 379
MIchelin map 988 fold 14 or 430 K 15
General plan of Florence on map 430,
in the Michelin Road Atlas Europe or the Michelin Red Guide Italia

The small town of Sesto Fiorentino is situated at the sixth *(sesto)* mile west of Florence, just as the neighbouring town of Quinto stands at the fifth mile. It has quite lost its medieval character since its industrial expansion based mainly on its reputation for the production of porcelain and ceramics.

★ **Museo Richard Ginori della porcellana di Doccia** ⓥ – *Viale Pratese 31.* These prestigious porcelain works, which were founded by the Ginori in 1735 in the nearby town of Doccia, were brought to Seso *(behind the museum)* in 1954. They have always produced remarkably fine pieces, because the Ginori have always employed the best specialists of the day, including an Englishman named Richard. The collection displayed in the museum traces the changes in taste from 18C Baroque to the present day – dinner services, vases, documents from the archives, wax and terracotta models.

SETTIGNANO*

Michelin Map 430 K 15 – General plan of Florence on map 430,
in the Michelin Road Atlas Europe or the Michelin Red Guide Italia

Settignano, situated on the hills north-east of Florence, is a small residential town steeped in memories of the past. It was here in the 15C that a large number of sculptors were born and that more modest stonecutters worked *pietra serena*, the bluish-grey stone used for so many of the architectural features in Florence. Settignano was the birthplace of two brothers, **Bernardo** and **Antonio Rossellino**, and of **Desiderio da Settignano**. Michelangelo was entrusted to a wet-nurse here and spent his childhood among the stonecutters. The brothers, **Benedetto** and **Giuliano da Maiano**, bear the name of the neighbouring hamlet where they were born. The beauty of the stony hillsides was appreciated very early on by the great families of Florence who had superb villas built throughout this area. **Boccaccio** *(qv)* set the beginning of his *Decameron* in the grounds of a country house at the foot of the hill here. In the 19C the area was fashionable with English high society; Bernard Berenson, the American art historian, had a villa restored in which he built up a fine art collection. In the 20C D'Annunzio chose this part of the world, where he himself had a villa, for his love affair with the great actress Eleonora Duse.

★ **Viale Gabriele D'Annunzio** – This long avenue winds out of Florence through **Coverciano** and up the hillside; the view reveals the beauty of the landscape and the magnificent country houses. Halfway up *(left of the road in a righthand bend)* stands the **villa Contri di Mezzaratta**, set high above the valley. It attracts attention because of its crenellated tower and the neo-medieval features that were characteristic of the end of the 19C.

The road leads to the heart of the village, Piazza Tommaseo, and the small **Church of l'Assunta** which was built in the 15C and altered in the following century.

From the square take the very narrow Via di San Romano; turn right into Via Rossellino; when the street bears right, go straight on and park (right) in front of the villa.

★ **Villa Gamberaia Gardens** ⊘ – *No 72; entrance on the right in front of a short vaulted passageway*. The original building was erected in the 14C by Benedictines who worked the surrounding land. It was acquired in the 17C and turned into a plain quadrangular villa, soon embellished with magnificent gardens, which were laid out with immense artistry. On the south side below the loggia is a formal layout of topiary work in cypress, yew and box, redesigned at the beginning of the century; it is semicircular in shape and enclosed by a hedge of cypress trees pierced by arched openings; it ends in a terrace from which there is a fine panoramic view of the Arno Valley and the hillsides clothed in silver olive groves. On the east side the grassy walks, which are set on different levels, are flanked by azaleas, camellias, hydrangeas and rhododendrons; there are groups of lemon trees in pots, grapefruit trees and mandarine trees, and also two grottoes decorated with shells, niches and statues.

Every year
the Michelin Red Guide Italia
revises its selection of starred restaurants
which also recommends culinary specialities and local wines

It also includes a selection of simpler restaurants
offering carefully prepared disches which are often regional specialities...
at a reasonable price

It is well worth buying the current edition

The 17 "contrade" of Siena

Although the city
has a coat of arms,
its true face
is reflected
in the colours
of the "contrade"

Wave

Shell

Porcupine

Eagle

Unicorn

Forest

Owl

Tortoise

Ram

She-wolf

Snail

Goose

Giraffe

Caterpillar

Dragon

Panther

Tower

SIENA★★★

Population 56 742
Michelin Map 988 fold 15 or 430 M 15/16.
Town plan in the Michelin Red Guide Italia. As the town centre is
closed to traffic, car parks are shown on the town plan below.

. . . .

Access

Visitors approaching Siena by **car** from the north (Florence) should take S2, the motorway *(Superstrada Firenze/Siena*: 68km – 42 miles) or S222 Via Chiantigiana (72km – 45 miles through the Chianti hills). To rejoin the motorway to Siena, follow the signs for *Tangenziale*.

Siena is linked by **rail** to Florence, Rome (via Chiusi) and seaside resorts as far south as Orbetello (via Grossetto). The railway station is on the north side of the city (Piazza Fratelli Rosselli); nearby is the bus station providing services into the city centre (nos 2, 3, 4, 6, 9 and 10); for information on bus services contact ☎ 0577/204246.

There is also a steam train service through Siena. For information and details of the route, contact the station ☎ 0577/280115.

There is a frequent **coach service** (morning and evening) between **Florence and Siena** provided by TRA-IN and SITA (☎ 0577/204245) – 75 minutes by the direct route; 2 hours 10 minutes via Poggibonsi. Departure point – the coach station near Santa Maria Novella railway station in Florence – and – Piazza San Domenico (in front of the basilica) in Siena.

Visiting and sightseeing

It is advisable to wear shoes which will not slip as the surface of the steps and streets is very shiny and some of the streets are very steep.

On Wednesday mornings a market is held at the foot of the Medici fortress (near the stadium). The city is then very lively but also very crowded and parking is more difficult than on other days.

The best place to enjoy an ice cream, a drink or a piece of Panforte *(qv)*, the Sienese speciality cake, is in Piazza del Campo, in Via Banchi di Sopra (**BZ**) or in Piazza Matteotti (**AY**) not far from the Lizza Gardens (one of the few parks in the city).

The *Enoteca Italiana (open 1500 to 2400; ☎ 0577/288497)* is a wine centre established in the bastions of the 16C Medici Fort. It sells only Italian *appellation contrôlée* wines which have been selected for their quality. The wine list, a book of some 140 pages, classifies the wines by region. Visitors can sample the wines and buy in cases of 3, 6, 12 or 24 bottles – vintages from 1970 to the most recent year without interruption. Orders are accepted from wine merchants.

. . . .

Siena is a mystic, gentle city of art and architecture with a passionate and generous soul, welcoming visitors with its motto which is inscribed above the Camollia Gate (north-west) – *"Cor magis tibi Seni pandit"* (Siena opens its heart even wider to you).

It is a Gothic city of yellowish-brown buildings – the "burnt Sienna" of paintboxes – set on three hills. The unhurried visitor will be able to enjoy the light dappling the pink brick and playing across the stones of the famous square and will have time to stroll between the mansions in the narrow streets and experience an atmosphere unlike that of any other city. The city embraces three steep hills of reddish clay, enclosed by extensive walls. Above the rippling lines of the biscuit-coloured rooftops rise the incomparably elegant tower of the Palazzo comunale and the nave of the vast cathedral, an unexpected façade of black and white stripes.

HISTORICAL NOTES

A city of uncertain origins – Nobody knows whether it was the Etruscans, the Gauls or the Romans who founded the original town. In the absence of any certainty, legend has replaced history and it is said that Siena was founded in the early days of the Roman era (8C BC) by Senius, son of Remus. This would explain the presence on the Sienese emblem of the she-wolf suckling the twins, Romulus and Remus. One fact, however, *is* certain. The site now occupied by the city was a small town in the days of the Republic of Rome and Caesar Augustus repopulated it (1C BC) by setting up a Roman colony here under the name of Sena Julia.

Medieval Siena – In the 12C Siena became an independent republic. Having prospered through its merchants, who were famous throughout Europe, and through its bankers, it became a threat to neighbouring Florence. At the same time political rivalry was rife between the two cities, Siena being a supporter of the Ghibelline faction while Florence supported the Guelfs *(qv)*. Until the 15C the history of the two cities, which had little in common, was marked by alternating success and failure. In 1230 the Florentines besieged Siena and catapulted manure and donkeys over the town walls. In 1258 Siena breached a treaty it had signed with Florence and opened its gates to Ghibelline exiles. The most memorable episode in this long struggle took place on 4 September 1260 on a small hill, a dozen or more miles to the east of the city, called **Montaperti**, where the Sienese, who had solemnly entrusted themselves to the protection of the Virgin Mary, suffered a bloody defeat at the hands of the Florentines.

This period of unrest – from the middle of the 13C to the middle of the 14C – was nevertheless the heyday of Siena. It was then that the most prestigious public buildings were erected together with most of its palaces and patrician mansions. The great plague which ravaged the Western world between 1348 and 1350 reduced the city's population by one-third. In the early years of the 15C internal struggles finally took the city into decline.

Although at first Siena accepted the peace-keeping role of Emperor Charles V and celebrated his arrival in the city in April 1536, the city then rebelled against his authority and placed itself under the protection of the King of France, Henry II. The town was occupied by imperial troops and defended by Blaise de Montluc, a French General from Gascony. It put up heroic resistance in which its womenfolk were also involved. Bread and wine were in short supply but the women organised veritable feasts. The city was bled white by the siege, which lasted from early in 1554 to April 1555. Four years later Siena was annexed to the Grand Duchy of Tuscany governed by Cosimo I of Florence.

Two great saints – **St Catherine** was born in Siena in 1347. She was the daughter of a dyer-fuller who had 25 children. According to tradition, she decided at the age of seven to devote her life not to a human but to a heavenly husband and she entered the Dominican Order when she was 16. Her mystical marriage with Christ was a favourite subject with artists. She should not be confused with St Catherine of Alexandria to whom a wedding ring was given, not by the adult Christ but by the Child Jesus. The golden legend of St Catherine of Siena is one of the most eventful in the hagiography. She had numerous visions and ecstasies and received the stigmata in Pisa in 1375. She also wrote a religious treaty. In 1377 she assisted in the return to Rome of the Papal court, which had been resident in Avignon since 1309. She died in Rome in 1380.

In the same year **St Bernard** was born in Massa Marittima. He too is greatly venerated by the Sienese. He gave up his university studies in order to help plague victims in the hospital of Santa Maria della Scala in Siena of which he became the general manager. At the age of 22 he entered the Franciscan Order. He founded the Congregation of Observants who complied strictly with the Rule laid down by St Francis and made the monastery of Osservanza *(qv)* to the north of Siena into a major centre for his teaching. St Bernard was an eloquent reformer who travelled throughout Italy preaching sermons filled with a degree of caustic sarcasm. Two of them, which he preached in Siena, have remained famous to this day. He died in 1440 in L'Aquila.

Piazza del Campo, Siena.

Administrative Structure – The medieval administrative structure has partly survived to this day. The three hills correspond to three urban districts *(terzi)* – di Città, di Camollia and di San Martino. Each district *(terzo)* was divided into 59 sub-districts *(contrade)* or parishes of which 17 still exist. At the head of each sub-district is an official *(capitano)*, who has administrative, judicial and territorial powers.

In the past the emblem of each district was borne on a standard or pennant which was the responsibility of the standard-bearer. Every citizen was required to take an oath of allegiance before the Cart of Freedom *(carroccio)*, the symbol of the community, which was taken into battle.

These days the 17 *contrade* spend the entire year in preparation for the *Palio (see below)*. Membership of the *contrade* is determined by birth. Each one has a centre containing a museum which displays the trophies it has won over the years, a church, a public fountain in the shape of its emblem, a band, stables and warehouses in which weapons used to be stored. Each *contrada* has its own local social life based on gastronomic evenings, dances and preparations for the *Palio*. The emblems of the 17 *contrade* represent one of the

17 virtues of Siena - the Porcupine is the symbol of sharpness, the She-wolf symbolises faithfulness, the Goose is perspicacity, the Forest is power, the Dragon ardour, the Giraffe elegance, the Wave symbolises joy, the Panther daring, the Eagle willingness to fight, the Snail prudence, the Tower is a symbol of resistance, the Tortoise is obstinacy, the Caterpillar is skill, the Ram perseverance, the Owl finesse, the Shell discretion and the Unicorn represents science.

The "Palio delle Contrade" - The *palio* is the banner awarded as the prize on a horse race. The festivities, which date from the 13C, are the most famous of their kind in Italy and are a splendid sight. The race is held twice a year on 2 July and 16 August but only 10 *"contrade"* take part in each competition so the 17 have to take it in turn to participate. During the days of preparation intrigue is rife and betting is heavy. The streets are draped in the colours of each *"contrada"*, young people practice throwing the flag, the edge of the Piazza del Campo is covered with sand to form the race track and dangerous corners are protected with mattresses. The outer edge is lined with tiers of seats but the centre, from which anybody can watch the race free of charge, is left open. Feelings run very high in the last two days before the race when there is a solemn drawing of lots in the Campo to see which horses are assigned to the participating *"contrade"*. The animals are then carefully prepared; doping is allowed. If a horse dies, the *"contrada"* that it represented has to retire from the race but its standard, set at half-mast, is entitled to take part in the opening procession and the horse's hooves are solemnly carried on a silver tray. The jockeys *(fantini)*, who are not Sienese, are accommodated within the *contrade* and watched day and night to ensure that they are not paid by a competitor to lose the race.

On the morning of the race a Mass is said in the church of each *contrada* and horse and rider are blessed. In the afternoon there is a lavish procession around the Campo involving all the representatives of the 17 *contrade* dressed in 15C costume and carrying their emblems while the flag-bearers *(alfieri)* brandish their pennants with great skill. Behind them come six black horses mounted by riders in mourning in memory of six *contrade* which no longer exist - Viper, Rooster, Oak Tree, Sword, Bear and Lion - and which were probably taken over by more powerful *contrade*. At the very end of the procession is the triumphal chariot, built according to the design of the ancient *carroccio*. The town guard of crossbowmen brings up the rear. The high spot of the festival occurs at the end of the afternoon when the famous *"corsa al palio"* is run. This is a dangerous horse race in which no holds are barred and it is all over within a matter of minutes, the time it takes the jockeys to ride bareback three times round the Campo.

S. Chirol

The winner receives the banner *(palio)* of the day, hence the name of the race; the banner bears a representation of the Virgin Mary which is painted by a leading artist especially for the occasion. After the race all the *"contrade"* continue the festivities in their streets and community centres where the dinner may be an occasion for feasting or bitterness depending on the result.

ART AND ARCHITECTURE IN SIENA

Whereas Florence was a great Renaissance city, Siena enjoyed its main period of artistic development during the flowering of Gothic art and has remained very conservative in this respect. The Gothic style was expressed here in a manner that was particularly elegant, affected and expansive.

Architecture – Although most of the architects who worked in Siena were born elsewhere, the Gothic style which developed, particularly in vernacular buildings, has certain specific characteristics – the combined use of brick and stone; double-arched openings on the lower levels of buildings consisting of a pointed arch with surbased arch below and known as **Sienese arches**; an abundance of windows – usually triple bays with slender colonnettes and tympani; merlons supported by a frieze of small arches to cap the top of buildings.

Religious architecture in Siena also had its own characteristics. Like the west front of Orvieto cathedral, which was designed by **Lorenzo Maitani**, the Sienese master *(see Michelin Green Guide Italy)*, the façade of Siena cathedral indicates the transition from the Tuscan Romanesque to the Flamboyant Gothic style, resulting in a rather affected architectural design.

Siena made its contribution to the Renaissance through a talented architect named **Francesco di Giorgio Martini** (1439-1502) who left very few traces of his artistry in the city of his birth but who worked in other towns in Tuscany, Umbria and the Marches, in particular in Urbino.

Sculpture – This art was originally a Pisan speciality and its greatest exponents were Nicola and Giovanni Pisano *(qv)* who came to work in Siena where they had a number of pupils.

Tino di Camaino, who was born in Siena *c*1280 and died in Naples in 1337, may have had a less strong personality than Giovanni, his master, but his talent was robust as well as delicate, and he too worked on the cathedral where his skills are most apparent in the complex tombs carved like reliquaries.

The leading figure, however, in Sienese sculpture in the 15C was **Jacopo della Quercia** (born *c*1371, died 1438) who rivalled the greatest artists of the day and who competed with Brunelleschi and Ghiberti for the commission to design the doors

Siena Cathedral.

for the Baptistery in Florence. He was trained in the Gothic tradition but was equally open to the Florentine Renaissance culture, and he combined both styles to produce a very personal synthesis. His austere and pure style, which is nevertheless vigorous and well-balanced, concealed an inherent irritability and a disorderly lifestyle. It was also very different from the exquisite gracefulness which had been the main feature of Sienese work until that time.

The Sienese School of Painting – It was mainly the Primitives in the 13C – 14C who earned Siena its reputation as a major city of art. Filled with fervent but calm piety, they painted hieratic figures against golden and engraved backgrounds, initially in a style strictly inspired by Byzantine art. Their expressiveness, in which beauty and tenderness are all-important, is often closely akin to mannerism. The fine drawing, vivid colours and taste for detail are reminiscent of the art of miniaturists.

The favourite subject of these artists was the Madonna and Child; it should be mentioned that for several centuries the people of Siena regarded the Virgin Mary as their supreme Saviour. There were so many representations of her in Siena in such similar attitudes that her image seems to have been mass-produced.

The first of the Sienese Primitives to make a name for himself was **Guido da Siena** who, in the second half of the 13C, produced a *Maestà* for the Palazzo comunale. It was, however, through **Duccio di Buoninsegna** that Siena made its brilliant entry into the pages of the history of art. The artist, who was born in Siena between 1250 and 1260 and died *c*1318, was to his native city what Cimabue was to Florence. He slipped from the Byzantine tradition to a new art form steeped in Gothic sensitivity; whereas in Cimabue, his contemporary, this transition resulted in the introduction of a sense of the dramatic, in Duccio it was less abrupt and resulted in an elegance that was a characteristic feature of Sienese art. His works were still impregnated with Byzantine atmosphere but they include an exquisite sense of line and colour and show the naïve grace and mannerist charm, together with the golden backgrounds inherited from Byzantine art, that were to characterise the Sienese School.

His pupil, **Simone Martini**, born *c*1285, was one of the great exponents of Gothic painting and his influence spread as far as Provence, Catalonia, Aragon, England, Flanders and Bohemia. He worked in the same style as his master but shed the constraints of Byzantine hieratic painting and tended instead towards a more natural art form. His colours have an unrivalled delicacy and his sinuous pure lines an unsurpassed elegance. As an artist, he showed mannered refinement and he has left us works steeped in unutterable gentleness and an almost musical lyricism. He was the favourite artist of Robert of Anjou who brought him to Naples. He settled in Avignon in 1339, becoming the official artist to the Papal court, and he died there in 1344. While in France he became friendly with Petrarch, another Tuscan exile, who had the same sort of artistic sensitivity and who brought the breath of lyricism to European culture. Foremost among Simone Martini's pupils were **Lippo Memmi**, his brother-in-law and assistant, and **Barna da Siena** (d *c*1380) whose cycle of frescoes in the collegiate church in San Gimignano show pathos and great vivacity.

The **Lorenzetti** brothers, who were contemporaries of Simone Martini, both trained with Duccio and were influenced by the expressive, tormented works of Giovanni Pisano, the sculptor, and the sober, naturalistic and outstandingly dramatic style of Giotto, without, however, losing the sense of colour and taste for detail that was so characteristic of the Sienese School. The work of **Piero** (born *c*1280), the elder of the brothers, was still close to the severity of Byzantine art but from Pisan sculpture he borrowed the way of depicting a Madonna seemingly linked to the Infant Jesus through a tender dialogue. **Ambrogio**, the younger brother, had a reputation for wisdom and was very well-known in Siena. He had a stronger personality than his elder brother and he was also more willing to accept Florentine art. He succeeded in freeing himself from all forms of constraint and in developing his own, personal style. As a true Sienese, he painted several pictures of the Madonna and the Virgin Mary in Majesty but he was most famous for his "civilian" fresco cycle in the Palazzo Pubblico. His landscapes express meticulous naturalism combined with a racy zest for life and exquisite sense of the fantastic. Both the brothers died of the plague in 1348.

The techniques of these masters of Gothic painting were continued in the second half of the 14C and later by a number of lesser artists such as **Lippo Vanni, Luca di Tommé** who was strongly influenced by Pietro Lorenzetti, **Bartolo di Fredi** who also worked on the frescoes in the collegiate church of San Gimignano and **Taddeo di Bartolo** (1362-1422). The 15C brought attractive and in some cases innovatory artists. While Florence was moving towards the Renaissance, Sienese art maintained a fundamental link with Gothic values. **Lorenzo Monaco** (1370 – *c*1425), a native of Siena, was still considered as a major artist of his day in Florence, where he taught Fra Angelico, with compositions that have all the intricacy of a miniaturist and all the colours of an illuminated manuscript and that made him one of the most brilliant exponents of the international Gothic style. **Giovanni di Paolo** (born *c*1403, died *c*1483) retained close ties with the Sienese tradition. Other artists, however, were more open to the Florentine influence. Stefano di Giovanni, also know as **Sassetta** (born c1400, died 1450) attempted to reproduce perspective while showing a benign ingenuity in his flowing figures and delightful harmonies of colour. His pupil, **Sano di Pietro** (1406-1481), continued to pay naïve but minute attention to detail; he also introduced a refreshingly new approach to the narrative aspect in his wonderful predellas.

It was Lorenzo di Pietro, better-known as **Vecchietta** (born c1410, died in 1480), who was responsible for a real change in style. He was a painter and sculptor and was in close contact with the Florentines. He introduced perspective into Sienese painting, rather late it is true, and gave it a new form of vigour. His most famous pupil was **Matteo di Giovanni** (born c1430, died in 1495) who created elegantly refined paintings of the Madonna as well as dramatic works that were full of movement. He also influenced **Francesco di Giorgio Martini** whose paintings reveal the attention to perspective handed on from the Florentines. His main characteristic, though, was his typically Sienese lyricism and gentleness.

In the 16C **Pinturicchio** from Umbria settled in Siena (1502) and created the brilliant decoration for the Libreria Piccolomini *(qv)*, thereby marking an artistic renaissance in the city. Siena was also the adopted home of **Il Sodoma** (1477-1549), Leonardo da Vinci's pupil who came originally from Lombardy. His works are steeped in rather theatrical pathos but they influenced the Sienese artist **Domenico Beccafumi** (born c1486, died c1551) and encouraged him to adopt the Mannerist style *(qv)* of which he became one of the greatest exponents in Tuscany.

★★★ PIAZZA DEL CAMPO (YZ) *Tour – 1 1/2 hours*

The "Campo" is one of the most famous squares in the world and the harmony of its buildings has rarely, if ever, been surpassed. It is a pink and white "shell" or "fan" set on a slight slope and is a consummate example of the "square-cum-drawing rooms" which are one of the main sights in any Italian city, representing rather less the point of convergence of city streets and rather more an enclosure in which life and history are lived to the full. It was in the Campo over the centuries that the great proclamations were heard by the citizens, that the factions whose fighting tore the city apart confronted one another, and that St Bernard addressed the people from a pulpit erected in front of the Palazzo Pubblico and railed against the frivolity of Sienese women and the destructive conflicts between rival parties.

In the mid 14C the square was paved with bricks within an outer circle of cobblestones. On the southeast side, also in brick and stone, is the long façade of the Palazzo Pubblico. From its centre radiate eight white lines dividing the Campo into nine sections, which symbolise the government "of the Nine" ie nine governors from among the craftsmen, traders and bankers who brought the city its greatest period of prosperity (1287-1355).

At the top of the square is the **Fonte Gaia** (Fountain of Joy), so-called because of the general joy that accompanied its inauguration in 1348. In 1419 it was decorated with marble panels by Jacopo della Quercia, which have been replaced by copies made in 1868. The originals, now displayed inside the Palazzo Pubblico, are in a poor state of repair.

Behind the fountain beneath a small tower *(right)* is the 13C Sansedoni Palace which was extensively altered at the end of the 19C.

★★★ Palazzo Pubblico ⊙

This is one of the finest vernacular buildings in Italy. It is exceptionally elegant and austere and it constitutes a synthesis of all the characteristics of the Sienese Gothic style. It served as a model for most of the other palaces in the city. Construction began at the end of the 13C and by the middle of the following century, it was almost complete, except for the second floor of the two wings, which was added in 1680. The pale travertine used for the lower section contrasts sharply with the yellow ochre of the remainder of the building. The large number of doors and windows along the ground floor and the slightly concave façade give an impression of lightness despite the size of the building. Two crenellated bell turrets, now empty, flank the top of the main building in the centre of which is a huge copper circle containing Christ's trigram (IHS – *Iesus Hominum Salvator* – Jesus Saviour of Mankind) which always accompanied St Bernard. The Sienese shield decorates the tympani of the trefoiled windows, each with three bays beneath a relieving arch.

Soaring heavenwards from the east end of the façade, crowned with a white stone belfry elegantly designed by Lippo Memmi, is the slender **Torre del Mangia** (88m – 286ft high). It took ten years to build and was only just finished when the Black Death broke out. Its name derives from the nickname of the first of the bellringers – *Mangiaguadagni* (he who eats all he earns). Visitors can climb to the top of the tower *(see below)*.

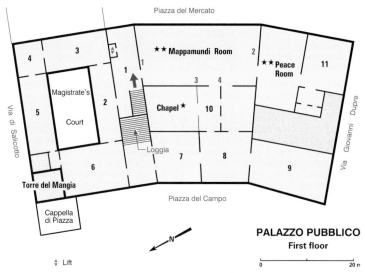

0   20 m

1. Landing – 18C ceramics
2. 16C-18C Foreign paintings
3-4. 16C-17C Sienese paintings
5. 17C-18C Sienese paintings and 17C-19C gold and silver ware
6. Risorgimento Room
7. Balìa Room
8. Ante chamber
9. Council Chamber
10. Ante chapel – 12C-17C gold and silver ware Chapel
   Mappamundi Room
   Peace Room
11. Pillar Room – 13C-15C Sienese painting

At the foot of the tower is the **Cappella di Piazza,** a chapel in the form of a loggia built in 1352 to express the gratitude of the people of Siena at the cessation of the plague. A century later it was altered and decorated in the Renaissance style.

The doorway *(right of the chapel)* leads into the narrow and austere courtyard, called the Magistrate's Court *(Cortile del Podestà),* of the Palazzo Pubblico. The palace has been the seat of successive goverments of Siena and still houses the local authority offices.

The interior of the palace was decorated by most of the great names in the Sienese School.

Tower ⊘ – *Access from the courtyard; visitors are not allowed to spend more than 20 minutes at the top.* From the top of the tower there is a superb **panoramic view★★** of the entire city with its amazing jigsaw puzzle of roofs the colour of burnt toast.

The view also extends over the surrounding countryside filled with gently-rolling hills.

First Floor – Former apartments of the governor *(podestà)* and members of the Council.

Sala del Risorgimento (6) – It gets its name from its decoration which was painted between 1886 and 1891 and which depicts the life of the first King of Italy, Victor-Emmanuel II.

Sala di Balìa (7) – This chamber is also known as the **Priors' Chamber** because, from 1445, it was the meeting-place of the influential magistrates who were members of the *Balìa,* a very old Sienese institution. Its walls, vaulted ceiling and dividing archway are covered with frescoes.

Between 1405 and 1407 Spinello Aretino painted the highly-descriptive frescoes depicting the struggle in the 12C between Pope Alexander III, who was born in Siena, and the Holy Roman Emperor, Frederick Barbarossa, in which the Pope was victorious. The most outstanding events were the naval battle in which the Venetians defeated the Imperial navy *(party wall with Room 8)* and *(opposite)* the Pope's return to Rome.

Sala del Concistoro (Council Chamber) (9) – The allegorical frescoes decorating the vault were painted *c*1530 by Domenico Beccafumi. The classical subjects all allude to the civic and patriotic virtues of the Sienese government.

Vestibollo della cappella (Ante-Chapel) (10) – Among the priceless pieces of gold and silver plate (12C-17C) is a small and intricately-worked gold rose tree by Simone da Firenze, which was given to the city by Pope Pius II Piccolomini.

★ **Cappella (Chapel)** – The superb wrought-iron **screen**★ is said to have been designed by Jacopo Della Quercia. The frescoes are by Taddeo di Bartolo narrating the *Life of the Virgin Mary* (1407-1414). The backs of the choir **stalls**★★ consist of wonderful marquetry panels illustrating the Creed, which are the work of Domenico di Niccolo, assisted by Matteo Vanni, over five years (1425-1429). Above the altar is a *Holy Family* by Il Sodoma.

★★ **Sala del Mappamondo (Mappamundi Room)** – Although this chamber was named after a rotating map of the world painted by Ambrogio Lorenzetti which was formerly attached to the wall beneath the equestrian portrait of Guido Riccio, it is famous for the two frescoes by Simone Martini.

The admirable **Virgin Mary in Majesty**★★ seated beneath a canopy and flanked by the Apostles, angels and saints (1), is an unexpected sight in a vernacular building. It was the artist's first known work, created in 1315 but badly damaged by the damp which has risen from a salt store below. It is unusual in that it was restored by the artist himself in 1321. The flowing composition, expressive faces, wonderfully fluid clothes, delicate colours and intricate decoration make this one of the most graceful and poetic examples of work from the Sienese Gothic period.

Opposite it is the famous **equestrian portrait of Guido Riccio da Fogliano**★★ (2). The Sienese General is portrayed between the two fortresses where he put down rebellions in 1328. Although the Republic of Siena paid for the artist to travel to the scene of the rebellions so that the background could be depicted accurately, the rugged chalky landscapes of the Maremma area seem unreal because of the contrast with the inky blue sky. On the other hand, the *Condottiere*, proudly sitting astride a horse that, like its rider, is covered with a rich piece of cloth on which the motifs are picked out in detail, is painted with a certain realism. The fresco immediately below the portrait, representing two men and a castle, was rediscovered early in the 1980's. It is thought to date from the early 14C and to be the last work by Duccio di Buoninsegna. The concentric circles left by the rotation of the old world map are clearly visible.

Other major artists also worked on the decoration of this chamber. On the same wall are two frescoes representing two saints painted by Il Sodoma. On one of the pillars St Catherine (3) was painted in 1461 by Vecchietta; on the next pillar (4) is St Bernard painted by Sano di Pietro in 1460.

★★ **Sala della Pace (Peace Room)** – This room contains a number of priceless paintings, unfortunately in a very poor condition. This chamber was used by the government of the Nine for their meetings and it is to them that Ambrogio Lorenzetti dedicated the two vast compositions painted between 1335 and

Effects of Good Government by Ambrogio Lorenzetti.

1340, illustrating the **Effects of Good and Bad Government**. In a style that is as lively as it is natural, the artist combined the noble and doctrinal tones inherent to allegorical painting with the detailed narrative style which he supported with great fervour and thus created a work that is predominantly didactic with scenes that are variously amusing or poetic. Not only was it unique in medieval times in that its inspiration was totally profane but it is also of inestimable artistic value and its documentary interest is priceless.

Good Government *(wall facing the window)* is represented by a noble old man dressed in the colours of Siena. Beside him are seated the cardinal virtues – Temperance, Justice, Fortitude and Prudence with Magnanimity and Peace; the room takes its name from Peace, one of the finest figures in the fresco, shown dressed in white and nonchalantly leaning. Above are the Theological Virtues – Faith, Hope and Charity. Justice is shown a second time, majestically seated on a throne *(extreme left of the scene)*. At her feet is Concord, with a plane in her lap, an allusion to the equality that must reign between the citizens depicted on the fresco in rows. They are all holding ropes, the symbol of agreement, running down from the scales of Justice.

The effects of Good Government *(above the door)* can be seen in town and country. Against the backdrop of Siena as it was in the Middle Ages with many towers, are a number of elegantly-dressed men and women on horseback. A tavern scene shows young men playing and young girls dancing. A clog-maker is at work in his workshop. Masons are building a house. The fields are depicted at the two best seasons of the year (spring and summer). The peasants are busy in the fields while noblemen set off to hunt wild boar.

Bad Government *(on the wall opposite the door)*, the most severely damaged fresco, shows figures representing the Vices surrounding Lucifer, who is sowing discord in the town where citizens are being arrested or killed. The countryside appears at it is in the dead seasons of the year (autumn and winter).

Sala dei Pilastri (11) – This room contains works by Sienese artists from the 13C, 14C and 15C including a *Maestà* by Guido da Siena *(righthand wall)* and a surprising *Massacre of the Holy Innocents* by Matteo di Giovanni *(opposite the door)*.

Loggia – From the corridor between the Balìa Room (**7**) and the Risorgimento Room (**6**), a flight of 51 steps leads up to a superb loggia containing the original fragments of the Fonte Gaia carved by Jacopo Della Querci. From the loggia, which looks down on the marketplace below, there is an extensive view southeast of the countryside, which reaches close in to the city between the urban districts of Santa Maria dei Servi *(left)* and San Agostino *(right)*.

SCALA

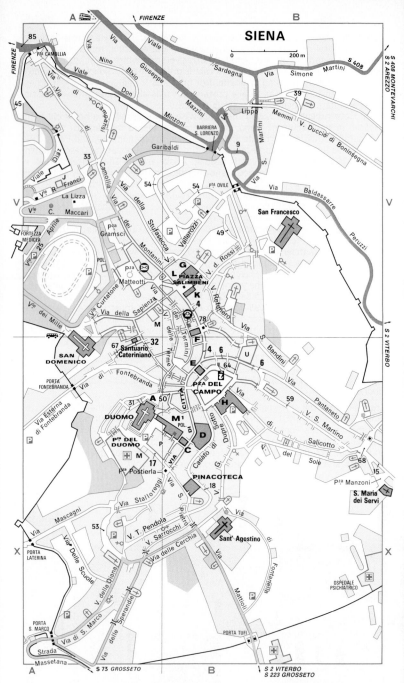

SIENA

0   200 m

Traffic restricted in town centre.

A	Battistero S. Giovanni
C	Palazzo Piccolomini
D	Palazzo Chigi-Saracini
E	Loggia dei Mercanti
F	Palazzo Tolomei
G	Palazzo Salimbeni
H	Palazzo Pubblico
K	Palazzo Spannocchi
L	Palazzo Tantucci
M¹	Museo dell'Opera Metropolitana

The main shopping streets ar printed in red
at the top of the street lists accompanying town plans

278

SIENA

Traffic restricted in town centre.

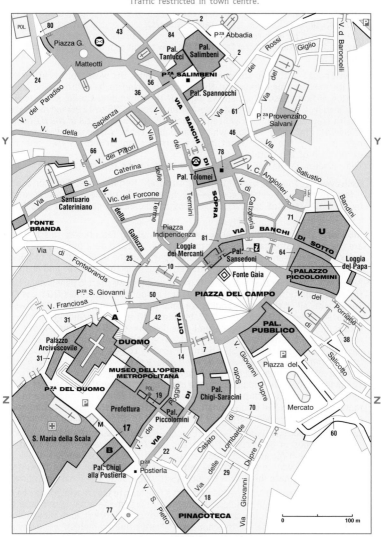

★★★ CATHEDRAL PRECINCT (z) *Tour - 2 hours*

The **Piazza del Duomo**★ (Cathedral Square) is situated at the top of the hill. The southwest side is lined by the long façade of the hospital of Santa Maria della Scala dating partly from the 13C; its name, St Mary of the Steps, is derived from the steps *(opposite)* leading up to the main entrance to the cathedral. On the two short sides are *(northwest)* the neo-Gothic Archbishop's Palace and *(southeast)* the 16C Prefecture.

The square is dominated by the famous cathedral with its bands of black and white marble.

★★★ Duomo (Cathedral)

The history of the cathedral is complex. The present building was begun in the middle of the 12C but was not completed until early in the 14C; the final work was mainly due to the Cistercian monks of San Galgano *(qv)* who sought inspiration in the design of their own abbey. In the 14C, when Siena was at the height of its prosperity, the citizens decided to create a much larger church in honour of the Virgin Mary, a cathedral which would be larger than the one in the rival city of Florence; the existing building would have become simply the transept of the new edifice. The work began in 1339 and was proceeding with great speed when it was suddenly interrupted in 1348 by the plague. Siena lost much of its manpower and decided to abandon the vast project. Some of the new building was deemed dangerous since the ground had been insufficiently prepared to take its weight and it was demolished. In the last quarter of the 14C, therefore, work began on the completion of the original cathedral – the upper section of the west front, raising the roof level of the nave, construction of the apse. The only relics of the grandiose 14C project are the arches of the nave and what was to be the façade of the new building *(south side of the present cathedral)*.

West Front – Although somewhat lacking in unity, the west front is attractive for its rich ornamentation and the gentle colouring in its marble. The lower section is Romanesque but shows signs of the impending Gothic style. It was designed by Giovanni Pisano who worked on it from 1285 to 1296 and decorated it with statues that have now been replaced by copies *(originals in the Cathedral Museum)*. The upper section, which was built a century later and was strongly influenced by the west front of the cathedral in Orvieto, shows the full exuberance of the Gothic style.

The mosaics on the gables date from the end of the last century.

Belltower – The belltower (1313) is austerely Romanesque. The horizontal effect created by the string courses of light and dark marble is counterbalanced by the impression of lightness created by the increasing number of bays from base to top.

Interior – The most characteristic and breathtaking features of this building are the densely alternating horizontal bands of light and dark marble, the short but very broad transept, the rectangular apse, and the large number of pillars which provide an infinity of different perspectives in the transept and chancel.

★★ **Pavement** – The pavement is unique. It is composed of 56 marble panels depicting figures from mythology (Sibyls, Virtues and allegories) and scenes from the Old Testament, all of them outstanding for their intricacy and liveliness. They were produced between 1369 and 1547 by some 40 artists, including Matteo di Giovanni, Pinturicchio and Beccafumi. The designs for 35 of the panels are due to Beccafumi's remarkable talent for drawing and decoration. Some of them have been restored; others have been replaced by copies. *60 % of the pavement is protected from excessive wear by a temporary floor which is moved from time to time so that all the panels can be admired in succession.*

The oldest panels were made using the *graffito* technique; they consist of white outlines on a black background and the details and reliefs are engraved in the marble then blackened using asphalt. From 1518 onwards, when Beccafumi took over the work, he used marquetry techniques with different coloured marbles.

Cappella della Madonna del Voto (A) – This Baroque chapel contains *(flanking the door)* marble statues of *St Jerome (right)* and *St Mary Magdalen (left)* carved by Bernini in the 17C. He also produced the altar and the two angels above it. The righthand wall in front of the entrance is covered with votive offerings, including a few hats hung here by jockeys *(fantini)* after the Palio (see above).

Sanctuary – The superb 16C marble altar has a fine bronze tabernacle, made c1470 by Vecchietta, and four candlesticks at the corners, made a few years later by Francesco di Giorgio Martini (the two lower candlesticks) and Giovanni di Stefano. The back panels of the choir **stalls**★★ are a fine example of woodcarving with marquetry. The ones at the end of the chancel date from the 16C; the ones on the sides, which are the finest, date from the 14C and were further embellished by wonderful marquetry panelling by Fra Giovanni da Verona (1503). The circular stained-glass window in the sanctuary depicts the Annunciation, the Coronation and the Death of the Virgin Mary. It was made in 1288 to designs by Duccio di Buoninsegna.

Capella di Sant'Ansano (B) – This chapel was dedicated to the first patron saint of Siena. Set in its pavement is the gravestone of Bishop Pecci carved by Donatello (1426); against the wall is a marble Gothic tomb (1318) by Tino di Camaino and his father, Camaino di Crescentino.

★★★ **Pulpit** – The splendid carved marble pulpit is a masterpiece by Nicola Pisano *(qv)* made from 1266 to 1268, six years after the one in the Baptistery in Pisa, with the assistance of Giovanni, his son, and a few other pupils such as Arnolfo di Cambio. The pulpit bears a resemblance to the earlier one but shows greater compliance with the Gothic tradition in its light design and flowing sculptures. The artist has used seven panels to depict episodes from the Life of Christ with the same sense of grandeur and power as on the pulpit in Pisa but with heightened drama – *(left to right)* the Nativity, the Adoration of the Magi, the Flight into Egypt and the Presentation of Jesus in the Temple, the Massacre of the Holy Innocents, the Crucifixion and the Last Judgement *(two panels)*. The various panels are separated by statues of prophets and angels. On the sill is a lectern shaped like an eagle, the emblem of St John. Between the trefoiled arches are seated female figures representing the Virtues. The pulpit is supported by nine marble, granite and porphyry columns; at the base of the central column is a group of·small figures representing the liberal arts.

Cappella di San Giovanni Battista (C) – This Renaissance chapel shaped like a rotunda contains a statue of St John the Baptist by Donatello (1457) in a niche *(below the window)*. The frescoes (restored) are by Pinturicchio.

4Libreria Piccolomini – A highly decorative marble doorway flanks the entrance to this very famous room, which was built c1495 on the orders of Cardinal Francesco Piccolomini to contain the library of Enea Silvia Piccolomini, his uncle, who had become Pope Pius II *(see Pienza)*.

On the floor and in the friezes round the ceiling is the Piccolomini emblem, the crescent moon set on a blue background. The room is of elegant proportions and all the walls were painted by Pinturicchio, who was brought to Siena from Umbria, to create works in honour of a Pope who had been archbishop of Siena for several years. The **frescoes**★★ which he produced between 1502 and 1509 have the detailed drawing typical of the art of the miniaturist and the brilliant colours of illuminated manuscripts. Using a variety of figures and architectural décors, he used his light, attractive narrative talents to illustrate the main episodes in the life of the Pope. The series of ten panels shows *(starting right*

281

of the window and going clockwise) his departure from Genoa to attend the Council of Basel, his return from the Council, his meeting with James I of Scotland, his consecration as a poet by Frederick III, his submission to Pope Eugene II, Enea at the betrothal of Emperor Frederick III and Eleonora of Aragon near the Camollia Gate, Pope Calixtus III presenting him with the cardinal's hat, his election as Pope, his decision to go to war against the Turks taken at the Congress in Mantua, the canonisation of Catherine of Siena, the welcome extended to the Christian fleet on its return from Turkey. The ceiling is richly decorated with allegories, mythological scenes and grotesques. A fine marble group representing *The Three Graces,* a 3C Roman sculpture showing the influence of the Greek tradition, stands in the centre of the room. The display cases beneath the frescoes contain 15C psalters.

Outside the Libreria *(on the right)* is the impressive **Piccolomini Altar,** a late 15C work with statues attributed to Michelangelo.

★★ Museo dell'Opera Metropolitana (Cathedral Museum) ⊙

The museum is housed in what was to be the south aisle of the new cathedral *(entrance beneath the great arch facing the south transept of the cathedral).*

Ground Floor – On each side of the gallery are statues by **Giovanni Pisano,** originally designed to decorate the west front of the cathedral. They include prophets, sages of Antiquity and sibyls and all are powerfully expressive pieces. Just beyond the gates in this room is the great *tondo* of the **Madonna and Child** by Donatello. Near the entrance are the bull and the lion – symbols of the Evangelists – and the she-wolf suckling Romulus and Remus, the emblem of Siena, also by Giovanni Pisano, assisted by his pupils. In the centre of the room is a superb **relief** representing the Virgin Mary, St Anthony the Abbot and a cardinal; it was carved by Jacopo della Quercia in the year of his death (1438).

First Floor – On this floor, admirably highlighted against the ambiant gloom, is the famous **Maestà** (Virgin Mary in Majesty) painted by Duccio towards the end of his life for the high altar in the cathedral. The reredos had narrative panels on both sides – they have now been separated – and was commissioned in 1308 by the city of Siena for a fee of 3000 gold florins. The artist worked on it for almost three years, after which the *Maestà,* which has remained his greatest masterpiece, was carried with much pomp and ceremony through cheering crowds from the painter's studio to the cathedral. In addition to the charm of its glistening golds, brilliant colours and fervent tenderness, the work is of outstanding interest for its effect on Sienese painting in later years. The Virgin Mary is set against a golden background, in accordance with medieval Byzantine tradition, and is pictured from the front, her face absolutely devoid of expression. Yet the work shows a certain flexibility – in the draping of the Virgin's clothes, which is a precursor of Gothic art and in the attitude of renunciation evident in the angels, which shows that the artist has moved away from the rigid compositions characteristic of the art of Byzantium.

The reverse side of the reredos *(left of the entrance)* originally consisted of some 40 panels which were sold off in 1771; some of them are now in London and New York. The 14 panels here depict episodes from Christ's Passion, with an exceptionally rich narrative style and a charming sense of observation.

In his work the *Birth of the Virgin Mary (against the wall to the right of the door)* Pietro Lorenzetti used a triptych in an unusual manner to depict a single scene. Beside it is the *Madonna and Child* by Duccio.

Reverse side of the *Maestà* by Duccio

1. Christ's entry into Jerusalem
2. Christ washing the Disciples' feet
3. The Last Supper
4. Jesus taking leave of the Apostles
5. Judas' pact
6. Jesus praying on the Mount of Olives
7. The kiss of Judas
8. Jesus before Annas, the High Priest
9. Peter denies Christ
10. Jesus before Caiaphas the High Priest
11. Jesus being mocked
12. Jesus brought before Pontius Pilate
13. Pontius Pilate's response to the Jews
14. Jesus before Herod
15. Jesus brought before Pontius Pilate again
16. Jesus being scourged
17. The Crown of Thorns
18. Pontius Pilate washing his hands
19. The climb to Calvary
20. The Crucifixion
21. The deposition from the Cross
22. The entombment
23. The Descent into Hell
24. The women at the tomb
25. Christ appears to Mary Magdalen
26. The pilgrims on the road to Emmaüs

15	16	19	20	22	24	26
14	17	18	20	21	23	25

1	2	5	7	8	11	13
1	3	4	6	9	10	12

Cathedral Treasury – *Mezzanine and second floor.* The most outstanding items displayed in the large chamber are the bellcote-shaped reliquary containing the head of St Galgan *(qv)* (centre of the room), a fine piece of *repoussé* silver-gilt work dating from the late 13C and decorated with scenes from the saint's life, the "Golden Rose Tree" *(display case against the end wall)* given by Pope Alexander VII Chigi in 1658 to the cathedral in Siena, his native city, and a superb 15C **altarcloth** *(against the lefthand wall)* embroidered in gold and silver thread with scenes from the Life of Christ; the Annunciation, Christ's Entry into Jerusalem, and the Last Supper are particularly fine.

Third Floor – In the room opposite the head of the stairs are some fine works by the Primitives including *(in the centre)* the **Madonna dagli occhi grossi** *(Madonna with the Large Eyes)* which gave its name to the room. This is one of the earliest Sienese paintings (early 13C) and its main features are the use of the light-relief technique and its touchingly clumsy execution. There is also a *St Bernard* by Sano di Pietro flanked by two scenes representing the saint preaching to the crowds in Piazza del Campo and Piazza San Francesco in Siena.

The other room *(right of the head of the stairs)* is hung with works by 16C-17C Italian artists including a *St Paul* by Beccafumi in which the background shows the saint's fall on the road to Damascus and his beheading. The *Sala dei Parati* contains richly-embroidered vestments.

At the far end are the steps *(about 150)* up to the top of the façade of the unfinished nave of the abandoned cathedral. From the top there is a magnificent **panoramic view★★**.

★ Battistero San Giovanni (A) ⓥ

The Baptistery of St John is beneath the apse of the cathedral. It was built in the early 14C. Its white marble façade (1382) was built in a more austere Gothic style than the cathedral but was never completed.

The interior *(ask the attendant at the entrance to switch on the lights)* is vaulted and has three aisles. It was decorated with frescoes in the 15C. In the centre stand the **font★★**, also 15C; it consists of a hexagonal basin decorated with gilded bronze panels capped by a delightful marble tabernacle; it is one of the most successful pieces of Tuscan sculpture from the transitional period between Gothic and Renaissance. It is said to have been designed by Jacopo della Quercia. Several masters worked on the panels round the basin depicting episodes from the life of John the Baptist. The scene depicting *Zachariah being expelled from the Temple (beside the altar)* was also by della Quercia. The *Birth of St John the Baptist (next on the right)* was by Turino di Sano, another Sienese sculptor. The *Preaching of John the Baptist* was by Giovanni di Turno, one of Jacopo della Quercia's pupils. The *Baptism of Jesus* and the *Arrest of John the Baptist* were carved by Lorenzo Ghiberti, the famous designer of the Paradise Door in the Baptistery in Florence. *Herod's Feast* was by Donatello, who created the effect of depth by the inclusion of more than one background. Donatello also carved two of the statues of the *Virtues* placed at each of the corners of the basin – *Faith* separating the two panels by Ghiberti and *Hope* before *Herod's Feast*.

★★★ PICTURE GALLERY (PINACOTECA) (Z) ⓥ *Tour – 2 hours*

The art gallery is housed in the **Buonsignori Palace★** (mid-15C). Its impressive red brick façade is similar to that of the Palazzo Pubblico. Although it contains very few works by Duccio and Simone Martini, the two great masters of the Sienese School, it is of outstanding interest for its extensive collections showing the development of Sienese painting from the 13C to the 16C.

For additional information, see The Sienese School of Painting in the introduction to the chapter on Siena.

Second Floor – This floor is devoted to the Primitives. *Begin on the right.*

Rooms 1 and 2 – The painted *Crucifixes* that used to decorate the Romanesque churches in the region were the only pictures in existence in the late 12C and early 13C. The first room contains two examples of these works, both of them of Byzantine inspiration as is obvious in their hieratic character and brilliant colouring. Christ is shown in triumph and not in suffering as was the case in later years. The first known artist from Siena was Guido da Siena. The three scenes from the Life of Christ *(wall opposite the door)* are among the earliest works on canvas attributed to his school.

The second room is almost entirely concerned with this great master, Guido da Siena. His works were all markedly Greek in style. The figures are shown from front view, although the heads are sometimes bent or seen from three-quarter view; the volume is suggested in the lines – the systematic emphasis of the ridge of the nose, the concentric lines used to suggest volume in the cheeks etc – and the folds or creases in the clothes are very marked and emphasised in dark

PICTURE GALLERY
Second floor

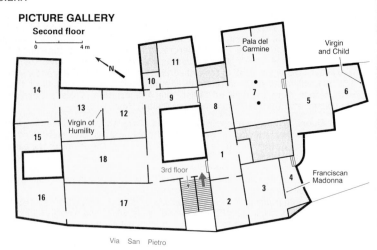

Via San Pietro

colours or gold. The extent to which the Byzantine influence lasted until the second half of the 13C is apparent in *St Francis (right of the door)* by Margaritone d'Arezzo, another Tuscan painter.

Rooms 3 and 4 – In some cases the end of the 13C was marked by a development in artistic techniques. Facial shapes were more gentle, the attitudes more natural and fabrics given greater volume. Niccolo di Segna *(Room 3)* sought to accentuate the natural features of his figures; the eyes are no longer heavily outlined and the hair and beards are softer. His large painting of the *Crucifixion (opposite the window)* shows a suffering Christ. Duccio is the supreme representative of the great period of Sienese painting. The delicate little **Franciscan Madonna** *(Room 4 – left of the door)* was one of his early works and it shows the solemnity and rigidity of expression typical of Byzantine art. There is, however, a foretaste of the flowing, graceful lines that were to characterise the Sienese School in later years in the slight bend in the Virgin Mary's body and the curl along the hem of her cloak. The master influenced a number of other artists, including Ugolino di Nerio.

Room 5 – Luca di Tommè and Bartolo di Fredi worked during the second half of the 14C, in the same style as the great masters (Simone Martini and the Lorenzetti brothers) but with additional refinement. An *Adoration of the Magi* by di Fredi *(righthand wall)* shows brilliant narrative skill and exquisite command of colouring. The golden sky has been reduced almost to nothing while the long procession is depicted in a wealth of minute and picturesque detail. The notion of landscape is suggested by two towns.

Room 6 – Simone Martini (d 1344) is represented by his **Virgin and Child** painted with a softness and purity rarely equalled. There is also his attractive polyptych of the *Blessed Agostino Novello*. The Madonnas painted by Lippo Memmi, his closest pupil, show something of his elegance and grace but they lack the vibrant lyricism that characterised the works of the great master of Sienese painting.

Room 7 – This room is also of outstanding interest for its remarkable series of works by the Lorenzetti brothers, who died of the plague in 1348. The great **Pala del Carmine** *(right of the door to Room 8)* was a reredos commissioned from Pietro, the elder brother, in 1329 by the Carmelites of Siena. Although the severe and impressive *Virgin Mary in Majesty*, shown full face and sitting very straight, is still rather stiff, the scenes on the predella depicting the history of the Carmelite Order show a very lively sense of narrative, supplemented by the landscapes and architectural perspectives.

The exquisite little *Virgin Mary in Majesty (opposite)* by Ambrogio, Pietro's brother, is a more precious and more refined piece of work which is also more tender, like his other representations of the Madonna, several of which are in the same room. Ambrogio also painted *two charming little views of a Town overlooking the Sea* and a *Castle on the Shores of a Lake* in which his Gothic grace is expressed in the extreme detail of the towers above the town and the graceful curve of the boat on the lake. Among the artists of Siena, he too was seen as a precursor since he introduced a search for perspective into his *Annunciation (same wall)*.

The golden *Assumption*, a work of unrivalled affectedness, was painted by the Master of Monte Oliveto who was strongly influenced by the monumental character of Pietro Lorenzetti's works. Most of the works on the lefthand side of the room are by this artist and by Paolo di Giovanni Fei.

Rooms 11 to 13 – Among the last Sienese Primitives to work in the late-Gothic style in the 15C were Taddeo di Bartolo *(Room 11)*, who died *c*1425 and who is represented here by an *Annunciation (righthand wall)*, and Giovanni di Paolo (*c*1403-1482), whose Mannerist tendencies are obvious in his *Assumption of the Virgin Mary surrounded by four Saints (Room 12, wall beside the door)* – the flowing garments, the slight bend in the knees of John the Baptist and the very obvious veins and the almost excessive suffering of the *Ecce Homo* and saints on the predella. His delightful **Virgin of Humility** *(Room 13 – left of the door)* is exquisitely unreal, with a long and sinuous outline, separated by a poetic curtain of rose trees from a minutely-detailed background.

Rooms 14 and 15 – In the 15C Sienese art was open to the innovations of the Renaissance while at the same time retaining the grace that is natural to the city of the *Palio*. In his religious paintings, Francesco di Giorgio Martini (1439-1502) shows the beginnings of the Florentine influence and in his descriptive landscapes there is an obvious fondness for Mantegna. Matteo di Giovanni (*c*1430-1495) had a vigorous drawing technique and he willingly accentuated and varied the attitudes and expressions of his figures; he produced a number of paintings of the *Madonna and Child (Room 14)* and an *Adoration of the Shepherds (Room 15)*.

Rooms 16 and 17 – Sano di Pietro (1406-1481) was a very prolific but not very innovatory artist. It was he, however, who remained most faithful to the Gothic style during this period. His great polyptych *(Room 16 – righthand wall)* shows a *Madonna and Child with Saints* in brilliant, refined colours; the drawing is of good quality. He also was the author of a number of exuberant polyptychs *(Room 17)* in the Gothic style.

Room 18 – The aesthetic innovations of the Florentine Renaissance are also evident in works by Vecchietta (*c*1400-1480) whose great coffered panel *(centre of the room)*, originally part of a relics chest *(arliquiera)*, shows a very obvious sense of perspective. In works by Girolamo di Benvenuto and Benvenuto di Giovanni, this new style is accompanied by a certain harshness.

Third Floor – The **Spannocchi Collection** consists of paintings from the 16C-17C of Flemish, Dutch and German origin (*St Jerome* by Dürer); from Venice (works by Paris Bordon, *Nativity* by Lorenzo Lotto) and from Lombardy, Emilia and Rome.

First Floor – Room 23 *(2nd room to the right beyond the courtyard)* contains a medallion *(tondo)* of *The Holy Family with the young St John* by Pinturicchio set against a background of gentle countryside suffused in the characteristic light of Umbrian skies.

The other two artists whose personality marked Sienese painting in the 16C, Beccafumi and Il Sodoma, are well represented. Among the outstanding works by Beccafumi is a **Birth of the Virgin Mary** *(below Room 13 on the 2nd floor)* in which the colours are daringly graduated; the main subject is set against a fairly dark background that seems to absorb the colours because of the unreal lighting. Il Sodoma painted the pathos-filled **Christ on the Column** *(below Room 15)* which is an amazingly beautiful work in aesthetic terms. The following room contains his large *Deposition from the Cross* on which the clothes look like sails swirling in the wind and the colours are rich and shimmering.

PICTURESQUE STREETS

★ **Via di Città** (Z) – *From Piazza Postierla (south of Piazza del Duomo) to Via Banchi di Sotto (north of Piazza del Campo)*. Like most of the streets in the historic city centre, this is a pedestrian precinct; together with Via Banchi di Sopra, it constitutes the main shopping street in Siena. Both streets are narrow and winding, cobbled and without pavements but they are lined with patrician houses and superb **palaces**★.

In **Via di Città** *(about half way from the southern end)* beyond several brick mansions is *(left)* **Palazzo Piccolomini**, also known as **Palazzo delle Papesse**, which now houses the offices of the Banco d'Italia. It was probably designed by Bernardo Rossellino and built of light-coloured stone in the second half of the 15C on the orders of Catherine Piccolomini, the sister of Pope Pius II (Enea Silvia Piccolomini). On the lower section of its stone façade it has marked rustication in the style of the Florentine Renaissance.

Almost opposite is the long and slightly-curved Gothic façade of the **Palazzo Chigi-Saracini** which was partially rebuilt in the 18C. The combination of stone and brick, the two rows of elegant triple-bay windows and the merlons along the top of the wall are all reminiscent of the Palazzo Pubblico. The building houses the *Accademia Chigiana*, a famous academy of music. It was from the top of its tower, since truncated, that the victory of Montaperti *(qv)* is said to have been proclaimed to the citizens.

At the north end of the street *(Croce del Travaglio)* is the **Loggia dei Mercanti** *(right)*, the Merchants' Loggia, which was the seat of the Commercial Court. It was built during the first half of the 15C and its architecture is Renaissance but its decoration – niches with statues – still bears traces of the Gothic style. Marble benches carved with low reliefs representing philosophers and generals from the days of Ancient Rome run along two of its sides. The upper storey was added in the 17C.

Via di Città leading out of Piazza del Campo.

* **Via Banchi di Sopra** (Y) – *North from the junction of Via di Città and Via Banchi di Sotto.* On the west side of Piazza Tolomei stands **Palazzo Tolomei**, dating from the early 13C, which now houses the Cassa di Risparmio di Firenze. This is the oldest privately-owned mansion in Siena. Its façade is built entirely of stone and has two rows of Gothic double-bay windows over an unusually high ground floor. It gives an impression of austerity but also of elegance. Robert of Anjou, King of Naples, stayed here in 1310.

Piazza Salimbeni★ is one of the most nobel squares in Siena and is lined on three sides by buildings in which three different styles of architecture are represented. On the east side is 14C **Palazzo Salimbeni** which was extensively restored in 1879. It has a light-coloured stone façade with a row of Gothic triple-bay windows, each capped by a pointed arch. It was named after an influential medieval Sienese family of merchants and bankers.

Building began on the **Palazzo Spannocchi** *(south side)* in 1470 to designs by the Florentine architect Giuliano da Maiano, for the treasurer to Pope Pius II Piccolomini. Its Renaissance façade with double bays and three rows of smooth rustication flanked by cornices is similar to the mansion built during the same period in Florence.

The **Palazzo Tantucci** *(north side)* was designed almost a century later by the Sienese architect, Riccio. All three house the departments of the famous **Monte dei Paschi**, a very ancient Sienese credit institution founded in 1472; its very existence was closely linked to the prosperity of Siena. Its name comes from the pastures (*pascoli* or *paschi*) in the Maremma *(qv)* region of Tuscany which in those days were owned by Siena. The income from the pastures guaranteed the financial viability of the credit institution. The Monte dei Paschi is now one of the foremost banks in Italy.

* **Via Banchi di Sotto** (Y) – *East from the junction of Via di Città and Via Banchi di Sopra.* This street, which skirts the north side of the mansions facing Piazza del Campo, includes the historic university of Siena *(left)*. Opposite is the white travertine façade of the **Palazzo Piccolomini★**. It was very probably Bernardo Rossellino, the architect of the Palazzo Ruccellai in Florence, who drew the plans for this fine Renaissance building and gave it its Florentine features – façade with light rustication becoming even less marked towards the top, small cornices emphasising the various levels, projecting roof with the coat of arms of the Piccolomini (crescent moon) set between the consoles. It houses the city archives.

The **loggia del Papa** *(right)* is a building with huge Renaissance arches supported by Corinthian columns. Its name recalls that it was built at the request of Pope Pius II Piccolomini.

* **Via del Capitano** (Z 17) – *From Piazza del Duomo southeast to Piazza Postierla (also known as Quattro Cantoni).* This is one of the finest street in Siena. **Palazzo Chigi alla Postieria** *(left no 1)* is a 16C building attributed to the Sienese architect Riccio. The late-13C **Palazzo del Capitano del Popolo** (B) (left nos 15-19), which was

extensively restored in the 19C, is a fine Gothic building of stone and brick in the Sienese style; the powerful and austere lower level has only three tall doorways and contrasts sharply with the top of the building which is relieved by a long row of Gothic double-bay windows, a cornice above tiny arches containing coats of arms and a row of merlons.

Via della Galluzza (Y) – *Northwest from Piazza del Campo.* This narrow, steeply-sloping street is one of the most picturesque medieval thoroughfares in Siena. It is lined with old brick houses incorporating unremarkable doors and windows and has eight arches, one of which includes an attractive triple bay.

ADDITIONAL SIGHTS

★ **Basilica di San Domenico** (AVX) – It was in this convent church near her home *(see below)* that St Catherine of Siena experienced her ecstasies. The church was built from the 13C - 15C in a powerful and austere Gothic style.
The T-shaped interior is spacious and well-lit, with a wide nave and very small chancel.
At the east end of the nave and on a slightly higher level is the *Capella delle Volte*, a chapel which contains *(above the altar)* the only authentic portrait of the saint, painted by one of her contemporaries, the Sienese artist, Andrea Vanni.
In **St Catherine's Chapel** *(mid-nave – right)* is the Renaissance marble **tabernacle**★ carved in 1466 by Giovanni di Stefano, another Sienese artist, which contains the saint's head. Il Sodoma painted the famous **frescoes**★ *(end wall and lefthand wall)* which depict scenes from her life – St Catherine in Ecstasy, St Catherine receiving the Stigmata, St Catherine helping a Condemned Man.
The modern stained-glass windows in the chancel were made in 1982 by B Cassinari.
The tabernacle and two angels *(high altar)* were carved in the 15C by Benedetto da Maiano. The delightful triptych of the *Madonna and Child surrounded by Saints (first chapel to the right)* is by Matteo di Giovanni, who also painted an exquisite *St Barbara between two Angels and two other Saints (second chapel to the left)*. In the lunette *(righthand wall)* is an *Adoration of the Magi*.

Santuario Cateriniano (St Catherine's Birthplace) (Y) – *Entrance Via Santa Caterina.* The saint's birthplace, which was turned into a sanctuary in 1465, now consists of a group of superimposed chapels, surrounded by other buildings. On the lower floor *(staircase left at the end)*, on the site of the dyeshop belonging to Catherine's father, there is now a church dedicated to the saint. On the upper floor are two chapels. The one *(left)*, on the site of the former kitchen, is richly decorated with wooden panelling decorated in blue and gold and a superb majolica pavement dating from the 17C. The other *(right)* contains the 13C painted Crucifix to which the saint is said to have been praying in Pisa when she received the stigmata.

★ **Fonte Branda** (Y) – Downhill from the basilica church of San Domenico is the unusual brick-built Branda Fountain, the oldest in the city. It was already in existence in 1080 but it was in 1246 that it acquired its present form, similar to the façade of Siena's Gothic mansions with its crenellated top and three arches as wide as doorways.

Basilica di San Francesco (BV) – On the very top of one of the three hills on which Siena is built stand the basilica church dedicated to St Francis, designed in the Gothic style but extensively restored (19C west front). It was in front of this church in 1425 that **St Bernard**, a Franciscan monk, preached one of his sermons, hence the small **chapel** *(right of the church)* bearing the three initials IHS on its façade. The basilica always flies the colours of the *contrade*. The building has a single, magnificently-wide **nave**★, in which the painted decor imitates the alternating black and white marble of the cathedral, and a chancel, flanked by small chapels. The church is lit by particularly fine narrative stained-glass windows.
Pietro Lorenzetti painted the fresco *(first chapel to the left of the altar)* representing the *Crucifixion*, and other frescoes *(third chapel)* are by his brother, Ambrogio, depicting *(righthand wall)* St Louis of Toulouse, great-nephew of St Louis and brother of Robert of Anjou, King of Naples, in front of Boniface VIII and *(opposite)* the Martyrdom of the Franciscans in Ceuta. This was the church chosen by Verdi for the first performance of his *Requiem*, with a choir of 400 singers, as is recorded on the plaque *(east end of the nave – lefthand side)*.

Sant'Agostino (BX) – St Augustine's Church dates from the 13C but has a Baroque interior (18C) redesigned by Vanvitelli.
The admirable **Adoration of the Crucifix**★ *(second altar to the right)*, set against a superb landscaped background, was painted in 1506 by Perugino. The Piccolomini Chapel *(door immediately beyond the altar)* contains some interesting **paintings**★ – a remarkably fresh fresco of the *Madonna with the Saints* by Ambrogio Lorenzetti and an *Adoration of the Magi* by Il Sodoma *(above the altar)*.

SIENA

Santa Maria dei Servi (BX) – The church presents an unfinished and rustic façade of brick at the top of a short avenue of cypress trees. Above it is an attractive Romanesque-Gothic belltower. From the top of the steps in front of the church, there is a magnificent **view**★★★ of the steeply-sloping hill on which the cathedral is built and of the rear of the Palazzo Pubblico.
The interior of the church is an unusual combination of Gothic and Renaissance styles but it also contains some outstanding **works of art**★ – a *Virgin Mary in Majesty* (1261) by the Florentine artist Coppo di Marcovaldo who was taken prisoner at Montaperti and is said to have painted this work *(second altar on the right)* in exchange for his freedom; a highly-expressive *Massacre of the Holy Innocents* by Matteo di Giovanni *(fifth altar)*; frescoes by Pietro Lorenzetti *(second chapel on the left of the chancel)* depicting *Salome's Dance* and the *Death of St John the Baptist (right)*; an *Adoration of the Shepherds* (1404) *(above the altar)* by Taddeo di Bartolo. A very gentle *Virgin Mary of Misericord* by Lippo Memmi *(end of the north transept)* is incorporated into another painting.

Convento dell'Osservanza – *3km – 2 miles north-east of Siena by S408 (to Montevarchi). After the level crossing, follow the yellow signs to Basilica Osservanza.* The **Observants Monastery**, which was founded by St Bernard *(qv)*, stands on a hilltop from which there is an attractive view of Siena.
The brick basilica, which was rebuilt in its 15C style after being destroyed in 1944, contains some interesting **works of art**★ – a terracotta *Coronation of the Virgin Mary* by Andrea Della Robbia *(second chapel on the left)*; a triptych of the *Madonna and Child* by Sano di Pietro *(first chapel on the left)*; a fine *Pietà (second chapel on the right)* carved by the Sienese sculptor, Giacomo Cozzarelli (1453-1515). Beneath the church is a huge crypt with groined vaulting.
Inside the monastery is St Bernard's cell containing his personal effects and a cast of his face made in 1443, one year before his death.

MICHELIN GUIDES

The Red Guides (hotels and restaurants)
Benelux – Deutschland – España Portugal – Main Cities Europe – France – Great Britain and Ireland – Italia – Suisse

The Green Guides (fine art, historical monuments, scenic routes)
Austria – California – Canada – England : the West Country – France – Germany – Great Britain – Greece – Ireland – Italy – London – Mexico – Netherlands – New England – New York – Paris – Portugal – Quebec – Rome – Scotland – Spain – Switzerland – Washington
... and the collection of regional guides for France

SINALUNGA

Population 11 587
Michelin map 988 fold 15 or 430 M 17

The old town stands high above the Chiana Valley, an area which used to be full of swamps and where malaria was rife. Since land improvement and the building of the railway, Sinalunga has expanded into the plain.
In the vast main square, **Piazza Garibaldi**, there are three 17C and 18C churches. The **Collegiata di San Martino**, at the top of a large flight of steps, was begun in the late 16C, on the site of the old fortress, using the stone from the castle. Inside *(right of the chancel)* the *Madonna and Child surrounded by two Saints and two Angels*, set on a golden background, is signed Benvenuto di Giovanni (1509).
From Piazza XX Settembre *(right of the church)* Via Mazzini leads to the historic town centre and the **Palazzo Pretorio**, decorated with coats of arms of the *Pretors* and of the Medici family who gained possession of the town in 1533; it has been altered on several occasions.

EXCURSIONS

Trequanda – *7km – 4 miles south-west of Sinalunga.* This is a small hilltop village which has retained some sections of its crenellated walls and a few remains of Cacciaconti Castle, including one huge round corner tower. The 13C **Church of San Pietro** has a very unusual rustic façade with an alternating checkerboard design of white travertine and brown-ochre local stone. The interior presents an *Ascension* by Il Sodoma *(righthand wall)* in a frame of carved and gilded *pietra serena*. Above the altar is a triptych by Giovanni di Paolo.

SORANO★

Population 4 172
Michelin Map 430 N 17

Sorano is a strange town, picturesquely set above the superb wooded limestone **Lente Gorge★** dotted with natural or man-made caves (Etruscan tombs). In the Middle

Ages it belonged to the Aldo-brandeschi family before passing into the hands of the Orsini family in 1293 and finally becoming part of the Grand Duchy of Tuscany in 1608.

The town is dominated by the half ruined Orsini Fortress built in the 15C and bearing coats of arms on the buttresses.

The 18C district, *Masso Leopoldino*, built on a flattened rock platform, provides a breathtaking view down into the gorge.

In the modern district there is a pleasant public park built in terraces from which there is an interesting view of the gorge, the town and the citadel.

Sorano.

SOVANA★

Michelin Map 430 O 16

Sovana was the birthplace of **Pope Gregory VII** (Ildebrando di Sovana) who was born *c*1020 and elected Pope in 1073. Although it is now a sleepy village, Sovana still boasts some interesting reminders of its glorious past.

At the east end of the long main street, paved with brick set out in a herringbone fashion, stand the ruins of the feudal fortress.

Halfway along is an elegant little square with a fountain and an old public washing place. The 12C church of **Santa Maria** has a typically-Romanesque interior and some 16C frescoes; the intricately-carved **ciborium★** dates from the 9C.

At the west end of the street, somewhat concealed, stands the **cathedral★**, a large Romanesque and Gothic construction. In the north wall is a delightful doorway and three narrow windows flanked by colonnettes. The semicircular apse is decorated with colonnades and low reliefs. The domed interior has quatrefoil pillars with amusing 12C capitals decorated in the Lombard style.

> **Etruscan graveyard** – *1.5km – 1 mile west of Sovana (direction San Martino).* Numerous Etruscan graves (7C-2C BC) dot the limestone cliffs flanking the road. The main ones are signed and can be reached by footpaths or by dark and narrow **gorges★** *(tagliate)* cutting into the cliffs, old Etruscan paths (several hundred yards long and some more than 30m – 98ft deep). Visitors can see several tombs – Tomba della Sirena (Mermaid's Tomb), which has a temple-shaped façade beneath a pediment carved in low relief with a mermaid motif; **Tomba Ildebranda**, the most interesting of all, which consists of a majestic set of terraces and caves surmounted by a temple with grooved pillars and the remains of low reliefs, within view of Sovana Cathedral; Tomba del Tifone, where the porch is decorated with a huge, shaggy head; Tomba Pola, a large right-angled hypogeum hollowed out of the cliff.

STIA

Population 3 000
Michelin map 988 fold 15 or 430 K 17

This village, once known as Palagio, lies at the confluence of the Stia and the Arno, which rises only a short distance away on Monte Falterona.

In Piazza Bernardo Tanucci, an attractive but narrow and elongated square, stands the 12C church of **Santa Maria Assunta,** which has been much altered over the years. The Romanesque interior with its nave and two aisles, divided by columns with fine decorative capitals, contains a number of interesting **works of art★**. The triptych of the *Annunciation (first chapel on the right)* is by Bicci di Lorenzo (141). There is a superb glazed terracotta tabernacle *(chapel to the right of the chancel)* by the della Robbias and a 14C wooden *Crucifix (centre of the apse).* The *Madonna and Child (chapel to the left of the chancel)* is by Andrea Della Robbia and the *Madonna and Child with two Angels (over the altar)* is by the Master of Varlungo. The early 15C painting of the *Assumption (above the altar in the north aisle)* is by the Master of Borgo alla Collina.

North-east of the village is the ancient castle that belonged to the Guidi, now totally restored in the neo-Gothic style popular in the late 19C. The **Museum of Contemporary Art** ⊘ *(second floor)* displays collections ranging from Futurism (1916) to the conceptual art of the present day. The common characteristic of the artists represented is their love of Tuscany.

EXCURSION

Porciano – *1.7km – 1 mile on the outskirts of Stia on S556 to Londa; turn right into a narrow road which climbs the hill.*
From the top there are some fine views of the castle.
The **castle** ⊘ in Porciano, which was built *c*1000, is considered to be one of the earliest residences of the Counts Guidi. It is surrounded by the medieval village and has retained its impressive tower and a few stretches of outer wall. The ground floor houses a Museum of Rural Art; on the first floor is a collection of ceramics discovered during archeological digs.

VALLOMBROSA★

Michelin map 988 fold 15 or 430 K 16

Vallombrosa was celebrated by Milton in *Paradise Lost* and by Lamartine. It is known for its abbey, its **natural beauty★**, its **views★★**, its magnificent pine forest and excursions in the Pratomagno range.

The convent ⊘ was founded *c*1028 by **Giovanni Gualberto**, a young Florentine nobleman, with a companion and the two hermits they met when they retired to this place. The Congregation of Vallombrosa was inspired by the Benedictines and was recognised in 1055 by Pope Victor II. Its founder was canonised in 1193. The monastery rapidly became influential because of the numerous gifts it received. It was altered several times during the centuries and now looks as it did in the 16C-17C. Its noble white façade with regularly-spaced windows framed in *pietra serena* was designed by Gherardo Silvani (1635-1640). In front of the building is a walled courtyard, dominated by a tall 13C belltower and *(right)* a 15C tower, the only surviving features of the earlier buildings.

The entrance leads to an inner courtyard and the church. Beneath the porch is a sculpture by Roberto Nardi (1990), *An Olive Tree for Peace,* depicting St John Gualberto and the wild game in Vallombrosa. The Baroque interior has a nave but no aisles. The *pietra serena* architrave beneath the organ loft dates from the Renaissance church.

Santuario della VERNA★

Michelin map 988 fold 15 or 430 K 17
Alt 1 128m – 3 666ft

In 1213 Monte Verna was given by Count Cattani from Chiusi in the Casentino to St Francis, who settled there with his brothers and received the stigmata there in 1224.

The sanctuary ⊘ is now a popular place of pilgrimage, owing to its atmosphere of serenity and meditation and its dramatic **position★** perched on the edge of sheer limestone cliffs among woods of pine, fir and beech trees.

10min on foot from first car park to the Friary.

Corridoio delle Stimmate – Every day the Franciscan brothers process along the **Corridor of the Stigmata** on their way to the Chapel of the Stigmata. The passage is decorated with frescoes by Baccio Bacci and *(at the end)* by Fra' Emmanuele da Como (late 17C). Halfway along the corridor is a door leading to the cave where St Francis used to sleep on a bare stone.

Cappella delle Stimmate – The **Chapel of the Stigmata** was built to preserve the place where the miracle occurred. On the end wall is a **Crucifixion** by Andrea della Robbia. The 15C choir stalls are decorated with marquetry (restored in the late 19C) depicting the saints, Popes and famous people who bore witness to St Francis' stigmata.

Near the chapel is the **precipice** *(37 steps)* down which, according to the *Fioretti,* the Devil tried to cast the saint.

Quadrante – The large square takes its name from the meridian *(quadrante)* that used to be carved on the wall of the church of Santa Maria degli Angeli.

Basilica – The church contains two works by Andrea Della Robbia in the two small temples next to the high altar – the Nativity *(right)* and the Annunciation *(left)*.

Santa Maria degli Angeli – The church contains two glazed terracotta pieces by Giovanni Della Robbia *(on the screen dividing the church in two)* and a terracotta altarpiece *(high altar)* by Andrea Della Robbia representing the *Assumption of the Virgin Mary*.

Sasso Spico – From the square a path *(88 steps)* lead down to an enormous rock where St Francis used to go and pray.

St Francis, Il Poverello (1182-1226)

Francis was the son of a wealthy Italian linen merchant of Assisi and a French mother. He had a brilliant mind; as a young man, being fond of society and fired with chivalrous ideals, he lived the life of a rich merchant's son. In 1202 he was taken prisoner during a border dispute with Perugia. On his return to Assisi he fell victim to a serious fever; during his illness he was touched by grace and decided to devote his life to prayer and the poor, hence his nickname – the poor man *(il poverello)*.

Francis had several visions of the Virgin Mary and Christ; the most famous one, when he received the stigmata, occurred at La Verna. He died in 1226, 16 years after setting up the Order of Minor Friars, a mendicant order, known as the Franciscans. Throughout his life of prayer and penitence, he attracted a large number of followers and he encouraged Clara, a young noble woman from Assisi, in her religious vocation; she founded the Order of Poor Clares. The real or legendary story of his life and the life of his followers was set down in an anonymous work in the 14C. It has now become famous and is called the *Fioretti*.

The simplicity of his lifestyle was evident in his language, which could be understood by even the poorest members of the community. This was vulgar Umbrian, in which he wrote the *Canticle of the Creatures* (1224), one of the first great poems in the Italian language. As a lover of beauty and nature, preaching love of all living creatures, he celebrated the value of Joy in the service of God and was nicknamed "God's juggler". The same simplicity can be seen in the joy with which he invented new and efficient ways of saving souls. He probably touched the hearts of the common people most effectively with his promotion of the Christmas crib.

VERSILIA *

Michelin map 988 fold 14 or 430 J 12 – K 12/13

Versilia is a district with a mild climate and contrasting landscapes lying between the sea coast and the mountains, which form a natural barrier against the north wind. The gently-rolling hills give way to the lush coastal plain which was formed in the Quaternary era by the alluvium deposited by the streams which tumbled down from the mountain peaks.

Along the coast is a string of superb resorts boasting fine sandy beaches (up to 100m – 108yds wide), which slope gently into the sea and are ideal for families with young children. In the distance one can see the Apuan Alps which give Upper Versilia the wonderful natural resources of white and red marble and slate. In the hinterland and on the mountains Nature has the upper hand and the traditional small villages, surrounded by olive and chestnut trees, provide a contrast to the crowded coast.

The Apuan Alps have been designated a **Country Park** which includes Camaiore, Pietrasante, Seravezza and Stazzema. The park is an ideal place for outdoor activities – rambling, climbing, gliding, pony trekking, mountain biking and pot-holing *(information is available from the tourist offices (APT) in the Versilia region)*.

1 **The Riviera** – *28km – 17.5 miles*

Viareggio – *See Viareggio*

North of Viareggio the coastline consists of an almost unbroken line of seaside resorts facing the Gulf of Genoa.

Lido di Camaiore – Lido di Camaiore is more modern and more of a family resort than Viareggio, its prestigious neighbour, but they are so close that they tend to run into one another. It has the same fine sandy beach, the same pine woods and a delightful esplanade along the front.

Beach huts, Forte dei Marmi.

The coast road then becomes more open and the vegetation more lush. The hotels are spaced further apart and are set about with vegetation. There is a splendid view of the Apuan Alps inland.

⌂⌂ **Marina di Pietrasanta** – Like Lido di Camaiore, this part of the shoreline, which includes the towns of **Focette, Motrone, Tonfano** and **Fiumetto,** is named after the village situated inland at the foot of the mountains.

The seaside resort has a long beach (over 5km – 3 miles), delightful paths through the pine woods, ideal for walking or cycling, and a wide range of sports amenities. There is also excellent night life.

On the outskirts of Marina di Pietrasanta, on the other bank of the Fiumetto, set slightly back from the beach, is **Versiliana Park** (about 80 hectares of woodland). Gabriele D'Annunzio was a regular visitor to the early-20C house. The park is traversed by pleasant paths and in summer it plays host to various cultural events.

⌂⌂⌂ **Forte dei Marmi** – This particularly elegant resort, which is set deep in a pine forest, is popular with artists and the Italian jet set. The beach has regular rows of delightful little cabins painted different colours. To the north

The Versilian Pievi

The Versilia district used to belong to Lombardy until it was annexed in the Middle Ages by Lucca which was seeking an outlet to the sea to facilitate its exports. The Romanesque churches *(pievi),* built in the 12C-13C, were therefore subject to Luccan influence as regards their structure and carved ornamentation. Their main features are their harmonious austerity, their smooth façades defined within a square, and their interiors with rafters.

the mountains of Liguria turn west towards the coast and plunge into the sea, marking the end of the gentle Versilian coastline.

Marina di Massa and **Marina di Carrara** – A somewhat deserted stretch of coast precedes these two resorts, which have a number of fine turn-of-the-century buildings. Between them is the harbour from which marble is exported with huge marble warehouses on the quayside.

② The Apuan Alps – *84km – 52 miles*

This route through Upper Versilia skirts **Monte Altissimo** in the heart of the Apuan Alps. The mountain contains particularly fine marble which is much sought-after for statues. It has been known for its excellence since the days of the Etruscans and Romans. Quarrying was abandoned in the Middle Ages but began again during the Renaissance with the encouragement of Pope Leo X, Lorenzo the Magnificent's son, who entrusted the enterprise to Michelangelo. There is a myth, echoed in the name of the neighbouring town of Pietrasanta (literally holy stone), which says that the marble was very difficult to reach and transport down the valley. Michelangelo worked here from 1515 to 1518 and one of the quarries still bears his name.

He selected the routes leading to the quarries from Seravezza and those for transporting the quarried marble down into the valley. Since then other quarries have been opened on the south and south-east sides of the mountain and the subsidiary activities can be seen from his proposed road – the cutting of marble into slabs of all sizes or into blocks and production of marble gravel chips.

Until recently Upper Versilia was also a mining district, producing lead, silver, mercury and iron.

★ **Pietrasanta** – *See Pietrasanta*

Take the main road (S1) northwest towards Massa; in Querceta turn inland; in Ripa turn left to Strettoia.

Beyond Strettoia the road climbs up to the Canale di Murli before descending again among the pines and vineyards beyond the watershed. Further on is a mountain pass on which stand the ruins of the **Castello Aghinolfi,** a castle said to have been commissioned by the Lombard king, Agilulfe, *c*600 AD. From the road, there is a fine view of the coast.

Beyond Capanne the road rejoins the Via Aurelia (S1) to Massa.

Massa – *See Massa.*

From Massa take SP4 east inland towards S Carlo.

The road leaves the coastal plain and runs through an area of natural beauty providing occasional panoramic views between the olive, chestnut and pine trees. The road passes through **San Carlo Terme, Altagnana** where there is a particularly superb view of the Apuan Alps, and **Antona**; beyond the mountain pass (**Passo del Vestito**) the road runs close by Arni. The scenery – mountains and vast expanses of grazing land – becomes increasingly grandiose.

At the junction (left to Castelnuovo di Garfagnana) bear right into SP10 to Seravezza and Pietrasanta.

In **Tre Fiumi** there is a succession of marble quarries. South of the **Galleria dei Cipollaio** (tunnel – about 1km – 1/2 mile long) the road is flanked *(right)* by **Monte Altissimo** (alt 1589m – 5164ft), the mountain that contains Michelangelo's famous quarry, easily recognisable for its jagged summit and slopes whitened by marble scree, and *(left)* by Monte Corchia, covered in chestnut trees.

At the junction by the River Vezza turn left; after 2km – 1 mile turn right into Ponte Stazzemese. Take the road to Stazzema (5km – 3 miles) with many bends and narrow places.

Stazzema (Alt 440m – 1 430ft) – The summit of Monte Procinto, which is as straight as a lookout tower, casts it shade over the narrow winding streets and flower-decked balconies of this village, which is a popular holiday resort owing to the surrounding cool chestnut forests and the proximity of the Apuan Alps which are ideal rambling country. Near the entrance to Stazzema stands the Romanesque church *(left)* of **Santa Maria Assunta** flanked by tall cypress trees. It was built on a spur of rock from which there is a delightful panoramic view. The church has a wonderful 14C ceiling.

Return downhill; in Ponte Stazzemese bear left and continue west down the Vezza Valley to Seravezza.

Seravezza – This village grew up at the confluence of two rivers – Serra and Vezza – hence its name. Since the early 16C its history has been closely linked to the quarrying of marble. When the Medici revived interest in this activity *(see above)*, Grand Duke Cosimo I commissioned a mansion, **Palazzo Mediceo**★ (1561-1565). In the centre of the splendid inner courtyard is a delightful well carved out of a single block of marble to represent a trout; it is said to be a copy of the fish caught by Marie-Christine of Lorraine in the River Vezza in 1603.

In the centre of Seravezza, which has a large number of bridges, stands the **Cathedral Church of Santi Lorenzo and Barnaba.** Construction began in 1422 and the cathedral was consecrated in 1569. It was badly damaged by bombs during the Second World War but has retained the early-16C marble font carved by Stagio Stagi, a local artist, and a lectern inset with marble.

South of Seravezza the road runs along the north bank of the River Vezza; turn left over the river into S439 to return to Pietrasanta.

③ **From the Apuan Alps to the Migliarino-San Rossore-Massaciuccoli Park** – *38km – 24 miles*

★ **Pietrasanta** – *See Pietrasanta*

Take S439 south towards Lucca; on the outskirts of Pietrasanta turn left.

Pieve dei Santi Giovanni e Felicità – *Left.* Among the olive trees stands the oldest church (9C) in the Versilia region. The west front includes a delightful late-14C rose window. There is small Gothic arcading at the top of the left wall and at the rear of the building. The very plain interior contains a few 14C frescoes and a pre-Romanesque sarcophagus.

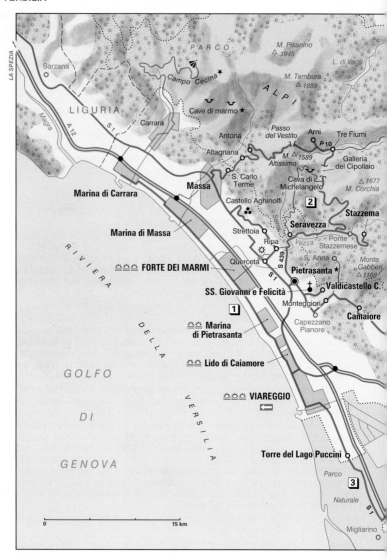

Continue up the valley to Valdicastello Carducci.

Valdicastello Carducci – It was here, at the foot of Monte Gabberi, that Giosuè Carducci, the poet, was born. His **birthplace** ⊘ *(casa natale)* houses a small museum with exhibits relating to his life.

Return to S439. After 3.5km – 2 miles turn left (shortly before Capezzano Pianore) towards S Lucia and Monteggiori.

The road climbs through olive groves and cypress trees to **Monteggiori,** a medieval village clinging to the mountainside. The cobbled streets *(pedestrians only)* lead to the hilltop from which there is a wonderful view of the valley and hills planted with vineyards and olive trees.

Continue by car to Camaiore following the direction S Anna di Stazzema (left at the first road junction) and Camaiore (right at the second junction).

Camaiore – This Roman village (Campus Major) is now a major farming and commercial centre set in the Camaiore basin at the foot of Monte Prana (alt 1 220m – 3 965ft). It has few reminders of its medieval past – the **Romanesque church of Santa Maria Assunta** (1278) flanked by a solid 14C campanile in Piazza S Bernardino da Siena which is decorated with a fine fountain. Beyond the 14C gate *(Follow signs to Badia and Cimitero; 1km – 1/2 mile from the centre)* stands the church of a Benedictine abbey *(badia)* founded in the 8C. The Romanesque church was completed in the 13C. The apse is surmounted by a majestic crenellated belltower with tracery in the form of arches. In front of it is a single arch, all that remains of the 13C crenellated wall which used to enclose the entire monastery.

From Camaiore take the road east towards Lucca. At the T-junction by a river, turn right to Massarosa. Continue for 5km – 3 miles.

In a bend *(right)* stands the Church of San Pantaleone di **Pieve a Elici**. It dates from the 11C and was built in the purest of Romanesque styles. Its austerity gives greater emphasis to the marble triptych (1470) above the high altar. Immediately beyond Pieve a Elici there is a view of the former Massaciuccoli Marshes – of the lake and the numerous canals which drain this area. The road winds through olive groves.

In Massarosa take S439 south across the plain to Quiesa. Turn right to Massaciuccoli.

The road passes through a resolutely modern area, unlike the small rural villages on the hilltop road. Beyond Quiesa the scenery becomes rural again. The old marshes are now divided into small parcels of land, growing vegetables and other crops interspersed with a few vines.

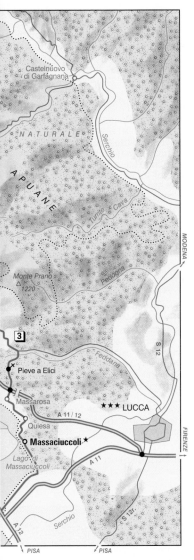

★ **Massaciuccoli** – This village, which gave its name to the neighbouring lake, has retained some links with the Roman era. At the entrance to the village are the walls *(right)* of a 1C and 2C **villa**. Beside it is the **Antiquarium** ⊘ which displays the various ceramics found on the site. A mosaic that once decorated the floor in one of the rooms is now in the elementary school *(opposite)*.

The impressive ruins of the **Roman baths**★ are set on a hilltop amid the olive trees *(left of the road; access on foot only along a path signed Zona archeologica)*. From in front of the church of San Lorenzo *(first on the left after the villa)* there is a fine **view**★ downhill over the baths and the lake to the sea.

Continue south and west; turn right into S1 (Via Aurelia) going north towards Viareggio; turn left to Torre del Lago.

This road crosses part of the **Migliarino-San Rossore-Massaciuccoli Country Park** including the lake (average depth 1.60m – just over 5 ft), the Massaciuccoli Marshes and all that remains of the ancient Pisan Forest which used to stretch uninterrupted from La Spezia (north) to Castiglioncello (south of Livorno). The lake is well stocked with fish and tortoises. Over 250 species of birds live and nest there or visit the lake during migration; some of the species are rare. The huge area of forest in the remainder of the park is indicative of the large-scale planting of parasol pines from the 16C onwards, despite the presence of other varieties.

Torre del Lago Puccini – It was here that **Puccini** (1858-1924), who was born in Lucca, composed most of his works – *La Bohème, Tosca, Madame Butterfly*. On the shores of the pleasant **Massaciuccoli Lake** stands his house, **Villa Puccini** ⊘, containing memorabilia relating to the composer, who is also buried here.

Return to Pietrasanta via Viareggio and Lido di Camaiore (tour no 1).

With this guide, use the appropriate Michelin Maps (scale 1 : 200 000) The common symbols make planning easier

Necropoli di VETULONIA★

Michelin Map 430 N 14

Vetulonia overlooks the Grosseto Plain. The huge **walls** are the only relics of the original citadel (6C-5C BC). It used to be one of the largest towns in northern Etruria and is mentioned by Diogenes of Halicarnassus and by Pliny. The archeological information indicates the way of life enjoyed by the citizens from the 8C-2C BC. The present town stands on the site as its Etruscan predecessor and the main place of interest is the necropolis.

Necropolis – *Follow the signs for Tombe etrusche; the track (800m – 866yds long) is rough but passable*. Among the most interesting remains is the **Tumulus della Pietrera** (7C BC), a grave consisting of two chambers, one above the other. The upper chamber is roofed with a pseudo-dome and has a quadrangular layout; the lower chamber, which has a pillar in the middle, was probably circular when first built. The **Tombe del Diavolino** (Litte Devil's Tomb) has a quadrangular chamber beneath a pseudo-dome; it still has the base of its central pillar.

The excavations in progress on the Greek and Etruscan-Roman town (north-east of the village) are also open to the public. They have uncovered a paved road which used to be lined by shops and houses.

VIAREGGIO☆☆☆

Population 57 563
Michelin map 988 fold 14 or 430 K 12 – Plan in the Michelin Red Guide Italia
For local map see Versilia

This is the main seaside resort in Versilia and one of the most popular in the whole of Italy. Viareggio is a small, modern town which became fashionable at the beginning of the 20C, a period from which it has retained a few fine 1920's houses and its long promenade, Via Giosué Carducci, elegantly lined with palm trees. The resort has a long and broad beach of fine sand; some parts are reserved for the residents of the seafront hotels. There is also a fairly busy fishing harbour.

The carnival in Viareggio is internationally famous for the procession of allegorical *papier mâché* floats, traditionally caricatures of Italian and international political figures.

Viareggio is also well-known for its **pine woods** *(east and west)*. The finer of the two is the western one, which is situated in the town centre. They are composed of maritime and parasol pines and offer a network of well-kept paths in an oasis of peace and tranquillity.

Canal Tour ⊘ – From Viareggio there are organised boat trips on the canals to the Massaciuccoli Lake *(see Versilia; Tour 3)* enabling visitors to enjoy the flora and fauna at close quarters.

Viale Giosué Carducci, Viareggio.

LARA PESSINA

VINCI★

Population 13 695
Michelin map 988 fold 14 or 430 K 14

It was near this village not far from Monte Albano in a landscape of olive trees and vines that the genius **Leonardo da Vinci** was born in 1452. He died in Amboise in France in 1519.

The medieval village perches on a hill. At the top is the pointed belltower of the parish church, opposite the 11C castle of the Counts Guidi, now the **museo Vinciano★** ⊙. It contains a collection of about 100 models of machinery built to the artist's plans and designs.

Leonardo da Vinci was born into a gentle and harmonious **landscape★★**, composed of the silver-leaved olive groves, the terraced plots, the rounded hills on the horizon, enhanced by the transparent light. The house thought to have been his **birthplace** *(casa natale)* ⊙ *(2.5km – 1 mile to the north of Vinci on the road to S Lucia and Faltognano; car park 50m – 54yds)* has a few 15C features – the fireplace, the stone sink and the family coat of arms in the main room; the paving in the lower room is also 15C.

Leonardo da Vinci, a universal genius (1452-1519)

Leonardo was an illegitimate child, born in Vinci, the village whose name he took as his own. He was a creative genius whose "gaze was four centuries ahead of its time". Very early on in life, he showed a gift for drawing, painting and science. In 1469 he travelled to Florence where he studied painting with Verrocchio. Florence did not, however, enable him to exploit his many talents and in 1482 he moved Milan where he entered the service of Ludovic the Moor and worked in every conceivable sector as painter, sculptor, civil and military engineer, hydraulics engineer, town planner, musician, organiser of festivities and special events. At the same time he continued his research into human anatomy, water, air, bird flight, physics and mechanical engineering. In 1499, owing to the fall of Ludovic the Moor, he was forced to leave Milan. Eventually, in 1516, after extensive travels, he found a patron worthy of his enormous intelligence, François I of France. His itinerant life was nonetheless very productive. He was a prolific and visionary engineer, an outstanding painter, the inventor of the famous *sfumato* technique – the light mist in which all his figures and landscapes acquire remarkable depth and relief and where light softly penetrates surfaces as if they were velvet.

VOLTERRA★★

Population 12 855
Michelin map 988 fold 14 or 430 L 14

Volterra, which is enclosed within Etruscan and medieval walls, stands on a hill between the Cecina and Era Valleys. It is set in an unusual and fascinating **landscape★★**. To the west the outline of the hill is broken by the grandiose **crags★** *(balze)* caused by erosion and rock falls. To the north the countryside is gentle and fertile.

The town was a Stone Age settlement and enjoyed a period of major prosperity during the days of the Etruscans. It became one of the 12 sovereign towns of the Etruscan confederation, before becoming a municipality *(municeps)* under Roman jurisdiction in the 3C BC. Although the general layout of Volterra is medieval, there are some Etruscan remains (Porta all'Arco, 4C BC walls) and Roman remains (theatre and other ruins).

One of the main industries of Volterra is the working of alabaster, a craft which dates from the 8C BC; there are many craft shops in the town.

To the west of the town are vast saltpans where table salt and soda are produced.

★★ **Piazza dei Priori** – The square is flanked by austere and sober mansions. The **Palazzo Pretorio** (13C) has twin-bay windows. Beside it rises a massive crenellated tower, which owing to the wild boar on its upper section is called *Porcellino* (Piglet). Opposite stands the 13C **Palazzo dei Priori** (H), decorated with the emblems of Florentine governors.

Take Via Turazza (along left side of the Palazzo dei Priori).

★ **Duomo** – The **cathedral** in picturesque Piazza S Giovanni, was built in the Pisan Romanesque style but has been altered on several occasions.

The nave is divided from the aisles by 16C monolithic columns with capitals. The coffered ceiling represents Paradise with the saints of Volterra and *(above the sanctuary)* the *Assumption of the Virgin Mary.*

The Addolorata Chapel *(left)* contains the *Procession of the Magi*, a fresco by Benozzo Gozzoli (1420-1497) serving as the background to a multicoloured terracotta crib by Zaccaria Zacchi da Volterra (1473-1544). Opposite this pleasing composition is another polychrome terracotta work by Zacchi, the *Adoration of the Magi*.

The *Annunciation (second altar to the left)* is by Albertinelli and Fra Bartolomeo della Porta (1498).

The pulpit *(between the aisle and nave)* has low reliefs by 12C Romanesque masters. The *Immaculate Conception (third altar to the left)* is by Niccolo Cercignani, better-known as il Pomarancio (*c*1530-1592).

The north transept contains the Inghirami (also called St Paul's Chapel) which displays the *Conversion of St Paul* by Il Dominici (1581-1641) and the *Martyrdom of St Paul* attributed to Guerchino (1591-1666). The wooden statue of the Virgin Mary is by the Sienese School (15C).

In the south transept is a touching 13C **Deposition from the Cross**★★ made of polychrome, silvered and gilded poplar wood. It represents Christ, Nicodemus, Joseph of Arimathaea, Mary and John, and is one of the best-preserved groups of its day. Its beauty comes from its colouring, the richness of the figures and the gentle overall harmony of the composition. The ladder and original Cross also contribute to its attractiveness.

Battistero – The octagonal **baptistery** dates from 1283. It has a marble doorway and one side decorated with white and green marble.

★ **Porta all'Arco (Arch Gate)** – This Etruscan archway, dating from the 4C BC, is built with huge quadrangular blocks of stone.

Return to Piazza dei Priori; take the street which slopes north and turn right into Via Buomparenti.

Via Buomparenti – The street contains the remarkable Buomparenti tower-houses which date from the 13C and are linked by a slender arch.

Pinacoteca (Art Gallery) ⊙ – *Via dei Sarti 1; in the Palazzo Minucci-Solaini*. The gallery has some interesing works of religious art by Tuscan masters of the 14C-17C – a *Madonna and Child* by Taddeo di Bartolo (*c*1362-1422); a superb *Annunciation* by Luca Signorelli (*c*1445-1523); a dramatic **Deposition from the Cross**★★ with stylised outlines by Rosso Fiorentino (1495-1540); a *Christ the Redeemer* by Domenico Ghirlandaio (1449-1494); 15C statues and paintings on wood dating from the 14C, among them a predella *(Marriage of the Virgin Mary)* by Benvenuto di Giovanni (1436-*c*1518).

Via dei Sarti – The street is lined with mansions, the most interesting of which are (no 1) the Palazzo Minucci-Solaini, now the art gallery, attributed to Antonio da Sangallo, and (no 37) the Palazzo Incontri, now the Palazzo Viti, which has a superb Renaissance façade designed by Ammannati.

Continue to Piazza San Michele.

The Romanesque west front of the church of San Michele is flanked (right) by an unusual tower-house.

Walk down Via Guarnacci.

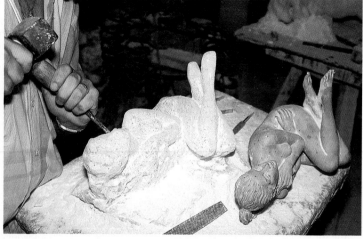

Alabaster craftsman at work.

G. Lucci/LAURA RONCHI

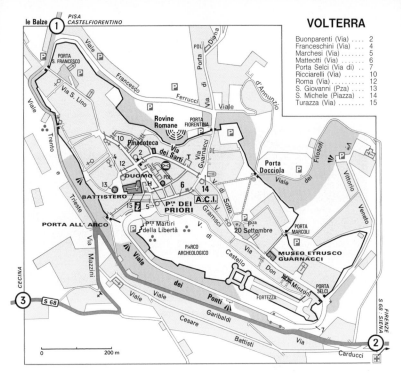

Buonparenti (Via) 2
Franceschini (Via) 4
Marchesi (Via) 5
Matteotti (Via) 6
Porta Selci (Via di) .. 7
Ricciarelli (Via) 10
Roma (Via) 12
S. Giovanni (Pza) 13
S. Michele (Piazza) .. 14
Turazza (Via) 15

Traffic restricted in town centre.

Porta Fiorentina at the bottom of the street leads to the **Roman ruins** *(rovine romane)* which date from the 1C BC. They can also be viewed from above from the street within the walls *(left of the gate)*.

Return to Piazza San Michele and descend the long flight of steps in Via di Docciola.

Porta di Docciola – The fortified gateway dates from the 13C. The Docciola Fountain was built in 1245.

Return up the steps to Piazza San Michele.
Turn left into picturesque Via Matteotti and left again into Via Gramsci.

The small church in Piazza XX Settembre contains a 16C terracotta *Assumption of the Virgin Mary* in the style of the della Robbias.

★ **Museo etrusco Guarnacci (Etruscan Museum)** ⊙ – In 1761 Monsignor Mario Guarnacci bequeathed his archeological collection and private library to the town. His extensive collection of Etruscan pieces is now displayed in chronological order, from the Villanovian period (8C BC) to the Hellenistic period (4C-1C BC), a time of extraordinary artistic creativity seen mainly in the tufa, alabaster and, more rarely terracotta, **cinerary urns**. Among the small bronze votive offerings is the famous Ombra della sera *(Evening Shadow)* (Room 22); it was named, probably by Gabriele D'Annunzio, because of the elongated pose of the body.

Etruscan Urn, Museo Guarnacci, Volterra.

SCALA

299

Volterra crags *(balze)*.

Viale dei Ponti – This promenade provides superb **views**★★ over the Metalliferous Mountains *(qv)*. Above it is the Fortezza, an impressive piece of military architecture now used as a prison and consisting of the Rocca Vecchia (14C) and the Rocca Nuova built in 1472 which comprises a keep and four corner towers.

The **cinerary urn** was a characteristic part of Etruscan funeral art in Volterra. After cremation, the ashes of the deceased were placed in the urn; the deceased, who had become immortal, was destined to partake of the banquet of the gods in the underworld. This vision of the hereafter explains why the urns have anthropomorphic covers on which the human figure is shown reclining, the usual position at banquets. Formerly funeral urns had pitched lids and a central beam.

The start of the *Palio* in Siena.

Practical
Information

Tourist information

The **Italian State Tourist Board** (Ente Nazionale Italiano per il Turismo – ENIT) has offices abroad and in Italy:

1 Princes Street, London W1R 8AY; ☎ 0171 408 1254, Fax 0171 493 6695 *(Open Mondays to Fridays, 0900 to 1700)*.

Suite 1565, 630 Fifth Avenue, New York, NY 10111; ☎ 245 4822.

Suite 550, 12400 Wilshire Boulevard, Los Angeles, California 90025; ☎ 820 0098.

Suite 1914, 1 Place Ville Marie, Montreal, Quebec; ☎ 866 7667/8/9.

The **Provincial Tourist Board** (ETP – Ente Provinciale per il Turismo) provides information on the whole region:

Dipartimento Turismo della Regione Toscana, 26 via di Novoli, Florence; ☎ 055-43 82 111.

The local **Tourist Information Centres** (APT – Azienda Promozione Turismo) provide brochures, maps and lists of hotels, youth hostels and camping sites free of charge. Their addresses and tel nos are given in the Admission Times and Charges chapter at the end of this guide and in the Michelin Red Guide Italia (Hotels and restaurants).

Public holidays – Public holidays *(giorni festivi)* are

> Saturdays and Sundays
> 1 and 6 January,
> Easter Sunday and Monday (lunedi dell'Angelo)
> 25 April (anniversary of liberation in 1945),
> 1 May,
> 15 August (Ferragosto),
> 1 November,
> 8, 25 and 26 December.

In Italy each town celebrates the feast day of its patron saint.
A working day is *giorno feriale.*

Time – The time in Italy is usually the same as in other European countries (one hour ahead of the United Kingdom) and changes during the last weekend in March and September between summer time *(ora solare)* and winter time *(ora legale).*

Museums – Most museums do not open on Mondays; on other days many close at 1400 and the ticket offices at 1330.
In many museums bags must be left in the cloakroom. Flash photography is usually not permitted.

Churches – The major cathedrals are open from 0700 to 1800 but most churches are closed between 1200 and 1600.
Visitors should be appropriately dressed: long trousers for men; no bare shoulders or very short skirts for women; those who do not observe this convention may be refused entry by the Verger or others in authority.
As many of the works of art are positioned high up, it is a good idea to take binoculars. Small change (L100 and L200 coins) is needed for the time switches.

Embassies and Consulates:

Australia – Via Alessandria 215, 00198 Rome; ☎ 06-83 27 21.

Canada – Via G B Rossi 27, 00161 Rome; ☎ 06-44 59 81.

Ireland – Largo Nazareno 3, Rome; ☎ 06-67 82 541, Fax 06-67 92 354.

UK – Lungarno Corsini 2, Florence; ☎ 055-21 25 94, 28 74 49, 28 41 33,
Via XX Settembre 80a, Rome; ☎ 06-48 25 441, 48 25 551, Fax 06-48 73 324.

USA – Lungarno Vespucci 38, Florence; ☎ 055-239 82 76, 21 76 05, 28 02 61, 28 40 88;
Via Veneto 119a, 00187 Rome; ☎ 06-46 741.

The annual Michelin Red Guide Italia
revises its selection of establishments which
– serve carefully prepared meals at a reasonable price
– include service on the bill or in the price of each dish
– offer a menu of simple but good food at a modest cost
– provide free parking
It is well worth buying the current edition

Travelling to and in Tuscany

Documents – Foreigners, including nationals of European Union (EU) countries, should be in possession of a valid identity card or **passport**.
Drivers must have a valid national or international **driving licence,** the vehicle's current **log book** and a **green card** for insurance.
As the UK is a member of the European Union, British subjects should obtain **medical form E111** from the Ministry of Social Security, Newcastle-upon-Tyne, before leaving home.

Customs – Information on customs regulations is obtainable from HM Customs, ☎ 0181 346 1144 or 0171 620 1313.

By air – Most international flights arrive at Galileo Galilei Airport in Pisa; there is a direct link (about one hour) to the centre of Florence by Alitalia coach or by train; direct access to the railway station from the airport.
International flights also land at Bologna Airport and Rome Airport.
A few international flights from 11 European cities land at Amerigo Vespucci Airport (4km – 2.5 miles northwest of Florence in Peretola) but this airport is used mainly for internal flights.

> British Airways: 156 Regent Street, London W1; ☎ 0171 434 4700;
> Galilei Airport, Primo Piano, Pisa; ☎ 050 40866; Reservations (freephone) 1670 14369 (Mondays to Fridays, 0900 to 1700).
> Alitalia: 27 Piccadilly, London W1; ☎ 0181 745 8200, Fax 0171 602 5584;
> Norwich Union House, 60/63 Dawson Street, Dublin 2; ☎ 01 677 5171; Piazza dell'Oro 1, Firenze; ☎ 055-27881, Fax 055-2788400;
> Florence Airport (Peretola) ☎ 055-216073;
> Galilei Airport, Primo Piano, Pisa; ☎ 050-48027.

By car – Michelin Map no 970 Europe (1/3 000 000), no 988 Italy (1/1 000 000) and no 430 Central Italy (1/4 000 000) or the Michelin Road Atlas Italia will make route planning easier.
Apart from the coastal roads from France (A10) and from Slovenia (A4), all roads from northern Europe into Italy go over the mountain passes, which may be blocked by snow in winter. Some passes are bypassed by tunnels.
Several motorways pass through Tuscany: A1 Milan – Naples, A11 Florence – Tyrrhenian coast and A12 Genoa – Livorno (Leghorn).
Italian **motorway tolls** can be paid with money or with the **Viacard,** a magnetic card with a value of L100 000, L50 000 and L20 000 which is sold in Italy at the beginning of the motorways, in Autogrill restaurants and in the offices of ACI (Automobile Club d'Italia), Via Marsala 8, 00185 Rome, ☎ 06-4477.
Seat belts are obligatory. Drivers must wear shoes, and carry spare lights and a red triangle to be displayed in case of a breakdown or accident. Emergency road service is provided by the ACI *(see above),* ☎ 116.
Speed limits: are 50kmph (built up areas), 90/110kmph (country roads), 130kmph (motorways). Petrol stations are usually open from 0700 to 1900 on the motorways and main roads. On minor roads they tend to close at lunchtime and on Sundays and rarely take credit cards.
In many towns in Tuscany traffic is banned from the centre *(zona a traffico limitato riservata ai veicoli autorizzati)* but there are car parks, some of which are free, or parking metres round the edge of the restricted area.
Motorways *(autostrade)* and dual carriageways *(superstrade)* are indicated by green signs; ordinary roads by blue signs; tourist sights by yellow signs.
Disabled people using their own vehicle must display the orange badge; further information from Radar, 25 Mortimer Street, London W1M 8AB, ☎ 0171 637 5400.

By train – The main line from Milan via Bologna to Rome passes through Prato, Florence and Arezzo, although not all trains stop in Prato and Arezzo. The west coast line from Genoa passes through Carrara, Viareggio, Pisa, Livorno and Grosseto.
There is also a network of slower trains serving the smaller towns.
Timetables are available at the Italian Tourist Office in London.
For tickets and prices apply to Wasteels Travel (adjacent to Platform 2 at Victoria Station), 121 Wilton Road, London SW1V 1JT. ☎ 0171 834 7066, Fax 0171 630 7628.

By coach – Coach services from Victoria Coach Station, London are organised by Eurolines, 52 Grosvenor Gardens, London SW1W 0AU, ☎ 0171 730 8235.

By bus – Information on the country bus services in Tuscany are available from
> SITA, Via Santa Caterina da Siena 15, Florence; ☎ 055-48 36 51
> CAP, Largo Fratelli Alinari 9, Florence; ☎ 055-21 46 37
> Lazzi, Piazza Stazione 4, Florence; ☎ 055-21 51 54
> TRA-IN, Via Trento 33, Poggibonsi; ☎ 0577-93 72 07.

Tickets for town buses, which are usually valid for a limited period (1 hour), should be bought before boarding from newspaper kiosks, tobacconists, bars, information office etc and stamped in the automatic machine on the bus.

Services

Telecommunications – The telephone service is organised by TELECOM ITALIA (formerly SIP). Each office has public booths where the customer pays at the counter after the call. There are phone boxes operated by phone cards and others operated by coins or even tokens. Phone cards are supplied by ČIT offices as well as tobacconists (sign bearing a white T on a black background). Phone calls cost less after 1830 and even less between 2200 and 0800.

For international calls dial: 00 + 61 for Australia

        00 + 1 for Canada

        00 + 64 for New Zealand

        00 + 44 for the UK

        00 + 1 for the USA

International calls can be made at main post offices.

For calls to other towns in Italy: dial 0 followed by the area code and the correspondant's number.

For calls from the UK to Italy: dial 00 39 followed by the area code and the correspondent's number.

Useful telephone numbers:

    113 general emergency services (equivalent of British 999)

     12 directory enquiries

     15 assisted operator service (reverse charge call)

    176 information in foreign languages

Post – In Italy post offices are open from 0830 to 1400 (1200 Saturdays and the last day of the month). Letters sent **poste restante** *(fermo posta)* can be collected from the main post office in any large town. Stamps are sold in post offices and tobacconists. The rates in Europe are: letters L850; postcards (few words only) L750.

Banks – Banks are usually open Monday to Friday, 0830 to 1330 and 1500 to 1600 but closed on Saturdays, Sundays and public holidays. Most hotels will change travellers' cheques. Money can be changed in post offices (except travellers' cheques), money-changing bureaux and at railway stations and airports. Commission is always charged.

The unit of currency is the lira which is issued in notes (L100 000, L50 000, L20 000, L10 000, L5 000, L2 000 and L1 000) and in coins (L500, L200, L100, L50 and L20).

Credit cards – Payment by credit card is widespread in shops, hotels and restaurants but rare at petrol stations. The Michelin Red Guide Italia and the Michelin Red Guide Europe indicate which credit cards are accepted at hotels and restaurants.

Pharmacies – A pharmacy *(farmacia)* is identified by a red and white cross. When it is closed it will advertise the names of the pharmacies on duty and a list of doctors.

Beaches – At the seaside there are supervised beaches where a fee is charged for umbrellas, chairs and sunbeds, and other beaches, which are free of charge but may be less well-maintained.

Accommodation

Hotels – The Michelin Red Guide Italia and the Michelin Red Guide Europe, which are revised each year, recommend a large selection of establishments together with their type, location, price, amenities and level of comfort.

Places marked with red symbols provide a particularly pleasant and restful stay.

Agritourism – For information about accommodation in farmhouses, from bed and breakfast to self-contained flats, is available from:

Associazione Nazionale per l'Agriturismo, l'Ambiente ed il Territorio, Via degli Sclavoia 6, 00196 Roma; ☎ 06-361 1051.

Agriturist, Associazione Regionale Toscana, Piazza San Firenze 3, Firenze; ☎ 055-287838

Turismo Verde Toscana; vai Verdi 5, Firenze; ☎ 055-2344 751

Terranostra Toscana, via dei Magazzini 2, Firenze; ☎ 055-280539 or 214430 *(Open daily except Saturdays, 0830 to 1330 and Mondays, Wednesdays and Friday, 1430 to 1730).*

Convents and monasteries – Convents offer accommodation at a reasonable price but close their doors at 2230. Information is available from the APT offices which will make a reservation at a particular convent.

Budget accommodation – Information about **Youth Hostels** in Italy and Tuscany is available from:

AIG (Associazione Italiana Alberghi per la gioventù), Via Cavour 44, Rome; ☎ 06-4871152.

Youth Hostels Association, Trevelyan House, 8 St Stephen's Hill, St Albans, Herts AL1 2DY

American Youth Hostel Inc, National Offices, P O Box 37613, Washington DC 20013-7613

or from the youth hostels in Tuscany itself:

Ostello della Gioventù, Zona Boscolungo, Via Brennero, **Abetone;** ☎ 0573-60117.

Ostello della Gioventù, Via Maffei 57, **Cortona;** ☎ 0575-601 392.

Ostello Villa Camerata, Viale Augusto Righi 2-4, **Florence;** ☎ 055-601 451.

Ostello della Gioventù, Via Brennero, Salicchi, **Lucca;** ☎ 0583-341 811.

Ostello della Gioventù, Via delle Fonti, **San Gimignano;** ☎ 0577-941 991.

Ostello della Gioventù, Via Fiorentina 89, **Siena;** ☎ 0577-52212, 56172.

Ostello del Chianti, Via Roma 137, **Tavarnelle Val di Pesa;** ☎ 055-807 7009.

Ostello della Gioventù, Via del Pogetto 3, **Volterra;** ☎ 0588-85577.

Student accommodation is available to students visiting on holiday as well as on courses; information from.....

Camping – Information about camp sites is available from:

Dipartimento Turismo della Regione Toscana, 26 via di Novoli, Florence; ☎ 055-43 82 111.

Touring Club Italiano, Corso Italia 10, 20122 Milano, ☎ 02-85 261;

Centro Internazionale Prenotazioni, Federcampeggio, Casella Postale 23, via V Emanuele II, Calenzano, 50041 Firenze; ☎ 055-882391, Fax 055-8825918;

Camping and Caravanning Club, Greenfields House, Westwood Way, Coventry CV4 8JH, ☎ 01203 694 995.

Electricity – The voltage is 220AC, 50 cycles per second; the sockets are for two-pin plugs. It is advisable to take an adaptor.

Shopping

Most shops are open from Mondays to Saturdays, 0800 to 1300 and 1600 to 1900. **Sizes** are not the same; for women an English 12 in clothes corresponds to an Italian size 44 and an English 5 in shoes corresponds to an Italian size 38; for men an English 40 in clothes corresponds to an Italian size 50, an English 15 in collar size to an Italian size 38, and an English size 8 in shoes corresponds to an Italian size 42.

In the past Tuscany had such a high reputation for its **art and craftsmanship** that the guilds to which the artists and craftsmen belonged were known by the Italian word *arti*. The high quality of Tuscan products is not in doubt.

For the specialities of Florence see the chapter on Florence.

Fine **fabrics** are the speciality of Florence, Prato and Lucca. High quality **leather goods** and **shoes**, which are produced in the Arno Valley, are on sale in the major towns and the spas.

In the field of the decorative arts Montelupo Fiorentino, Cafaggiolo (north of Florence) and Sesto Fiorentino are famous for *ceramics;* Siena and Cortona for earthenware – the blue and yellow decoration of plates and dishes recalls the beautiful pieces of old Majolica on display in the museums.

Impruneta is the most important place for **terra cotta** but there are several manufacturers further south in the Chianti region; as well as tiles, bricks and other building materials, they produce great flower pots and troughs of every shape and size, decorated with flutes, putti and garlands.

Volterra specialises in sculpting **alabaster** – carved figures, chess sets, table lamps, bowls and dishes – which are on sale not only in Volterra but also in Pisa because Volterra is in the district of Pisa.

There are a number of regional **food products** which travel well – olive oil, balsamic vinegar and wine – and others which should be enjoyed more immediately – raw ham *(prosciutto crudo),* sausages *(salsiccie),* sheep's milk cheese *(pecorino).*

Throughout the year in Tuscany there are **antique** and **second-hand sales** where all sorts of unusual objects are sold – old furniture, glassware, silver, lace and glazed pottery. The most famous of these markets *(mercatini)* is the one in Arezzo which may be the inspiration for all the others.

Arezzo – *First weekend in the month; in Piazza Grande.* Large selection of objects and furniture.

Prato – *Holy Saturday, 8 September and at Christmas;* ☎ *0574-42 841; around Piazza del Comune.* Particularly good for linen and old books.

Montelupo – *Sunday before 25 April and third Sunday in October.* ☎ *0571-91 74.* Antiques Fair.

Porto Santo Stefano – *15 to 17 April, 28 to 29 July and 25 to 26 August;* ☎ *055-24 76 279.* 19C and early 20C Tuscan furniture, engravings of seascapes.

Orbetello – *13 to 17 August;* ☎ *055-24 76 279; in the Municipal Gardens.* Antiques Fair.

Marina di Grosseto – *Third Saturday of each month between May and October;* ☎ 055-24 75 279. Bric-à-brac.

Food and Drink

Restaurants, cafés and bars – The Michelin Red Guide **Italia** and the Michelin Red Guide **Europe**, which are revised each year, recommend a large selection of **restaurants** offering Italian and Tuscan specialities. Stars (from 1 to 3) indicate restaurants where the cooking is of a particularly high quality.

Before the meal has been ordered the waiter will bring a basket of bread and a flask of **bread sticks** – long narrow tubes of bread, very dry like rusks, made of flour, salt and olive oil – each make varies slightly in flavour from the others.

A traditional meal consists of:

a starter or hors d'œuvre (*antipasto* – cooked meat, raw or cooked vegetables, salad, soup),

a first course (*primo piatto* – pasta in many different forms – *see below*).

a main course (*secondo piatto* – meat or fish accompanied by a side dish (*contorno*) of vegetables or salad, cheese (*formaggio*) or dessert (*dolce* – fresh fruit, cake, pudding or icecream),

coffee (*caffè*).

Italian cakes.

Pasta – Pasta may be homemade (*fatta in casa*) or manufactured (*pasta asciuta*) and comes in many shapes and sizes, which are traditional or of recent invention:

cannelloni – thick rolls filled with a meat or other sauce (baked);

farfalle – butterfly-shaped pasta;

fettuccine – long flat ribbons of pasta, a Roman speciality;

fusilli – spiral-shaped pasta;

lasagne – large squares of pasta arranged in alternate layers of pasta and meat sauce flavoured with tomato and parmesan (baked);

maccheroni – small hollow tubes of pasta;

ravioli – little cushions filled with spinach and ricotta (cheese) and cooked in butter and sage or tomato sauce;

spaghetti – traditional long thin laces of pasta;

tagliatelle – long flat ribbons of pasta (usually called fettuccine in Rome);

tortellini – parcels of pasta filled with meat or cheese which are delicious served in broth.

Drinks – In **bars** it is usual to pay the cashier who supplies a ticket which is then presented to the barman who does not handle money.

Wine – Wine is usually ordered from the menu in a bottle (*bottiglia*) or a half-bottle (*mezza bottiglia*) but many restaurants offer red / white wine in a jug (*vino rosso /*

bianco in caraffa) – a half litre *(mezzo litro),* a quarter litre *(un quartino)* – or from the owner's cellar *(vino della casa).* For information about local wines see the chapter on Wine in the Introduction.

Beer – Beer *(birra)* is served in bottles or on draught *(alla spina);* the main makes in Italy are Moretti, Forst and Peroni.

Fruit juice – A particularly refreshing drink is freshly pressed orange juice *(spremuta di arance),* not to be confused with fizzy orangeade *(aranciata).*

Water – Although tap water is served *(acqua del robineto),* it is usual to order sparkling or still mineral water *(acqua minerale gassata or naturale).*

Coffee – Italians drink coffee frequently throughout the day. An *espresso* is very strong and barely half fills a small cup. For a longer drink ask for *caffè lungo* or *alto* or *Americano. Caffè corretto* has been "corrected" with brandy or any other liqueur. *Caffelatte* is coffee served with warm milk, not to be confused with *caffè macchiato* which is served in a small cup with only a dash of cold milk.
Cappuccino or *cappuccio* is similar to coffee with milk but the milk is frothy and sprinkled with cocoa. Italians also serve decaffeinated coffee *(decaffinato or caffè Haag).*

In summer sweetened cold coffee without milk *(caffè freddo)* and with milk *(caffelatte freddo)* are refreshing and stimulating.

Ice-creams – The fame of Italian ice-cream *(gelato)* is of long date; it is best to buy the home-made variety from a specialist establishment *(gelateria).* The range of flavours is vast: *stracciatella,* ice-cream with chocolate chips; *gianduia* is creamy milk chocolate flavoured with hazelnuts; *bacio* is a milk chocolate ice-cream; *fior di latte (panna* is very similar) is made with full cream; *crema* is flavoured with vanilla; *tiramisù* recalls the flavour of coffee cake; *cassata,* a Sicilian speciality in the form of an ice-cream cake. There are also many exciting fruit flavours – mango, fig *(fico),* peach *(pesca),* apricot *(albicocca),* melon *(melone),* pistacchio *(pistacchio),* hazelnut *(nocciola),* walnut

Ice-cream.

(nocci), strawberry *(fragola),* berries *(frutta di bosco)* and lemon sorbet *(limone).*

Snacks – In small towns and villages the local food shop or delicatessen *(pizzicheria)* can provide what is necessary for a simple meal – bread, cold meat, cheese, tomatoes, fruit, bottled water and wine.
Some places will make up **sandwiches**. For a filling try cooked or raw ham *(prosciutto cotto* or *crudo)* cut wafer thin and accompanied by artichoke hearts, tomatoes, tiny mushrooms, spinach or egg plant *(melanzane). Mortadella* is very popular, also anchovies and fromage frais such as *mozzarella* or *stracchino.*
Italian sandwiches come in three typical shapes:

    la schiacciata – round dough base sprinkled with salt, olive oil and various mixtures and cut in slices;

    il tramezzino – triangular sandwich made of bread cut diagonally;
    il panino – a long or round roll.

Many bakeries offer portions of different sorts of bread, such as bread with olives, or slices of pizza *(trancia di pizza).* The latter can also be bought in a bar where large pizzas are cooked on great metal hot plates and cut into portions *(trancie).*

Touring in Tuscany

The tours shown on the **Touring Programmes Map** at the front of the guide are described here in detail.

1 Famous cities – *300km – 186 miles (12 days including 4 days in Florence).* This tour includes the most famous sights and is therefore appropriate for people who are visiting Tuscany for the first time. It provides a varied view of the countryside around Florence and follows the main road (S2) through the Chianti Hills and the minor roads round San Gimignano.

2 Mountains of marble – *300km – 186 miles.* This part of the region is mainly mountainous but also includes the Versilia Riviera along the coast and the cities of Pisa and Lucca. It gains its living from the marble quarries in the Apuan Alps which on the north side are linked with the foothills of the Apennines by the Magra river valley in the Lunigiana region and by the Serchio river valley in the Gargagnana region.

3 North of Florence – *200km – 124 miles.* The rich hinterland north of Florence is a district of high hills which includes Fiesole, the Sieve valley and the Mugello district.

4 Casentino and Pratomagno – This district has been shaped by the middle reaches of the River Arno and consists of mountains which are neither harsh nor inhospitable. Their soft and rounded contours seem to be conducive to meditation in view of the number of religious communities which were founded in the district and later spread to other regions – La Verna, Camaldoli, Vallombrosa.

5 The Upper Tiber Valley to Val di Chiana – *250km – 155 miles.* This tour includes the great Etruscan city, Arezzo, the major works by Piero della Francesca who spent many years of his life in the district, as well as the peaceful landscape of the upper Tiber Valley and the high hills of the Val di Chiana.

6 Siena and the countryside south of the city – *200km – 124 miles.* Starting from the medieval glory of Siena, the tour passes through the peaceful Sienese countryside – rolling hills, strange peaks streaked by mud-slides, the valley of the Orcia and the valley of the Arbia, dotted with art treasures, hill villages, splendid abbeys and a rare fortress.

7 Mineral resources of Tuscany (**Metalliferous Hills and the Isle of Elba**) – *400km – 248 miles.* This region contains rich mineral deposits which were known to the Etruscans; it has a varied and surprising character, some attractive towns and the beautiful ruins of the Cistercian abbey of San Galgano.

8 Southern Tuscany – *450km – 280 miles.* This region is sparsely populated and attracts few visitors except to the beautiful coastline. The summit of Monte Amiata, which is often snow-capped, contrasts with the flat land of the Maremma, which used to consist largely of marshland. Nature lovers will be attracted by its wildness, which the Etruscans tried to tame.

Spas

Tuscany is the region of Italy where most of the spa towns are situated. The springs have attracted visitors since time immemorial. Some are in the open air like the hot waterfall outside Terme di Saturnia; others have been channelled into elegant buildings where medical treatments are available.

The charm and elegance of Chianciano, Saturnia (east of Grosseto) and Montecatini are known beyond the borders of Italy. These spas were at the height of their fame in the 19C and early 20C, when people took holidays in the elegant surroundings of fine architecture and landscaped gardens.

A selection of these spa towns is shown on the Places to Stay Map (at the front of the guide). A complete list is available from the Italian Tourist Office (ENIT – *see above*); it provides supplementary information about the type of facilities available (drinking water, hot baths, mud baths, underground or surface baths, accommodation).

In most centres a medical examination is necessary before embarking on certain types of treatment and the costs vary according to what is involved.

Tettuccio Baths, Montecatini Terme.

Recreation

Archery

Compagnia Arcieri Matilde di Toscana, via Amendola 35, 55049 Viareggio (Lucca); ☎ 0584-98 96 20.
1a Campagnia Arcieri Mugello, loc. Corte, 50032 Borgo San Lorenzo (Firenze); ☎ 055-84 57 273.
Società Arcieri Val di Sieve, via Aretina 4, 50065 Pontassieve (Firenze); ☎ 055-83 15 477.
Arcobaleno Sport, 50039 Vicchio (Firenze); ☎ 055-8448638.
1a Compagnia Arcieri Ugo di Toscana, via Nuova de'Caccini 4, 50121 Firenze; ☎ 055-2340792.
Campagnia Arcieri Pisani, via Don Bosco 26, 56100 Pisa; ☎ 050-55 32 32.
Compagnia Arcieri Dino Sani, piazza Bartelloni 34, 57100 Livorno; ☎ 0586-406006.
Compagnia Arcieri del Leon Passante, viale Carducci 27, 57028 Suvereto (Livorno); ☎ 0565-828036.
Compagnia Arcieri Palagio Fiorentino, via Tintoria 11, 52017 Stia (Arezzo); ☎ 0575 58 21 38.
Società Arcieri, via Sa Antonino 19, 52043 Castiglion Firoentino (Arezzo); ☎ 0575-658627.
Club Arcieri, via Garibaldi 170, 52100 Arezzo; ☎ 0575 32 04 18.
Compagnia Arcieri Senesi, via Nenni 4, 53100 Siena; ☎ 0577 22 02 42.
Compagnia Arcieri Arcobaleno, 53021 Abbadia S Salvatore (Siena); ☎ 0577-778396.
Compagnia dell'Arco Porsenna, via Tegumento 25b, 53043 Chiusi (Siena); ☎ 0578-274072.
Compagnie Maremma Arcieri, via Lago di Varano, 558100 Grosseto.

Ballooning

Chianti Balloon Club, loc. Podere il Porto, 53010 Pianella (Siena); ☎ 0577-363232 or 363152.

Canoeing

Federazione Italiana Canoa, borgo Ognissanti 39, 50123 Firenze; ☎ 055-23 02 874.
Società Canottieri Velocior, ul Italia (porto mercantile), 19100 La Spezia; ☎ 0187-30 025.
Club Val di Magra, 54011 Aulla, Massa Carrara; ☎ 0187-40 96 03.
Associazione canoa Giunti, via Chianesi 12, 55049 Viareggio (Lucca); ☎ 0584-39 59 64.
Kaiak Airone UISP, via Machiavelli 26, 55049 Viareggio (Lucca); ☎ 0584-96 36 96.
Cooperativa Il Lago, 55030 Vagli di Sotto (Lucca); ☎ 0583-66 40 57.
Cooperativa La Fanaccia, 50000 Gramolazzo (Lucca); ☎ 0583-61 04 50.

Fuori Rotta, loc. Fabriche di Carregine, 55021 Bagni di Lucca (Lucca); ☎ 0583-85 802.
Società Canottieri Arno, via da Padule 2, 56122 Pisa.
Kaiak di mare (AKM), via Leonardo da Vinci 6, 55132 Firenze; ☎ 055-319384
Arcobaleno Sport, loc. lago di Montelleri, 50039 Vicchio (Firenze); ☎ 055-84 48 638.
Unione Canottieri, via Calabria 10, 57100 Livorno.
Canoa Club, viale Corti, 57010 Castellanselmo (Livorno).
Fuori Rotta Centro Kaiak in Mare, 57032 Capraia Isola (Livorno).
Valle del Farma, via Fontebranda 56, 53100 Siena.
Circolo Ombrone, 58040 Istia d'Ombrone (Grosseto); ☎ 0564-40 91 52.
Centro canoe alla Barca, via Cavour 9, 58100 Grosseto; ☎ 0564-41 20 00.

Caving

Gruppo Speleologico Apuano, piazza Mazzini 13, 54100 Massa (Massa Carrara).
Club Speleologico, via Repubblica 27, 51026 Maresca (Pistoia).
Unione Speleologica Pratese, via Ricasoli 7, 50047 Prato; ☎ 0574-22004.
Speleo Club Prato, via Galceti 74, 50047 Prato.
Gruppo Speleo Grotta del vento, loc. Trimpello, 50000 Fornovolasco (Lucca); ☎ 0583-722024.
Gruppo Speleologico Garfagnana, via Vittorio Emanuele, 55032 Castelnuovo Garfagnana (Lucca).
Gruppo Speleologico Versiliese, Palazzo oroni, 55054 Pietrasanta (Lucca).
Gruppo Speleologico, via S Stefano 22, 56100 Pisa.
Speleoclub Talpe, via 1 Maggio 90a, 56100 Pontedera (Pisa).
Gruppo Speleologico Pipistrelli, via S Andrea a Sveglia 13, 50014 Fiesole (Firenze); ☎ 055-540676.
Gruppo Speleologico Fiorentino, via Torre del Gallo 30, 50125 Firenze; ☎ 055-2299979.
Gruppo Speleoarcheologico Livornese, via Ricci 109, 57100 Livorno; ☎ 0586-802294.
Gruppo Speleologico Aretino, via S Giovanni Decollato 37, 52100 Arezzo; ☎ 0575-355849.
Gruppo Speleologico Valtiberina, viale Diaz 6, 52037 Sansepolcro (Arezzo).
Associazione Speleologica Senese, via S Marco 157, 53100 Siena.
Gruppo Naturalistico Maremmano, via Petrarca 57, 58046 Marina di Grosseto (Grosseto).

Cycling

Bicycle hire *(noleggio)* can be a good way of touring some of the cities, such as Lucca, to see the sights.
Club La Colombiera ARCI, via Carbone 10, 19100 La Spezia.
MTB 90 Team, via Azzi 6/8, 50032 Castelnuovo Garfagnana (Lucca).
MTB Giornale di Barga, 55051 Barga (Lucca); ☎ 0583-72 30 03 (Sig Galeotti).
Ciclo Club Vellutini, 55050 Filecchio (Lucca).
MTB Garfagnana, 55032 Castelnuovo Garfagnana; ☎ 0583-62 217.
Federazione Ciclistica Italiana, via Panciatichi 11, 51100 Pistoia; ☎ 0573-21066.
Lega Ciclismo UISP, viale Adua 74, 51100 Pistoia.
MTB Club Le Ruote, via Montalese 131, 50045 Montemurlo (Pistoia); ☎ 0574-798164.
MTB Casa dello Sport, piazza San Marco 13, 50047 Prato; ☎ 0574-606206.
Gruppo Ciclistico, via Villani, 50033 Firenzuola (Firenze).
Lega Ciclismo UISP/MTB, via Bocchi 32, 50126 Firenze; ☎ 055-68 50 25.
Federazione Ciclistica Italiane, piazza Stazione 2, 50123 Firenze; ☎ 055-28 39 26.
Gruppo MTB, via Don Minzoni, 50052 Certaldo (Firenze).
Veloetruria MTB Alta Val di Cecina, via Gramsci, 56045 Pomarance (Pisa); ☎ 0588-63060.
MTB CRAL/CNR, via S Apollinare 2, 56100 Pisa.
MTB Libertas, via Vietta 6, 56011 Calci (Pisa).
Ciclomoda Tracker Bike, via Romagnola Ovest 459, 56021 Cascina (Pisa).
Team Bike, via Pantalone 13, 57122 Livorno.
Grizzly MTB Club, via Galilei 36, 57025 Piombino (Livorno).
Velo Club, c.so Italia 94, 57027 San Vincenzo (Livorno).
Gruppo Protezione Civile, viale Kennedy 4, 57036 Porto Azzurro (Livorno); ☎ 0565-92 02 02.
Gruppo Costa dei Gabbiani, stradone S Fermo 13, 57031 Capoliveri (Livorno); ☎ 0565-96 84 02.
MTB Club Casentino, via Carlo Marx, 52012 Bibbiena (Arezzo); ☎ 0575-59 42 31.
Iron Team, via Vittorio Veneto 33, 52100 Arezzo; ☎ 0575-90 24 06.
Free Bikers Club Ripa della Luna, via Martin Luther King 203, 52037 Sansepolcro (Arezzo); ☎ 0575-73 56 54.
Federazione Ciclistica Italiana, via Cassia Nord 32, 53100 Siena; ☎ 0577-52 505.

Lega Ciclismo UISP, via Vallerozzi 77, 53100 Siena; ☎ 0577-47 522.
Club Biancaneve, piazza Garibaldi 25a, 58033 Castel del Piano (Grosseto).
Team MTB Aquilaia, via Ricasoli 1, 58031 Arcidosso (Grosseto); ☎ 0564-96 65 34.
Spazio Bici, via Settembrini 15, 58100 Grosseto; ☎ 0564-49 63 03.
Tecnobike Team, via Alighieri 1e, 58022 Follonica (Grosseto); ☎ 0566-45 012.

Equestrian Sports

APTE, via Ceccardi 41, 54031 Carrara (Massa Carrara); ☎ 0585-77 71 27.
Cooperative Colle Argegna, 55030 Giuncagnano (Lucca); ☎ 0583-61 11 82.
Centro Ippico Valdilago, 55052 Fornaci di Barga (Lucca); ☎ 0583-75 89 49.
Sport Club Il Ciocco, 55020 Castelnuovo Pascoli; ☎ 0583-71 91.
Società Ippica Viareggina, viale Comparini, 55049 Viareggio (Lucca); ☎ 0584-39 11 76.
Centro Ippico Lucchese, loc. Ai Rocchi, 55100 Lucca; ☎ 0583-59 581.
Circolo Ippico Val di Nievole, via Poggiolina Bassa 4, 50130 Serravalle; ☎ 0573-51055.
Circolo Ippico Pistoiese, via Puglianese, 51100 Pistoia; ☎ 0573-477284.
Centro Ippico La Querce, via la Querce 357, 50045 Montemurlo (Prato); ☎ 0574-682138.
Centro Ippico Selvapiana, 50040 Cantagallo (Prato); ☎ 0574-956045.
Lega Equitazione, via Bocchi 32, 50126 Firenze; ☎ 055-68 50 25 or 68 50 31.
APTE, via Montopolo 11, 50026 Casciano Val di Pesa (Firenze); ☎ 055-828824.
Azienda Vallebona, via di Grignano 32, 50065 Pontassieve (Firenze); ☎ 055-83 97 246.
Equitrekking, loc. Campestri, 50039 Vicchio (Firenze); ☎ 055-84 90 003.
Centro Ippico, loc. Montefreddi, 50030 Pietramala (Firenze).
Centro Ippico, via Amendola 10, 50050 Montaione (Firenze); ☎ 0571-63 166.
Casina della Burraia, loc. S Luigi 67, 52010 Subbiano (Arezzo); ☎ 0575-59 65 55.
Centro Ippico Il Violino, loc. Gricignano, 52037 Sansepolcro (Arezzo); ☎ 0575-720323.
Centro Ippico S Apollinare, loc. S Apollinare, 52036 Pieve S Stefano (Arezzo); ☎ 0575-79911.

Maremma horses.

Unione Popolare Sport Equestre, loc. Ossaia, 52040 Montanino di Cortona (Arezzo); ☎ 0575-67500.
Azienda Agricola La Selva, loc. La Selva 13, 52045 Foiano della Chiana (Arezzo); ☎ 0575-640079.
APTE, via S Pietro 19, 56011 Calci (Pisa); ☎ 050-93 75 90.
APTE, via M Adriatico 49, 57012 Caletta (Livorno); ☎ 0586-75 43 19.
Centro Ippico California, via Melograni 2, 57020 Bibbona (Livorno); ☎ 0586-60 02 94.
Circolo UAK Il Pettirosse, via Cibo 12, 57032 Capraia Isola (Livorno).
Fattoria Casablance, loc. Montepescini, 53016 Murlo (Siena).
Fattoria La Bagnaia, 53100 S Rocco a Pilli (Siena); ☎ 0577-817592.
Cavalieri Val d'Orcia, str. Foce e Fornace 24, 53042 Chianciano (Siena).
Rifigio Prategiano, 58026 Montieri (Grosseto); ☎ 0566-99 77 03.
Centro Ippico Amiata Horsy's, via Chiassi di Castello 1, 58037 S Fiora (Grosseto); ☎ 0564-97 81 54.
Centro Ippico Le Sugherine, 58021 Bagno di Gavorrano (Grosseto); ☎ 0566-84 49 06.
Circolo Cavalcanti di Maremma, via Stazione 19, 58011 Capalbio (Grosseto).
Centro Ippico Hippomaremma, via Talamino 51, 58100 Grosseto.

313

Mountaineering

Scuola di Alpinismo Lunigiana verticale, piazza Labindo, 54013 Fivizzano (Massa Carrara).
Scuola di Alpinismo Monte Forato, viale Michelangelo 47, 55042 Forte dei Marmi (Lucca).
Scuola di Alpinismo Roccandagia, Cortile Carrara 18, 55100 Lucca; ☎ 0583-582669.
Gruppo Sci Alpinistico La Focolaccia, Cortile Carrara 18, 55100 Lucca; ☎ 0583-582669.
Scuola di Alpinismo Alpi Apuane, via Cisanello 4, 56100 Pisa; ☎ 050-94792.
CAI, via S Fortunata 31, 57100 Livorno; ☎ 0586-897785.
Climbing the Elba, via Badi Sugarello 19, 57031 Capoliveri (Livorno).
CAI, via XXVII Aprile 6, 51500 Pistoia; ☎ 0573-365582 or 25851.
Scuola di Alpinismo Guido Rossa, via Ricasoli 7, 50047 Prato; ☎ 0574-22004.
Scuola di Alpinismo Tita Piaz, via Studio 5, 50122 Firenze; ☎ 055-2398580.
Guide Alpine AGAI, via Torre degli Agli 65, 50127 Firenze; ☎ 055-431974.
Gruppo Speleologico Aretino, via S Giovanni Decollato 37, 52100 Arezzo; ☎ 0575-355849.

Para-gliding

Toscana Parapente, Casella Postale 17, 51021 Abetone (Pistoia).
Parapendio Città di Prato, via Fra Bartolomeo 265, 50047 Prato.
Volo Libero Versilia, CP 155, 55045 Pietrasanta (Lucca).
Scuola di Volo Libero Fly TEN, via Quasimodo, 55020 Diecimo (Lucca); ☎ 0583-83 90 27.
Aeroclub, loc. Tassignano, 55012 Capannori (Lucca); ☎ 0583-93 60 62 or 93 55 01.
Volo Libero Versilia, C P 155, 55045 Pietrasanta (Lucca).
Gruppo Lisi, via Palazzetto 19, 56100 S Giuliano Terme (Pisa).
Volovelistico Mugello, Aeroclub sez. paracadutisti, loc. Figliano, 50031 Barberino di Mugello (Firenze).
Aero Club L Gori, via del Termine 12, 50145 Peretola (Firenze); ☎ 055-31 73 12.
Star Flying, viale Petrarca 143, 57124 Livorno.
Aeroclub, loc. Aeroporto, 57034 La Pila (Livorno).
Aeroclub Aeroporto, sez Paracadutisti, loc. Ampugnano, 53018 Sovicille (Siena).
Azienda Agricola Plan dei Casali, loc. Pianetti, 58050 Montemerano (Grosseto); ☎ 0564-60 26 25 or 60 29 93.

Rambling and Trekking

Walking is one of the best ways of exploring Tuscany. Organised walking tours are available in the United Kingdom from:
Ramblers Holidays Ltd, Box 43, Welwyn Garden City, Herts AL8 6PQ; ☎ 01707 331 133, Fax 01707 333 276.
Alternative Travel Group Limited, 69-71 Banbury Road, Oxford OX2 6PE; ☎ 01865 513 333.
Information is available in Italy from:
CAI, piazza Labindo, 54013 Fivizzano (Massa Carrara).
CAI, piazza Unità d'Italia, 54027 Pontremoli (Massa Carrara); ☎ 0187-830714.
Servizio Guide Scuola di Trekking, via Monte Carboni, 54035 Fosinovo (Massa Carrara); ☎ 0187-68411 or 68465.
WWF, via Resistenza 76, 54011 Aulla (Massa Carrara); ☎ 0187-420212.
CAI, piazza Mazzini 13, 54100 Massa (Massa Carrara); ☎ 0585-488081; also via Giorgi 4, 54033 Carrara (Masssa Carrara).
WWF, Palazzo Uffici, 54100 Massa (Massa Carrara); ☎ 0585-857922.
Cooperative del Turismo Verde, via Pacinotti 14, 54100 Massa (Massa Carrara); ☎ 0585-45440.
CAI, via Vittorio Emanuele, 55023 Castelnuovo Garfagnana (Lucca); ☎ 0583-65092.
CAI, Cortile Carrara 18, 55100 Lucca; ☎ 0583-582669.
CAI, via XXVII Aprile 6, 51100 Pistoia; ☎ 0573-365582.
CAI, via Repubblica 27, 51026 Maresca (Pistoia); ☎ 0573-648801.
WWF, via Medici del vascello 5, 51016 Montecatini Terme Pistoia).
CAI, via Ricasoli 7, 50047 Prato; ☎ 0574-22004.
Gruppo Trekking Bisenzio, 50048 Vernio (Prato); ☎ 0574-950237.
Associazione Italiana Trekking, piazza Etrusca 10, 50061 Compiobbi (Firenze); ☎ 055-6594167.
Club Alpino Italiano, via Algeri, 50065 Pontassieve (Firenze); ☎ 055-2398580.
Polisportiva Mugello '88, 50031 Barberino di Mugello (Firenze).
Gruppo Escursionistico Vicchiese, 50039 Vicchio (Firenze); ☎ 055-848688 or 844 146.
Gruppo Escursionistico Fiesole, via Ponte alla Badia, 50014 Fiesole (Firenze); ☎ 055-599568.

CAI, via Tanucci 7, 52017 Stia (Arezzo); ☏ 0575-58891.
CAI piazza Varchi 1, 52045 Montevarchi (Arezzo).
Coop Euroservizi, 52010 Badia Prataglia (Arezzo); ☏ 0575-21658 or 559020.
CAI, via S Giovanni Decollato 37, 52100 Arezzo; ☏ 0575-355849.
CAI, viale Diaz 6, 52037 Sansepolcro (Arezzo).
CAI, via Studio 5, 50122 Firenze; ☏ 055-2398580 or 211731.
Gruppo Trekking Firenze, piazza S Gervasio 12, 50126 Firenze; ☏ 055-585320.
Centro Naturalistico Europeo, via S Francesco di Paola 10, 50100 Firenze; ☏ 055-223984.
WWF, via Lucardese 99, 50025 Montespertoli (Firenze).
Gruppo Trekking Dodo, 50052 Certaldo (Firenze); ☏ 055-664133
CAI, via Cisanello 4, 56100 Pisa; ☏ 050-94792.
WWF, via S Martino 10b, 56100 Pisa; ☏ 050-41144.
CAI, via S Fortunata 31, 57123 Livorno; ☏ 0586-897785.
WWF, via Corsica 27, 57100 Livorno.
Cooperativa ARDEA, Servizio Accompagnatori, via Pescatori 18, 57100 Livorno; ☏ 0586-881 382.
Cooperativa Parco Naturale Isola di Gorgona, via Solferino 94, 57122 Livorno; ☏ 0586-888318.
CAI, viale Mazzini 95, 53100 Siena; ☏ 0577-270666.
CAI, via Roma 18, 58100 Grosseto; ☏ 0564-21022 or 410368 or 29253.
Amiata Trekking (Servizio Guide), piazza Fratelli Cervi 21, 53021 Abbadia S Salvatore (Siena); ☏ 0577-777751 or 778539.
Lega Ambiente ARCI, piazza Zuavi 15, 58100 Grosseto; ☏ 0564-27886.
Follonica Trekking Club, via Bicochi 86, 58022 Follonica (Grosseto); ☏ 0566-45407.
WWF, via Umberto I 1, 58013 Giglio Porto (Grosseto).
WWF, piazza Socci, 58024 Massa Marittima (Grosseto).

Sailing and Sailboarding

The marinas which are marked on Michelin Map 430 (⚓) have been selected for their facilities. It is advisable to consult the weather forecast before setting sail.
Club nautico, 54036 Marina di Carrara (Massa Carrara); ☏ 0586-78 51 50.
Circolo della Vela, 54037 Marina di Massa (Massa Carrara); ☏ 0585-24 00 00.
Associazione Surfisti Italiani Versilia, via Nino Bixio 30, 55049 Viareggio (Lucca); ☏ 0584-55 074.
Circolo della Vela, loc. Darsena, 55049 Viareggio (Lucca).
Gruppo Vela LNI Arno, viale d'Annunzio 250, 56013 Marina di Pisa (Pisa); ☏ 050-36 652.
Circolo Nautico, loc. Porticciolo, viale Nazario Sauro 12, 57126 Livorno; ☏ 0586-80 73 54.
Yacht Club, molo Mediceo 21, 57123 Livorno; ☏ 0586-896142 or 894123.
Circolo Nautico, via Toniolo 9, 57024 Donoratico (Livorno); ☏ 0565-74 57 94.
Club del Mare, via Generale Micelli 2, 57034 Marina di Campo (Livorno); ☏ 0565-97 69 42.
Circolo Velico, Banchina IV Novembre 25, 57036 Porto Azzurro (Livorno).

Punta Ala in the Maremma.

Club Velico Molo di Levante, C P 9, 58043 Castiglione della Pescaia (Grosseto); ☎ 0564-93 70 98.
Circolo della Vela, via Marina 2, 58010 Talamone (Grosseto); ☎ 0564-88 72 45.
Yacht Club, loc. Porto, 58040 Punta Ala (Grosseto); ☎ 0564-92 11 17 or 92 22 52.

Sub-Aqua

CDS Sub-Maldive, via de Sanctis 1, 50136 Firenze.
Federazione Italiana Attività Subacquee, via Aurelia 640, 57012 Castiglioncello (Livorno).
Spazio Sub, viale Caprera 17, 57123 Livorno.
Gruppo A Millemaci, via Cagliari 39, 56100 Pisa.
Capraia Diving Service, via Assunzione 72, 57032 Capraia Isola (Livorno).
Sporting Club Lacona Sub, 57030 Lacona (Livorno).
Sirena Diving Center, loc. Enfola, 57037 Portoferraio (Livorno).

Books and films

History

A Traveller's History of Italy by Valerio Lintner (Windrush Press, Gloucestershire 1989)
The Merchant of Prato - Daily Life in a Medieval Italian City by Iris Origo (Peregrine Books 1963)
War in Val d'Orcia by Iris Origo (Century Hutchinson 1985)
A Tuscan Childhood by Kinta Beevor (Penguin Books 1993)
Etruscan Places by D H Lawrence (Olive Press 1986)
The Rise and Fall of the House of Medici by Christopher Hibbert (Penguin 1979)

Art

Painting and Experience in 15C Italy by Michael Baxandall (OUP 1990)
Benvenuto Cellini – Autobiography, translated by George Bull (Penguin 1980)
The Art of the Renaissance by Peter and Linda Murray (Thames and Hudson 1963)
Art and Architecture in Italy 1250-1400 by John White (Pelican History of Art 1987)
Artistic Theory in Italy 1450-1600 by Anthony Blunt (OUP 1962)
Hall's History of Ideas and Images in Italian Art by James Hall (John Murray)
The Agony and the Ecstasy by Irving Stone (Mandarin 1989)

General

La Terra in Piazza by Alan Dundes and Alessandro Falassi (University of California Press 1975)
The Prince by Nicolo Machiavelli, translated by Bruce Penman (Dent Everyman 1992)
Tuscany by Jonathan Keates, photography by Charlie Waite (Mitchell Beazley)
Travelling in Italy with Henry James edited by Fred Kaplan (Hodder)

Cookery

Leaves from our Tuscan Kitchen by Janet Ross (Penguin 1990)
Italian Food by Elizabeth David (Penguin 1984)
The Essentials of Classic Italian Cooking by Marcella Hazan (Pan)

Novels

Where Angels Fear to Tread by E M Forster (Penguin Books 1976)
A Room with a View by E M Forster (Penguin Books 1980)
Enchanted April by Elizabeth von Arnim (Virago 1986)
Summer's Lease by John Mortimer (Penguin Books 1988)
Romola by George Eliot (OUP 1994)
Pinocchio by Carlo Lorenzini Collodi (Cape 1988)
The Divine Comedy by Dante (OUP 1993)
The Decameron by Boccacio, translated by David Wallace (OUP 1991)

Films

The best films made in Tuscany are the work of Italian film-makers who understand and express the essence of this region. Obviously those who do it best are themselves Tuscans like Mauro Bolognini, who was born in Pistoia in 1922, or the Taviani brothers, who were born in 1929 and 1931 in San Miniato to which they often return.

1953 *La Provinciale* by Mario Soldati – about provincial Tuscany near Lucca
1961 *La Viaccia* by Mauro Bolognini – about Florence
1965 *Vaghe stelle dell'Orsa* by Luchino Visconti – about Volterra and the *balze*
1970 *Metello* by Mauro Bolognini – about Florence and its workers' movement from the end of the 19C to the great strikes in 1920
1979 *Il Prato* by the Taviani brothers – about San Gimignano and its towers
1982 *La Notte di San Lorenzo* by the Taviani Brothers – a film about an episode in the Second World War which could have been fatal to their home village, San Miniato, (re-named San Lorenzo in the film) which records the rural and agricultural life of the 1940s
1985 *Room with a View* by James Ivory, exploration of Florence by young English men and women early in the 20C which ends in marriage
1987 *Good Morning Babilonia* by the Taviani Brothers – about the work of three sculptors on the Camposanto in Pisa before leavng to try their luck in the United States early in the 20C
1988 *Domani, Domani* by Daniele Luchetti – about rural Tuscany in the 19C
1994 *Con gli occhi chiusi* (With closed eyes) by Francesca Archibugi – about the Sienese countryside in the early 20C
1983 *Nostalgia* by Tarkovsky – partially set in Bagno Lignoni
1968 *Romeo and Juliet* by Zeffirelli – partially set in Pienza
1991 *Enchanted April* BBC Films
1995 *Piccola storia d'amore* by Bernardo Bertolucci

LARA PESSINA

Carnival in Viareggio.

Calendar of Events

Carnival (Shrove Tuesday)	
Viareggio	Procession of floats *(see Viareggio)*.
Santa Croce sull'Arno ...	Procession of floats.
Easter Sunday	
Florence	Scoppio del Carro *(see Florence)*.
Prato	Presentation of the Holy Girdle *(see Prato)*.
2nd Sunday after Easter	
San Miniato	Kite festival *(Festa degli Aquiloni)*: Kites are flown from the fortress esplanade (non-competitive tournament), followed by a historic pageant through the streets of the town and the launch of a hot-air balloon.
April to late Summer	
Lucca	Sagra Musicale Lucchese *(see Lucca)*.
1 May	
Prato	Presentation of the Holy Girdle *(see Prato)*.
20 May or following Sunday	
Massa Marittima	Balestro del Girifalco *(see Massa Marittima)*.
May-June	
Pisa	Historic Regatta of Maritime Republics *(see Pisa)*.
May/June	
Florence	Music in May *(see Florence)*.
Corpus Christi (June)	
Fucecchio	"Infiorita del Corpus Domini": streets decorated with flowers.
Mid-June to August	
San Gimignano	San Gimignano Summer Fair *(Estate Sangimignanese)* on Piazza Duomo: lyrical works, prose, ballet, concerts, cinema.
16 June	
Pisa	Luminara di San Ranieri *(see Pisa)*.
17 June	
Pisa	Historic regatta in honour of St Ranieri *(see Pisa)*.
3rd Sunday in June	
San Quirico d'Orcia	"Festa del Barbarossa" *(see San Quirico d'Orcia)*.
24 June	
San Miniato	St John's Day Bonfires *(see San Miniato)*.
24 June and following days	
Florence	Calcio storico fiorentino *(see Florence)*.
Last Sunday in June	
Pisa	Gioco del Ponte *(see Pisa)*.
July and August	
Siena	Master classes given by famous soloists at the Accademia Chigiana.
2 July	
Siena	Palio delle Contrade *(see Siena)*.
2nd fortnight in July	
San Miniato	Drama festival organised by the Popular Drama Institute *(see San Miniato)*.
Siena	Siena Music Week (operas and chamber music), concerts given by the famous Accademia Musicale Chigiana.
25 July	
Pistoia	Bear Joust *(see Pistoia)*.

Carrara . . . . "Simposio": international open-air event in the town centre in which some 20 sculptors are each given the chance to create a work in public.

San Miniato . . . . International Puppet Theatre Festival: "La Luna è azzurra".

Massa Marittima . . . . Balestro del Girifalco *(see Massa Marittima)*.

Prato . . . . Presentation of the Holy Girdle *(see Prato)*.

Siena . . . . Palio delle Contrade *(see Siena)*.

Montepulciano . . . . "Bravio delle botti": two men from each urban district push the barrel *(botte)* weighing some 80kg-175lb up the steep streets to the cathedral. The banner (bravio) representing the town of Montepulciano is awarded to the winning team.

Arezzo . . . . Saracen's Joust *(see Arezzo)*.

Pescia . . . . Biennial Flower Show.

Florence . . . . Rificolona Festival *(see Florence)*.

Prato . . . . Presentation of the Holy Girdle to the congregation to celebrate the birth of the Virgin Mary: huge procession in period costume *(see Prato)*.

Lucca . . . . Luminara di Santa Croce *(see Lucca)*.

Volterra . . . . "Astiludio": fair with demonstrations of flag throwing.

Sansepolcro . . . . Cross-bow contest *(see Sansepolcro)*.

Impruneta . . . . Grape Festival *(festa dell'Uva)*: one of the largest festivals in the Chianti region with a procession of floats.

Impruneta . . . . Fiera di San Luca *(see Impruneta)*.

Montalcino . . . . Thrush Festival (Sagra del Tordo): historic pageant, traditional costumed ball *(il Trescone)*, archery competition and evening banquet at the fortress.

Empoli . . . . Busoni Piano Festival *(see Empoli)*.

San Miniato . . . . Grand white truffle fair *(see San Miniato)*.

Florence . . . . Antique Toy Fair.

San Quirico d'Orcia . . . . . Oil Fair.

Prato . . . . Presentation of the Holy Girdle to the congregation *(see Prato)*.

Glossary

On the road and in town

a destra	right	neve	snow
a sinistra	left	parcheggio	parking
annulare	ring road	passaggio a livello	level crossing
banchina	roadside, soft verge	passo	mountain pass
binario	station platform	pericolo	danger
corso	street	piazza	square
discesa	descent	piazzale	small square
dogana	customs	senso unico	one-way
fermata	bus stop	stazione	station
fiume	river	stretto	narrow
frana	landslip	strada in alestimento	road works
ghiaccio	frost	uscita	exit
ingresso	entrance	viale	avenue
largo	broad street	vietato	forbidden
lavori in corso	building works in progress		

Sights

abbazia	abbey	lungomare	seafront
affreschi	frescoes	mercato	market
aperto	open	navata	nave
cappella	chapel	palazzo	palace, mansion
casa	house	passeggiata	walk
castello	castle	piano	floor
chiesa	church	quadro	picture
chiostro	cloister	(in) restauro	restoration in progress
chiuso	closed		
città	city	rivolgersi a	refer to
civico	civic, municipal	rocca	fortress, castle
convento	convent, monastery	rovine, ruderi	ruins
cortile	courtyard	sagrestia	sacristy
dintorni	environs	scala	steps, ladder
duomo	cathedral	scavi	excavations
funicolare, funivia	cable-car	seggiovia	chair-lift
giardini	gardens	spiaggia	beach
gola	gorge	tesoro	treasury
lago	lake	torre	tower

Common phrases

Yes, no	Si, no	enough	basta
Sir	Signore	much	molto
Madam	Signora	less	meno
Miss	Signorina	a little	poco
Good morning	buon giorno	large, big	grande
good evening	buona sera	small, little	piccolo
goodbye	arriverderci	all	tutto, tutti
yesterday	ieri	dear	caro
today	oggi	how much ?	quanto costa ?
tomorrow	domani	the way to ?	la strada per ?
morning	mattina	where ?	dove ?
evening	sera	when ?	quando ?
afternoon	pomeriggio	where is ?	dov'è ?
please	per favore	what is the time?	che ore sono ?
thank you	grazie	can one visit ?	si puo visitare ?
pardon	scusi	I do not understand	non capisco

Figures and numbers

0	zero	10	dieci	20	venti
1	uno	11	undici	30	trenta
2	due	12	dodici	40	quaranta
3	tre	13	tredici	50	cinquanta
4	quattro	14	quattordici	60	sessanta
5	cinque	15	quindici	70	settanta
6	sei	16	sedici	80	ottanta
7	sette	17	diciassette	90	novanta
8	otto	18	diciotto	100	cento
9	nove	19	diciannove	1 000	mille

Admission times and charges

As admission times and charges are liable to alteration, the information printed below - valid for 1995 - is for guidance only.

Order: The information is listed in the same order as in the Sights Section of the guide.

⊙: Every sight for which times and charges are listed below is indicated by the symbol ⊙ after the title in the Sights Section of the guide.

Dates: The dates given are inclusive. The list of main public holidays appears in the Practical Information section.

Times: The clocks change in spring and autumn dividing the year into summer time (ora solare) and winter time (ora legale).
Ticket offices usually shut 30min before closing time; only exceptions are mentioned below.
Most churches do not admit visitors during services and are closed during the afternoon siesta.
It is advisable to make an early start in the day as many museums are shut in the afternoon.
It is also advisable to check before setting out as many sights are being restored, some over a period of several years. Some museums may be completely or partially closed for restoration or for lack of staff.

Charge: The charge given is for an individual adult. Concessionary rates may be available for families, children, students, old-age pensioners and the unemployed. Many places offer special rates for group bookings provided they are made in advance. For some sights and museums admission is free during Heritage week (Settimana dei Beni Cultuali) in December.

Telephone: Telephone numbers are preceded by an area dialling code (prefisso) - in front of the oblique stroke; omit the zero when dialling from abroad.

Tourist Information Centres: The addresses and telephone numbers of the local Tourist Information Centres, indicated by the symbol ⓑ, are given opposite the names of the main towns.

TUSCAN VILLAS (Introduction)

Villa de Cetinale – Visits by appointment.

Villa di Poggio Imperiale – Open by appointment only; apply by telephone between 1000 and 1200. ☎ 055/220151.

Villa Rospigliosi a Lamporecchio – Part of a seminary. To visit apply in advance. ☎ 0573/803432 (Signor Taddei).

Villa del Trebbio – Open by appointment Tuesdays and Thursdays, 1100 to 1200. ☎ 055/8458793 (Associazione Turismo e Ambiente).

A

ABBADIA SAN SALVATORE   ⓑ via Mentana 97, 53021; ☎ 0577/778608

ABETONE   ⓑ via Marconi 28, San Marcello Pistoiese; ☎ 0573/630145

Excursion

San Marcello Pistoiese: Museo Ferruciano – Open July and August, daily, 0930 (1000 Sundays and public holidays) to 1230 and 1600 (1700 Sundays and public holidays) to 1900; September to June, Thursdays and Saturdays, 1500 to 1700. L1 000. ☎ 0573/630439.

ANGHIARI

Museo statale di Palazzo Taglieschi – Open 0900 to 1830. Closed 1 January, 1 May and 25 December. No admission charge. ☎ 0575/788001.

ARCIPELAGO TOSCANO

Isola del Giglio – Ferry from Porto San Stefano to Giglio Porto (1 hour) daily. Information from Toremar-agenzia Cavero, via Umberto I. ☎ 0564/809349.

Isola di Giannutri – Ferry from Porto San Stefano or from Isola del Giglio in summer daily, in winter less frequently. Information from Navalgiglio, via Privinciale 31, Isola del Giglio. ☎ 0564/812920 (Porto San Stefano) or 809309 and 809469 (Isola del Giglio).

Capraia – Ferry from Livorno daily. Information from Toremar, via Calafati 6, Livorno. ☎ 0586/896113.

AREZZO
🛈 piazza Risorgimento 116, 52100; ☎ 0575/23952

Casa del Vasari – Open 0900 to 1900. Closed 1 January, Easter Sunday, 1 May, 15 August and 25 December. No admission charge. Ring at the door.

Museo d'arte medievale e moderna – Open 0900 to 1900. Closed 1 January, 1 May and 25 December. L8 000. ☎ 0575/300301.

Museo archeologico – Open 0900 to 1400 (1300 Sundays and public holidays). Closed 1 January, 1 May and 25 December. L8 000. ☎ 0575/20882.

Saracen joust, Arezzo.

ARTIMINIO

Villa medicea la Ferdinanda: Museo archeologico etrusco – Open all year, Sundays to Tuesdays and Thursdays and Fridays, 0900 to 1300 (1230 Sundays and public holidays), Saturdays, 1500 to 1900. L5 000. ☎ 055/8718124.

Excursions

Comeana: Tomba di Montefortini – Open daily except Mondays, 0800 to 1900 (1400 in winter). No admission charge.

ASCIANO

Museo di arte sacra – Open on request by applying to the parish of Sant'Agata. ☎ 0577/718207.

Museo archeologico – Open 15 June to 15 September, daily except Mondays, 1000 to 1230 and 1630 to 1830; otherwise, 1000 to 1230. L3 000; combined ticket with the Museo Amos e Giuseppe Cassioli L5 000.

Museo Cassioli – Open 15 June to 15 September, daily except Mondays, 1000 to 1230 and 1630 to 1830; mid-September to mid-June, 1000 to 1230. L3 000; combined ticket with the Museo Archeologico L5 000.

B

BARGA

Excursions

Castelvecchio Pascoli: Casa di Giovanni Pascoli – Guided tour (30min) summer, daily except Mondays, 1000 to 1300 and 1500 to 1830; winter, 1000 to 1300 and 1430 to 1700. L5 000. ☎ 0583/723352.

Grotta del Vento – Guided tour (1 hour) all year, daily at 1000, 1100, 1200, 1400, 1500, 1600, 1700, 1800; in winter except public holidays (2 hours) at 1100, 1500, 1600, 1700 and (3 hours) at 1000, 1400. L10 000 (1 hour); L18 000 (2 hours); L25 000 (3 hours). Information from ☎ 0583/722024.

BUONCONVENTO

Museo d'arte sacra della Val d'Arbia – Open Tuesdays and Thursdays, 1000 to 1200, Saturdays, 1000 to 1200 and 1600 to 1800, Sundays and public holidays, 0900 to 1300. L2 500. ☎ 0577/806012.

C

CAMALDOLI

Eremo – Open weekdays, 0830 to 1115 and 1500 to 1800; Sundays and public holidays, 0830 to 1045 and 1500 to 1800.

CAMPIGLIA MARITTIMA

Scavi (Archeological Excavations) – Open daily except Saturdays, Sundays and public holidays, 0800 to 1700. Make appointment the day before by calling 0565/83911. No admission charge.

CAPALBIO

Excursion

Giardino dei Tarrocchi (Tarot Gardens) – Open in summer, Monday to Saturday, 1500 to 1930. Advance notice advisable. ☎ 0564/895032.

CAPRESE MICHELANGELO

Museo Michelangiolesco – Open 0900 to 1200 and 1500 to 1700. No admission charge. ☎ 0575/793912.

CARRARA

🛈 Lungomare Vespucci 24, 54037 Marina di Massa; ☎ 0585/240046 or 542344 or 243636

Museo del marmo (Marble Museum) – Open April to October, daily except Sundays and public holidays, 1000 to 1300 and 1600 to 1900; November to March, daily except Sundays and public holidays, 1000 to 1300 and 1400 to 1700. L4 000. ☎ 0585/845746.

CASTAGNETO CARDUCCI

Museo archivio Giosuè Carducci – Open mid-June to late September, daily except Mondays, 1730 to 1930 and 2030 to 2300. No admission charge. ☎ 0565/77068 or 778411.

CASTELFIORENTINO

Raccolta Comunale d'Arte – Open all year, Tuesdays, Thursdays, Saturdays, 1600 to 1900, Sundays and public holidays, 1000 to 1200 and 1600 to 1900. Closed 1 February, in August and 25 December. L3 000. ☎ 0571/64019.

CASTELLO

Villa di Castello – Open all year, daily, 0900 to 1930 (1830 April, May and September; 1730 March and October; 1630 November to February). Closed 1 January, 1 May and 25 December. L4 000 (ticket also valid for Villa della Petraia). ☎ 055/454791.

Villa della Petraia – Same admission charges and times as Villa di Castello. ☎ 055/451208.

CASTIGLION FIORENTINO

Pinacoteca – Open 1 April to 30 September, daily except Mondays, 1000 to 1230 and 1600 to 1830; 1 October to 30 March, daily except Mondays, 1000 to 1230 and 1530 to 1800. L2 000. ☎ 0575/658042-3.

Chiesa del Gesù – Open Sunday mornings. Further information available from the priest. ☎ 0575/658080.

CECINA

Museo archeologico – Open 16 June to 15 September, Tuesdays to Saturdays, 1700 to 1900, Sundays and public holidays, 0900 to 1200; 16 September to 15 December and 15 January to 15 June, Tuesdays, Thursdays and Fridays, 1500 to 1800. L3 000. ☎ 0586/660411.

Excursions

Rosignano Marittimo: Museo archeologico – Open last week in June to mid-September, daily except Mondays, 1730 to 2330; otherwise, Tuesdays to Fridays, 0900 to 1400, Saturdays and Sundays and public holidays, 1600 to 1900. L5 000. ☎ 0586/799232.

CERRETO GUIDI

Villa medicea – Open daily, 0900 to 1900 (1400 Sundays and public holidays). L4 000. ☎ 0571/55707.

CERTALDO

Casa museo di Boccaccio – Open 1000 to 1230 and 1500 to 1900. Closed 25 December. No admission charge. ☎ 0571/664208.

Palazzo Pretorio – Open 26 March to 26 September, daily except Mondays, 1000 to 1230 and 1630 to 1930; 27 September to 25 March, daily except Mondays, 1000 to 1200 and 1530 to 1800. L2 500. ☎ 0571/661219.

CETONA

Museo civico per la preistoria del Monte Cetona – Open 1 June to 30 September, daily except Mondays, 0900 to 1300 and 1700 to 1900; 1 to 15 October, daily except Mondays, 0900 to 1300 and 1600 to 1800; 16 October to 31 May, Saturdays, 1600 to 1800, Sundays and public holidays, 0930 to 1230. L3 500 (ticket also valid for Belverde). ☎ 0578/238004-239143.

Excursion

Belverde Caves – Guided tour 1 July to 15 October, daily except Mondays, 0900 to 1230 and 1600 to 1900. Museum ticket also valid for this visit. ☎ 0578/227667.

CHIANCIANO TERME   🚩 via Sabatini 7, 53042; ☎ 0578/63538

Chianciano Vecchia: Museo di arte sacra – Open June to October, daily except Sundays and Mondays, 1000 to 1200 and 1600 to 1900; November to May by request only, 1000 to 1200 and 1500 to 1700. L3 000. ☎ 0578/30378.

IL CHIANTI

San Casciano in Val di Pesa: Museo di arte sacra – Open May to September, Saturdays, 1730 to 1930, Sundays and public holidays, 1000 to 1230 and 1630 to 1930; October to April, Saturdays, 1630 to 1900, Sundays and public holidays, 1000 to 1230 and 1600 to 1900. No admission charge. ☎ 055/8228220 (Signor Lumachi).

Badia a Passignano (Abbey) – Guided tour by appointment, Saturday afternoons and Sundays. ☎ 055/8071622.

Sant'Appiano: Antiquarium – Open April to September, Saturdays and Sundays, 1500 to 1900.

Brolio Castle – Open 0900 to 1230 and 1430 to 1800. L4 000. ☎ 0577/747104 or 747156.

Castelnuovo Beradenga: Villa Chigi Park – Open 1 April to 30 September, Sundays and holidays, 1000 to 2000 (1700 October to March). No admission charge. ☎ 0577/355453.

CHIUSI   🚩 via Petrarca 3; ☎ 0578/21663

Museo archeologico (e tombe etrusche) – Open 0900 to 1400 (1300 Sundays and public holidays). Closed 1 January, 1 May, 25 December. L4 000. ☎ 0578/20177.

Museo della cattedrale – Open 1 June to 15 October, 0930 to 1245 and 1630 to 1930; 16 October to 31 May, 0930 to 1245 (also Sundays and public holidays, 1600 to 1900). Closed at Easter and Christmas. L3 000. ☎ 0578/226490.

Excursion

Catacombe di Santa Mustiola e di Santa Caterina – Guided tour (1 hour) of one tomb daily at 1100; Sundays and public holidays advance booking essential. Coach departs from Museo della Cattedrale. L6 000. ☎ 0578/226490.

COLLE DI VAL D'ELSA

Museo archeologico Bianchi Bandinelli – Open May to September, daily except Mondays, 1000 to 1200 and 1600 to 1800 (1900 Saturdays, Sundays and public holidays); October to April, Tuesdays to Fridays, 1530 to 1730, Saturdays, Sundays and public holidays, 1000 to 1200 and 1500 to 1800. L3 000. ☎ 0577/920490.

Museo civico – Open April to September, Tuesdays to Fridays, 1700 to 1900, Saturdays, 1000 to 1200 and 1700 to 1900, Sundays and public holidays, 1000 to 1200 and 1600 to 1900; October to March, Tuesdays to Fridays, 1530 to 1730, Saturdays, Sundays, public holidays, 1000 to 1200 and 1530 to 1830. L3 000.

COLLODI

Villa Garzoni (Castle and gardens) – Open 21 March to 31 October, 0800 to sunset; 1 November to 20 March, 0900 to sunset. L10 000. The castle may be closed in 1995.

Parco di Pinocchio – Open 0830 to sunset. ☎ 0572/429342 or 429613.

CORTONA 🛈 via Nazionale 72; ☎ 0575/630352

Palazzo comunale (Sala del Consiglio) – Open daily except Sundays and public holidays, 0900 to 1300. Apply the previous day by telephone or ask for the keys on the upper floor of the palace during office hours. ☎ 0575/6371.

Museo dell'Accademia etrusca – Open April to September, daily except Mondays, 1000 to 1300 and 1600 to 1900; October to March, daily except Mondays, 0900 to 1300 and 1500 to 1700. L5 000. ☎ 0575/637235 or 630415.

Museo diocesano – Open all year, daily except Mondays, 0900 to 1300 and 1500 to 1830 (1700 October to March). L5 000.

San Domenico – Open 0900 to 1200 and 1530 to 1900 (1700 in winter). When closed, ring the bell.

Excursions

Le Celle – Open 0730 to 1200 and 1330 to 1900. ☎ 0575/603362.

Abazzia di Farneta – Guided tour by the priest; advance notice of at least one day advisable. ☎ 0575/610010.

COSA

Ansedonia: Museo-Antiquarium – Open May to September, 0900 to 1900, otherwise, 0900 to 1400. No admission charge. ☎ 0564/881421.

Scavi (Excavations) – Open all year, 0900 to 2000 (1700 October to April). No admission charge. ☎ 0564/881421.

For historical information on the region consult the table and notes in the Introduction

E

Isola d'ELBA 🛈 Calata Italia 26, 57037 Portoferraio; ☎ 0565/914671

Portoferraio: Villa dei Mulini – Open all year, daily, 0900 to 1900 (1400 in winter; 1330 Sundays and public holidays). Closed 1 January and 1 May. L8 000 (ticket also valid for the Villa Napoleone di San Martino).

Monte Capanne – Access by cable-car *(cabinovia)* August, 1000 to 1215 and 1400 to 1830 (1900 last cable-car from the summit); Easter to July and September to October, 1000 to 1245 and 1430 to 1800 (1830, May and June, last cable-car from the summit). L16 000 Return.

Marciana: Archeological museum – Open 15 June to 15 September, Mondays to Fridays, 0900 to 1300 and 1600 to 1900; Saturdays and public holidays, 0900 to 1300. L3 000. ☎ 0565/901215.

Villa Napoleone di San Martino – Same charges and admission times as for the Villa dei Mulini de Portoferraio (see above). ☎ 0565/914688.

EMPOLI

Museo della Collegiata – Open Thursdays to Saturdays, 0900 to 1200 and 1600 to 1900; Sundays and public holidays, 1000 to 1200 only. Closed 1 January, Easter Sunday, 15 August and 25 December. L4 000, ticket also valid for Santo Stefano. ☎ 0571/76284.

Excursion

Montelupo Fiorentino: Museo archeologico e della ceramica – Open daily except Mondays, 0900 to 1200 and 1430 to 1900. Closed Easter Sunday, 15 August and 25 December. L5 000, child L3 500. ☎ 0571/51087.

F

FIESOLE

Convento di S Francesco: Church and museum of the Franciscan missions – Open in summer, Mondays to Saturdays, 0900 to 1230 and 1500 to 1900, Sundays and public holidays, 0900 to 1100 and 1500 to 1900; in winter, Mondays to Saturdays, 0930 to 1230 and 1500 to 1800, Sundays and public holidays, 0900 to 1100 and 1500 to 1800. No admission charge; donation welcome. ☎ 055/59477.

Archeology Zone - Museo archeologico – Open 0900 to 1900 (1800 Tuesdays and in winter). L5 000. ☎ 055/59477.

Antiquarium Costantini – Open daily except Tuesdays, 0900 to 1800. Closed 1 January, 1 May, Easter Sunday, 15 August and 25 December. L5 000. ☎ 055/59477.

Museo Bandini – Open in summer, daily except Tuesdays, 0930 (1000 in winter) to 1300 and 1500 to 1900 (1800 in winter). L5 000; combined ticket with Antiquarium Costantini L6 000. ☎ 055/59477.

FIRENZE (Florence)   🚻 via Manzoni 16, 50121; ☎ 055/23320
No admission charge to the city museums for children under 12

Duomo (Cathedral) – Open 1000 (1300 Sundays) to 1700.

Dome – daily except Sundays, 1000 to 1730. Closed 1 and 6 January, Maundy Thursday to Easter Sunday, 24 June, 15 August, 1 November, 8, 25 and 26 December. L5 000. ☎ 055/230 2885.

Belltower (Campanile) – Open April to October, 0900 to 1930; November to March, 0900 to 1700. Closed 1 January, Easter Sunday and at Christmas. L5 000 ☎ 055/2302885.

Baptistery (Battistero) – Open 1330 to 1800; Sundays and public holidays, 0900 to 1300. ☎ 055/230 2885.

General view of Florence.

Museo dell'Opera del Duomo – Open April to October, daily except Sundays, 0900 to 1930 (1800 in winter; 1300 public holidays in winter). Closed 1 January, Easter Sunday and at Christmas. L5 000. ☎ 055/2302885.

Palazzo Vecchio – Open Mondays to Wednesdays, Fridays and Saturdays, 0900 to 1900, Sundays and public holidays 0800 to 1300. Closed 1 January, Easter Sunday, 1 May, 15 August and 25 December. L8 000. ☎ 055/27681.

Galleria degli Uffizi – Open daily except Mondays, 0900 to 1900 (1400 Sundays and public holidays). Closed 1 January, 1 May and 25 December. L12 000. ☎ 055/23885.

Palazzo Pitti – **Galleria Palatina:** Open daily except Mondays, 0900 to 1400. L12 000. ☎ 055/216673. **Appartamenti reali:** in summer same times as the Galleria Palatina; in winter, by appointment. L12 000. ☎ 055/2388611. **Galleria d'Arte Moderna:** Open daily except Mondays, 0900 to 1400. L4 000. ☎ 055/287096. **Museo degli Argenti:** Open daily except Mondays and public holidays, 0900 to 1400. L8 000. ☎ 055/212557-2388658. **Galleria del Costume:** Open daily except Mondays, 0900 to 1400. Closed 1 May and 25 December. L8 000. ☎ 055/212557.

Giardino di Boboli – **Gardens:** Open all year, daily except first and last Monday in the month, 0900 to 1930 (1630 in winter). L4 000. ☎ 055/213440. **Museo delle Porcellane:** Closed.

Palazzo e museo del Bargello – Open daily except Mondays, 0900 to 1400; 25 April to 15 August, possible alternate closure with other museums; information by telephone. Closed 1 January, 1 May and 25 December. L8 000. ☎ 055/2388606.

San Lorenzo – **Church:** Open 0700 to 1200 and 1530 to 1730. **Biblioteca Medicea Laurenziana:** Open daily except Sundays and public holidays, 0900 to 1300. No admission charge. ☎ 055/210760 or 214443. **Cappelle Medicee:** Open daily except Mondays, 0900 to 1400. Closed 1 January, Easter Sunday, 1 May and 25 December. **Drawings attributed to Michelangelo:** Access variable; information from the ticket office. L9 000. ☎ 055/2388602.

Palazzo Medici Riccardi – Open Mondays, Tuesdays and Thursdays to Saturdays, 0900 to 1300 and 1500 to 1800, Sundays and public holidays, 0900 to 1300. Closed 1 January, 1 May, 15 August and 25 December. L6 000. ☎ 055/2760526 or 2760340.

Convento e museo di San Marco – Open daily except Mondays, 0900 to 1400. Closed 1 January, 1 May and 25 December. L8 000. ☎ 055/2388608.

Galleria dell'Accademia – Open daily except Mondays, 0900 to 1900 (1400 Sundays and public holidays and in winter); summer times may apply all year. Closed 1 January, 1 May and 25 December. L12 000. ☎ 055/2388612.

Santa Maria Novella – **Church:** Open Sundays, 1530 to 1700, Mondays to Saturdays, all day. Guided tours available 0700 to 1130 and 1500 to 1800. ☎ 055/210113. **Monumental cloisters:** Open Sundays and public holidays, 0800 to 1300, Mondays to Thursdays and Saturdays, 0900 to 1400. Closed 1 January, Easter Sunday, 1 May, 15 August and 25 December. L4 000. ☎ 055/282187.

Santa Croce – **Church:** Open in summer, Mondays to Saturdays, 0800 to 1830, Sundays and public holidays, 0800 to 1230 and 1500 to 1830; in winter, Mondays to Saturdays, 0800 to 1230 and 1500 to 1830, Sundays and public holidays, 1500 to 1800. **Cloisters, the Pazzi Chapel and Museo dell'Opera di S Croce:** Open March to September, daily except Wednesdays, 1000 to 1230 and 1430 to 1830; October to February, daily except Wednesdays, 1000 to 1230 and 1500 to 1700. Closed 1 January and 25 December. L3 000. ☎ 055/244619 or 2342289.

Santa Maria del Carmine: Cappella Brancacci – Open daily except Tuesdays, 1000 (1300 Sundays and public holidays) to 1630. L5 000. ☎ 055/288671.

Passeggiata ai Colli (Piazzale Michelangelo) – Buses nos 12 and 13 operate clockwise and anticlockwise on the circular route (Viale dei Colli) starting from the terminus at Santa Maria Novella and passing through Piazzale Michelangelo south of the river; useful central stops are Piazza del Duomo, Teatro Comunale, Museo della Scienza and Boboli Gardens (Porta Romana entrance).

Forte di Belvedere – Open in summer, 0900 to 2000, in winter, 0900 to 1630. No admission charge. ☎ 055/2342822.

Museo della Casa fiorentina antica – Open daily except Mondays, 0900 to 1400. L4 000.

Palazzo Rucellai: Museo di storia della fotografia – Open daily except Wednesdays, 1000 to 1930 (2330 Fridays and Saturdays). Closed in August; 25 December. L8 000. ☎ 055/218975.

Santissima Annunziata Church – Open 0730 to 1230 and 1600 to 1900.

Ospedale degli Innocenti: Art Gallery – Open daily except Wednesdays, 0830 to 1400 (1330 Sundays and public holidays). Closed 1 January, Easter Sunday, 1 May, 15 August and 25 December. L3 000. ☎ 055/2479317.

Orsanmichele – Open 0800 to 1200 and 1500 to 1830.

Cenacolo di Santo Spirito – Open daily except Mondays, 1000 to 1300. Closed 1 January, Easter Sunday, 1 May, 15 August and 25 December. L3 000. ☎ 055/2398483.

Cenacolo di Sant'Apollonia – Open daily except Mondays, 0900 to 1400. Closed 1 January, 1 May and 25 December. Donation. ☎ 055/2388607.

Ognissanti - Church: Open 0800 to 1200 and 1600 to 1900. **Cenacolo:** Open all year except August, Mondays, Tuesdays and Saturdays, 0900 to 1200. No charge.

Cenacolo di Fuligno – Open Mondays to Saturdays, 0900 to 1200 and 1500 to 1700; Sundays and public holidays, 0900 to 1200. Closed 1 January, Easter, 1 May, 15 August, 25 December. L4 000. Information from Sezione Didattica degli Uffizi. ☎ 055/284272.

Cenacolo di San Salvi – Open Tuesdays to Saturdays, 0900 to 1400; Sundays and public holidays, 0900 to 1300. L4 000.

Crocifissio del Perugino – Open 0900 to 1200 and 1700 to 1900. Donation. ☎ 055/2478420.

Chiostro dello Scalzo – Open Mondays to Thursdays, 0900 to 1300. Ring the doorbell. Donation.

Sinagoga – Open April to September, Sundays to Thursdays, 1000 to 1300 and 1400 to 1700, Fridays, 1000 to 1300; October to March, Mondays to Thursdays, 1100 to 1300 and 1400 to 1700, Fridays and Sundays, 1000 to 1300. ☎ 055/245252.

Museo Archeologico – Open daily except Mondays, 0900 to 1400 (1300 Sundays and public holidays). L8 000. ☎ 055/23575.

Casa Buonarroti – Open daily except Tuesdays, 0930 to 1330. Closed 1 January, Easter Sunday, 25 April, 1 May, 15 August and 25 December. L8 000. ☎ 055/241752.

Opificio delle Pietre dure – Open daily except Sundays and public holidays, 0900 to 1400. L4 000. ☎ 055/210102 or 289414. Detailed commentary in various languages available on request.

Museo di Storia della Scienza – Open daily except Sundays and public holidays, 0930 to 1300; also Mondays, Wednesdays and Fridays, 1400 to 1700. Closed 24 June. L10 000. ☎ 055/293493.

Museo Marino Marini – Open June to August, daily except Tuesdays, 1000 to 1300 and 1600 to 1900; September to May, daily except Tuesdays, 1000 to 1300 and 1500 to 1800. Closed 1 May and 25 December. L5 000. ☎ 055/219432.

Museo Bardini – Open daily except Wednesdays, 0900 to 1400 (1300 Sundays and public holidays). Closed 1 January, Easter Sunday, 1 May, 15 August and 25 December. L5 000. ☎ 055/2342427.

Museo La Specola – Via Romana, 17. Open daily except Wednesdays, 0900 to 1200 (1300 Sundays). Closed 1 January, Easter Sunday, the week of 15 August and 24 to 26 December. L6 000. ☎ 055/222451.

Museo Stibbert – Open 0900 to 1300. L5 000. ☎ 055/486049.

Museo storico topografico "Firenze com'era" – Open daily except Thursdays, 1000 to 1300. Closed 1 January, Easter Sunday, 1 May, 15 August and 25 December. L3 000. ☎ 055-2398483.

Casa di Dante – Open in summer daily except Tuesdays, 0930 to 1300; in winter 1000 to 1600 (1400 Sundays). L5 000.

Excursions

Quinto Alto: Tomba etrusca della Montagnola – Open 15 April to 30 September, Tuesdays and Thursdays, 1000 to 1300, Saturdays and Sundays, 1000 to 1300 and 1700 to 1900; October to 14 April, Saturdays and Sundays, 1000 to 1300. No charge. ☎ 055/44961.

Villa Demidoff Park – Open May to last Sunday in September, Thursdays to Sundays, 1000 to 2000. L5 000. Advance notice advisable. ☎ 055/409427 (caretaker) or 055/2760538 (Park Official).

Convento del Monte Senario – Open 0900 to 1200 and 1500 to 1900.

G

GALLUZZO

Certosa del Galluzzo – Guided tour (45min) daily except Mondays, 0900 to 1200 and 1500 to 1900 (1800 Sundays and public holidays; 1700 in winter). Donation.

GROSSETO   🅾 via Monterosa 206, 58100; ☎ 0564/454510 or 454527

Museo diocesano – Open 1 June to 30 September, daily except Mondays, 1000 to 1300 and 1500 to 1900; May and 1 October to 15 November, daily except Mondays, 1000 to 1200 and 1500 to 1800. ☎ 0564/615568.

I

IMPRUNETA

Museo del Tesoro – Open June to September, Saturdays, Sundays and public holidays, 1000 to 1300 and 1630 to 2000, Thursdays and Fridays, 1000 to 1300; October to May, Sundays and public holidays, 1000 to 1300 and 1500 to 1830, Fridays, 1000 to 1300, Saturdays, 1500 to 1800. Closed Easter Sunday and at Christmas. L2 000. ☎ 055/2011700.

The annual Michelin Red Guide Italia
revises its selection of establishements which
– serve carefully prepared meals at a reasonable price
– include service on the bill or in the price of each dish
– offer a menu of simple but good food at a modest cost
– provide free parking
It is well worth buying the current edition

L

LIVORNO   🅾 piazza Cavour 6, 57100; ☎ 0586/899111

Bottini dell'Olio (Oil Pits) – Apply to the Ufficio Cultura; ☎ 0586/820517.

Aquarium – Open March to September, daily except Mondays, 0930 to 1230 and 1600 to 1900; February and October, 0930 to 1230 and 1500 to 1800; November to January, 0930 to 1230 and 1430 to 1730. Closed 1 January, Easter Sunday, 1 May, 15 May, 15 August and 25 December. L2 500. ☎ 0586/805504.

Museo civico G Fattori – Villa Mimbelli, via Jacopo in Acquaviva. Open daily except Mondays and public holidays, 1000 to 1300 and 1600 to 1900. L8 000. ☎ 0586/808001.

Museo Pietro Mascagni – Open Thursdays and Saturdays, 1000 to 1300 and 1600 to 1900. Closed public holidays. No admission charge. ☎ 0586/852695.

Excursion

Montenero Sanctuary – Open 0630 to 1230 and 1430 to 1900 (1800 in winter).

LUCCA   🅾 piazza Guidiccioni 2, 55100; ☎ 0583/491205

Museo della cattedrale – Open May to September, daily except Mondays, 1000 to 1800 (1900 Saturdays, Sundays and public holidays); October and March, daily except Mondays, 1000 to 1800; November to February, daily except Mondays, 1000 to 1600 (1700 Saturdays, Sundays and public holidays). L5 000. ☎ 0583/490530.

Battistero e chiesa dei Santi Giovanni e Reparata – Open June to September, daily except Mondays, 1000 to 1800; October to May, daily except Mondays, 1000 to 1300 and 1500 to 1800. Closed Easter Sunday morning and 25 December. Guided tour (20min) of excavations available. Church L1 000; church and excavations L5 000. ☎ 0583/490530.

Guinigi Tower – Open March to September, 0900 to 1930; otherwise, 1000 to 1630 (1800 October). Closed 25 December. L4 500. ☎ 0583/48524.

Pinacoteca – Open daily except Mondays, 0900 to 1900 (1400 Sundays and public holidays). Closed 1 January, 1 May and 25 December. L8 000. ☎ 0583/55570.

Casa natale di Puccini – Open all year, daily except Mondays, 1000 (1100 October to March) to 1300 and 1500 to 1800 (1700 October to March). Closed 1 January and 25 December. L3 000. ☎ 0583/584028. Guided tour.

Museo Nazionale di Villa Guinigi – Open daily except Mondays, 0900 to 1900 (1400 Sundays and public holidays and also in winter). Closed 1 January, 1 May and 25 December. L4 000. ☎ 0583/46033.

San Michele, Lucca.

S. Chirol

Excursions

Villa Reale di Marlia – Guided tour (1 hour) March to November, daily except Mondays at 1000, 1100, 1500, 1600, 1700 and 1800. L8 000. ☎ 0583/30108 or 30009.

Camigliano: Villa Torrigiani – Guided tour March to October, daily except Tuesdays, 1000 to 1200 and 1500 to sunset. L12 000 (villa and park), L7 000 (park). ☎ 0583/928041.

Segromigno: Villa Mansi – Open May to September, daily except Mondays, 0930 to 1230 and 1430 to 1900; October to April, daily except Mondays, 1000 to 1300 and 1430 to 1800. Closed 25 December. L7 000 (park and villa). ☎ 0583/920096.

LUCIGNANO

Palazzo comunale museo – Open daily except Mondays, 0930 to 1300 and 1500 to 1930 (1830 in winter). Closed 25 December. L5 000. ☎ 0575/836128.

LUNIGIANA

Aulla: Natural History Museum – Open daily except Mondays, 0900 to 1200 and 1500 to 1800. L3 000. ☎ 0187/400252.

Equi Terme: Caves – Open 15 July to 30 September, Mondays to Saturdays, 1000 to 1200 and 1500 to 1700, Sundays and public holidays, 1000 to 1900; 1 October to 14 July, Sundays and public holidays, 1000 to 1200 and 1400 and 1700. Admission price not available.

Villafranca in Lunigiana: Ethnography Museum – Open June to September, daily except Mondays, 0900 to 1200 and 1600 to 1900; October to May, daily except Mondays, 0900 to 1200 and 1500 to 1700 (1800 Saturdays, Sundays and holidays). Closed 1 January, Easter Sunday and 25 December. L5 000. ☎ 0187/493417 or 494400.

Pontremoli: Museum of Statues and Steles – Open June to September, daily except Mondays, 0900 to 1200 and 1600 to 1900; October to May, daily except Mondays, 0900 to 1200 and 1400 to 1700. L3 000.

Respect the life of the countryside

Drive carefully on country roads

Protect wildlife, plants and trees

M

MAGLIANO IN TOSCANA

Necropolis – Apply to Mr Vasco Vellati; ☎ 0564/592297.

MAREMMA

Alberese: Parco naturale della Maremma – Guided tours from the Centre for visits to the park (Centro Opene del Parco) Wednesdays, Saturdays and Sundays at 0700 (to **San Rabano Abbey**) and at 0800 and 1600 (to the **Torri**). Guided tour (forest and wild life), daily, 0730 to 1000 and 1600 to 1800. Guided tour of the pinewoods and marshes of the Maremma (it is advisable to visit early in the morning or late in the afternoon). Times may vary according to the seasons and number of participants. L7 500 (including guide and transport); L4 500 (for guide book on the forest and wild life). Ticket office and information at the Centro Visite del Parco; ☎ 0564/407098.

MASSA CARRARA   🛈 Lungomare Vespucci 24, Marina di Massa; ☎ 0585/240046

MASSA MARITTIMA

Palazzo del Podestà (Archeological Museum) – Open all year, daily except Mondays, 1000 to 1230 and 1530 to 1900 (2300 16 July to 31 August; 1700 October to March). L5 000. ☎ 0566/902289.

Fortezza del Senesi et Torre del Candeliere – Open 16 July to 31 August, daily except Mondays, 1000 to 1300 and 1600 to 2000; 1 April to 15 July and September, daily except Mondays, 1100 to 1300 and 1630 to 1900. L2 500. ☎ 0566/902289.

Museo di storia e arte delle miniere – Open 16 July to 31 August, daily except Mondays, 1000 to 1230 and 1530 to 1900; 1 April to 15 July and September, daily except Mondays, 1000 to 1100 and 1530 to 1700. L2 500. ☎ 0566/902289.

Antico frantoio – Guided tour April to September, daily except Mondays, 1000 to 1230 and 1530 to 1900. L2 000. ☎ 0566/902289.

San Francesco – Open all year, 0830 to 2000 (1730 in winter). ☎ 0566/902641.

Museo della Miniera – Guided tour (40min) 16 July to 31 August, daily except Mondays at 1000, 1030, 1100, 1130, 1200, 1530, 1600, 1630, 1700, 1730, 1800 and 1830; 1 April to 15 July and September daily except Mondays at 1010, 1100, 1150, 1540, 1630, 1720 and 1820; October to January and March at 1000, 1030, 1100, 1130, 1530 and 1600. L5 000. ☎ 0566/902289.

MONTALCINO

Rocca – Access via the wine cellar; open summer, 0900 to 1300 and 1430 to 2000; winter, 0900 to 1300 and 1400 to 1800.

Museo civico e diacesano – Open all year, daily except Mondays, 0930 (1000 October to April) to 1300 and 1530 (1500 October to April) to 1700. L3 500. ☎ 0577/848135.

MONTECATINI TERME   🛈 viale Verdi 66/A; ☎ 0572/772244

Museo dell'Accademia d'Arte – Open April to October, Mondays, Wednesdays and Fridays, 1600 to 1930; November to March, on written application to the Accademia d'Arte, viale Diaz 6, 51016 Montecatini Terme (Pistoia).

MONTE OLIVETO MAGGIORE

Abbazia – Open 0915 to 1200 and 1515 to 1745 (1700 in winter). ☎ 0577/707106.

MONTEPULCIANO   🛈 via Ricci 9; ☎ 0578/758687

Palazzo comunale: Tower – Open daily except Sundays and public holidays, 0800 to 1300. No charge. Ask the attendant for access (staircase straight and narrow). ☎ 0578/757442.

Museo Civico – Open April to October, daily except Mondays and Tuesdays, 0930 to 1300 and 1500 to 1800; otherwise by request. L3 000. ☎ 0578/716943.

MUGELLO

San Piero a Sieve: San Martino fortress – Closed for restoration. ☎ 055/848432 (Town Hall).

Vicchio: Museo Beato Angelico – Open Thursdays to Sundays, 1500 to 1900; other days by appointment. ☎ 055/8497026. L1 000.

Vespignano: Casa natale di Giotto – Open Thursdays to Sundays, 1500 to 1900; other days by appointment. ☎ 055/8497026. L1 000.

MURLO

Antiquarium di Poggio Civitate – Open May to September, daily, 0930 to 1230 and 1500 to 1830 (1900 Saturdays, Sundays and public holidays); also July and August, 2100 to 2300; October to March, Tuesdays to Fridays, 0930 to 1230 and 1430 to 1700, Saturdays, Sundays and public holidays, 0930 to 1230 and 1500 to 1730. L5 000. ☎ 0577/814099 or 814213.

P

PESCIA

Gipsotea Libero Andreotti – Open 4 April to 8 November, Wednesdays, Fridays and the last Sunday in the month, 1600 to 1900, Saturdays, 1000 to 1300; 9 November to 3 April, Wednesdays, Fridays and the last Sunday in each month, 1500 to 1800, Saturdays, 1000 to 1300. No charge. ☎ 0572/490057.

PIENZA

Museo del duomo – Open summer 1000 to 1300 and 1600 to 1800; winter 1000 to 1300 and 1500 to 1700. ☎ 0578/748549.

Museo Piccolomini – Guided tour (20min) in summer, daily except Mondays, 1000 to 1230 and 1600 to 1900; in winter, daily except Mondays, 1000 to 1200 and 1500 to 1800. Closed November. L3 500. ☎ 0578/748503.

PIETRASANTA

Museo archeologico – Open Tuesdays to Thursdays, 0900 to 1200, Saturdays, 1500 to 1800, Sundays 1000 to 1230. No admission charge.

San Biago e Sant'Antonio (or della Misericordia) Church – Open 0830 to 1200 and 1500 to 1800. ☎ 0584/70055.

PISA

🛈 piazza del Duomo; ☎ 050/560464
🛈 Lungarno Mediceo 42, 56100 Pisa; ☎ 050-541800 or 542344

Torro pendente – Apply to the Opera della Primaziale Pisana for information on the reopening of the Leaning Tower to the public ☎ 050/561820.

Duomo – Open March to October, Mondays to Saturdays from 1000, Sundays from 1300. L2 000; no charge (November to February). ☎ 050/561820.

Battistero – Open April to September, 0800 to 2000; March and October, 0900 to 1800; November to February, 0900 to 1700. Closed 1 January and 25 December. L8 000 (ticket also valid for another monument in Piazza dei Miracoli); L12 000 (including Museo dell'Opera, Camposanto and Museo delle Sinopie). ☎ 050/561820.

Camposanto – Open April to September, 0800 to 2000; March and October, 0900 to 1800; November to February, 0900 to 1700. Closed 1 January and 25 December. L8 000 (ticket also valid for another monument in the Piazza dei Miracoli); L12 000 (including Museo dell'Opera, Battistero and Museo delle Sinopie). ☎ 050/561820.

Museo delle Sinopie – Open April to September, 0800 to 2000; March and October, 0900 to 1800; November to February, 0900 to 1700. Closed 1 January and 25 December. L8 000 (ticket also valid for another monument in Piazza dei Miracoli); L12 000 (including Museo dell'Opera, Camposanto and Battistero). ☎ 050/561820.

Museo delle'Opera del Duomo – Open April to September, 0800 to 2000; March and October, 0900 to 1800; November to February, 0900 to 1700. Closed 1 January and 25 December. L8 000 (ticket also valid for another monument in Piazza dei Miracoli); L12 000 (including Battistero, Camposanto and Museo delle Sinopie). ☎ 050/561820.

Museo Nazionale di San Matteo – Open daily except Mondays, 0900 to 1900 (1300 Sundays and public holidays). Closed 1 January, 1 May and 25 December. L8 000. ☎ 050/541865.

Excursions

Certosa di Pisa – Guided tour (1 hour) all year, daily except Mondays, 0900 to 1800 (1200 Sundays and public holidays; 1600 in winter), every hour. Closed 1 January, Easter Monday, 1 May and 25 December. L8 000.

Museo di storia naturale (Natural History Museum) – Open July to September, Wednesdays and Fridays to Sundays, 1000 to 1300 and 1500 to 1900 (2330 Saturdays), Tuesdays and Thursdays, 1700 to 2330; October to June, daily except Mondays, 0900 to 1300 and 1430 to 1900. Closed 1 January, 1 to 10 June, 18 to 25 December and 31 December. L5 000. ☎ 050/937751.

PISTOIA

Duomo: Chapel of the altar of San Jacopo – Open 0800 to 0945 and 1030 to 1200; no visiting during mass on Sundays at 0900, 1030, 1200 and 1800. ☎ 0573/25095 or 0573/24063 (Signor Rafanelli).

Battistera di San Giovanni in Corte – Open all year, Tuesdays to Saturdays, 0900 to 1200 and 1630 (1530 October to March) to 1830; Sundays and public holidays, 0900 to 1200. ☎ 0573/25095.

Palazzo dei Vescovi – Open Tuesdays and Thursdays, 0830 to 1300 and 1530 to 1700, Fridays, 0830 to 1300 and 1430 to 1800. Guided tours available (1 hour) at 0830, 1000, 1130 and 1530; also Fridays at 1430 and 1645. L5 000. ☎ 0573/3691.

Chiesa del Tau – Open Mondays to Saturdays, 0800 to 1400. ☎ 055/218741 (Soprintendenza ai beni architettonici).

Palazzo del Tau – Open Tuesdays to Saturdays, 0900 to 1300 and 1500 to 1900, Sundays and public holidays, 0900 to 1230. Closed 1 January, Easter Sunday, 1 May, 15 August and 25 December. L4 000; Saturdays no charge. ☎ 0573/30285 or 31332.

Frieze, Ospedale del Ceppo, Pistoia.

Museo Civico – Open Tuesdays to Saturdays, 0900 to 1300 and 1500 to 1900, Sundays and public holidays, 0900 to 1230. Closed 1 January, Easter Sunday, 1 May, 15 August and 25 December; the afternoons of 6 January, Easter Monday, 1 November, 8 and 26 December. L5 000. ☎ 0573/371214.

POGGIO A CAIANO

Villa – Open all year, 0900 to 1930 (1730 October; 1400 November to April). Closed 1 January, 1 May and 25 December. L4 000. ☎ 055/877012.

POPPI

Castello – Open in summer, 0930 to 1230 and 1530 to 1900; in winter, 0930 to 1230 and 1430 to 1730. L3 000 in winter, L5 000 in summer. ☎ 0575/529964 and 520120.

Zoo – Open 0900 to 2000 (1700 in winter). L7 000. ☎ 0575/504541 or 504542.

POPULONIA

Necropolis – Guided tour (1 hour) 0900 to 2000 (1800 April and 29 September to mid-October; 1700 mid-October to 31 March).

Museo Gaspari – Apply to the pottery shop. L2 500. ☎ 0565/29338 and 29436.

PRATO

Museo dell'opera del Duomo – Open Mondays and Wednesdays to Saturdays, 0930 to 1230 and 1500 to 1800, Sundays and public holidays, 0930 to 1230. Closed 1 January, Easter Sunday, 1 May, 15 August and 25 December. L5 000 (ticket also valid for Galleria comunale). ☎ 0574/29339.

Palazzo Pretorio: Galleria comunale – Same admission times and charges as the Museo dell'Opera del Duomo. ☎ 0574/452302.

Castello dell'Imperatore – Open Mondays and Wednesdays to Saturdays, 0930 to 1230 and 1500 to 1830, Sundays and public holidays, 0930 to 1230. Closed Easter Sunday, 1 May, 15 August, 8 September and 25 December. No charge. ☎ 0574/38207 or 452355 or 452303.

San Francesco: Cappella Migliorati – Open 0630 to 1200 and 1600 to 1900.

Museo d'Arte Contemporanea Luigi Pecci – Open daily except Tuesdays, 1000 to 1900. ☎ 0574/570620.

R

ROMENA

Pieve – Apply to the house on the other side of the road except at meal times.

Castello – Open in summer, 0900 to 1200 and 1500 to 1800; in winter, 0900 to 1200 and 1500 to sunset. Tip the caretaker.

ROSELLE

Scavi (Excavations) – Open May to August, 0730 to 2030; March, April, September and October, 0830 to sunset; November to February, 0900 to 1730. No admission charge. ☎ 0564/402403.

S

SAN GIMIGNANO
🖪 piazza del Duomo 1; ☎ 0577/940008

Collegiata di S Maria Assunta: Capella Santa Fina – Open April to September, 0930 to 1230 and 1500 to 1800; October to March, 0930 to 1230 and 1500 to 1730. Closed 1 and 31 January, Easter Sunday, 1 May and 25 December. L3 000. ☎ 0577/940316.

Museo d'arte sacra (Museum of Sacred Art) – Open April to September, daily except Mondays, 0930 to 1930; October to March, daily except Mondays, 0930 to 1230 and 1430 to 1730.

Museo Etrusco (Etruscan Museum) – Same opening times as the Museo d'arte sacra.

Palazzo del Popolo: Museo civico – Open April to September, 0930 to 1930; March and October, daily except Mondays, 0930 to 1830; November to February, daily except Mondays, 0930 to 1330 and 1400 to 1630. Closed 1 and 31 January, Easter Sunday, 1 May and 25 December. L6 000. ☎ 0577/940340.

Museo di Arti e Mestieri – Open 0930 to 1230 and 1430 to 1830. Closed 1 and 31 January, Easter Sunday, 1 May and 25 December. L4 000.

SAN GIOVANNI VALDARNO

Basilica di Santa Maria delle Grazie: Museo – Open in summer, daily except Mondays, 0600 to 1900; in winter, daily except Mondays, 1500 to 1800; also Thursdays and Saturdays, 1000 to 1200. No admission charge.

SAN MINIATO

Museo diocesano d'Arte Sacra – Open Easter to 31 December, daily except Mondays, 0900 to 1200 and 1630 to 1900; 1 January to Easter, Saturdays, Sundays and public holidays, 1000 to 1200 and 1500 to 1730. L2 000.

SAN QUIRICO D'ORCIA

Excursion

Rocca di Tintinnano – Open 21 June to 30 September, daily, 1000 to 1300 and 1500 to 1930; 1 October to 20 June, Saturdays, Sundays and public holidays, 1000 to 1300 and 1430 to 1800. Closed 25 December. Tours by appointment during the week in winter. ☎ 0577/887363. L3 000.

SANSEPOLCRO
🖪 piazza Matteotti; ☎ 0575/740536

Museo civico – Open June to September, 0900 to 1330 and 1430 to 1930; October to May, 0930 to 1300 and 1430 to 1800; at Easter, 0900 to 1300. Closed on 1 January, 15 August and 25 December. L7 000; no admission charge at Easter, the second Sunday in September and 12 October. ☎ 0575/732218.

Excursion

Monterchi Cemetery Chapel – Open daily except Mondays, 0900 to 1300 and 1400 to 1900 (1800 in winter). L5 000.

SANT'ANTIMO

Abbey – Open Mondays to Saturdays, 1030 to 1230 and 1500 to 1830, Sundays, 0900 to 1030 and 1500 to 1800. **Gregorian mass:** Mondays to Saturdays at 0900, Sundays at 1100.

SAN VIVALDO

Sacro Monte – Guided tour by the Brothers Mondays to Saturdays, 0900 to 1100 and 1500 to sunset; Sundays and public holidays, 1300 to sunset. Advance notice advisable. ☎ 0571/680114.

SESTO FIORENTINO

Museo Richard Ginori della porcellana di Doccia – Open Tuesdays, Thursdays and Saturdays, 0900 to 1300 and 1530 to 1830. Closed public holidays and in August. L5 000. ☎ 055/4210451.

SETTIGNANO

Villa Gamberaia Gardens – Open in summer, daily except Saturdays, Sundays and public holidays, 0800 to 1200 and 1300 to 1900 (1700 in winter). Either ring the bell and wait a long time for the gardener or give advance notice of visit. ☎ 055/697205.

SIENA ⓘ via di Città 43, 53100; ☎ 0577/42209

Palazzo Pubblico – Open 15 March to 15 November, 0930 to 1930 (1330 Sundays and public holidays); otherwise, daily except Sundays and public holidays, 0930 to 1330. Closed 1 January, Easter Sunday, 1 May and 25 December. L6 000. ☎ 0577/292226 or 292232.

Mangia Tower – Open 16 June to 15 September, 1000 to 1900 (1800 16 April to 15 June and 16 September to 15 October; 1700 15 March to 15 April and 16 October to 15 November; 1630 26 to 31 December; 1330 1 January to 14 March and 16 November to 24 December). Closed on 1 January, Easter Sunday, 1 May and 25 December. L4 000.

Duomo – Open 0730 to 1930 (1700 1 November to 15 March).

Museo dell'Opera Metropolitana – Open 16 March to 30 September, 0900 to 1930 (1800 October); 1 November to 15 March, 0900 to 1330. Closed 1 January and 25 December. L5 000. ☎ 0577/283048.

Unfinished transept of Siena Cathedral.

P. Someley/DIAF

Battistero – Open 16 March to 30 September, 0900 to 1930 (1800 October); 1 November to 15 March, 1000 to 1300 and 1430 to 1700. Closed 1 January and 25 December. L3 000. ☎ 0577/283048.

Pinocateca (Picture Gallery) – Open July to September, 0800 to 1900; otherwise, 0830 to 1330 and after 1430 whenever a large enough group has gathered. Closed January 1, 2 May and 25 December. L8 000. ☎ 0577/286143 or 281161.

STIA

Museum of Contemporary Art – Open June to September, Saturdays, Sundays, holidays and day preceding holidays, 1600 to 1900; otherwise, by request. ☎ 0575/58673 or 58673 (Town Hall) or ☎ 0575/583388 (caretaker). L3 000.

Excursion

Porciano Castle – Open 15 August to 15 October, Sundays, 1000 to 1200 and 1500 to 1900. ☎ 0575/582635 (Signora Faminia Goretti).

V

VALLOMBROSA

Monastery – Guided tour in summer, Tuesdays and Thursdays at 1000.

LA VERNA

Monastery – Open 0700 to 1900. ☎ 0575/599356.

VERSILIA

Valdicastello: Casa natale du Giosuè Carducci – Open mid-June to mid-September, daily except Mondays, 1700 to 2000; 16 September to 15 June, Saturdays, 0900 to 1200, Sundays and public holidays, 1500 to 1800. Closed 1 January, Easter Sunday, 25 April, 1 May and 25 December. No admission charge. ☎ 0584/791122.

Massaciuccoli: Antiquarium – Open mid-September to mid-June, Sundays, 0930 to 1230 and 1500 to 1800, Saturdays, 1500 to 1800, other days except Mondays, by appointment; mid-June to mid-September, Sundays, 0900 to 1230 and 1700 to 2000, Tuesdays to Saturdays, 1700 to 2000. Closed Easter Sunday and 25 December. ☎ 0584/975480.

Migliarino-San Rossore-Massaciuccoli Country Park – via Aurelia 4, 56100 Pisa. ☎ 050-525500.

Torre del Lago Puccini: Villa Puccini – Open daily except Mondays, 1000 and 1200 and 1500 to 1700. L5 000. ☎ 0584/341445.

VIAREGGIO
🚩 viale Carducci 10, 55049; ☎ 0584/962233 or 48881

Information on sporting activities or guided tours of the region (Versilia and the lake Massaciuccoli area) available from the Tourist Office.

VINCI

Museo Vinciano – Open 0930 to 1900 (1800 in winter); Easter Sunday, 1 May and 15 August, 1400 to 1900. Closed 1 January and 25 December. L5 000. ☎ 0571/56055.

Casa natale di Leonardo – Open in summer, daily except Wednesdays, 0930 to 1300 and 1530 to 1800; Easter Sunday, 1 May and 15 August, 1400 to 1900; in winter, daily except Wednesdays, 0930 to 1300 and 1430 to 1700. Closed 1 January and 25 December. No admission charge. ☎ 0571/56055.

VOLTERRA
🚩 via G Turazza 2; ☎ 0588/87580

Pinacoteca – Open 16 March to 1 November, 0930 to 1300 and 1500 to 1830; 2 November to 15 March, 0900 to 1330. Closed 1 January and 25 December. L6 000; L10 000 including admission to city museums and Roman ruins. ☎ 0588/87580.

Museo etrusco Guarnacci – Open 16 March to 1 November, 0930 to 1300 and 1500 to 1830; 2 November to 15 March, 0900 to 1400. Closed 1 January and 25 December. L10 000, L20 000 (family maximum 4). Ticket also valid for city museums and Roman ruins.

Index

San Gimignano . . . . Place, sight, tourist region
Machivelli . . . . Personality, event, technical term
Numbers in *italics* . . . . . Admission Times and Charges
Numbers in **bold** . . . . Main entry
Isolated places – abbeys, burial sites, castles, caves, churches, country houses, islands, lakes, mountains, Roman baths, ruins, viewpoints – are listed under their proper names.

Notes

Notes

MANUFACTURE FRANÇAISE DES PNEUMATIQUES MICHELIN

Société en commandite par actions au capital de 2 000 000 000 de francs

Place des Carmes-Déchaux – 63 Clermont-Ferrand (France)

R.C.S. Clermont-Fd B 855 200 507

© Michelin et Cie, Propriétaires-Éditeurs 1996

Dépôt légal Février 1996 – ISBN 2 06-159701-7 – ISSN 0763-1383

Printed in the EU 01-96

Photocomposition : MAURY Imprimeur S.A., Malesherbes

Impression et brochage : KAPP LAHURE JOMBART, Évreux

Illustration de la couverture par Gérard RADEGONDE/Michel GUILLOT

MANUFACTURE FRANÇAISE DES PNEUMATIQUES MICHELIN

Société en commandite par actions au capital de 2 000 000 000 de francs

Place des Carmes-Déchaux – 63 Clermont-Ferrand (France)

R.C.S. Clermont-Fd B 855 200 507

© Michelin et Cie, Propriétaires-Éditeurs 1996

Dépôt légal Février 1996 – ISBN 2 06-159701-7 – ISSN 0763-1383

Printed in the EU 10-96/1

Photocomposition : MAURY Imprimeur S.A., Malesherbes

Impression et brochage : KAPP LAHURE JOMBART, Évreux

Illustration de la couverture par Gérard RADEGONDE/Michel GUILLOT